HIDD

Coast of California

HIDDEN ®

Coast of California

Including San Diego, Los Angeles,
Santa Barbara, Monterey, San Francisco,
and Mendocino

Ray Riegert

ELEVENTH EDITION

Ulysses Press ®
BERKELEY, CALIFORNIA

Published by: ULYSSES PRESS
        P.O. Box 3440
        Berkeley, CA 94703
        www.ulyssespress.com

ISSN 1523-5769
ISBN10: 1-56975-595-7
ISBN13: 978-1-56975-595-2

Printed in Canada by Transcontinental Printing

20 19 18 17 16

UPDATE AUTHOR: Carolyn Patten
MANAGING EDITOR: Claire Chun
PROJECT DIRECTOR: Elyce Petker
COPYEDITOR: Lee Micheaux
EDITORIAL ASSOCIATES: Laurel Shane, Ruth Marcus, Lauren Harrison
TYPESETTER: Lisa Kester
CARTOGRAPHY: Pease Press
INDEXER: Sayre Van Young
COVER PHOTOGRAPHY: Robert Holmes Photography
ILLUSTRATOR: Victor Ichioka

Distributed by Publishers Group West

For Keith and Alice

What's Hidden?

At different points throughout this book, you'll find special listings marked with a hidden symbol:

◀ HIDDEN

This means that you have come upon a place off the beaten tourist track, a spot that will carry you a step closer to the local people and natural environment of the Coast of California.

The goal of this guide is to lead you beyond the realm of everyday tourist facilities. While we include traditional sightseeing listings and popular attractions, we also offer alternative sights and adventure activities. Instead of filling this guide with reviews of standard hotels and chain restaurants, we concentrate on one-of-a-kind places and locally owned establishments.

Our authors seek out locales that are popular with residents but usually overlooked by visitors. Some are more hidden than others (and are marked accordingly), but all the listings in this book are intended to help you discover the true nature of the Coast of California and put you on the path of adventure.

Write to us!

If in your travels you discover a spot that captures the spirit of the Coast of California, or if you live in the region and have a favorite place to share, or if you just feel like expressing your views, write to us and we'll pass your note along to the author.

We can't guarantee that the author will add your personal find to the next edition, but if the writer does use the suggestion, we'll acknowledge you in the credits and send you a free copy of the new edition.

ULYSSES PRESS
P.O. Box 3440
Berkeley, CA 94703
E-mail: readermail@ulyssespress.com

Contents

Maps

OUTDOOR ADVENTURE SYMBOLS

The following symbols accompany national, state and regional park listings, as well as beach descriptions throughout the text.

Camping

Hiking

Biking

Horseback Riding

Swimming

Snorkeling or Scuba Diving

Surfing

Waterskiing

Windsurfing

Canoeing or Kayaking

Boating

Boat Ramps

Fishing

ONE

The Coast of California

California. The word comes from an old Spanish novel about a mythic island populated by Amazons and filled with gold. It was, according to the author, "very near to the terrestrial paradise." The first part of this magical land to be explored, and the area which still symbolizes the California dream, is the coast.

Stretching 1100 miles along the rim of the Pacific, it is a wildly varied region with sharp mountains and velvet beaches, barren sand dunes and rich estuaries. Los Angeles, San Francisco, and San Diego, three of the nation's largest cities, are here, together with the old mission centers of Santa Barbara and Monterey. There are small fishing towns and international shipping ports, Victorian neighborhoods and oceanfront mansions.

Powerfully influenced by early Spanish culture, the coast today is responding to a fresh influx of Mexican immigrants as well as a growing Asian population. It is a region both at the edge of the continent and at the cutting edge of the global shift toward Asia and the Pacific Rim.

The California shore is also one of the most popular travel destinations in the world. Tens of millions of visitors explore its byways and beaches every year. *Hidden Coast of California* is an attempt to make the entire area accessible to everyone.

For those seeking the good life, each chapter describes the hotels, restaurants, shopping places, and night-owl roosts that dot every town along the coast. There is information on transportation, bicycling, and water sports. Then, when the spirit of adventure takes hold, there are descriptions of secluded beaches, remote hiking trails, and sightseeing spots both famous and unknown.

Beginning in San Francisco, *Hidden Coast of California* explores Northern California first and then moves on to Los Angeles and the southern coast. San Francisco is described as a port city, with special emphasis on its Pacific shoreline and magnificent bay. The North Coast chapter, extending from Marin County all the way to the Oregon border, ranges through redwood forest, along twisting country roads, and high above sharp ocean cliffs.

Then, venturing south from San Francisco, the North Central Coast and South Central Coast chapters contain a string of oceanfront mission towns—Santa Cruz,

Monterey, San Luis Obispo, Santa Barbara and Ventura—as well as the magnificent coastline of Big Sur.

The many faces of Los Angeles are uncovered to reveal Long Beach with its
island neighborhood and industrial complex, the tumbling Palos Verdes Peninsula,
the blond-haired surf cultures of the South Bay, bohemian Venice, and ultra-chic
Malibu. Moving south into Orange County, the book scopes out the surfing scene
at Huntington Beach, then sweeps through Newport Beach and Laguna Beach.
Finally, it takes in the sparkling bays and historic neighborhoods of San Diego.

The entire coastline is a land of rare opportunity, where visitors can stay in
art deco hotels or quaint country inns, bivouac on the beach or dine on fresh California cuisine. A multicultural extravaganza as well as a region of extraordinary
beauty, the California Coast is a place for creative travelers, those anxious to
combine the easy life of cities with the challenges of the open ocean in a place very
near indeed to "the terrestrial paradise."

▼ ▼ ▼ ▼ ▼ ▼ ▼ ▼ ▼ ▼ ▼ ▼ ▼ ▼ ▼

The Story of the Coast

GEOLOGY

Things are never what they seem. Trite
though that adage might be, it perfectly fits
the California Coast. Lined with softly roll-
ing hills and bounded by a pacific sea, the shoreline is actually a
head-on collision between the edge of the ocean and the rim of
North America.

Two tectonic plates, those rafts of land that float upon the
earth's core, meet in California. Here the North American Plate
and the Pacific Plate push against each other in a kind of international arm wrestle. Between them, under colossal pressure from
both sides, subject at any moment to catastrophic forces, lies the
San Andreas fault, villain of the 1906 San Francisco earthquake.

Things were not always as they are. About 150 million years
ago, the coast rested where the Sierra Nevada mountains reside
today. Then the North American Plate shifted west, riding rough-
shod over the Pacific Plate, compressing and folding the earth
upward to create the Coast Ranges, and moving the continent
100 miles westward.

Just 25 million years ago, a blink of the eye in geologic time,
the Pacific Plate shifted north along the San Andreas fault, creating
the Central Coast from what had been part of Baja. This northerly
movement continued, building pressures of unimaginable mag-
nitude, and formed the Transverse Range five million years ago.

As a result of this continental shoving match, modern-day California comprises three distinct regions. In the south, the Peninsular Range, built of granite, runs from the tip of Baja to the Los
Angeles basin.

After a journey of a thousand miles along the Pacific coast,
the chain is broken by the Transverse Ranges, those unusual
mountain formations which run east and west rather than north
to south. Formed of 1.7-billion-year-old gneiss, among the oldest

rock in North America, the mountains reach to Point Conception, the geographic dividing point between Northern and Southern California.

To the north rise the Coast Ranges, a series of sharp mountains which resume the march from south to north. Built of shale, sandstone, and other sedimentary rocks, the Coast Ranges extend all the way up the San Francisco peninsula, through Northern California to Oregon.

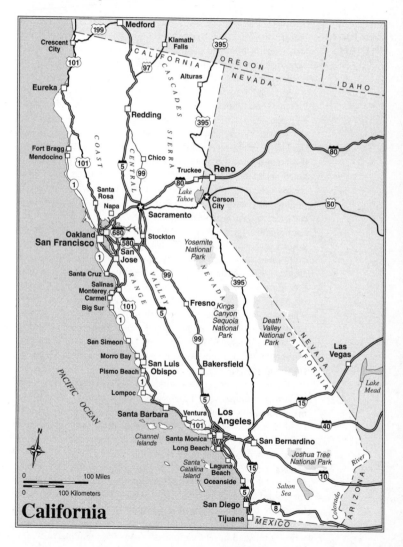

California

Today the San Andreas fault reaches the coast just south of San Francisco, then cuts north through Stinson Beach, Bodega Bay, and Point Arena, before heading seaward from Shelter Cove. Meanwhile the Pacific Plate, carrying Los Angeles, is shifting north along the North American Plate, which holds San Francisco, at a pace that should position the rival cities next to each other in about ten million years. Anyone planning to hitch a ride north should pack extra sandwiches and prepare for a long wait at the side of the road.

AMERICAN INDIANS

Before the advent of European settlers as many as 300,000 American Indians inhabited California. Of the 50 groups present, 16 lived along the coast and on offshore islands. Far to the south were the Diegueño; the Chumash occupied the South Central Coast while Costanoan Indians dominated the North Central Coast. North of San Francisco the coast Miwok, Pomo, and Athabascan language groups held sway. In the northwest corner of the state the Wiyot, Yurok, and Tolowa fished offshore waters.

They were hunter-gatherers, relying on the seemingly boundless resources of the ocean, picking wild plants, and stalking indigenous animals. Primitive by comparison with the agricultural tribes of the American Southwest, coastal tribes chipped obsidian points for arrows, fished with hooks and nets, and used harpoons to spear migrating salmon.

Dwellings were basic, dome-shaped, and fashioned from woven grasses and wooden poles. Each village included storehouses, a ceremonial lodge, burial grounds, and individual quarters, as well as a *temescal*, or sweat lodge, that served as a kind of American Indian men's club.

Men did the hunting, women gathered and cooked, and everywhere village life centered around the family. Polygamy was practiced and wives were purchased. The religious life of the community was conducted by shamans, who "cured" diseases by sucking out the illness. In some places jimsonweed was used to induce visions and became the basis of a cult.

Richer and more sophisticated than inland tribes, the coastal Indians themselves varied greatly. Language barriers were all but insurmountable. There were 21 different language families in California, further divided into dialects, often mutually unintelligible. Natives of San Diego could not understand Indians a few miles away in San Luis Rey.

Yet they fought less than American Indians elsewhere on the continent and went to battle for revenge rather than plunder. When they did war—fighting with clubs, bows, and rocks—they were known to torture enemies and slaughter women and children.

Among the more advanced coastal tribes were the Chumash, who established an elaborate system of trade. Sailing in woodplanked canoes called *tomols*, they commuted to the Channel Islands and bartered with neighbor tribes. Other American Indians used tule balsa canoes built from rushes; and along the open, rocky coast around Humboldt Bay, the northwestern California tribes hollowed canoes from redwood trunks.

These northerly tribes, greatly influenced by the rich cultures of the Pacific Northwest, hunted sea lions, spearing them with harpoons that carried barbed points of bone and antler. They also developed social classes and, like the Chumash, established a more elaborate social system.

Otherwise they were much like the tribes all along the California Coast, weaving beautiful baskets, making ceramics, and fashioning jewelry from shell and coral. They gambled, smoked tobacco, and used beads as currency. And everywhere they looked to the sea as provider and destroyer, drawing their livelihoods from its waters. They fished, canoed, dove, and gathered shellfish—rich, plentiful quantities of shellfish, which archaeologists later found in refuse mounds 30 feet deep, mounds that represented thousands of years of simple life along the California Coast.

DISCOVERY AND EXPLORATION If the story of the world starts at the creation, the history of California begins with Juan Rodriguez Cabrillo. The year was 1542 and Cabrillo, a Portuguese navigator in the employ of the Spanish crown, sailed north from Mexico, pressing forward the boundaries of empire. Seeking the elusive Northwest Passage, he tacked up the coast of Baja, landing in San Diego, then pushed on to Santa Catalina Island, Point Conception, Monterey, and Point Reyes.

For years Spanish conquistadors in Mexico had pursued El Dorado, a mythic land ruled by a king whose people covered him in gold dust. Francisco Vasquez de Coronado trekked off seeking the Seven Cities of Cibola while from his base in Mexico City Hernan Cortes sent expeditions north from Mexico City in pursuit of untold wealth. Though they found neither fabulous kings nor gilded cities, Cabrillo had discovered a new land, Alta California, which he promptly claimed for the Spanish crown.

HISTORY

KILL THE CARTOGRAPHER!

Sebastian Vizcaíno, who charted and named much of the California coast, so grossly exaggerated the harbor of Monterey that his mapmaker was eventually hanged. Vizcaíno's 1602 story of this perfect port proved so distorted that when Juan Gaspar de Portolá, exploring California by land in 1769, saw Monterey, he failed entirely to recognize it.

To world powers, even unpromising land is a prize to be coveted. The British, determined to thwart Spanish conquests in the New World, harried the Spanish and encouraged privateers to plunder their galleons. Sir Francis Drake, the most famous of these adventurers, happened upon the coast in 1579, possibly landing at Point Reyes and, naturally, claiming the territory for England.

This outpost of empire, known to the British as Nova Albion, proved more significant to the Spanish. Since their ships, laden with luxurious goods from the Philippines, passed California en route to Mexico, they began seeking ports of call. In 1587 Pedro de Unamuno anchored at Morro Bay. Eight years later Sebastian Rodriguez Cermeño, a daring seaman, swept down the coast past Cape Mendocino, lost his ship to a ferocious storm in Drake's Bay, then pressed on with 70 men in an open launch.

THE MISSIONS To the early explorers, all California was one grand disappointment. It was a region that promised rich gold discoveries, but delivered none, was rumored to contain a Northwest Passage, but did not, and which was desolate, dangerous, and difficult to reach. The British virtually ignored it and the Spanish took more than two centuries to even begin colonizing the place.

Then in 1769, as Juan Gaspar de Portolá and Padre Junípero Serra ventured north to establish the first mission in San Diego, the California dream began. Portolá continued on to Los Angeles, and following a route which would become the fabled El Camino Real, reached San Francisco Bay, perhaps the first explorer to discover the site. Later Captain Juan Bautista de Anza opened the territory farther north.

But it was Father Serra, the hard-driving Franciscan missionary, who penned the early chapter in the history of the coast. Between 1769 and 1823, he and his successor, Padre Fermin Francisco de Lasuen, established a chain of 21 missions from San Diego to Sonoma. Fortified with presidios, they became the backbone of Spain's Colonial empire.

Serra's dream of a New World became a nightmare for American Indians. Devastated by European diseases, they were forcibly converted to Catholicism and pressed into laboring on the missions. While their slaves were dying in terrible numbers, the Spanish, dangerously overextended, were beleaguered with other problems throughout the empire. In 1821 Mexico declared its independence and Alta California, still numbering only 3000 settlers, was lost.

MANIFEST DESTINY Abandoned and ignored for centuries, the California Coast was becoming an increasingly vital area. British ships had re-entered the Pacific in force and by 1812 the Russians, lured by the region's rich fur trade, built Fort Ross on the Sonoma coast. More important, the United States, asserting itself as a commercial power, was dispatching New England harpooners in pursuit of California gray whales. Whaling stations were built in San Diego, Palos Verdes, and farther north along the coast in Monterey and Bolinas.

Meanwhile the Mexican government secularized the missions in 1833, distributed the land to early settlers and American Indians, and ushered in the era of the *ranchos*. These generous land grants, often measuring 75 square miles and lining the narrow coastal strip once occupied by the missions, became huge cattle ranches. Merchants from New England traded pewter, copper, and jewels for animal skins as a lucrative trade developed. Richard Henry Dana, sailing along the coast in 1834, immortalized the industry in *Two Years Before the Mast*.

> In the 19th century, cattle hides came to be known as "California banknotes."

Gazing round him at the rich ocean and undeveloped shore, Dana remarked that "In the hands of an enterprising people, what a country this might be!" The thought was occurring increasingly among Americans, who tried unsuccessfully to buy California from Mexico. Manifest Destiny was on the march, wagon trains were crossing the Sierra Nevada with pioneers, and even the interior valleys were filling with Americans.

Finally in 1846 American settlers, with assistance from the United States government, fomented the Bear Flag Revolt. Colonel John Charles Fremont seized San Francisco while Commodore John D. Sloat took Monterey. Just two years before precious metal was finally found in Spain's fabled land of gold, the stars and stripes flew over California.

THE GOLD RUSH On January 28, 1848, a hired hand by the name of James Marshall discovered gold in the Sierra foothills, revealing how near the Spanish had come to their vision. But the yellow metal that lured and eluded the conquistadors proved to be located not along the coast they had settled but far to the interior.

The California Dream was realized. For anyone with courage and ambition, it represented a chance to blaze trails and become rich in the flash of a fortuitous find. Gold became the currency of Manifest Destiny, drawing 100,000 people across an implacable land and creating a civilization on the fringes of a continent.

San Francisco became the capital of that civilization. The town's population exploded with prospectors and a wild Barbary Coast ghetto grew along the Bay. Over 500 businesses sold liquor; gambling, drugs, and prostitution were rampant; gangs roamed the boom town and iron-fisted vigilance committees enforced law and order. Sailors were shanghaied and failed prospectors committed suicide at the rate of 1000 per year.

The North Coast, filled with lumber needed in the gold mines, also flourished. Mills and settlements by the hundreds were established and every cove became a shipping port. Mendocino, Fort Bragg, Eureka, and other timber towns soon dominated the area.

The Gold Rush not only brought prospectors and loggers to Northern California: many of America's finest writers were soon mining literary material. Mark Twain arrived during the 1860s, as did local colorist Bret Harte. Ambrose Bierce excoriated everyone and everything in his column for William Randolph Hearst's *Examiner*. In 1879, Henry George published a book in San Francisco called *Progress and Poverty*, which propounded a revolutionary system of taxation. Robert Louis Stevenson explored the Bay Area a few years later, and Jack London used it as a setting for his adventure tales.

THE INDUSTRIAL AGE   By the time the continental railroad connected the California Coast with the rest of the country in 1869, Southern California trailed far behind its northern counterpart. Los Angeles, the largest town in the region, numbered 6000 people. During the 1870s the south began to rise. The Southern Pacific railroad linked San Pedro and Santa Monica with the interior valleys where citrus cultivation was flourishing. Southern California's rich agriculture and salubrious climate led to a "health rush." Magazines and newspapers romanticized the region's history and beauty, leading one writer to proclaim that "if the Pilgrim fathers had landed on the Pacific Coast instead of the Atlantic, little old New York wouldn't be on the map."

> By 1850, about 500 ships, whose fickle crews had deserted for the gold fields, lay abandoned in San Francisco Bay.

San Diego, Santa Monica, and Santa Barbara became fashionable resort towns, and the port of San Pedro expanded exponentially, making Los Angeles a major shipping point. Around the turn of the century Henry Huntington, nephew of railroad baron Collis P. Huntington, established the Pacific Electric Railway Company. Within a few years this ruthless and creative businessman revolutionized the beach towns of Los Angeles. Buying tracts along the coast, then extending his red trolley line to one coastal town after another, Huntington became wealthier than even his uncle, creating in the process a land boom and population explosion up and down the coast.

The fishing industry, developed by the Chinese between 1860 and 1880, proved as lucrative as tourism and shipping. While Huntington was wresting control of the coast, local Portuguese, Japanese, Italians, and Yugoslavs were forcing the Chinese from the offshore fishing grounds.

When oil was discovered early in the 20th century, Southern California also became a prime drilling region. Oil wells sprang up along Huntington Beach, Long Beach, and San Pedro, adding to coastal coffers while destroying the aesthetics of the shore. The Signal Hill field in Long Beach, tapped by Shell Oil in the 1920s, became the richest oil deposit in the world and Los Angeles became the largest oil port. Little wonder that by 1925, flush with petroleum just as the age of the automobile shifted into gear, Los Angeles also became the most motor-conscious city in the world. The Pacific Coast Highway was completed during the 1930s, "auto camps" and "tourist cabins" mushroomed, and motorists began exploring the California Coast in unprecedented numbers.

MODERN TIMES   Meanwhile San Francisco, long since recovered from the horrific 1906 earthquake that shattered the San Andreas fault and rocked the coast, was becoming a strategic military area. During World War II the Navy also developed port facilities in San Diego. Coastal defense bases grew at Camp Pendleton, Vandenberg, Point Mugu, Fort Ord and in Marin County.

This rush to protect the coast turned into a kind of social mania in 1942 when the United States government, in one of the most racist acts in its history, ordered the "relocation" of 93,000 Japanese Americans. Stripped of their rights, they were removed from coastal regions where, it was charged, they could aid the Japanese Empire. In fact the only attack on the coast occurred when a lone submarine lobbed a few shells at an oil field near Santa Barbara, doing minor damage to a wooden pier.

After the war, development of another sort became the order of the day. Homes and businesses sprouted up along the entire coastline. Los Angeles became the nation's second largest metropolis, and California, 80 percent of whose residents live within 30 miles of the coast, became the most populous state.

This unbridled development, combined with the 1969 Santa Barbara oil spill and plans for a controversial nuclear power plant in Diablo Canyon, led to the creation of the California Coastal Commission. Established by California voters in 1972, this watchdog agency has succeeded in slowing development and preserving the natural beauty of the shoreline.

Also in 1972, Congress established the Golden Gate National Recreation Area in and around San Francisco. Then, just six years later, it created the Santa Monica Mountains National Recreation Area in Southern California.

The years from the 1970s to the early 1990s were marked by both natural disasters and cultural accomplishments. On nature's side of the balance, drought conditions prevailed all along the coast during the mid-'70s and for a five-year span beginning in the 1980s. El Niño, a warm ocean current, disrupted weather patterns during this period and forced southern marine life species to migrate north. Then in 1989 a monstrous earthquake struck the San

Francisco Bay Area, followed by other destructive temblors on the North Coast in 1992 and in the Los Angeles region in 1994.

Culturally, the era saw the 1984 Olympics come to Los Angeles and the state-of-the-art Monterey Bay Aquarium open along the Central Coast. The California Conservation Corps began its crucial environmental work in 1976, and during the next decade Congress provided legislation for Channel Islands National Park and a marine sanctuary around the Farallon Islands. Then, during the 1990s, the U.S. Army moved out of the Presidio, a spectacular 1400-acre park in San Francisco. This entire complex, with its historic structures and forested hills, became part of the Golden Gate National Recreation Area.

By the time the conservation movement began to flex its muscle, however, California had already demonstrated—through its tourism, ports, oil deposits, aircraft industry, construction trade, and fishing fleet—that the gold sought centuries before by Spanish explorers did not lie in the hills, but along the state's extraordinary coastline.

The Life of the Coast

FISH & FISHING

The poet William Butler Yeats wrote of "the mackerel-crowded seas," oceans filled with a single species. Along California's lengthy coastline, in the shallow waters alone, over 250 kinds of fish thrive. Most are small, exotically colored creatures, which in an entire lifetime barely venture from their birthplace. Others, like the king salmon and steelhead trout, live off the Northern California coast until summer and fall, then run upstream for miles to spawn in freshwater.

Among California's other well-known species are halibut, surf perch, and rockfish, found along the entire coast, and gamefish like barracuda, yellowtail, and bonito, which inhabit the kelp beds of Southern California. There are also bluefin tuna, albacore, and Yeats' fabled mackerel.

Most famous of all is the shark, 30 species of which prowl California's coastal waters and bays. While none particularly savor human flesh, all but a few are carnivores, and do periodically leave their teeth in divers and surfers. The great white shark, a fearful beast which grows to 25 feet in length, is now a common resident along the coast, where it feeds on sea lions, seals, and sea otters.

Methods for catching these different species are about as numerous as the fish themselves. There's surf casting, rock fishing, poke-pole fishing in tidepools, trolling and deep-sea fishing from party boats. Fishing licenses are required of everyone over 16 years old, except people fishing from public piers. Regulations and information can be obtained from the Department of Fish and Game. ~ 1416 9th Street, 12th floor, Sacramento, CA 95814; 916-653-7664. To obtain a license call 916-227-2271.

Crustaceans and mollusks, those hard-shelled characters we usually encounter only in biology class and later in life on the dinner table, abound along the California coast. Among the crustaceans are lobsters, crabs, prawns, and shrimps, while the local mollusks include mussels, oysters, squid, clams, and abalone.

California spiny lobsters live on the coast of Southern California, inhabiting rock crevices by day and foraging at night for mollusks and fellow crustaceans. Rock crabs, another crusty crustacean, dine in turn on abalone, picking apart their shells. In the endless chain of carnivorous consumption, rock crabs, particularly the large Dungeness variety, end up in local restaurants.

Most common among the mollusks is the mussel, a black-shelled creature that grows in clumps along rocks and pilings. Several species of oyster inhabit the area, the most common being the Pacific oyster, introduced from Japan. Then there are the squid, considered shellfish because of their small internal shells. Caught at night with the help of floodlights, they are among the region's most important commercial catches.

Several species of clams proliferate along the coast, such as soft-shell, gaper, geoduck, bent-nosed, and Washington clams, which inhabit the mud flats of bays and lagoons. Along the gravel areas of the bays are little-neck clams, also known as rock cockles. And on the beaches of Humboldt and Del Norte counties reside razor clams, known for their delicious flavor and frustrating ability to rapidly bury themselves beneath the sand.

One of the state's best known shellfish is the Pismo clam, a species characterized by a thick, gray-white shell marked with annual bands. Living as long as 35 years and growing up to seven inches in diameter, they flourish along the San Luis Obispo coast, favoring cold, turbulent water rich in nutrients and oxygen.

Beds of these bivalves once lined the shore, serving as a staple in the diet of Coastal American Indians. In 1914 bag limits were 200 per person, but by 1947 commercial clamming was outlawed. Today sport clamming is still permitted though heavy storms have seriously diminished the beds. Easily located, Pismo clams reside no more than six inches beneath the sand in water

GRUNION RUNS

Grunion actually climb onto land to lay their eggs. These small silvery fish come ashore between March and August after particularly high tides. The females anchor themselves in the sand and lay as many as 3000 eggs, which are hatched by surf action. During these grunion runs, common from Morro Bay south, the fish are so plentiful they can be caught by hand.

about three feet deep at low tide. To catch them, clammers work parallel to the shore, probing the sand every two inches with a clam fork.

Favorite food among the sea otters, and at gourmet restaurants, is red abalone. Of some 100 abalone species worldwide, only Pacific varieties grow to significant size; the red abalone, reaching 13 inches in length, is the largest. Marked by jet-black tentacles and a red fringe along the shell, they hold tenaciously to offshore rocks, many clinging to the same stone their entire lives.

Back in the 1930s abalone were harvested commercially in Northern California and great piles of their shells lined the road between Monterey and Castroville. In those days three million a year were taken, many processed in factories along Cannery Row. Today commercial harvesting occurs only in Southern California, but amateur divers still gather them everywhere along the coast.

Prized for their delicious meat, abalone also have beautiful shells with mother-of-pearl interiors that cast iridescent colors. Coastal American Indians used abalone shells for barter and one tribe, the Ohlone, or abalone people, took their name from this valuable shellfish.

TIDEPOOLS   It's a climactic scene in that Hollywood classic *Chinatown*. Jack Nicholson, portraying a 1930s-era private eye, is about to accuse John Huston of murdering his own partner. But Huston, a deceitful and powerful businessman playing the innocent, waxes sentimental about the dead friend. His partner, Hollis Mulwrey, had been water commissioner, a great man who early in the century brought water to the Los Angeles basin, transforming a dusty town into a metropolis. Yet Hollis was a simple man, sensitive to nature, and loved the sea.

"Hollis was always fascinated by tidepools," Huston intones. "Do you know what he used to say? 'That's where life begins— sloughs, tidepools.'" As Huston knows, tidepools are also where life ends: he murdered Mulwrey by drowning him in one.

Poor Hollis' fascination with tidepools is shared by everyone. These rocky pockets, exposed to view at low tide, are microcosms of the world. Delicately poised between land and sea, they are a frontier dividing two wildly varied environments.

Life flourishes here, but living is not easy. Denizens of tidepools are exposed to air twice a day during low tide. They must adapt to dehydration, the heat of the sun, and the effects of the atmosphere. Rain brings fresh water to a saline environment, disturbing the precious equilibrium. Waves, particularly during severe storms, wreak havoc with reefs. Exceptionally high or low tides upset the rhythm of air and water exposure.

It is this balance between time in the air and water that differentiates the tidal life forms. Tidepools, or intertidal areas, are

Ocean
Safety

For swimming, surfing, and skindiving, few places match the California Coast. With endless miles of white sand beach, it attracts aquatic enthusiasts from all over the world. Many water lovers, however, never realize how awesome the sea can be. Particularly in California, where waves can reach significant heights and currents often flow unobstructed, the ocean is sometimes as treacherous as it is spectacular. People drown every year on California beaches, others are dragged from the surf with serious injuries, and countless numbers sustain minor cuts and bruises.

These accidents can be entirely avoided if you relate to the ocean with a respect for its power as well as an appreciation of its beauty. All you have to do is heed a few simple guidelines. First, never turn your back on the sea. Waves come in sets: one group may be small and quite harmless, but the next set could be large enough to sweep you out to sea. Never swim alone.

Don't try to surf, or bodysurf, until you're familiar with the sports' techniques and precautionary measures. Be very careful when the surf's high.

If you do get caught in a rip current, do not swim *against* it: swim *across* it, parallel to the shore. These currents, running from the shoreline out to sea, can often be spotted by noting their ragged-looking surface water and foamy edges.

When stung by a jellyfish, apply vinegar to the affected area, leave it on the sting for 10 or 20 minutes, then rinse it off with alcohol. Old Hawaiian remedies, which are reputedly quite effective, involve applying urine or green papaya. If you step on the sharp, painful spines of a sea urchin, soak the affected area in very hot water for 15 to 90 minutes. Another remedy calls for applying urine or undiluted vinegar. If any of these preliminary treatments do not work, consult a doctor.

Oh, one last thing. The chances of encountering a shark are about as likely as sighting a UFO. But should you meet one of these ominous creatures, stay calm. He'll be no happier to see you than you are to confront him. Simply swim quietly to shore. By the time you make it back to terra firma, you'll have one hell of a story to tell.

divided into four zones, which parallel the beach and vary in their distance from shore.

The splash zone, dampened by mist and occasional large waves, rests far up along the beach and is inhabited by green algae and small snails. Below it lies the upper intertidal zone, an area covered only during high tide. Here barnacles, chitons, and limpets cling to rocks, closing tight during low tide to preserve moisture.

Covered by water twice a day, the middle intertidal zone is home to mussels and rock weed. Since mussels grow in clumps, they form a biological community in themselves, sheltering varieties of plants and animals, some of which spend their entire lives in a single clump.

Starfish, which generally inhabit the low intertidal zone, feed on these mussels, prying open the stubborn shells with their powerful suctioned tentacles. This fourth region, uncovered only when the ocean deeply recedes during minus tides, supports the most diverse life forms. Sea urchins, abalone, and anemones flourish here, as do crabs, octopus, and chitons, those oval-shaped mollusks that date back to before the age of dinosaurs.

COASTAL PLANT LIFE

From the rim of the sea to the peaks of surrounding mountains, the coastline is coated with a complex variety of plant life. Several plant communities flourish along the shore, each clinging to a particular niche in the environment. Blessed with a cooler, more moderate climate near the ocean, they are continually misted by sea spray and must contend with more salt in their veins.

On the beaches and along the dunes are the herbs, vines, and low shrubs of the coastal strand community. Among their numbers are beach primrose, sand verbena, beach morning-glory, and sea figs, those tenacious succulents that run along the ground sprouting magenta flowers and literally carpeting the coast. Characterized by leathery leaves that retain large quantities of water, they are the plant world's answer to the camel.

Around the mud flats and river mouths grow rushes, pickleweed, tules, cord grass, and other members of the salt marsh community. Low, shrubby plants growing in clumps, these hearty fellows are inundated by tides and able to withstand tremendous concentrations of salt.

Coastal sage scrub inhabits a broad swath from above the water line to about 3000 feet elevation. White and black sage, wild buckwheat, and California sagebrush belong to this community of short, tough plants.

The chaparral community grows in thick, often impenetrable stands along the hillsides and mountains. These scrub oak, manzanita, and Christmas holly bushes lend a distinct character to the fabled rolling hills of California. Down along the rivers and creeks resides the riparian community whose members range from willow, alder, and big-leaf maple to redwood and Douglas fir.

There are wildflowers everywhere—violets, lilies, irises, azaleas, wild roses, and of course California poppies, the state flower. Buttercups, with their shiny yellow petals, are abundant. Growing from the coast right out to the desert are the lupines, silky bushes with whorled flowers that stand straight as bottlebrushes.

The cactus family is represented by the prickly pear with its sharp spines and yellow blossoms; and there are nasty thickets of gorse, poison hemlock, and tenacious thistles. Several species of fern occupy coastal bluffs, descending to the very edge of the beach. In addition to serrated sword ferns and giant horsetails, these include California lace ferns and Saint Catherine's lace, with petals like finely woven textiles.

Then there are the trees—lofty Monterey pine; the rare Torrey pine that grows only in San Diego County and on an offshore island; oak, laurel, maple, and alder; fir, spruce, and cedar. The fabled Monterey cypress inhabits a picturesque region along the Monterey coast, the only place in the world it is found. Giant redwoods, the tallest trees on earth, grow in awesome groves along the coastal fog belt, living for centuries and reaching 350 foot heights.

And don't forget the tree that has no branches and sheds little shade, but is the foremost symbol of California—the palm tree. There are Pindo palms from Paraguay, European hair palms, plume palms from Brazil, blue palms, Mexican fan palms, and the Erythea. Among the most common are the California fan palm, largest native palm in the continental United States, and the date palm, which lines many California streets and is nicknamed "pineapple palm" for its trunk's resemblance to the tropical fruit.

SEABIRDS

Somehow the mud flats of San Francisco Bay are the last place to go sightseeing, particularly at high tide, after the flood has stirred the ooze. But it is at such times that birdwatchers gather to view flocks of as many as 60,000 birds.

LOOK, BUT DON'T TOUCH

When you go searching for tidepool creatures remember, even out here in the wild, there are a few rules of the road. Collecting plants and animals, including dead ones, is strongly discouraged and in some places entirely illegal. Follow the old adage and look but don't touch. If you do turn over a rock or move a shell, replace it in the original position; it may be someone's home. Also watch out for big waves and exercise caution—it can be dangerous out there.

The California shore is one of the richest bird habitats anywhere in North America. Over 500 species are found across the state, many along the coast and its offshore islands.

Coastal species fall into three general categories—near-shore birds like loons, grebes, cormorants, and scoters, which inhabit the shallow waters of bays and beaches; offshore birds, such as shearwaters, which feed several miles off the coast; and pelagic or open-ocean species like albatross and Arctic terns, which fly miles from land and live for up to 30 years.

A kind of streamlined hawk, the peregrine falcon is one of the fastest birds alive, capable of diving at 200 miles an hour to prey on ducks, coots, and terns.

Joining the shore birds along California's beaches are ducks, geese, and other waterfowl. While waterfowl dive for fish and feed on submerged vegetation, near-shore birds use their sharp, pointed beaks to ferret out inter-tidal animals. Both groups flee the scene each year, flying north in spring to Canada and Alaska or south in autumn to Mexico and Central America, along the Pacific flyway, that great migratory route spanning the western United States.

Some birds, like canvasback ducks, loons, and Arctic terns, fly a route entirely along the coast. Others finish wintering in California and make a beeline due east. The short-tailed shearwater, one of the world's smallest but greatest travelers, leaves everything far behind. Breeding off the coast of Australia, this incredible bird flies a figure eight around the Pacific, skirting California and covering 20,000 miles.

Ospreys inhabit large nests which can often be seen high in shoreline trees. Also known as fish hawks, these are handsome birds with brown head crowns and six-foot wingspans. Ever the gentle creature, ospreys nab fish by circling over the ocean, then diving talons first into the water.

Whistling swans, white birds with black bills and yellow eyespots, arrive in California from the Arctic every November. Residing until March, they build nests and breed cygnets before returning to colder climes.

Among the most beautiful birds are the egrets and herons. Tall, slender, elegant birds, they live from January until July in Bolinas and other coastal towns, engaging in elaborate courtship rituals. Together with more common species like sea gulls, sandpipers, and pelicans, they turn travelers into birders and make inconvenient times, like the edge of dawn, and unusual places, like swamps, among the most intriguing possibilities California has to offer.

MARINE MAMMALS

Few animals inspire the sense of myth and magic associated with the marine mammals of California. Foremost are the ocean-going animals like whales, dolphins, and porpoises, members of the unique Cetacean order that left the land 30 million years ago for the alien world of the sea. Six species of seals and sea lions also inhabit the coast, together with sea otters, those playful creatures that delight visitors and bedevil fishermen.

While dolphins and porpoises range far offshore, the region's most common whale is a regular coastal visitor. Migrating 12,000 miles every year between the Bering Sea and Baja Peninsula, the California gray whale cruises the shoreline each winter (see "Whale Watching" in Chapter Eight). Measuring 50 feet and weighing 40 tons, these distinguished animals can live to 50 years of age and communicate with sophisticated signaling systems.

The seals and sea lions that seem to loll about the shoreline are characterized by small ears and short flippers equipped for land travel. Fat and sassy, they have layers of blubber to keep them warm and loud barks to inform tourists who's king of the rookery.

Even people who never venture to the ocean have seen California sea lions, those talented circus performers. Occupying the entire coast, particularly around Santa Barbara, they stay offshore for months at a time, landing only during breeding season.

Harbor seals differ from these showmen in an inability to use their hind flippers for land travel. Not to be upstaged, they sport beautiful dark coats with silver and white spots from which they borrow their second name, leopard seals. Like other pinnipeds, harbor seals feed on fish, shellfish, and squid. Largest of all the pinnipeds are the Northern elephant seals, those ugly but lovable creatures that grow to 16 feet and weigh three tons. Characterized by a huge snout, they come ashore only to molt, mate, and give birth. Breeding season, beginning in December, is the best time to watch these waddling characters. The males wage fierce battles to establish who will be cock of the walk. A few weeks after the males finish their tournament the females arrive.

"Sentence first," said the Queen of Hearts in *Alice's Adventures in Wonderland*, "verdict afterwards." In the upside-down world of the elephant seal, birth comes first, then breeding. Within days of arriving onshore, the females give birth to 75-pound pups. Three weeks later the mothers breed with their mates, conceiving pups that will be born eight months later.

Every California visitor's favorite animal is the sea otter. A kind of ocean-going teddy bear, they are actually members of the weasel family, weighing up to 85 pounds, measuring about four feet in length, and characterized by thick fur, short paws used for feeding and grooming, and webbed hind feet that serve as flippers. Intelligent critters, sea otters are quite capable of using tools—rocks with which they pry tenacious shellfish from the ocean bottom and hammer open shells. Voracious eaters, sea otters feed on abalone, sea urchins, and crabs, consuming as much as 25 percent of their body weight daily.

Like many other California marine mammals, sea otters were hunted to near extinction by 19th-century fur traders. Today the animals have made a remarkable recovery, populating the coast from the Channel Islands to Monterey. Inhabiting kelp beds where they are often difficult to spot, these sleek animals can best be seen during feeding their time in early morning and late afternoon. Watch carefully for the hungry sea gulls that patiently circle kelp beds in search of sea otter scraps. Then look for a reddish-black animal, relaxing on his back, tapping a rhythm with a rock and abalone shell, his mouth curved in a cunning smile.

Traveling the Coast

SEASONS

The California Coast extends all the way from Mexico to Oregon. Along this entire expanse the weather corresponds to a Mediterranean climate with mild temperatures year-round. Since the coastal fog creates a natural form of air conditioning and insulation, the mercury rarely drops below 40° or rises above 70°. The ocean air creates a significant amount of moisture, keeping the state's average humidity in the neighborhood of 65 percent and making some areas, particularly Northern California, seem somewhat colder than the thermometer would indicate. September and October are the hottest months, and December and January the coolest.

Spring and particularly autumn are the ideal times to make a visit. During winter, the rainy season brings overcast days and frequent showers. Summer is the peak tourist season, when voluminous crowds can present problems. Like spring, summer is also a period of frequent fog; during the morning and evening, fog banks from offshore blanket the coast, burning off around midday.

Since most winter storms sweep in from the north, rainfall averages and the length of the rainy season diminish as you head southward. Crescent City receives 70 inches of rain annually, San Francisco averages about 20 inches, and San Diego receives only 10 inches of rain a year. Inversely, temperatures vary widely from north to south: Eureka ranges from an average temperature of 47° in January to 57° during August, while down south, San Diego rises from 55° to 70° during the same months.

CALENDAR OF EVENTS

JANUARY

San Francisco   During the end of January or early February, the Chinese New Year features an extravagant parade with colorful dragons, dancers, and fireworks.

South Central Coast   The Hang Gliding Festival in Santa Barbara features contests and demonstrations by local pilots. Stars and stargazers gather for **Santa Barbara's International Film Festival.**

North Coast   The **World Championship Crab Races and Crab Feed** takes place in Crescent City; if you forget to bring your own, you can rent a racing crab. Who said California lacks culture?

North Central Coast   The **AT&T Pebble Beach National Pro-Am**, an annual golf tournament, swings into action along the Monterey Peninsula.

South Central Coast   New Orleans–style jazz accompanies a parade and costume ball at the San Luis Obispo **Mardi Gras**.

Orange Coast   Along the coast, crowds gather for seasonal grunion runs.

San Diego Coast   **Mardi Gras** festivities take to the streets in San Diego's Historic Gaslamp Quarter.

San Francisco   Bands, politicians, and assorted revelers parade through the city on the Sunday closest to March 17, marking **St. Patrick's Day**.

North Coast   Mendocino and Fort Bragg host a **Whale Festival** with whale-watching, cruises, art shows and winetasting.

South Central Coast   Santa Barbara's **Whale Festival** near Stearns Wharf includes Coast Guard cutter tours, whale-watching cruises, art shows, and winetasting.

Orange Coast   The **Fiesta de las Golondrinas** commemorates the return of the swallows to Mission San Juan Capistrano. In Dana Point, the **Festival of the Whales** features a concert series, sporting competitions, sand castle workshops, and a street fair.

San Diego Coast   The **Ocean Beach Kite Festival and Parade**, with contests for flying and decorating kites, takes place at Ocean Beach.

San Francisco   Japantown's **Cherry Blossom Festival** features parades, tea ceremonies, theatrical performances, and martial arts displays. The **San Francisco International Film Festival** offers a wide selection of cinematic events at participating theaters throughout the city. Cowboys celebrate at the **Grand National Rodeo, Horse & Stock Show**.

North Coast   The two-day wildlife festival at Lower Lake, **Heron Days**, features boat rides to heron rookeries on Clear Lake, nature walks, slide shows, and fun for the kids.

North Central Coast   Enjoy amazing ocean views as you jog along Highway 1 in the **Big Sur International Marathon**, featuring a fun run and relay race so everyone can participate.

Los Angeles Coast   Race car buffs head to the **Toyota Grand Prix** in Long Beach.

San Diego Coast   The **Santa Fe Market** in Old Town features Southwestern and American Indian arts, crafts, and demonstrations. **MotorCars on MainStreet** in Coronado features 150 pre-1972 automobiles.

FEBRUARY

MARCH

APRIL

MAY

San Francisco   Over 70,000 hearty souls (soles?) run the **Bay to Breakers Foot Race**, many covering the seven-and-a-half mile course in elaborate costumes.

South Central Coast   Food, exhibits, and dancing highlight the Italian celebration, **I Madonnari**, held in Santa Barbara.

San Diego Coast   Carlsbad hosts the spring observance of the semi-annual **Village Faire**, with hundreds of exhibits, an elephant ride, petting zoo, and countless food stands. In Old Town, the **Annual Fiesta Cinco de Mayo** celebration is highlighted by mariachis, traditional Mexican folk dancers, food, and displays.

JUNE

San Francisco   The **San Francisco Lesbian, Gay, Bisexual, Transgender Pride Parade**, with its colorful floats and imaginative costumes, marches down Market Street to the Civic Center. June launches the performances of the two-month-long **Stern Grove Midsummer Music Festival**, which showcases international music and dance, vocal ensembles, opera, and jazz.

North Central Coast   An annual Portuguese fete in Ferndale since 1871, the **Portuguese/Holy Ghost Celebration** falls on the seventh Sunday after Easter and commemorates the end of an Old Country famine with free food and wine, a parade, and dances. Monterey presents the **Monterey Wine Festival**, with winetasting, gourmet food, and cooking demonstrations.

South Central Coast   A parade and many other festivities highlight Santa Barbara's **Summer Solstice Celebration**.

San Diego Coast   The **La Jolla Festival of the Arts and Food Faire** starts its two-day event that benefits San Diego's physically challenged.

JULY

San Francisco   Here, at Fisherman's Wharf, and throughout Northern California, firework displays commemorate the **Fourth of July**. The **Chronicle Marathon** begins in Golden Gate Park, then winds for 26.2 past many of the city's sights before heading back to the Park.

North Central Coast   Beginning in July and continuing through August, the **Carmel Bach Festival** includes recitals, weekend matinees, and evening concerts of classical and baroque music.

Los Angeles Coast   Every Thursday evening from July through August the **Santa Monica Pier Twilight Dance Series** features a variety of live music from reggae to Western swing.

Orange Coast   The **Festival of Arts Pageant of the Masters**, one of Southern California's most notable events, opens in Laguna Beach.

San Diego Coast   The **San Diego Symphony Summer Pops** begins its series of evening concerts. The **Del Mar Race** season, which features parties, concerts and daily horse racing, starts in July and runs through Labor Day weekend.

San Francisco The **SF Jazz Summerfest** produces a two-month-long series of free jazz concerts on Thursday evenings.

North Central Coast Pebble Beach sponsors the **Blackhawk Historic & Classic Car Exposition**, a classic auto show featuring pre- and postwar cars. Check out Santa Cruz for the **Aloha Outrigger Races & Polynesian Festival**, which features novice outrigger races and Polynesian food, dance, music, and more. Salinas celebrates its four-day **Steinbeck Festival** with walking tours, lectures, films, and plays.

Remember, everywhere along the coast requires a raincoat between November and March.

South Central Coast Santa Barbara rounds up everyone for a rodeo, open-air food markets, a children's parade, and live entertainment at the five-day-long **Old Spanish Days**. Polo players from around the world gather in Santa Barbara for the prestigious **Pacific Coast Open**.

Los Angeles Coast Surfers hang ten at the **International Surf Festival** on Hermosa, Manhattan, Torrance, and Redondo beaches.

San Diego Coast Crowds in costume liven up San Diego's 20 miles of coastline during the **Midnight Madness Fun Bicycle Run**. Chamber music concerts, lectures, and workshops are all part of the three-week **SummerFest La Jolla**.

San Francisco This month for music is marked by the opening of the **San Francisco Opera** and the **San Francisco Symphony**, as well as the annual **Blues Festival** and **Opera in the Park**. **Comedy Celebration Day** is a free "comedy concert" in Golden Gate Park featuring standups from around the world. The **San Francisco Jazz Festival** kicks off in late September to present two month's worth of concerts, dance, performances, and tributes to the masters.

North Central Coast It's the magic month for the internationally renowned **Monterey Jazz Festival**.

San Diego Coast **Old Town Fiestas Patrias** celebrates its Hispanic heritage with food, crafts, and music.

San Francisco **Columbus Day** is marked by a parade, a bocce ball tournament, and the annual blessing of the fishing fleet. The **Castro Street Fair** features food, art, and loads of quirky San Francisco culture.

North Central Coast The fun-filled **Art and Pumpkin Festival** in Half Moon Bay features pie-eating contests, food booths, and crafts exhibits.

South Central Coast   Pismo Beach, the "clam capital of the world," presents its annual **Pismo Beach Clam Festival** with feasting, live entertainment, and arts-and-crafts booths.

NOVEMBER   **San Francisco**   Several fairs and festivals kick off the holiday season. One notable event is the **Harvest Festival and Christmas Crafts Market.**
North Coast   Mendocino hosts a **Thanksgiving Festival** complete with refreshments and crafts booths.
San Diego Coast   Carlsbad hosts the year's second **Village Faire** (see May listing).

DECEMBER   **San Francisco**   The **Great Dickens Christmas Fair**, which goes from Thanksgiving to Christmas, and the **Holiday Festival of Lights** commemorate the holiday season. There are also **Christmas Parades** in many towns throughout Northern California.
Southern California   During the holidays Newport Beach marks the season with a **Christmas Boat Parade**. San Diego, San Luis Obispo, and other Southland cities celebrate the Mexican yuletide with **Las Posadas.**

▼▼▼▼▼▼▼▼▼▼▼
Before You Go

VISITORS CENTERS

Several agencies provide free information to travelers. The **California Office of Tourism** will help guide you to areas throughout the state. ~ 480 9th Street, Suite 4800, Sacramento, CA 95812; 916-444-4429, 800-862-2543; www.visitcalifornia.com. The **San Francisco Visitors Information Center** is an excellent resource for San Francisco. ~ Hallidie Plaza, Lower Level, Powell and Market streets; 900 Market Street, San Francisco, CA 94101; 415-391-2000; www.sfvisitor.org. For information on the North Coast counties between San Francisco and Oregon, you should contact the **Redwood Empire Association.** ~ 1925 13th Avenue #103, Oakland, CA 94606; 800-619-2125; www.redwoodempire.com. For the Los Angeles area, the **Los Angeles Visitors and Convention Bureau** can help. ~ 333 South Hope Street, 18th floor, Los Angeles, CA 90071; 213-624-7300, 800-228-2452; www.visitlanow.com. The **San Diego Convention and Visitors Bureau** can provide information on the San Diego area. ~ 1040¹/₃ West Broadway, San Diego, CA 92101; 619-236-1212; www.sandiego.org. Also consult local chambers of commerce and information centers, which are mentioned in the various area chapters.

PACKING   There are two important guidelines when deciding what to take on a trip. The first is as true for the California Coast as anywhere in the world—pack light. Dress styles here are relatively informal and laundromats and dry cleaners are frequent. The airlines allow two suitcases and a carry-on bag; try to take one suitcase and perhaps a small accessory case.

The second rule is to prepare for cool weather, even if the closest you'll come to the mountains are the bluffs above the beach. While the coastal climate is temperate, temperatures sometimes descend below 50°. Even that might not seem chilly until the fog rolls in and the ocean breeze picks up. A warm sweater and jacket are absolute necessities. In addition to everyday garments, pack shorts year-round for Southern California.

Overnight accommodations along the California Coast are as varied as the region itself. They range from highrise hotels and neon motels to hostels and bed-and-breakfast inns. One guideline to follow with all of them is to reserve well in advance.

LODGING

Check through each chapter and you're bound to find something to fit your budget and personal taste. Neon motels offer bland facilities at low prices and are great if you're economizing or don't plan to spend much time in the room. Larger hotels often lack intimacy, but provide such conveniences as restaurants and shops in the lobby. My personal preference is for historic hotels, those slightly faded classics that offer charm and tradition at moderate cost. Bed-and-breakfast inns present an opportunity to stay in a homelike setting. Like hostels, they are an excellent way to meet fellow travelers; unlike hostels, California's country inns are quite expensive.

Six species of seals and sea lions inhabit the coast, together with sea otters, those playful creatures that delight visitors and bedevil fishermen.

To help you decide on a place to stay, I've described the accommodations not only by area but also according to price (prices listed are for double occupancy during the high season; rates may decrease in low season). *Budget* hotels are generally less than $90 per night for two people; the rooms are clean and comfortable, but not luxurious. *Moderate* price hotels run $90 to $150, and provide larger rooms, plusher furniture, and more attractive surroundings. At *deluxe*-priced accommodations, expect to spend between $150 and $250 for a homey bed and breakfast or double in a hotel or resort. You'll usually find spacious rooms, a fashionable lobby, a restaurant, and a group of shops. If you want to spend your time (and money) at the very finest hotels, try an *ultra-deluxe* facility, which will include all the amenities and cost more than $250.

It seems as if the California Coast has more restaurants than people. To establish a pattern for this parade of dining places, I've organized them according to location and cost. Restaurants listed offer lunch and dinner unless otherwise noted.

DINING

Within a particular chapter, the restaurant listings are categorized geographically and each individual restaurant entry describes the establishment as budget, moderate, deluxe, or ultra-deluxe in price.

Dinner entrées at *budget* restaurants usually cost $10 or less. The ambience is informal-café style and the crowd is often a local one. *Moderate* price restaurants range between $10 and $20 at dinner and offer pleasant surroundings, a more varied menu, and a slower pace. *Deluxe* establishments tab their entrées from $20 to $30, featuring sophisticated cuisines, plush decor, and more personalized service. *Ultra-deluxe* dining rooms, where $30 will only get you started, are gourmet gathering places where cooking (one hopes) is a fine art form and service a way of life.

> Be aware that many bed-and-breakfast inns do not allow children. Call ahead to check on an accommodation's policy.

Breakfast and lunch menus vary less in price from restaurant to restaurant. Even deluxe kitchens usually offer light breakfasts and lunch sandwiches, placing them within a few dollars of their budget-minded competitors. These early meals can be a good time to test expensive restaurants.

TRAVELING WITH CHILDREN

Visiting California with kids can be a real adventure, and if properly planned, a truly enjoyable one. To ensure that your trip will feature the joy, rather than the strain of parenthood, remember a few important guidelines.

Children under age six or under 60 pounds must be in approved child restraints while riding in cars/vans. The back seat is safest.

Use a travel agent to help with arrangements; they can reserve spacious bulkhead seats on airlines and determine which flights are least crowded. Bring everything you need on board—diapers, food, toys, and extra clothes for kids and parents alike. If the trip to California involves a long journey, plan to relax and do very little during the first few days.

Always allow extra time for getting places. Book reservations well in advance and make sure the hotel has the extra crib, cot, or bed you require. It's smart to ask for a room at the end of the hall to cut down on noise.

Even small towns have stores that carry diapers, food, and other essentials; in larger towns and cities, convenience stores are often open all night (check the Yellow Pages for addresses).

Hotels often provide access to babysitters. Also check the yellow pages for state licensed and bonded babysitting agencies.

A first-aid kit is always a good idea. Ask your pediatrician for special medicines and dosages for colds and diarrhea.

DISABLED TRAVELERS

California stands at the forefront of social reform for the disabled. During the past decade, the state has responded with a series of progressive legislative measures addressing the needs of the blind, wheelchair-bound, and others.

The **Department of Motor Vehicles** provides special parking permits for the disabled. Many local bus lines and other public transit facilities are wheelchair-accessible ~ 1377 Fell Street, San Francisco; 800-777-0133; www.dmv.ca.gov.

There are also agencies in California assisting persons with disabilities. For information about the San Francisco Bay area, contact the **Center for Independent Living,** a self-help group that has led the way in reforming access laws in California. ~ 2539 Telegraph Avenue, Berkeley, CA 94704; 510-841-4776; www.cil berkeley.org. Other organizations on the coast include the **Westside Center for Independent Living.** ~ 12901 Venice Boulevard, Los Angeles, CA 90066; 800-851-9245; www.wcil.org. In San Diego, contact **The Access Center.** ~ 1295 University Avenue, Suite 10, San Diego, CA 92103; 619-293-3500; www.a2isd.org.

The **Society for Accessible Travel & Hospitality** (SATH) is an organization that can provide information. ~ 347 5th Avenue, Suite 605, New York, NY 10016; 212-447-7284; www.sath.org, e-mail sathtravel@aol.com. Or try **Flying Wheels Travel.** ~ 143 West Bridge Street, P.O. Box 382, Owatonna, MN 55060; 507-451-5005; www.flyingwheelstravel.com. Or consult the comprehensive guidebook, *Access to the World—A Travel Guide for the Handicapped,* by Louise Weiss (Henry Holt & Company, Inc.).

Be sure to check in advance when making room reservations. Many hotels and motels feature facilities for those in wheelchairs.

SENIOR TRAVELERS

The California Coast is an ideal spot for older vacationers. The mild climate makes traveling in the off-season possible, helping to cut down on expenses. Many museums, theaters, restaurants, and hotels offer senior discounts (requiring a driver's license, Medicare card, or other age-identifying card). Be sure to ask your travel agent when booking reservations.

The AARP offers travel discounts and provides referrals for escorted tours. ~ 601 E Street NW, Washington, DC 20049; 888-687-2277; www.aarp.com. For those 55 or over, **Elderhostel** offers numerous educational programs in California. ~ 11 Avenue de Lafayette, Boston, MA 02111; 800-454-5768; www.elderhostel.org.

Be extra careful about health matters. Bring any medications you use, along with the prescriptions. Consider carrying a medical record with you—including your current medical status and medical history, as well as your doctor's name, phone number, and address. Also be sure to confirm that your insurance covers you away from home.

WOMEN TRAVELING ALONE

Traveling solo grants an independence and freedom different from that of traveling with a partner, but single travelers are more vulnerable to crime and should take additional precautions. An option for those who are alone but prefer not to be is to join a tour group.

It's unwise to hitchhike and probably best to avoid inexpensive accommodations on the outskirts of town; the money saved does not outweigh the risk. Bed and breakfasts, youth hostels and YWCAs are generally your safest bet for lodging, and they also foster an environment ideal for bonding with fellow travelers. Lodging in a major hotel in a safe area is a fine option, as well.

Keep all valuables well-hidden and hold on to cameras and purses. Avoid late-night treks or strolls through undesirable parts of town, but if you find yourself in this situation, continue walking with a confident air until you reach a safe haven. A fierce scowl never hurts.

These hints should by no means deter you from seeking out adventure. Wherever you go, stay alert, use your common sense and trust your instincts.

Northern California boasts nearly 900 women's organizations, including, National Organization of Women (NOW) chapters, business networking clubs, artists' and writers' groups, and one-of-a-kind organizations ranging from the New African Women for Self-Determination in Oakland to the Women's Mountain Bike & Tea Society (WOMBATS) in Fairfax. In the Los Angeles, Orange County, and Ventura County areas, consult the **Women's Yellow Pages.** ~ 818-995-6646; www.referral-guide.com. Feminist bookstores are also good sources of information.

Emergency services, including rape crisis and battered women's hotlines, can be found in local phone books or by calling directory assistance. A good place to start when seeking information about other resources is the local women's center, often affiliated with a university. Among them are **University of California–Santa Cruz Women's Center** (Cardiff House, University of California, Santa Cruz; 831-459-2072) and **University of California–San Francisco Center for Gender Equity** (100 Medical Center Way, San Francisco; 415-476-5222). For more hints, get a copy of *Safety and Security for Women Who Travel* (Travelers' Tales).

GAY & LESBIAN TRAVELERS

The California Coast offers countless opportunities for gay and lesbian travelers to unwind, or wind up, in an atmosphere of tolerance. Without doubt, San Francisco is one of the premier gay and lesbian vacation spots in the country. The Castro Street and Polk Street neighborhoods, as well as the South of Market district, are all major gay areas. Each offers gay-owned and gay-friendly lodging, restaurants, and nightspots. (See the "Gay Neighborhoods" and "South of Market" sections in Chapter Two.) In many ways, the entire city is a gay-friendly enclave. Gays and lesbians constitute a powerful voting block in local politics, and a gay supervisor currently serves on the Board of Supervisors.

For weekly updates on the gay community, pick up a *Bay Area Reporter*, which focuses on local news, arts, and entertainment. ~

415-861-5019. *SF Frontiers* is a biweekly, publishing articles of interest to the gay and lesbian community. ~ www.frontiersnews magazine.com. The monthly *San Francisco Bay Times* deals with gay issues and doubles as a resource guide. ~ 415-626-0260.

One of the largest of its kind, the **San Francisco Lesbian, Gay, Bisexual, and Transgender Community Center** (LGBT) offers a plethora of services from health and legal referrals to lodging and activity suggestions. ~ 1800 Market Street; 415-865-5555; www.sfcenter.org, e-mail info@sfcenter.org. The **Billy DeFrank** LGBT **Community Center** in San Jose, has lots of information online. ~ www.defrank.org.

See "Gay-friendly travel" in the index for gay- and lesbian-friendly establishments along the California coast.

If you find yourself in need of medical or legal help there are several resources available. **San Francisco AIDS Foundation Hotline** is the area's very best resource for counseling and referrals. ~ 415-863-2437, 800-367-2437 (within California). The AIDS **Nightline** staffs operators from 5 p.m. to 5 a.m. ~ 415-434-2437, 800-628-9240. **Community United Against Violence Support Hotline** is available 24 hours a day to assist gay, lesbian, transgender, and bisexual people who have been physically assaulted. ~ 415-333-4357.

Despite its name, **The Women's Building** is a community center with bulletin boards loaded with information and job listings for gays, lesbians, and bisexuals. ~ 3543 18th Street #8, San Francisco; 415-431-1180; www.womensbuilding.org. Medical attention for lesbian and transgender women can be had at **Lyon-Martin Women's Health Services**. ~ 1748 Market Street, Suite 201, San Francisco; 415-565-7667; www.lyon/martin.org, e-mail info@lyon-martin.org.

Although Southern California is often known for its social and political conservatism, the tolerance that accompanies the booming entertainment industry makes certain areas inviting and exciting for gay and lesbian travelers. For more information on hotels, shops, restaurants, and nightclubs catering to gay and lesbian travelers, see the "Long Beach" section in Chapter Six and the "Laguna Beach" section in Chapter Seven.

After arriving in town, visitors may want to make their first stop the **Los Angeles Gay & Lesbian Center**, a resource center with informative bulletin boards, brochures, counseling, and, for the long-term visitor, job placement services. Should you get slapped with one of L.A.'s famous jaywalking tickets, they also offer legal services. ~ 1625 North Schrader Boulevard, Los Angeles; 323-993-7400, www.gay-lesbian-center.org. Pick up a copy of *iN* magazine, which comes out twice a month—almost as often as the average Sunset Strip pedestrian—and covers the goings-on in L.A. County. ~ 8235 Santa Monica Boulevard, West Hollywood; 323-848-2200; www.inmagla.com. Also look for the biweekly *Frontiers*

Magazine; it's full of movie, theater, and club reviews that cover the area between San Francisco and San Diego. ~ 5657 Wilshire Boulevard, Suite 500, Los Angeles, CA 90036; 323-848-3220; www.frontiersnewsmagazine.com. Women may consult *Lesbian News*, a monthly publication based in L.A. that covers the Southern California entertainment scene. Along with reviews, interviews, health, and travel, the magazine has a comprehensive club guide and calendar of events. ~ P.O. Box 55, Torrance, CA 90507; 800-458-9888; www.lesbiannews.com.

Book reservations in advance: the California coast is an extremely popular area, particularly in summer, and facilities fill up quickly.

Farther south, San Diego's Hillcrest district is the focus of that city's gay scene, with guesthouses, stores, and cafés. (See "San Diego Gay Scene" in Chapter Eight.) In San Diego, get a copy of *Gay & Lesbian Times*, a weekly publication with local and world news, business, sports, weather, and arts sections. It also contains a calendar of events and a directory of gay-friendly businesses and establishments. ~ 1730 Monroe Avenue, Suite A, San Diego; 619-299-6397, fax 619-299-3430; www.gaylesbiantimes.com. **The Lesbian, Gay, Bisexual, Transgender Community Center** offers referrals for those seeking drop-in counseling, mental health services, or support groups—or stop by on Tuesday nights for bingo. Closed Sunday. ~ 3909 Center Street, San Diego; 619-692-2077; www.thecentersd.org.

FOREIGN TRAVELERS

Passports and Visas   Foreign visitors need a passport and tourist visa to enter the United States. Furthermore, in 2007, tighter U.S. Department of Homeland Security regulations now mandate that all those traveling to the U.S. by air, including U.S. citizens, must show a valid passport to enter or reenter the U.S. This requirement will expand to include those entering by land and sea by January 2008. Contact your nearest U.S. Embassy or Consulate well in advance to obtain a visa and to check on any other entry requirements.

Customs Requirements   Foreign travelers are allowed to carry in the following: 200 cigarettes (1 carton), 50 cigars, or 2 kilograms (4.4 pounds) of smoking tobacco; one liter of alcohol restricted to checked luggage for personal use only (you must be 21 years of age to bring in alcohol); and US$100 worth of duty-free gifts that can include an additional quantity of 100 cigars (except Cuban). As of August 2006, the maximum amount of liquid permitted in carry-on luggage is 3 oz. All containers with liquids must be enclosed in a 1-quart plastic bag. You may bring in any amount of currency, but must fill out a form if you bring in over US$10,000. Carry any 90-day supply of prescription drugs in clearly marked containers. (You may have to produce a written prescription or doctor's statement for the custom's officer.) Meat or meat products, seeds, plants, fruits, and narcotics are not allowed to be brought into the United States. Contact the **United States Customs and Border Protection** for further information. ~ 1300 Pennsylvania Avenue NW, Washington, DC 20229; 202-354-1000; www.cbp.gov.

Driving   If you plan to rent a car, an international driver's license should be obtained before arriving in the United States. Some car rental agencies require both a foreign license and an international driver's license. Many also require a lessee to be at least 25 years of age; all require a major credit card. Seat belts are mandatory for the driver and all passengers. Children under the age of 6 or under 60 pounds should be in the back seat in approved child-safety restraints.

Currency   United States money is based on the dollar. Bills generally come in denominations of $1, $2, $5, $10, $20, $50, and $100. Every dollar is divided into 100 cents. Coins are the penny (1 cent), nickel (5 cents), dime (10 cents), and quarter (25 cents). Half-dollar, dollar coins, and $2 bills are rarely used. You may not use foreign currency to purchase goods and services in the United States. Consider buying traveler's checks in dollar amounts. You may also use credit cards affiliated with an American company such as Interbank, Barclay Card, VISA, and American Express.

Electricity and Electronics   Electric outlets use currents of 110 volts, 60 cycles. To operate appliances made for other electrical systems, you need a transformer or other adapter. Travelers who use laptop computers for telecommunication should be aware that modem configurations for U.S. telephone systems may be different from their European counterparts. Similarly, the U.S. format for videotapes is different from that in Europe; National Park Service visitors centers and other stores that sell souvenir videos often have them available in European format on request.

Weights and Measures   The United States uses the English system of weights and measures. American units and their metric equivalents are: 1 inch = 2.5 centimeters; 1 foot (12 inches) = 0.3 meter; 1 yard (3 feet) = 0.9 meter; 1 mile (5280 feet) = 1.6 kilometers; 1 ounce = 28 grams; 1 pound (16 ounces) = 0.45 kilogram; 1 quart (liquid) = 0.9 liter.

▼ ▼ ▼ ▼ ▼ ▼ ▼ ▼ ▼ ▼ ▼ ▼ ▼

Outdoor Adventures

CAMPING

The state oversees 277 camping facilities. Amenities at each campground vary. There is a day-use fee of $4 to $14 per vehicle. Campsites range from about $11 up to $25 (a little less in off season). For a complete listing of all state-run campgrounds, send for *California Escapes* published by the **California Department of Parks and Recreation**. ~ P.O. Box 942896, Sacramento, CA 94296; 916-653-6995, 800-777-0369; www.parks.ca.gov. Reservations for campgrounds can be made by calling 800-444-7275.

For general information on National Park campgrounds, contact the **National Park Service**. ~ Golden Gate National Parks, Fort Mason, Building 201, San Francisco, CA 94123; 415-561-4700; www.nps.gov/goga. To reserve a National Park campsite call the park directly or call 800-365-2267.

In addition to state and national campgrounds, the California Coast offers numerous municipal, county, and private facilities. See the "Beaches & Parks" sections in each chapter for the locations of these campgrounds.

PERMITS   **Wilderness Permits**   For camping and hiking in the wilderness and primitive areas of national forests, a wilderness permit is required. Permits are largely free and are issued for a specific period of time, which varies according to the wilderness area. You can obtain permits from ranger stations and regional information centers, as described in the "Beaches & Parks" sections in each chapter. Information is available through the **U.S. Forest Service**. ~ 1323 Club Drive, Vallejo, CA 94592; 707-562-8737, fax 707-562-9130; www.fs.fed.us/r5.

Fishing Licenses   For current information on the fishing season and state license fees, contact the **California Department of Fish and Game**. ~ 1416 9th Street, Sacramento, CA 95814; 916-445-0411; www.dfg.ca.gov.

TWO

San Francisco

 It is a city poised at the end of the continent, civilization's last fling before the land plunges into the Pacific. Perhaps this is why visitors demand something memorable from San Francisco. People expect the city to resonate along a personal wavelength, speak to them, fulfill some ineffable desire at the center of the soul.

There is a terrible beauty at the edge of America: the dream begins here, or ends. The Golden Gate Bridge, that arching portal to infinite horizons, is also a suicide gangplank for hundreds of ill-starred dreamers. Throughout American history, those who crossed the country in search of destiny ultimately found it here or turned back to the continent and their own past.

Yet San Francisco is only a city, a steel-and-glass metropolis mounted on a series of hills. With a population of about 799,000, it covers 47 square miles at the tip of a peninsula bounded by the Pacific Ocean and San Francisco Bay. A gateway to Asia, San Francisco supports a multicultural population with large and growing concentrations of Chinese, Latinos, African Americans, Italians, Filipinos, Japanese, and Southeast Asians.

The myth of San Francisco originates not only from its geography, but also from its history. If, as early Christians believed, the world was created in 4004 B.C., then the history of San Francisco began on January 28, 1848. That day a hired hand named James Marshall discovered gold in California. Year One is 1849, a time etched in the psyche of an entire nation. The people swept along by the mania of that momentous time have been known forever since as "'49ers." They crossed the Rockies in covered wagons, trekked the jungles of Panama, and challenged the treacherous seas around Cape Horn, all because of a shiny yellow metal.

Gold in California was the quintessence of the American Dream. For anyone with courage and ambition, it represented a chance to blaze trails, expand a young nation, and become rich in the flash of a fortuitous find.

During the Gold Rush, a Barbary Coast ghetto grew along the Bay. Over 500 businesses sold liquor; gambling, drugs, and prostitution were rampant; gangs roamed the boomtown and iron-fisted vigilance committees enforced law and order. Sailors were shanghaied and failed prospectors committed suicide at the rate of 1000 per year.

Amid all the chaos, San Francisco grew into an international city. Ambitious Americans, displaced Mexicans, indentured Chinese, itinerant Australians, and Chilean immigrants crowded its muddy streets. The populace soon boasted over a dozen newspapers, published in a variety of languages. Because of its multicultural population, and in spite of periodic racial problems, San Francisco developed a strong liberal tradition, an openness to the unusual and unexpected, which prevails today.

Allen Ginsberg, Jack Kerouac, Gary Snyder, and other Beat poets began haunting places like Caffe Trieste and the Co-Existence Bagel Shop in the 1950s.

Of course, San Francisco's most famous encounter with the unexpected came on April 18, 1906. Dream turned to nightmare at 5:12 that morning as a horrendous earthquake, 8.3 on the Richter scale, rocked and buckled the land. Actually, the infamous San Francisco earthquake owed its destructive ferocity more to the subsequent fires than the seismic disturbance. One of the few people killed by the earthquake itself was the city's fire chief. Gas mains across the city broke and water pipes lay shattered. Within hours, 50 separate fires ignited, merged, and by nightfall created firestorms that tore across the city. Three-quarters of San Francisco's houses were destroyed in the three-day holocaust, 452 people died, and 250,000 were left homeless.

The city whose municipal symbol is a phoenix rising from the ashes quickly rebuilt. City Hall and the Civic Center became part of a resurrected San Francisco. The Golden Gate and Bay bridges were completed in the 1930s, and during World War II the port became a major embarkation point for men and materiel. A city of international importance, San Francisco was the site for the signing of the United Nations charter in June 1945.

It entered the post–World War II era at the vanguard of American society. San Francisco's hallmark is cultural innovation. This city at the continent's edge boasts a society at the edge of thought. During the 1950s it became the Beat capital of the world. The Beats blew cool jazz, intoned free form poems, and extolled the virtues of nothingness.

Not even Kerouac was prepared for San Francisco's next wave of cultural immigrants. This mecca for the misplaced became a mystical gathering place for myriads of hippies. The Haight-Ashbury neighborhood was the staging area for a movement intent on revolutionizing American consciousness.

By the 1970s San Francisco was becoming home to a vital and creative minority, gay men and women. The city's gay population had increased steadily for decades; then, suddenly, San Francisco's open society and freewheeling lifestyle brought an amazing influx of gays. In 1977, Supervisor Harvey Milk became the nation's first outfront gay to be elected to a major municipal post. That same year the city passed a landmark gay rights ordinance. With an advancing population that today numbers perhaps 200,000, gays became a powerful social and political force.

Throughout the 1980s, '90s, and into the 21st century, San Francisco has retained a gay supervisor whose constituency remains an integral part of the city's life. A multi-cultural society from its early days, San Francisco remains a city at the edge, open to experiment and experience. The national media still portray the region as a kind of open ward, home to flakes and weirdos. They point to events like the mayoral election in which a character named Jello Biafra, then a singer for a punk band called the Dead Kennedys, polled over three percent of the vote.

The city does sometimes seem to contain as many cults as people, but it also boasts more than its share of artists and activists. The national ecology movement, which began in this area with the pioneering work of John Muir, also flourishes here. This is headquarters for dozens of concerned organizations.

There are some problems: during the last few decades, San Francisco's skyline has been Manhattanized, crowded with clusters of dark skyscrapers. The AIDS epidemic has taken a terrible toll, particularly among the area's gay population. And the city has allowed its port to decline. Most cargo ships travel across the Bay to Oakland, while San Francisco's once great waterfront is being converted into gourmet restaurants and chic shopping malls. It is a city in love with itself, trading the mundane business of shipping for the glamorous, profitable tourist industry.

In October 1989, television viewers across America who had tuned in for the third game of the World Series between the San Francisco Giants and neighboring Oakland Athletics in Candlestick Park witnessed a 7.1-level earthquake that rocked the stadium and rolled through Northern California, leaving 67 dead and causing more than $10 billion in damage. As with previous disasters, however, San Francisco quickly rose from the rubble to achieve a new level of prosperity. The rebuilding process provided ideal investment opportunities for the new money flooding the Bay Area thanks to booming high-tech companies in nearby Silicon Valley. Condemned warehouses were bulldozed to make way for luxury condominium and office complexes. Artsy, affordably run-down districts were transformed almost overnight into yuppie enclaves of richly renovated Victorian mansions, their former carriage houses converted to garage space for Lexuses and BMWs. Ultimately, Candlestick Park itself was abandoned by the Giants in favor of a new, state-of-the-art ballpark in another part of the city. But by the turn of the 20th century, the dot-com crash hit hard, knelling a death blow for much of SF's computer industry. Technology continues to be an important sector, though it has lost its explosive and vibrant nature.

Perhaps Rudyard Kipling was right. He once called the place "a mad city—inhabited for the most part by perfectly insane people." William Saroyan saw it as "a city that invites the heart to come to life . . . an experiment in living." The two thoughts do not contradict: San Francisco is madly beautiful, a marvelous and zany place. Its contribution to the world is its lifestyle.

The people who gravitate here become models—some exemplary, others tragic—for their entire generation. Every decade San Francisco moves further out along the edge, maintaining a tradition for the avant-garde and iconoclastic that dates back to the Gold Rush days. The city is a jigsaw puzzle that will never be completed. Its residents, and those who come to love the place, are parts from that puzzle, pieces that never quite fit, but rather stand out, unique edges exposed, from all the rest.

Text continued on page 38.

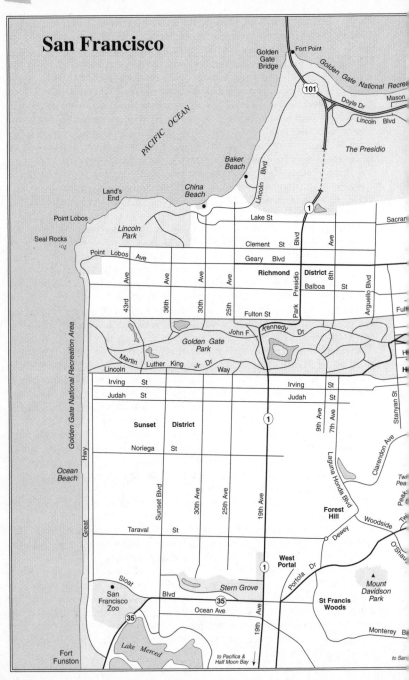

San Francisco

PACIFIC OCEAN

Golden Gate Bridge

Fort Point

Golden Gate National Recre...

101

Doyle Dr

Mason

Lincoln Blvd

The Presidio

Baker Beach

Lincoln Blvd

China Beach

Land's End

Lake St

Sacram...

Point Lobos

Lincoln Park

Seal Rocks

Clement St

Blvd

Ave

Point Lobos Ave

Geary Blvd

Richmond District 8th

Presidio

Arguello Blvd

Ful...

Ave

Ave

Ave

Ave

Balboa St

43rd

36th

30th

25th

Fulton St

John F Kennedy Dr

Golden Gate Park

Martin Luther King Jr Dr

Lincoln Way

Irving St

Irving St

Judah St

Judah St

Stanyan St

Sunset District

9th Ave

7th Ave

Clarendon Ave

Noriega St

Laguna Honda Blvd

Twi...
Pea...

Hwy

Ocean Beach

Sunset Blvd

30th Ave

25th Ave

19th Ave

Forest Hill

Peak...

Woodside

Tw...

Great

Taraval St

Dewey

O'Shau...

West Portal

Portola Dr

Mount Davidson Park

Sloat

Stern Grove

Fort Funston

San Francisco Zoo

Blvd

35

St Francis Woods

Ocean Ave

19th Ave

Monterey B...

35

Lake Merced

to Pacifica &
Half Moon Bay

to San...

Golden Gate National Recreation Area

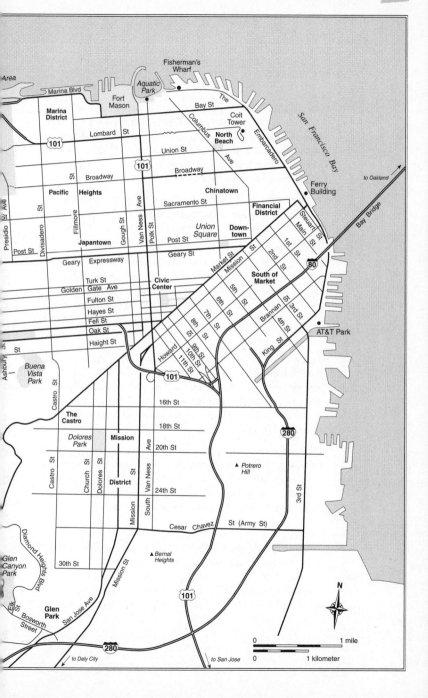

Three-day Weekend

San Francisco

Day 1
- Starting at the **San Francisco Visitor Information Center**, find your way to some of the city's most unique areas—**Chinatown, North Beach** and **Fisherman's Wharf**. You can see all these and more along the **Barbary Coast Trail** (pages 52–53), or, if urban hiking isn't your idea of a good time, you can reach all three areas on the Powell-Mason **cable car**.

- In these areas of the city, you're never far from a great place for lunch. Try a dim sum restaurant in Chinatown, an Italian café in North Beach, or a sidewalk seafood cocktail stand on Fisherman's Wharf.

- Evening is the time to discover why San Francisco enjoys a reputation for the best restaurants and live theater on the West Coast. Out-of-towners—to find out about upcoming stage productions ahead of time and get phone numbers for reservations, check www.sfweekly.com or the "pink section" at www.sfgate.com/chronicle.

Day 2
- Pack a picnic lunch and head for **Golden Gate Park** (page 96). With three world-class museums plus a thousand acres of formal gardens, meadows, lakes, forests, and spectacular vistas, it's easy to while away a whole day here. Weather permitting, the best way to tour the park is on a bicycle; rentals are available at shops near the east end of the park.

- Dine out at another tempting restaurant this evening. Afterwards, there are limitless possibilities for evening entertainment. Feeling adventuresome? For a look at another element that makes San Francisco unique, check out the gay and lesbian nightclub scene. Straight people are welcome in most places.

Day 3
- This could be the perfect day for a spending spree. You might start at Union Square, surrounded by department stores and art galleries, and then move on to more esoteric districts like North Beach, Japantown, and the Haight, or to such exclusive—and expensive—shopping enclaves as Union Street and Upper Fillmore.

- If shop-'til-you-drop isn't your idea of fun, consider a boat trip from Fisherman's Wharf. It could be a harbor tour, a visit to Alcatraz, or an excursion to Angel Island.

- Round out your San Francisco culinary experience with a climactic splurge at one of the city's top restaurants, such as **Boulevard** (page 60), the **Empress of China** (page 66), or **Restaurant Gary Danko** (page 80).

- Leave your heart in San Francisco and come back soon.

IF YOU ONLY HAVE ONE DAY

If you have only one day free for San Francisco sightseeing, hit the highlights using the Day 1 itinerary above.

Downtown

Visit any city in the world and the sightseeing tour will begin in a vital but nebulous area called "Downtown." San Francisco is no different. Here, Downtown is spelled Union Square (Geary and Stockton streets), a tree-dotted plot in the heart of the city's hotel and shopping district. Lofty buildings bordering the area house major department stores while the network of surrounding streets features many of the city's poshest shops and plushest hotels.

SIGHTS

Union Square's most intriguing role is as San Francisco's free-form entertainment center. On any day you may see a brass band high-stepping through, a school choir singing the world's praises, or a gathering of motley but talented musicians or mimes passing the hat for bus fare home.

Cable cars from the nearby turnaround station at Powell and Market streets clang past en route to Nob Hill and Fisherman's Wharf. So pull up a patch of lawn and watch the world work through its paces, or just browse the Square's hedgerows and flower gardens.

While you're here, you'd be wise to stop by the **San Francisco Visitor Information Center** for some handy brochures. Closed Sunday November through April. ~ Hallidie Plaza, Lower Level, Powell and Market streets; 415-391-2000; www.onlyinsanfrancisco.com.

At street level you'll see the **Flood Building**, which overlooks the Powell Street BART station and houses The Gap. This was the only downtown building besides the U.S. Mint to survive the 1906 earthquake intact.

Then you can head off toward the city's high voltage Financial District. Appropriately enough, the route to this pinstriped realm leads down **Maiden Lane**, headiest of the city's high-heeled shopping areas. Back in Barbary Coast days, when San Francisco was a dirty word, this two-block-long alley-way was wall-to-wall with bawdy houses. But today it's been transformed from redlight district to ultra-chic mall. Of particular interest among the galleries and boutiques lining this pedestrian-only thoroughfare is the building at **140 Maiden Lane**. Designed by Frank Lloyd Wright in 1948, its circular interior stairway and other unique elements foreshadow the motifs he later used for the famous Guggenheim Museum.

LODGING

BUDGET LODGING The cheapest accommodations in town are found in the city's Tenderloin district. Situated between Union Square and the Civic Center, this area is an easy walk from restaurants and points of cultural interest. The Tenderloin is a sometimes dangerous, sleazy neighborhood filled with interesting if menacing characters, the kind of place you stay because of the low rents rather than the inherent charm. Still, if the spirit is willing, the

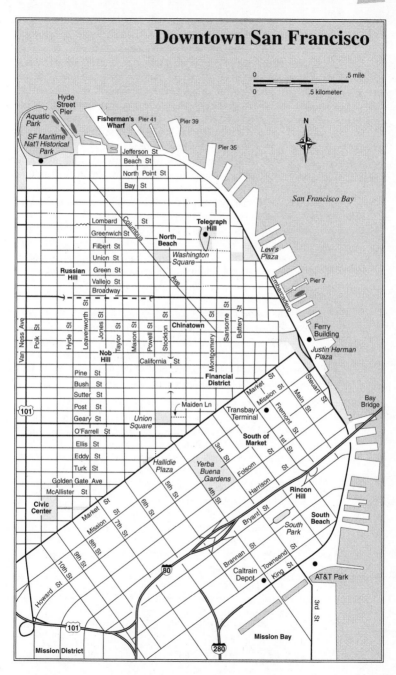

Downtown San Francisco

0 .... .5 mile
0 .... .5 kilometer

N

Hyde Street Pier

Aquatic Park

SF Maritime Nat'l Historical Park

Fisherman's Wharf   Pier 41   Pier 39

Pier 35

Jefferson St

Beach St

North Point St

Bay St

San Francisco Bay

Lombard St

Greenwich St

Columbus

Filbert St

Union St

North Beach

Telegraph Hill

Washington Square

Levi's Plaza

Russian Hill

Green St

Vallejo St

Broadway

Ave

Pier 7

Embarcadero

St

Hyde St

Leavenworth St

Jones St

Taylor St

Mason St

Powell St

Stockton St

Montgomery St

Sansome St

Battery St

Chinatown

Van Ness Ave

Polk St

Nob Hill

California St

Ferry Building

Justin Herman Plaza

Pine St

Bush St

Sutter St

Post St

Maiden Ln

Geary St

Union Square

O'Farrell St

Ellis St

Eddy St

Turk St

Golden Gate Ave

McAllister St

101

Financial District

Market St

Mission St

Steuart St

Main St

Fremont St

1st St

Transbay Terminal

South of Market

Bay Bridge

Hallidie Plaza

Yerba Buena Gardens

3rd St

4th St

Folsom St

Harrison St

Rincon Hill

South Beach

Civic Center

Market St

Mission St

5th St

6th St

7th St

8th St

9th St

10th St

Howard St

Bryant St

South Park

Brannan St

Townsend St

Caltrain Depot

King St

AT&T Park

80

3rd St

101

Mission District

280

Mission Bay

purse will certainly be appreciative. Just don't flaunt the purse—
or camera, for that matter.

Hostelling International—Downtown is *the* place if you are
looking for budget accommodations in the heart of the city. There
are 32 private rooms as well as shared rooms with four bunks per
room; a kitchen is available for guests to use.
Internet access is also available. Continental breakfast included. ~ 312 Mason Street; 415-788-5604,
fax 415-788-3023; www.norcalhostels.org, e-mail
downtown@sfhostels.org.

Union Square is a scene—
where the rich and power-
ful come to view the
merely talented, where
panhandlers sometimes
seem as plentiful as
pigeons.

For native funk at rock bottom rates consider the
Adelaide Inn. Billed as "Old-World charm less than
two blocks from Union Square," it is an 18-room, family-operated establishment. There is a small lobby plus a
coffee room and kitchen for the guests. The room prices,
with continental breakfast included, are friendly to the pocketbook. Rooms are small, tidy, and plainly furnished; each is
equipped with a sink and television; bathrooms are shared. Most
important, the inn is located in a prime downtown location, not
in the Tenderloin. ~ 5 Isadora Duncan Place; 415-441-2261, fax
415-359-1940.

The **Grant Hotel** is basic and clean. The furniture is in good
condition and the hotel is well maintained, and a friendly, helpful staff makes this 76-room hotel a pleasant place to stay. Every
room has a color TV; continental breakfast is included. ~ 753
Bush Street; 415-421-7540, 800-522-0979, fax 800-686-8063;
www.granthotel.net, e-mail contact@granthotel.net.

MODERATE LODGING   In my opinion the best hotel buys in San
Francisco are the middle-range accommodations. These usually
offer good location, comfortable surroundings, and reasonable
service at a cost that does not leave your pocketbook empty.
Happily, the city possesses a substantial number of these facilities, the best of which are listed below.

Vantaggio Suites Cosmo is another European-style hotel. The
lobby here is a fresh, bright place hung with crystal and dotted
about with potted plants. Upstairs the private rooms are brilliantly coordinated and possess an air of artistry with their
gallery prints, floral drapes, and wicker furniture. ~ 761 Post
Street; 415-614-2400, fax 415-614-2500; www.vantaggiosuites.
com, e-mail vantaggio@covad.net.

European elegance at reasonable cost: that's what the **Hotel
Beresford** has offered its clientele for years. You'll sense a touch
of class immediately upon entering the richly decorated lobby.
There's a historical flair about the place, highlighted by the ad-
joining White Horse Tavern and Restaurant, with its Olde
England ambience. Upstairs the individually wall-papered rooms

are outstanding—wooden headboards, comfortable furnishings, small refrigerators, and a marble-top vanity in the bathroom. Complimentary continental buffet. All this, just two blocks from Union Square. If you can beat it, let me know how. ~ 635 Sutter Street; 415-673-9900, 800-533-6533, fax 415-474-1317; www.beresford.com, e-mail info@beresford.com.

The brilliant polished wood facade of the **Savoy Hotel** provides only a hint of its luxurious interior. The lobby is the first word in elegance with black and white marble floors, brass fixtures, and dark woods. The rooms at this lavish but affordable hotel second the invitation of the lobby. Sporting a French-country motif, they blend floral prints with attractive wood furniture. An afternoon wine-and-cheese reception is included. Add a tile bath-shower, goosedown featherbeds, plus wi-fi access, and you have one very noteworthy hotel. ~ 580 Geary Street; 415-441-2700, 800-227-4223, fax 415-441-0124; www.thesavoyhotel.com, e-mail sanfrancisco@hotelca.com.

The Touchstone Hotel sits smack-dab in the center of the theater district, but even more important, it is located over David's Delicatessen, one of the best delis in town. The lobby is nearly non-existent, but the rooms are attractively done in modern deco style, with warm woods and white duvets. This hotel is immaculately clean, and anyone would be hard-pressed to find a speck of dust anywhere. The rate includes a complimentary breakfast and discounts for the deli. This place is a true original. ~ 480 Geary Street; 415-771-1600, 800-620-5889, fax 415-931-5442; www.thetouchstone.com, e-mail johnsen2004@yahoo.com.

DELUXE LODGING   If your wallet is willing, the city's deluxe-priced hotels are waiting. Among them are several that I suggest you consider.

The **Beresford Arms** is a sister hotel to the Beresford in more than name. Featuring a similar antique lobby, the Beresford Arms has gracefully decorated its public area with a crystal chandelier, leather-tooled tables, stuffed armchairs, and an old grandfather clock. Casting that same European aura, rooms often feature mahogany dressers and headboards as well as the expected amenities like wall-to-wall carpeting, tile tubs, and spacious closets and VCRs with movie rentals at the desk. All at the same prices as the Beresford. The Arms has suites with whirlpools, kitchenettes, and wet bars. ~ 701 Post Street; 415-673-2600, 800-533-6533, fax 415-929-1535; www.beresford.com, e-mail info@beresford.com.

The upscale **Nob Hill Hotel** boasts rooms and suites decorated in Victorian style, appointed with antiques and marble bathrooms. In addition, suites are equipped with wet bars and hot tubs. There's a complimentary wine tasting every evening. Continental breakfast included. ~ 835 Hyde Street; 415-885-2987, 877-662-4455,

fax 415-921-1648; www.nobhillhotel.com, e-mail nobhill@nob
hillhotel.com.

The **Carlton Hotel** features a rich lobby with marble floors,
brass wall sconces, and a fireplace. The rooms have been decorated with pieces from around the world and are reasonably
priced. A morning town car takes guests to downtown shopping.
Though located about five blocks from Union Square, the
Carlton is highly recommended and is a certified green business.
~ 1075 Sutter Street; 415-673-0242, 800-922-7586, fax 415-
673-4904; www.hotelcarltonsf.com, e-mail carltonres@jdvhospi
tality.com.

From its marble and glass exterior to its 111 rooms with
cobalt carpet and steel headboards, **Hotel Diva** is glossy, clean,
high-tech, and hip. It's also comfortable, with luxury linens, wi-
fi access, CD players, a Starbucks next door, and a consistently
warm and helpful staff. There are even two sweetly chic suites
for children and a collection of mini offices for guest use. ~ 440
Geary Street; 415-885-0200, 800-553-1900, fax 415-346-6613;
www.hoteldiva.com, e-mail reservations@personalityhotels.com.

Another upscale establishment is the **Hotel Union Square**.
Built early in the 20th century to accommodate visitors to the
Panama–Pacific International Exposition, this 131-plus room
hotel has been exquisitely decorated. Mystery writer Dashiell
Hammett and playwright Lillian Hellman, who reportedly once
frequented the place, might recognize it even today. The lobby is
done in 1930s art deco style. The old speakeasy is reputed to
have included a secret "chute entrance" from Ellis Street. Walls
upstairs have been sandblasted to expose original brick and the
rooms are decorated in rich colors with cherrywood furniture. ~
114 Powell Street; 415-397-3000, 800-553-1900, fax 415-885-
3268; www.hotelunionsquare.com, e-mail reservations@person
alityhotels.com.

ULTRA-DELUXE LODGING   In lower Pacific Heights, a mile or
two from the Downtown district, stands **The Majestic**. As a hotel
this five-story structure dates from 1902 when The Majestic opened
as one of the city's first grand hotels. It underwent several incarnations before finally being reincarnated as The Majestic. The
current 58-room establishment features a bar and attractive lobby.
Some rooms are strikingly appointed with canopied beds, European antiques, and marble bathrooms. Rates start in the deluxe
range. ~ 1500 Sutter Street; 415-441-1100, 800-869-8966, fax
415-673-7331; www.thehotelmajestic.com, e-mail info@thehotel
majestic.com.

Elegance *and* style? That would be the **White Swan Inn**. A six-
story, English-style building with curved bay windows, the White

Swan was originally built in 1908 as a small hotel. Today it is a fashionable bed and breakfast with a living room, library, solarium, and small courtyard. The decorative theme, reflected in the garden, wallpapers, and art prints, is English. Each room contains a fireplace, television, telephone with voicemail, wet bar, coffeemaker, and private bath. Like the public rooms, they are all beautifully appointed. ~ 845 Bush Street; 415-775-1755, 800-999-9570, fax 415-775-5717; www.whiteswaninnsf.com, e-mail white swan@jdvhospitality.com.

The **Hotel Rex** is one of those quirky kinds of places that sets itself apart from more ordinary hostelries. The lobby looks like a library, where you long to spend the evening curled up in front of the fireplace, with a glass of sherry and an antique book chosen from the hundreds on shelves around the room. The rooms have a modern edge with a Provençal color-scheme and artwork from local artisans on the walls. ~ 562 Sutter Street; 415-433-4434, 800-433-4434, fax 415-433-3695; www.thehotelrex.com, e-mail jlim@jdvhospitality.com.

Opened in 2000, the **Orchard Hotel** exhibits the polished graces of a much-older hostelry: vaulted ceilings, marble baths, arched entryways, muted colors. But the amenities included in all of the 104 rooms and suites immediately reveal its true age: DVD and CD players, cordless phones, and internet connection in addition to minibars, safes, hairdryers, robes, and coffeemakers. You'll also find a restaurant, a bar, and an exercise room on-site. ~ 665 Bush Street; 415-362-8878, 888-717-2881, fax 415-362-8088; www.theorchardhotel.com.

Close to Union Square and the Chinatown gates, the **Hotel des Arts** is both installation art gallery and hotel. Hundreds of ever-changing paintings are hung throughout the space. Many of the 51 tiny rooms have been decorated by emerging international artists such as L.A. graffiti muralist Buff Monster, whose giant

NOTHING STAID IN THIS HOTEL

From the wild and crazy lobby with its dervish chairs to the sapphire theater curtains in all 140 rooms, the **Hotel Triton** is a place with a sense of humor. If you are seeking a hotel with a fantasy mural, furniture that appears to undulate, iridescent throw pillows, starburst light fixtures, and room service from several trendy restaurants, look no further. Several of its suites were designed by celebrities (think Carlos Santana and Jerry Garcia). An added plus is its proximity to Chinatown. ~ 342 Grant Avenue; 415-394-0500, 800-800-1299, fax 415-394-0555; www.hoteltriton.com.

pink toe graphic adds whimsy and makes up for the lack of furniture. Standard rooms have shared baths and all have refrigerators, microwaves, and wi-fi access. A complimentary continental breakfast is served. ~ 447 Bush Street; 415-956- 3232, 800-956-4322, fax 415-956-0399; www.sfhoteldesarts.com, e-mail reservations@sfhoteldesarts.com.

Once inside the 21-story **JW Marriott San Francisco**, some guests simply cannot believe there are 337 rooms and suites here; the ambience is more like that of an intimate small hotel. Guest rooms have fine furnishings, custom cabinetry, and distinctive arched windows. Despite their size, they feel cozy, almost too much so. Oversized marble baths and attentive valet service are extra indulgences at this ultra-deluxe-priced hotel one block west of Union Square. ~ 500 Post Street; 415-771-8600, 800-228-9290, fax 415-398-0267; www.marriott.com.

Accommodations at the 25-story **Hotel Nikko** exude *shibui*, a Japanese word that expresses elegant simplicity. Smooth-edged contemporary furnishings and natural colors. Rates include access to business services and fitness facilities, including a glass-enclosed rooftop swimming pool. ~ 222 Mason Street; 415-394-1111, 800-248-3308, fax 415-394-1106; www.hotelnikko sf.com, e-mail reservations@hotelnikkosf.com.

DINING   Whether they are hungry or not, Dashiell Hammett fans always track down **John's Grill**. It's the restaurant that detective Sam Spade popped into during a tense scene in *The Maltese Falcon*. Today the wood-paneled walls, adorned with memorabilia and old photos, still breathe of bygone eras. Waiters dress formally, the bartender gossips about local politicians, and the customers

AUTHOR FAVORITE

When a travel writer is reduced to writing about a hotel's hallways, the establishment is either problematic or exceptional. Corridors at **The Inn at Union Square** are fashionably done along their entire length with mirrors and brass wall sconces, and most rooms leading off the halls are equipped with a brass lion-head door knocker. All that brass is a polisher's nightmare, but adds immeasurably to the charm of this pocket hotel. The entire inn numbers only 30 rooms, so intimacy is a primary consideration here. There is a small lobby with a fireplace on most floors where wine and evening hors d'oeuvres are served. Rooms are plush and cozy with quilted bedspreads, wooden headboards, and antique Georgian furnishings. In sum, a marvelous establishment, one of the city's finest small hotels. ~ 440 Post Street; 415-397-3510, 800-288-4346, fax 415-989-0529; www.unionsquare.com, e-mail inn@unionsquare.com. ULTRA-DELUXE.

sink onto bar stools. The menu features broiler and seafood dishes as well as a nostalgic platter of chops, baked potato, and sliced tomato (what Spade wolfed down on that fateful day). Live jazz nightly. No lunch on Sunday. ~ 63 Ellis Street; 415-986-3274, fax 415-982-2583; www.johnsgrill.com. MODERATE TO DELUXE.

Sushi Man is a matchbox sushi bar with matchless style. If that's not evident from the plastic sushi displays in the window, then step inside. The tiny wooden bar is decorated with serene silk screens and fresh flowers. Owner Ryo Yoshioka has earned a deserved reputation for his sushi creations. There's *sake* (smoked salmon) and *mirugai* (clam), as well as sashimi. Dinner only. ~ 731 Bush Street; 415-981-1313, fax 415-668-3214. MODERATE.

Maiden Lane used to be a perfect spot for slumming; today it's a fashionable shopping district. But there's one place along the high-priced strip that brings back the easy days. **Bistro 69** is an unassuming restaurant/café serving an array of sandwiches, salads, homemade pastas, Mediterranean dishes, and mouth-watering pastries. Dine alfresco or pull up a chair inside this recently remodeled brick-walled establishment. Local newspapers routinely give this joint high marks. At lunch there will likely be a line out the door. Also open for breakfast. Closed Sunday September through November and January through May. ~ 69 Maiden Lane; 415-398-3557, fax 415-981-3735. BUDGET.

It is the rare restaurateur who can please both Los Angeles and San Francisco, but that's exactly what Wolfgang Puck has done in bringing his talents north to **Postrio**. Puck's innovative food pairings, such as grilled quail with spinach and soft ravioli and seared ahi with Indian coconut curry, compete for attention with a stunning dining room and impressive art collection. Reserve far in advance. Breakfast also served. ~ 545 Post Street; 415-776-7825, fax 415-776-6702; www.postrio.com, e-mail mail@postrio.com. DELUXE TO ULTRA-DELUXE.

After dining at **Tempura House**, you'll understand why the Financial District crowd goes out of its way to eat there. What's delivered to your table looks exactly like the plastic meals displayed in the front window, and everything's delicious. Tempura is the specialty of the house, but the grilled fish, sukiyaki, and sushi also rate highly. ~ 529 Powell Street; 415-393-9911. MODERATE.

Cortez is like a skewed Mondrian painting brought to life. Oversized mobiles fashioned from hanging globe lamps, illuminated panels, and occasional primary color splashes provide edgy contrast to the earthy, Mediterranean-inspired menu. These small plates are best shared with friends. Favorites include the New Zealand lamb and asparagus with lemon bernaise and cripsy sunchokes. The desserts are sinful. Dinner only. ~ 550 Geary Street; 415-292-6360, fax 415-673-7080; www.cortezrestaurant.com, e-mail info@cortezrestaurant.com. DELUXE.

Indonesia Restaurant has developed a loyal following among the many San Franciscans who have lived or traveled in Indonesia. And for good reason. The complex and diverse flavors in this tiny, crowded hole-in-the-wall establishment tantalize the taste buds. Such favorite dishes as *gado-gado*, *soto ayam*, beef curry, *mie goreng*, *rendang*, and *sate* are included on the menu, as well as many others. ~ 678 Post Street; 415-474-4026, fax 415-858-8095. BUDGET.

Gatsby would feel right at home in **Bix**, a glamorous, '30s-style supper club with live jazz at night, white-jacketed bartenders, classic martinis, and a stunning mahogany bar. Lunch and dinner items change daily. Fresh seasonal entrées might include grilled rack of lamb with spring vegetable couscous, truffled pecorino cheeseburger, or American Kobe steak. ~ 56 Gold Street; 415-433- 6300, fax 415-433-4574; www.bixrestaurant. com, e-mail info@bixrestaurant.com. ULTRA-DELUXE.

Another small and romantic dining room, **Masa's** is one of my favorite San Francisco restaurants. Elite yet understated, the decor is a mix of dark woods, softly colored upholstered chairs, and floral arrangements. Changing daily, the contemporary French menu might include filet mignon with foie gras mousse and black truffles, roasted squab with wild rice risotto, or sautéed medallions of fallow deer with caramelized apples and zinfandel sauce. Dinner only. Jackets required. Reservations highly recommended. Closed Sunday and Monday. ~ 648 Bush Street; 415-989-7154, fax 415-989-3141; www.masasrestaurant.com, e-mail info@masasrestaurant.com. ULTRA-DELUXE.

Craving authentic Italian pizza, but don't want to trek out to North Beach? Hit up **Uncle Vito's**. It's casual, homestyle Italy

DEEP-SEA DINING

In addition to being a dining extravaganza, **Farallon** is a total immersion experience. Step into this uniquely designed restaurant and it's like plunging beneath the waves; every aspect of the decor reflects an aquatic motif. Light fixtures resembling jellyfish hang suspended two stories overhead, handrails look like tendriling kelp, and bar stools stand on octopus tentacles. The Gothic arches in the dining room (called, naturally, the "Pool Room") sport mermaid mosaics and sea urchin light fixtures. After easing into a booth, you can order from a menu laden with seafood dishes. The menu, which changes every few weeks, might feature Atlantic black bass, poached sea scallops, parchment roasted monkfish, or, for those who don't get the point—grilled filet of beef. No lunch on Sunday and Monday. ~ 450 Post Street; 415-956-6969, fax 415-834-1234; www.farallon restaurant.com, e-mail pdr@farallonrestaurant.com. ULTRA-DELUXE.

with what some San Franciscans claim are the best pies around. Everyone has a favorite, and pasta dishes are available, too. ~ 700 Bush Street; 415-391-5008. BUDGET.

Union Square quite simply is *the* center for shopping in San Francisco. First of all, this grass-and-hedgerow park (located between Post and Geary, Stockton and Powell streets) is surrounded by department stores. **Macy's** is along one border. ~ 170 O'Farrell Street; 415-397-3333. **Saks Fifth Avenue** guards another. ~ 220 Post Street; 415-986-4300. **Neiman-Marcus**, the Texas-bred emporium, claims one corner. ~ 150 Stockton Street; 415-362-3900. Once the haven of European specialty boutiques, Union Square is becoming a hot address among sport-shoes shops, entertainment-company merchandising centers, and mass-appeal clothing stores.

SHOPPING

Of course, that's just on the square. Beyond the plaza are scads of stores, including those along **Maiden Lane**. One notable Maiden Lane shop is **Xanadu Gallery Folk Art International**, offering icons, folk sculptures, baskets, pottery, and other crafts from Africa, Oceania, Latin America, and Asia, as well as antique jewelry from India and gem-quality Baltic amber from Poland and Denmark. Closed Sunday and Monday. ~ FLW building, 140 Maiden Lane; 415-392-9999; www.xanadugallery.us, e-mail info@xanadugallery.us.

Along Stockton, one of the streets radiating out from the square, you'll find a number of prestigious shops.

Then if you follow Post, another bordering street, there's **Crocker Galleria**, a glass-domed promenade lined with fashionable shops. A center for well-heeled business crowds, the mall showcases designer fashions and elegant gifts. Closed Sunday. ~ 50 Post Street; 415-393-1505; www.shopatgalleria.com.

Farther along, you'll find **Gump's**, which features fine jewelry, objets d'art, and imported decorations for the home. If you get bored looking through the antiques, china pieces, and oriental art, you can always adjourn to the Crystal Room. ~ 135 Post Street; 415-982-1616, fax 415-984-9361; www.gumps.com.

While you're in the epicenter of high-end San Francisco shopping, an excellent stop is **H&M**, a hip department store recently upgraded on the fashion totem pole by their line "M by Madonna." Styles are sleek and posh, but prices are surprisingly affordable. ~ 150 Post Street; 415-986-0156; www.hm.com.

For a vicarious "rich and famous" experience, take a stroll through **Giorgio Armani** at Union Square. This boutique is one of only eleven American stores carrying the designer's premier Black Label line. Formalwear and sportswear are elegantly displayed under the tutelage of attentive salespeople, who discreetly disclose the cost of the apparel. Closed Sunday. ~ 278 Post Street; 415-434-2500, fax 415-434-2546; www.giorgioarmani.com.

The streets all around host a further array of stores. You'll encounter jewelers, dress designers, boutiques, furniture stores, tailor shops, and more. So take a gander—there's everything out there from the unexpected to the bizarre.

Braunstein/Quay Gallery is an outstanding place to view the work of local artists. Owner Ruth Braunstein "embodies the brash, irreverent, and irrepressible energy of the San Francisco art world." This contemporary gallery also exhibits works from other parts of the world. Closed Sunday and Monday except by appointment. ~ 430 Clementina Street; 415-278-9850.

San Francisco's answer to Boston's famous Filene's Basement discount apparel chain is **Loehmann's**, a clothing store with low-priced designer clothes. ~ 222 Sutter Street; 415-982-3215.

You've never seen a mall quite like the **Westfield San Francisco Centre.** The 2006 addition of a nearly 400,000-square-foot, multilevel Bloomingdale's, complete with sparkling checkered floors and chandeliers, established the center as an authoritative shopping headquarters. Also added were a movie theater, a gourmet food court with international cuisine and an entire grocery store, and over 100 high-fashion boutiques. The older part of the center is not too shabby either: six stacked spiral escalators ascend through an oval-shaped, marble-and-granite atrium toward the retractable skylight. Tinkling music from a grand piano welcomes patrons to the five-story Nordstrom that tops the west section. ~ Market Street between 4th and 5th streets; 415-512-6776, fax 415-512-6770; www.westfield.com/sanfrancisco.

NIGHTLIFE Since its rowdy Gold Rush days, San Francisco has been renowned as a wide-open town, hard-drinking and easygoing. Today there are over 2000 places around the city to order a drink, including saloons, restaurants, cabarets, boats, private clubs, and even a couple of hospitals. There's a bar for every mood and each occasion.

When looking for nightlife, it is advisable to consult the *SF Bay Guardian*, the *SF Weekly*, *the Onion*, or the "Datebook" (commonly called the "pink section") in the Sunday *San Francisco Chronicle* for current shows and performers. However you decide to spend the evening, you'll find plenty of possibilities in this city by the Bay.

San Francisco's answer to a Scottish pub is **Edinburgh Castle**, a cavernous bar complete with dart board. There are chandeliers hanging from the ceiling, heavy wooden furniture, and convivial crowds—Scotland incarnate. ~ 950 Geary Street; 415-885-4074; www.castlenews.com.

The **Warfield Theatre**, owned by promotion giant Live Nation, brings in top groups from around the country. Live Nation produces other shows regularly throughout the Bay Area. ~ 982 Market Street; 415-775-7722; www.livenation.com.

The lovely **Empire Plush Room** in the York Hotel caters to an upscale clientele and draws big-name cabaret acts. Cover. ~ 940 Sutter Street; 415-885-6800; www.plushroom.com.

Built in 1910, the Beaux Arts–style **Geary Theater** features a sky lobby. This state historic landmark is home of the **American Conservatory Theater,** or ACT, the biggest show in town. It's also one of the nation's largest resident companies. The season runs from September to July, and the repertory is traditional, ranging from Shakespeare to French comedy to 20th-century drama. Closed Monday. ~ Geary Theater, 415 Geary Street; 415-749-2228, fax 415-439-2322; www.act-sf.org.

The "On Broadway" theater scene in San Francisco is on Geary Street, near Union Square; while the "Off Broadway," or avant-garde drama, is scattered around the city.

The **Curran Theatre** brings Broadway musicals to town. ~ 445 Geary Street; 415-551-2000; www.shnsf. com. **Golden Gate Theatre** attracts major shows and national companies. Built in 1922, the theater is a grand affair with marble floors and rococo ceilings. ~ 1 Taylor Street, at the corner of 6th and Market streets; 415-551-2000. Among the city's other playhouses is the **Marines Memorial Theatre.** ~ 609 Sutter Street; 415-771-6900; www.marinesmemorialtheatre.com. Close to the Civic Center is the **Orpheum Theatre.** ~ 1192 Market Street; 415-551-2000.

On the other side of the Downtown district, to the southwest, rises the Civic Center, the architectural pride of the city. The prettiest pathway through this municipal meeting ground begins in United Nations Plaza at Fulton and Market streets.

Civic Center

Every Wednesday and Sunday the **United Nations Plaza** is home to the **Heart of the City Farmers' Market,** an open-air produce fair that draws farmers from all over Northern California. ~ 415-558-9455.

SIGHTS

A notable stop is the city's new eco-friendly energy-efficient **Federal Building,** which stands 18 stories tall. With floor-to-ceiling windows, the spacious structure was designed to allow for natural air and light. The public can get a close-up look at this modern edifice at the 11th floor open-air sky garden, which is dotted with pedestrian bridges and benches. Security checks to enter are rigorous, but worth the hassle. ~ 7th and Mission streets.

To experience one of the country's most modern information centers, saunter on over to the main branch of the **San Francisco Public Library** in its $104.5 million headquarters that opened in 1996. Exemplifying the fact that libraries are not just about books anymore (in fact, critics charge that the architectural splendor and special features have resulted in a lack of shelf space), the main branch's facilities include 512 electronic workstations with free connection to the internet. Among the library's 11 special-interest research centers are the San Francisco History Center, the Gay and Lesbian Center, and the Art, Music and Recreation Center. ~ 100 Larkin Street; 415-557-4400, fax 415-557-4205; www.sfpl.lib.ca.us, e-mail webmail@sfpl.org.

With its bird-whitened statues and gray-columned buildings, the **Civic Center** is the domain of powerbrokers and political leaders; ironically, its grassy plots and park benches also make it the haunt of the city's homeless. Guided tours of the Civic Center begin at the San Francisco Public Library. ~ Tour information, 415-557-4266; www.sfcityguides.org.

As you pass the reflecting pool and formal gardens of **Joseph L. Alioto Performing Art Piazza**, an area often used for outdoor events and named in honor of one of San Francisco's most beloved mayors, you'll see **City Hall**, open after a three-year, $300 million renovation during which it was lifted from its foundation and set on 600 steel-and-rubber base insulators designed to make it earthquake-proof. Its gold-leafed dome is 307 feet tall—the fifth-tallest domed building in the world, 20 feet taller than the U.S. Capitol. It also surpasses other government centers in technology, with interactive touch screens that let supervisors vote, call staff, and retrieve documents during meetings. Free guided tours of City Hall are offered Monday through Friday. ~ 1 Dr. Carlton B. Goodlett Place. ~ 415-554-6023; www.sfgov.org.

Across from City Hall and housed in a historic 1917 Beaux Arts building, the **Asian Art Museum** features major pieces from China, Tibet, Japan, Korea, Iran, Syria, and throughout the continent. This institution is the largest museum in the country devoted exclusively to Asian art. Some of the 14,000-plus pieces date back 6000 years. Admission. ~ 200 Larkin Street; 415-581-3500, fax 415-581-4700; www.asianart.org.

Centerstage of the Civic Center is the **War Memorial Opera House**, home of one of the world's finest opera companies as well as the San Francisco Ballet Company. Considered by such performers as Placido Domingo to be one of the world's finest opera houses and called "the most attractive and practical building of its kind in the U.S." by *Time Magazine*, the grandiose building's interior features lofty romanesque columns, a gold-leafed proscenium and a five-story-high ceiling. Although conceived in 1918 as a tribute to the nation's World War I veterans, the opera house was not completed until 1932. Perhaps its finest moment came in 1945, when the opera house and adjacent Veterans Auditorium (now Herbst Theatre) hosted the signing of the United Nations Charter and the first official sessions of the U.N. ~ 301 Van Ness Avenue at Grove Street.

The two blocks of Polk Street within the Civic Center were renamed Dr. Carlton B. Goodlett Jr. Place in honor of the San Francisco civil rights leader who died in 1997.

To the left, that ultramodern glass-and-granite building is the **Louise M. Davies Symphony Hall**, home of the San Francisco Symphony. Through the semicircle of green-tinted glass, you can peer into one of the city's most glamorous buildings. Or if you'd prefer to be on the inside gazing out, tours of the hall and its cultural cousins next door are given Monday from 10 a.m. to 2 p.m. Admission. ~ Van Ness Avenue and Grove Street; information, 415-552-8338.

One of the best places in town to appreciate the city's rich cultural tradition is the **San Francisco Performing Arts Library and Museum**. The collection covers San Francisco's musical and theatrical heritage with photos, programs, books, and audio and visual recordings. Recent exhibitions include a retrospective on *Madame Butterfly*, a survey of Chinese opera in the U.S., and a centennial tribute to Broadway composer Irving Berlin. Library open Wednesday through Saturday; galleries open Tuesday through Saturday. Researchers should call the librarian in advance. ~ Veterans Building, 401 Van Ness Avenue; 415-255-4800, fax 415-255-1913; www.sfpalm.org, e-mail info@sfpalm.org.

LODGING

A two-story motor court flanking a pool courtyard, spacious rooms and suites with a '50s bungalow theme, a chic southeast Asian restaurant and lounge . . . can this be the heart of San Francisco? It is, and it's the **Phoenix Hotel**, just a long block from Civic Center. Concierge services and a rock-and-roll clientele may make the Phoenix the hippest inn in town. ~ 601 Eddy

◄ HIDDEN

Civic Center

Turk St

101

St

Van Ness Ave

Polk St

Golden Gate Ave

Franklin

Larkin St

Hyde St

Leavenworth St

Jones St

McAllister St

Gough St

Fulton St

Veterans Building

City Hall

Civic Center

Asian Art Museum

United Nations Plaza

Stevenson St

7th St

Federal Bldg

War Memorial Opera House

San Francisco Public Library

N

Louise M. Davies Symphony Hall

Grove St

Hayes St

Market St

8th St

Mission St

Fell St

101

9th St

10th St

0   .25 mile

0   .25 kilometer

Text continued on page 54.

WALKING TOUR

The Barbary Coast Trail

This thoroughly urban "trail" blazed along San Francisco's sidewalks introduces you to some of the city's best-known districts on an easy four-mile trek. Because of stoplights and storefronts, city hiking takes longer than country hiking, so allow four to five hours for the whole route. The Barbary Coast Trail is marked by well-worn circular bronze plaques embedded in the sidewalks, each with one arrow pointing where you're coming from and another pointing the way you want to go.

DOWNTOWN   If you're driving, the nearest lots are between Harrison and Market on 5th Street. Start at the intersection of Powell and Market—location of the cable car turnaround, the Powell Street BART station, and the **San Francisco Visitor Information Center** (page 38). Walk three blocks north on Powell Street to **Union Square** (page 38). Stroll through the square to cross the intersection at the corner of Post and Stockton streets. Half a block south, facing the square, is the entrance to **Maiden Lane** (page 38). Walk a block east through this narrow alley lined with cafés and boutiques to Grant Avenue and turn north (left). Proceed three blocks on Grant to the Chinatown gate.

CHINATOWN   Stroll three blocks along Chinatown's tourist-tacky **Grant Avenue** (page 62), past **St. Mary's Square** and **Old St. Mary's Church**, California's oldest cathedral. Turn west (left), go half a block, and turn north (right) onto **Waverly Place** (page 64) and plunge into the real heart of Chinatown. You can't get lost—directly east is the Transamerica Building, the city's tallest, visible from every streetcorner; you can pick up the Barbary Coast Trail again in front of it. Wander down Waverly, past ornate tong buildings and Taoist temples. Walk two blocks to Washington Street, turn west (left) and go half a block, turning north (right) into **Ross Alley** (page 64), home of the **Golden Gate Fortune Cookie Factory**. At the north end of the alley, turn east (right) down Jackson Street for a block. Turn south (right) on Grant to the corner of Washington and the landmark **Bank of Canton** with its elaborate facade and triple pagoda roof. Go one block south on Washington, crossing Lum Place, to historic **Portsmouth Square** (page 63), the city's original town plaza. Strolling across the square to Clay Street, turn east (left) half a block to Kearny Street, south (right) one block to Commercial Street, and east (left) on Commercial. There you'll find the **Chinese Historical Society of America** (page 61). Turn left onto Montgomery Street.

TAKE A BREAK IN THE WOODS   Officially, the Barbary Coast Trail takes you along Montgomery Street past the west side of the **Transamerica Building** (the "Pyramid Building") but why not detour to **Redwood Park**, one of the city's shadiest and most peaceful spots, on the building's east side? Back on Montgomery, walk north to Jackson Street and turn east (right).

IMAGINE THE BARBARY COAST   San Francisco's oldest historic district, **Jackson Square** occupies the site of the old Barbary Coast. During the gold rush, stage star Sarah Bernhardt called it "the most fascinatingly wicked place on earth." Leveled by the 1906 earthquake, the Barbary Coast tried to re-establish its houses of ill repute but ultimately became infested by lawyers—notably tort king Melvin Belli, whose worn red-brick former office building still dominates the block. At Jackson Street, turn east (right) and walk one block, passing across the street from the the ornate **Hotaling Buildings** (445–473 Jackson). The trail turns north (left) on Balance Street and goes a short distance to Gold Street, site of the first assay office during the Gold Rush. Turning east (right) on Gold, go to Sansome Street, turn north (left) and walk one block to Pacific Avenue. Turn west (left) and walk two blocks to Columbus Avenue. The copper-sheathed seven-story flatiron building at **916 Kearny**, where Pacific, Columbus, and Kearny meet, is the headquarters for filmmaker Francis Ford Coppola's **Zoetrope Studios**.

NORTH BEACH   Walk northwest (right) up Columbus Street, passing such historic Beat hangouts as **City Lights Bookstore** (page 68) and **Vesuvio Café** (page 68) before crossing **Broadway** with its strip clubs and porn houses. Three more blocks up Columbus, through a mixed Italian and Chinese neighborhood, brings you to **Washington Square** (page 70). Rest in the park, then proceed one block east on Union Street, turn north (left) on Grant, and go two blocks north. Here, if you're feeling athletic, you can climb the steps to the 495-foot summit of **Telegraph Hill** and ride the elevator up **Coit Tower** (page 69) for a great view of the city. The designated route skips the hill and continues three more blocks up Grant, past hidden **Jack Early Park**, to Francisco Street; turn east (right) into the cul-de-sac, then north (left) down a flight of stairs to Kearny Street. Continue two more blocks north to the Embarcadero.

THE WATERFRONT   You don't need the Barbary Coast Trail markers to find your way west along the waterfront. Just turn left from Kearny onto the Embarcadero, passing **Pier 39** (page 76), and follow the throngs of sightseers, street vendors, and silver-painted mimes down **Fisherman's Wharf** to **Aquatic Park** (page 78).

CABLE CARS   The **Powell-Hyde Cable Car** turnaround is at Hyde and Beach streets, between **The Cannery** (page 78) and **Ghirardelli Square** (page 78). Anticipate a half-hour wait in line—possibly much more on weekends and in summer. The cable car climbs steeply up and down **Russian Hill** and **Nob Hill** before reaching Powell and Market streets, where this tour began. If you wish to stop at the **Cable Car Museum** (page 65) or other sights along the way, you can get off and on the cable car on the same ticket.

Street; 415-776-1380, 800-248-9466, fax 415-885-3109; e-mail pw@jdvhospitality.com. MODERATE.

Located on the border between the city's stately Civic Center and unwashed Tenderloin district, **Shih Yu-Lang Central** YMCA has singles and doubles with shared baths. In traditional Y-style, the rooms are as clean as they are sterile; they are scantily furnished and tend to be cramped. But for these prices—which include a continental breakfast and free use of the sunroof, pool, sauna, steam room, weight room, laundry, aerobics area, and basketball and racquetball courts—who's complaining? ~ 220 Golden Gate Avenue; 415-345-6700, fax 415-885-5439; www.ymcasf. org, e-mail hotel@ymcasf.org. BUDGET.

Located right on the edge of the Civic Center, the **Hotel Renoir** is one of the more economical spots to rest. The lobby is lined with Renoir prints and decorated in gold and soft peach colors. There's a Brazilian restaurant, a lounge and a friendly ambience about the place. The only detraction is its location on busy Market Street and proximity to the city's Tenderloin district. Rooms are reasonably well furnished. The accommodations I saw featured wall-to-wall carpeting, color televisions, steam heat, plush furniture, and tile bathrooms with shower-tub combinations. ~ 45 McAllister Street; 415-626-5200, 800-576-3388, fax 415-626-0916; www.renoirhotel.com, e-mail info@renoirhotel.com. MODERATE TO DELUXE.

DINING

This area spotlights several outstanding dining rooms. One of the best in my opinion is **Hayes Street Grill**, situated within strolling distance of the opera and symphony. Specializing in fresh fish dishes, they also serve grilled porkchops, dry-aged steak, and escarole. Excellent food. No lunch on the weekend. ~ 320 Hayes Street; 415-863-5545, fax 415-863-1873; www.hayes streetgrill.com. DELUXE.

Few, if any, places in the Hayes Valley gourmet ghetto are more popular than **Caffe Delle Stelle**. Sheer shades grace the windows, and photographs adorn the walls of this quirky, cute Tuscan

◆◆◆

CLASSROOM CUISINE

With two restaurants, the **California Culinary Academy** offers everything from a half pint of delicious potato salad to a global buffet. Here students under faculty supervision hone their talents. Located in a skylit neoclassic hall, the Carême Room serves three-course lunches and dinners as well as buffets. Closed Saturday through Monday. ~ 625 Polk Street; 415-771-3500, 800-739-9700, fax 415-771-2194; www.baychef. com. DELUXE.

trattoria. Conversation buzzes, but it's not too loud to enjoy an intimate discussion of your own. The cuisine is Italian country cooking, and meals begin with fresh bread and a bowl of *pan-sanela*, a dip made from olive oil, bread, tomato juice, and spices. Entrées include a selection of pastas, baked chicken, roasted salmon fillet, and daily specials like ravioli barbarossa stuffed with arugula, ricotta, and walnuts in a basil sauce. ~ 395 Hayes Street; 415-252-1110, fax 415-863-5224. MODERATE.

Max's Opera Café serves a variety of fare that ranges from smoked barbecued ribs to California cuisine, but the standouts are the thick pastrami, corned beef, and turkey breast sandwiches accompanied by tangy coleslaw and potato salad. Low-carb dinner and sugar-free dessert menus available. A lively bar area features occasional impromptu entertainment by the staff, some of whom are budding tenors and sopranos. ~ 601 Van Ness Avenue; 415-771-7301, fax 415-474-9780; www.maxsworld.com. MODERATE.

A café setting that features brass fixtures, pastel walls, bentwood furniture, and Asian artwork make **Thepin** an inviting Thai establishment. The fare, ranging from red curry duck to marinated prawns and chicken breast, is also a winner. Specialties include sliced chicken and shrimp with spinach in peanut sauce, marinated filet of salmon in curry sauce, and sliced green papaya salad with tomatoes and chili pepper. No lunch on Saturday, closed Sunday. ~ 298 Gough Street; 415-863-9335, fax 415-863-9276. BUDGET TO MODERATE.

SHOPPING

Hayes Valley lies directly west of the Civic Center and has as its focus the block bounded by Hayes, Franklin, Grove, and Gough streets.

F. Dorian specializes in crafts from all over the world including ethnic and contemporary items. Although their selection varies, you may be lucky enough to find antique Filipino furniture, Indian oil lamps, Indonesian diary boxes, and exotic jewelry. ~ 370 Hayes Street; 415-861-3191; www.fdorian.com.

Just a few blocks away lies **Opera Plaza** (at Van Ness and Golden Gate avenues), an atrium mall with shops, restaurants, and a movie theater collected around a courtyard and fountain. It's a pretty place to sit and enjoy the day.

NIGHTLIFE

San Francisco is rich culturally in its opera, symphony, and ballet, located in the Civic Center area. Since tickets to major theatrical and other cultural events are expensive, consider buying day-of-performance tickets from TIX **Bay Area** in Union Square, on Powell Street between Geary and Post. Open from 11 a.m. until just before showtime, they sell tickets at half-price on the day of the show and full price for future events. Closed Monday.

~ 415-433-7827; www.tixbayarea.com, e-mail tba@theatrebay area.org.

San Francisco takes nothing quite so seriously as its opera. The **San Francisco Opera** is world class in stature and invites operatic greats from around the world to perform. As a result, tickets sell out quickly. Standing-room only tickets are always available, and at just $10 are a steal (if your legs are up to it). The international season begins in mid-September and runs through June. The box office is closed on Sunday during performance season and weekends during off-season. ~ 301 Van Ness Avenue; 415-864-3330, fax 415-626-1729; www.sfopera.com.

The **San Francisco Symphony** stands nearly as tall on the world stage. The season extends from September through July. Michael Tilson Thomas conducts, and guest soloists have included Jessie Norman and Itzhak Perlman. ~ Davies Hall, Van Ness Avenue and Grove Street; 415-864-6000, fax 415-554-0108; www.sfsym phony.org.

The **San Francisco Ballet**, performing since 1933, is the nation's oldest professional ballet, and one of the finest. Featuring *The Nutcracker* during December, the company's official season runs at the Opera House from January until May. In addition to original works, they perform classic ballets. The box office is only open on performance days. ~ 301 Van Ness Avenue; 415-865-2000, fax 415-865-0740; www.sfballet.org, e-mail sfbmail@sf ballet.org.

Over at the **Great American Music Hall**, a vintage 1907 building has been splendidly converted to a nightclub featuring a variety of entertainers. Included in the lineup are international acts such as Jimmy Cliff, Bonnie Raitt, and Shawn Colvin. ~ 859 O'Farrell Street; 415-885-0750, fax 415-885-5075; www.gamh. com, e-mail info@gamh.com.

Embarcadero

The Embarcadero is where the city's skyscrapers meet the Bay. This waterfront promenade has become increasingly appealing since the 1989 earthquake, which resulted in the dismantling of a freeway that once ran along the bayfront. Today the vistas are unobstructed and the strip is wide open for wandering.

Back in Gold Rush days, before the pernicious advent of landfill, the entire area sat beneath fathoms of water and went by the name of Yerba Buena Cove. Matter of fact, the hundreds of tall-masted ships abandoned here by crews deserting for the gold fields eventually became part of the landfill.

Nature is rarely a match for the shovel. The Bay was pressed back from around Montgomery Street to its present perimeter. As you head down from the Financial District, walk softly; the

world may be four billion years old, but the earth you're tread-
ing has been around little more than a century.

Fittingly enough, the first place encountered is **Embarcadero**   **SIGHTS**
Center, a skein of five skyscrapers rising sharp and slender along
Sacramento Street to the foot of Market Street. This $645 mil-
lion complex, oft tagged "Rockefeller Center West," features a
three-tiered pedestrian mall that links the buildings together in a
labyrinth of shops, restaurants, fountains, and gardens.

That blocky complex of cement pipes from which water pours
in every direction is not an erector set run amok. It's **Vaillancourt**
Fountain, situated smack in the Hyatt's front yard. The surrounding patchwork of grass and pavement is **Justin Herman Plaza**, a
perfect place for a promenade or picnic. Craft vendors with en-
graved brass belt buckles, silver jewelry, and beanbag chairs have
made the plaza their storefront and skaters have made it their
playground. It's also the starting point for the monthly roving bicycle protest known as Critical Mass.

Just across the road, where Market Street encounters the Embarcadero, rises San Francisco's answer to the Statue of Liberty.
Or what was the city's answer at the turn of the 20th century,
when the clock tower of the **Ferry Building** was as well-known
a landmark as the Golden Gate Bridge is today. Back then there
were no bridges, and 100,000 ferryboat commuters a day poured
through the portals of the world's second-busiest passenger terminal. Built in 1898, the old landmark has made a comeback
with a complete renovation. Now the building houses a plethora
of shops and restaurants and a bustling **farmers market** on
Tuesday and Saturday. Afternoon or evening tours of the building are available through City Guides (415-557-4266; www.sfcity
guides.org) on Tuesday, Thursday, and Saturday.

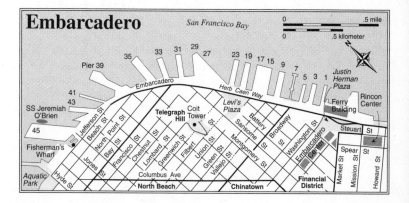

Embarcadero
San Francisco Bay

You might want to walk the ramp that leads up to the **World Trade Center**, on Embarcadero at the foot of Market Street. It's lined with Covarrubias' murals that were preserved from the 1939 Golden Gate International Exposition. They look like those maps in your old sixth grade social studies book: one vividly depicts "the people of the Pacific" with aborigines sprouting up from the Australian land mass and seraped Indians guarding the South American coast. Another pictorial geography lesson features the Pacific economy with salmon swimming off the North American shore and rice bowls growing in China.

One positive result of the horrendous 1989 Loma Prieta earthquake was the demolition of the Embarcadero Freeway, a longtime eyesore that ran like a concrete scar through the waterfront area. Now that the freeway is gone, there is a lighter and brighter look to the area, with palm trees planted along the Embarcadero and more expansive views of the Bay Bridge and Treasure Island. In 1996, the city named the pedestrian promenade that parallels the boulevard **Herb Caen Way**, in honor of San Francisco's famous gossip columnist who died in 1997. At the same time, a new neighborhood is fast growing up around and to the south of lower Market Street with apartments, restaurants, nightspots, and a Saturday-morning farmers' market. A popular gathering spot for locals, especially at noontime, is the **Rincon Center**, which features a cluster of eateries offering everything from Korean noodles to Indian curries. The eateries surround a central indoor courtyard dining area and spectacular, rainfall-like fountain. ~ 101 Spear Street; 415-777-4100.

The Rincon Annex is a restored 1930s post office with magnificent WPA murals glorifying science and technology.

Stretching from either side of the Ferry Building are the rows of **shipping piers** that once made San Francisco a fabulous harbor. Today much of the commerce has sailed across the Bay to the Port of Oakland. To recapture San Francisco's maritime era, head north on Embarcadero from the Ferry Building along the odd-numbered piers. The city looms to your left and the Bay heaves and glistens before you. This is a world of seaweed and fog horns where proverbial old salts still ply their trade. Blunt-nosed tugboats tie up next to rusting relics from Guadalcanal. There are modern jet ferries, displaying the latest aeronautical curves and appearing ready at any moment to depart from the water for open sky. The old, big-girthed ferries have been stripped of barnacles, painted nursery colors, and leased out as office space; they are floating condominiums.

Along this parade of piers you'll see cavernous concrete wharves astir with forklifts and dockhands. Locomotives shunt with a clatter, trucks jockey for an inside post, and container cranes sweep the air. Other piers have fallen into desuetude, rust-caked wharves propped on water-rotted pilings. The only common denominators in this odd arithmetic progression of piers are the seagulls and pelicans whitening the pylons.

Across from Pier 23, **Levi's Plaza** features a grassy park ideal for picnicking; just beyond Pier 35 there's a waterfront park with a wonderful vantage for spying on the ships that sail the Bay. ~ 1155 Battery Street.

The Embarcadero continues along the waterfront all the way to Fisherman's Wharf. Joggers, skaters, and skateboarders all favor this long smooth stretch of Herb Caen Way.

The lobby of the **Hyatt Regency**, on the corner of Market and California streets, features a towering atrium that rises 170 feet— a triangular affair lined with a succession of interior balconies that ascend to a skylighted roof. Along one side, plants cascade in a 20-story hanging garden, while another wall is designed in a zigzag shape that gives the sensation of being inside a pyramid. Fountains and flowering plants are all about, glass capsule elevators scale the walls, and sun flecks splash in through the roof. The 800-plus large, fashionable guest rooms, accented with tall green plants and fresh-cut flowers, come with business-oriented amenities such as two telephones, voice mail and computer hookups, as well as such luxury touches as hairdryers, plush robes and optional turndown service. Most rooms have exterior balconies, and many have bay views. ~ 5 Embarcadero Center; 415-788-1234, fax 415-398-2567; www.hyatt.com. ULTRA-DELUXE.

LODGING

Just one block from the Embarcadero and convenient to the Financial District, the **Hotel Griffon** offers 62 attractive rooms and suites appointed with modern art, window seats, oversized mirrors, and, in a few cases, Bay views and terraces. A cozy lobby features a reading nook and fireplace, and there's an adjacent fitness center. An expanded continental breakfast is included. ~ 155 Steuart Street; 415-495-2100, 800-321-2201, fax 415-495-3522; www.hotelgriffon.com, e-mail reservations@hotel griffon.com. ULTRA-DELUXE.

On the same block is **Harbor Court Hotel**, where some of the 131 rooms and suites also offer marine views. Guest accommodations are small but attractively appointed with dramatic prints, modern furnishings, and canopied beds. The lobby is large and comfortable, and ideal for leisurely afternoons. Complimentary wine is served in the evening. You can also relax at the health club and indoor pool adjacent to the hotel. ~ 165 Steuart Street; 415-882-1300, 866-792-6283, fax 415-882-1313; www.harbor courthotel.com. DELUXE TO ULTRA-DELUXE.

The eight-story **Hotel Vitale** offers 185 guest rooms, eight suites, and six studios—each styled in natural, contemporary motifs, and many with Bay views. Amenities include 24-hour room service, twice-daily housekeeping, high-speed internet, spa-styled bathrooms, and flatscreen TVs with DVD players. The Vitale also has a waterfront restaurant, outdoor café, a spa with outdoor soaking tubs, fully equipped business center, fitness center, and free yoga classes. ~ 8 Mission Street; 415-278-3700, 888-890-8688, fax 415-278-3750; www.hotelvitale.com, e-mail bookvitale@jdv hospitality.com. ULTRA-DELUXE.

DINING

Consistently ranked among the city's top restaurants, **Boulevard** is the brainchild of famed San Francisco chef Nancy Oakes and interior designer Pat Kuleto. Belle epoque decor unifies three distinct seating areas—a casual central section around an open kitchen where you can watch the chefs at work, a front bar, and a more formal back dining area. The food is as chic as the decor, and the menu changes regularly. Representative entrées have included glazed quail, vanilla-cured pork loin and grilled ahi tuna in ginger salsa. There's also an exceptional list of hard-to-find California wines. No lunch on weekends. ~ 1 Mission Street; 415-543-6084; www.boulevardrestaurant.com, e-mail info@boulevardres taurant.com. ULTRA-DELUXE.

San Francisco's modern version of camp is **Fog City Diner**. It is the most upscale diner you've ever seen. Check out the exterior with its art-deco curves, neon lights, and checkerboard tile. Then step into a wood-and-brass paneled restaurant that has the feel of a club car on the Orient Express. Featuring California cuisine, the menu changes frequently, but might include ahi tartare with jalepeño and cilantro, or seared halibut with asparagus and garlic noodles. Everything is à la carte, including the Fog City T-shirts. What can I tell you except to book a reservation in advance. ~ 1300 Battery Street; 415-982-2000, fax 415-982-3711; www.fog citydiner.com, e-mail fogcitydiner@aol.com. MODERATE TO DELUXE.

HIDDEN ►

Head on down to **Pier 23 Cafe**, a little shack between Fisherman's Wharf and downtown, for unique waterfront dining. The place is funky but nice, with white tablecloths and linen napkins on the tables. Dine inside or on the huge back patio overlooking the bay. This restaurant specializes in seafood and offers several fish specials daily. The deep-fried calamari appetizer and the oven-roasted crab with garlic, parsley, and butter dipping sauce are two of the most popular items on the menu. ~ Pier 23; 415-362-5125; www.pier23cafe.com, e-mail pier23cafe@aol.com. MODERATE.

SHOPPING

Shoppers along the Embarcadero head for the **Embarcadero Center**, located on Sacramento Street near the foot of Market Street. It's a vaulting glass-and-concrete "town" inhabited by stores and restaurants. This multifaceted mall consists of the lower three levels of five consecutive skyscrapers. You pass from one building to the next along corridors that open onto a galaxy of shops. Verily, what Disneyland is for kids, Embarcadero Center is to shoppers. The place has positively everything. There are bookstores, bakeries, jewelry stores, gift bazaars, newsstands, and camera shops. There's even a "general store," plus dozens of restaurants, cocktail lounges, and espresso bars, a luggage shop, a store devoted entirely to nature, and on and on and on in labyrinthine fashion.

NIGHTLIFE

The Holding Company is crowded with young professionals on the make. Closed Saturday and Sunday. ~ 2 Embarcadero Center; 415-986-0797.

Over at the Hyatt Regency, there's a revolving rooftop bar, **The Equinox.** A glass-encased elevator whisks you to this aerie, where you can pull up a window seat and watch the world spin. ~ 5 Embarcadero Center; 415-788-1234.

Pier 23 Cafe is a funky roadhouse that happens to sit next to the San Francisco waterfront. The sounds emanating from this saloon are live jazz, reggae, salsa, and blues. Highly recommended to those searching for the simple rhythms of life. There's music nightly; Wednesday evening features a salsa class. Cover. ~ Embarcadero and Pier 23; 415-362-5125; www.pier23cafe.com.

Chinatown

It's the largest Chinatown outside Asia, a spot that older Chinese know as *dai fao*, Big City. San Francisco's Chinatown also ranks as the city's most densely populated neighborhood. Home to more than 14,000 of the city's 153,000 Chinese, this enclave has been an Asian stronghold since the 1850s. Originally a ghetto where Chinese people were segregated from San Francisco society, the neighborhood today opens its arms to burgeoning numbers of immigrants from a host of Asian nations.

CHINATOWN—A DIFFERENT PERSPECTIVE

Just off the notorious Columbus/Broadway intersection lies a museum that will open wide your perspective on Chinatown's history. The **Chinese Historical Society of America** graphically presents the history of San Francisco's Chinese population. In the museum is a magnificent collection of photos and artifacts re-creating the Chinese experience from the days of pig-tailed "coolies" to the recent advent of ethnic consciousness. Wide in scope, the museum is a treasure house with a helpful and congenial staff. Closed Sunday and Monday. Admission. ~ 965 Clay Street; 415-391-1188, fax 415-391-1150; www.chsa.org, e-mail info@chsa.org.

On the surface, this pulsing, noisy, chaotically colorful 70-square-block stretch projects the aura of a tourist's dream—gold and crimson pagodas, stores brimming with exquisite silks and multicolored dragons, more restaurants per square foot than could be imagined, roast ducks strung up in shop windows next door to Buddhist temples and fortune cookie factories.

But Chinatown is far more than a tourist mecca. This crowded neighborhood is peopled with families, powerful political groups, small merchants, poor working immigrants and rising entrepreneurs molding a more prosperous future. Although the "city within a city" that Chinatown once symbolized now encompasses less than a quarter of San Francisco's Chinese people, it's still a center of Chinese history, culture, arts, and traditions that have lived for thousands of years.

In appropriately dramatic fashion, you enter Chinatown through an arching gateway bedecked with dragons. Stone lions guard either side of this portal at Grant Avenue and Bush Street.

SIGHTS

To stroll the eight-block length of Chinatown's **Grant Avenue** is to walk along San Francisco's oldest street. Today it's an ultramodern thoroughfare lined with Chinese arts-and-crafts shops, restaurants, and Asian markets. It's also one of the most crowded streets you'll ever squeeze your way through. Immortalized in a song from the musical *Flower Drum Song*, Grant Avenue, San Francisco, California, U.S.A., is a commotion, a clatter, a clash of cultures. At any moment, a rickety truck may pull up beside you, heave open its doors, and reveal its contents—a cargo of chinaware, fresh produce, or perhaps flattened pig carcasses. Elderly Chinese men lean along doorways smoking fat cigars, and Chinatown's younger generation sets off down the street clad in sleek leather jackets.

At the corner of California Street, where cable cars clang across Grant Avenue, rises the lovely brick structure of **Old St. Mary's Church**. Dating to 1854, this splendid cathedral was originally built of stone quarried in China. Just across the way in **St. Mary's Square**, there's a statue of the father of the Chinese Republic, Dr. Sun Yat Sen, crafted by San Francisco's foremost sculptor, Beniamino Bufano. You might take a hint from the crowds of businesspeople from the nearby financial center who bring their picnic lunches to this tree-shaded plaza.

Next you'll encounter **Nam Kue School**. With an iron fence, mullioned doors, and pagoda-like facade, it's an architectural beauty ironically backdropped by a glass-and-concrete skyscraper. ~ 755 Sacramento Street.

As you walk along Grant Avenue, with its swirling roof lines and flashing signs, peek down **Commercial Street**. This curious brick-paved street permits a glimpse into "hidden" Chinatown. Lined with everything from a noodle company to a ginseng shop, this tightly packed street also holds the **Mow Lee Shing Kee & Co.**, Chinatown's second-oldest establishment. ~ 774 Commercial Street.

After you've immersed yourself in Chinese history, head down to **Portsmouth Square** (Kearny and Washington streets) for a lesson in the history of all San Francisco. Formerly the city's central plaza, it was here in 1846 that Yankees first raised the Stars and Stripes. Two years later, the California gold discovery was announced to the world from this square. At one corner of the park you'll find the bronze statue of a galleon celebrating the ocean-going Robert Louis Stevenson. Today this gracious park is a gathering place for old Chinese men playing chess and practicing tai chi. From the center of the plaza, a sky bridge arches directly into the **Chinese Culture Center**, with its displays of Chinese art. Closed Sunday and Monday. ~ 750 Kearny Street; 415-986-1822, fax 415-986-2825; www.c-c-c.org, e-mail info@c-c-c.org.

Now that you've experienced the traditional tour, you might want to explore the hidden heart of Chinatown. First take a stroll along **Stockton Street**, which runs parallel to, and one block

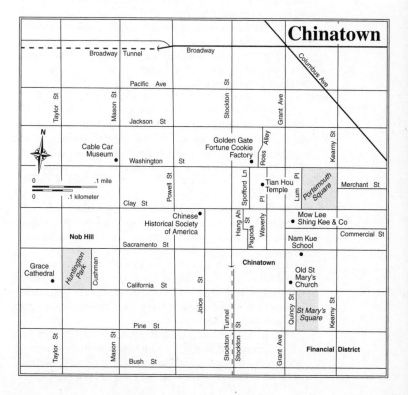

above, Grant Avenue. It is here, not along touristy Grant Avenue, that the Chinese shop.

The street vibrates with the crazy commotion of Chinatown. Open stalls tumbling with vegetables cover the sidewalk, and crates of fresh fish are stacked along the curb. Through this maze of merchandise, shoppers press past one another. In store windows hang Peking ducks, and on the counters are displayed pigs' heads and snapping turtles. Rare herbs, healing teas, and chrysanthemum crystals crowd the shelves.

The local community's artwork is displayed in a fantastic **mural** that covers a half-block between Pacific and Jackson streets.

To further explore the interior life of Chinatown, turn down Sacramento Street from Stockton Street, then take a quick left into Hang Ah Street. This is the first in a series of alleyways leading for three blocks from Sacramento Street to Jackson Street. When you get to the end of each block, simply jog over to the next alley.

HIDDEN ▶ A universe unto themselves, these **alleyways of Chinatown** are where the secret business of the community goes on, as it has for over a century. Each door is a barrier beyond which you can hear the rattle of mah-jongg tiles and the sounds of women bent to their tasks in laundries and sewing factories.

Along Hang Ah Street, timeworn buildings are draped with fire escapes and colored with the images of fading signs. As you cross Clay Street, at the end of Hang Ah Street, be sure to press your nose against the glass at **Grand Century Enterprise**. Here the ginseng and other precious roots sell for hundreds of dollars a pound. ~ 858 Clay Street; 415-392-4060, fax 415-392-4063.

The next alley, **Spofford Lane**, is a corridor of painted doorways and brick facades occasionally humming with the strains of Chinese melodies. It ends at Washington Street where you can zigzag over to **Ross Alley**. This is the home of the **Golden Gate Fortune Cookie Factory**. At this small family establishment you can watch your fortune being made. ~ 56 Ross Alley; 415-781-3956.

The last segment in this intriguing tour will take you back to **Waverly Place**, a two-block stretch leading from Washington Street to Sacramento Street. Readers of Dashiell Hammett's mystery story, *Dead Yellow Women*, will recall this spot. It's an enchanting thoroughfare, more alley than street. At first glance, the wrought-iron balconies draped along either side of Waverly evoke images of New Orleans. But not even the French Quarter can boast the beauty contained in those Chinese cornices and pagoda swirl roof lines.

Prize jewel in this architectural crown is **Tian Hou Temple**. Here Buddhists and Taoists worship in a tiny temple overhung with fiery red lanterns. There are statues portraying battlefields and country landscapes; incense smolders from several altars.

From the pictures along the wall, Buddha smiles out upon the believers. They in turn gaze down from the balcony onto Chinatown's most magical street. ~ 125 Waverly Place.

Just uphill from Chinatown stands the **Cable Car Museum**, a brick goliath that houses the city's cable cars. The museum here provides a great opportunity to see how these wood-and-steel masterpieces operate. The system's powerhouse, repair, and storage facilities are here, as are the 14-foot diameter sheaves which neatly wind the cable into figure-eight patterns. The museum also has on display three antique cable cars from the original cable car company. Video displays show footage of the 1906 earthquake and a ride down Market Street before the quake. ~ 1201 Mason Street; 415-474-1887, fax 415-929-7546; www.ca blecarmuseum.org.

DINING

Chinatown is one of the best places in the city to find exceptional food at rock-bottom prices. Look for it at the kind of plain-looking places where most of the diners appear to be from the neighborhood and children roam around as freely as if they were at home. A good example is **Hon's Wun Tun House**, where spotless formica, shared tables and counter seating set the stage for noodle dishes and soups as tasty as they are affordable. Closed Sunday. ~ 648 Kearny Street; 415-433-3966, fax 415-433-1506. BUDGET.

Among budget restaurants, **Sam Wo** is a San Francisco classic. Dining in this jook house is a rare adventure. The entrance is also the kitchen, and the kitchen is just a corridor filled with pots, stovepipes, cooks, and steamy smells. Sam Wo's menu is extensive and the food is quite good for the price. ~ 813 Washington Street; 415-982-0596. BUDGET.

Concealed along one of Chinatown's back alleyways, the **Pot Sticker** has the feel of a local secret, part social club, part takeout place serving neighborhood families, and so exotic that it seems a world apart from the more touristy restaurants of Grant

◀ HIDDEN

AUTHOR FAVORITE

My favorite dim sum restaurant is tucked away in an alley above Grant Avenue. Personalized but unpretentious, more cozy than cavernous, **Hang Ah Tea House** is a rare find. Enter the dining room with its Chinese wood carvings and fiberglass tables. Serving a full Mandarin cuisine as well as dim sum portions, it warrants an exploratory mission into the alleys of Chinatown. ~ 1 Hang Ah Street; 415-982-5686. BUDGET.

Avenue. Specializing in its namesake—meat-filled dumplings that are first steamed and then fried—the Pot Sticker also offers a full menu of Mandarin-style dishes. ~ 150 Waverly Place; 415-397-9985, fax 415-397-3829. MODERATE.

For luxurious dining in the heart of Chinatown, no place matches the **Empress of China**. Set on the top floor of the China Trade Center, with nothing between you and heaven, it is a culinary temple. Dining rooms are adorned with carved antiques and the maitre'd dons a tuxedo. Lunch at this roof garden restaurant begins with appetizers like Shanghai dumplings and walnut prawns, then graduates to lichee chicken and Manchurian beef. Dinner is the true extravagance. The menu includes a royal variety of chicken, duck, lamb, shellfish, pork, and beef dishes. There are also unique selections like baby quail flambé, Dungeness crab in ginger and onion sauce, and almond pressed duck. ~ 838 Grant Avenue; 415-434-1345, fax 415-986-1187; www.empressofchinasf.com, e-mail info@empressofchinasf.com. DELUXE TO ULTRA-DELUXE.

Rudyard Kipling, Jack London, and Robert Louis Stevenson once wandered the grounds of Portsmouth Square.

Of course, the ultimate Chinatown experience is to dine dim sum style. Rather than choosing from a menu, you select dishes from trundle carts laden with steaming delicacies. A never-ending convoy of waitresses wheels past your table, offering plates piled with won tons, pork tidbits, and Chinese meatballs. It's up to you to create a meal (traditionally breakfast or lunch) from this succession of finger-size morsels.

Many dim sum establishments are cavernous restaurants, sparsely decorated like cafeterias. But each has a particular personality and generates warmth from the crowds passing through. Do not be fooled by the neon facades, for an Asian adventure waits within these dining palaces. You should be careful about prices, however: most dim sum courses cost only $2 or $3, but it's easy to lose count as you devour dish after dish. Figure that the restaurants noted below will be moderate in price, unless you become a dim sum addict.

The brightly lit yellow sign outside **Gold Mountain Restaurant** attracts its share of tourists and passersby. Nonetheless, this clean and modern dining room serves trusty claypot specialties, traditional seafood and noodles, and dim sum at lunch. Try the three treasures in black bean sauce, a colorful dish with red bell peppers, eggplant and stuffed tofu. ~ 644 Broadway near Powell Street; 415-296-7733. BUDGET TO MODERATE.

Overlooking Portsmouth Square on the second story of a nondescript building, the **Oriental Pearl** serves sophisticated, gourmet dim sum, a step above the usual Chinatown teahouse. Here dim sum is ordered from a menu, allowing diners to concentrate on conversation and cuisine, rather than being distracted by the contents of passing carts. Such treats as shrimp and scallop dumplings, pork buns, and chicken meatballs emerge hot and fresh from the kitchen. White tablecloths, mahogany chairs, and classical Chinese music make this a quiet oasis from the busy streets of Chinatown below. ~ 760–778 Clay Street; 415-433-1817, fax 415-433-4541; www.orientalpearlsf.com. BUDGET TO DELUXE.

Styled like a teahouse, **Lichee Garden** limits glitzy decor and concentrates on excellent, authentic Cantonese cuisine. The tables are consistently crowded with Chinese families who have come to rely on the over 60 fresh dim sum dishes that are prepared daily. Pork, beef, duck, seafood, or vegetarian dim sum options are available, along with full lunch and dinner menus, which boast all the traditional favorites. ~ 1416 Powell Street; 415-397-2290; licheegarden.ypguides.net. MODERATE.

SHOPPING

Shopping in Chinatown brings you into immediate contact with both the common and the unique. If you can slip past the souvenir shops, many of which specialize in American-made "Chinese products," you'll eventually discover the real thing—Chinese arts and crafts as well as Asian antiques.

Grant Avenue is the neighborhood's shopping center, but local Chinese favor **Stockton Street**. My advice is to browse both streets as well as the side streets between. Some of the city's best bargains are right here in Chinatown.

NIGHTLIFE

Li Po, a dimly lit Chinatown bar, is complete with incense, lanterns, and carved statuary, plus an incongruous jukebox featuring some Caucasian favorites mixed in with the Chinese music. The potions they mix here are powerful and exotic; the place has an air of intimacy. ~ 916 Grant Avenue; 415-982-0072.

North Beach

It's a region of contrasts, a neighborhood in transition. North Beach combines the sex scene of neon-lit Broadway with the brooding intellect and Beat heritage of Grant Avenue and Columbus Street. Traditionally an Italian stronghold, North Beach still retains its fabulous pasta palaces and bocce ball courts, but it's giving way to a growing influx of Chinese residents.

Introductions to places should be made gradually, so the visitor comes slowly but certainly to know and love the area. In touring North Beach, that is no longer possible, because the logical spot to begin a tour is the corner of Broadway and Montgomery streets, at night when the neon arabesque of Broadway is in full glare.

SIGHTS   Broadway, you see, has long been San Francisco's answer to Times Square, a tawdry avenue that traffics in sex. While the neighborhood is steadily changing, it still features strip joints, peekaramas, and X, Y, Z-rated theaters—a modern-day Barbary Coast.

After you've dispensed with North Beach's sex scene, your love affair with the neighborhood can begin. Start at **City Lights Bookstore.** Established in 1953 by poet Lawrence Ferlinghetti, City Lights is the old hangout of the Beat poets. Back in the heady days of the '50s, a host of "angelheaded hipsters"—Allen Ginsberg, Jack Kerouac, Gary Snyder, and Neal Cassady among them—haunted its book-lined rooms and creaking staircase. Today the place remains a vital cultural scene and gathering point. It's a people's bookstore where you're invited to browse, carouse, or even plop into a chair and read awhile. You might also check out the paintings and old photographs, or perhaps the window display in this official national landmark. More than fifty years after the Beats, the inventory here still represents a who's who in avant-garde literature. ~ 261 Columbus Avenue; 415-362-8193, fax 415-362-4921; www.citylights.com, e-mail staff@citylights.com.

Vesuvio Café next door was another hallowed Bohemian retreat. ~ 255 Columbus Avenue; 415-362-3370; www.vesuvio. com. Then head up nearby Grant Avenue to the **Caffe Trieste**, at the corner of Vallejo Street. With its water-spotted photos and funky espresso bar, the place has changed little since the days when bearded bards discussed cool jazz and Eisenhower politics. ~ 601 Vallejo Street; 415-392-6739, fax 415-982-3045; www. caffetrieste.com.

You're on "upper Grant," heart of the old Beat stomping grounds and still a major artery in the city's Italian enclave. You're also only a block from the **Beat Museum,** home to memorabilia from Lawrence Ferlinghetti, Allen Ginsberg, Jack Kerouac, and their buddies. The Beat Generation Walking Tours visit the bars and coffeehouses where these icons spent both their days and nights. Regular poetry readings, open mic nights, and concerts feature new voices. Closed Monday. ~ 540 Broadway; 831-372-4911; www.thebeatmuseum.org.

Chinatown is at your back now, several blocks behind, but you'll see from the Chinese script adorning many shops that the Asian neighborhood is sprawling into the Italian. Still remaining, however, are the cafés and delicatessens that have lent this area its Mediterranean flair since the Italians moved in during the late 19th-century.

Beyond Filbert Street, as Grant Avenue continues along the side of Telegraph Hill, the shops give way to Italian residences and Victorian houses. When you arrive at **Lombard Street,** look to your left and you'll see the sinuous Lombard, labeled "The

Crookedest Street in the World." Then turn right as Lombard carries you up to the breeze-battered vistas of Telegraph Hill.

Named for the semaphore station located on its height during the 1850s, **Telegraph Hill** was a Bohemian haunt during the 1920s and 1930s. Money moved the artists out; today, this hillside real estate is among the most desirable, and most expensive, in the city.

Poking through the top of Telegraph Hill is the 180-foot-high **Coit Tower** (admission for elevator to observation platform). Built in 1933, this fluted structure was named for Lillie Hitchcock Coit, a bizarre character who chased fire engines and became a fire company mascot during the 1850s. Lillie's love for firemen gave rise to stories that the phallic tower was modeled after a fire hose nozzle. Architectural critics scoff at the notion. Some of the nation's most outstanding **WPA murals** decorate Coit Tower's interior. Done as frescoes by New Deal artists, they sensitively depict the lives of California laborers.

Upstaging these marvelous artworks is the view from the summit. That sinewy structure to the right is the **Bay Bridge**, which

North Beach

stretches for eight and one quarter miles, the world's longest steel bridge. It is interrupted in its arching course by **Yerba Buena Island** and **Treasure Island**, the latter a manmade extension created for the 1939 Golden Gate International Exposition. The Bay Bridge's gilded companion to the left is the **Golden Gate Bridge**. Between them lies San Francisco Bay. Tugs and freighters slide past in search of mooring. Fog horns groan. From this aerie the distant sloops and ketches look like children's toys blown astray in a pond puffed with wind.

It's hard to imagine that Washington Square was a tent city back in 1906. The great earthquake and fire totally devastated North Beach, and the park became a refuge for hundreds of homeless.

The island moored directly offshore is **Alcatraz**, named for the pelicans that still inhabit it, but known for the notorious prisoners who have long since departed its rocky terrain. Looming behind America's own Devil's Island is **Angel Island**. That high point on the horizon, between the Golden Gate and Angel Island, is **Mt. Tamalpais**, crown jewel in Marin County's tiara. Across the water, where the Bay Bridge meets terra firma, are the East Bay cities of **Berkeley** and **Oakland**. Behind you, past the highrise cityscape, the hills and streets of San Francisco sweep out toward the sea.

Now that all San Francisco has been spread before you like a tableau, it's time to descend into the hidden crannies of the city. Unlike Coit Tower, there will be no elevator to assist on the way down, but then again there won't be any tourists either.

After exiting Coit Tower, turn right, cross the street, and make your way down the brick-lined staircase. In the middle of San Francisco, with wharves and factories far below, you have just entered a countrified environment. Ferns and ivy riot on either side of the **Greenwich Steps**, while vines and conifers climb overhead.

HIDDEN ▶

HIDDEN ▶

At the bottom of the steps, turn right, walk a short distance along Montgomery Street, then head left down the **Filbert Steps**. Festooned with flowers and sprinkled with baby tears, the steps carry you into a fantasy realm inhabited by stray cats and framed with clapboard houses. Among the older homes are several that date to the 1870s; if you follow the Napier Lane Boardwalk that extends from the steps, there are falsefront buildings from which sailors reportedly once were shanghaied.

Retracing your tracks back up the steps, then descending the other side of Filbert Street, you'll arrive at **Washington Square**, between Filbert and Stockton streets in the heart of North Beach. Nestled between Russian and Telegraph hills, this is the gathering place for San Francisco's "Little Italy." In the square, old Italian men and women seek out wooden benches where they can watch the "young people" carrying on. From the surrounding delis and cafés you might put together a picnic lunch, plant yourself on the lawn, and catch this daily parade. But if you come early in the morning, you will see evidence of the slow transition North Beach is undergoing: 50 or more Chinese and Westerners practice tai chi in the square.

Saints Peter & Paul Catholic Church anchors one side of the square. Its twin steeples dominate the North Beach skyline. The façade is unforgettable, an ornate affair upon which eagles rest in the company of angels. The interior is a wilderness of vaulting arches hung with lamps and decorated in gilt bas-relief. Tourists proclaim its beauty. For my taste, the place is overdone; it drips with architectural jewelry. Everything is decoration, an artistic happening; there is no tranquility, no silent spot for the eye to rest. ~ Filbert Street, between Powell and Stockton streets; 415-421-5219, fax 415-421-1831; www.stspeterpaul.san-francisco.ca.us, e-mail info@stspeterpaul.sanfrancisco.ca.us.

LODGING

As a nighttime visit to North Beach will clearly indicate, this neighborhood was not made for sleeping. The "love acts" and encounter parlors along Broadway draw rude, boisterous crowds until the wee hours.

But if noise and neon have a soporific effect upon you, or if you have some bizarre and arcane need to know what sleeping on the old Barbary Coast was like, check out **Europa Hotel**. The price is certainly right, and you get a clean, carpeted room and shared bath. ~ 310 Columbus Avenue; 415-391-5779, fax 415-391-0499. BUDGET.

Or better yet, retreat a little farther from Broadway to the **Hotel Bohème** and take a step back into North Beach history. This European pensione–style hotel has been decorated to reflect the Beat-generation era, complete with a black-and-white photo retrospective. Poet Allen Ginsberg even stayed here. Rooms feature antique wardrobes, tile bathrooms, and black iron beds. Ask for one of the rooms in the back, which are quieter than those along busy Columbus Avenue. ~ 444 Columbus Avenue; 415-433-9111, fax 415-362-6292; www.hotelboheme.com, e-mail info@hotelboheme.com. DELUXE.

◀ *HIDDEN*

DINING

Dining at **Helmand** is like visiting the home of an upper-class Afghani family. Lush handmade Afghan carpets, beautiful chandeliers, and paintings add a touch of elegance, and the food is first-rate. You can feast on grilled rack of lamb, roasted chicken, and many vegetarian dishes. *Aushak*, Afghan ravioli stuffed with leeks and topped with ground beef marinated in yogurt, can be habit-forming. A true find among the sleazy strip joints of Broadway. No lunch Saturday through Monday. ~ 430 Broadway; 415-362-0641, fax 415-362-0862, www.helmandrestaurantsanfrancisco.com. MODERATE.

Some of the best pizza in town is served at **Tommaso's Neapolitan Restaurant,** where the chefs bake in an oak-fired oven. The creations they prepare have resulted in this tiny restaurant being written up in national magazines. As soon as you walk in you'll realize it's the food, not the surroundings, that draws the attention. Entering the place is like stepping down into a grotto. The walls are lined with booths and covered by murals; it's dark, steamy, and filled with inviting smells. Filmmaker Francis Ford Coppola drops by occasionally, as should every pizza and pasta lover. Dinner only. Closed Monday. ~ 1042 Kearny Street; 415-398-9696, fax 415-989-9415. MODERATE.

At least once during a North Beach visit, you should dine at a family-style Italian restaurant. Dotted all around the neighborhood, these establishments have a local flavor unmatched by the area's chic new restaurants. A good choice is **Capp's Corner,** a local landmark adorned with celebrity photos, more celebrity photos, and a few photos of celebrities. The prix-fixe dinner includes soup, salad and an entrée. Among the dishes are osso buco, linguini with steamed mussels and clams, and lamb shanks. ~ 1600 Powell Street; 415-989-2589, fax 415-989-2590. MODERATE.

A big blue neon moosehead marks the entrance to **Moose's,** located on Washington Square. Owner Ed Moose, a San Francisco icon who has dominated the restaurant scene for decades, oversees a warm, inviting dining room that is part of the city's history. It even features a cardboard figure of former *San Francisco Chronicle* columnist Herb Caen, pen and pad in hand, gazing down on the assembled. There's an open kitchen, done in stainless steel and dark wood, and a menu that runs the gamut from the trademark Mooseburger (actually made from quality ground beef, but mooselike in its hugeness) to haute cuisine such as foie gras with apples and huckleberry jus and a cheese course with walnut bread. Dinner only. Brunch served Saturday and Sunday. ~ 1652 Stockton Street; 415-989-7800; www.mooses. com. DELUXE TO ULTRA-DELUXE.

Dessert in North Beach means Italian ice cream, and few places make it better than **Gelato Classico.** Creamy and thick, Italian ice cream is made without air, so it's denser and more delicious than other ice cream. At Gelato Classico they also use fresh fruit and other natural ingredients to guarantee great taste. If you try it in summer, you can have fresh strawberry, blackberry, burgundy cherry, or raspberry. During the rest of the year, they serve a host of flavors ranging from coppa mista and banana to good old chocolate and vanilla (made, of course, from vanilla beans). *Viva Italia!* ~ 576 Union Street; 415-391-6667.

The heart of North Beach beats in its cafés. Gathering places for local Italians, the neighborhood's coffee houses are also literary scenes. Step into any of the numerous cafés dotting the district and you're liable to hear an elderly Italian singing opera or see an aspiring writer with notebook in one hand and espresso cup in the other.

The best North Beach breakfasts are the continental-style meals served in these cafés. But any time of day or night, you can order a croissant and cappuccino, lean back, and take in the human scenery. Foremost among these people-watching posts is **Caffe Trieste**, the old Beatnik rendezvous. ~ 601 Vallejo Street; 415-392-6739, fax 415-982-3045; www.caffetrieste.com. Another prime location is **Caffe Puccini**, with heavenly homemade *tiramisu*. ~ 411 Columbus Avenue; 415-989-7033. Right on Washington Square is the popular **Mario's Bohemian Cigar Store Cafe**. ~ 566 Columbus Avenue; 415-362-0536, fax 415-362-0112.

The *New Yorker* once called **Hunan Restaurant** "the best Chinese restaurant in the world." Those are pretty big words, hard to substantiate this side of Beijing. But it's certainly one of the best San Francisco has to offer. Understand now, we're talking cuisine, not ambience. The atmosphere at Hunan is characterized by noise and crowds; there is a bar and a contemporary-style dining room adorned with color photographs. But the food will transport you to another land entirely. It's hot, spicy, and delicious. From the dining room you can watch masterful chefs working the woks, preparing pungent sauces, and serving up bean curds with meat sauce, Hunan scallops, and a host of other delectables. A culinary experience well worth the price. ~ 924 Sansome Street; 415-956-7727. BUDGET.

SHOPPING

Shopping in North Beach is a grand escapade. As you browse the storefronts here, do like the Sicilians and keep an eye out for Italian treasures such as the hand-painted ceramics and colorful wallhangings still brightening many a home in old Italia.

Biordi Art Imports provides the Italian answer to gourmet living. Specializing in Italian ceramics, the place is loaded. There are hand-painted pitchers from Florence and De Simone folk art from Palermo, and hand-painted dinnerware, wall mirrors framed

AUTHOR FAVORITE

A diverse crowd packs the tables and barstools at **Vesuvio Café**, a major North Beach scene, rich in soul and history. The place hasn't changed much since the Beat poets haunted it during the days of Eisenhower. Kerouac, Corso, Ginsberg, and the crew spent their nights here and their days next door at City Lights Bookstore. ~ 255 Columbus Avenue; 415-362-3370, fax 415-362-1613; www.vesuvio.com.

in ceramic fruit, hand-painted umbrella stands and other high-kitsch items. Walking through this singular shop is like browsing an Italian crafts fair. Closed Sunday. ~ 412 Columbus Avenue; 415-392-8096; www.biordi.com, e-mail info@biordi.com.

No North Beach shopping spree would be complete without a visit to **A. Cavalli & Company**. Operating since 1880, this family business caters to all sorts of local needs. They offer an assortment of Italian cookbooks as well as records and tapes ranging from Pavarotti to Italian new wave. Cavalli's also stocks Italian travel posters, Puccini opera prints, Italian movies on DVD, and magazines from Rome. ~ 1441 Stockton Street; 415-421-4219.

Ooma stands for "Objects of My Affection," and it's packed with affordable and trendy finds — flirty jersey skirts and dresses, trendy handbags, chic shoes, bright swimsuits, and a good selection of unusual jewelry. Stock changes frequently. Closed Monday. ~ 1422 Grant Avenue; 415-627-6963; www.ooma.net.

NIGHTLIFE North Beach, the old Beatnik quarter, is the area for slumming. It's door-to-door with local bars and nightclubs, not to mention the few topless and bottomless joints that still remain along Broadway.

Spec's Twelve Adler Museum Café is a bohemian haunt. There's nary a bald spot on the walls of this literary hangout; they're covered with all manner of mementos from bumperstickers to a "walrus' penis bone." A great place to get metaphysical. ~ 12 Adler Place; 415-421-4112.

To step uptown, just walk down the hill to the **San Francisco Brewing Company**. Built the year after the 1906 earthquake, it's a mahogany-paneled beauty with glass lamps and punkah wallah fans. Legend tells that Jack Dempsey once worked here as a bouncer. It's also the first pub in San Francisco to brew its own beer on the premises. Live jazz several nights a week. ~ 155 Columbus Avenue; 415-434-3344; www.sfbrewing.com, e-mail brewmaster@sfbrewing.com.

Club Fugazi features an outlandish musical revue, *Steve Silver's Beach Blanket Babylon*, which has been running since 1973 (although the script is frequently updated). The scores and choreography are good, but the costumes are great. The hats—elaborate, multilayered confections—make Carmen Miranda's adornments look like Easter bonnets. Cover. Closed Monday and Tuesday. ~ 678 Green Street (Beach Blanket Babylon Boulevard); 415-421-4222; www.beachblanketbabylon.com, e-mail bbb@beachblanketbabylon.com.

Bimbo's 365 Club, a snazzy North Beach institution since 1951, showcases an eclectic mix of live music from jazz and rock to French pop. Call for a list of events. Cover. ~ 1025 Columbus Avenue; 415-474-0365; www.bimbos365club.com.

A wide-open bar with bright murals and a small dancefloor, **Mojitos** offers low-priced drinks and tapas in a lively, Latin American atmosphere. A deejay spins a mix of hip-hop, '80s rock, and Cuban music all night. Locals crowd the place on Tuesdays for the $2-dollar Tuesday menu specials. Closed Monday. ~ 1337 Grant Avenue; 415-398-1120.

Fisherman's Wharf

Places have a way of becoming parodies of themselves—particularly if they possess a personal resonance and beauty or have some unique feature to lend the landscape. People, it seems, have an unquenchable need to change them.

Such is the fate of Fisherman's Wharf. Back in the 19th century, a proud fishing fleet berthed in these waters and the shoreline was a quiltwork of brick factories, metal canning sheds, and woodframe warehouses. Genoese fishermen with rope-muscled arms set out in triangular-sailed *feluccas* that were a joke to the west wind. They had captured the waterfront from the Chinese and would be supplanted in turn by Sicilians. They caught sand dabs, sea bass, rock cod, bay shrimp, king salmon, and Dungeness crab. Salt caked their hands, wind and sun gullied their faces.

Today the woodplanked waterfront named for their occupation is hardly a place for fishermen. It has become "Tourist's Wharf," a bizarre assemblage of shopping malls and penny arcades that make Disneyland look like the real world. The old waterfront is an amusement park with a wax gallery, a Ripley's museum, and numerous trinket shops. The architecture subscribes to that modern school which makes everything look like what it's not—there's pseudo-Mission, ready-made antique Victorian, and simulated falsefront.

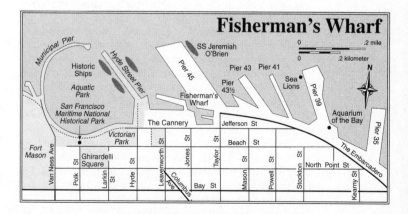

But salt still stirs the air here and fog fingers through the Bay. There are sights to visit along "the Wharf." It's a matter of recapturing the past while avoiding the plastic-coated present. To do that you need to follow a basic law of the sea—hug the shoreline.

SIGHTS

On the corner of Embarcadero and Beach Street, **Pier 39** itself is an elaborately laid-out shopping mall catering primarily to tourists who spill over from neighboring Fisherman's Wharf. In addition to a plethora of waterfront shops and restaurants, Pier 39 features jugglers, yo-yo champs, and other entertainers who delight the crowd with their sleight of hand.

The central attraction at Pier 39 is the colony of **sea lions** that has taken up residence on the nearby docks. Numbering 400 at times, these thousand-pound pinnipeds are a cross between sea slugs and sumo wrestlers. They began arriving in 1989, taking over a marina, causing a ruckus, and creating the greatest stench this side of a sardine factory. But when Pier 39 attracted over 10 million people the next year, placing it behind Orlando's Walt Disney World and Anaheim's Disneyland as the most popular tourist spot in the country, the local merchants decided to welcome the smelly squatters as permanent residents. On weekends, you can join docents from the Marine Mammal Center for free educational talks about the sea lion's habitat. Meet at the K Dock at Pier 39's west marina. Advance reservations required. ~ 415-289-7330, fax 415-289-7333; www.tmmc.org, e-mail edu@tmmc.org.

For an up-close look at other residents of the San Francisco Bay, including sharks and fish, go to **Aquarium of the Bay**. Journey along moving walkways through a 300-foot-long transparent tunnel into two giant two-story tanks. These tanks contain rays, salmon, crabs, jellyfish, eels, and more than 150 examples of the six shark species found in surrounding waters. Touch live seastars and other shoreline creatures in the Touch the Bay area. Admission. ~ Pier 39; 415-623-5300, 888-732-3483, fax 415-623-5324; www.aquariumofthebay.com, e-mail info@aquariumofthebay.com.

Among Pier 39's attractions is **Forbes Island**, a 10-foot-long fantasyland complete with live palm trees, a sand beach, a waterfall, and a 40-foot-tall lighthouse with an observation deck. This self-propelled 700-ton motor vessel in disguise offers dishes like roasted rack of lamb with artichokes and olives. Closed Monday and Tuesday. Admission. ~ Pier 39; 415-951-4900; www.forbes island.com.

Pier 45 is a working wharf, bleached with bird dung and frequented by fishing boats. From here it's a short jog to the docks on Jefferson Street, located between Jones and Taylor streets. The remnants of San Francisco's fishing fleet lies gunnel to gunnel here. The *Nicky-J*, *Whacky Jacky*, *Butchy B*, *Phu Quy*, *Hai Tai Loc*, and an admiralty of others cast off every morning around 4 a.m.

to return in late afternoon. With their brightly painted hulls, Christmas tree rigging, and roughhewn crews, they carry the odor and clamor of the sea.

At the intersection of Taylor Street and the Embarcadero is the **Musée Mécanique**, a collection of vintage mechanical amusements dating to a simpler time. You can still put in your change and see them do their thing. ~ Pier 45; 415-346-2000; www.museemechanique.com.

On a given day there might be jugglers, clowns, or other entertainers performing free at Pier 39.

Docked at Pier 45 at the Embarcadero is the **S.S. Jeremiah O'Brien**, one of two 2751 World War II Liberty Ships to remain in original condition (the other is docked in Baltimore). A beamy hulk, the *Jeremiah O'Brien* numbers among its combat ribbons the D-Day invasion of Normandy. Visitors may walk the decks of the old vessel, explore the sailors' quarters, descend into the depths of the engine room, and chat with a volunteer crew member. Call ahead for tour information. Admission. ~ 415-544-0100, fax 415-544-9890; www.ssjeremiahobrien.org.

Fish Alley is a nostalgic nook. Just duck into the narrow corridor next to Castagnola's Restaurant on Jefferson Street and walk out towards Scoma's Restaurant. Those corrugated metal sheds lining the docks are fish-packing operations. The fleet deposits its daily catch here to be processed for delivery to restaurants and markets. This is an area of piers and pilings, hooks and hawsers, flotsam and fish scales, where you pay a price to recapture the past: as you work farther into this network of docks, approaching nearer and nearer the old salty truths, you'll also be overwhelmed by the putrefying stench of the surrounding businesses.

◀ *HIDDEN*

For a breather, it's not far to the Hyde Street Pier, where history is less offensive to the nose. Here you'll find the **San Francisco Maritime National Historical Park**. Docked along the pier are historic ships. You can board the *Eureka*, an 1890 paddlewheeler that ferried commuters between San Francisco and Sausalito for almost 30 years. Recently the largest floating wooden structure on earth, it served as police headquarters for the crime-fighting crew on TV's now-defunct "Nash Bridges." To walk this pier is to stride back to San Francisco's waterfront at the turn of the 20th century. The *Eppleton Hall* is an old paddlewheeler and the *Alma* a "scow schooner" with a flat bottom and square beam. A three-masted merchant ship built in Scotland in 1886, the *Balclutha* measures 301 feet. This steel-hulled craft sailed around Cape Horn 17 times in her youth. She loaded rice in Rangoon, guano in Callao, and wool in New Zealand. Today the old ship's cargo boasts exhibits and a hold full of memories. Stop by the Small Boat Shop and watch volunteers work on restoration projects or try your hand at knot-tying and block-and-tackle work. A visitors center is located across from the Hyde Street

Pier. Admission to board the ships. ~ 415-447-5000, fax 415-556-1624; www.nps.gov/safr.

The nearby **San Francisco Maritime Museum,** in case you mistook it for a ferryboat run aground, is actually an art-deco building designed to resemble the bridge of a passenger liner complete with wildly colorful murals along the first floor. Onboard there's a weird collection of body parts from old ships plus models, scrimshaw displays, and a magnificent photo collection. But perhaps the neatest exhibit is "Sparks, Waves and Wizards." Using a live feed from the U.S. Coast Guard, visitors can use a telescope to spot a vessel entering the Golden Gate, find the ship on a computer screen, and with a click of a button pull up all sorts of information, from vessel speed to cargo contents. The museum is closed for renovations until 2009. ~ Beach and Polk streets; 415-561-7100, fax 415-556-6293; www.nps.gov/safr.

All these nautical showpieces are anchored in **Aquatic Park,** which sports a lovely lawn that rolls down to one of the Bay's few sandy beaches. A mélange of sounds and spectacles, the park has a bocce ball court where you'll encounter old Italian men exchanging stories and curiously eyeing the tourists. There are street vendors galore. If that's not enough, you can watch the Powell and Hyde Street cable cars being turned around for their steep climb back up Nob Hill. Or catch an eye-boggling glimpse of San Francisco Bay. Alcatraz lies anchored offshore, backdropped by one of the prettiest panoramas in this part of the world.

Of course no tour of Fisherman's Wharf is complete without a stop at **The Cannery,** a shopping center with 30 specialty shops. ~ Jefferson and Leavenworth streets; 415-771-3112.

Be sure to stop at **Ghirardelli Square,** former site of the chocolate factory, which has been converted into an open-air shopping courtyard. ~ 900 North Point Street; 415-775-5500; www.ghiradellisq.com. For more information, see "Shopping" below.

LODGING Fisherman's Wharf contains more hotels than fishermen. Most facilities here are overpriced and undernourished. I'm only going to mention a few, since I think you'll do much better financially and experience San Francisco more fully in a downtown or neighborhood hotel.

The first is **The Wharf Inn,** which has 51 moderate-size rooms. Unlike its nearby competitors, free onsite parking is included. The place is clean and bright, offering the same type of facility you could have downtown at a lesser cost. In an area of pricey hotels, The Wharf Inn has some of the best rates around. ~ 2601 Mason Street; 415-673-7411, 877-275-7889, fax 415-776-2181; www.wharfinn.com, e-mail info@wharfinn.com. DELUXE TO ULTRA-DELUXE.

Cruising the Bay

Ground zero (water zero?) for the Alcatraz Cruises—which sponsors Bay cruises, Alcatraz tours, and ferry service to Angel Island, Sausalito, and Tiburon—is Pier 33 near Fisherman's Wharf. ~ 415-981-7625; www.alcatrazcruises.com, e-mail rich_weidman@nps.gov.

The trip to **Alcatraz** is highlighted with a National Park Service tour of the infamous prison. Originally a fort and later a military prison, Alcatraz gained renown as "The Rock" when it became a maximum security prison in 1934. Al Capone, "Machine Gun" Kelly, and Robert "Birdman of Alcatraz" Stroud were among its notorious inmates. On the tour, you'll enter the bowels of the prison, walk the dank corridors, and experience the cage-like cells in which America's most desperate criminals were kept. Be sure to tune in to the audio cassette tour of former guards and prisoners remembering their time at The Rock.

The prison closed in 1963; then in 1969 a group of American Indians occupied the island for almost two years, claiming it as Indian territory. Today Alcatraz is part of the Golden Gate National Recreation Area.

A cruise to **Angel Island State Park** is a different adventure entirely. Unlike "The Rock," this star-shaped island is covered with forest and rolling hills. During previous incarnations it has served as a military installation, quarantine station, immigration center, and prisoner of war camp. Today, the largest true island in San Francisco Bay is a lacework of hiking and biking trails and flowering meadows. For an overview stop by the Visitors Center at Ayala Cove. Here you'll find a diorama and map of the island, historical exhibits, a self-starting 20-minute video that reviews the history of the island and the light fixture from an old lighthouse. You can trek five miles around the island or climb to the top for 360° views of the Bay Area.

Deer graze throughout the area and there are picnic areas galore. It's a perfect spot for a day in the sun. Along the way you can visit the small Immigration Station Museum, which is dedicated to the history of the island's early immigration station. Touching photographs document the story of this "West Coast Ellis Island." The museum is closed for renovation until February 2007. Except for the visitors center, which is open year-round, the buildings on Angel Island are open weekends only April through October (and for group tours). A tram operates on weekends in the summer. (The entrance fee is included in the ferry price; however, there is a $15 day-use fee if you bring your own boat.) ~ 415-435-5390; www.angelisland.org.

Lodging in the **Sheraton Fisherman's Wharf,** a sprawling 529-room facility, feature spacious rooms tastefully furnished in Sheraton fashion, plus room service and nightly turndown service. The hotel has other alluring features like a tiled entranceway, liveried doormen, swimming pool, and an attractive gift shop. ~ 2500 Mason Street; 415-362-5500, 800-325-3535, fax 415-956-5275; www.sheratonatthewharf.com. ULTRA-DELUXE.

The **Hyatt at Fisherman's Wharf** is a 313-room luxury retreat that is faced in antique brick and illuminated through skylights. It comes complete with a pool, a spa, and a fitness center. ~ 555 North Point Street; 415-563-1234, 800-233-1234, fax 415-749-6122; www.hyatt.com. ULTRA-DELUXE.

Smaller in scale than the Hyatt, the 221-room **Tuscan Inn Best Western** is richly decorated and more intimate. This Italian-style boutique hotel features a garden court and an Italianate lobby complete with fireplace. ~ 425 North Point Street; 415-561-1100, 800-648-4626, fax 415-561-1199; www.tuscaninn.com, e-mail sales@tuscaninn.com. DELUXE TO ULTRA-DELUXE.

DINING

Dining at Fisherman's Wharf usually means spending money at Fisherman's Wharf. The neighborhood's restaurants are over-priced and over-touristed. If you look hard enough, however, it's possible to find a good meal at a fair price in a fashionable restaurant. Of course, the easiest way to dine is right on the street, at one of the **seafood cocktail stands** along Jefferson Street. An old wharf tradition, these curbside vendors began years ago feeding bay fishermen. Today they provide visitors an opportunity to sample local catches like crab, shrimp, and calamari. ~ BUDGET.

PERFORMANCE CUISINE

Dinner at **Restaurant Gary Danko**, San Francisco's top-rated restaurant in the current Zagat guide, is an extravaganza. The eponymous owner, who once built stage sets, envisions each evening as a "performance" featuring a "multi-act meal." The restaurant setting is certainly dramatic enough—with contemporary paintings on taupe walls and a decor that combines oak panels, plantation-style shutters and pin-spot lights to create an intimate but active atmosphere. The seasonal cuisine focuses on freshness and includes signature dishes like lamb loin and roast lobster. They also boast an exceptional wine cellar, special tea service, and a granite cheese cart for which they are renowned. It's a special place for special occasions. Highly recommended. Dinner only. ~ 800 North Point Street; 415-749-2060, fax 415-775-1805; www.garydanko.com, e-mail info@garydanko.com. ULTRA-DELUXE.

Situated between the Wharf and North Beach, **Cafe Francisco** enjoys the best of both worlds—it's strolling distance from the water and possesses a bohemian flair. A great place for light and inexpensive meals, this trendy café serves salads and sandwiches for lunch. Breakfast at the espresso bar ranges from a continental repast to bacon and eggs. Decorated with changing exhibits by local artists, it attracts a local crowd. ~ 2161 Powell Street; 415-397-2602; www.cafefrancisco.com, e-mail julie@cafe francisco.com. BUDGET.

The **Eagle Café** is another old-timer. It's so much a part of San Francisco that plans to tear the place down years ago occasioned a public outcry. Instead of flattening the old woodframe building, they lifted it—lock, stock, and memories—and moved it to the second floor of the Pier 39 shopping mall. Today it looks like an ostrich at a beauty pageant, a plain all-American café surrounded by glittering tourist shops. The walls are covered with faded black-and-white photos, Eagle baseball caps, and other memorabilia. Actually, the bar is more popular than the restaurant. Who wants to eat when they can drink to old San Francisco? The bar is open all day and into the night. ~ Pier 39; 415-433-3689, fax 415-434-9253. BUDGET TO MODERATE.

At **Butterfly**, your meal is combined with live jazz or deejay music. The excellent food is California-Asian fusion (think coriander and porcini–crusted salmon). The decor is cool and modern, studded with glass and floor-to-ceiling windows with views of the bay. ~ Pier 33; 415-864-8999; www.butterflysf.com, e-mail info@butterflysf.com. MODERATE TO DELUXE.

Alioto's started as a fresh fish stall in 1925, added a seafood bar in 1932, and is still one of the best places to pick up fresh crab and shrimp cocktails. Upstairs, diners choose a just-caught fish special served with veggies and hot sourdough. The tiramisu and the view to the bay are delicious. ~ #8 Fisherman's Wharf (Taylor and Jefferson streets); 415-673-0183; www.aliotos.com. MODERATE.

Would you believe a hidden restaurant in tourist-mobbed Fisherman's Wharf? **Scoma's** is the place. Seafood is the password to this chummy restaurant. There's *cioppino alla pescatore*, a Sicilian-style broth; *calamone alla anna*, squid prepared "in a totally different manner"; or just plain old sole, snapper, shrimp, or scallops. There's lobster tail, too, and Dungeness crab. ~ Pier 47 near the foot of Jones Street; 415-771-4383, fax 415-775-2601; www.scomas.com. DELUXE TO ULTRA-DELUXE.

◀ HIDDEN

Crisp, clean, and classy is the way to describe **McCormick & Kuleto's**, a popular seafood restaurant in Ghirardelli Square. Natural woods predominate, white tablecloths adorn the tables, and faux tortoiseshell lamps hang from the high ceilings, but the focus of attention is the incredible view of the bay from the floor-to-ceiling windows. The extensive menu changes daily depending on what fish is available and includes such specialties as crab cakes, seafood pastas, seared ahi, alder-smoked salmon, and mesquite-grilled bass fillet. There's also a very lengthy wine list. ~ 900 North Point Street; 415-929-1730, fax 415-567-2919; www.mccormickandkuletos.com. DELUXE TO ULTRA-DELUXE.

Albona Ristorante Istriano is a high-heeled hole-in-the-wall, a small but fashionable restaurant serving Venetian and Central European dishes. The interior is a mélange of beveled mirrors, white linen tablecloths, burgundy banquettes, and fresh flowers. The menu, not to be upstaged, includes sauerkraut braised with prosciutto, pan-fried gnocchi, and exotic entrées like braised rabbit with juniper berries and *brodetto alla Veneziana* (fish stew). Valet parking is available. Dinner only. Closed Sunday and Monday. ~ 545 Francisco Street; 415-441-1040, fax 415-441-5107. MODERATE.

SHOPPING   Fisherman's Wharf is a shopper's paradise . . . if you know what you're doing. If not, it's a fool's paradise. This heavily touristed district houses a mazelike collection of shops, malls, arcades, and galleries. Most of them specialize in high-priced junk. How someone can arrive in the world's most splendid city and carry away some trashy trinket to commemorate their visit is beyond me. But they do. Since you're certainly not the type searching out an "I Got Crabs at Fisherman's Wharf" T-shirt, the best course is to go where the natives shop.

Though its wooden boardwalks and clapboard buildings look promising, **Pier 39** proves hardly the place for bargains or antiques. It's a haven for tourists and features gift stores that range from cutesy card shops to places selling ceramic unicorns. There are restaurants and stores galore, plus an amusement arcade. Kids often enjoy the carnival atmosphere here. ~ Embarcadero and Beach Street; 415-981-7437.

My main objection is to the ticky-tacky shops. Every year, however, millions of tourists disagree with me. They flock to this two-tiered mall, popping in and out of the more than 110 shops and enjoying the ersatz early-20th-century atmosphere.

One noteworthy exception to Pier 39's tourist-oriented selection of shops is **The Golden Gate National Park Store**, the only bookshop I know that comes with a view of sea lions basking in the sun. It offers a complete selection of travel, hiking, and wildlife books and also sells educational toys, American Indian arts and crafts, and other gifts. ~ Pier 39; 415-433-7221.

For locally crafted goods, be sure to watch for the **street vendor stalls**. Located along Beach Street between Hyde and Larkin, and on side streets throughout the area, they offer hand-fashioned wares with homemade price tags. You'll find jewelry, leather belts, statuary, framed photos of the bay city, tie-dye shirts, kites, and anything else the local imagination can conjure.

Before people buy anything in the City, they go to **Cost Plus World Market** and see if it's there. If so, it's cheaper; if not, maybe they don't really need it. You'll find ceramics, wallhangings, and a host of other items. There are temple rubbings from Thailand, Indian mirrorcloths, scenic San Francisco posters, household furnishings, clothes, gourmet foods, wine, etc. Everything under the sun, at prices to brighten your day. ~ 2552 Taylor Street; 415-928-6200; www.costplusworldmarket.com.

Another popular spot among San Franciscans is the old brick canning factory on Jefferson and Leavenworth streets. Thanks to innovative architects, **The Cannery** has been transformed into a tri-level marketplace dotted with interesting shops. The central plaza, with its olive trees and potted flowers, contains picnic tables, several cafés, and snack kiosks, and features free daily entertainment. Among the dozens of shops are many selling handcrafted originals. ~ 415-771-3112; www.thecannery.com, e-mail info@thecannery.com.

The chocoholics who don't know will be delighted to discover that the home of Ghirardelli chocolate, **Ghirardelli Square**, has been converted into yet another shopping complex. This early 20th–century factory is another example of old industrial architecture being turned to contemporary uses. Around the factory's antique chocolate-making machines are myriad shops varying from designer outlets to sundry stores. There are also import stores, boutiques, and a creamery where you can order your favorite ice cream creation with gobs of Ghirardelli chocolate on top. ~ 900 North Point Street; 415-775-5500; www.ghirardellisq.com, e-mail info@ghirardellisq.com.

NIGHTLIFE

Don't know any local people, but still like to party? Head for Lou's Pier 47 Restaurant and Blues Club, have a meal, and dance the afternoon and night away. For eats, there are sandwiches, burgers, pastas, and fried, grilled, or sautéed fish and seafood. The bands that play each week in the glass-enclosed nightclub

AUTHOR FAVORITE

The **Eagle Café** appears like some strange bird that has landed in the wrong roost. All around lies touristville, polished and preening, while the Eagle remains old and crusty, filled with waterfront characters. Old photos and baseball caps adorn the walls, and in the air hang age-old memories. ~ Pier 39; 415-433-3689.

upstairs play mostly rhythm-and-blues but you can also hear Motown and light rock occasionally. The music begins around 4 p.m. daily. Cover. ~ 300 Jefferson Street; 415-771-5687; www. louspier47.com.

Buena Vista Café, situated near Fisherman's Wharf, is popular with local folks and tourists alike. There's a fine old bar and friendly atmosphere, and the place claims to have introduced America to the Irish coffee. ~ 2765 Hyde Street; 415-474-5044.

▼ ▼ ▼ ▼ ▼ ▼ ▼ ▼ ▼ ▼ ▼ ▼ ▼ ▼

Golden Gate National Recreation Area

One of San Francisco's most spectacular regions belongs to us all. The Golden Gate National Recreation Area, a 74,000-acre metropolitan park, draws about 20 million visitors annually. A place of natural beauty and historic importance, this magnificent park stretches north from San Francisco throughout much of the Bay Area. In the city itself, the Golden Gate National Recreation Area forms a narrow band around the waterfront. It follows the shoreline of the Bay from Aquatic Park to Fort Mason to the Golden Gate Bridge. On the ocean side it encompasses Land's End, an exotic and untouched preserve, as well as the city's finest beaches.

SIGHTS   The most serene way to begin exploring the Golden Gate National Recreation Area is via the **Golden Gate Promenade**. This three-and-a-half-mile walk will carry you across a swath of heaven that extends from Aquatic Park to the shadows of the Golden Gate Bridge.

Just start in the park and make the short jaunt to the **Municipal Pier**. This hook-shaped cement walkway curls several hundred yards into the Bay. As you follow its curving length, a 360-degree view unfolds—from the Golden Gate to the Bay Bridge, from Mt. Tamalpais to Alcatraz to downtown San Francisco. The pier harbors fisherfolk and seagulls, crabnetters and joggers; few tourists seem to make it out here.

From the pier it's uphill and downstairs to **Fort Mason Center**, a complex of old wharves and tile-roof warehouses that was once a major military embarkation point. Fort Mason today is the cultural heart of avant-garde San Francisco. This National Historic Landmark houses theaters, museums, and a gourmet vegetarian restaurant, and hosts thousands of programs and events. ~ Marina Boulevard and Buchanan Street; 415-441-3400, fax 415-441-3405; www.fortmason.org, e-mail contact@fortmason.org.

Nearly all the arts and crafts are represented—several theater groups are home here; there is an on-going series of workshops in dance, creative writing, painting, weaving, printing, sculpture, music, and so on. A number of environmental organizations also have offices in the center. As one brochure describes, "You can

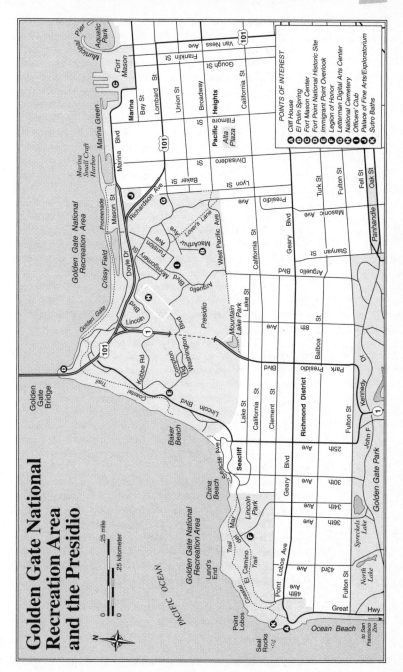

Golden Gate National Recreation Area and the Presidio

POINTS OF INTEREST

- Ⓐ Cliff House
- Ⓑ El Polin Spring
- Ⓒ Fort Mason Center
- Ⓓ Fort Point National Historic Site
- Ⓔ Immigrant Point Overlook
- Ⓕ Legion of Honor
- Ⓖ Letterman Digital Arts Center
- Ⓗ National Cemetery
- Ⓘ Officers' Club
- Ⓙ Palace of Fine Arts/Exploratorium
- Ⓚ Sutro Baths

PACIFIC OCEAN

N

0   25 mile
0   25 kilometer

see a play, stroll through a museum or gallery, learn how to make poetry films, study yoga, attend a computer seminar, or find out about the rich maritime lore of San Francisco."

Museo ItaloAmericano presents samplings of Italian artistry. The museum is dedicated to displaying the works of Italian and Italian-American artists and culture. The permanent collection features the work of several artists, some of whom have made San Francisco their home for years. Docent-led group tours available by appointment. Closed Monday except by appointment. Admission. ~ Building C; 415-673-2200, fax 415-673-2292; www.museoitaloamericano.org, e-mail sf museo@sbcglobal.net.

At Fort Point, if you follow the spiral granite staircase to the roof, you'll stand directly beneath the Golden Gate Bridge and command a sentinel's view out into the Pacific.

Now that you're fully versed in the arts, continue on the shoreline to the **Marina**, along Marina Boulevard. (The remainder of the tour can be completed by car, though walking is definitely the aesthete's and athlete's way.) Some of this sailor-city's spiffiest yachts are docked along the esplanade.

Nearby **Marina Green**, a stretch of park paralleling the Bay, is a landlubber's haven. Bicyclers, joggers, jugglers, sunbathers, and a world of others inhabit it. The park's most interesting denizens are the kitefliers who fill the blue with a rainbow of soaring colors.

Continue on past a line-up of luxury toys—boats with names like *Haiku, Sea Lover, Valhalla,* and *Windfall.* When you arrive at the far end of that small green rectangle of park, you'll have to pay special attention to your navigator; you're on Marina Boulevard at the corner of Yacht Road; if going by car, proceed directly ahead through the U.S. Army gate and follow Mason Street, Crissy Field Avenue, and Lincoln Boulevard, paralleling the water, to Fort Point; if on foot, turn right onto Yacht Road, then left at the waterfront, and follow the shoreline toward the Golden Gate Bridge.

Before doing either, you have an alluring detour in store. Turn left at Yacht Road, cross Marina Boulevard, and proceed to that magnificent Beaux-Arts monument looming before you. It's the **Palace of Fine Arts**, a domed edifice built of arches and shadows. Adorned with molded urns and bas-relief figures, it represents the only surviving structure from the 1915 Panama–Pacific International Exposition. Happily, it borders on a sun-shivered pond. The pond in its turn is peopled by mallards and swans, as well as pintails and canvasbacks from out of town. Together, the pool, the pillars, and surrounding park make this one of the city's loveliest spots for sitting and sunning.

But enough for detours; we were embarked on a long march to the bridge. If you cheated and drove, you're already at Fort Point, and we'll catch up with you later; otherwise you're on foot, with the Bay at your side and the Golden Gate dead ahead. This is a land where freighters talk to foghorns, and sloops scud along soundlessly. The waterfront is a sandy beach, a rockpile in seeming upheaval, then beach again, sand dunes, and occasional shade trees. That wooded grove rising to your left is the Presidio; those bald-domed hills across the Bay to the right are the Marin Headlands, and the sharp-rising buildings poking at your back are part of the San Francisco skyline. You'll pass a Coast Guard Station and a fishing pier before arriving at the red brick fort that snuggles in the arch of the Golden Gate Bridge.

Modeled on Fort Sumter and completed around the time Confederate forces opened fire on that hapless garrison, **Fort Point National Historic Site** represents the only brick fort west of the Mississippi. With its collection of cannons and Civil War–era exhibits, it's of interest to history buffs. Open Friday through Sunday. Call for hours and information on guided tours and special programs. ~ End of Marine Drive; 415-556-1693, fax 415-561-4390; www.nps.gov/fopo.

From Fort Point, a footpath leads up to the observation area astride the **Golden Gate Bridge**; if driving, take Lincoln Boulevard to the vista point. By whichever route, you'll arrive at "The Bridge at the End of the Continent." Aesthetically, it is considered one of the world's most beautiful spans, a medley of splayed cable and steel struts. Statistically, it represents one of the longest suspension bridges anywhere—6450 feet of suspended concrete and steel, with twin towers the height of 65-story buildings and cables that support 200 million pounds. It is San Francisco's emblem, an engineering wonder that has come to symbolize an entire metropolis.

If you're game, you can walk across, venturing along a dizzying sidewalk out to one of the most magnificent views you'll ever experience. The Bay from this height is a toy model built to scale; beyond the bridge, San Francisco and Marin, slender arms of land, open onto the boundless Pacific.

The Golden Gate Promenade ends at the bridge, but Lincoln Boulevard continues along the cliffs that mark the ocean side of San Francisco. There are **vista points** overlooking the Pacific and affording startling views back toward the bridge. After about a mile you'll reach **Baker Beach**, a wide corridor of white sand. Ideal for picnicking and sunbathing, this lovely beach is a favorite among San Franciscans. ~ Off Lincoln Boulevard on Gibson Road. Adventurers can follow this strand, and the other smaller beaches with which it connects, on a fascinating walk back almost all the way to the Golden Gate Bridge. With the sea unfolding on one side and rocky crags rising along the other, it's definitely worth a little sand in the shoes. As a final reward, there's a **nude beach** ◄ HIDDEN on the northern end, just outside the bridge.

Lincoln Boulevard transforms into El Camino del Mar, which winds through Sea Cliff, one of San Francisco's most affluent residential neighborhoods. This exclusive area has something to offer the visitor in addition to its scenic residences—namely **China Beach** (formerly known as James Phelan Beach). More secluded than Baker, this pocket beach is backdropped by a rocky bluff atop which stand the luxurious plate-window homes of Sea Cliff. Named for the Chinese fishermen who camped here in the 19th century, the beach has a dilapidated beach house and restroom facilities. (To get there, turn right on 25th Avenue, left on Sea Cliff Avenue, then follow until it dead ends.)

Continuing on El Camino del Mar as it sweeps above the ocean, you'll come upon San Francisco's prettiest museum. With its colonnaded courtyard and arching entranceway, the **Legion of Honor** is modeled after a gallery in Paris. In fact, a mini pyramid mirroring the one at the Louvre sits in the courtyard, letting light into the gallery below. Appropriately, it specializes in European art and culture. The exhibits trace European aesthetic achievements from ancient Greek and Roman art to the religious art of the Middle Ages to Renaissance painting, the Baroque and Rococo periods, and the Impressionists of the 19th and 20th centuries. Closed Monday. Admission. ~ Lincoln Park, 34th Avenue and Clement Street; 415-750-3600, fax 415-750-3656; www.legion ofhonor.org.

After you've drunk in the splendid view of city and Bay from the museum grounds, head downhill on 34th Avenue past the golf course, turn right on Geary Boulevard, which becomes Point Lobos Avenue, then turn right on to El Camino del Mar and follow it to the end. (Yes, this is the same street you were on earlier; no, I'm not leading you in circles. It seems that years ago land-

IT'S HANDS-ON TIME HERE

If education is on your mind, note that the Palace of Fine Arts houses the **Exploratorium**. A great place to bring children, this "hands-on" museum, with imaginative exhibits demonstrating the principles of optics, sound, animal behavior, etc., was once deemed "the best science museum in the world" by *Scientific American*. It's an intriguing place with constantly changing temporary exhibits and permanent displays that include a "distorted room" lacking right angles and an illusionary mirror into which you seemingly pass. Also check out the Tactile Dome (reservations required; separate admission), a pitch-black crawl-space of textural adventures. Closed Monday and selected holidays. Admission. ~ Marina Boulevard and Lyon Street; 415-397-5674, fax 415-561-0370; www.exploratorium.edu.

slides collapsed the midriff of this highway, leaving among the survivors two dead-end streets known forever by the same name.)

This is **Land's End,** a thumb-like appendage of real estate that ◀ HIDDEN San Francisco seems to have stolen from the sea. It is the nearest you will ever approach to experiencing San Francisco as the Costanoan Indians knew it. Hike the trails that honeycomb the hillsides hereabout and you'll enter a wild, tumbling region where winds twist cypress trees into the contours of the earth. The rocks offshore are inhabited by slithering sea creatures. The air is loud with the unceasing lash of wave against shoreline. Land's End is San Francisco's grand finale—a line of cliffs poised at the sea's edge and threatening imminently to slide into eternity.

From the parking lot located at the end of El Camino del Mar, walk down the steps that begin at the U.S.S. *San Francisco* Memorial Flagpole, and head east on the trail to the water. That dirty blonde swath of sand is a popular **nude beach,** perfectly sit- ◀ HIDDEN uated here in San Francisco's most natural region.

(Note: While hiking the footpaths in the region, **beware!** Land's End is plagued by landslides and foolish hikers. Remain on the trails. Exercise caution and this exotic area will reward you with eye-boggling views of Marin's wind-chiseled coast.)

Continuing down Point Lobos Avenue, at the corner where the road turns to parallel the Pacific Ocean, rest the ruins of the **Sutro Baths.** From the configuration of the stones, it's a simple trick to envision the foundation of Adolf Sutro's folly; more difficult for the mind's eye is to picture the multitiered confection that the San Francisco philanthropist built upon it in 1896. Sprawling across three oceanfront acres, Sutro's baths could have washed the entire city. There were actually six baths total, Olympian in size, as well as three restaurants and 500 dressing rooms—all con- tained beneath a stained-glass dome.

Towering above them was the **Cliff House,** a Gothic castle that survived the earthquake only to be consumed by fire the next year. Following several reincarnations, the Cliff House houses two restaurants, two bars, a lounge, and a gift shop. Three observa- tion decks jut over the rocky edge of the continent; from this crow's nest you can gaze out over a sweeping expanse of ocean. ~ 1090 Point Lobos Avenue; 415-386-3330, fax 415-387-7837; www.cliffhouse.com, e-mail info@cliffhouse.com.

A controversy once surrounded the **Camera Obscura,** the camera-shaped kiosk near the Cliff House. The National Park Service, which leases the land on which this venerable old-time tourist attraction stands, wanted to tear the building down and move the camera's inner workings to a visitors center. Public out- cry resulted in the addition of the Camera Obscura to the National Register of Historic Places, which protects it perma- nently. So rest assured that you'll be able to stand inside this dark chamber and watch as a rotating lens and mirror, based on a 16th-century design by Leonardo da Vinci, projects a panoramic view that takes in the Cliff House, the Sutro Baths and the Golden Gate Bridge, and **Seal Rocks**, which lie just offshore. (The seals for which the rocks were named have all moved to Pier 39 at Fisherman's Wharf, but other sea lions take up residence on the rocks during the spring months.) Closed in inclement weather. Admission. ~ 1096 Point Lobos Avenue; 415-750-0415; www.giantcamera.com, e-mail sfgiantcamera@yahoo.com.

Below the Cliff House, extending to the very end of vision, is the Great Highway. The salt-and-pepper beach beside it is **Ocean Beach**, a slender ribbon of sand that decorates three miles of San Francisco's western perimeter. Remember, this is San Francisco—land of fog, mist, and west winds—beachwear here more often consists of sweaters than swimsuits. The water, sweeping down from the Arctic, is too cold for mere mortals; only surfers and polar bear swimmers brave it. Nevertheless, to walk this strand is to trek the border of eternity. American Indians called San Francisco's ocean the "sundown sea." If you'll take the time some late afternoon, you'll see that the fiery orb still settles nightly just offshore.

At the intersection of Skyline and Lake Merced boulevards lies **Lake Merced**, a U-shaped reservoir that has the unusual distinction of once having been salt water. Bounded by the Harding Park golf links and hiking trails, it provides a pretty spot to picnic. If you decide to pass up the hang gliding at Fort Funston, you might rent a rowboat or canoe at the clubhouse here and try a less nerve-jangling sport. The lake is stocked with catfish and trout.

Heading back along the Great Highway, you'll encounter the **San Francisco Zoo**. Countless changes have taken place over the past few years as part of an ambitious rebuilding program. The longtime main entrance on Sloat Boulevard has moved to the Great Highway and a new Entry Village now greets visitors. The newest exhibit is a one-acre grizzly bear habitat with a meadow and a 20,000-gallon pool. Guests can stroll up Zoo Street and visit

sights

AUTHOR FAVORITE

Located on Skyline Boulevard at the far end of Ocean Beach, **Fort Funston** is the prettiest stretch to stroll. The fort itself is little more than a sequence of rusting gun emplacements, but there is a half-mile nature trail here that winds along cliffs overlooking the sea. It's a windblown region of dune grass and leathery succulent plants, with views that span San Francisco and alight on the shore of Marin. Hang gliders dust the cliffs of Fort Funston, adding another dramatic element to this spectacle of sun and wind.

the African Savanna, a three-acre habitat housing giraffes, antelope, and birds. Guests can continue on to the Lemur Forest, while Puente al Sur ("bridge to the south") brings together such South American species as the giant anteater, tapir, and capybara. There's a children's zoo, home to the Meerkat and Prairie Dog exhibits, as well as an extensive facility for classes and educational programs. Other unique exhibits include Gorilla World, one of the world's largest gorilla habitats; Koala Crossing, one of the few zoo habitats of this teddy bear–like marsupial; and the Primate Discovery Center, a home for rare and endangered apes, monkeys, and lemurs. The daily (except Monday) big-cat feeding at the Lion House is especially popular. More than most zoos, this one goes out of its way to prove it's not just for kids. Besides a full calendar of events for children and families, the zoo sponsors adults-only mating season parties, including a popular Valentine's Day Woo at the Zoo sex tour. Admission. ~ 47th Avenue and Sloat Boulevard; 415-753-7080; www.sfzoo.org, e-mail webmaster@sfzoo.org.

Say the word "hostel" and the first pictures to come to mind are spartan accommodations and shabby surroundings. At **Hostelling International–San Francisco–Fisherman's Wharf** that simply is not the case. Set in Fort Mason, an old military base that is now part of a magnificent national park, the hostel overlooks San Francisco Bay. In addition to eye-boggling views, the facility is within walking distance of the Marina district and Fisherman's Wharf. The hostel itself is contained in a Civil War–era infirmary and features a living room, kitchen, and laundry, as well as a café that offers stunning views of the bay. The rooms, carpeted and quite clean, are dorm-style with 4 to 24 bunk beds in each. Rates also include a continental breakfast. No smoking or alcohol-imbibing; strict noise curfew at 11:00 p.m. Free walking tours, music, and movies are offered. Reservations recommended. ~ Fort Mason, Building 240, Bay and Franklin streets; 415-771-7277, fax 415-771-1468; www.norcalhostels.org, e-mail fishermanswharf@sf hostels.com. BUDGET.

LODGING

If you're seeking a hotel near the ocean, removed from the hubbub of downtown San Francisco, consider **Seal Rock Inn**. Perched on a bluff overlooking the Pacific, it's located just outside the Golden Gate National Recreation Area, a stone-skip away from Ocean Beach and Golden Gate Park. The 27 guest rooms are spacious, easily sleeping four people. Furnishings and decor are unimaginative but quite comfortable; the rooms are carpeted wall-to-wall and equipped with televisions and phones. Also, a godsend in this region of frequent fog, some rooms have fireplaces. These are a little extra, as are rooms featuring mini-kitchenettes and panoramic ocean views. ~ 545 Point Lobos Avenue; 415-752-8000, 888-732-5762, fax 415-752-6034; www.seal

San Francisco, Family-Style

San Francisco can be a great vacation spot for travelers with children. Plan ahead and allow plenty of time; many of the places that kids find the most fun are widely dispersed around the city. Here are some family-tested recommendations:

CHINATOWN   Ride the Powell-Hyde cable car to Chinatown to see the **Golden Gate Fortune Cookie Factory** (page 64) and the nearby **Cable Car Museum** (page 65).

FISHERMAN'S WHARF   See the historic ships in **Aquatic Park** (page 78) at Fisherman's Wharf. Then take a walk among the sharks at **Aquarium of the Bay** (page 76).

rockinn.com, e-mail reservations@sealrockinn.com. MODERATE TO DELUXE.

San Francisco's first motel is a 24-room art-deco beauty. Built in 1936, the same year as the Golden Gate Bridge, the **Ocean Park Motel** has modern furnishings and cedar paneling. In addition to attractive rooms with microwaves and refrigerators (some with kitchens) and large family suites, it offers guests an outdoor hot tub, garden courtyard, and small playground. Dogs are welcome (extra fee). ~ 2690 46th Avenue; 415-566-7020, fax 415-665-8959; www.oceanparkmotel.com, e-mail ocnprk36@aol.com. MODERATE.

DINING   One of San Francisco's most popular vegetarian restaurants is incongruously situated in an old waterfront warehouse. With pipes exposed and a metal superstructure supporting the roof, **Greens at Fort Mason** possesses the aura of an upscale airplane hangar. But this eatery, run by the Zen Center, has been deftly furnished with burlwood tables, and there's a view of the Golden Gate out of the warehouse windows. The lunch menu includes vegetable brochettes fired over mesquite charcoal, pita bread stuffed with hummus, grilled tofu, soups, and daily specials. Dinner menu is à la carte Monday through Friday, pre-set on Saturday. The menu changes daily: a typical multicourse repast would be soft polenta with grilled portobello mushrooms; spinach linguine with artichokes, shiitake mushrooms, pine nuts, rosemary, and parmesan; Tunisian salad; eggplant soup; Gruyère tart; lettuce salad; tea; and dessert. Reservations recommended for lunch and dinner. No lunch on Monday, brunch but no dinner on Sunday.

SF'S WEST COAST   Head out to San Francisco's west coast to visit two different kid-pleasers: the **Exploratorium** (page 88) and the **San Francisco Zoo** (page 90).

METREON   Although some moms report that their media-savvy kids are unimpressed with other Metreon attractions, two places not to miss are the adjacent **Zeum** and the **1906 Charles Looff Carousel** on the Rooftop at Yerba Buena Gardens (page 109).

THE HAIGHT   Fool your kids into learning while they have a blast at the **Randall Museum**. Interactive exhibits focus on the culture of San Francisco, from science to art. Audience-participation animal sessions are held Saturday at noon. There's a playground adjacent to the museum. Closed Sunday and Monday. ~ 199 Museum Way; 415-554-9600, fax 415-554-9609; www.randallmuseum.org, e-mail info@randallmuseum.org.

~ Fort Mason Center, Building A; 415-771-6222, fax 415-771-3472; www.greensrestaurant.com. MODERATE TO DELUXE.

In a city famed for its amazing array of ethnic restaurants, there's only one place where you can try Tibetan cuisine. **Taste of the Himalayas** provides it, as well as Nepalese and Indian dishes. The minute you wrap your taste buds around any item served here, you'll know you're not in Kansas any more. Go for the *momos* (dumplings with veggies or meat) or the *alu bhanta* (Himalayan-style eggplant with potatoes). The warm, friendly staff, mainly Tibetan refugees, and the authentic decorative touches make a meal here a memorable experience. ~ 2420 Lombard Street; 415-674-9898. MODERATE.

Try as you might to escape the trodden paths, some places in the world are simply inevitable. Such a one is the Cliff House, a historic structure at the edge of the sea that is positively inundated with tourists. Still, the **Bistro at the Cliff House** offers great views of the Sutro Baths, the Marin coastline, and the Golden Gate Bridge. The breakfast and lunch menu boasts omelettes as well as soups and sandwiches. At dinner there are pasta dishes, several seafood selections, and a few chicken, steak, or lamb entrées. **Sutro's**, a more formal two-story dining room, offers an upscale seafood menu for lunch and dinner. ~ 1090 Point Lobos Avenue; 415-386-3330; www.cliffhouse.com, e-mail info@cliffhouse.com. MODERATE TO DELUXE.

For a tad less expensive meal than at the nearby Cliff House, head uphill a few steps to **Louis'**, a cliffside café that's been family-owned since 1937. The dinners, served with soup or salad, include New York steak, prawns, scallops, and hamburger steak.

Breakfast and lunch are similar all-American affairs. Add a post-card view of the Sutro Baths and Seal Rocks and you have one hell of a bargain. Limited dinner hours during winter. ~ 902 Point Lobos Avenue; 415-387-6330. MODERATE.

Seafood lovers start lining up early at the popular **Pacific Café** in the outer Richmond District where the wait for a table is soothed by a complimentary glass of wine and convivial talk. Then it's time to sink into a high-backed wooden booth and ponder the daily specials, which always include a wide assortment of grilled fresh fish and frequently ahi tuna garnished with wasabe butter, crab cakes, and garlic-infused steamed mussels. Dinner only. ~ 7000 Geary Boulevard; 415-387-7091. MODERATE.

Leave your shoes at the door and step into Southeast Asian elegance. **Khan Toke Thai House** offers all the culinary and aes-thetic delights of fine dining without the hefty price. Sunken-floor seating, intricate wood carvings, and gold inlay transform the interior into an exotic locale. Try the fried tofu appetizer with peanut sauce, green curry chicken, or any of their other Thai de-lights. Ask for a spot in the back and get your own secluded table. Reservations suggested. Dinner only. ~ 5937 Geary Boule-vard; 415-668-6654. MODERATE.

NIGHTLIFE   The **Magic Theatre** has premiered several plays by Pulitzer Prize–winning dramatist Sam Shepard, who was playwright-in-residence here for several years. Plays by new playwrights are performed nearly year-round. ~ Fort Mason Center, Building D; 415-441-8822; www.magictheatre.org.

▼ ▼ ▼ ▼ ▼ ▼ ▼ ▼ ▼ ▼
The Presidio

What was previously the oldest active military base in the country is now part of the country's largest urban national park. The Presidio is also a National Historic Landmark. It was established by the Spanish in 1776 and taken over by the United States in 1846. Civil War troops trained here, and the Sixth Army established the base as its headquarters. Even when it was a military base, the Presidio had the feel of a coun-try retreat. Hiking trails snake through the 1400 acres of undu-lating hills sprinkled with acacia, madrone, pine, and redwood trees, and there are expansive bay views. Although still under de-velopment, there are plans for new hiking trails, museums, edu-cation centers, and conference facilities.

SIGHTS   The best way to explore the Presidio is by stopping first at the **Visitor Center**. The folks here are very knowledgeable; they'll provide you with a map and information about free public pro-grams. The center is temporarily located at the **Officers' Club**, a tile-roof, Spanish-style structure. It includes part of the original 1776 Presidio, one of the first buildings ever constructed in San

Francisco. ~ Building 50, Moraga Avenue; 415-561-4323, fax 415-561-4310; www.nps.gov/prsf.

The **National Cemetery**, with rows of tombstones on a grassy knoll overlooking the Golden Gate Bridge, is San Francisco's salute to the nation's war dead. ~ Lincoln Boulevard.

The remainder of our Presidio tour is of a more natural bent. There's **El Polin Spring**, where, as the brass plaque proclaims, "the early Spanish garrison attained its water supply." History has rarely been made in a more beautiful spot. The spring is set in a lovely park surrounded by hills upon which eucalyptus trees battle with conifers for strategic ground. Hiking trails lead down and outward from this enchanted glade. ~ Located at the end of MacArthur Avenue.

◄ HIDDEN

The newly opened **Immigrant Point Overlook** features stone benches and terraces, and affords outstanding views of the Pacific Ocean and the Golden Gate Bridge. ~ Washington Boulevard between Central Magazine and Compton roads.

Mountain Lake Park, stationed along the Presidio's southern flank, is another idyllic locale. With grassy meadows and wooded walkways, it's a great place to picnic or stroll. The lake itself, a favorite watering hole among ducks visiting from out of town, is skirted with tule reeds and overhung with willows. There's also a playground here. ~ Lake Street between 8th and Funston avenues.

The Presidio's newest addition centers around the **Letterman Digital Arts Center**. This 865,000-square-foot office complex (one of the largest developments in San Francisco history) is now home to employees of Lucasfilm, Ltd. George Lucas, of *Star Wars* fame, has extended his Marin-based digital media firm southward across the Golden Gate. This sprawling campus also includes open acreage and beautiful views of the bay. ~ Corner of Lyon Street and Lombard Street.

The base's prettiest walk is actually in civilian territory along the **Presidio Wall** bordering Lyon Street. Starting at the Lombard Street Gate, where two cannons guard the fort's eastern entrance,

THE LAST STAND

The battle lines are drawn at **Lover's Lane**. March, or even stroll, along this narrow pathway, and review these armies of nature. On one side, standing sentinel straight, out-thrust arms shading the lane, are the eucalyptus. Mustered along the other front, clad in darker uniforms, seeming to retreat before the wind, are the conifer trees. Forgetting for a moment these silly games soldiers play, look around. You are standing in an awesome and spectacular spot, one of the last forests in San Francisco. ~ In the southeast corner of the Presidio.

walk uphill along Lyon Street. That wall of urbanity to the left is the city's chic Union Street district, breeding place for fern bars and antique stores. To the right, beyond the Presidio's stone enclosure, are the tumbling hills and towering trees of the old garrison.

After several blocks, Lyon ceases to be a street and becomes a staircase. The most arduous and rewarding part of the trek begins; you can follow this stairway to heaven, which happens to be Broadway, two heart-pounding blocks above you. Ascend and the city falls away—the Palace of Fine Arts, Alcatraz, the Marina, all become landing points for your vision. Closer to hand are the houses of San Francisco's posh Pacific Heights district, stately structures looming several stories and sprawling across the landscape. When you reach the stone steps at the top of Broadway, they will still rise above, potent and pretentious, hard contrast to the Presidio's leafy acres.

DINING   Creative California cuisine may be everywhere you look in San Francisco, but rarely will you find it served in such a restfully sylvan setting as at the **Presidio Café**, located in the clubhouse of the Presidio Golf Course. The indoor dining area features an exposed-beam cathedral ceiling, a massive stone fireplace, and picture windows looking out on the golf course, while the outdoor area is sandwiched between the links and the forest. The menu features specialty sandwiches. Prices are reasonable, and there's ample free parking. Hours are late morning to afternoon, with appetizers served until evening. (Hours vary slightly on weekends.) ~ 300 Finley Road (at the Arguello gate); 415-561-4661 ext. 203; www.presidiogolf.com. MODERATE.

Golden Gate Park

It is the Central Park of the West. Or perhaps we should say that Central Park is New York's answer to Golden Gate Park. It extends from the Haight-Ashbury neighborhood, across nearly half the width of the city, all the way to the ocean. With its folded hills and sloping meadows, its lakes and museums, Golden Gate is everyone's favorite park.

Once an undeveloped region of sand dunes, the park today encompasses over 1000 acres of gardens, lawns, and forests. The transformation from wasteland to wonderland came about during the late-19th and early-20th centuries through the efforts of a mastermind named John McLaren. A gardener by trade, this Scotsman could rightly be called an architect of the earth. Within his lifetime he oversaw the creation of the world's largest human-made park.

What he wrought was a place that has something to suit everyone: there are tennis courts; lawn bowling greens; hiking trails; byways for bicyclists, rollerskaters, skateboarders, even unicyclists; a nine-hole golf course; an archery field; flycasting pools; playgrounds; fields for soccer and football; riding stables; even checker pavilions. Facilities for renting bikes and skates are located just outside the park along Haight and Stanyan streets.

Or, if you'd prefer not to lift a finger, you can always pull up a shade tree and watch the parade. The best day to visit Golden Gate Park is Sunday when many of the roads in the eastern end of the park are closed to cars but open to skaters, jugglers, cyclists, troubadours, mimes, skateboarders, impromptu theater groups, sun worshippers, and anyone else who feels inspired.

Touring the park should be done on another day, when you can drive freely through the grounds. There are two roads spanning the length of the park. Each begins near Stanyan Street on the east side of Golden Gate Park and runs about four miles westward to the Pacific. The best way to see this area is to travel out along John F. Kennedy Drive and back by Martin Luther King, Jr. Drive, detouring down the side roads that lead into the heart of the park.

The first stop along John F. Kennedy Drive lies immediately after the entrance. That red-tile building is **McLaren Lodge**, park headquarters and home base for maps, brochures, pamphlets, and information. ~ Stanyan and Fell streets; 415-831-2700, fax 415-221-8034; www.parks.sfgov.org.

SIGHTS

The glass palace nearby is the **Conservatory of Flowers**. Built in 1878 and Victorian in style, it houses a plant kingdom ruled by stately palm trees and peopled with tropical flowers, pendent ferns, and courtly orchids. The Conservatory makes for a stunning photo op. Closed Monday. Admission. ~ John F. Kennedy Drive; 415-666-7001; www.conservatoryofflowers.org.

Just down the street is **Rhododendron Dell**. A lacework of trails threads through this 20-acre garden; if you're visiting in early spring, when the rose-hued bushes are blooming, the dell is a concert of colors.

Just beyond this garden beats the cultural heart of Golden Gate Park. Located around a tree-studded concourse are the de

AUTHOR FAVORITE

If you're like me, you won't be in Golden Gate Park more than an hour or two before museum fatigue sets in and all the art starts looking like kindergarten craft. It's time for the **Japanese Tea Garden**. Here you can rest your heavy eyes on carp-filled ponds and handwrought gateways. There are arch footbridges, cherry trees, bonsai gardens, and, of course, a tea house where Japanese women serve jasmine tea and cookies. Admission.

Young Museum, Academy of Sciences, and Japanese Tea Garden. The **de Young Memorial Museum** first opened in 1895; an earthquake in 1989 closed its doors until 2005, when it re-opened in a contemporary copper structure with a 144-foot-high twisting tower. A new sculpture garden and thoughtful landscaping create a feast for the eyes. Skylit courts, floor-to-ceiling windows, and avant-garde free-standing furniture bring a modern touch to the interior. Exhibits trace the course of American art from colonial times to the mid-20th century, including an important collection of colonial-era art donated by the Rockefellers; the Art of the Americas gallery features ancient art from Central and South America as well as North American art of the past 400 years. There's also an intriguing display of works from Africa and Oceania. The de Young has one of the largest collections in the nation. Admission. ~ 415-750-3600, fax 415-750-7386; www.thinker.org, e-mail guestbook@famsf.org.

All these cultural gathering places cluster around a **Music Concourse.**

Just to the southeast of the Music Concourse is the new home of the **California Academy of Sciences**, a natural history museum lauded as "the Smithsonian of the West." A new piazza with views of the park sits at the heart of the building and the Steinhart Aquarium has expanded to include the Tank of Giants, for huge sea bass and halibut and the California Kelp Forest, home to schools of rainbow-colored fish. A four-story rainforest, planetarium, and penguins in their natural habitat make this a joy for the family. Admission. ~ 55 Concourse Drive; 415-321-8119; www.calacademy.org.

You can get back on John F. Kennedy Drive and resume your self-guided tour by continuing to **Stow Lake**. This is a donut-shaped body of water with an island as the hole in the middle. From the island's crest you can gaze across San Francisco from Bay to ocean. Or, if an uphill is not in your day's itinerary, there's a footpath around the island perimeter that passes an ornate Chinese pagoda. There are also rowboats, pedalboats, and electric motorboats for rent, and a small snack bar.

Next along John F. Kennedy Drive you'll pass **Rainbow Falls**. That monument at the top, from which this cascade appears to spill, is **Prayerbook Cross**, modeled after an old Celtic cross.

This is followed close on by a chain of meadows, a kind of rolling green counterpoint to the chain of lakes that lie ahead. **Speedway Meadow** and **Lindley Meadow** offer barbecue pits and picnic tables; both are fabulous areas for sunbathing.

Spreckels Lake is home to ducks, seagulls, and model sailboats. Nearby is the **Buffalo Paddock**, where American bison still roam, though within the confines of a barbed wire fence.

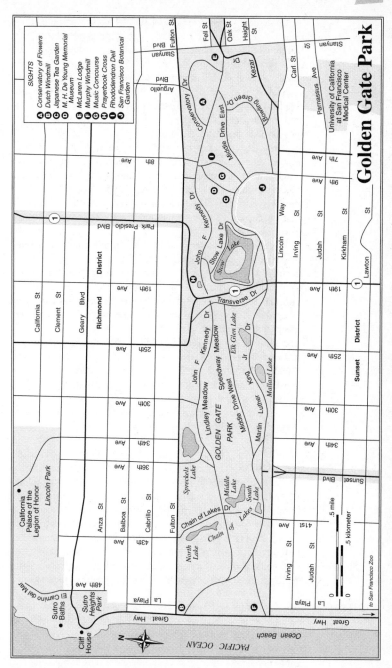

SIGHTS

- Ⓐ Conservatory of Flowers
- Ⓑ Dutch Windmill
- Ⓒ Japanese Tea Garden
- Ⓓ M. H. De Young Memorial Museum
- Ⓔ McLaren Lodge
- Ⓕ Murphy Windmill
- Ⓖ Music Concourse
- Ⓗ Prayerbook Cross
- Ⓘ Rhododendron Dell
- Ⓙ San Francisco Botanical Garden

Golden Gate Park

Immediately beyond is the **Chain of Lakes**, a string of three reservoirs stretching the width of the park, perpendicular to John F. Kennedy Drive. Framed by eucalyptus trees, they offer hiking paths around each shoreline. As you circumnavigate these baby lakes, you will notice they are freckled with miniature islands. Each lake possesses a singular personality: North Lake is remarkable for its hip-deep swamp cypress; Middle Lake features an island tufted with willows; and South Lake, tiniest of the triplets, sprouts bamboo along its shore.

If these ponds be babies, the great mother of them all rests nearby. Where the road meets the Pacific you'll come upon the **Dutch Windmill**, a regal structure built in 1903. With its wooden struts and scale-like shingles, it stares into the face of the sea's inevitable west winds. The Dutchman's cousin, **Murphy Windmill**, which is currently under renovation, lives several hundred yards down the coast.

From here at continent's edge, it's a four-mile trip back through the park along Martin Luther King, Jr. Drive. After picking it up at Murphy Windmill, you'll find that this softly curving road passes lakes and forests, meadows and playgrounds. More importantly, it borders **San Francisco Botanical Garden**, a place specially made for garden lovers. The garden is a world within itself, a 55-acre flower quilt stitched together by pathways. Over 7000 species peacefully coexist here—dwarf conifers and sprawling magnolias, as well as plants from Asia, the Andes, Australia, and America. There is a "redwood trail" devoted to native California plants, a "garden of fragrance" redolent of flowers, and a Japanese strolling garden. It's a kind of park within a park, a glorious finale for your visit to this park within a city. ~ 415-661-1316, fax 415-661-3539; www.sfbotanicalgarden.org.

Gay Neighborhoods

▼▼▼▼▼▼▼▼▼▼▼▼▼▼

San Francisco's gay neighborhoods center around Castro Street, Polk Street, and in the South of Market area. The city's lesbian community focuses along Valencia Street in the Mission District. With a population that today numbers perhaps 200,000, the community has become a powerful social and political force. In 1977, Supervisor Harvey Milk became the nation's first openly gay man elected to a major municipal post. Since then, despite the AIDS epidemic, San Francisco has retained gay supervisors and the gay community has remained an integral part of the city's life.

SIGHTS

The **San Francisco Lesbian Gay Bisexual Transgender Community Center** ("the Center" for short) houses 11 non-profit organizations and is a major meeting point for the LGBT community, as well as their friends and families. Each week more than 2,000 people use their services and the hundreds of meetings and events encompass education, arts and social events, programs for children and youth, health screening and referrals. ~ 1800 Market Street; 415-865-5555, fax 415- 865-5501; www.sfcenter. org, e-mail info@sfcenter.org.

Throughout the Castro and Polk districts are numerous hotels catering primarily to gay travelers. Others in these areas serve a wide-ranging clientele, including many gay guests.

LODGING

There are several hotels located in the center of the action. The first is the **Inn on Castro**, an eight-room bed and breakfast housed in an old Victorian. A class establishment all the way, the inn adds subtle touches like fresh flowers. Each room is decorated in a different fashion, and the house atmosphere is comfortable and personal. Most rooms have private baths. Because of its popularity, the hotel recommends reservations. ~ 321 Castro Street; phone/fax 415-861-0321; www.innoncastro.com, e-mail innkeeper@innoncastro.com. MODERATE TO DELUXE.

A charming 1870s Victorian B&B, **24 Henry** is right in the middle of the Castro on a quiet little side street. The ten guest rooms have high ceilings, period furniture, and comfortable beds. Just three have private baths and all have wi-fi access. The TV is in the parlor, where breakfast is served. ~ 24 Henry Street; 415-864-5686, 800-900-5686, fax 415-864-0406; www.24henry. com, e-mail reservations@24henry.com. BUDGET TO MODERATE.

Several blocks from Castro Street is **The Willows Bed and Breakfast Inn**, a beautiful 12-room facility that attracts both gay and straight guests. Each room has been furnished with antique wooden pieces and adorned with French art prints (while all have a contemporary mini-fridge). The trademark of this cozy hostelry, however, is the willow-branch furniture designed expressly for the Inn. It's personal touches like this that make it a special place.

VISIT A PAINTED LADY

Those in search of the quintessential "Painted Lady" Victorian will not want to miss **Chateau Tivoli**, a dazzling three-story 1892 mansion resplendent with gold leaf, stained-glass windows, and elaborate woodwork. Many of the rooms and suites are named for famous painted ladies of San Francisco, including actress Lola Montez and flapper Aimee Crocker. Accommodations consist of nine rooms and suites. Two have a shared bath, and some have marble bathrooms. The clientele is both straight and gay. Wine and cheese are served in the afternoon, and champagne brunch on Sunday is included in the rates. Non-smoking. ~ 1057 Steiner Street; 415-776-5462, 800-228-1647, fax 415-776-0505; www.chateautivoli.com, e-mail mail@chateautivoli.com. MODERATE TO ULTRA-DELUXE.

Shared bath. ~ 710 14th Street; 415-431-4770, 800-431-0277, fax 415-431-5295; www.willowssf.com, e-mail vacation@willowssf. com. MODERATE TO DELUXE.

A lovingly restored 1909 Edwardian mansion, **The Parker Guest House** has 21 rooms with hardwood or tile floors, lots of light, and warm wood furnishings. All but the smallest queen room have private baths and all have wi-fi access. There are extensive gardens, two lounges with a piano and fireplace, a library, and a steam room. ~ 520 Church Street; 888-520- 7275, fax 415-621-4139; www.parkerguesthouse.com, e-mail info@parker guesthouse.com. MODERATE TO DELUXE.

The **Inn San Francisco** resides in a 19th-century world. Set in a grand four-story Victorian, this splendid mansion has been furnished entirely with period pieces. There are gilded mirrors and beveled glass in the parlors, wall sconces and marble sinks in many rooms, as well as other antique flourishes. The rooftop sundeck provides a great view of the city, and an English garden in the back has a gazebo and hot tub. Room prices in this elegant establishment all include a full buffet breakfast; the moderate prices are for shared bath; some deluxe rooms have private facilities; ultra-deluxe rooms come with jacuzzis. The clientele is both gay and straight. ~ 943 South Van Ness Avenue; 415-641-0188, 800-359-0913, fax 415-641-1701; www.innsf.com, e-mail innkeeper@innsf.com. MODERATE TO DELUXE.

Midway between Castro Street and the Haight-Ashbury neighborhood is the **Metro Hotel**. Appealing to a mixed clientele, there are 24 rooms, a small lobby, an adjoining café downstairs, and an English garden. The guests rooms are carpeted wall-to-wall, furnished with oak pieces, and decorated with wallhangings. Each has a private bath (shower only) and color television with cable. Set in a white Victorian building, it is clean and comfortable. Free wireless internet. ~ 319 Divisadero Street; 415-861-5364, fax 415-863-1970; www.metrohotelsf.com, e-mail metrohotelsf @sbcglobal.net. BUDGET TO MODERATE.

DINING

Over in the Castro Street neighborhood, **Luna** is a good choice. You can dine indoors or outside on a tree-studded patio. They feature a breakfast menu that includes poached eggs, omelettes, and eggs Benedict. Lunch consists of hamburgers, sandwiches, salads, and pasta. The restaurant serves dinner as well. ~ 558 Castro Street; 415-621-2566. MODERATE.

Anchor Oyster Bar is a hole-in-the-wall café that happens to serve delicious shellfish. There are oysters on the half shell, steamed clams and mussels, seafood cocktails, and various daily specials. Recommended for lunch or dinner. No lunch on Sunday. ~ 579 Castro Street; 415-431-3990. MODERATE.

Unique Bookstores

San Francisco has a long tradition of supporting unusual, often quirky bookstores, large and small. Yes, these days you'll find bookselling behemoths Borders, Barnes & Noble, and B. Dalton downtown, but serious readers still head for personality-packed independent shops.

For used books and magazines, try **McDonald's Bookshop** in the Tenderloin. This musty warren of crowded aisles could keep you browsing for hours. It boasts more than a million books and a vast array of magazines that dates back to the 1920s, including a complete selection of *Life*, which began publication in 1936. There are also hundreds of old photos and a collection of James Dean pictures and books. Closed Sunday and Monday. ~ 48 Turk Street; 415-673-2235; e-mail mcdonaldsbookshop@prodigy.net.

For guidebooks, language instruction manuals and CDs, maps, luggage, and a host of other travel accessories, try **Get Lost Travel Books**. ~ 1825 Market Street; 415-437-0529; www.getlostbooks.com.

A destination for discriminating book lovers for more than 40 years, **Green Apple Books** sells, buys and trades new and used books, CDs, and DVDs in virtually every genre. ~ 506 Clement Street; 415-387-2272; www.greenapplebooks.com.

San Francisco's most famous independent bookshop, **City Lights Bookstore** in North Beach stocks both the traditional and the avant-garde. Within the hallowed confines of this oddly shaped store is a treasure trove of magazines on arts and politics, plus books on everything from nirvana to the here and now. Once a roosting place for Beat writers like Allen Ginsberg, Jack Kerouac, and Neal Cassady, it still remains a vital gathering point for local artists. The book selection is unique, featuring many contemporary poetry and prose volumes that are unavailable elsewhere. More importantly, City Lights is a place where you're welcome to pull up a chair and immerse yourself in conversation or classic literature *and* they're open daily until midnight. ~ 261 Columbus Avenue; 415-362-8193, fax 415-362-4921; www.citylights.com, e-mail staff@citylights.com.

Located in the heart of the Castro, **A Different Light** carries the most popular titles for and about the lesbian, gay, bisexual, and transgender community. ~ 489 Castro Street; 415-431-0891; www.adlbooks.com.

To appease your sugar cravings, stop in at **Sweet Inspiration**. Though the café doesn't sport a particularly Castro-esque vibe, it has the most delectable cakes and pastries around. The slices are so huge, you'll have to share. Try the cheesecake, tiramisu, or fresh fruit tart. ~ 2239 Market Street; 415-621-8664. BUDGET.

Exceptionally popular with the locals, **Cafe Flore** has a partially enclosed outside patio and sidewalk, where diners can watch life in the Castro go by. Inside, the floor is tiled, the atmosphere casual and relaxed. You order at the window from a blackboard menu listing soups, pastas, sandwiches, and burgers. There's also a full bar and an espresso bar. ~ 2298 Market Street; 415-621-8579, fax 415-934-8579; www.cafeflore.com. BUDGET TO MODERATE.

A good place after a late movie at the Castro Theater is **Orphan Andy's**, one of the few San Francisco restaurants open 24 hours. Decorated with a colorful 1950s diner theme with a counter and leatherette booths, Orphan Andy's serves good burgers, sandwiches, omelettes, and other classic coffee-shop fare. ~ 3991 17th Street; 415-864-9795. BUDGET TO MODERATE.

Open for breakfast and lunch, catering to a mixed clientele, and particularly popular with women, is **Just For You**. This diner just outside the Potrero Hill district has counter service and tables and is decorated with artwork by local artists. The cuisine is a mix of American and Cajun, with cornmeal pancakes and grits for breakfast, hamburgers and crabcake sandwiches at lunch. ~ 732 22nd Street; 415-647-3033; www.justforyoucafe.com. MODERATE.

Dollar for dollar, the best dining spot along Polk Street is **Swan Oyster Depot**. It's a short-order place serving fresh prawns, crabs, lobster, shrimp, and oysters, all displayed in trays out front. The place consists simply of a counter lined with stools and is almost always packed. The depot opens at 8 a.m. and closes at 5:30 p.m. Closed Sunday. ~ 1517 Polk Street; 415-673-1101. MODERATE.

HIDDEN ▶ There are about a thousand restaurants in San Francisco named Hunan, and the second most popular name seems to be Cordon Bleu. The place claiming to be the original **Cordon Bleu Vietnamese Restaurant** is a simple café-style establishment serving a few good Southeast Asian dishes. There are imperial rolls, shish kabobs and five-spice roast chicken. No lunch on Sunday. Closed Monday. ~ 1574 California Street; 415-673-5637. BUDGET.

SHOPPING   The Castro Street shopping district stretches along Castro from 19th Street to Market Street, then continues for several blocks on "Upper Market"; there are also several interesting stores along 18th Street. The entire area is surprisingly compact, but features a variety of shops. Together with Polk Street, it represents the major gay shopping area in San Francisco.

Polk Street is wall to wall with designer fashion shops, boutiques, and all manner of clothing outlets. The central gay area stretches from Post Street to Washington Street, but savvy shoppers will continue on to Union Street, since several intriguing stores lie on the outskirts of the neighborhood.

At the **Tibet Shop** are *sili* bangles, painted lanterns, Buddha figurines, prayer beads, and monastic incense. This wonderful little shop also has vests, skirts, dresses, shirts, and jackets made in Nepal, Tibet, and Bhutan. ~ 4100 19th Street; 415-982-0326.

Good Vibrations, a sex toy, book, and video emporium designed in the late 1970s especially for women, has become a Bay Area institution. The store sells erotic literature, self-help sex books, feminist erotica, videos and sex education films, and an unbeatable array of vibrators and electric massagers. A highlight of the store is an antique vibrator museum with some rather unusual items like a cranked version that looks like a rolling pin. ~ 603 Valencia Street; 415-522-5460, 800-289-8423; www.good vibes.com, e-mail customerservice@goodvibes.com.

One example of San Francisco's wide-open tradition is the presence of almost 200 gay bars in the city. There's everything here from rock clubs to piano bars to stylish cabarets. Some are strictly gay, others mix their customers, and some have become so popular that straights have begun to take them over from gays.

NIGHTLIFE

There are a dozen or so bars in the Castro Street area, many open from early morning until the wee hours. Among the nicest is **Twin Peaks Tavern** with its overhead fans and large windows overlooking the street. ~ 401 Castro Street; 415-864-9470.

Nearby, you'll find **The Stud**, everybody's favorite gay bar. Everybody in this case includes aging hippies, multihued punks, curious straights, and even a gay or two, all packed elbow to armpit into this pulsing club. Cover on most nights. Occasionally closed on Monday. ~ 399 9th Street; 415-863-6623; www. studsf.com.

SHOPPING FOR A GOOD CAUSE

Shopping at **Under One Roof** is like giving to a good cause. This store is underwritten by individuals and corporations, so 100 percent of the profits are donated to dozens of AIDS service organizations. It sells a wide selection of items, including candles, soaps, lotions, candy, T-shirts, jewelry, and gay and lesbian books. Most of the personnel are volunteers.
~ 549 Castro Street; 415-503-2300, fax 415-503-2301; www.under oneroof.org.

The scene is different down the street at the **The Eagle Tavern**, a Levis and leather bar when there is live music. Cover on Thursday. ~ 398 12th Street; 415-626-0880; www.sfeagle.com.

Closer to the Castro you'll find the **Lexington Club**, a mellow nightspot especially popular with lesbians. There's a pool table, a jukebox, and, perhaps most significantly, two women's restrooms. Closed Sunday. ~ 3464 19th Street; 415-863-2052; www.lexing tonclub.com.

For women who are ready to relax, there's **Osento Bath House**, a quiet and comfortable Japanese-style bath for women. There are also massage and sauna facilities and a sun deck for lounging and picnicking. Open from noon to midnight. Fee. ~ 955 Valencia Street; 415-282-6333; www.osento.com.

Cafe du Nord is *the* hip hangout for gays and straights alike. Built in 1907, the historic building's past life as a speakeasy is still visible in its bordello-red interior and dim lighting. Sidle up to the 40-foot mahogany bar or hunker down in a separate room where there's live entertainment most nights. ~ 2170 Market Street; 415-861-5016; www.cafedunord.com.

Nicest of all the Polk Street neighborhood bars is **Kimo's**. With mirrors and potted palms all around, it's a comfortable atmosphere. Cover for live music. ~ 1351 Polk Street; 415-885-4535.

The **N'Touch** has a disco dancefloor plus video monitors. There's always a lively Asian crowd here. With flashing lights and ample sound, it's a good spot for dancing and carousing and watching the go-go boys. Most nights have shows or other entertainment. Occasional cover. ~ 1548 Polk Street; 415-441-8413; www.ntouchsf.com.

Plays with gay, bisexual, transgender, and lesbian themes are the focus of **Theatre Rhinoceros**, an acclaimed company that presents performances at two theaters, Rhino's Mainstage and Rhino's Studio. ~ 2926 16th Street; 415-861-5079; www.therhino.org.

San Francisco's answer to off-off-Broadway is **The Marsh Theater**, a small, informal theater billed as a "breeding ground for new performances," which offers plays and spoken-word entertainment. Monday nights are reserved for performers trying out new work. ~ 1062 Valencia Street; 415-826-5750; www.the marsh.org.

South of Market

In the 1970s, South of Market, popularly known as SOMA, had the reputation as one of the most unattractive and unsafe neighborhoods in the city. Filled with residential hotels, vacant warehouses, and seedy bars, it was long ignored by many of the city's residents. This neglect presented an opportunity for those who wanted to be isolated, and SOMA became a hub for the gay-bathhouse crowd and the gay-leather crowd.

During the '80s SOMA metamorphosed again. Gay bathhouses were closed in a sweeping move by government officials and replaced by trendy nightclubs; gay-leather bars with names like "The Arena" converted into popular dance clubs with names like the "DNA Lounge."

The underutilized warehouses then brought in a different countercultural crowd—artists. Modeling themselves after the residents of New York City's SOHO (South of Houston) district, Bay Area artists converted SOMA warehouses into combination live/work spaces featuring art galleries, music studios, and performance spaces. Many of San Francisco's most creative people still live and display (or perform) in small galleries and theaters throughout SOMA.

Ephemeral as ever, SOMA next burst into another transitional phase, flaunting its formerly low-profile cyber-art industry with the promotional flair of a P. T. Barnum. Centering on Yerba Buena Gardens as the town square of the area, developers quickly packed the blocks between Market Street and Moscone Convention Center with family-oriented entertainment attractions, many of them showcasing interactive media.

Meanwhile, decrepit old hotels and office buildings in the surrounding neighborhood were replaced by upscale live/work complexes as builders petitioned City Hall for exemptions from San Francisco's strict anti-growth regulations, claiming that more condominiums and office suites in SOMA were needed to keep high-tech companies from moving elsewhere. Today, the artist and gay communities are being squeezed out of SOMA block by block. And

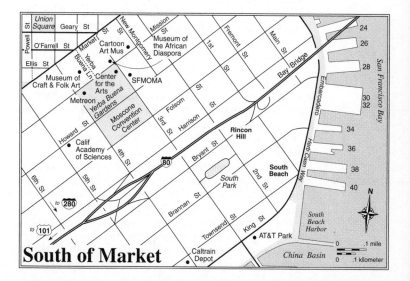

South of Market

oddly enough, all this urban redevelopment is meeting with less public protest than the traffic and noise associated with the big, glitzy nightclubs that are replacing the local leather bars of old.

Still, there are many restaurants and cafés that offer a true SOMA twist to their atmosphere and menu. Don't be surprised if your café table has a computer hooked up to the internet, or the restaurant you're dining at has decor created during the slow hours before lunch.

SIGHTS   Named for George Moscone, the San Francisco mayor who was assassinated in 1978, **Moscone Convention Center** is a mammoth convention center that extends across 11 acres. With restaurants, hotels, apartments, and stores encircling it like satellites, the center is the dominant feature in San Francisco's fastest-changing district. ~ Howard Street between 3rd and 4th streets.

An important addition to the area is **Yerba Buena Gardens**, a project that was 30 years in the making but has proven to be worth the wait by providing a forum for the visual and performing arts as well as some much-needed green space.

One component of the ten-acre complex located on top of the underground Moscone Convention Center is the **Yerba Buena Center for the Arts** with two buildings, one designed by the acclaimed Japanese architect Fumihiko Maki. It includes three galleries devoted to visual arts and high-tech installations, as well as a screening room for video and film. A large multipurpose room called "The Forum" hosts special events. In addition, a 755-seat theater offers a diverse lineup of music, dance, and performance art. Closed Monday. Admission.

Softening the contemporary hard edges of Yerba Buena is a five-and-a-half-acre esplanade of gardens and outdoor public art. A focal point of Yerba Buena Gardens is the **Martin Luther King Jr. Memorial**, a graceful waterfall spilling over Sierra granite. Behind the waterfall are a series of 12 thick glass panels etched with quotations drawn from speeches Dr. King made in San Francisco. Each quote is paired with a translation into a different language, including Chinese, Spanish, Hebrew, and Swahili, and representing the origins of the city's major ethnic groups. ~ 415-978-2787, fax 415-978-9635; www.ybca.org, e-mail comments@ ybca.org.

The **San Francisco Museum of Modern Art** is one of the top-ten most-visited museums in the United States. The building, designed by Swiss architect Mario Botta, is a Modernist work of art in itself, distinguished by a tower finished in alternating bands of black and white stone. Inside are three large galleries and more than 20 smaller ones, totaling 50,000 square feet. The second floor displays selections from the museum's permanent collection. The third-floor gallery features photographs and works on paper. The top two gallery floors accommodate special exhibitions and large-scale art from the museum's collection. Closed Wednesday. Admission. ~ 151 3rd Street; 415-357-4000, fax 415-357-4037; www.sfmoma.org.

A peculiar blend of theme park and shopping mall, the **Metreon** combines San Francisco's largest motion picture complex (15 screens plus an IMAX theater), six restaurants, play areas based on children's books, a futuristic video arcade, and 11 retail stores, plus plenty of high-tech advertising. The self-styled "entertainment center" looks like a giant concrete cube from the outside and stands four stories tall to accommodate the 50-by-100-foot IMAX screen. Almost everything here is associated with Sony's entertainment and technology empire and supported by sponsorships from other huge corporations, and many of the management team members are veterans of Disney, so don't be surprised if you feel like you've stepped into the world's largest advertisement for corporate America. If you're traveling with kids, the Metreon is a must-see—sort of. Among the multimedia "tie-ins" is the 175-seat Action Theatre featuring anime movies and live performances Friday through Sunday. You gotta be a teen to fully appreciate the **Playstation Store**, where you can try the latest video games played against opposing teams instead of against the computer. A standout here is the **International Spy Shop**, which sells gadgets that would impress James Bond. Meanwhile, mom and dad can play with the latest high-tech toys at the Sony and Cell Pro retail outlets. ~ 4th and Mission streets; 415-3537-3400, 800-638-7366; www.metreon.com, e-mail information@metreon.com.

> If your attention wanders during a game at AT&T Park, don't blame your team: it may be the food. In addition to basic hot dogs, there's Caribbean food, fruit smoothies, microbrews, and sushi. You *are* in San Francisco, after all.

Just over a second-floor walkway from the Metreon, on top of the Moscone Convention Center, the **Rooftop at Yerba Buena Gardens** presents another collection of family-oriented attractions, this time created not by megacorporations but by the San Francisco Redevelopment Agency. The high-tech draw here is **Zeum**, an art-and-technology center that offers hands-on, behind-the-scenes experiences in animation, video production, digital photography, web page design, 3-D modeling, and stage set design and production. Closed Monday and Tuesday during the school year; closed Monday in summer. Admission. ~ 4th and Howard streets; 415-820-3320; www.zeum.org.

In striking contrast to the futuristic Zeum is the antique **1906 Charles Looff Carousel**, originally the centerpiece of San Francisco's former Playland-at-the-Beach amusement park. The large, beautifully restored carousel has all-white horses that gleam like new. Admission. ~ 4th and Howard streets; 415-777-2800.

In addition, the rooftop complex includes the **Yerba Buena Ice Skating Center** (admission), an Olympic-size ice rink with huge windows overlooking the San Francisco skyline to create the feel of skating outdoors, and the adjoining 12-lane **Yerba Buena Bowling Center**. ~ 750 Folsom Street; 415-820-3532; www.skate bowl.com.

In 2005, the city finished construction of **Yerba Buena Lane**, a spiffy pedestrian mall connecting Mission and Market between 3rd and 4th streets. In addition to functioning as a convenient walkway from BART to Yerba Buena Gardens and Moscone Convention Center, the streetscape acts as a retail corridor and includes a dozen cafés, restaurants, and retailers.

A magnate for artistic ventures of all sorts, the area plays host to numerous museums, including the **Museum of Craft & Folk Art**. Exhibitions range from Cook Island quilts to San Simeon architect Julia Morgan's craftware. You'll also want to visit the gift shop, where they sell native and tribal goods, as well as a wide variety of jewelry and contemporary craft. Closed Monday. Admission. ~ 51 Yerba Buena Lane; 415-227-4888, fax 415-227-4351; www.mocfa.org, e-mail store@mocfa.org.

Another museum planning to relocate to Yerba Buena Lane is the **Contemporary Jewish Museum**, which will showcase scholarly and artistic work relating to the Jewish experience. This new $43 million facility—slated for completion in Spring 2008—will consist of 60,000 square feet of exhibition spaces and include an education center, auditorium, café, and museum shop. ~ 415-344-8800, fax 415-344-8815; www.jmsf.org.

Nearby is the 20,000-square-foot **Museum of the African Diaspora**, which offers film screenings, traveling and media-based exhibits, live music, and colloquiums and panels on a wide variety of topics central to the African diaspora. Closed Monday and Tuesday. ~ St. Regis Hotel and Residences, 685 Mission Street; 415-358-7200; www.moadsf.org.

HIDDEN ►   Also located in the Yerba Buena neighborhood, the **Cartoon Art Museum** features rotating exhibits of cartoon art in all its various incarnations: newspaper strips, political cartoons, comic

THREE BABES AND A BUS

If you find SF's nightlife options overwhelming, **3 Babes and a Bus** allows you a taste of different scenes, from '70s disco and Top-40 to salsa and R&B. For a flat fee, this nightclub-touring company takes care of the driving and cover charges while ensuring priority entry to a number of clubs on this four-hour tour. Reservations recommended. ~ 415-552-2582, 800-414-0158; www.threebabes.com, e-mail info@threebabes.com.

books, and animation are amply represented. Highlights include a children's gallery and a bookstore. One of only two museums of its kind in the United States, this rare treat should not be missed. Closed Monday. Admission. ~ 655 Mission Street; 415-227-8666, fax 415-243-8666; www.cartoonart.org, e-mail office@cartoonart.org.

The recently rechristened AT&T Park is situated on the south side of the South of Market warehouse district, along the China Basin waterfront and readily accessible from the Embarcadero or Route 280. Baseball's San Francisco Giants left 3Com Park (known as Candlestick Park until a Silicon Valley conglomerate bought the naming rights) in favor of this more cost-efficient facility, which has just over one-half the seating capacity. The $319 million ballpark features classic architecture inspired by Wrigley Field and Fenway Park, together with state-of-the-art lighting and electronics and an innovative seating alignment that provides the best possible views of the field from most seats. Speaking of views, fans also find themselves surrounded by a panorama of the San Francisco skyline, the Bay, and the distant East Bay Hills. Just outside the stadium, a wharfside promenade near center field lets passersby view ball games knothole-style. Tours (fee), offered at 10:30 a.m. and 12:30 p.m. daily except game days, include looks at the press box and the dugout. ~ King Street between 2nd and 3rd streets; 415-972-2400.

LODGING

The W Hotel provides trendy types upscale accommodations done in sleek Euro-Asian style. In addition to the usual high-end conveniences, special touches include goose-down duvets, complimentary boutique toiletry packs, in-room "munchie boxes," and "whatever, whenever" service. Rooms are spacious enough to launch a start-up inside. ~ 181 3rd Street; 415-777-5300, 888-625-5144, fax 415-817-7823; www.whotels.com. ULTRA-DELUXE.

The St. Regis Hotel and Residences is a bit more than just a hotel. First, the bottom 20 floors of the 40-story building indeed provide guest rooms: 269 in total, including 46 suites. These unusually spacious rooms (up to 3200 square feet) include first-rate amenities such as deep soaking tubs, original art, 42-inch plasma TVs, Wi-Fi, and great views. The building's top floors, however, are reserved for those who just couldn't leave: 102 privately owned condominiums and penthouses. The premises also include four levels of underground parking, a restaurant, spa, café, and two lounges. ~ 125 3rd Street; 415-284-4000, fax 415-284-4100; www.stregis.com/sanfrancisco. ULTRA-DELUXE.

DINING

If you're looking to nosh on a bagel, burgers, sandwich, or salad while your duds spin around in the suds, drop by Brain Wash. This innovative address combines a café with a laundromat.

Check out their cheap ($3.99) breakfasts Monday through Friday. ~ 1122 Folsom Street; 415-861-3663; www.brainwash. com, e-mail contact@brainwash.com. BUDGET.

There's another side to San Francisco beyond the bridge-dotted skyline and bustling capitalism; past the elaborate Victorians and winding streets; behind the inline skaters and Sunday strollers. It's a world of camp and fashion, where the drinks are mixed, the music is intoxicating, the clothing is sleek, and the men are women. Welcome to **AsiaSF**. Make no mistake, the food is good: grilled seafood, chicken satay, "baby got back" ribs and other Asian-influenced entrées. But no one comes for the food. They come for the "gender illusionists"—men you'd swear on your partner were women—performing cabaret numbers on a red runway when they're not filling water glasses. After dinner, work off the calories in the state-of-the-art danceclub downstairs. ~ 201 9th Street; 415-255-2742; www.asiasf.com. DELUXE.

A hotspot not far from the Yerba Buena Gardens complex is **Restaurant Lulu**, a noisy warehouse-sized restaurant that draws in crowds at lunch and dinner for superb meats and chicken prepared on a brick rotisserie. Also noteworthy are the shellfish selections such as iron skillet–roasted mussels and Dungeness crab with garlic. Reservations recommended. ~ 816 Folsom Street; 415-495-5775, fax 415-495-7810; www.restaurantlulu.com. MODERATE TO ULTRA-DELUXE.

HIDDEN ► **South Park Café** is a sunny and cheery dining spot facing, as its name suggests, South Park. With only a long zinc bar and a few tables, it is a popular gourmet dining spot known for its imaginative salads and daily meat and fish specials. Closed Sunday. No lunch Saturday; no dinner Monday. ~ 108 South Park; 415-495-7275, fax 415-495-7295; www.southparkcafesf.com. MODERATE TO DELUXE.

NIGHTLIFE SOMA is the epicenter of San Francisco's nightclub scene, and "something for everybody" seems to be the motto. For some live acoustic sounds from local bands or deejay-spun jazz, check out **Brain Wash**. There's always something happening at this hip café that also doubles as a . . . laundromat! Wednesday is "spoken word" night, Thursday is comedy night, and Friday and Saturday feature live bands. ~ 1122 Folsom Street; 415-861-3663; www. brainwash.com.

Icon Ultra Lounge takes an evening martini to new heights of sophistication with elaborate decor, plush seating, and an atmosphere geared toward young professionals. ~ 1192 Folsom Street; 415-626-6043. For upscale drinks in a fashionably low-brow setting, head to **Wish Bar and Lounge**, where deejays spin hits nightly. ~ 1539 Folsom Street; 415-278-9474.

There is only one thing in the world better than a rocking nightclub: two rocking nightclubs. That's what you get over at 3rd and Harrison streets. On Friday **the X** jumps to the sound of Top-40, hip-hop, R&B, and house; and on Thursday, it's 18+ hip-hop night at **City Nights**. Cover. ~ 715 Harrison Street; 415-339-8686; www.sfclubs.com.

The DNA **Lounge** has lasted much longer than most trendy clubs. The scene is high-decibel with a mixed crowd clearly born to dance. And dance they do, all over this two-story club. There's also occasional live music. Cover. ~ 375 11th Street; 415-626-1409; www.dnalounge.com.

A self-proclaimed "trailer-trash bistro," **Butter** serves up a host of snacks and drinks—all to the sound of a funky house beat provided by deejays. Just follow the 30-something model-chic hipsters in always-fashionable black. Closed Sunday and Monday. ~ 354 11th Street; 415-863-5964; www.smoothasbutter.com.

Some of the classic Bay Area rock and blues performers appear at **Slim's**, possibly because entertainer Boz Scaggs is an owner. But there is also a hefty line-up of alternative rock bands, so the crowd could be gray- or green-haired at this all-ages club. Usually a cover. ~ 333 11th Street; 415-255-0333; www.slims-sf.com.

An important member of the city's group of small theaters is the **Asian American Theater Company**, which represents the city's burgeoning Asian community. ~ 690 5th Street, Suite 211; 415-543-5738; www.asianamericantheater.org.

Outdoor Adventures

SPORT-FISHING

If you hanker to spend a day deep-sea fishing for rock cod, bass, salmon, and other gamefish, check out **Wacky Jacky**, which takes you out on her 50-foot *Delta*, often heading out to the Farallon Islands in search of salmon. Also offers private tours. ~ Fisherman's Wharf, Berth 1; 415-586-9800. Bring a lunch and dress warmly.

SAILING & NATURE CRUISES

Some of the world's most challenging sailing can be found on San Francisco Bay. Spend a Sunday morning cruising the Bay on a motorized yacht with **Signature Hospitality Group**, which has a luxury 150-foot yacht. The two-hour Sunday brunch excursion

STOP TRAFFIC

If you find yourself on a bike on the last Friday of the month, head over to Justin Herman Plaza at 5:30 p.m. and join **Critical Mass** for a huge group ride. This slow-paced, moderate bike expedition lasts about two hours; the route varies each time, but expect to bring traffic to a halt as you maneuver through thoroughfares and up inclines with hundreds of other two-wheelers.

is available from April to October. ~ Pier 39; 415-788-9100, 800-292-2487; www.signaturesf.com.

From the deck of the **Oceanic Society**'s 56-foot vessel you'll observe elephant seals and sea lions, dolphins, puffins, porpoises, and humpback, blue, and gray whales also frequent the waters. Day-cruises to the Farallon Islands are offered mid-May through November; whale-watching tours go from December until mid-May. Reservations required. ~ Fort Mason Center, Building E; 415-474-3385, 800-326-7491, fax 415-474-3395; www.oceanic society.org.

HANG GLIDING

If you like to soar the skies, try hang gliding. There is a site at Fort Funston (Skyline Boulevard at the far end of Ocean Beach). For lessons in paragliding, contact **Merlin Flight School**. Flights offer views of the coastline. ~ 415-456-3670; www.merlinflight school.com, e-mail wally@merlinflightschool.com. If you're not ready to test those wings, you'll find it's fun just to watch.

SKATING

When weekends roll around, several hundred folks are apt to don inline skates and rollerskates and careen along the sidewalks and streets of Golden Gate Park. John F. Kennedy Drive, on the east side of the park, is closed to cars on Sundays and holidays. It's great exercise, and a lot of fun to boot. Rentals are available near the park at **Purple Skunk**. Closed Monday. ~ 5820 Geary Boulevard between 22nd and 23rd avenues; 415-668-7905; www.purpleskunk.com. You can also rent on the park's north side from **Golden Gate Park Skates and Bikes**. ~ 3038 Fulton Street at 6th Avenue; 415-668-1117.

JOGGING

In a city of steep hills, where walking provides more than enough exercise, jogging is nevertheless a favorite pastime. There are actually places to run where the terrain is fairly level and the scenery spectacular. Most popular are the Golden Gate Bridge, the Presidio Highlands, Glen Canyon Park Trail, Ocean Beach, Golden Gate Park, and Angel Island.

Parcourses, combining aerobic exercises with short jogs, are located at Justin Herman Park (the foot of Market Street near the Ferry Building; half course only), Marina Green (along Marina Boulevard near the foot of Fillmore Street), Mountain Lake Park (Lake Street between 8th and Funston avenues), and the Polo Field in Golden Gate Park.

SWIMMING

Although the air temperature remains moderate all year, the ocean and bay around San Francisco stay cold. If you're ready to brave the Arctic current, join the hearty swimmers who make the plunge regularly at Aquatic Park. Many of these brave souls belong to either the **Dolphin Club** or the **South End Rowing Club**.

San Francisco, Step by Step

San Francisco is a city made for walkers. Appropriately, it offers a number of walking tours that explore various neighborhoods and historical spots.

Chinese Heritage Walks, conducted by the Chinese Culture Center, reveal the true Chinatown. They also offer a **Culinary Walk** that visits markets and herb shops, then stops for lunch in a dim sum restaurant. Reservations required. Fee. ~ Holiday Inn at the corner of Kearny and Washington streets; 415-986-1822; www.c-c-c.org, e-mail info@c-c-c.org.

Wok Wiz Walking Tours, led by cookbook author Shirley Fong-Torres and staff, features local markets, herbal pharmacies, temples and other attractions. A dim sum lunch is optional. This two-and-a-half-hour walk is a convenient way to get acquainted with Chinatown's historical and culinary world. Fee. Tours gather at the Hilton Hotel. Reservations required ~ 750 Kearny Street; 650-355-9657; www.wokwiz.com, e-mail shirley@wokwiz.com.

City Guides, a volunteer organization sponsored by the Friends of the San Francisco Public Library, offers free tours of various locations throughout the city. They include separate tours of Pacific Heights Victorians, Historic Market Street, North Beach, Nob Hill, Coit Tower, and other points of interest. For information on times and starting places, call 415-557-4266; www.sfcityguides.org, e-mail tours@sfcityguides.org.

The **Haight-Ashbury Flower Power Walking Tour** explores the neighborhood made famous during the hippie era of the 1960s. Along with sites from the Summer of Love, the tour takes a longer look back at the area's Victorian architecture stemming from the days when the once-rural Haight was a weekend resort. Fee. ~ P.O. Box 17016, San Francisco, CA 94117; 415-863-1621; www.hippygourmet.com, e-mail hasf525@aol.com.

Experience San Francisco's gay community by **Cruisin' the Castro** with host Trevor Hailey. Approximately four hours long, this entertaining walking tour includes a visit to the 1922 vintage Castro Theater, Harvey Milk's camera shop, and a lunch stop. Reservations required. Gay-friendly (but all are welcome). No tours January through May; no tours Sunday and Monday. Fee. ~ 415-255-1821; www.webcastro.com/castrotour, e-mail cruisinthecastro@yahoo.com.

Both clubs are open to the public (on alternating weekdays, call for open dates) and provide saunas and showers for a small fee (bring your own towel and swimgear). Closed Sunday and Monday. ~ Dolphin Club: 502 Jefferson Street; 415-441-9329. South End Rowing Club: 500 Jefferson Street; 415-776-7372.

SURFING

West of Golden Gate Park there are several spots along San Francisco's wide, sandy **Ocean Beach**; however, the conditions vary seasonally and, because of strong rip currents, this is not a place for beginners. **Fort Point**, located on the bay side of the Golden Gate Bridge's south tower, is another surf break in the city. Fast-flowing currents moving out the Gate make this another spot for experts only.

GOLF

For the earthbound, golf can be a heavenly sport in San Francisco. Several courses are worth checking out. With two separate tee boxes, the **Glen Eagles Golf Course at McLaren Park** features a nine-hole course that's hilly and narrow. This public course rents power carts. ~ 2100 Sunnydale Avenue; 415-587-2425. **Golden Gate Park Golf Course** is a short but tricky nine-hole course close to the ocean. They rent pull carts and clubs at this public course. ~ 47th Avenue and Fulton Street; 415-751-8987. **Harding Park Golf Course** is considered to be one of the finest public courses in the country. There is an 18-hole course and a 9-hole course. Power carts are available for rent, as well as golf clubs. ~ 99 Harding Road; 415-661-1865. The 18-hole **Presidio Golf Course**, the only golf course in a U.S. national park, was originally built in 1895 for Army officers to use and doubled as a drill field for troop reviews. Opened to civilians in 1995, it has quickly gained a reputation as one of the finest public courses in Northern California. Cart and club rentals are available. ~ Presidio; 415-561-4664; www.presidiogolf.com.

TENNIS

With more than 150 free public courts, San Francisco could easily be called The City of Nets. **Golden Gate Park** has 21 courts. There *is* a fee to play, however. ~ John F. Kennedy and Middle drives. In the Marina try the four lighted courts at the **George Moscone Playground**. ~ Chestnut and Buchanan streets. A popular spot in the Mission is **Dolores Park**, with six lighted courts. ~ 18th and Dolores streets. On Nob Hill the three courts at the **Alice Marble Memorial Playground** are recommended. ~ Greenwich and Hyde streets. In Chinatown try the one lighted court at the **Chinese Playground**. ~ Sacramento Street and Waverly Plaza. Over in North Beach the **North Beach Playground** has three lighted courts. ~ Lombard and Mason streets. For more information on all city courts call the San Francisco Parks and Recreation Department. ~ 415-831-6302.

San Francisco is not a city designed for cyclers. Some of the hills   **BIKING**
are almost too steep to walk and downtown traffic can be gruel-
ling. There are places, however, that are easy to ride and beautiful
as well. **Golden Gate Park**, the **Golden Gate** ◆◆◆◆◆◆◆◆◆◆◆◆◆◆◆◆◆◆◆◆
Promenade, and **Lake Merced** all have excellent   Among the city's most
bike routes.   dramatic rides is the
   The **Sunset Bikeway** begins at Lake Merced Boule-   bicyclists' sidewalk
vard, then carries through a residential area and past   on the Golden Gate
views of the ocean to the Polo Field in Golden Gate Park.   Bridge.
Bike Rentals Near Fisherman's Wharf is **Blazing**
Saddles Bike Rentals, with mountain bikes, hybrids, and
tandems. ~ 1095 Columbus Avenue; 415-202-8888;
www.blazingsaddles.com. Located nearby, **Bike and Roll** rents
comfort and touring hybrids. ~ 734 Lombard Street; 415-771-
8735, 888-544-2453; www.bicyclerental.com. Near the southeast
corner of Golden Gate Park is **Avenue Cyclery**, which rents mountain bikes, hybrids, and kids' bikes. ~ 756 Stanyan Street; 415-
387-3155. The **Angel Island Company** rents 21-speed mountain
bikes and junior bikes to explore that state park's paved paths.
~ Angel Island; 415-897-0715; www.angelisland.com.

The major highways leading into San Francisco are   ▼▼▼▼▼▼▼▼▼▼
Route 1, the picturesque coastal road, **Route 101**, Cali-   **Transportation**
fornia's coastal north–south thoroughfare, and **Route**
80, the transcontinental highway that originates on the East Coast.   **CAR**

San Francisco International Airport, better known as SFO, sits 15   **AIR**
miles south of downtown San Francisco off Routes 101 and 280.
A major destination from all points of the globe, the airport is
always bustling. ~ www.flysfo.com.
   Most domestic airlines fly into SFO, including Alaska Airlines,
American Airlines, Continental Airlines, Delta Air Lines, Hawaiian
Airlines, Northwest, and United Airlines.
   International carriers are also prominent here: Air Canada,
British Airways, China Airlines, Japan Airlines, Lufthansa,
Mexicana, Philippine Airlines, Singapore Airlines, TACA Inter-
national Airlines, and Virgin Atlantic have regular flights into
San Francisco's airport.
   The SFO **Ground Transportation Information Service** is a free
service that will help you plan your way to and from the airport
via buses, shuttles, taxis, limousines, and more. ~ There's an information booth in the baggage claim area of each SFO terminal.
   BART (650-992-2278) runs from the airport to all its destinations. Or, to travel from the airport to downtown San Francisco, **Supershuttle** provides door-to-door service. ~ 415-558-
8500; www.supershuttle.com. Or catch a **San Mateo County**
Transit, or **SamTrans**, bus (800-660-4287) to the Transbay Ter-

minal (425 Mission Street). Taxi and limo service are also available, or try **Lorrie's Airport Service**. ~ 415-334-9000; www.lorries-shuttles.com.

BUS

Greyhound Bus Lines (800-231-2222) services San Francisco from around the country. Buses arrive and depart from the Transbay Terminal. ~ 425 Mission Street; 415-495-1569; www.greyhound.com.

An alternative to Greyhound is the **Green Tortoise**, a New Age company with a fleet of funky buses. Each is equipped with sleeping platforms that allow travelers to rest as they cross the country. The buses stop at interesting sightseeing points en route. The Green Tortoise, an endangered species from the '60s, travels to and from the East Coast, Grand Canyon, Alaska, Baja Mexico, and elsewhere. It provides a mode of transportation as well as an experience in group living. ~ 494 Broadway; 415-956-7500; www.greentortoise.com, e-mail tortoise@greentortoise.com.

TRAIN

For those who prefer to travel by rail, **Amtrak** has train service via the "Coast Starlight," "California Zephyr," and "San Joaquin." These trains arrive at and depart from the Emeryville train station, with connecting bus service to San Francisco's Ferry Building, where Market Street meets the Embarcadero. ~ 5885 Horton Street, Emeryville; 800-872-7245; www.amtrak.com.

CAR RENTALS

The easiest way to explore San Francisco is by foot or public transit. Driving in San Francisco can be a nightmare. Parking spaces are rare, parking lots expensive. Then there are the hills, which require you to navigate along dizzying inclines while dodging cable cars, trollies, pedestrians, and double-parked vehicles. The streets of San Francisco make Mr. Toad's wild ride look tame.

If you do decide to rent a car, most major rental agencies have franchises right at the airport. These include **Alamo** (800-462-5266), **Avis Rent A Car** (800-331-1212), **Budget Rent A Car** (800-527-0700), **Dollar Rent A Car** (800-800-4000), **Enterprise Rent A Car** (800-261-7331), **Hertz Rent A Car** (800-654-3131), **National** (800-227-7368) and **Thrifty Car Rental** (800-847-4389).

PUBLIC TRANSIT

San Francisco is a city where public transit works. To get anywhere in the city, call **San Francisco Muni** and an operator will direct you to the appropriate mode of public transportation. ~ 415-673-6864 or 311; www.sfmta.com.

Over 90 bus lines travel around, about, and through the city. Trolley buses, street cars, light-rail subways, and cable cars also crisscross San Francisco. Most lines operate daily (with a modified schedule on weekends and holidays). Free transfers allow a 90-

minute stopover or connection to two more lines. Exact fares are required. For complete information on the Muni system, purchase a copy of the "Muni Street and Transit Map" from the Visitor Information Center (900 Market Street; 415-391-2000), the Information Desk at City Hall, or local bookstores and corner groceries.

Unlike San Francisco's classic cable cars, the **Bay Area Rapid Transit System**, or BART, operates streamlined cars that zip beneath the city's streets. The system travels from Downtown to the Mission District, Glen Park, and SFO. It also runs under the San Francisco Bay to the cities of Oakland, Berkeley, and other parts of the East Bay. Trains run every 8 to 20 minutes depending on the time of day. BART opens at 4 a.m. (6 a.m. on Saturday and 8 a.m. on Sunday) and closes at midnight every night. ~ 650-992-2278; www.bart.gov.

Many surrounding communities feature transportation services to and from San Francisco. To the north, **Golden Gate Transit** provides both bus and ferryboat service. ~ 415-923-2000; www.goldengatetransit.org. South of San Francisco, **San Mateo County Transit**, or **SamTrans**, offers bus service as far south as Palo Alto. ~ 800-660-4287; www.samtrans.com. In addition, **Caltrain** provides daily commuter service from San Jose to San Francisco with stops along the way. ~ 4th and Townsend streets; 800-660-4287; www.caltrain.com. Across the Bay, **Alameda–Contra Costa Transit**, or **AC Transit**, carries passengers from Oakland, Berkeley, and other East Bay cities to the Transbay Terminal in San Francisco. ~ 510-839-2882; www.actransit.org. For more information on ferry services, see the "Transportation" section in Chapter Three.

CABLE CARS

Cable cars, those clanging symbols of San Francisco, are *the* way to see this city of perpendicular hills. This venerable system covers a ten-mile section of downtown San Francisco.

The cable car was invented in 1873 by Andrew Hallidie and works via an underground cable that travels continuously at a speed of nine and a half miles per hour. Three of the system's original twelve lines still operate year-round. The Powell–Mason and Powell–Hyde cars travel from the Downtown district to Fisherman's Wharf; the California Street line runs east to west and passes through Chinatown and Nob Hill.

TAXIS

Cabs are plentiful, but flagging them down can be tricky—it's best to call by phone. The main companies are **DeSoto Cab Company** (415-970-1300), **Luxor Cabs** (415-282-4141), **Veteran's Taxi Cab Company** (415-552-1300), and **Yellow Cab** (415-626-2345).

THREE

North Coast

When visitors to San Francisco seek a rural retreat, paradise is never far away. It sits just across the Golden Gate Bridge along a coastline stretching almost 400 miles to the Oregon border. Scenically, the North Coast compares in beauty with any spot on earth.

There are the folded hills and curving beaches of Point Reyes, Sonoma's craggy coast and old Russian fort, plus Mendocino with its vintage towns and spuming shoreline. To the far north lies Redwood Country, silent domain of the world's tallest living things.

Along the entire seaboard, civilization appears in the form of fishing villages and logging towns. Matter of fact, a lot of the prime real estate is saved forever from developers' heavy hands. California's Coastal Commission serves as a watchdog agency protecting the environment.

Much of the coast is also preserved in public playgrounds. Strung like pearls along the Pacific are a series of federal parks—Golden Gate National Recreation Area, Point Reyes National Seashore, and Redwood National Park.

The main highway through this idyllic domain is Route 1. A sinuous road, it snakes along the waterfront, providing the slowest, most scenic route. Paralleling this road and following an inland course is Route 101. This superhighway streaks from San Francisco to Oregon. It is fast, efficient, and at times boring. In the town of Leggett, Route 1 merges into Route 101, which continues north through Redwood Country.

Route 1 runs through San Francisco into Marin County, passing Sausalito before it branches from Route 101. While the eastern sector of Marin, along San Francisco Bay, is a suburban sprawl, the western region consists of rolling ranch land. Muir Woods is here, featuring 1000-year-old redwoods growing within commuting distance of the city. There is Mt. Tamalpais, a 2571-foot "sleeping maiden" whose recumbent figure has been the subject of numerous poems.

According to some historians, Sir Francis Drake, the Renaissance explorer, landed along the Marin shore in 1579, building a fort and claiming the wild region for dear old England. The Portuguese had first sighted the North Coast in 1543 when they espied Cape Mendocino. Back then Coastal Miwok Indians inhabited Marin, enjoying undisputed possession of the place until the Spanish settled the interior valleys during the early 1800s.

To the north, in Sonoma County, the Miwok shared their domain with the Pomo Indians. After 1812 they were also dividing it with the Russians. The Czar's forces arrived in California from their hunting grounds in Alaska and began taking large numbers of otters from local waters. The Russians built Fort Ross and soon proclaimed the region open only to their shipping. Of course, these imperial designs made the Spanish very nervous. The American response was to proclaim the Monroe Doctrine, warning foreign powers off the continent.

By the 1830s the Russians had decimated the otter population, reducing it from 150,000 to less than 100. They soon lost interest in the area and sold their fort and other holdings to John Sutter, whose name two decades hence would become synonymous with the Gold Rush.

Many of the early towns along the coast were born during the days of the '49ers. Established to serve as pack stations for the mines, the villages soon turned to lumbering and fishing. Today these are still important industries. About seven percent of California's land consists of commercial forest, much of it along the coastal redwood belt. Environmentalists continue to battle with the timber interests as they have since 1918 when the Save-the-Redwoods League was formed.

The natural heritage they protect includes trees that have been growing in California's forests since before the birth of Christ. Elk herds roam these groves, while trout and steelhead swim the nearby rivers. At one time the forest stretched in a 30-mile-wide swath for 450 miles along the coast. But in little more than a century the lumber industry has cut down over 90 percent of the original redwoods. Presently, 87,000 acres of ancient trees remain, over 90 percent of which are protected in parks. The fate of one unprotected grove, the Headwaters Forest in Humboldt County, which contains the world's largest privately owned stand of old-growth redwoods, has been an emotional issue, resulting in the arrest of scores of protesters during the past several years. The federal government has recently purchased 7500 acres of old-growth and second-growth redwoods in the forest from the Pacific Lumber Company.

Another, much younger, cash crop is marijuana. During the '60s and early '70s, Mendocino and Humboldt counties became meccas for counterculturalists intent on getting "back to the land." They established communes, built original-design houses, and plunged into local politics. Some also became green-thumb outlaws, perfecting potent and exotic strains of sinsemilla for personal use and black-market sale. They made Northern California marijuana famous and helped boom the local economy. In 1996, California voters passed Proposition 215, an initiative legalizing the use of marijuana for medical purposes. Although 38 other states already had similar laws, and the herb had actually been available to cancer patients prior to the Reagan administration, marijuana was not currently available to patients anywhere because it was (and still is) prohibited by federal law. When bars where the recreational herb was actually dispensed for medical purposes began to open in San Francisco, the U.S. Drug Enforcement Administration was quick to close them down. The California statute reached the U.S. Supreme Court for a final determination of its legality and that of similar laws in other states across the country, in 2001, but the ruling, which deemed that state and federal laws need not conform with each other, only served to continue the dissonance. Despite occasional Federal raids, pot clubs flourish throughout California.

The North Coast has become home to the country inn as well. All along the Pacific shoreline, bed and breakfasts serve travelers seeking informal and relaxing accommodations. Local artisans have also proliferated while small shops have opened to sell their crafts.

The great lure for travelers is still the environment. This coastal shelf, tucked between the Coast Ranges and the Pacific, has mountains and rivers, forests and ocean. Once the habitat of Yuki, Athabascan, Wiyot, Yurok, and Tolowa Indians, it remains an adventureland for imaginative travelers. Winters are damp, mornings and evenings sometimes foggy, but the weather overall is temperate. It's a place where you can fish for chinook and salmon, go crabbing, and scan the sea for migrating whales. Or simply ease back and enjoy scenery that never stops.

Marin Coast

As frequently photographed as the Golden Gate Bridge, the coast of Marin County consists of rolling ranch lands and spectacular ocean bluffs. It extends from San Francisco Bay to Tomales Bay, offering groves of redwoods, meadows filled with wildflowers, and miles of winding country roads.

SIGHTS

An exploration of this vaunted region begins immediately upon crossing the **Golden Gate Bridge** on Route 101. There's a vista point at the far north end of the bridge affording marvelous views back toward San Francisco and out upon the Bay. (If some of your party want to start off with an exhilarating walk across the bridge, drop them at the vista point on the city side and pick them up here a little later.)

Once across the bridge, take the first exit, Alexander Avenue; then take an immediate left, following the sign back toward San Francisco. Next, bear right at the sign for Marin Headlands.

For what is literally a **bird's-eye view** of the Golden Gate Bridge, go three-tenths of a mile uphill and stop at the first turnout on the left. From here it's a short stroll out and up, past deserted battery fortifications, to a 360° view point sweeping the Pacific and Bay alike. You'll practically be standing on the bridge, with cars careening below and the tops of the twin towers vaulting above you.

Continue along Conzelman Road and you will pass a series of increasingly spectacular views of San Francisco. Ahead the road will fall away to reveal a tumbling peninsula, furrowed with hills and marked at its distant tip by a lighthouse. That is **Point Bonita**, a salient far outside the Golden Gate. After proceeding to the point, you can peer back through the interstices of the bridge to the city or turn away from civilization and gaze out on a wind-tousled sea.

Text continued on page 126.

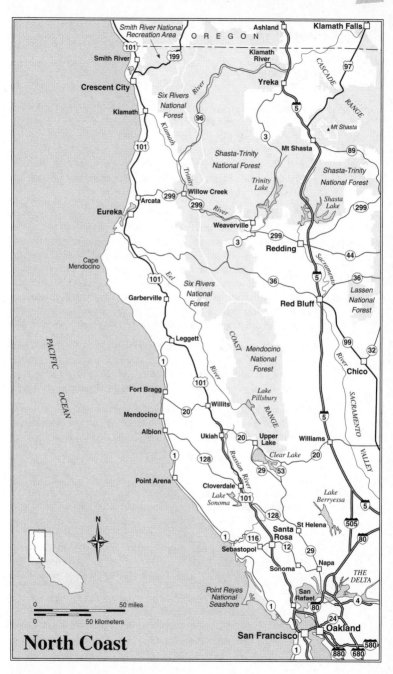

North Coast

North Coast

Day 1 From San Francisco, cross the Golden Gate Bridge. After the bridge, take Route 1 to the **Marin Headlands**, with increasingly spectacular views along the way. For an even more scenic and not much longer drive, turn north (left) at the crest of the Marin Peninsula onto Panoramic Highway, which takes you through deep forest in **Mt. Tamalpais State Park** (page 140) before rejoining Route 1 at Stinson Beach on the peninsula's west coast.

It's a 150-mile drive along Route 1 to Mendocino, which may not sound like far (except on Saturdays, when heavy traffic can slow highway speeds to a crawl, giving passengers plenty of extra time to enjoy the scenery), but allow all day to get there. The two-lane highway is often winding and sometimes steep, and it passes through numerous 25-mph small towns. Most of these towns have restaurants where you can stop for lunch, or you may prefer to picnic in one of no less than 35 beautiful beaches and coastal parks along the way, all of them ideal for relaxing hours of hiking and enjoying nature.

Check into your hotel in the **Mendocino** area for two nights. Lodging tends to be pricey in Mendocino establishments such as the landmark **Stanford Inn by the Sea** (page 153) and less so in nearby Fort Bragg at places like the lovely **Weller House** (page 155).

Dine at one of the Mendocino coast's many fine restaurants, such as the **Café Beaujolais** (page 158) or the **MacCallum House Restaurant** (page 158), where you'll experience gourmet dining at its finest with a wide range of entrée prices.

Day 2 Continue north on Route 1 for another 50 miles to join Route 101 at Leggett. This is Redwood Country, and although you could take Route 101 all the way to Redwood National Park, another 150 miles north, this would mean more driving than most people prefer to do on a three-day trip. Instead, why not take time to explore **Richardson Grove State Park** (page 164), drive the **Avenue of the Giants** (page 164), and hike in **Humboldt Redwoods State Park** (page 164)?

From Humboldt Redwoods State Park, loop west to Honeydew and south to Shelter Cove for a glimpse of California's **Lost Coast** (page 167). Protected from civilization by the towering sea cliffs and steep, treacherous slopes of the King Range, as well as by reclusive marijuana farmers, this is one of California's most thoroughly hidden corners.

Return to Route 101 at Garberville and retrace your route to your hotel in the Mendocino area for dinner and a well-earned night's rest.

Day 3 Spend the morning exploring more of the beaches and headlands along the Mendocino coast. One good bet is **Russian Gulch State Park** (page 162) just north of Mendocino, where you'll find lofty vistas, a waterfall, and a sheltered beach. Another is **MacKerricher State Park** (page 163), one of the region's best, encompassing a cross-section of coastal environments that includes an ocean beach, sand dunes, high lookouts, a lush forest, and marshes that provide an edenlike habitat for an abundance of birds. South of Mendocino, the hiking trails of **Van Damme State Park** (page 162) take you from the beach through a pygmy pine forest to a verdant fern canyon and a pungent meadow of skunk cabbage.

In early or mid-afternoon, by taking Route 20 east from Noyo (between Mendocino and Fort Bragg) you can rejoin fast Route 101 at Willits and be back in San Francisco within four hours. This return route takes you through the heart of the Russian River wine country.

By the time you hit the freeway traffic waiting to cross the Golden Gate Bridge to the city, you may find that you've left your heart in Mendocino.

Nature writes in big letters around these parts. You're in the **Marin Headlands** section of **Golden Gate National Recreation Area**, an otherworldly realm of spuming surf, knife-edge cliffs, and chaparral-coated hillsides. From Point Bonita, follow Field Road, taking a left at the sign for the **Marin Headlands Visitors Center**, where you can pick up maps and information about the area, or make a camping reservation. ~ 415-331-1540, fax 415-331-6963; www.nps.gov/goga.

Walk along **Rodeo Beach**, a sandy corridor separating the Pacific from a tule-fringed lagoon alive with waterfowl. Miles of hiking trails lace up into the hills (see the "Hiking" section at the end of this chapter). At the far end of the beach you can trek along the cliffs and watch the sea batter the continent.

At the nearby **Marine Mammal Center** are seals, sea lions, and other marine mammals who have been found injured or orphaned in the ocean and brought here to recuperate. Center workers conduct rescue operations along 600 miles of coastline, returning the animals to the wild after they have gained sufficient strength. ~ 1065 Fort Cronkhite; From Alexander Avenue take Conzelman Road and follow the signs; 415-289-7325, fax 415-289-7333; www.marinemammalcenter.org, e-mail sales@tmmc.org.

SAUSALITO　Sausalito is a shopper's town: galleries, boutiques, and antique stores line Bridgeway, and in several cases have begun creeping uphill along side streets. **Plaza Vina del Mar** (Bridgeway and El Portal), with its elephant statues and dramatic fountain, is a grassy oasis in the midst of the commerce. Several strides seaward of this tree-thatched spot lies **Gabrielson Park**, where you can settle on a bench or plot of grass at water's edge.

Then continue along the piers past chic yachts, delicate sloops, and rows of millionaires' motorboats. To get an idea of the inland pond where the rich sail these toys, check out the U.S. Army Corps of Engineers **Bay Model**. Built to scale and housed in a two-acre warehouse, this hydraulic model of the San Francisco Bay and Delta is used to simulate currents and tidal flows. A self-guided map and audio tour leads you around the mini-Bay. You can watch the tide surge through the Golden Gate, swirl around Alcatraz, and rise steadily along the Berkeley shore. The tidal cycle of an entire day takes 15 minutes as you witness the natural process from a simulated height of 12,000 feet. Also part of the permanent exhibit is a display portraying Sausalito during World War II, when it was converted into a mammoth shipyard that produced almost 100 vessels in three years. Call ahead to make sure the model will be operating. Closed Sunday and Monday in winter. Closed Monday only the rest of the year. ~ 2100 Bridgeway, Sausalito; 415-332-3871, fax 415-332-0761; www.spn.usace.army.mil/bmvc.

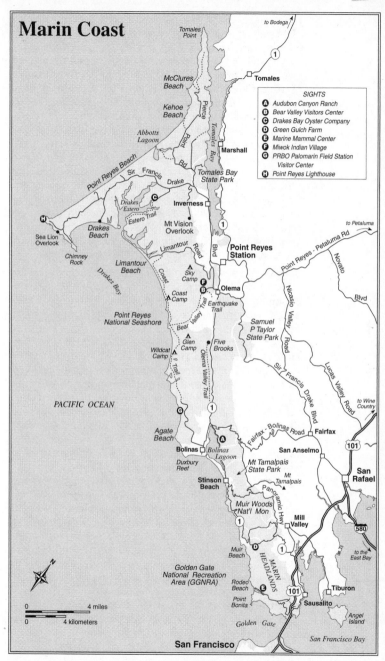

Marin Coast

SIGHTS
- **A** Audubon Canyon Ranch
- **B** Bear Valley Visitors Center
- **C** Drakes Bay Oyster Company
- **D** Green Gulch Farm
- **E** Marine Mammal Center
- **F** Miwok Indian Village
- **G** PRBO Palomarin Field Station Visitor Center
- **H** Point Reyes Lighthouse

to Bodega

Tomales Point

McClures Beach

Kehoe Beach

Abbotts Lagoon

Pierce Point Rd

Tomales

Marshall

Tomales Bay

Point Reyes Beach

Sir Francis Drake

Tomales Bay State Park

Drakes Estero

Inverness

Estero Trail

Mt Vision Overlook

Sea Lion Overlook

Drakes Beach

Chimney Rock

Limantour

Limantour Beach

Point Reyes Station

Point Reyes - Petaluma Rd

to Petaluma

to Wine Country

Novato Blvd

Drakes Bay

Coast Trail

Sky Camp

Coast Camp

Olema

Earthquake Trail

Point Reyes National Seashore

Bear Valley Trail

Glen Camp

Five Brooks

Samuel P Taylor State Park

Nicasio Valley Road

Sir Francis Drake Blvd

Lucas Valley Road

Wildcat Camp

Olema Valley Trail

Fairfax - Bolinas Road

Fairfax

San Anselmo

101

PACIFIC OCEAN

Agate Beach

Bolinas

Bolinas Lagoon

Duxbury Reef

Stinson Beach

Mt Tamalpais State Park

Mt Tamalpais

Panoramic Hwy

San Rafael

Muir Woods Nat'l Mon

Mill Valley

580

to the East Bay

Golden Gate National Recreation Area (GGNRA)

Muir Beach

Rodeo Beach

Point Bonita

MARIN HEADLANDS

101

Tiburon

Sausalito

Angel Island

Golden Gate

San Francisco Bay

San Francisco

0   4 miles

0   4 kilometers

N

Imagine a cluster of eight historic buildings and more than 100 hands-on activities all devoted to children ages six months to eight years. Throw in a 2.5 acre sea cave, a performing-arts theater, and an indoor/outdoor "Tot Spot" for infants and toddlers and what you have is a place called the **Bay Area Discovery Museum**. Closed Monday. Admission. ~ 557 McReynolds Road, East Fort Baker, Sausalito; 415-339-3900, fax 415-339-3905; www.baykidsmuseum.org, e-mail contact@badm.org.

I heartily recommend the quarter-mile self-guided tour through the **Richardson Bay Audubon Center and Sanctuary**. It will provide an inkling of what Marin was like before the invention of cars and condominiums. During the winter months harbor seals can be seen in sanctuary waters. You can wander through dells and woodlands, past salt marshes and tidepools. Also contained on the property is **Lyford House**, a magnificent Victorian that commands a strategic spot on the shore of Richardson Bay. ~ 376 Greenwood Beach Road, Tiburon; 415-388-2524; www.tiburon audubon.org, e-mail richardsonbaycenter@audubon.org.

SAUSALITO TO POINT REYES   From Sausalito follow Route 101 north a few miles, then pick up Route 1. You'll be on the northern leg of one of the most beautiful roads in America. With its wooded sanctuaries and ocean vistas, Route 1 is for many people synonymous with California.

When Route 1 forks after several miles, turn right on Panoramic Highway toward Muir Woods and Mt. Tamalpais; the left fork leads to Stinson Beach, but that comes later. It's uphill and then down to **Muir Woods National Monument**, a 560-acre park inhabited by *Sequoia sempervirens*, the coast redwood. Though these forest giants have been known to live over two millennia, most enjoy a mere four-to-eight-century existence. In Muir Woods they reach 260 feet, while farther up the coast they top 360 feet (with roots that go no deeper than 10 feet!). Admission. ~ 415-388-2596, fax 415-389-6957; www.nps.gov/muwo.

Back up on Panoramic Highway, the road continues through Mt. Tamalpais State Park en route to **Mt. Tamalpais'** 2571-foot peak. Mt. Tam, as it is affectionately known, represents one of the Bay Area's most prominent landmarks. Rising dramatically between the Pacific and the Bay, the site was sacred to Indians. Even today some people see in the sloping silhouette of the mountain the sleeping figure of an Indian maiden. So tread lightly up the short trail that leads to the summit. You'll be rewarded with a full-circle view that sweeps across the Bay, along San Francisco's miniature skyline, and out across the Pacific. Contrary to rumor, on a clear day you cannot see forever, but you can see north toward Redwood Country and east to the Sierras.

Continue on Panoramic Highway as it corkscrews down to Stinson Beach. Better yet, take the longer but more spectacular route to Stinson: backtrack along Panoramic to where the fork originally separated from Route 1 (Shoreline Highway). Turn right and head north on Route 1.

Shortly, a turnoff will lead down to **Green Gulch Farm**, a 115-acre Zen retreat tucked serenely in a coastal valley. Residents here follow a rigorous program of work and meditation. There is a temple on the grounds and guests are welcome to tour the organic farm. Sunday is the best day to visit since a special meditation program and speaker is offered then. Closed January. ~ 1601 Shoreline Highway, near Muir Beach; 415-383-3134, fax 415-383-3128; www.sfzc.org, e-mail ggfoffice@sf2c.org.

It's not far to **Muir Beach**, where you'll find a crescent-shaped cove with sandy beach. Though swimming is not advised, this is a good spot for picnicking. About a mile farther up the road, follow the "vista point" sign to **Muir Beach Overlook**. Here you can walk out along a narrow ridge for a view extending from Bolinas to the coastline south of San Francisco. It's an outstanding place for whale watching in winter. Matter of fact, this lookout is so well placed it became a site for World War II gun batteries, whose rusty skeletons remain.

You have entered a realm that might well be called the Land of a Thousand Views. Until the road descends to the flat expanse of Stinson Beach, it follows a tortuous route poised on the edge of oblivion. Below, precipitous cliffs dive to the sea, while above the road, rock walls edge upward toward Mt. Tamalpais. Around every curve another scene opens to view. Before you, Bolinas is a sweep of land, an arm extended seaward. Behind, the San Francisco skyline falls away into the past. If God built highways, they'd look like this.

Stinson Beach, that broad sandy hook at the bottom of the mountain, is one of Northern California's finest strands. Anglers

AUTHOR FAVORITE

Facts can't convey the feelings inspired by the towering coast redwoods at **Muir Woods National Monument**. You have to move among them, walk through Muir's Cathedral Grove where redwoods form a lofty arcade above the narrow trail. It's a forest primeval, casting the deepest, most restful shade imaginable. Muir Woods has the double-edged quality of being the redwood forest nearest to San Francisco. It can be horribly crowded. Since silence and solitude are vital to experiencing a redwood forest, plan to visit early or late in the day, and allow time to hike the more remote of the park's six miles of trails. For more information, see page 128.

haunt the rocks along one end in pursuit of blenny and lingcod, while birdwatchers are on the lookout for sandpipers, shearwaters, and swallows. Everyone else comes for sand, surf, and sun.

Birdwatchers also flock to **Audubon Canyon Ranch**, located astride Route 1 on Bolinas Lagoon. Open on weekends and holidays from mid-March to mid-July (or by appointment), the ranch includes four canyons, one of which is famed as a rookery for egrets and herons. From the hiking trails here you can see up to 90 bird species as well as gray fox, deer, and bobcats. ~ Route 1; 415-868-9244, fax 415-868-1699; www.egret.org, e-mail acr@egret.org.

Bolinas Lagoon is also a bird sanctuary. Great egrets, ducks, and great blue herons make this one of their migratory stops. A colony of harbor seals lives here permanently and is joined in summer by migrating seals from San Francisco.

To reach the next point of interest you'll have to pay close attention. That's because you're approaching **Bolinas**. To get there from Route 1, watch for the crossroad at the foot of the lagoon; go left, then quickly left again and follow the road along the other side of the lagoon; take another left at the end of the road.

There should be signs to direct you. But there probably won't be. Not because the state neglected them or highway workers forgot to put them up. It seems that local residents subscribe to the self-serving philosophy that since Bolinas is beautiful and they got there first, they should keep everyone else out. They tear down road signs and discourage visitors. The rest of Northern California is fair game, they seem to say, as long as Bolinas is left as some sort of human preserve.

The place they are attempting to hide is a delightful little town that rises from an S-shaped beach to form a lofty mesa. There are country roads along the bluff that overhangs the beach.

Whether you stroll the beach or hike the highlands, you'll discover in the houses here a wild architectural array. There are domes, glass boxes, curved-roof creations, huts, ranch houses, and stately brown-shingle designs.

Bolinas, abutting on the Point Reyes National Seashore, is also a gateway to the natural world. Follow Mesa Road for several miles outside town and you'll encounter the PRBO **Palomarin Field Station Visitor Center**, where scientists at a research station study a bird population of over 200 species. ~ www.prbo.org.

The award-winning **Bolinas Museum** features exhibits on the history of the Marin coast, including displays of Miwok Indian artifacts and Coastal Marin Artist's Gallery shows, which present the work of Marin County painters and sculptors. Open Friday through Sunday and by appointment. ~ 48 Wharf Road,

Bolinas; 415-868-2006, fax 415-868-0607; www.bolinasmu
seum.org, e-mail info@bolinasmuseum.org.

On the way back to town take a right on Overlook Drive,
then a right on Elm Road; follow it to the parking lot at road's end.
Hiking trails lead down a sharp 160-foot cliff to **Duxbury Reef**,   ◀ HIDDEN
a mile-long shale reef. Tidepool-watching is great sport here at
low tide: starfish, periwinkles, abalone, limpets, and a host of
other clinging creatures inhabit the marine preserve. Back in 1971
a huge oil spill endangered this spectacular area, but volunteers
from all around the state worked day and night to save the reef
and its tenacious inhabitants. Just north of this rocky preserve is
Agate Beach, an ideal spot to find agates, driftwood, and glass
balls (however, no collecting is permitted).

Back on Route 1, continue north through Olema Valley, a
peaceful region of horse ranches fringed by forest. Peaceful, that
is, until you realize that the **San Andreas Fault**, the global suture
that shook San Francisco back in 1906, cuts through the valley.
As a matter of fact, the highway you are travel-
ing parallels the fault line. During the great
quake, houses collapsed, trees were uprooted, and
fences decided to mark new boundaries.

Over 45 percent of
North America's bird
species have been
sighted at Point
Reyes.

As you turn off Route 1 onto Sir Francis Drake
Boulevard headed for the Point Reyes Peninsula, you'll
be passing from the North American Plate, one of the
six tectonic plates on which the entire earth's surface rides,
to the Pacific Plate, which extends across the ocean. It is
the pressure formed by the collision of these two great land masses
that causes earthquakes. No sign will notify you as you cross this
troubled geologic border, no guide will direct you along the rift
zone. If you're like the people who live hereabouts, within 15
minutes of crossing over you'll have forgotten the fault exists.
Especially when you see what is served on the Pacific Plate.

POINT REYES NATIONAL SEASHORE   Point Reyes National Seashore, with 88 miles of shoreline, is without doubt one of the
finest seaside parks on any of the world's six plates. It is a realm
of sand dunes and endless beaches, Scottish-type moors and
grassy hillsides, salt marshes and pine forests. Bobcats, mountain
lions, fox, and elk inhabit its wrinkled terrain, while harbor seals
and gray whales cruise its ragged shoreline. More than 45 percent
of North American bird species have been spotted here. The
seashore also supports dairies and cattle ranches. In 1995, fire
ripped through Point Reyes, burning 12,000 acres. However, all
areas have since been cleared and await your exploration. All
trails listed here and in the "Hiking" section are open and additional trails lead through the charred area, giving you a close-up
look at the awesome healing power of nature.

The first stage in exploring this multifeatured preserve involves a stop at the **Bear Valley Visitors Center**. Here you can obtain maps, information, and camping permits. ~ Bear Valley Road; 415-464-5100, fax 415-663-8132; www.nps.gov/pore. A short hike from the center will lead you to a **Miwok Indian Village**, where the round-domed shelters and other structures of the area's early inhabitants have been re-created. There is also an earthquake trail where you can see evidence of the San Andreas fault.

Most points of interest lie along Sir Francis Drake Boulevard, which rolls for miles through the park. It will carry you past the tiny town of **Inverness**, with its country inns and ridgetop houses, then out along **Tomales Bay**. Like the Golden Gate, this finger-shaped inlet is a drowned river valley.

Deeper in the park, a side road twists up to Mount Vision Overlook, where vista points sweep the peninsula. At **Drakes Bay Oyster Company**, along another side road, workers harvest the rich beds of an estuary. The farm is a conglomeration of slap-dash buildings, house trailers, and rusty machines. The shoreline is heaped over with oyster shells and the air is filled with pungent odors. Raw oysters are for sale. Even if you don't care for them, you might want to visit anyway. After all, when was the last time you saw an oyster farm? ~ 17171 Sir Francis Drake Boulevard, Inverness; 415-669-1149, fax 415-669-7272.

A brass plate, purportedly left by Drake, was discovered near San Francisco Bay in 1936; later it was believed that the plate had been first located near Drakes Bay and then moved; finally the plate was deemed a counterfeit.

The main road continues over folded hills that fall away to reveal sharp bluffs. Farm animals graze through fields smothered in wildflowers. There are ocean vistas stretching along miles of headland.

On **Drakes Beach** you can picnic and beachcomb. Or gaze at the surrounding cliffs and wonder whether they truly resemble the White Cliffs of Dover. In that question resides a story told by one school of historians and vehemently denied by others. It seems that in 1579 the English explorer Sir Francis Drake anchored somewhere along the Northern California coast. But where? Some claim he cast anchor right here in Drakes Bay, others say Bolinas Lagoon, even San Francisco Bay. Find out more at the **Ken Patrick Visitor Center**, which also features aquarium and interactive computer displays. Saturday and Sunday only. ~ 415-669-1250.

Point Reyes Beach (also known as "North Beach" and "South Beach"), a windy ten-mile-long strip, is an ideal place for whale watchers. From there, it's not far to the end of Point Reyes' hammerhead peninsula. At one tip is **Chimney Rock**, a sea stack formed when the ocean eroded away the intervening land mass, leaving this islet just offshore. On the way to Chimney Rock you'll pass an **overlook** that's ideal for watching sea lions; then from Chimney Rock, if the day is clear, you'll see all the way to San Francisco.

At the other tip is **Point Reyes Lighthouse**, an 1870s beacon located at the foggiest point on the entire Pacific coast. The treacherous waters offshore have witnessed numerous shipwrecks, the first occurring way back in 1595. The original lighthouse, constructed to prevent these calamities, incorporated over a thousand pieces of crystal in its intricate lens. A modern beacon eventually replaced this multifaceted instrument, although the antique is still on view. The old lighthouse and an accompanying information center are still open to the public Thursday through Monday, weather permitting (lighthouse is inaccessible during winds exceeding 40 m.p.h.). ~ 415-669-1534.

From Olema you can continue north on Route 1 or follow a looping 25-mile detour through the region's **pastoral interior**. On ◄ *HIDDEN* the latter, Sir Francis Drake Boulevard leads east past bald-domed hills and isolated farms. Livestock graze at the roadside while overhead hawks work the range. Grassland gives way to dense forest as you enter the realms of **Samuel P. Taylor State Park**. Then the road opens again to reveal a succession of tiny, woodframe towns.

At San Geronimo, turn left on Nicasio Valley Road. This carries you farther into the pastoral region of west Marin, which varies so dramatically from the county's eastside suburban enclaves. Indeed, the inland valleys are reminiscent more of the Old West than the busy Bay Area. At the Nicasio Reservoir, turn left onto Point Reyes–Petaluma Road and follow it to Sir Francis Drake Boulevard, closing the circle of this rural tour.

From Olema, Route 1 continues north along Tomales Bay, the lovely fjord-shaped inlet. Salt marshes stretch along one side of the road; on the other are rumpled hills tufted with grass. The waterfront village of **Marshall** consists of fishing boats moored offshore and woodframe houses anchored firmly onshore. Then the road turns inland to **Tomales**, another falsefront town with clapboard church and country homes. It continues past paint-peeled barns and open pastureland before turning seaward at Bodega Bay.

Green Gulch Farm, a Zen meditation center and organic farm, of- **LODGING** fers a guest residence program. Located on a 115-acre spread in a lovely valley, it's a restful and enchanting stop. Enroll in the Guest ◄ *HIDDEN* Practice Retreat Program, available between Sunday and Thursday with a three-night minimum. The schedule involves meditation, chanting, and bowing as well as morning chores and includes all meals (vegetarian, of course). Or you can simply rent a room by the night (at deluxe prices including meals) in their 12-room guest house. With nearby hiking trails and beaches, it's a unique place. Closed in January ~ 1601 Shoreline Highway near Muir

Beach; 415-383-3134, fax 415-383-3128; www.sfzc.org, e-mail ggfdirector@sfzc.org. MODERATE TO DELUXE.

Most folks grumble when the fog sits heavy along the coast. At **The Pelican Inn**, guests consider fog part of the ambience. Damp air and chill winds add a final element to the Old English atmosphere at this seven-chamber bed and breakfast. Set in a Tudor-style building near Muir Beach, The Pelican Inn re-creates 16th-century England. There's a pub downstairs with a dart board on one wall and a fox-hunting scene facing on another. The dining room serves country fare like meat pies, prime rib, and bangers. Upstairs the period-print bedrooms contain time-honored antique furnishings including canopied beds. Highly recommended; reserve well in advance. ~ 10 Pacific Way, Muir Beach; 415-383-6000, fax 415-383-3424; www.pelicaninn.com, e-mail innkeeper@pelicaninn.com. DELUXE TO ULTRA-DELUXE.

Smiley's Schooner Saloon and Hotel, located in the rustic town of Bolinas, is a three-minute walk to the beach. Accommodations are clean and nicely refurbished. The rooms are done in a rose color with antiques and have no radio, TV, phones, or other newfangled inventions. Six guest rooms are in the bungalows behind the saloon while two are above the bar. Light sleepers be forewarned: The bar downstairs is a favorite haunt of late-night revelers. ~ 41 Wharf Road, Bolinas; 415-868-1311, fax 415-868-0502; www.coastalpost.com/smileys, e-mail editor@coastalpost.com. MODERATE.

There's also **Grand Hotel,** a tiny business where the two rooms share a bath and a kitchen. The proprietor also serves as a referral service for other places in town, so check with him about local accommodations. ~ 15 Brighton Avenue, Bolinas; 415-868-1757. BUDGET.

Within Point Reyes National Seashore, the **Hostelling International—Point Reyes Hostel** provides low-rent lodging. In addition to 44 dorm-style accommodations, the hostel has a patio,

AUTHOR FAVORITE

Sometimes location is everything. That—plus a lively young clientele—is why I recommend the **Marin Headlands Hostel**. Also known as Golden Gate Hostel, the lodging is ideally located in the spectacular Marin Headlands section of the Golden Gate National Recreation Area. Housed in two historic woodframe buildings, this hostel's 104 dormitory-style accommodations go for low prices. There are kitchen and laundry facilities available, a game room, a living room, and a few private rooms. Reservations are advised. ~ Fort Barry, Building 941; 415-331-2777, 800-909-4776 ext. 168, fax 415-331-3568; www.norcalhostels.org. BUDGET.

kitchen and a living room with a wood-burning stove. Perfect for explorers, it is situated two miles from the ocean near several hiking trails. The hostel is closed from 10 a.m. to 4:30 p.m. Reservations recommended. ~ Point Reyes National Seashore; Box 247, Point Reyes Station, CA 94956; phone/fax 415-663-8811, 800-909-4776 ext. 168; www.norcalhostels.org. BUDGET.

The **Blackthorne Inn** is an architectural extravaganza set in a forest of oak, bay trees, and Douglas fir. The four-level house is expressive of the flamboyant "woodbutcher's art" building style popular in the 1970s. Using recycled materials and heavy doses of imagination, the builders created a maze of skylights, bay windows, and French doors, capped by an octagonal tower. A spiral staircase corkscrews up through this multitiered affair to the top deck, where an outdoor hot tub overlooks the canyon. There are four bedrooms, all with private baths. Each room has been personalized; the most outstanding is the "Eagle's Nest," occupying the glass-encircled octagon at the very top of this Aquarian wedding cake. ~ 266 Vallejo Avenue, Inverness Park; 415-663-8621, fax 415-663-8635; www.blackthorneinn.com, e-mail susan@blackthorneinn.com. ULTRA-DELUXE.

Nearby in Inverness there's **Motel Inverness**, commanding a location along Tomales Bay that would be the envy of many well-heeled hostelries. Unfortunately, the architect who designed it faced the rooms toward the road, not the water. Only the newly-added honeymoon suite overlooks Tomales Bay. Guests can, however, enjoy views of the bay in the motel's common room, which also features a billiards table. The guest rooms come equipped with color televisions and cable. The entire motel is a nonsmoking establishment. ~ 12718 Sir Francis Drake Boulevard, Inverness; 415-669-1081, 888-669-6909; www.motelinverness.com, e-mail reservations@motelinverness.com. MODERATE.

Situated on 15 quiet country acres, the **Inverness Valley Inn** offers an affordable retreat in the increasingly upscale Point Reyes area. Scattered over the well-groomed grounds are five contemporary A-frame buildings, each housing large, light, and airy rooms complete with kitchenettes, barbecues, and private patios. A pool, hot tub, and, of course, tennis courts round out the amenities. Perfect for families and active couples, the inn is a stone's throw away from secluded coves, spectacular hiking trails, and excellent kayaking. And if you forgot your tennis rackets, the friendly owners will be glad to provide them. Pet-friendly. ~ 13275 Sir Francis Drake Boulevard, Inverness; 415-669-7250, 800-416-0405; www.invernessvalleyinn.com, e-mail info@invernessvalleyinn.com. DELUXE.

Another favorite bed and breakfast lies along the flagstone path at **Ten Inverness Way**. The place is filled with pleasant surprises, like fruit trees and flowers in the yard, a hot tub, a library, and a warm living room with stone fireplace. The five bedrooms are small but cozy, carpeted wall-to-wall, and imaginatively decorated with hand-fashioned quilts; all have private baths. It's a short stroll from the house to the shops and restaurants of Inverness. Another special treat: tea and fresh-baked cookies are served in the afternoon, and wine and cheese in the evening. ~ 10 Inverness Way, Inverness; 415-669-1648, fax 415-669-7403; www.ten invernessway.com, e-mail inn@teninvernessway.com. DELUXE.

As country living goes, it's darn near impossible to find a place as pretty and restful as Point Reyes. People with wander in their hearts and wonder in their minds have been drawn here for years. Not surprisingly, country inns sprang up to cater to star-struck explorers and imaginative travelers. A good source for information on these local hostelries is **Point Reyes Lodging**, which offers 24-hour information on a dozen or so inns and cottages in coastal Marin. ~ 415-663-1872, 800-539-1872; www.ptreyes.com.

DINING

From the Marin Headlands region, the nearest restaurants are in the bayside town of Sausalito. Then, progressing north, you'll find dining spots scattered throughout the towns and villages along the coast.

Stinson Beach sports several restaurants; my favorite is the **Sand Dollar Restaurant**, with facilities for dining indoors or on the patio. At lunch this informal eatery serves hamburgers and sandwiches. At dinner there are fried prawns, fresh fish dishes, and pasta; they also serve vegetarian and meat dishes. With a fireplace and random artwork on the wall, it is a cozy local gathering point. ~ 3458 Route 1, Stinson Beach; 415-868-0434, fax 415-868-0159. MODERATE.

Bring the kids and the dogs—**Bolinas Coast Café** is warm, welcoming, and casual. Specialties such as house-made pizza, tomato-fennel seafood stew, and linguini and clams use local organic produce, locally caught fish and shellfish, local dairy, and chemical-free meats. In the summer, the chefs barbecue oysters and salmon on the front patio. Breakfast on weekends. Closed Monday. ~ 46 Wharf Road, Bolinas; 415-868-4924, fax 415-868-0660; www.bolinascafe.com. MODERATE.

HIDDEN ▶

The **Station House Café** comes highly recommended by several local residents. Maybe it's the artwork along the walls or the garden patio. Regardless, it's really the food that draws folks from the surrounding countryside. The dinner menu includes fresh oysters, plus chicken, steak, and fish dishes. There are also daily chef's specials, such as salmon with a dill-smoked salmon sauce. Dinners are served with their signature piping hot popovers. The Station House also features a complete breakfast menu; at lunch time there are light crêpe, pasta, and seafood dishes, plus sandwiches and salads. Closed Wednesday. ~ 11180

Main Street, Point Reyes Station; 415-663-1515; www.station housecafe.com. MODERATE.

Priscilla's Pizzeria & Cafe, a woodframe café in the center of tiny Inverness, serves delicious pizza and pasta as well as soups and salads. The place has a touch of city style in a country setting; there are overhead fans and an espresso machine. Closed Tuesday. ~ 12781 Sir Francis Drake Boulevard, Inverness; 415-669-1244. BUDGET TO MODERATE.

The best shopping spot in all Marin is the town of Sausalito. Here you can stroll the waterfront along Bridgeway and its side streets, visiting gourmet shops, boutiques, and antique stores. One of the Bay Area's wealthiest towns, Sausalito sports few bargains, but it does host an assortment of elegant shops.

SHOPPING

Several shops in the mini-mall at 660 Bridgeway are worth a browse. **Jewelry by the Bay**, a one-of-a-kind boutique, features contemporary women's fashions and jewelry. ~ Sausalito; 800-266-0660.

If the weather's nice take a stroll through the **Claudia Chapline Gallery and Sculpture Garden**. Featuring a variety of mixed media and three roomy skylight galleries, it's a great place to pick up an interesting work of art. Open Saturday and Sunday, or by appointment. Appointment only December through March. ~ 3445 Shoreline Highway, Stinson Beach; 415-868-2308; www.cchapline.com.

Stinson Beach Books may be located in a small town, but it handles a large variety of books. Compressed within the confines of the place is an array of travel books, field guides, bestsellers, novels, children's books, etc. It's a great place to stop before that long, languorous day at the beach. Closed Tuesday from January through May. ~ 3455 Shoreline Highway, Stinson Beach; 415-868-0700.

Gallery Route One spotlights sculptures, photographs, and paintings by contemporary regional artists. There's also mixed-media environmental art exhibits. Closed Tuesday. ~ 11101 Route 1, Point Reyes Station; 415-663-1347.

TOMALES BAY'S GOURMET OYSTERS

Shacks and storefronts along Tomales Bay sell fresh local oysters, barbecued or on the half-shell. Most oysters in the Point Reyes area are Pacific oysters, imported from Japan in the 1930s to replace local oysters that had disappeared from San Francisco Bay because of pollution. Tomales Bay is one of the few areas where the smaller, sweeter Olympia oyster native to the Bay Area is still harvested. Gourmets consider Olympic oysters a special delicacy.

The showroom at **Susan Hayes Handwovens** is a gorgeous tumble of the colored suedes, leathers, and handwoven textiles used to make coordinating separates. Custom orders are the specialty. There's also a wide selection of beautiful hats, gloves, handbags, and jewelry. Closed Monday and Tuesday. ~ 80 4th Street, Point Reyes Station; 415-663-8057; www.susanhayeshandwovens.com, e-mail shays@svn.net.

There are small shops scattered about all along the coast, but the best selection of arts and crafts is located around Point Reyes.

Shaker Shops West is a marvelous store specializing in reproductions of Shaker crafts, particularly furniture. In addition to rag rugs, candlesticks, and woven baskets, there are beautifully handcrafted boxes. The Early American household items range from cross-stitch needlepoint to tinware. Touring the store is like visiting a mini-museum dedicated to this rare American community. Open Friday and Saturday, and by appointment. ~ 5 Inverness Way, Inverness; 415-669-7256, 800-474-2537; www.shakershops.com, e-mail shaker@shakershops.com.

NIGHTLIFE   When the sun goes down in Bolinas, you are left with several options. Sleep, read, curl up with a loved one, fade into unrelieved boredom, or head for **Smiley's Schooner Saloon**. Since local folks often follow the latter course, you're liable to find them parka-to-parka along the bar. They come to shoot pool, listen to weekend live music, and admire the lavish wood-panel bar. Smiley's, after all, is the only show in town—and one of the longest continuously operating saloons in California (since 1851). Occasional cover. ~ 41 Wharf Road, Bolinas; 415-868-1311.

Local folks in Point Reyes Station ease up to a similar wooden bar at **Old Western Saloon** practically every night of the week. But on Friday, Saturday, and alternating Sundays, when the place features live rock, blues, country—you name it—and dancing 'til the wee hours, the biggest crowds of all arrive. Occasional cover. ~ 11201 Route 1, Point Reyes Station; 415-663-1661.

BEACHES & PARKS   **KIRBY COVE** 🚶 🚴 🐎 🎣 ⛵ This pocket beach, located at the end of a one-mile trail, nestles in the shadow of the Golden Gate Bridge. The views from beachside are unreal: gaze up at the bridge's steel lacework or out across the gaping mouth of the Gate. When the fog's away, it's a sunbather's paradise; regardless of the weather, this cove is favored by those who like to fish. Facilities include a picnic area and toilets. ~ The beach is located in the Marin Headlands section of the Golden Gate National Recreation Area. Take the first exit, Alexander Avenue, after crossing the Golden Gate Bridge. Then take an immediate left, following the sign back toward San Francisco. Next, bear right at the sign for Marin Headlands. Follow Conzelman Road three-tenths of a mile to a turnout where a sign will mark the trailhead; 415-331-1540, fax 415-331-6963; www.nps.gov/goga.

▲ There are four campsites for tents only; $25 per night. Reservations are required: 877-444-6777. Closed November through March.

UPPER FISHERMAN'S BEACH 🚲 🐎 ♨ This is a long, narrow corridor of sand tucked under the Marin Headlands. With steep hills behind and a grand view of the Golden Gate in front, it's a perfect place for naturists and nature lovers alike. It is a popular beach for nudists, although not officially recognized as such. It cannot be found on maps or atlases, but local folks and savvy travelers know it well (some call it "Black Sands"). There are no facilities here. ~ Located in the Marin Headlands section of the Golden Gate National Recreation Area. Follow the directions to Kirby Cove trailhead (see listing above). Continue on Conzelman Road for two and a third miles. Shortly after passing the steep downhill section of this road, you'll see a parking lot on the left with a trailhead. Follow the trail to the beach.

◀ *HIDDEN*

RODEO BEACH 🏃 🚲 🐎 🏄 ♨ A broad sandy beach, this place is magnificent not only for the surrounding hillsides and nearby cliffs, but also for the quiescent lagoon at its back. Given its proximity to San Francisco, Rodeo Beach is a favorite among the natives. The beach has restrooms, cold-water showers, and a picnic area. Pets on leashes are allowed. Beware of the strong undercurrents and rip tides. ~ Located in the Marin Headlands section of the Golden Gate National Recreation Area. After crossing Golden Gate Bridge on Route 101, take the first exit, Alexander Avenue. Bear right on Alexander Avenue, then go left on Bunker Road. Follow this road to Rodeo Beach; 415-331-1540, fax 415-331-6963; www.nps.gov/goga.

▲ Though not permitted on the beach, camping is available at three campgrounds in the area. They are hike-in campgrounds, ranging from 100 yards to 3 miles. There are five sites at Haypress, three sites at Hawkcamp, and three sites at Bicentennial. No water, no fires, and no pets. These campgrounds are for tents only, all are free, but reservations and permits are required. Call the information number above for more details.

MUIR WOODS NATIONAL MONUMENT 🏃 If it weren't for the crowds, this redwood preserve would rank little short of majestic. Designated a national treasure by President Theodore Roosevelt in 1908, it features stately groves of tall timber. There are six miles of hiking trails, a snack bar, a gift shop, and restrooms. Day-use fee, $3. ~ Off Route 1 on Panoramic Highway, about 17 miles north of San Francisco; 415-388-2596, fax 415-389-6957; www.nps.gov/muwo.

MT. TAMALPAIS STATE PARK 🏃 🚴 🐎 Spectacularly situated between Mt. Tamalpais and the ocean, this 6300-acre park offers everything from mountaintop views to a rocky coastline. More than 50 miles of hiking trails wind past stands of cypress, Douglas fir, Monterey pine, and California laurel. Wildlife abounds. The countryside draws nature lovers and sightseers alike. The park's facilities include picnic areas, restrooms, a refreshment stand, and a visitors center (open weekends only). Every year since 1913 a mountain play has been staged in the amphitheater. Parking fee, $6. ~ Follow Route 1 north through Mill Valley; turn right on Panoramic Highway, which runs along the park border; 415-388-2070, fax 415-388-2968.

> Salmon run the creeks at Muir Woods from November to April. The best viewing times are a few days after a heavy storm.

▲ There are 16 tent sites at Pantoll Park Headquarters (415-388-2070); facilities in this well-shaded spot include picnic areas, restrooms, and running water; $15 per night. There's also camping at Frank Valley Horsecamp (800-444-7275), located near Muir Beach in the southwest end of the park. You'll find picnic tables, pit toilets, and running water. Reservations are required and can be obtained at park headquarters. For information on Steep Ravine Environmental Camp see the listing below.

MUIR BEACH 🏃 🚴 🐎 🏄 ⛵ Because of its proximity to San Francisco, this spot is a favorite among local people. Located at the foot of a coastal valley, Muir Beach forms a semicircular cove. There's a sandy beach (with a rough surf) and ample opportunity for picnicking. Other than picnic tables the facilities are limited to toilets. ~ Route 1, about 16 miles north of San Francisco; 415-388-2596, fax 415-389-6957; www.nps.gov/muwo.

STEEP RAVINE ENVIRONMENTAL CAMP Set on a shelf above the ocean, this outstanding site is bounded on the other side by sharp slopes. Contained within Mt. Tamalpais State Park, it features a small beach and dramatic sea vista. This is a good place for nature study. ~ Located along a paved road off Route 1, about one mile south of Stinson Beach. Turn at the sign; 415-388-2070, fax 415-388-2968.

▲ There are six tent sites ($15 per night) and ten rustic cabins ($75 per night). Reservations can be made up to six months in advance for cabins; call 800-444-7275.

HIDDEN ▶   **RED ROCK BEACH** 🏖 🏄 One of the area's most popular nude beaches, this pocket beach is wall-to-wall with local folks on sunny weekends. Well protected along its flank by steep hillsides, Red Rock is an ideal sunbathers' retreat. There are no facilities here. ~ Part of Mt. Tamalpais State Park, Red Rock is located off Route 1 about one mile south of Stinson Beach. Watch for a large (often crowded) parking area on the seaward side of the highway. Follow the steep trail down to the beach.

STINSON BEACH PARK ⚓ 🏊 🚻 ⛱ 🅿 One of Northern California's finest beaches, this broad, sandy corridor curves for three miles. Backdropped by rolling hills, Stinson also borders beautiful Bolinas Lagoon. Besides being a sunbather's haven, it's a great place for beachcombers and birdwatchers. To escape the crowds congregating here weekends, stroll up to the north end of the beach. You'll find a narrow sand spit looking out on Bolinas. You still won't have the beach entirely to yourself, but a place this beautiful is worth sharing. Because of currents from Bolinas Lagoon, the water at Stinson Beach Park is a little warmer than elsewhere along the Northern California Coast (but it's still brisk by Atlantic Coast standards). There are picnic areas with barbecues, a snack bar, outdoor showers and restrooms; lifeguards in summer. If you dare swim anywhere along the North Coast, it might as well be here, where the waters are a tiny bit warmer. ~ Located along Route 1 in the town of Stinson Beach, 23 miles north of San Francisco; 415-868-0942, 415-868-1922 (weather).

BOLINAS BEACH 🚶 🚴 ⚓ 🏊 ⛱ 🅿 Beginning near Bolinas Lagoon and curving around the town perimeter, this salt-and-pepper beach provides ample opportunity for walking. A steep bluff borders the beach. In the narrow mouth of the lagoon you can often see harbor seals and waterfowl. There are no facilities but the town of Bolinas is within walking distance. ~ Located at the end of Wharf Road in Bolinas.

AGATE BEACH AND DUXBURY REEF You could spend the whole day at Agate Beach gazing at the beautiful variety of stones under your feet. (Collecting is not permitted.) At low tide, Duxbury Reef to the south is also outstanding for tidepool gazing. Both are highly recommended for adventurers, daydreamers, and amateur biologists. There are portable restrooms. ~ From Olema–Bolinas Road in Bolinas, go up the hill on Mesa Road, left on Overlook Drive, and right on Elm Road. Follow Elm Road to the parking lot at the end; take the path down to the ocean; 415-499-6387, fax 415-499-3795.

HAGMAIER POND ⚓ Favored by swimmers and nude sun-bathers, this miniature lake offers a variation from nearby ocean beaches. It's fringed with grassland and bounded by forest, making it an idyllic spot within easy reach of the highway. There are no facilities. ~ On Route 1 go three and a half miles north of the Bolinas turnoff (at the foot of Bolinas Lagoon). You'll see a shallow parking lot on the right side of the highway. A dirt road leads uphill several hundred yards to the lake; take the first left fork.   ◄ HIDDEN

SAMUEL P. TAYLOR STATE PARK 🚶 🚴 🐎 ⚓ Located several miles inland, this redwood facility provides an opportunity to experience the coastal interior. The place is heavily wooded and offers close to 2900 acres to roam. In addition to the campgrounds, there are hiking trails and a creek. Wildflowers adorn the park entrance and gentle hiking trails. The park has picnic areas, restrooms, and showers. Parking fee, $6. ~ Located on Sir Francis Drake Boulevard, east of Route 1 and six miles from Olema; 415-488-9897, fax 415-488-4315.

▲ There are 60 sites, 25 for tents only (no hookups); $18 to $20 per night. Reservations are required from Memorial Day through Labor Day; call 800-444-7275.

POINT REYES NATIONAL SEASHORE 🚶 🚲 🐎 ⚓ 🎣 🛶 One of the great natural features of Northern California, this 72,000-acre park contains everything from wind-blown beaches to dense pine forests. No traveler should miss it. The park's facilities include three visitors centers, picnic areas, restrooms, and 140 miles of hiking trails. ~ Off Route 1, about 40 miles north of San Francisco; 415-464-5137, fax 415-663-8132; www.nps.gov/pore.

▲ You may camp in any of four campgrounds, which are all accessible only by hiking trails or bikes. Sky Camp, with 12 primitive sites, sits on the side of Mt. Wittenberg, commanding stunning views of Drakes Bay. Wildcat Camp rests on a bluff above a pretty beach; there are 8 primitive sites. Glen Camp lies in a forested valley and has 12 primitive sites. Coast Camp nestles in a meadow near the beach; there are 14 primitive sites. Each camp is equipped with toilets, non-potable water, and picnic areas. Wood fires are not allowed; plan to bring alternate campfire materials. Permits are required; camping fee is $15 per night. You are limited to four nights in the park. Reservations are strongly recommended. For reservations call 415-663-8054 between 9 a.m. and 2 p.m. Monday through Friday, or download a camping form from the website and fax to 415-464-5149. Permits can be obtained Monday through Friday until 2 p.m. at Bear Valley Visitors Center.

LIMANTOUR BEACH 🛶 This white-sand beach is actually a spit, a narrow peninsula pressed between Drakes Bay and an estuary. It's an exotic area of sand dunes and sea breezes. Ideal for exploring, the region shelters over 350 bird species. There's good (but cold) swimming and fishing seaside. The only facilities are toilets. ~ Once in Point Reyes National Seashore, follow Limantour Road to the end.

▲ None, but the Point Reyes Youth Hostel is located on the road to Limantour.

TOMALES BAY STATE PARK 🚶 🛶 ⚓ This delightful park, which abuts on Point Reyes National Seashore, provides a warm, sunny alternative to Point Reyes' frequent fog. The water, too, is warmer here in Tomales Bay, making it a great place for swimming, as well as fishing and boating. Or check out the self-guided nature trail for a description of the relationship between American Indians and local plants. The virgin grove of Bishop pine is a special treat. Rimming the park are several sandy coves; most accessible of these is Heart's Desire Beach, flanked by bluffs and featuring nearby picnic areas. From Heart's Desire a self-guided nature trail goes northwest to Indian Beach, a long stretch of white sand fringed by trees. Hiking trails around the park lead to other secluded beaches, excellent for picnics and day hikes. Dogs are restricted to the upper picnic area and must be kept on a leash. The park has picnic areas and restrooms. Day-use fee, $6. ~ From Route 1 in Olema take Sir Francis Drake Boulevard to Inverness. From Inverness it's another eight miles. When Sir Francis Drake forks, take the right fork, which becomes Pierce Point Road. Then follow Pierce Point Road to the park; 415-669-1140, fax 415-669-1701.

SHELL BEACH Actually part of Tomales Bay State Park, this pocket beach is several miles from the park entrance. As a result, it is often uncrowded. A patch of white sand bordered by steep hills, Shell Beach is ideal for swimming and picnicking. No dogs allowed. The only facilities are toilets. ~ Once in Point Reyes National Seashore, take Sir Francis Drake Boulevard one mile past Inverness, then turn right at Camino del Mar. The trailhead is located at the end of this street; follow the trail three-tenths of a mile down to the beach.

MARSHALL BEACH This secluded beach on Tomales Bay is a wonderful place to swim and sunbathe, often in complete privacy. The beach is a lengthy strip of white sand fringed by cypress trees. ~ Once in Point Reyes National

AUTHOR FAVORITE

Of the many beautiful beaches in Point Reyes National Seashore, **McClures Beach** is by far my favorite. It is a white-sand beach protected by granite cliffs that stand like bookends on either flank. Tidepool watching is a great sport here; if you arrive during low tide it's possible to skirt the cliffs along the south end and explore a pocket beach next door. But don't let a waxing tide catch you sleeping! Swimming is dangerous here; surf fishing, birdwatching, and driftwood gathering more than make up for it. Quite simply, places like this are the reason folks visit Northern California. The only facilities are toilets (at the trailhead). ~ Located in Point Reyes National Seashore at the end of Pierce Point Road. A steep trail leads a half-mile down to the beach. ~ 415-464-5100.

Seashore, take Pierce Point Road. Immediately after passing the entrance to Tomales Bay State Park, turn right onto the paved road. This road travels uphill, turns to gravel and goes two and six tenths miles to a gate. From the gate you hike one and a half miles along the road/trail to the beach.

Walking the steps between the Point Reyes Lighthouse and its observation platform is equivalent to ascending a 30-story building.

▲ Boat-in camping allowed on the beach; be sure to pack out everything you packed in. For information call 415-663-8054.

ABBOTTS LAGOON 🏃 Because of its rich waterfowl population and beautiful surrounding dunes, this is a favorite place among hikers. From the lagoon it's an easy jaunt over the dunes to Point Reyes Beach. The only facilities are toilets. ~ Once in Point Reyes National Seashore, take Pierce Point Road. The trailhead is located along the roadside, two miles past the turnoff for Tomales Bay State Park; follow the trail one mile to the lagoon.

KEHOE BEACH 🏃 ⛵ Bounded by cliffs, this strand is actually the northern end of ten-mile-long Point Reyes Beach. It's a lovely place, covered with wildflowers in spring and boasting a seasonal lagoon. The isolation makes it a great spot for explorers. The only facilities are toilets (at the trailhead). ~ Once in Point Reyes National Seashore, take Pierce Point Road. The trailhead is along the roadside four miles past the turnoff for Tomales Bay State Park; follow the trail a half-mile to the beach.

POINT REYES BEACH ⛵ It will become wonderfully evident why this is nicknamed "Ten Mile Beach" when you cast eyes on this endless sand swath. A great place for whale watching, and fishing, this is not the spot for swimming. Sharks, riptides, and unusual wave patterns make even wading inadvisable. Also the heavy winds along this coastline would chill any swimmer's plans. But that does not detract from the wild beauty of the place, or the fact you can jog for miles along this strand (also referred to as North Beach and South Beach). Restrooms are the park's only facilities. ~ Located off Sir Francis Drake Boulevard, about 14 miles from park headquarters.

DRAKES BEACH 🏊 ⛵ Edged by cliffs, this crescent beach looks out upon the tip of Point Reyes. Since it's well protected by Drakes Bay, this is a good swimming spot. It also provides interesting hikes along the base of the cliffs to the inlet at Drakes Estero. Facilities include picnic areas, restrooms, a visitors center, and a snack bar open weekends only during off-season. ~ Located off Sir Francis Drake Boulevard, 15 miles from park headquarters.

OLEMA RV RESORT & CAMPGROUND This roadside camping park has facilities for trailers and tent campers. The price, however, ain't cheap—$25 to $28 for a tent and two people ($35 to $38 for RV sites). That will buy a plot of ground in a grassy area. It's not exactly the great outdoors, but the place is strategically situated along Route 1 near the turnoff for Point Reyes National Seashore. There are picnic areas, restrooms, showers, a playground, a post office, and a laundromat. ~ 10155 Route 1, Olema; 415-663-8106, fax 415-663-8135; www.olemaranch.com, e-mail ed@olemaranch.com.

▲ There are 230 tent/RV sites (full hookups available); $40 to $60 per night.

▼▼▼▼▼▼▼▼▼▼▼▼

Sonoma and Mendocino Coast

Just north of Marin County lie the coastlines of Sonoma and Mendocino, beautiful and still lightly developed areas. Placid rangeland extends inward while along the shoreline, surf boils against angular cliffs. Far below are pocket beaches and coves; offshore rise dozens of tiny rock islands, or sea stacks. The entire coast teems with fish—salmon and steelhead—as well as crabs, clams, and abalone. Rip currents, sneaker waves, and the coldest waters this side of the Arctic make swimming inadvisable. But the landscape is wide open for exploration, enchanting and exotic.

SIGHTS

Jenner, Mendocino, and Fort Bragg are among the small towns along this endless coastline, but the first place you'll come to is a somewhat different type of community. In fact the fishing village of **Bodega Bay** might look vaguely familiar, for it was the setting of Alfred Hitchcock's eerie film *The Birds*. It's questionable whether any cast members remain among the population of snowy egrets, but the Bay still supports a variety of winged creatures. Conservation efforts have encouraged a comeback among the endangered brown pelicans and blue herons. Serious Hitchcock fans in search of familiar structures from the movie can take a short side trip inland along the Bay Highway to the town of **Bodega**. Here they'll find the old Potter schoolhouse and the church from the film.

In Bodega Bay, at **Lucas Wharf**, and elsewhere along this working waterfront, you can watch fishermen setting off into the fog every morning and hauling in their catch later in the day. ~ Route 1 and Smith Brothers Lane, Bodega Bay.

For a rustic detour, follow Coleman Valley Road when it departs from Route 1 north of Bodega Bay. It weaves through farmland and offers great views of ocean and mountains, and leads to the forest-rimmed village of **Occidental**.

When Route 1 winds up to the woodframe town of **Jenner** (population 170, elevation 19), where the broad Russian River meets the ocean, you can take Route 116 up the river valley to the fabled Russian River resort area and the town of Guerneville.

The Russians for whom the river is named were explorers and trappers sailing down the Pacific coast from Russian outposts in Alaska. They came in search of sea otters and in hope of opening trade routes with the early Spanish settlers. In 1812 these bold outlanders went so far as to build **Fort Ross**, a wooden fortress overlooking the sea. The old Russian stronghold, 13 miles north of Jenner, is today a state historic park. Touring the reconstructed fort you'll encounter a museum, an old Russian Orthodox chapel, a stockade built of hand-tooled redwood, barracks and officers' houses, and two blockhouses (one seven-sided and another eight-sided). Together they provide an insight into an unusual chapter in California history. Admission. ~ 707-847-3286, fax 707-847-3601; e-mail fria@mcn.org.

From Jenner north through Fort Ross and beyond, Route 1 winds high above the coast. Every curve exposes another awesome view of adze-like cliffs slicing into the sea. Driving this corkscrew route can jangle the nerves, but the vistas are soothing to the soul. With the exception of scattered villages, the coastline remains undeveloped. You'll pass sunbleached wooden buildings in the old town of Stewarts Point. Then the road courses through **Sea Ranch**, a development bitterly opposed by environmentalists, which nevertheless displays imaginative contemporary-design houses set against a stark sea.

Just north of Point Arena, a side road from Route 1 leads out to **Point Arena Lighthouse**. The original lighthouse, built in 1870, was destroyed in the 1906 San Francisco earthquake, which struck Point Arena even more fiercely than the bay city. The present beacon, rebuilt shortly afterwards, rises 115 feet from a narrow peninsula. The lighthouse is open for tours. The views, by definition, are outstanding. Open from 10 a.m. to 4:30 p.m. Memorial Day to Labor Day and from 11 a.m. to 3:30 p.m. the rest of the year. Admission. ~ 707-882-2777; e-mail palight@mcn.org.

In Mendocino County, the highway passes through tiny seaside villages. **Elk**, **Albion**, and **Little River** gaze down on the ocean from rocky heights. The coastline is an intaglio of river valleys, pocket beaches, and narrow coves. Forested ridges, soft and green in appearance, fall away into dizzying cliffs.

The houses that stand amid this continental turmoil resemble Maine saltboxes and Cape Cod cottages. In the town of **Mendocino**, which sits on a headland above the sea, you'll discover New England incarnate. Settled in 1852, the town was built largely by Yankees who decorated their village with wooden towers, Victorian homes, and a Gothic Revival Presbyterian church. The town, originally a vital lumber port, has become an artists' colony. With a shoreline honeycombed by beaches and a villagescape capped with a white church steeple, Mendocino is a mighty pretty corner of the continent.

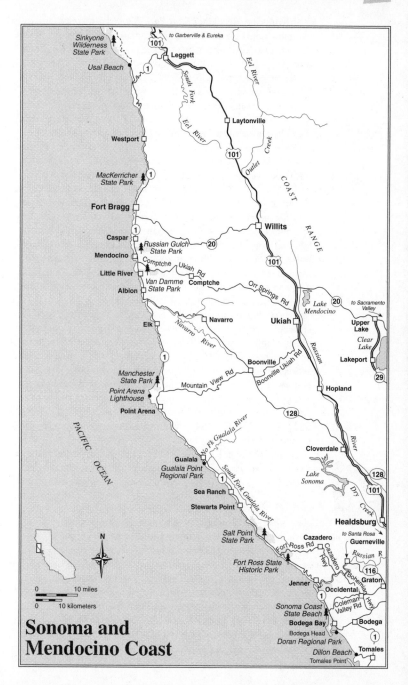

Sonoma and Mendocino Coast

Mendocino Headlands State Park, located atop a sea cliff, offers unmatched views of the town's tumultuous shoreline. From the bluffs you can gaze down at placid tidepools and wave-carved grottoes.

In the park is the historic **Ford House**, an 1854 home with a small museum that also serves as a visitors center for the park. ~ 735 Main Street, Mendocino; 707-937-5397.

The best way to experience this antique town is by stopping at the **Kelly House Museum**. Set in a vintage home dating from 1861, the museum serves as an historical research center (open Tuesday through Friday from 9 a.m. to 4 p.m.; admission). The museum is open daily year-round. ~ 45007 Albion Street, Mendocino; 707-937-5791, fax 707-937-2156; e-mail staff@mendocinohistory.org.

Among Mendocino's intriguing locales are the **Chinese Temple**, a 19th-century religious shrine located on Albion Street (open by appointment only); the **Presbyterian Church**, a national historic landmark on Main Street; and the **MacCallum House**, a Gingerbread Victorian on Albion Street, which has been reborn as an inn and restaurant. Another building of note is the **Masonic Hall**, an 1865 structure adorned with a hand-carved redwood statue on the roof. ~ Ukiah Street.

Then after meandering the side streets, stop at the **Mendocino Art Center**. Here exhibits by painters, potters, photographers, textile workers, and others will give an idea of the tremendous talent contained in tiny Mendocino. Nearly 300 one- to six-day workshops in ceramics, sculpture, computer arts, and textiles are offered annually. There's a pretty garden and a gift shop, and the complex also houses a local theater company. ~ 45200 Little Lake Street, Mendocino; 707-937-5818, 800-653-3328, fax 707-937-1764; www.mendocinoartcenter.org, e-mail mendoart@mcn.org.

North of town, on the way to Fort Bragg, stop at **Jug Handle State Reserve**. Here you can climb an ecological stairway which

AUTHOR FAVORITE

Maybe it's just the name, but I have to rank the ride on the **Skunk train** through the redwoods as one of my favorite scenic rail trips. You can board the train near the center of Fort Bragg for a half-day ride aboard a steam or diesel engine or a diesel-powered railcar. Dating from 1885, the Skunk was originally a logging train; today it also carries passengers along a 40-mile route through mountains and redwoods to the inland area of Northspur and back. For information, contact Sierra Railroad. Reservations recommended. ~ Fort Bragg; 707-964-6371, 800-866-1690, fax 707-964-6754; www.skunktrain.com, e-mail skunk45@adelphia.net.

ascends a series of marine terraces. On the various levels you'll encounter the varied coast, dune, and ridge environments that form the area's diverse ecosystem. ~ Along Route 1 about one mile north of Caspar; 707-937-5804, fax 707-937-2953.

For a thoroughly delightful stroll to the sea, meander through the **Mendocino Coast Botanical Gardens**. This coastal preserve, with three miles of luxuriant pathways, is "a garden for all seasons" with something always in bloom. The unique Northern California coastal climate is conducive to heathers, perennials, fuchsias, and rhododendrons, which grow in colorful profusion here. Trails lead past gardens of camellias, ferns, and dwarf conifers to a coastal bluff with vistas up and down the rugged shoreline. Admission. ~ 18220 North Route 1, Fort Bragg; 707-964-4352, fax 707-964-3114; www.gardenbythesea.org, e-mail info@gardenbythesea.org.

North of Fort Bragg, Route 1 runs past miles of sand dunes and traverses several small towns. Then, after having followed the coast all the way from Southern California, it abruptly turns inland. The reason is the mysterious Lost Coast of California. Due north, where no highway could possibly run, the King Range vaults out of the sea, rising over 4000 feet in less than three miles. It is a wilderness inhabited by black bears and bald eagles, with an abandoned lighthouse and a solitary beach piled with ancient Indian shellmounds.

LODGING

Though bed-and-breakfast prices are generally high, Northern California's inns are unparalleled in intimacy and personal care.

Located a few miles east of Bodega Bay, the **Inn at Occidental** is a charming Victorian homestead encircled by a wide porch bedecked with potted plants and white wicker rockers. The 16 guest rooms feature fireplaces, spa tubs, antiques, and original artwork. There is also a separate cottage with a full kitchen and two master suites. A full breakfast is included, as are afternoon wine and cheese. ~ 3657 Church Street, Occidental; 707-874-1047, 800-522-6324, fax 707-874-1078; www.innatoccidental.com, e-mail innkeeper@innatoccidental.com. ULTRA-DELUXE.

Situated on six secluded acres of apple orchards, rose gardens, and redwood trees, **The Applewood Inn** is a destination built for romance and repose. This Mediterranean-style villa—painted in the lovely, muted pink of the roses in the garden—surrounds a quiet courtyard and murmuring fountain. The inn's 19 rooms are equal to the grounds, attractively appointed with a blend of modern comforts and antique designs. Private patios, double showers and tile fireplaces will surely coax you into romance and relaxation. ~ 13555 Route 116, Guerneville; 707-869-9093, fax 707-869-9170; www.applewoodinn.com. DELUXE TO ULTRA-DELUXE.

A prime Jenner resting spot is **Jenner Inn and Cottages**, a bed and breakfast overlooking the river. Several buildings comprise the spread: you can rent a room, a suite, even a cottage. Many rooms have fireplaces and hot tubs, all have private decks. The rooms are lovingly decorated with antiques and comfy furnishings. Full breakfast included. ~ 10400 Route 1, Jenner; 707-865-2377, 800-732-2377, fax 707-865-0829; www.jennerinn.com, e-mail innkeeper@jennerinn.com. MODERATE TO DELUXE.

A fair bargain can be found along the coast at **Fort Ross Lodge**, two miles north of the old Russian fort. Overlooking the ocean, this 22-unit establishment consists of a cluster of wood-frame buildings. The rooms have ocean views; the ceilings are knotty pine, and the varied decor includes everything from wicker to antique furniture. There are TVs, DVD players, refrigerators, patios equipped with grills, and private baths in all rooms, plus a community sauna and hot tub. ~ 20705 Route 1, Jenner; 707-847-3333, 800-968-4537, fax 707-847-3330; www.fortrosslodge.com. moderate to ultra-deluxe.

Several lodges along the California coast reflect in their architecture the raw energy of the surrounding sea. Such a one is **Timber Cove Inn**. Set on 26 acres and elemental in style, it is a labyrinth of unfinished woods and bald rocks. The heavy timber lobby is dominated by a walk-in stone fireplace and sits astride a Japanese pond. The 50 guest rooms are finished in redwood with beams and columns exposed; they look a bit old and dated for my taste, but they do afford marvelous views of the mountains and open sea. Many have decks, fireplaces, and hot tubs. All have TVs and phones. Timber Cove, fittingly, rests on a cliff directly above the ocean. Raccoons are a common sight; if you have critter issues you might want to steel yourself before wandering the grounds at night. Restaurant and lounge. ~ 21780 North Route 1, 15 miles north of Jenner; 707-847-3231, 800-987-8319, fax 707-847-3704; www.timbercoveinn.com. MODERATE TO ULTRA-DELUXE.

Set on a plateau above the ocean, **Stillwater Cove Ranch** is set on lovely grounds and populated with peacocks. Formerly a boys' school, this complex of buildings has been transformed into a restful retreat. Accommodations are varied and include single rooms, large kitchenettes, and a cottage with a fireplace. Even the dairy barn can house guests: it's been converted to a bunkhouse with kitchen. Stillwater Cove is certainly worth checking into. Closed for one week around Christmas. ~ 22555 Route 1, 16 miles north of Jenner; 707-847-3227. BUDGET TO MODERATE.

Mar Vista Cottages at Anchor Bay is a community of 12 separate cottages scattered around nine acres of oceanview property. Each is an old woodframe affair with a sitting room and kitchen as well as a bedroom and bathroom. Several are equipped with decks, fireplaces, or wood stoves. A soaking tub and barbecue facility on the property are surrounded by trees; a short path leads across Route 1 to the beach. Guests can harvest their own organic greens and fruit from the garden and fetch fresh eggs from the hens. Completely nonsmoking. Pets welcome. ~ 35101 South Route 1, Gualala; 707-884-3522, 877-855-3522, fax 707-884-4861; www.marvistamendocino.com, e-mail renata@marvista mendocino.com. DELUXE TO ULTRA-DELUXE.

Built in 1903, the **Gualala Hotel** is a massive two-story struc-   ◄ *HIDDEN*
ture. It's an old clapboard affair, fully refurbished, that includes a bar and dining room. The 19 rooms upstairs are small, but the wallpaper, decor, and old-time flourishes give the place a comfy traditional feel, making it a rare find on the North Coast. Because of the downstairs restaurant/bar, it can get noisy at times. ~ 39301 Route 1, Gualala; 707-884-3441. BUDGET TO MODERATE.

Every one of the 16 rooms at **Seacliff Inn** stares straight at the Pacific Ocean, and some days you can see whales rubbing their bellies on the sandbar. Accommodations are simple but entirely comfortable, with everything you need for an atmospheric retreat: fireplaces, private decks, two-person whirlpool tubs with ocean views, downy king-size beds and plush comforters, coffee makers, and refrigerators stocked with complimentary champagne. The staff treats you like family. ~ 39140 South Route 1, Gualala; 707-884-1213, 800-400-5053, fax 707-884-1731; www.seacliffmotel.com, e-mail information@seacliffmotel.com. MODERATE TO DELUXE.

Country inns of this genre are quite abundant farther north. Near the town of Mendocino there are numerous bed and breakfasts, some outstanding. The seaside towns of Elk, Albion, Little River, Mendocino, and Fort Bragg each house several.

Among the more renowned is **Harbor House Inn**. Set on a rise overlooking the ocean, the house is built entirely of redwood.

AUTHOR FAVORITE

Sea Ranch Lodge is the ultimate Sonoma coast retreat. Miles of secluded beaches and hiking trails, fields of wildflowers, and beautiful bluffs make this resort a perennial favorite. The lodge, which wears its weathered wood siding with dignity, offers 20 rooms with ocean or ridge views. The decor emphasizes earth tones that blend in with the natural surroundings. There is a bar with a solarium, a store, and nearby hiking and biking trails. ~ 60 Sea Walk Drive, Sea Ranch; 707-785-2371, 800-732-7262, fax 707-785-2917; www.searanchlodge.com, e-mail reservations@ searanchlodge.com. ULTRA-DELUXE.

The living room alone, with its fireplace and exposed-beam ceiling, is an architectural feat. The house was modeled on a design exhibited at San Francisco's 1915 Panama–Pacific Exposition. Of the ten bedrooms and cottages, all are beautifully and individually decorated, many with ocean views, fireplaces, and antique appointments. The gardens are gorgeous, with paths leading down to the private beach. Rates include breakfast and dinner. The inn is closed the first two weeks in December. ~ 5600 South Route 1, Elk; 707-877-3203, 800-720-7474, fax 707-877-3452; www.theharborhouseinn.com, e-mail innkeeper@theharborhouseinn.com. ULTRA-DELUXE.

A message in a guest room diary at **Elk Cove Inn** reads: "A view, with a room." The view is of knobby coast and simmering surf of ice blue and shaggy dunes falling away. The room is perfect for watching it all: a comfortable cabin with dramatic beamed ceiling, gas fireplace at the foot of your featherbed, carafe of port waiting on the nightstand. In the morning the proprietor lays out an elaborate buffet—coffee cakes, corned beef hash—in the main 1883 Victorian house, a short walk from the four bluff-top cabins. There are seven guest rooms in the main house, some with dormer windows overlooking ocean, others with views of the riotous gardens. Four luxurious spa suites and an outdoor hot tub complete the picture. ~ 6300 South Route 1, Elk; 707-877-3321, 800-275-2967, fax 707-877-1808; www.elkcoveinn.com, e-mail innkeeper@elkcoveinn.com. DELUXE TO ULTRA-DELUXE.

Heritage House was constructed in 1877 and reflects the New England architecture popular then in Northern California. Most guests are housed in duplex cottages that overlook the rocky coastline. All of these 47 rooms have fireplaces and private decks. ~ 5200 North Route 1, Little River; 707-937-5885, 800-235-5885, fax 707-937-0318; www.heritagehouseinn.com, e-mail info@heritagehouseinn.com. ULTRA-DELUXE.

Baby Face Nelson is reputed to have hidden in the old farmhouse that today serves as the Heritage House's reception and dining area.

The New England–style farmhouse that has transformed into **Glendeven** dates even further back, to 1867. The theme is country living, with a meadow out back and dramatic views of the ocean and headlands nearby. The sitting room is an intimate affair with comfortable armchairs set before a brick fireplace. In the rooms you're apt to find a bed with wooden headboard, an antique wardrobe, and colorful orchids. Glendeven is as charming and intimate as a country inn can be. A full breakfast is delivered to your room. Closed first two weeks of January. ~ 8205 North Route 1, Little River; 707-937-0083, 800-822-4536; www.glendeven.com, e-mail innkeeper@glendeven.com. DELUXE TO ULTRA-DELUXE.

The **Little River Inn**, centered in a quaint 1850s-era house, has expanded into a mini-resort with 66 units, a restaurant, tennis courts, a day spa, a lounge, and a nine-hole golf course. Intimacy may be lacking, but the inn boasts a variety of rooms, from simple to super luxurious, and almost all afford grand ocean views. Pets welcome. ~ 7901 North Route 1, Little River; 707-937-5942, 888-466-5683, fax 707-937-3944; www.littleriverinn.com, e-mail lri@mcn.org. MODERATE TO ULTRA-DELUXE.

Auberge Mendocino overlooks Van Damme State Park, with trails that deliver you instantly to rocky coast and the shiny bald heads of grey seals. Six rooms, three suites, a cottage, and a vacation rental home are extra spacious and decorated with pastel walls, folded linen draperies, antique dressers, and woodburning hearths. Music streams through the living room. Breakfast, featuring savory items like fresh seasonal fruit, frittatas and herbed cheese omelettes, is served by candlelight in the elegant dining room. Some rooms are pet-friendly. ~ 8200 North Route 1, two miles south of Mendocino; 707-937-0088, 800-347-9252, fax 707-937-3620; www.aubergemendocino.com, e-mail innkeeper@ aubergemendocino.com. ULTRA-DELUXE.

A minute from downtown Mendocino, set right where Big River meets the ocean, **Stanford Inn by the Sea** is both woodsy and New Agey. The rambling lobby is paneled in Ponderosa pine and looks across to Pacific headlands while llamas and geese roam terraced lawns. Families love it here, and pets are welcome. There's kayaking and redwood outrigger canoeing down Big River, and mountain biking along Pacific cliff trails. Couples go for the handsome, intimate rooms with Lexington furnishings, woodburning fireplaces, VCRs (the inn stocks 5000 videos), and DVD players. You'll also find a wonderful greenhouse pool with gardens of palms and bougainvillea, and water that's bathtub-warm year-round. Yoga classes are offered, as is massage. ~ Route 1 and Comptche Ukiah Road, Mendocino; 707-937-5615, 800-331-8884, fax 707-937-0305; www.stanfordinn.com, e-mail info@stanfordinn.com. ULTRA-DELUXE.

Set in a falsefront building which dates to 1878, the 51-room **Mendocino Hotel** is a wonderful place, larger than other nearby country inns, with a wood-paneled lobby, two restaurants, and living quarters adorned with antiques. There are rooms in the hotel with both private and shared baths as well as quarters in the garden cottages out back. ~ 45080 Main Street, Mendocino; 707-937-0511, 800-548-0513, fax 707-937-0513; www.mendocino hotel.com, e-mail info@mendocinohotel.com. MODERATE TO ULTRA-DELUXE.

The queen of Mendocino is the **MacCallum House Inn**, a Gingerbread Victorian built in 1882. The place is a treasure trove of antique furnishings, knickknacks, and other memorabilia. Many of the rooms are individually decorated with rocking chairs, quilts, and wood stoves. Positively everything—the carriage house, barn, greenhouse, gazebo, even the water tower—has been converted into a guest room. Full breakfast included. Pet-friendly. ~ 45020 Albion Street, Mendocino; 707-937-0289, 800-609-0492, fax 707-937-2243; www.maccallumhouse.com, e-mail info@mac callumhouse.com. MODERATE TO ULTRA-DELUXE.

The neighboring **Sweetwater Spa & Inn** offers a variety of accommodations, including cozy watertower rooms and private suites. Breakfast, afternoon coffee and tea, and evening wine and cheese are included. ~ 44840 Main Street, Mendocino; 800-300-4140; www.sweetwaterspa.com, e-mail lodging@sweetwaterspa. com. MODERATE TO ULTRA-DELUXE.

The nearby **Sea Gull Inn** has nine guest accommodations, some with ocean views. In a land of pricey hotels, this B&B establishment is a rarity. Choose to stay in the main house or in the cottage set in the garden. ~ 44960 Albion Street, Mendocino; 707-937-5204, 888-937-5204, fax 707-937-3550; www.seagull bb.com, e-mail seagull1@mcn.org. BUDGET TO DELUXE.

Set on two landscaped acres overlooking Mendocino village and the coast, the **Joshua Grindle Inn** is a 19th-century New England–style farmhouse with ten spacious rooms, all with sitting areas, and some with woodburning fireplaces, whirlpool tubs, and ocean views. A separate two-bedroom home is also available. An inviting gathering spot during evening hours, the parlor offers a cheerful fire and an antique pump organ. Full breakfast included. ~ 44800 Little Lake Road, Mendocino; 707-937-4143, 800-474-6353; www.joshgrin.com, e-mail stay@josh grin.com. DELUXE TO ULTRA-DELUXE.

If upon seeing the New England–style **Hill House Inn** you're suddenly inspired to compile detective notes on a typewriter, don't be alarmed. This 44-room bed and breakfast set amid Victorian gardens was the site of the 1980s television series *Murder, She Wrote*. These days the elegant lodging boasts ocean view suites furnished with antiques and fireplaces; some with whirlpool tubs. In-room massage is available. Pet-friendly. ~ 10701 Palette Drive, Mendocino; 707-937-0554, 800-422-0554; www.hillhouseinn.com. DELUXE.

For women guests only, **Sallie & Eileen's Place** offers a studio A-frame cottage and a spacious cabin three miles from Mendocino. The studio has a fireplace, a kitchen area, and a sunken tub, while the cabin, which can sleep up to six, has a loft bedroom, a woodstove, a deck, a full kitchen, and a private backyard. Pets allowed with a nominal extra fee. ~ Box 409, Mendocino, CA 95460; 707-937-2028, fax 707-937-2918; www.seplace.com, e-mail innkeeper@seplace.com. MODERATE.

Built with virgin redwood timbers salvaged from Big River, the **Brewery Gulch Inn** is the ultimate bed and breakfast, oozing romance, luxury, and privacy. Perched on a bluff overlooking Smuggler's Cove, it's designed so each of its ten arts-and-crafts-style guest rooms has views of the crashing surf from private decks. Rooms are fitted with down comforters, fireplaces, and wi-fi access. The huge gourmet breakfasts feature specialties such as pra-line pecan pancakes doused in vanilla-bourbon syrup. ~ 9401 Coast Highway 1 North, Mendocino; 800-578-4454, fax 707-937-1279; www.brewerygulchinn. com, e-mail innkeeper@brewerygulchinn.com. MODERATE TO DELUXE.

> The Weller House is home to the tallest land structure in Fort Bragg: a historic water tower.

Right in the center of Fort Bragg and only blocks away from galleries and shops sits **The Atrium**. This lovely yellow Victorian inn offers ten charming rooms, each well-appointed and well-maintained. The indoor garden provides a serene resting spot, while those looking for outdoor scenery will be delighted by the proximity to the town's botanical gardens. An afternoon bever-age service and a full breakfast are included. ~ 700 North Main Street, Fort Bragg; 707-964-9440, 800-278-8392, fax 707-964-1770; www.atriumbnb.com, e-mail info@atriumbnb.com. MOD-ERATE TO DELUXE.

The **Weller House**, originally built in 1886, is now on the National Registry of Historic Places. The property boasts a 900-square-foot redwood-paneled ballroom, six-person hot tub, and English gardens. It's a great place for relaxing in one of nine an-tique-decorated guest rooms, and even better place for exploring the lavish surroundings. ~ 524 Stewart Street, Fort Bragg; 877-893-5537; www.wellerhouse.com, e-mail innkeeper@weller house.com. MODERATE TO DELUXE.

DINING

For the best meal hereabouts (or for that matter, anywhere about), head for **River's End Restaurant**. Situated at that mo-mentous crossroad of the Russian River and Pacific Ocean (and commanding a view of both), this outstanding little place is a restaurant with imagination. How else do you explain a dinner menu that ranges from *médallions* of venison to racklettes of elk to coconut-fried shrimp? Not to mention good service and a se-lection of over 150 local wines. River's End is a great place for ocean lovers and culinary adventurers. Closed Monday through Thursday in winter. Closed January and first two weeks of February. ~ 11048 Route 1, Jenner; 707-865-2484 ext. 111, fax 707-865-9621; www.ilovesunsets.com, e-mail dine@rivers-end. com. MODERATE TO DELUXE.

The **Salt Point Bar and Grill** features a small restaurant serv-ing breakfast, lunch, and dinner. The menu relies heavily on sea-food—halibut, oysters, prawns—but also includes chicken, steak, and other dishes. At lunch, enjoy a variety of salads, sandwiches, or seafood selections. Breakfast offers an array of omelettes. ~ 23255 North Route 1, 17 miles north of Jenner; phone/fax 707-847-3234; www.saltpointlodgebarandgrill.com. MODERATE TO DELUXE.

The 1903 **Gualala Hotel** has an attractive dining room with a menu that varies from braised lamb shank to pan-seared duck breast. Stops along the way include linguini puttanesca, salmon, and New York steak. What makes dining here really special is the old hotel with its big front porch and antique decor. ~ 39301 Route 1, Gualala; 707-884-3441. MODERATE.

Okay, so **St. Orres** is yet another California-cuisine restaurant. But it's the only one you'll see that looks as if it should be in Russia rather than along the California coast. With its dizzying spires, this elegant structure evokes images of Moscow and old St. Petersburg. The kitchen provides an everchanging menu of fresh game and fish dishes with an emphasis on organic, locally grown food. The fixed-price menu will include hot and chilled soups, poached salmon, rabbit, rack of lamb, stuffed wild boar, and several seasonal specialties. Even if you're not interested in dining, it might be worth a stop to view this architectural extravaganza. Dinner and occasional brunch. Closed Tuesday and Wednesday during winter. ~ 36601 Route 1, Gualala; 707-884-3303, fax 707-884-1840; www.saintorres. com, e-mail saintorres@yahoo.com. ULTRA-DELUXE.

Arena Cove Bar & Grill looks out on a pier as well as a series of ocean bluffs. With a hand-carved bar and woodplank dining room, it's a local seafood restaurant serving fresh salmon, sautéed prawns, and raw oysters. If oysters and homemade clam chowder don't interest you, there are steaks and chops at this good-ol'-style eating place. ~ 790 Port Road, Point Arena; 707-882-2100, fax 707-882-2762. MODERATE TO DELUXE.

Although the dining room at **Harbor House Inn** mainly serves guests at this bed and breakfast, there are three extra tables for two people each evening. A fire in the fireplace will keep you warm and cozy on a cold coastal night, and in the summer you can watch the sunset over the ocean out of the huge windows. The chef prepares a set menu, served at 7 p.m., with entrées such as salmon, pork tenderloin, or halibut. A vegetarian meal can also be prepared with advance notice. Reservations are required. ~ 5600 South Route 1, Elk; 707-877-3203, 800-720-7474, fax 707-877-3452; www.theharborhouseinn.com, e-mail innkeeper@the harborhouseinn.com. ULTRA-DELUXE.

The **Albion River Inn**, set high on a cliff above the Albion Cove and the ocean, is a plate-glass dining spot serving California cuisine, and specializing in otherworldly ocean views. Entrées include grilled ginger-lime prawns, oven-roasted quail, and grilled filet mignon in a sauce of pancetta, wild mushrooms and caramelized onions, and can be perfectly paired with a selection from their award-winning wine list. Dinner only. ~ 3790 North Route 1, Albion; 707-937-1919, 800-479-7944, fax 707-937-2604; www. albionriverinn.com, e-mail innkeepers@albionriverinn.com. MODERATE TO ULTRA-DELUXE.

The Ravens provides a gourmet vegetarian alternative to the many seafood restaurants along the coast. On the vegan dinner menu, look for citrus polenta with sautéed garden greens and cashew cream sauce, tofu portabella with lemon tahini sauce, and, for the adventurous, quinoa enchiladas. Pizzas and pastas are also available. Breakfasts include a variety of omelette and pancake dishes. ~ Stanford Inn by the Sea, Route 1 and Comptche Ukiah Road, Mendocino; 707-937-5615, 800-331-8884, fax 707-937-0305; www.ravensrestaurant.com, e-mail info@stanfordinn.com. MODERATE TO DELUXE.

> At Stanford Inn by the Sea, "biodynamic" nurseries provide fare for the inn's outstanding vegetarian menus.

A morning ritual for locals and visitors alike is to climb the rough-hewn stairs to the loft-like **Bay View Café** for coffee, French toast, or fluffy omelettes. On sunny afternoons, the deck overlooking Main Street and the coastal headlands makes an ideal lunch spot, especially for fish and chips or a jalapeño chile burger. Dinner only on Friday and Saturday in winter. ~ 45040 Main Street, Mendocino; 707-937-4197, fax 707-937-2884. BUDGET TO MODERATE.

At the **Mendocino Hotel** you can enjoy California-style cuisine in the main dining room or out in the "garden room." The menu represents a mix of meat and seafood entrées such as prime rib, free-range chicken, and local salmon. The ambience in this 19th-century building evokes Mendocino's early days. ~ 45080 Main Street, Mendocino; 707-937-0511, 800-548-0513; www. mendocinohotel.com, e-mail reservations@mendocinohotel.com. DELUXE TO ULTRA-DELUXE.

Situated in a cozy little house, the **Moosse Café** offers imaginative seasonal dishes and organically grown comfort food. Try their seafood dishes or pasta special. Finish with a homemade dessert. ~ 390 Kasten Street, Mendocino; 707-937-4323, fax 707-937-3611; www.themoosse.com, e-mail manager@themoosse. com. MODERATE TO DELUXE.

For French and California cuisine, **955 Ukiah Street** is an address worth noting. Candles, fresh flowers, and impressionist prints set the tone here. Serving dinner only, it prepares brandied prawns, red snapper in phyllo pastry, roast duck, and calamari. For the diet-conscious, they also offer lighter dishes. Dinner only. Closed Monday through Wednesday. ~ 955 Ukiah Street, Mendocino; 707-937-1955, fax 707-937-5138; www.955restaurant.com. DELUXE.

The dining rooms of the 1882 **MacCallum House Restaurant** are beautiful, the walls and ceilings covered with carved redwood and fir, the tables glittering with firelight and candlelight. Everything on the menu is excellent. Start with a huckleberry and basil mojito and duck tamales steamed in banana leaves. Then try the Petrale sole with jasmine rice and cilantro buerre blanc or the filet mignon with cabernet reduction sauce and blue cheese popover. There's a lighter café menu served in the bar. Breakfast and dinner only. ~ 45020 Albion Street, Mendocino; 707-937-0289; www.maccallumdining.com, e-mail info@maccallumhouse.com. DELUXE TO ULTRA-DELUXE.

Mendo Bistro is Fort Bragg's best-kept secret. True to his stomping grounds, the chef/owner exclusively uses local produce, seafood, free-range meat, beer and wine. Fresh-made pastas, breads, and desserts also have a prominent place on his menu. A local favorite, Mendo Bistro offers diners a casual, elegant atmosphere with a picturesque view of Fort Bragg's historic downtown. ~ 301 Main Street, Fort Bragg; 707-964-4974, fax 707-964-4949; www.mendobistro.com, e-mail eat@mendo bistro.com. MODERATE TO DELUXE.

Fort Bragg's favorite dining spot is easy to remember—**The Restaurant**. Despite the name, this is no generic eating place but a creative kitchen serving excellent dinners. It's decorated with dozens of paintings by local artist Olaf Palm, lending a sense of the avant-garde to this informal establishment. The Restaurant's menu offers seasonal entrées like sautéed prawns, salmon, rockfish, steaks ,and vegetarian selections. Everything is house-made down to the stocks and dressings by chef/owner Jim Larsen. Choose from a selection of house-made desserts, including ice creams and sorbets. Dinner only. Closed Tuesday and Wednesday. Closed first week of November and first two weeks of March. ~ 418 North Main Street, Fort Bragg; 707-964-9800; www.therestaurantfortbragg.com, e-mail info@therestaurantfortbragg.com. MODERATE TO DELUXE.

AUTHOR FAVORITE

Mendocino's best-known dining room is well deserving of its renown. **Café Beaujolais**, situated in a small antique house on the edge of town, serves designer dishes, which I try to sample on a regular basis. Dinner, served seven nights a week, is ever changing. They serve a global menu featuring local organic produce, wild and sustainably cultured seafoods, humanely raised meats, and more than 50 varieties of wine available by the glass. Excellent cuisine. No lunch Monday and Tuesday. ~ 961 Ukiah Street, Mendocino; 707-937-5614; www.cafebeaujolais.com, e-mail cafebeau@mcn.org. DELUXE.

In the New England–style town of Mendocino you'll discover a shopper's paradise. Prices are quite dear, but the window browsing is unparalleled. Housed in the town's old Victorians and Cape Cod cottages is a plethora of shops. There are stores specializing in soap, seashells, candles, and T-shirts; not to mention bookstores, potters, jewelers, art galleries, and antique shops galore. Most shops are located along Mendocino's woodframe Main Street, but also search out the side streets and passageways in this vintage town.

SHOPPING

One particularly noteworthy gallery is the **William Zimmer Gallery**, which houses an eclectic collection of contemporary and traditional arts and crafts. ~ 10481 Lansing Street, Mendocino; 707-937-5121. Be sure to also check out **Highlight Gallery**, featuring, among other things, displays of handmade furniture, contemporary art, jewelry, ceramic, glass, and woodwork. ~ 45052 Main Street, Mendocino; 707-937-3132. The **Mendocino Art Center** houses numerous crafts studios as well as art studios. ~ 45200 Little Lake Street, Mendocino; 707-937-5818.

Books are the order of the day at the **Gallery Bookshop Bookwinkle's Children's Books**. ~ Main and Kasten streets, Mendocino; 707-937-2665.

There's music four nights a week at the **Caspar Inn**. This downhome bar room spotlights deejays, local bands as well as groups from outside the area. Hit it on the right night and the joint will be rocking. If you've overdone your partying by the end of the night, ask management about the rooms they have available. Cover for live music. ~ 14957 Caspar Road, Caspar; 707-964-5565; www.casparinn.com.

NIGHTLIFE

For a night on the town, enjoy a quiet drink at the **Mendocino Hotel**. You can relax in a Victorian-style lounge or in an enclosed garden patio. ~ 45080 Main Street, Mendocino; 707-937-0511.

For a pint of Guinness, a game of backgammon, local characters and friendly chit chat, slip into **Patterson's Pub**. The pub is small, in keeping with its Irish persona, and furnished in dark wood and brass. There's occasional live entertainment. ~ 10485 Lansing Street, Mendocino; 707-937-4782.

DILLON BEACH Located at the mouth of Tomales Bay, this beach is popular with boaters and clammers. The surrounding hills are covered with resort cottages, but there are open areas and dunes to explore. There are picnic areas and restrooms, groceries, boat rentals, and fishing charters. Day-use fee, $5. ~ From Route 1 in Tomales take Dillon Beach Road west for four miles.

BEACHES & PARKS

▲ Located nearby, Lawson's Landing (707-878-2443) has open-meadow tent/RV camping (no hookups); $20 to $22 per night. Take note: This campground hosts hundreds of trailers. Call in December and January for closures; they may lock the gates if it's too wet.

DORAN REGIONAL PARK

This peninsular park is situated on a sand spit between Bodega Harbor and Bodega Bay. With a broad sand beach and good facilities, it's an excellent spot for daytrippers and campers alike. You can explore the tidal flats or fish up on the jetty. There are picnic areas, restrooms, and showers. Day-use fee, $5 to $6. ~ Off Route 1 in Bodega Bay; 707-875-3540, fax 707-875-2171; e-mail groupwise@sonoma-county.org.

▲ There are 134 tent/RV sites (no hookups); $19 per night.

BODEGA HEAD There are pocket beaches here dramatically backdropped by granite cliffs. A good place to picnic and explore, this is also a favored whale-watching site. There are restrooms and showers located in nearby Westside Park. ~ Off Route 1 in Bodega Bay along Bay Flat Road.

▲ Westside Park has 47 tent/RV sites (no hookups); $16 per night for Sonoma County residents and $18 for nonresidents. ~ 707-875-3540.

SONOMA COAST STATE BEACH

This magnificent park extends for 19 miles between Bodega Head and the Vista Trail. It consists of a number of beaches separated by steep headlands; all are within easy hiking distance of Route 1. The beaches range from sweeping strands to pocket coves and abound with waterfowl and shorebirds, clams, and abalone. The park headquarters and information center is at Salmon Creek Beach, where endless sand dunes backdrop a broad beach. Schoolhouse Beach is a particularly pretty pocket cove bounded by rocky cliffs; Portuguese Beach boasts a wide swath of sand; Blind Beach is rather secluded with a sea arch offshore; and Goat Rock Beach faces the town of Jenner and is decorated with offshore rocks. Pick your poison—hiking, tidepooling, birdwatching, whale watching, camping, picnicking, fishing—and you'll find it waiting along this rugged and hauntingly beautiful coastline. Bodega Dunes, Salmon Creek Beach, Schoolhouse Beach, Goat Rock, Portuguese Beach, and Wrights Beach have restrooms; Bodega Dunes and Wrights Beach also feature picnic areas. Day-use fee, $6. ~ Located along Route 1 between Bodega Bay and Jenner; 707-875-3483, fax 707-875-3876.

▲ At Bodega Dunes, there are 98 tent/RV sites (no hookups); $25 per night. At Wrights Beach, there are 27 tent/RV sites (no hookups); $35 per night. Reservations are required; call 800-444-7275. At Pomo Canyon and Willow Creek you'll find

31 walk-in primitive sites; $15 per night; closed December through March.

FORT ROSS REEF CAMPGROUND 🚶 🚴 🛶 🎣 🛥 Set in a canyon surrounded by bluffs, this facility is beautifully located near the ocean and features a redwood grove. It is a state park with spectacular surroundings and gorgeous views. There are picnic areas and restrooms. Day-use fee, $6. ~ 19005 Route 1, 12 miles north of Jenner; watch for a cluster of white barns on the west side of the highway; 707-847-3286, fax 707-847-3601.

▲ There are 20 tent/RV sites (no hookups); $15 per night. Closed November through March. Depending on the weather, fires may not be allowed.

STILLWATER COVE REGIONAL PARK 🚶 🛶 🛥 Situated amid pine trees on a hillside above the ocean, this is a small park with access to a beach. The canyon trail leads up to the restored (but closed) Fort Ross Schoolhouse. There are picnic areas, restrooms, and showers. Day-use fee, $5. ~ Route 1, about 16 miles north of Jenner; 707-847-3245, fax 707-847-3325.

▲ There are 22 tent/RV sites (no hookups); $19 per night. Reservations must be made at least ten days in advance; 707-565-2267.

OCEAN COVE STORE AND CAMPGROUND 🚶 🚴 🛶 🛥 This privately owned campground has sites on a bluff above a rocky shoreline. Anglers catch everything from salmon to rockfish. The scenery is mighty attractive, and the campsites are well removed from the road. There are hot showers and portable toilets. ~ Route 1, about 17 miles north of Jenner; 707-847-3422, fax 707-847-3624; www.oceancove.org.

▲ There are 150 tent/RV sites (no hookups); $19 per night; $2 extra for dogs. Closed December through March.

SALT POINT STATE PARK 🚶 🚴 🛶 🛥 Extending from the ocean to over 1000 feet elevation, this 6000-acre spread includes coastline, forests, and open range land. Along the shore are weird honeycomb formations called tafoni, caused by sea erosion on coastal sandstone. Up amid the stands of Douglas fir and Bishop pine there's a pygmy forest, where unfavorable soil conditions have caused fully mature redwoods to reach only about 20 feet in height. Blacktail deer, raccoons, mountain lions, and bobcats roam the area. Miles of hiking trails lace the park, including one through a rhododendron reserve. There are picnic areas and restrooms. Day-use fee, $6. ~ Route 1, about 20 miles north of Jenner; 707-847-3221, fax 707-847-3843.

▲ There are three campgrounds here with 108 tent/RV sites (no hookups); $25 per night. Reservations are required from April to October; call 800-444-7275.

> After the fall rains, chanterelles and other favored mushrooms abound at Salt Point. Pickers beware: carefully identify anything you plan to eat, since some mushrooms can be fatal.

GUALALA POINT REGIONAL PARK 🏃 🏊 🚣 ⛵ Located where the Gualala River meets the ocean, this charming place has everything from a sandy beach to redwood groves. Across the river, there are kayak and canoe rentals. There are picnic areas, restrooms, and an information center. Day-use fee, $5. ~ Located along Route 1 due south of Gualala; 707-785-2377, fax 707-785-3741.

▲ There are 19 tent/RV sites (no hookups), 1 hiker/biker site, 6 walk-in sites; $19 per night. Reservations: 707-565-2267; sonomacounty.org/parks.

MANCHESTER STATE PARK 🏃 🎣 ⛵ This wild, windswept beach extends for miles along the Mendocino coast. Piled deep with driftwood, it's excellent for hiking. There are picnic areas, restrooms, and an information center. ~ Located along Route 1, about eight miles north of Point Arena; 707-937-5804, fax 707-937-2953.

▲ There are 18 tent/RV sites (no hookups) and 10 primitive, hike-in environmental sites; $15 per night; first-come, first-served. Reservations: 800-444-7275.

VAN DAMME STATE PARK 🏃 🚲 🚣 ⛵ Extending from the beach to an interior forest, this 2069-acre park has several interesting features: a "pygmy forest" where poor soil results in fully mature pine trees reaching heights of only six inches to eight feet; a "fern canyon" smothered in different species of ferns; and a "cabbage patch" filled with that fetid critter with elephant ear leaves—skunk cabbage. This park is also laced with hiking trails and offers excellent beachcombing opportunities. Facilities include a visitors center, picnic areas, restrooms, and showers. Day-use fee, $6 for the fern canyon. ~ Route 1, about 30 miles north of Point Arena, or three miles south of Mendocino; 707-937-5804, fax 707-937-2953.

▲ There are 74 tent/RV sites (no hookups); $20 to $25 per night. The upper campground is closed in winter. Reservations are essential during the summer: 800-444-7275.

MENDOCINO HEADLANDS AND BIG RIVER BEACH STATE PARKS 🏃 🎣 🚣 ⛵ These adjoining parks form the seaside border of the town of Mendocino. And quite a border it is. The white-sand beaches are only part of the natural splendor. There are also wave tunnels, tidepools, sea arches, lagoons, and 360-degree vistas that sweep from the surf-trimmed shore to the prim villagescape of Mendocino. The only facilities are restrooms; private canoe rental nearby. ~ Located in the town of Mendocino.

RUSSIAN GULCH STATE PARK 🏃 🚲 🐎 🚣 ⛵ Set in a narrow valley with a well-protected beach, this park has numerous features. There are marvelous views from the craggy headlands, a waterfall, and a blowhole that rarely blows. Rainbow and steelhead trout inhabit the creek while hawks and ravens circle the forest. There are picnic areas, restrooms, and showers. Day-use fee, $6. ~ Located along Route 1, two miles north of Mendocino; 707-937-5804, fax 707-937-2953.

▲ There are 30 tent/RV sites (no hookups); $20 to $25 per night. Reservations: 800-444-7275.

MACKERRICHER STATE PARK 🏃 🚴 🐎 🏊 🏕 🚤 🚣

Another of the region's outstanding parks, this facility features a crescent of sandy beach, dunes, headlands, a lake, a forest, and wetlands. Harbor seals inhabit the rocks offshore and over 90 bird species frequent the area. The park has picnic areas, restrooms, and showers. ~ Along Route 1, about three miles north of Fort Bragg; 707-937-5804, fax 707-937-2953.

▲ There are 140 tent/RV sites (no hookups), 10 walk-in and 8 hike-and-bike sites ($3 per night, per person); $20 to $25 per night. Reservations: 800-444-7275.

Redwood Country

Near the nondescript town of Leggett, Route 1 joins Route 101. Logging trucks, those belching beasts that bear down upon you without mercy, become more frequent. You are entering Redwood Country.

This is the habitat of *Sequoia sempervirens*, the coastal redwood, a tree whose ancestors date to the age of dinosaurs and which happens to be the world's tallest living thing. These "ambassadors from another time," as John Steinbeck called them, inhabit a 30-mile-wide coastal fog belt stretching 450 miles from the Monterey area north to Oregon. Redwoods live five to eight centuries, though some have survived over two millennia, while reaching heights over 350 feet and diameters greater than 20 feet.

There is a sense of solitude here uncapturable anywhere else. The trees form a cathedral overhead, casting a deep shade across the forest floor. Solitary sun shafts, almost palpable, cut through the grove; along the roof of the forest, pieces of light jump across

AUTHOR FAVORITE

sights Don't miss **Clarke Historical Museum**, with its outstanding collection of Northern California American Indian artifacts. Here are twined baskets, ceremonial regalia, and a dugout redwood canoe. It provides a unique insight into this splendid Humboldt Bay region before the age of gold pans and axe handles. There is also the museum's Victorian section, featuring items from the Gold Rush and the timber and maritime industries. Closed Sunday and Monday. ~ 240 E Street, Eureka; 707-443-1947, fax 707-443-0290; www.clarkemuseum.org, e-mail cclarke@humboldt1.com.

the treetops, poised to fall like rain. Ferns and a few small animals are all that survive here. The silence and stillness are either
transcendent or terrifying. It's like being at sea in a small boat.

SIGHTS

The Redwood Highway, Route 101, leads north to the tallest,
densest stands of *Sequoia sempervirens*. At **Richardson Grove
State Park** the road barrels through the very center of a magnificent grove. A short nature trail leads through this virgin timber,
though the proximity of the road makes communing with nature
seem a bit ludicrous.

North of Garberville, follow the **Avenue of the Giants**, a 32-
mile alternative route that parallels Route 101. This two-lane
road winds along the Eel River south fork, tunneling through
dense redwood groves. Much of the road is encompassed by
Humboldt Redwoods State Park, a 52,000-acre preserve with
some of the finest forest land found anywhere—17,000 acres are
virgin-growth redwood. Park headquarters contains a nice visitors center. ~ 707-946-2409, fax 707-946-2326; www.humboldt
redwoods.org, e-mail hrsp@humboldtredwoods.org.

Farther along is **Founder's Grove**, where a nature trail loops
through a redwood stand. The forest is dedicated to early Save-the-
Redwoods League leaders who were instrumental in preserving
thousands of redwood acres, particularly in this park. Nearby
Rockefeller Forest has another short loop trail that winds through
a redwood grove. Avenue of the Giants continues through towns
that are little more than way stations and then rejoins Route 101,
which leads north to Eureka.

It's not far to **Cape Mendocino**, the westernmost point in the
contiguous United States. Here you'll have broad views of the
ocean, including the menacing shoals where countless ships have
been slapped to timber. Next, the road curves up through forest
and sheep-grazing lands before rolling down to the gentle pastureland near the unique town of Ferndale.

A Victorian-style hamlet set in the Eel River valley, **Ferndale**
is so perfectly refurbished it seems unreal. Main Street and nearby
thoroughfares are lined with Gothic Revival, Queen Anne, East-
lake, and Italianate-style Victorians, brightly painted and blooming with pride. Tragedy struck this picturesque town in April 1992
when a 7.1-level earthquake and several powerful aftershocks
rocked the entire area. Since then local residents have devotedly
rebuilt the quaint Main Street district with its boutiques and gift
shops and other affected neighborhoods. The film *Outbreak*, starring Dustin Hoffman, was shot in Ferndale.

The best way to see the town is by stopping first at the **Ferndale Museum**. Here is an ever-changing collection of antiques
and memorabilia from the region, plus an old blacksmith shop.
There are sometimes maps available for self-guided walking

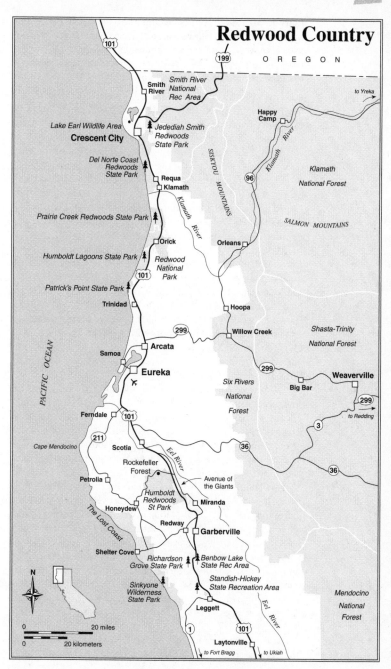

Redwood Country

OREGON

101

199

to Yreka

Smith River National Rec Area

Smith River

Happy Camp

Lake Earl Wildlife Area

Crescent City

Jedediah Smith Redwoods State Park

Klamath River

SISKIYOU MOUNTAINS

Klamath National Forest

96

Del Norte Coast Redwoods State Park

Requa

Klamath

SALMON MOUNTAINS

Prairie Creek Redwoods State Park

Klamath River

Orick

Orleans

Humboldt Lagoons State Park

Redwood National Park

101

Patrick's Point State Park

Trinidad

Hoopa

Shasta-Trinity National Forest

299

Willow Creek

Arcata

Samoa

299

Eureka

Weaverville

Six Rivers National Forest

Big Bar

299

to Redding

PACIFIC OCEAN

Ferndale

101

3

211

Cape Mendocino

Scotia

Eel River

36

Rockefeller Forest

Avenue of the Giants

36

Petrolia

Humboldt Redwoods St Park

Miranda

The Lost Coast

Honeydew

Redway

Garberville

Shelter Cove

Richardson Grove State Park

Benbow Lake State Rec Area

Standish-Hickey State Recreation Area

Mendocino National Forest

N

Sinkyone Wilderness State Park

Leggett

Eel River

0   20 miles

1

0   20 kilometers

101

Laytonville

to Fort Bragg   to Ukiah

tours of this historic community. It's an architectural wonder that shouldn't be missed. Closed Monday during summer and Monday and Tuesday during winter. Admission. ~ 515 Shaw Avenue, Ferndale; phone/fax 707-786-4466; www.ferndale-museum.org, e-mail museum@ferndale-museum.org.

EUREKA Eureka's roughly 26,000 inhabitants make it the largest town on the Northern California coast. Founded in 1850, the town's first industry was mining; the name "Eureka!" came from an old gold mining exclamation meaning "I found it."

Today fishing and lumbering have replaced more romantic occupations, but much of the region's history is captured in points of interest. Stop at the **Greater Eureka Chamber of Commerce** on the way into town for maps, brochures, and information. Closed on the weekends in winter. ~ 2112 Broadway, Eureka; 707-442-3738, 800-356-6381, fax 707-442-0079; www.eurekacham ber.com, e-mail chamber@eurekachamber.com.

Make certain to ask at the Chamber of Commerce for the **architectural tour** map. Eureka has over 100 glorious Victorian homes ranging from understated designs to the outlandish **Carson Mansion**, a multilayered confection that makes other Gothic architecture seem tame. It was built in the 1880s by William Carson, a wealthy lumber merchant with the same need for ostentation that afflicted the robber barons on San Francisco's Nob Hill. The Carson Mansion is a private club, but you can drive by and view its distinctive architecture. ~ 2nd and M streets, Eureka.

HIDDEN ► Of a more subdued nature are the **covered bridges** on the southern outskirts of town. To reach them from Route 101, take Elk River Road two miles to Berta Road or three miles to Zanes Road (there is a wooden span covering both). You'll enter a picture of red barns and green pasture framed by cool, lofty forest. The bridges, crossing a small river, evoke Vermont winters and New Hampshire sleigh rides.

Fort Humboldt is also stationed at this end of town. Built in the early 1850s to help resolve conflict between gold settlers and indigenous tribes of Yurok, Hoopa, Wiyot, and Mattole Indians; it has been partially restored. In addition to re-creating Army life (experienced here by a hard-drinking young officer named Ulysses S. Grant), the historic park displays early logging traditions. There's a drafty logger's cabin, a small lumber industry museum, a military museum displaying Army artifacts, a museum of American Indian artifacts, and a couple of remarkable old steam engines. ~ 3431 Fort Avenue, Eureka; 707-445-6567, fax 707-441-5737.

Nearby **Sequoia Park** provides a nifty retreat from urban life. Tucked into its 52-acre preserve is a petting zoo (closed Mon-

The Lost Coast

There are alternate routes to Eureka leading along the perimeter of California's Lost Coast region. One of the state's most remote wilderness areas, it is a tumbling region of extraordinary vistas. Here the King Range, with its sliding talus and impassable cliffs, shoots 4087 feet up from the ocean in less than three miles. No road could ever rest along its shoulder. The place has been left primitive, given over to mink, deer, river otter, and black bear; rare bald eagles and peregrine falcons work its slopes.

The range extends about 35 miles. Along the shore is a wilderness beach from which seals, sea lions, and porpoises, as well as gray and killer whales, can be seen. There's also an abandoned lighthouse and the skeletons of ships wrecked on the rocks.

To reach this remote area, from Route 101 near Redway take Briceland–Thorne Road, which turns into Shelter Cove Road as it winds through the King Range.

Shelter Cove is a tiny bay neatly folded between sea cliffs and headlands. A point of embarkation for people exploring the Lost Coast, it has a few stores, restaurants, and hotels. Stock up here: The rest of this backcountry jaunt promises little more than a couple of stores.

Outside Shelter Cove you can pick up Kings Peak Road or Ettersburg–Honeydew Road, which connect with Wilder Ridge Road and lead to the general store town of **Honeydew**. This is a prime marijuana growing region and a colony of laidback locals is bound to be sitting on the stoop swapping tales.

Mattole Road heads northeast, meandering along the Mattole River, to another forest hamlet, **Petrolia**. Nestled in a river valley and marked by a white-steeple church, the town is a scene straight from a Norman Rockwell painting. Hawks glide overhead. Old men rock on their front porches.

Next, **Mattole Road** ascends a succession of plateaus to a ranch land of unpainted barns and broad shade trees, then noses down to the coastline and parallels the waves for perhaps five miles. Here the setting is Scottish. Hillsides are grazed by herds of sheep and covered with tenacious grasses that shake in the sea wind. The gray sand beach is covered with driftwood. Along the horizon peaks rise in jagged motions, seemingly thrust upward by the lash of the surf.

day), a picnic area, a playground, and a thick stand of redwoods.
~ W Street between Glatt and Madrone streets, Eureka.

Then head to **Old Town**, Eureka's answer to the nation's gentrification craze. This neighborhood was formerly the local bowery; the term "skid row" reputedly originated right here. It derived from the bums residing beside the nearby "skid roads," along which redwood logs were transported to the waterfront. Now the ghetto is gilded: old Victorians, woodframe warehouses, brick buildings, and clapboard houses have been rebuilt and painted striking colors. Stylish shops have sprung up and restaurants have opened.

At the foot of F Street in Old Town, where the bowery meets the bay, the vintage motor vessel **Madaket** departs. For several well-invested dollars, you'll sail past an egret rookery, oyster beds, pelican roosts, ugly pulp mills, and the town's flashy marina. The cruises are weather-dependent; always call ahead. Closed October through April. Admission. ~ Eureka; 707-445-1910, fax 707-442-0514.

Heading north from Eureka there are two towns worth noting. **Arcata**, home of Humboldt State University, is a student town with an outstanding collection of old Victorians. For a self-guided architectural tour, obtain a map at the **Arcata Chamber of Commerce**. ~ 1635 Heindon Road, Arcata; 707-822-3619, fax 707-822-3515; www.arcatachamber.com, e-mail arcata@arcata chamber.com.

Trinidad, one of the area's oldest towns, perches above a small port. Sea stacks and sailboats lie anchored offshore, watched over by a miniature lighthouse. For a tour of the pocket beaches and rocky shores lining this beautiful waterfront, take a three-mile trip south from town along Scenic Drive.

Next is **Redwood National Park**, a fitting finale to this lengthy coastal journey. Park of parks, it's a necklace strung for over 33 miles along the coast. Among its gems are secluded beaches, elk herds, and some of the world's tallest trees.

First link in the chain is the **Redwood National and State Park Visitors Center**. ~ 119441 Route 101, Orick; 707-464-6101 ext. 5265, fax 707-488-5335. In addition to information, the center issues permits for **Tall Trees Grove**. A one-and-one-third-mile hike leads to a redwood stand boasting some of the loftiest of all California's redwoods. **Lady Bird Johnson Grove**, located off Bald Hill Road on a one-mile trail, represents another magnificent cluster of ancient trees.

Another side road, Davison Road (day-use fee), leads along remote **Gold Bluffs Beach** eight miles to Fern Canyon. Here angular walls 50 feet high are covered with rioting vegetation.

Redwood National Park encompasses three state parks—Prairie Creek Redwoods, Del Norte Coast Redwoods, and Jedediah Smith Redwoods. Just after the main entrance to the first you'll pass **Elk Prairie**, where herds of Roosevelt elk graze across open meadows. Immediately past the entrance, Cal Barrel Road, another short detour, courses through dense redwood forest.

Also plan to turn off onto **Coastal Drive**, a gravel road paral-   ◀ HIDDEN
leling Route 101. Its numerous turnouts expose extraordinary ocean vistas. The road snakes high above the coast before empty-ing onto the main highway near the mouth of the Klamath River.

The Del Norte section of the park reveals more startling sea views en route to Crescent City, where the **main park headquarters** is located. ~ 1111 2nd Street, Crescent City; 707-464-6101, fax 707-464-1812. There is travel information aplenty at the head-quarters and at the **Crescent City–Del Norte County Chamber of Commerce** building just across the street. Closed on weekends in winter. ~ 1001 Front Street, Crescent City; 707-464-3174, 800-343-8300, fax 707-464-9676; www.northerncalifornia.net, e-mail chamber@northerncalifornia.net.

Woodlands, wetlands, grasslands—you'll find them all at **Lake**   ◀ HIDDEN
Earl Wildlife Area. This preserve also offers secluded sand dunes and a sufficient number of bird species, over 300 at last count, to make it look like it was created by the Audubon Society. One of the finest birdwatching spots on the North Coast, this Pacific Flyway destination is the place to see hawks, falcons, bald eagles, Canada geese, and canvasback ducks. As many as 51,000 Aleutian Canadian geese stop here in the spring to fatten up before their 3000-mile non-stop flight back to the Aleutian Islands. Closed weekends. ~ Old Mill Road, three miles north of Crescent City; 707-464-2523, fax 707-464-2871; e-mail lakeearlwla@dfg.ca.gov.

Route 101 north to Route 199 leads to the park's Jedediah Smith section with its mountain vistas and thick redwood groves. The Smith River, rich in salmon and steelhead, threads through the region. For further details on this remote area check with the **Hiouchi Information Center.** Closed mid-September to mid-June. ~ Route 199, four miles east of Route 101; 707-464-6101, fax 707-464-1812.

❖❖❖

NORTH COAST BEACON

Perched on a rocky island off Route 101 in Crescent City is **Battery Point Lighthouse,** an 1856 stone and masonry structure that is one of the best preserved original lighthouses on the Pacific Coast, and the fifth-oldest on the West Coast. At low tide from April through September visitors can walk across a spit of sand and rock to the lighthouse for tours of the house, the lantern room, and a small museum. Closed Monday and Tuesday, and weekdays from October through March. Admission. ~ Crescent City; 707-464-3089.

LODGING   One of Northern California's finest old lodges is the imposing, Tudor-style **Benbow Inn**. Located astride the Eel River, this regal retreat is bounded by lawns, gardens, and umbrella-tabled patios. The structure itself is a bold three-story manor in the English country tradition. The lobby, paneled in carved wood and adorned by ornamental molding, is a sumptuous sitting area with a grand fireplace. Jigsaw puzzles lie scattered on the clawfoot tables and rocking horses decorate the room. The dining area and lounge are equally elegant. Guest quarters offer such flourishes as quilted beds with wooden headboards, hand-painted doors, period wall-prints, marble-topped nightstands, and complimentary sherry. Visitors also enjoy tea and scones in the afternoon and evening hors d'oeuvres. ~ 445 Lake Benbow Drive, Garberville; 707-923-2124, 800-355-3301, fax 707-923-2122; www.benbowinn.com, e-mail benbow@benbowinn.com. DELUXE TO ULTRA-DELUXE.

The cheapest lodging I've found in the southern redwoods area is **Johnston Motel**. Unlike the region's big-tag caravansaries, this 14-unit facility has rooms at budget prices. Don't expect a lot of shine. The plain rooms are small but comfortable. ~ 839 Redwood Drive, Garberville; 707-923-3327, fax 707-923-2108. BUDGET.

Not that I have anything against Johnston's; it's just that Garberville is not my idea of paradise. For a few well-spent dollars more you can rent a room in any of several motels along redwood-lined Avenue of the Giants. **Miranda Gardens Resort** is a good choice. This 16-unit resort has everything from one- and two-person cottages to cabins with fully equipped kitchens. Some accommodations include whirlpools. All cabins boast a private patio or deck, some overlooking Redwood State Park. The place features a heated swimming pool, playground, and market. The facilities are tucked into a redwood grove with lush gardens, and the rooms are partially paneled in redwood. Continental breakfast during summer. ~ 6766 Avenue of the Giants, Miranda; 707-943-3011, fax 707-943-3584; www.mirandagardens.com, e-mail info@mirandagardens.com. MODERATE TO DELUXE.

HIDDEN ▶   Way out in Shelter Cove, at the southern end of California's remote Lost Coast, is the **Shelter Cove Beachcomber Inn**, which consists of three buildings with six units. Three rooms have kitchens and woodburning stoves; all seem to be lovingly cared for. All come with barbecue grills and patios, almost all with ocean views. Considering that the price tag on this luxury is reasonable and that Shelter Cove is one of the coast's most secluded hideaways, the Beachcomber Inn is well worth the effort. ~ 412 Machi Road, Shelter Cove; 707-986-7551, 800-718-4789; www.sojourner2000.com. BUDGET TO MODERATE.

HIDDEN ▶   **Mattole River Organic Farms Country Cabins** offers full-facility cottages complete with kitchenettes. Each is plain but comfortably furnished and most feature a sitting room and a bedroom. This rustic colony sits amid shade trees and is backdropped by forested hills. ~ 42354 Mattole Road, Honeydew; phone/fax 707-629-3445, 800-845-4607; e-mail iansigman@hotmail.com. MODERATE.

The cheapest lodging of all is in the neon motels along Route 101 on the outskirts of Eureka. Many advertise room rates on highway signs along the southern entrance to town. **Sunrise Inn and Suites** is perhaps the best of these. Because it is centrally located, guests can walk to Old Town and other points of interest. The rooms are simple but very clean, with carpeting and king or queen beds. Nearly half have jacuzzi tubs. ~ 129 4th Street, Eureka; phone/fax 707-443-9751, 800-404-9751. MODERATE.

> Coast redwoods are one of just a few species that transpire, a process that allows them to create their own rain (one tree can produce 500 gallons a day).

For country-inn sensibility in an urban environment, **Old Town Bed & Breakfast Inn** comes highly recommended. Just a couple blocks from Eureka's fabled Carson Mansion, this four-bedroom house dates from 1871. It's a Victorian structure with a winding staircase and a wealth of antiques. Plushly carpeted and adorned with patterned wallpaper, the house has been beautifully redecorated; there's also a library/media room The cost includes a full country-style breakfast. ~ 1521 3rd Street, Eureka; 707-443-5235, 888-508-5235, fax 707-442-4390; www.oldtownbnb.com, e-mail info@oldtownbnb.com. MODERATE.

Another of Eureka's spectacular bed and breakfasts is **Carter House**, one of the finest Victorians I've ever seen. This grand old four-story house is painted in light hues and decorated with contemporary artwork, lending an airy quality seldom found in vintage homes. The place is beautiful: light streams through bay windows; oriental rugs are scattered across hardwood floors; there are sumptuous sitting rooms, and oak banisters that seemingly climb forever. In the seven rooms are antique nightstands and armoires, beds with bold wooden headboards, ceramic pieces, and original local artwork. Two private cottages with fireplaces, spa tubs, and full kitchens are also available. The price includes a full breakfast, complimentary wine, and cookies before bedtime. ~ 301 L Street, Eureka; 707-445-1390, 800-404-1390, fax 707-444-8067; www.carterhouse.com, e-mail reserve@carterhouse.com. MODERATE TO ULTRA-DELUXE.

Mark and Christi Carter added the 23-room **Hotel Carter** to their lodging empire a number of years ago. Its pale pine furniture and moss green-colored walls offer a refreshing counterpoint to the Carter House across the street. Accommodations are quite spacious; some have fireplaces and whirlpool baths. Complimentary breakfast is served in the ground-floor dining room, where colorful dhurrie rugs and silver candleholders add an elegant touch. ~ 301 L Street, Eureka; 707-444-8062, 800-404-1390, fax 707-444-8067; www.carterhouse.com, e-mail reserve@carterhouse.com. ULTRA-DELUXE.

Time-travel to the turn of the 20th century at **Abigail's Elegant Victorian Mansion**, an 1888 manse with a classic gingerbread exterior. This opulent B&B offers four guest rooms with richly ornamental Victorian decor. You can wander into the Turkish Sitting Room and catch one of 700 period films, or check out the gramophones playing pre-1930 popular music. The stay here also comes with the option of participating in a variety of sporting and recreational opportunities, including tennis, croquet, and a five-hour backcountry wilderness safari ride on four-wheelers. ~ 1406 C Street, Eureka; 707-444-3144; www.eureka-california.com, e-mail info@eureka-california.com. DELUXE.

Built in 1905 by a local department store magnate, **The Daly Inn** is now an elegant bed and breakfast. Surrounded by colorful Victorian gardens, this picture-perfect inn has three comfortable rooms and two spacious suites, all furnished in early-20th-century antiques. A full breakfast and evening hors d'oeuvres are included in the rate. ~ 1125 H Street, Eureka; 707-445-3638, 800-321-9656, fax 707-444-3636; www.dalyinn.com, e-mail innkeeper@dalyinn.com. MODERATE.

For an extra dash of history in your nightly brew, there's the **Shaw House Bed & Breakfast** in nearby Ferndale. It's only fitting to this bed and breakfast that Ferndale is an island in time where the Victorian era still remains. The Shaw House, built in 1854, is the oldest home in town and is on the National Historic Register. A library, two parlors, a dining room, and balconies are available to guests, and the home is furnished throughout with precious antiques. All rooms have private baths. Tea and cookies are served in the afternoon. ~ 703 Main Street, Ferndale; mailing address: P.O. Box 1369, Ferndale, CA 95536; 707-786-9958, 800-557-7429, fax 707-786-9758; www.shawhouse.com, e-mail stay@shawhouse.com. MODERATE TO ULTRA-DELUXE.

A Carpenter Gothic creation, the Shaw House Bed & Breakfast was modeled on Hawthorne's *House of the Seven Gables.*

In a town chockablock with precious Victorians, one of the most precious of all is **The Gingerbread Mansion**. Turrets and gables, an intimate garden, interesting antiques, and a delicious homemade breakfast are among the features; but what you'll find particularly special about this bed and breakfast are the bathrooms. One has mirrored ceilings and walls; another, his-and-hers clawfoot tubs set near a tiled gas fireplace. The 11 distinct accommodations (4 are top-floor suites), are comfortably cozy. Afternoon tea and Godiva turn-down chocolates (port, too, for suite guests) are additional touches. ~ 400 Berding Street,

Ferndale; 707-786-4000, 800-952-4136, fax 707-786-4381; www.
gingerbread-mansion.com, e-mail innkeeper@gingerbread-man
sion.com. DELUXE TO ULTRA-DELUXE.

Set in a quiet residential neighborhood within walking distance
of downtown, the **Lady Anne** has five antique-appointed rooms
in a 1888 Queen Anne–style home. You can sit on the porch or
in a chair in the front yard and watch the world go by, or play
the grand piano and guitars in one of the inn's two parlors. ~ 902
14th Street, Arcata; 707-822-2797; www.humboldt1.com/la
dyanne, e-mail ladyanne@humboldt1.com. MODERATE.

You will be hard pressed anywhere along the coast to find a
view more alluring than that of **Trinidad Bay Bed & Breakfast**.
This New England–style shingle house, set in a tiny coastal town,
looks across Trinidad Bay, past fishing boats and sea rocks, seals
and sandy beaches, to tree-covered headlands. Two of the country-style rooms are equipped with standard furnishings, private
entrances, and come with a delivered breakfast. There is a fireplace and a living room for guests to share. Rates include breakfast. ~ Edwards and Trinity streets, Trinidad; 707-677-0840;
www.trinidadbaybnb.com. DELUXE.

Turtle Rocks Oceanfront Inn is located four and a half miles
north of town on a rocky bluff overlooking seastacks that provide a refuge for barking seals. Decorated with seashells, driftwood, turtle figurines, and fresh flowers, the contemporary bed
and breakfast has six spacious guest rooms, each with a sitting
area with facing divans, a king-size bed, a private bath, and a private glass-paneled deck that's picture-perfect for whale-watching
in spring or fall and enjoying sunsets any time of year. Trinidad
State Beach and Trinidad Head Trail are close by, and Patrick's
Point State Park, with its rock headlands and promontories, is
less than a mile's walk. Rates include a full gourmet breakfast. ~
3392 Patrick's Point Drive, Trinidad; 707-677-3707; www.turtle
rocksinn.com, e-mail innkeeper@turtlerocksinn.com. ULTRA-
DELUXE.

Hostelling International—Redwood National Park, set in a
1908 settler's house, provides basic dormitory-style accommodations; there are two private rooms for couples. It's across the
highway from a beach and features a laundry room, kitchen facilities, and a common room. Closed Monday through Wednesday in November, December, and February. Closed January. ~
14480 Route 101 at Wilson Creek Road, Klamath; 707-482-
8265, 888-464-4872 ext. 552, fax 707-482-4665; www.red
woodhostel.org, e-mail info@redwoodhostel.com. BUDGET.

Farther north in Crescent City, along the scimitar strand that
gave the town its name, is **Crescent Beach Motel**. This 27-unit
motel has plate-glass views of the ocean. Rooms are small but
decorated with oak furniture and a blue-green color scheme. They

have TVs, and most rooms have those oh-so-priceless sea vistas.
~ 1455 Route 101 South, Crescent City; 707-464-5436, fax 707-464-9336; www.crescentbeachmotel.com. MODERATE.

DINING Personally, my favorite dining place in these parts is the **Benbow Inn**. This Tudor lodge serves meals in a glorious dining room that will make you feel as though you're feasting at the estate of a British baron. The dinner menu relies on local produce and herbs grown in the inn's own garden. Though the menu changes seasonally, you are likely to find such items as lamb, salmon, scallops, and filet of beef. Breakfast and dinner served year round; lunch served June to mid-September. ~ 445 Lake Benbow Drive, Garberville; 707-923-2124, 800-355-3301, fax 707-923-2122; www.benbowinn.com, e-mail benbow@benbowinn.com. ULTRA-DELUXE.

Proceeding north along the Avenue of the Giants, you'll encounter cafés in tiny towns like Miranda, Myers Flat, Weott, and Pepperwood. Most are tourist-oriented businesses, adequate as way stations, but undistinguished and slightly overpriced.

Non-chain eateries in Scotia are limited, so your best bet is to head half a mile over the Scotia Bridge to the popular **DJs Burger Bar** in Rio Dell. Locals gather here for chicken and beef tacos, BLTs, hot dogs, and the always popular bacon-cheeseburger-with-fries special. DJs has also been known to play host to regional festivities, such as Classic Car Night. ~ 509 Wildwood Avenue, Rio Dell; 707-764-2924. BUDGET.

The historic Old Town section of Eureka, a refurbished neighborhood of stately Victorians, supports several good restaurants. **Restaurant 301** in the Hotel Carter offers fresh, inventive gourmet food, with imaginative entrées such as teriyaki-bourbon portobello mushroom and coffee-dusted venison medallions. The menu changes seasonally but usually features fish, meat, and vegetarian

AUTHOR FAVORITE

In the southern redwoods region you'll be hard pressed to find a better restaurant than **Woodrose Café**. T'aint much on looks—just a counter, some tables and chairs, and a small patio out back. But the kitchen folk cook up some potent concoctions. That's why the place draws locals in droves. The breakfast menu offers buckwheat pancakes, lox and bagels, and spinach-and-feta-cheese omelettes. At lunch they make homemade soups, organic salads, sandwiches, and tofu burgers; no dinner served. The Woodrose Café is a good reason to visit otherwise drab Garberville. No lunch on Saturday and Sunday. ~ 911 Redwood Drive, Garberville; 707-923-3191. BUDGET TO MODERATE.

dishes. Prix-fixe multicourse meals, complete with wine pairings for each course, are also available. Breakfast and dinner. Call for winter hours. ~ In the Hotel Carter, 301 L Street, Eureka; 707-444-8062, 800-404-1390, fax 707-444-8067; www.carter house.com. DELUXE TO ULTRA-DELUXE.

A meal at the **Sea Grill** is a chance to enjoy fine dining in a historic 1876 storefront. The place has an airy Victorian feel about it, with lots of peachy pastels, fabric drapes, and an antique mahogany bar. Oil paintings created by local artists add to the atmosphere. Chicken, steak, and seafood dishes are the specialties here. No lunch Saturday through Monday. Closed Sunday. ~ 316 E Street, Eureka; 707-443-7187, fax 707-825-9223. MODERATE TO DELUXE.

For Asian fare there's **Samurai Restaurant**, a simple dining room appointed with Japanese antiques and folk art. The menu includes seafood, standard sukiyaki, tempura, and teriyaki dishes. There's a large selection of imaginative sushi. You can also try the "Treasure Ship," a sampler of five different entrées. Dinner only. Closed Sunday and Monday. ~ 621 5th Street, Eureka; 707-442-6802. MODERATE.

For a dining experience lumberjack-style, there's **Samoa Cook-house** just outside Eureka. A local lumber company has opened its chow house to the public, serving three meals daily. Just join the crowd piling into this unassuming eatery, sit down at a school cafeteria–style table and dig in. You'll be served redwood-size portions of soup, salad, meat, potatoes, vegetables, and dessert—you can even ask for seconds. Ask for water and they'll plunk down a pitcher, order coffee and someone will bring a pot. It's noisy, crowded, hectic, and great fun. Reduced rates for children and seniors. ~ Samoa Road, Samoa; 707-442-1659, fax 707-442-1699; www.humboldtdining.com/cookhouse. MODERATE.

◀ HIDDEN

The **Seascape Restaurant** is small and unassuming. There are only about three dozen tables and booths at this seafood dining room. But the walls of plate glass gaze out upon a rocky headland and expansive bay. Situated at the foot of Trinidad Pier, the local eating spot overlooks the town's tiny fishing fleet. The dishes, many drawn from surrounding waters, include halibut, rock cod, salmon, crab, and shrimp. Landlubbers dine on filet mignon. Lunch and breakfast menus are equally inviting. ~ Trinidad Pier, Trinidad; 707-677-3762, fax 707-677-3921; www. cheraeheightscasino.com. MODERATE TO DELUXE.

From Trinidad to the Oregon border the countryside is sparsely populated. Crescent City is the only town of real size, but you'll find nondescript cafés in such places as Orick, Klamath, and Smith River.

Crescent City—like the entire North Coast—is seafood country. Best place around is **Harbor View Grotto**, a family restaurant with an ocean view. This plate-glass eatery features a long inventory of ocean dishes—whole clams, fried prawns or oysters, scallops, red snapper, salmon, cod, halibut, and so on, not to mention the seafood salads and shrimp cocktails. There are also a few meat dishes (prime rib and steak) plus an assortment of sandwiches, chicken, and pasta dishes. Worth a stop. ~ 150 Starfish Way, Crescent City; 707-464-3815, fax 707-464-3875. MODERATE.

SHOPPING In Ferndale, a picturesque Victorian town south of Eureka, there's a covey of intriguing shops. The community has attracted a number of artisans, many of whom display their wares in the 19th- and early-20th-century stores lining Main Street. There are shops selling needlework, stained glass, and kinetic sculptures; others deal in ironwork, used books, and handknits. There are even stores specializing in "paper treasures," boots and saddles, dolls, and "nostalgic gifts." All are contained along a three-block section that more resembles a living museum than a downtown shopping district.

Eureka, too, has been gentrified. Most of the refurbishing has occurred in Old Town, where stately Victorians, falsefront stores, and tumbledown buildings have been transformed into sparkling shops and art galleries. Window browse down 2nd and 3rd streets from C Street to H Street and you're bound to find several inviting establishments. Of particular interest is the F Street corridor, which is becoming a nexus for the arts. The crown jewel is the Humboldt Arts Council's **Morris Graves Museum of Art**, featuring seven galleries of local fine arts. Closed Monday through Wednesday. ~ 636 F Street, Eureka; 707-442-0278, fax 707-442-2040; www.humboldtarts.org.

NIGHTLIFE Now don't misunderstand—California's northern coast and redwood region are wild and provocative places. It's just that the word "wild" up here is taken in the literal sense, as in wilderness and wildlife. Somehow the urban meaning of crazy nights and endless parties was never fully translated.

The **Benbow Inn** features a fine old lounge with carved walls and an ornate fireplace. A pianist adds to the intimacy. ~ 445 Lake Benbow Drive, Garberville; 707-923-2124.

Entertaining for almost three decades, the **Ferndale Repertory Theater** puts on a variety of plays and musicals year-round in an old movie theater. ~ 447 Main Street, Ferndale; 707-786-5483; www.ferndale-rep.org.

BEACHES & PARKS THE "LOST COAST" 🚶 🚲 🐎 🎣 ⛱ 🛶 ⚓ 🎣 California's coastal Route 1 is one of the greatest highways in America. Beginning in Southern California, it sweeps north through Big

Sur, Carmel, San Francisco, and Mendocino, past ocean scenery indescribably beautiful. Then it disappears. At the foot of Redwood Country, Route 1 quits the coast and turns into Route 101.

The region it never reaches is California's fabled "Lost Coast." Most of the region is now protected as the King Range National Conservation Area. Four major trails traverse it: Cooskie Creek Trail is 11.9 miles of coastal prairie areas; King Crest Trail, which climbs the main coastal ridge for 11.5 miles, with views of the ocean and Eel River Valley; the nine-mile-long Chemise Mountain trail; and the 24-mile-long Lost Coast Trail along the wilderness beach. Before you go, it's good to get trail information from the King Range ranger station. ~ 707-986-5400.

One of the wettest areas along the Pacific Coast, King Range gets about 100 inches of rain a year. The precipitation is particularly heavy from October to April. Summer carries cool coastal fog and some rain. Weather permitting, it's a fascinating region to explore—wild and virgin, with the shellmounds of American Indians who inhabited the area over a century ago still scattered on the beach.

Motels, restaurants, groceries, and boat rentals are available in Shelter Cove, at the south end of the Conservation Area. To get there from Garberville on Route 101, Shelter Cove Road leads to nearby Redway and then southwest to Shelter Cove. About 15 miles down this road, Kings Peak Road forks northwest, paralleling the Conservation Area, to Ettersberg and Honeydew. Just before Kings Peak Road, Chemise Mountain Road turns off into Nadelos and Wailaki campgrounds.

▲ There are numerous tent/RV campgrounds (no hookups): Wailaki is for RVs and tents, Nadelos for tents only. Fees range from free to $8 per night. For information contact the Arcata Field Office, U.S. Bureau of Land Management, 1695 Heindon Road, Arcata, CA 95521; 707-825-2300, fax 707-825-2301; www.ca.blm.gov/arcata, e-mail caweb330@ca.blm.gov.

SINKYONE WILDERNESS STATE PARK 🚶 🐎 ⚓ This 7500-acre park below the southern tip of the King Range is known for the narrow and steep winding dirt roads leading to its interior. For

---

BE PREPARED

Keep in mind that the "Lost Coast" is a wilderness area and not a heavily monitored state park. Hikers and campers need to bring water or water purifiers, sturdy hiking boots, and insect repellent. If you want to hike the beach, use a tide table; hikers often get trapped for hours by the tides. Mountain bikers should stick to the area east of King Range. Black Sands Beach is closed to motorized vehicles.

this reason trailers and RVs are discouraged from entering the park—especially since there are no RV facilities. Featuring old-growth redwood groves and clear-cut prairies, the park hugs the southern section of the Lost Coast. The ranch house and visitors center are a mere 200 yards from awe-inspiring bluffs. Other facilities include picnic tables and pit toilets. Keep an eye out for the majestic Roosevelt elk who inhabit Sinkyone Wilderness State Park. Day-use fee, $6. ~ Located 30 miles west of Redway on Briceland Road or 50 miles north of Fort Bragg on County Road 431; phone/fax 707-986-7711.

▲ There are 16 drive-in sites at Usal Beach and 17 hike-in sites at Needle Rock for tents only; $15 per night. All of the north end sites are hike-in only.

STANDISH-HICKEY STATE RECREATION AREA
Near the southern edge of Redwood Country, this 1000-acre park primarily consists of second-growth trees. The single exception is a 1200-year-old giant named after the Mayflower pilgrim, Captain Miles Standish. The forest here also has Douglas fir, oak, and maple trees. The south fork of the Eel River courses through the area, providing swimming holes and fishing spots (catch-and-release only). There are picnic areas, restrooms, and showers. Day-use fee, $6. ~ Located along Route 101, two miles north of Leggett; 707-925-6482, fax 707-925-6402.

▲ There are 99 tent/RV sites (no hookups) and 63 tent sites; $15 to $20 per night. Reservations recommended during summer; call 800-444-7275.

RICHARDSON GROVE STATE PARK The first of the virgin redwood parks, this 2300-acre facility features a grove of goliaths. For some bizarre reason the highway builders chose to put the main road through the heart of the forest. This means you won't miss the redwoods, but to really appreciate them you'll have to disappear down one of the three hiking trails that loop through the grove. The south fork of the Eel River flows through the park, providing swimming and trout fishing opportunities. In the summer there are weekend campfires and kids' programs. The park has an information center, picnic areas, restrooms, and showers. Day-use fee, $6. ~ Route 101, about 18 miles north of Leggett; 707-247-3318, fax 707-247-3308.

▲ There are 176 tent/RV sites (no hookups); $20 per night. Reservations: 800-444-7275.

BENBOW LAKE STATE RECREATION AREA One of the less desirable parks in the area, this facility fronts the Eel River near the dam that creates Benbow Lake. The lake is usually full and suitable for boating from July 1 to mid-September; it's a good idea to call first. Motorized boats are not allowed. Route 101 streams through the park's center, disrupting an otherwise idyllic scene. Nevertheless, there's good swimming and fishing in the river-lake. In summer there are weekend campfires and kids' programs here. There are picnic areas, restrooms, and showers. Day-use fee, $6. ~ Route 101, about 23 miles north of Leggett; 707-923-3238, fax 707-247-3300.

▲ There are 75 tent/RV sites (two have hookups) along the river; $15 to $20 per night. Closed in winter. Reservations: 800-444-7275.

HUMBOLDT REDWOODS STATE PARK One of the state's great parks, it is set within a 20-million-year-old forest. The park is a tribute to early conservationists who battled lumber interests in an effort to save the area's extraordinary trees. Today more than 100 miles of hiking trails lead through redwood groves and along the south fork of the Eel River. Within the park's 35-mile length there are also opportunities for swimming, biking, horseback riding (you must provide your own horse), fishing, or tree gazing. Facilities include an information center, picnic areas, restrooms, and showers. Day-use fee, $6. ~ Located along the Avenue of the Giants between Miranda and Pepperwood; 707-946-2409, fax 707-946-2618; www.humboldtredwoods.org.

▲ There are four different campgrounds (only one in the winter) with a total of 256 tent/RV sites (no hookups); $20 per night. (The best, most private sites are, appropriately enough, at Hidden Springs Campground.) There are also five hike-in camps. Reservations: 800-444-7275.

CLAM BEACH COUNTY PARK There's a broad expanse of beach here with good views of surrounding headlands. As its name suggests, this place was once known for its clams; unfortunately for mollusk-lovers, clamming has all but disappeared from these parts in the last few years. Still, it's a lovely local park. Horseback riders must provide their own horses. There's a picnic area and toilets. ~ Located along Route 101, about 15 miles north of Eureka; 707-445-7652, fax 707-445-7409.

Drop by the reconstructed Yurok Indian village at Patrick's Point State Park, where rangers will tell you about life on the coast before the Europeans showed up.

▲ There is a number of open-ground tent/RV sites here (no hookups); $10 per night. No reservations accepted.

PATRICK'S POINT STATE PARK This 650-acre park is particularly known for Agate Beach, a long crescent backdropped by wooded headlands. It's one-third of a mile from the main parking area. There are tidepools to explore, sea lions and seals offshore, and several miles of hiking trails. Leave Fido at home—dogs aren't allowed on the beach or trails. The facilities here include picnic areas, restrooms, and showers. Day-use fee, $6. ~ Off Route 101, about 25 miles north of Eureka; 707-677-3570, fax 707-677-9357.

▲ There are 124 tent/RV sites (no hookups); $20 per night. Reservations are recommended in the summer; call 800-444-7275.

HUMBOLDT LAGOONS STATE PARK 🏃 🏊 🚣 🛶 🛶 🚤 🛶

A 2000-acre facility, this beach park is full of surprises. The main entrance leads to a sandy beach tucked between rocky outcroppings and heaped with driftwood. Behind the beach an old lagoon has slowly transformed into a marsh of brackish water. Add the two areas together and you come up with a splendid park. Catch-and-release fishing at Stone Lagoon is good for cutthroat trout. Toilets and a visitors center are the only facilities. ~ Off Route 101, about 31 miles north of Eureka; 707-488-2169.

▲ There are 12 environmental hike-in and boat-in sites; $12 per night.

REDWOOD NATIONAL AND STATE PARKS 🏃 🚲 🏇 🛶 🛶

🛶 Actually four parks in one, this 105,516-acre giant encompasses Prairie Creek Redwoods, Del Norte Coast Redwoods, Jedediah Smith Redwoods state parks and Redwood National Park. Together they stretch over 33 miles along the coast from Orick to the Crescent City region. Within that span, one of California's wettest areas (69 inches of rain yearly in Del Norte), are hidden beaches, ocean cliffs, deep redwood forests, and mile on mile of hiking trails.

Along the coast are wind-scoured bluffs and gently sloping hills. The beaches range from sandy to rocky; because of the rugged terrain in certain areas, some are inaccessible. In addition to beaches, many streams—including Prairie Creek, Redwood Creek, Klamath River, Mill Creek, and the Smith River—traverse this series of parks.

How far back in time do redwoods go? Far enough to be present on earth at the same time as dinosaurs!

Hikers and redwood lovers will find that several spectacular groves lie adjacent to Routes 101 and 199. Others can be reached along uncrowded trails. Tan oak and madrone grow around the redwoods, while farther inland there are Jeffrey pine and Douglas fir.

Birdwatchers will encounter mallards, hawks, owl, shorebirds, quail, and great blue herons. The mammal population ranges from shrews and moles to rabbit and beaver to blacktail deer, Roosevelt elk, and an occasional bear. Along the coast live river otters and harbor seals. These and other features make the parks a natural for swimming, fishing, canoeing, and kayaking.

Facilities include information centers, picnic areas, restrooms, and showers. Day-use fee, $6 at campgrounds. ~ Located along Route 101 between Orick and Crescent City; Jedediah Smith Redwoods State Park is along Route 199, nine miles east of Crescent

City. The park headquarters is at 1111 2nd Street, Crescent City; 707-464-6101, fax 707-464-1812; www.nps.gov/redw.

▲ In the national park, there are four hike-in campgrounds: Nickel Creek, with five sites; Flint Ridge and Demartin, each with ten sites; and Little Bald Hills has four sites and one group site. All are free and completely primitive. The incorporated state parks offer more campgrounds. **Prairie Creek Redwoods State Park** offers 75 tent/RV sites (no hookups); $20 per night. **Jedediah Smith Redwoods State Park** has 106 tent/RV sites (no hookups); $20 per night. And at **Del Norte Coast Redwoods State Park** you will find 145 tent/RV sites (no hookups); $20 per night. ~ In winter, sites are on a first-come, first-served basis. Call for reservations: 800-444-7275.

Outdoor Adventures

SPORT-FISHING

All along the coast, charter boats depart daily to fish for salmon, Pacific snapper, or whatever else is running. Most companies leave the dock at 6 a.m. and return by 3:30 p.m.

MARIN COAST If you hanker to try your luck for salmon, contact **Caruso's Sportfishing**. ~ Harbor Drive, Sausalito; 415-332-1015. **Loch Lomond Live Bait House** sells bait and tackle. They cruise the bay for striper, halibut, and sturgeon. ~ Loch Lomond Marina, San Rafael; 415-456-0321.

SONOMA AND MENDOCINO COAST **Bodega Bay Sportfishing** operates four boats. Besides salmon charters, they run charters for halibut, rock cod, ling cod, albacore, and crab, as well as bird-watching trips. Whale-watching cruises run January through April, and in the summer there are sunset cruises. ~ 1410 Bay Flat Road, Bodega Bay; 707-875-3344; www.usafishing.com. Whatever your sportfishing tastes, **Anchor Charter Boats** aims to please. Besides the usual rockfish, tuna, salmon, and whale-watching excursions, they'll also take you on extended trips, or out for a funeral. ~ North Harbor Drive, Wharf Restaurant, Fort Bragg; 707-964-4550; www.anchorcharterboats.com.

REDWOOD COUNTRY For deep-sea fishing trips in search of tuna, salmon, rockfish, or halibut, contact **Full Throttle Sportfishing**. Bait and all gear are provided. ~ Woodley Island Marina, 601 Startare Drive, Eureka; 707-498-7473; www.fullthrottle sportfishing.com, e-mail gary@fullthrottlesportfishing.com.

SAILING

Nothing is more visually stunning than the sight of the sailboats on a clear, breezy San Francisco morning. Don't miss the experience of capturing the wind and drinking in endless vistas.

MARIN COUNTY In the North Bay, try **Cass' Rental Marina**. In addition to running a sailing school, they rent keel sloops. ~ 1702

Bridgeway, Sausalito; 415-332-6789; www.cassmarina.com. For charters on San Francisco Bay call **Ocean Voyages**, which has luxury vessels. ~ 1709 Bridgeway, Sausalito; 415-332-4681, 800-299-4444; www.oceanvoyages.com.

KAYAKING   Your trip will take on a new dimension as you paddle among seals and seagulls, along the cityfronts and through the harbors of the world's largest landlocked bay. There are several small companies that cater to kayakers and would-be kayakers of all physical and financial abilities. While the most convenient place to paddle is on the bay itself, there are also stellar locations to the north in Marin County.

MARIN COUNTY   To paddle across Richardson Bay under the bright silvery moon, contact **Sea Trek Ocean Kayaking Center**. They also do trips to Angel Island and guided tours all over Northern California, teach classes, and rent all the equipment you'll need. ~ Schoonmacher Point Marina, Sausalito; 415-488-1000; www.seatrekkayak.com.

RIVER RUNNING   With the Eel, Klamath, Smith, and Trinity rivers traversing many of the North Coast's parks, you're never far away from these mysterious fog-filled areas full of natural vegetation and wildlife.

All Outdoors Adventure Trips offers professionally guided rafting excursions ranging from Class I to Class V. Trips are half-day to three-day affairs, with all food and lodging included. ~ 1250 Pine Street, Suite 103, Walnut Creek; 925-932-8993, 800-247-2387; www.aorafting.com.

In addition to running trips on the Stanislaus, Kaweah, American, and Yuba rivers (Class I to Class V), **Beyond Limits** can arrange kayak and canoe trips. ~ P.O. Box 215, Riverbank, CA 95367; 800-234-7238; www.rivertrip.com.

The **Redwoods & Rivers** rafting company has half-day to five-day trips on the Trinity, South Fork Eel, Upper Eel, Lower Klamath, and Cal Salmon rivers for all levels, plus kayaking lessons and drift-boat fishing. ~ P.O. Box 606, Big Bar, CA 96010; 800-429-0090; www.redwoods-rivers.com, e-mail redriver@redwoods-rivers.com.

GOLF   From Marin to the Oregon border you'll find several clubs where it's relatively easy to get tee times.

SONOMA AND MENDOCINO COAST   On the Sonoma Coast, **Bodega Harbor Golf Links** is hilly and scenic. Part of the 18-hole course meanders around a freshwater marsh. ~ 21301 Heron Drive, Bodega Bay; 707-875-3538; www.bodegaharborgolf.com.

REDWOOD COUNTRY   In the home of that lofty tree, I recommend **Eureka Golf Course**, an 18-hole course nestled in red-

Whale Watching

I t is the world's longest mammal migration: 6000 miles along the Pacific coast from the Bering Sea to Baja California, then back again. The creatures making the journey measure 35 to 50 feet and weigh 40 tons. During the entire course of their incredible voyage they neither eat nor sleep.

Every year from mid-December to early February, the California gray whale cruises southward along the Northern California coast. Traveling in groups numbering three to five, these magnificent creatures hug the shoreline en route to their breeding grounds.

Since the whales use local coves and promontories to navigate, they are easy to spot from land. Just watch for the rolling hump, the slapping tail, or a lofty spout of spuming water. Sometimes these huge creatures will breach, leaping 30 feet above the surface, then crashing back with a thunderous splash.

The best crow's nests from which to catch this aquatic parade are Muir Beach Overlook, Chimney Rock at Point Reyes National Seashore, Bodega Head State Park, Sonoma Coast State Beach, Salt Point State Park, Mendocino Headlands State Park, Shelter Cove or Trinidad Head in Humboldt County, and Point St. George up near Crescent City. Visitors to California's Central Coast also enjoy this annual event.

Several outfits sponsor whale-watching cruises. During the winter and early spring, **Oceanic Society Expeditions** offers gray whale migration tours, which are led by qualified naturalists. June through November, full-day Farallon Islands trips to see humpback and blue whales are provided. Weekends only. ~ Fort Mason Center, Quarters 35, San Francisco; 415-474-3385, fax 415-474-3395; www.oceanic-society.org. For a close look at our fellow mammals from January through April, contact the **Boat House**. ~ 1445 Route 1, Bodega Bay; 707-875-3495.

California gray whales live to 40 or 50 years and have a world population numbering about 21,000. Their only enemies are killer whales and humans. They mate during the southern migration one year, then give birth at the end of the following year's migration. The calves, born in the warm, shallow waters of Baja, weigh a ton and measure about 16 feet. By the time they are weaned seven months later, the young are already 26 feet long.

Blue whales, humpback whales, dolphins, and porpoises also sometimes visit the coast. Gray whales can be seen again from March to mid-May, though farther from shore, during their return migration north. So keep an eye peeled: that rocky headland on which you are standing may be a crow's nest in disguise.

woods. There's a pro shop, a driving range, a putting green, a restaurant, and carts. ~ 4750 Fairway Drive, Eureka; 707-443-4808; www.playeureka.com. In Crescent City, the challenging nine-hole **Del Norte Golf Course** is set amidst redwoods. ~ 130 Club Drive, Crescent City; 707-458-3214.

TENNIS

The best bet for finding a tennis court without staying at the most expensive hotels is to call the local parks and recreation department.

REDWOOD COUNTRY   In Eureka, you can play at **Highland Park**. ~ Highland and Glen streets. **Hammond Park** has two courts. ~ 14th and E streets, Eureka; 707-441-4226. In Crescent City there are four lighted courts available. ~ 301 West Washington Boulevard. For information on courts call 707-464-6141.

RIDING STABLES & PACK TRIPS

Riding along the hauntingly beautiful North Coast is not an experience easily forgotten.

MARIN COAST   There are few prettier places to ride than Point Reyes National Seashore, where you can canter through rolling ranch country and out along sharp sea cliffs. **Five Brooks Stables** conducts mounted tours of this extraordinary area. Reservations required. ~ 8001 Route 1, Olema; 415-663-1570.; www.five brooks.com.

BIKING

Two-wheeling north of San Francisco is an invigorating sport. Not only is the scenery magnificent, but the accommodations aren't bad either. Many state and national parks sponsor campgrounds where cyclists and hikers can stay for a nominal fee.

Route 1 offers a chance to pedal past a spectacular shoreline of hidden coves, broad beaches, and sheer headlands. Unfortunately, the highway is narrow and winding—for experienced cyclists only.

MARIN COAST   Point Reyes National Seashore features miles of bicycling, particularly along Bear Valley Trail.

SONOMA AND MENDOCINO COAST   Other popular areas farther north include the towns of Mendocino and where level terrain and beautiful landscape combine to create a cyclist's haven.
Bike Rentals   In Mendocino **Catch a Canoe and Bicycles Too!** rents and sells state-of-the-art equipment. ~ Coast Highway 1 at Comptche-Ukiah Road; 707-937-0273. Located on the bicycle migration route between Canada and Mexico. **Fort Bragg Cyclery** rents bikes and does full-service repairs. ~ 221-A North Main Street, Fort Bragg; 707-964-3509.

HIKING

To call California's North Coast a hiker's paradise is an understatement. After all, in San Francisco and north of the city is the

Golden Gate National Recreation Area. Together with continuous county, state, and national parks it offers over 100,000 acres to be explored.

Within this ambit are trails ranging from trifling nature loops to tough mountain paths. The land varies from tidal areas and seacliffs to ranch country and scenic mountains. In the far north are the giant redwood forests, located within national parks and featuring networks of hiking trails.

All distances listed for hiking trails are one way unless otherwise noted.

MARIN COAST The **Marin Headlands**, a region of bold bluffs and broad seascapes, contains many hiking paths in its unpredictable landscape.

The moderate **Kirby Cove Trail** (1 mile) leads from Conzelman Road down to a narrow beach. The views of San Francisco en route provide a lot of adventure for a short hike.

The moderate **Wolf Ridge Loop** (5 miles) begins at Rodeo Beach, follows the Coastal Trail and Wolf Ridge Trail, then returns along Miwok Trail. It ascends from a shoreline environment to heights with sweeping views of both San Francisco and Mt. Tamalpais.

The easy **Tennessee Valley Trail** (2 miles) winds along the valley floor en route to a small beach and cove. The trailhead sits off Route 1 at the end of Tennessee Valley Road.

About 45 miles of trails loop through **Mt. Tamalpais State Park** (415-388-2070, fax 415-388-2968). These link to a 200-mile network of hiking paths through Muir Woods National Monument and Golden Gate National Recreation Area. Explorers are rewarded with a diverse terrain, startling views of the entire Bay Area, and a chance to hike within commuting distance of San Francisco. Most trails begin at Pan Toll Park Headquarters. Here you can pick up trail maps ($1) and descriptions from which to devise your own combination loop trails, or consult with the rangers in planning anything from an easy jaunt to a rugged trek.

> The thick bark of a redwood—up to a foot wide in places—essentially makes the tree fireproof.

Dipsea Trail (7.1 miles) is a favorite moderate path beginning in Mill Valley and heading along rolling hills, past sea vistas, then ending near Stinson Beach. The easiest way to pick up the trail is in Muir Woods, about a 3.5 miles from the Mill Valley trailhead.

Matt Davis Trail (3.8 miles) descends 1200 feet from Pan Toll Park Headquarters to Stinson Beach; you'll encounter deep woods, windswept knolls, and views of San Francisco and Point Reyes.

Steep Ravine Trail (2.8 miles), true to its name, angles sharply downward from Pan Toll Park Headquarters through a redwood-studded canyon, then joins the Dipsea Trail.

Redwood Creek Trail (2.5 miles) loops through several re-markable redwood stands. A favorite with tourists, this easy trail begins near Muir Woods park headquarters and is often crowded. So it's best hiked either early or late in the day.

There are numerous other trails that combined form inter-esting loop hikes. For instance, from Bootjack picnic area in Mt. Tamalpais State Park, you can follow **Bootjack Trail** down a steep canyon of redwood and Douglas fir to Muir Woods, then take **Ben Johnson Trail** back up to Pan Toll Park Headquarters. From there it's a half-mile walk back to Bootjack. This 4.2-mile moderate circle tour carries through relatively isolated sections of Muir Woods.

For a more challenging (9.4 miles) circular trek to the top of Mt. Tamalpais, begin at Pan Toll Park Headquarters. Along Old Stage Road you'll encounter Mountain Home, an inn located along Panoramic Highway. Follow **Old Railroad Grade**. This will lead to West Point Inn, a cozy lodging place for hikers. From here you climb to the road that goes to East Peak, one of Mt. Tamalpais' three summits. If you choose to go on down the rocky **Fern Creek Trail**, you'll encounter Old Railroad Grade once more. En route are flowering meadows, madrone stands, chaparral-cloaked hillsides, and mountaintop views.

POINT REYES NATIONAL SEASHORE   Within its spectacular 72,000-acre domain, this park contains over 140 miles of hiking trails plus four hike-in campsites. The trails form a latticework across forests, ranch lands, and secluded beaches and along sea cliffs, brackish inlets, and freshwater lakes. Over 350 bird species inhabit the preserve. Black-tailed deer, Eurasian fallow deer, and spotted axis deer abound. You might also encounter raccoons, weasels, rabbits, badgers, bobcats, even a skunk or two.

Most trailheads begin near **Bear Valley Visitors Center**, Palo-marin, Five Brooks, or Estero. For maps and information check with the rangers at the visitors center. ~ 415-464-5100, fax 415-464-5149; www.nps.gov/pore.

Hikers can learn about the nearby San Andreas Fault on the short **Earthquake Trail** (.6 mile) that begins from the Bear Valley Visitors Center and leads along the original rupture of the 1906

AUTHOR FAVORITE

A hike along the two-mile **Hiouchi Trail** in Del Norte Coast Redwoods State Park, with its huckleberries, trilliums, and rhododendrons, is one of the best ways I know to beat the big-city blues and get back in touch with nature. This nature trail goes right through a burned-out redwood; it also affords scenic vistas along the Smith River.

earthquake. The ground here shifted over 16 feet during that terrible upheaval.

Woodpecker Trail (.7 mile) is an easy self-guiding trail with markers explaining the natural environment. The annotated path leads to a horse "museum" set in a barn.

Bear Valley Trail (4.1 miles), also beginning near the visitors center, courses through range land and wooded valley to cliffs overlooking the Pacific Ocean. The park's most popular trail, it is level and may unfortunately be crowded with hikers and bicyclists.

Coast Trail (15.9 miles) runs between Palomarin (near Bolinas) and Limantour Beach. Hugging the shoreline en route, this moderate, splendid trail leads past four freshwater lakes and two camping areas, then turns inland to Hostelling International's lodge.

Olema Valley Trail (5.3 miles) parallels Route 1 as it tracks a course along the infamous San Andreas Fault. Originating from Five Brooks, it alternates between glades and forest while beating a level path to Dogtown. Moderate.

Estero Trail (8.6 miles) shadows the shoreline of Drakes Estero and provides opportunities to view local waterfowl as well as harbor seals, sea lions, and bat rays.

REDWOOD COUNTRY There are more than 100 miles of hiking and riding paths within **Humboldt Redwoods State Park**. Many lead through dense redwood stands, others meander along the Eel River, and some lead to the park's hike-in camps.

Founder's Grove Nature Trail (.5 mile) tunnels through a virgin redwood forest that once boasted the national champion coastal redwood. Though a storm significantly shortened the 362-foot giant, it left standing a cluster of equally impressive neighbors.

Rockefeller Loop Trail (.5 mile) ducks into a magnificent grove of old-growth redwoods.

There are also longer trails leading deep into the forest and to the top of 3379-foot Grasshopper Peak.

Comprising three distinct state parks and extending for miles along California's northwestern corner, **Redwood National and State Parks'** diverse enclave offers adventure aplenty to daytrippers and mountaineers alike. There are over 150 miles of trails threading the parks, leading through dense redwood groves, along open beaches, and atop wind-buffeted bluffs. ~ 707-464-6101, fax 707-464-1812.

Yurok Loop Trail (1 mile), with its berry patches and wildflowers, begins near the terminus of Coastal Trail.

Enderts Beach Trail (.5 mile), south of Crescent City, features tidepools, seaside strolling, and primitive camping. It also offers access to the moderate **Coastal Trail** (8.2 miles), an old roadway that cuts through forests of redwood, alder, and spruce and features glorious ocean views.

Within **Prairie Creek Redwoods State Park** there are numerous trails to enjoy.

Redwood Creek Trail (9 miles) leads from a trailhead two miles north of Orick to Tall Trees Grove, home of the world's tallest trees. There is backcountry camping en route; permits available at the trailhead.

Tall Trees Trail (1.6 miles) provides a shorter route to the same destination.

Lady Bird Johnson Grove Nature Loop Trail (1 mile) winds through ancient redwood country.

The moderate **Rhododendron Trail** (7.8 miles) begins at park headquarters and continues along the eastern ridge of the park, which is filled with rhododendrons.

James Irvine Trail (4.3 miles) goes from the Prairie Creek visitors center along a redwood ridge to Fern Canyon. For a longer loop (10.3 miles), hike south on Gold Bluffs Beach, then pick up Miner's Ridge Trail. This last trail follows a corduroy mining road used early in the century.

The **Fern Canyon Trail** (.8 mile) courses along a gulch dripping with vegetation.

The easy **Coastal Trail** (5 miles) begins at Fern Canyon and parallels Gold Bluffs Beach.

The moderate **West Ridge Trail** (7.1 miles) traces a sharp ridgetop through lovely virgin forest, ending at the Butler Creek backpacking camp.

The **Revelation Trail** (.3 mile), a marvelous innovation, contains handrails and a tape-recorded description of the surroundings for the blind. For those of us gifted with sight, it provides a fuller understanding of the scents, sounds, and textures of a redwood forest.

Cathedral Trees Trail (1.4 miles) heads along streams and meadows to elk country.

Brown Creek Trail (1.2 miles), reputedly one of the park's prettiest hikes, leads along streams and through old redwood stands.

Del Norte Coast Redwoods State Park offers several areas ideal for short hikes. **Coastal Trail** (4 miles), located south of the state park, begins at Klamath River Overlook. In addition to ocean vistas, it offers a moderate walk through a spruce and alder forest, plus glimpses of sea lions, whales, and numerous birds.

Damnation Creek Trail (2.1 miles), a strenuous ancient Yurok Indian path, winds steeply down from Route 101 to a hidden cove and beach.

Hobbs Wall Trail (3.8 miles) leads through a former lumberjacking region.

Alder Basin Trail (1 mile) meanders along a stream through stands of willow, maple, and alder.

Farther north, **Jedediah Smith Redwoods State Park** has a number of trails to hike.

Stout Grove Trail (.5 mile) highlights several spots along its short easy course: a 340-foot redwood tree, swimming and fishing holes, plus rhododendron regions.

Hatton Trail (.3 mile) tours an ancient redwood grove.

Nickerson Ranch Trail (.8 mile) leads through a corridor of ferns and redwoods.

Transportation

When traveling by car you can choose the ever-winding, spectacular coastal **Route 1**, which provides some of the prettiest scenery this side of Shangri-la. Or take **Route 101**, the faster, more direct freeway that follows an interior route.

CAR

AIR

Arcata/Eureka Airport in McKinleyville is served by United Airlines and Horizon Air. On a bluff above the Pacific, this is one of the most beautiful small fields in California. **Humboldt Transit Authority** provides roughly hourly service (Monday through Friday) from Eureka and Arcata to the airport. There's limited service on Saturday. ~ 133 V Street, Eureka; 707-443-0826; www.hta.org.

BUS

Greyhound Bus Lines (800-231-2222; www.greyhound.com) travels the entire stretch of Route 101 between San Francisco and Oregon, including the main route through Redwood Country. ~ 707-545-6495; www.greyhound.com.

CAR RENTALS

It's advisable to rent an auto in San Francisco rather than along the North Coast. There are more rental agencies available and prices are lower. At the Arcata/Eureka Airport you can rent from **Avis Rent A Car** (800-331-1212), **Hertz Rent A Car** (800-654-3131), and **National Car Rental** (800-227-7368).

PUBLIC TRANSIT

Golden Gate Transit has bus service between San Francisco and Sausalito. It also covers Route 101 from San Francisco to Santa Rosa. ~ 415-923-2000; www.goldengate.org.

From Santa Rosa you can pick up coastal connections on **Mendocino Transit Authority**, which travels Route 1 from Bodega Bay to Point Arena. There's only one bus a day in either direction. ~ 800-696-4682; www.4mta.org.

Public transportation from San Francisco to Marin can become a sightseeing adventure when you book passage on a **Golden Gate Transit** ferry boat. ~ 415-455-2000.

FOUR

North Central Coast

 If the North Central Coast were an oil painting, it would portray a surf-laced shoreline near the bottom of the frame. Pearly beaches and bold promontories would occupy the center, while forested peaks rose in the background. Actually, a mural would be more appropriate to the subject, since the coastline extends 150 miles from San Francisco to Big Sur. The artist would paint two mountain ranges parallel to the shore, then fill the area between with a patchwork of hills, headlands, and farmland.

Even after adding a swath of redwoods along the entire length of the mural, the painter's task would have only begun. The Central Coast will never be captured—on canvas, in print, or in the camera's eye. It is a region of unmatched beauty and extraordinary diversity.

Due south of San Francisco is Half Moon Bay, a timeless farming and fishing community founded by Italians and Portuguese during the 1860s. The oceanside farms are so bountiful that Half Moon Bay dubs itself the pumpkin capital of the world, and Castroville, farther south, claims to be the artichoke capital. While local farmers grow prize vegetables, commercial fishing boats comb the entire coast for salmon, herring, tuna, anchovies, and cod.

In the seaside town of Santa Cruz, on the other hand, you'll encounter a quiet retirement community that has been transformed into a dynamic campus town. When the University of California opened a school here in the 1960s, it created a new role for this ever-changing place. Originally founded as a Spanish mission in 1791, Santa Cruz became a lumber port and manufacturing center when the Americans moved in around 1849. Then in the late 19th century it developed into a tourist resort filled with elaborate Victorian houses.

Like every place on the Central Coast, Santa Cruz is reached from San Francisco along Route 1, the tortuous coast road that twists past sandy coves and granite cliffs. Paralleling it is Route 101, the inland freeway that leads through the warm, dry agricultural regions of the Salinas Valley. Between these two roadways rise the Santa Cruz Mountains, accessible along Routes 35 and 9. Unlike the low-lying coastal and inland farming areas, this range measures 3000 feet in elevation and is filled with redwood, Douglas fir, alder, and madrone.

Different still is the Monterey Peninsula, a fashionable residential area 125 miles south of San Francisco. Including the towns of Monterey, Pacific Grove, and Carmel, this wealthy enclave is a far cry from bohemian Santa Cruz. If Santa Cruz is an espresso coffeehouse, Monterey is a gourmet restaurant or designer boutique.

Farther south lies Big Sur, the most unusual area of all. Extending from the Monterey Peninsula for 90 miles along the coast, and backdropped by the steep Santa Lucia Mountains, it is one of America's most magnificent natural areas. Only about 1000 residents live in this rugged region of bald crags and flower-choked canyons. None but the most adventurous occupy the nearby Ventana Wilderness, which represents the southernmost realm of the coastal redwoods. Once a nesting place for rare California condors, Ventana is still home to wild boar, black bear, and mountain lion.

The Esselen Indians, who inhabited Big Sur and its mountains, took Spanish names to avoid being slaughtered during the missionary period. In recent years, they have been organizing to make the state of California recognize their tribal status. Together with the Costanoans, who occupied the rest of the Central Coast, the Esselen may have been here for 5000 years. By the time the Europeans happened upon California, about 10,000 American Indians lived near the coast between San Francisco and Big Sur. Elk and antelope ranged the region. The American Indians also hunted sea lions, gathered seaweed, and fed on oysters, abalone, clams, and mussels.

Westerners did not settle Big Sur until after 1850, and Route 1 did not open completely until 1937. During the 1950s, novelist Henry Miller became the focus of an artists' colony here. Jack Kerouac trekked through the area, writing about it in several of his novels. Other Beat poets, lured by Big Sur's dizzying sea cliffs and otherworldly vistas, also cut a path through its hills.

Over 300 years before settlers arrived in Big Sur, Monterey was already making history. As early as 1542, Juan Rodríguez Cabrillo, a Portuguese explorer in Spanish employ, set anchor off nearby Pacific Grove. Then in 1602 Sebastian Vizcaíno came upon the peninsula again and told a whale of a fish story, grandly exaggerating the size and amenities of Monterey Bay.

His account proved so distorted that Gaspar de Portolá, leading an overland expedition in 1769, failed to recognize the harbor. When Father Junípero Serra joined him in a second journey the next year, they realized that this gentle curve was Vizcaíno's deep port. Serra established California's second mission in Monterey, then moved it a few miles in 1771 to create the Carmel Mission. Neither Serra nor Portolá explored the Big Sur coast, but the Spanish were soon building yet another mission in Santa Cruz.

In fact, they found Santa Cruz much easier to control than Monterey. By the 1820s, Yankee merchant ships were plying Monterey waters, trading for hides and tallow. This early American presence, brilliantly described in Richard Henry Dana's classic *Two Years Before the Mast*, climaxed in 1846 during the Mexican War. Commodore John Sloat seized the town for the United States. By 1849, while

Big Sur was still the hunting ground of American Indians, the adobe town of Monterey had become the site of California's constitutional convention.

An added incentive for these early adventurers, and modern-day visitors as well, was the climate along the Central Coast. The temperature still hovers around 67° in summer and 57° during winter; Santa Cruz continues to boast 300 sunny days a year. Explorers once complained of foggy summers and rainy winters, but like today's travelers, they were rewarded with beautiful spring and fall weather.

Perhaps that's why Monterey became a tourist mecca during the 1880s. Of course the old Spanish capital also developed into a major fishing and canning region during the early 20th century. It was then that John Steinbeck, the Salinas-bred writer, added to the already rich history of Monterey with his novels and stories. Much of the landscape that became known as "Steinbeck Country" has changed drastically since the novelist's day, and the entire Central Coast is different from the days of Serra and Sloat. But the most important elements of Monterey and the Central Coast—the foaming ocean, open sky, and wooded heights—are still here, waiting for the traveler with a bold eye and robust imagination.

South of San Francisco

An easy drive from the city, the coast south of San Francisco is full of surprises. You might see gray whales, watch the sea lions at Año Nuevo State Reserve, or visit one of the rural towns that dot this shoreline. The area along Route 1 between San Francisco and Santa Cruz also sports numerous beaches, bed-and-breakfast inns, and country roads that lead up into the Santa Cruz Mountains.

SIGHTS   Preceding the beauty, however, is the beast. The road south from San Francisco leads through one of America's ugliest towns. In fact, **Daly City** is the perfect counterpoint to the bay city: it is as hideous as San Francisco is splendid. If Tony Bennett left his heart in San Francisco, he must have discarded a gallbladder in Daly City. This town was memorialized in Malvina Reynolds' song, "Little Boxes," which describes its "ticky tacky" houses and over-developed hillsides.

No matter, this suburban blight soon gives way to Route 1, which cuts through Pacifica and curls into the hills. As the road rises above a swirling coastline you'll be entering a geologic hotspot. The **San Andreas Fault**, villain of the 1906 and 1989 earthquakes, heads back into shore near Pacifica. As the road cuts will reveal, the sedimentary rock along this area has been twisted and warped into bizarre shapes. At **Devil's Slide**, several miles south of Pacifica, unstable hillsides periodically collapse into the sea.

Now that I have totally terrified you, I should add that this is an area not to be missed. Drive carefully and you'll be safe to enjoy the outstanding ocean vistas revealed at every hairpin turn in this

Text continued on page 196.

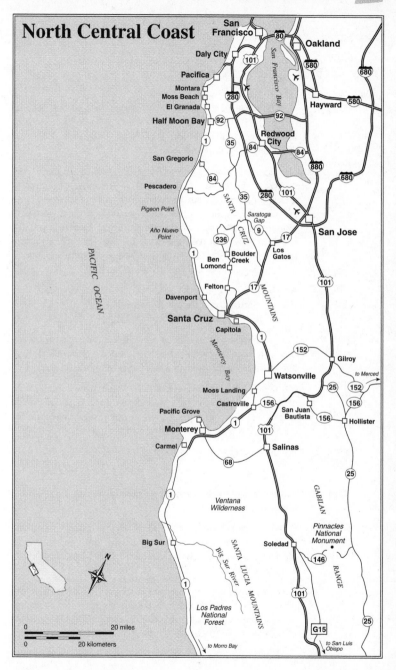

North Central Coast

North Central Coast

Day 1
- From San Francisco, follow the San Andreas earthquake fault south on Route 280 to the Routes 35/92 exit, and stay on Route 92 for seven miles to **Half Moon Bay**. Allow one-half to one hour depending on traffic conditions.

- Take coastal Route 1 south to Santa Cruz, a distance of 40 miles that takes about an hour to drive. Along the way you'll discover almost a dozen great beaches along with hidden fishing and farming villages, headlands, marshy estuaries, and sand dunes. Take your pick among such spots as **Pescadero State Beach** (page 204) and **Año Nuevo State Reserve** (page 198) for a mellow morning walk. In this world, it's hard to believe you're just over the hill from the big cities of San Francisco and San Jose.

- Arriving in Santa Cruz, if it's a summer day or weekend, be sure to visit the **Santa Cruz Beach Boardwalk** (page 207), one of the last old-fashioned amusement parks.

- Later in the afternoon, continue down Route 1, skirting **Monterey Bay**. This 30-mile stretch is four-lane divided highway all the way, but you're never far from an opportunity for a beach break.

- **Monterey** has accommodations in all price ranges. If money is no object, you'll find an array of ultra-deluxe resorts in nearby **Pacific Grove** and **Carmel**. Any of these towns makes a fine base for exploring the coast and the Sierra de Salinas.

- Take a **walking tour of Monterey** (page 228) before dinner.

Day 2
- Visit the fabulous **Monterey Bay Aquarium** (page 227). Allow at least two hours.

- Follow Route 1 down the coast to **Big Sur** (page 249), one of the most spectacular scenic drives anywhere. Scattered restaurants offer lunch possibilities, while four scenic state parks provide perfect picnic spots.

- You could spend the rest of the day continuing to explore your way down Route 1, which winds between the sea and Los Padres National Forest for another 65 miles to San Simeon. Or you could choose to return to Carmel and head into the Santa Lucia Mountains to unwind in the hot springs at the **Tassajara Zen Mountain Center** (page 253).

• Return to your Monterey area lodging for the evening.

Day 3 • Pack a picnic lunch.

• Drive inland from Carmel along pastoral Carmel Valley Road (Route G16) to Greenfield; take Route 101 north for 10 miles to Soledad. Turn east on Route 146 and go 13 miles to the west entrance of **Pinnacles National Monument** (page 248). Allow one and a half to two hours for the drive.

• Equipped with good hiking boots and plenty of water, explore the wild stone wonderland of Pinnacles.

• The return trip to San Francisco via Route 101 takes two hours (unless you encounter traffic snarls in Silicon Valley—a distinct possibility any day of the week).

winding roadway. Rocky cliffs, pocket beaches, and erupting surf open to view. There are sea stacks offshore and, in winter, gray whales cruise the coast.

At the village of **Montara**, you will pass an old lighthouse whose utility buildings have been converted to a youth hostel. As the road descends toward Moss Beach, precipitous rock faces give way to gentle slopes and placid tidepools. Then in Half Moon Bay a four-mile-long white-sand beach is backdropped by new homes built on farmlands.

Half Moon Bay is what happens when the farm meets the sea. It's a hybrid town, half landlubber and half old-salt. They are as likely to sell artichokes here as fresh fish. The town was named for its crescent beach, but thinks of itself as the pumpkin capital of the world. In October, this San Francisco suburb bedroom community hosts the **Art & Pumpkin Festival**, which draws over 300,000 people. At times the furrowed fields seem a geometric continuation of ocean waves, as if the sea lapped across the land and became frozen there. It is Half Moon Bay's peculiar schizophrenia, a double identity that lends an undeniable flair to the community.

From Half Moon Bay, a connecting road leads to Route 35 and Route 9, providing an alternate course to Santa Cruz; this will be covered below, in the "Santa Cruz Mountains" sightseeing section of this chapter. For now, let's stay on Route 1, which continues south, poised between the mountains and the sea.

HIDDEN ► On the southern outskirts of Half Moon Bay, watch for the **Higgins–Purisima Road**, a country lane that curves for eight miles into the Santa Cruz Mountains, returning to Route 1. This scenic loop passes old farmhouses and sloping pastures, mountain meadows and redwood-forested hills. Immediately upon entering this bumpy road, you'll spy a stately old New England–style house set in a plowed field. That will be the **James Johnston House**, a saltbox structure with sloping roof and white clapboard facade. Dating back to 1853 and built by an original '49er, it is the oldest house along this section of coastline. The house is open to the public from January through September, the third Saturday of the month, or by appointment. ~ 650-726-0329; www.johnstonhouse.org, e-mail questions@johnstonhouse.org.

The farming plus fishing spirit of Half Moon Bay prevails as Route 1 continues south. A short distance from the highway, you'll encounter **San Gregorio**, a weather-beaten little town. Once a resort area, today it reveals a quaint collection of sagging roofs and unpainted barns. Be sure to drop by the **San Gregorio General Store**, a classic general store that's been around since the 1890s. You'll find live music here on weekend mornings. ~ Corner of Stage Road and Route 84, San Gregorio; 650-726-0565; www.sangregoriostore.com.

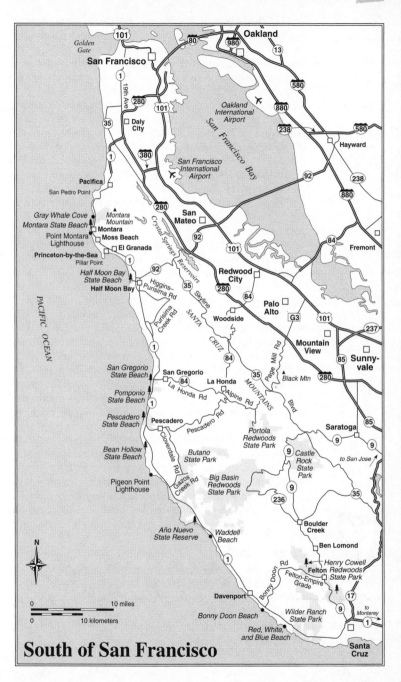

South of San Francisco

Pescadero represents another timeworn town hidden a short way from Route 1. It's a woodframe hamlet of front-porch rocking chairs and white-steeple churches. The name translates as "fisherman," but the Portuguese and Italian residents are farmers, planting artichokes, Brussels sprouts, beans, and lettuce in the patchwork fields surrounding the town.

A family-owned farm open to the public, **Phipps** offers a nursery, pottery studio, child-friendly barnyard and a market selling dried beans, herbs, and other products grown on the premises. During the summer visitors can pick several varieties of berries. Admission. ~ 2700 Pescadero Creek Road, Pescadero; 650-879-0787, 650-879-1032, fax 650-879-1622; www.phippscountry. com, e-mail phippscountry@earthlink.net.

The beacon several miles south is **Pigeon Point Lighthouse**, a 110-foot sentinel that's one of the nation's tallest lighthouses. The point gained a nasty reputation during the 19th century when one ship after another smashed on the rocks. In fact, Pigeon Point is named for the *Carrier Pigeon*, a Yankee clipper that wrecked on the rocks here in 1854. The lighthouse went up in 1872, and originally contained a 1000-piece lens. Doubling as a youth hostel, it now warns sailors while welcoming travelers.

The Ohlone Indians highly valued the region around **Año Nuevo State Reserve** for its abundant fish and shellfish population. It was here they experienced their first contact with whites in 1769 when Juan Gaspar de Portolá trekked through en route to his discovery of San Francisco Bay. Today, visitors come to Año Nuevo to observe the elephant seals who return to breed each year from December through March. (For further information, see "Beaches & Parks" below.) ~ 650-879-2025, fax 650-879-2031.

From here to Santa Cruz, the road streams past bold headlands and magnificent seascapes. There are excellent beaches to explore and marvelous vista points along the way. You'll also discover rolling farmlands where giant pumpkins grow at the edge of the sea.

About two miles north of Santa Cruz along Route 1 you'll discover **Wilder Ranch State Park**. This 8000-acre spread has 30

AUTHOR FAVORITE

Miles of sand dunes border **Año Nuevo State Reserve**, an enchanting park that contains an offshore island where two-ton elephant seals breed in winter. With its tidepools, exotic bird population, sea lions, and harbor seals, the reserve is a natural playground. My favorite time to visit is during the mating season of the elephant seals from December to March. See above for more information.

acres that have been designated a "cultural preserve" because of the historic houses found on the property. Hiking trails allowing horses and bikes wind throughout. In addition to an 1839 adobe, the complex features a Greek Revival farmhouse dating to 1859 and an 1897 Queen Anne Victorian. You can also tour the out-lying barns and workshops portraying life on a turn-of-the-20th-century dairy farm, which this once was. Go on a weekend to see a living-history demonstration and the working Pelton water-wheel, used during the Gold Rush to operate mining equipment. Open Thursday through Sunday, and occasionally other week-days; call for hours. Parking fee. ~ 831-423-9703, 831-426-0505.

LODGING

If there were a hotel on the site of **Hostelling International— Point Montara Lighthouse**, it would easily charge $300 a night. Set on a bluff overlooking the ocean, on one of those dramatic points always reserved for lighthouses, the hostel charges down-to-earth prices (and requires a morning chore). The daily fee buys you a bunk in a cozy dorm-style room. Couple and family rooms are also available. There is a kitchen, a common room, and laundry facilities in this old lightkeeper's house. This is a good spot for whale watching (November through April). Reservations are strongly recommended. ~ Route 1 at 16th Street, Montara; 650-728-7177, 888-464-4872, fax 650-728-7058; www.norcal hostels.org, e-mail himontara@norcalhostels.org. BUDGET.

The Seal Cove Inn, located 30 minutes south of San Fran-cisco and six miles north of Half Moon Bay, is the perfect place to sojourn for one more night before heading farther afield. The decor has been freshly refurbished in a modern European style, but the setting is pure Californian, with seals, whales, long white beaches, and towering cypress trees sharing the surrounding acreage. ~ 221 Cypress Avenue, Moss Beach; 650-728-4114, 800-995-9987, fax 650-728-4116; www.sealcoveinn.com, e-mail sealcoveinn@sealcoveinn.com. DELUXE TO ULTRA-DELUXE.

The Cape Cod look has become very popular with estab-lishments in the Half Moon Bay area. One of the foremost, **Pillar Point Inn** is a fully modern bed and breakfast cloaked in 19th-century New England disguise. Overlooking the harbor, this 11-room inn combines VCRs, DVD players, televisions, and re-frigerators with traditional amenities like featherbeds, window seats, and fireplaces. Every guest room has a private bath, and there's a deck overlooking the waterfront. Breakfast is a full-course affair. ~ 380 Capistrano Road, Princeton-by-the-Sea; 650-728-7377, 800-400-8281, fax 650-728-8345; www.pillar pointinn.com, e-mail reservations@pillarpointinn.com. DELUXE.

Sitting right above the beach a few miles north of Half Moon Bay is the 54-room **Beach House**. This contemporary facility, de-signed in the style of a New England summer home, features "lofts" that include patios, fireplaces, and private balconies. One of the most comfortable hotels along this stretch of coastline, it creates a sense of easy elegance. There's a lobby with fireplace, a heated pool and a jacuzzi, not to mention a succession of beautiful sunsets just beyond your patio door. Complimentary continental breakfast. ~ 4100 North Cabrillo Highway, P.O. Box 129, Half Moon Bay; 650-712-0220, 800-315-9366, fax 650-712-0693; www.beach-house.com, e-mail view@beach-house.com. MODERATE TO ULTRA-DELUXE.

Among lodgings on this stretch of coastline, **San Benito House** is a personal favorite. Set in a 1905 building, it's a 12-room bed-and-breakfast inn with adjoining bar and restaurant. The less expensive rooms are small but quite nice. One room I saw featured a brass light fixture, hanging plants, quilted beds, framed drawings, and wood furniture. There are both shared and private baths. Add a sauna plus a country-inn ambience and you have a bargain at the price. ~ 356 Main Street, Half Moon Bay; 650-726-3425; www.sanbenitohouse.com, e-mail inquiries@sanbenitohouse.com. MODERATE TO DELUXE.

The blue clapboard home of an early merchant in Half Moon Bay is now a bed-and-breakfast inn called the **Zaballa House**. Within the 1859 structure, the oldest in town, are 14 charming rooms, some with fireplaces and large whirlpool tubs. A friendly, unpretentious atmosphere prevails throughout, with guests encouraged to put their feet up in the parlor and relax with a good book. All guests enjoy a full breakfast and afternoon wine and cheese. ~ 324 Main Street, Half Moon Bay; 650-726-9123; www.zaballahouse.net, e-mail zaballahouse@earthlink.net. MODERATE TO DELUXE.

Comparable to the low-cost lodging at Montara is **Hostelling International—Pigeon Point Lighthouse**. It has a similarly dramatic windswept setting above the ocean. The rooms are in sev-

AUTHOR FAVORITE

One of the finest country inns along the entire Central Coast is **Mill Rose Inn**. This inn, built in 1902, is adorned with hand-painted wallpapers, European antiques, and colorful tiles throughout. The grounds resemble an English garden and include an enclosed gazebo with a jacuzzi and flagstone patio. Each of the six guest rooms is brilliantly appointed; even the least expensive displays an antique armoire, European featherbed, and marble-top dresser covered with old-style combs and brushes. The sitting room and spacious dining room are equally elegant. ~ 615 Mill Street, Half Moon Bay; 650-726-8750, 800-900-7673, fax 650-726-3031; www.mill roseinn.com, e-mail info@millroseinn.com. ULTRA-DELUXE.

eral shared cottages with kitchens, living rooms, and accommodations for couples. Rates, as in other American Youth Hostels, are budget, and a chore is requested. Guests have access to a private, clifftop hot tub for a small fee. Set beneath California's second tallest lighthouse on a beautiful shoreline, the hostel is a charming place to stay. Four private rooms are available for an additional charge. Reservations strongly advised; couples should call four to six months in advance. ~ Route 1 at Pigeon Point Road, Pescadero; 650-879-0633, 888-464-4872, fax 916-443-4763; www.norcalhostels.org. BUDGET.

The recently refurbished **Roadhouse Restaurant & Inn** boasts a sparse decor featuring bare white walls and clean, environmentally sound modern furniture in dark woods. The eight rooms have extra-thick mattresses and private baths. Oceanfront views, wine-tastings, and massages give it a singular appeal. ~ 31 Davenport Avenue, Davenport; 831-426-8801, fax 831-426-8830; www.davenportroadhouse.com, e-mail info@davenportroad house.com. DELUXE.

DINING

Nick's Restaurant has been operated by the same Greek-Italian-American family for more than eight decades and is still pulling in the Pacifica crowds. Wood sculptures of sea life decorate the walls, but the main attraction is the million-dollar view of Rockaway Beach. Nick's is known for its grilled crab sandwiches, sautéed prawns, and fettuccine angelina. ~ 100 Rockaway Beach, Pacifica; 650-359-3900, fax 650-359-5624, www.nicks restaurant.net. DELUXE.

For dinner overlooking the ocean, there's nothing quite like **Moss Beach Distillery**. The place enjoys a colorful history, dating back to Prohibition days, when this area was notorious for supplying booze to thirsty San Francisco. Today it's a bustling plate-glass restaurant with adjoining bar and an indoor/outdoor patio with an incredible ocean view. The menu includes fresh seafood, gulf shrimp and Chicago steaks. The bootleggers are long gone, but those splendid sea views will be here forever. Brunch served on Sunday. Closed first three weeks of December. ~ 140 Beach Way, Moss Beach; 650-728-5595, fax 650-728-8135; www.moss beachdistillery.com. ULTRA-DELUXE.

Speaking of seafood, **Barbara's Fishtrap** down on Half Moon Bay has some of the lowest prices around. Set in and around a small woodframe building smack on the bay, this unpretentious eatery features several fresh fish dishes daily. "The trap," as the locals call it, is liable to be serving fresh sea bass, local halibut, and salmon, as well as steak sandwiches and shellfish. Calamari rings are a specialty. Friendly, local, inexpensive—and highly recommended. ~ 281 Capistrano Road, Princeton-by-the-Sea; 650-728-7049, fax 650-728-2519. MODERATE.

Mezza Luna offers an authentic taste of Southern Italy with contemporary dishes that include a variety of pastas with home-made sauces, fresh seafood, lamb and veal. A favorite is the homemade, half-moon–shaped ravioli in a tomato cream sauce. The ambience is wonderful as well: terracotta- and salmon-colored walls, arched windows, and tile floors resemble a true Italian trattoria. ~ 459 Prospect Way, Princeton-by-the-Sea; 650-728-8108, fax 650-728-8201; www.mezzalunabythesea.com, e-mail dinner@mezzalunabythesea.com. MODERATE TO ULTRA-DELUXE.

Once past Half Moon Bay, restaurants become mighty scarce. Practically anything will do along this lonesome stretch south; but rather than just anything, you can have **Duarte's Tavern**. Open since 1894, this restaurant and tavern has earned a reputation all down the coast for delicious food. There's a menu filled with meat and fish entrées, omelettes, and sandwiches. They also serve a variety of homemade desserts, and there's a full bar. Personally, I recommend trying the artichoke soup and olallieberry pie. Breakfast, lunch, and dinner daily. ~ 202 Stage Road, Pescadero; 650-879-0464, fax 650-879-9460; www.duartestavern.com. MODERATE.

NIGHTLIFE There's jazz, classical or world music most Sunday afternoons at the **Bach Dancing and Dynamite Society**. Situated beachfront off Route 1 about two miles north of the Route 92 intersection, it's renowned for quality sounds. See website for dates. ~ Miramar Beach, off Medio Road, Half Moon Bay; 650-726-4143, fax 650-726-3134; www.bachddsoc.org, e-mail info@bachddsoc.org.

The **Davenport Roadhouse at the Cash Store Bar** offers a mellow café-like setting. ~ 1 Davenport Avenue, Davenport; 831-426-4122; www.davenportroadhouse.com.

AUTHOR FAVORITE

I find the countrified atmosphere at **Davenport Roadhouse at the Cash Store Restaurant** a perfect match to the hearty, homestyle meals served here. It's decorated with colorful wall rugs, handwoven baskets, and fresh flowers. The cuisine at this eatery ranges from steak and eggs to grilled vegetable panini to gourmet pizzas made in a wood-burning oven. More ordinary fare—such as omelettes, hamburgers, and seafood—is also on the agenda. They also feature dinner specials such as salmon, lamb, and Cornish game hen. Breakfast, lunch, and dinner daily. ~ 1 Davenport Avenue, Davenport; 831-426-8801; www.davenportroad house.com, e-mail info@davenportroadhouse.com. MODERATE TO DELUXE.

GRAY WHALE COVE This white-sand crescent is a well-known clothing-optional beach. Tucked discreetly beneath steep cliffs, it is also a beautiful spot. The undertow is strong, so swimming is not advised. The only facilities are toilets. ~ Located along Route 1 three miles south of Pacifica. Watch for the parking lot on the east side of the highway. Cautiously cross the highway and proceed down the staircase to the beach; 650-726-8819.

MONTARA STATE BEACH Though this half-mile beach may be a haven to nude sunbathers, police controls have been known to pass out tickets. Volleyball players and frisbee throwers can be found everywhere. Backdropped by a rocky bluff, it's a very pretty place. Advanced surfers ride the swells. Visitors can go biking and horseback riding on McNee Ranch on the east side of the highway. The only facilities here are primitive toilets and parking is limited. ~ The beach is located along Route 1 seven miles south of Pacifica. There is a trail leading to the beach from Route 1 and 2nd Street in Montara; 650-726-8820, 800-444-7275, fax 650-726-8816.

JAMES V. FITZGERALD MARINE RESERVE Boasting the best facilities among the beaches in the area, this park also has a sandy beach and excellent tidepools. It's a great place to while away the hours watching crabs, sea urchins, and anemones. Since there are houses nearby, this is more of a family beach than the freewheeling areas to the immediate north and south. And since it is a reserve, there is no collecting of anything (even rocks). There are restrooms and a picnic area. Day-use fee, $6. ~ Off Route 1 in Moss Beach about eight miles south of Pacifica; 650-728-3584.

HALF MOON BAY STATE BEACH (OR FRANCIS BEACH) Despite a four-mile-long sand beach, this park receives only a guarded recommendation. Half Moon Bay is a working harbor, so the beach lacks the seclusion and natural qualities of other strands along the coast. Of course, with civilization so near at hand, the facilities here are more complete than elsewhere. Also, Francis Beach is part of a chain of beaches that you can choose from, including Venice Beach, Roosevelt Beach, and Dunes Beach. Personally, I pick the last. Surfers head to the sandy beach break at Francis Beach and below Half Moon Bay jetty. Restrooms or toilets are available at all four beaches; picnic areas at Francis Beach. No dogs allowed. Day-use fee, $6. ~ All four park segments are located along Route 1 in Half Moon Bay; 650-726-8820, fax 650-726-8816.

▲ There are 50 tent/RV sites (no hookups) and 3 additional tent sites at Francis Beach, available during the summer only; $25 per night. Hiker/biker camp available at Francis; $3 per night. Reservations: 800-444-7275.

HIDDEN ▶ **SAN GREGORIO STATE BEACH** 🚶 🏊 🎣 ⛴ There is a white-sand beach here framed by sedimentary cliffs and cut by a small creek. Star of the show, though, is the nearby private nude beach (admission) north of the state beach, reputedly the first and one of the nicest beaches of its type in California. There are picnic areas and toilets at the state beach, no facilities at the nude beach. Day-use fee, $6. ~ Located along Route 1 about 15 miles south of Half Moon Bay. Entrance to the nude beach is several hundred yards north of the state beach entrance; 650-879-2170, fax 650-879-2172.

Spanish explorer Gaspar de Portolá dropped anchor at San Gregorio in October 1769.

POMPONIO STATE BEACH 🚶 🎣 ⛴ Less appealing than its neighbor to the north, this park has a white-sand beach that's traversed periodically by a creek. There are headlands on either side of the beach. Facilities include picnic areas and toilets. Day-use fee, $6. ~ Route 1, about 16 miles south of Half Moon Bay; 650-879-2170, fax 650-879-2172.

PESCADERO STATE BEACH 🚶 🎣 ⛴ Backed by sand dunes and saltwater marsh, this lovely park also features a wide beach. There are tidepools to the south and a wildlife preserve across the highway. Steelhead run annually in the streams here, while deer, blue herons, and egrets inhabit the nearby marshland. Rangers sometimes lead guided tours (call for availability). There are picnic areas and toilets. ~ Route 1, about 19 miles south of Half Moon Bay; 650-879-2170, fax 650-879-2172.

BEAN HOLLOW STATE BEACH 🚶 🎣 ⛴ The small sandy beach here is bounded by rocks, so sunbathers go elsewhere while tide-pool watchers drop by. Particularly interesting is nearby Pebble Beach, a coarse-grain strand studded with jasper, serpentine, agates, and carnelians. The stones originate from a quartz reef offshore and attract rockhounds by the pack. But don't take rocks away—it's illegal. Also not to be missed is the blufftop trail between Bean Hollow and Pebble Beach, from which you can espy whales and seals in season. Facilities include a picnic area and toilets. ~ Located along Route 1 about 21 miles south of Half Moon Bay; Pebble Beach is about a mile north of Bean Hollow; 650-879-2170, fax 650-879-2172.

BUTANO STATE PARK 🚶 🚴 ⛴ This inland park, several miles from the coast, provides a welcome counterpoint to the beach parks. About 3600 acres, it features a deep redwood forest, including stands of virgin trees. Hiking trails traverse the territory. Not as well known as other nearby redwood parks, Butano suffers less human traffic. The park has picnic areas and rest-rooms. Day-use fee, $6. ~ Located 22 miles south of Half Moon Bay. Coming from the north on Route 1, go 20 miles south of

Half Moon Bay; turn left (east) on Pescadero Road, and then right on Cloverdale Road about four and a half miles to the park. Or, coming from the south, turn right (east) on Gazos Creek Road (two miles south of Pigeon Point Lighthouse) and then left on Cloverdale Road; 650-879-2040.

▲ There are 21 drive-in sites and 18 walk-in sites; $25 per night. Camping by reservation only from Memorial Day to Labor Day: 800-444-7275.

AÑO NUEVO STATE RESERVE 🏃 🏄 🚣 Awesome in its beauty, abundant in wildlife, this park is one of the most spectacular on the California coast. It consists of a peninsula heaped with sand dunes. A miniature island lies just offshore. There is a nature trail for exploring. Seals and sea lions inhabit the area; loons, hawks, pheasants, and albatrosses have been spied here. But most spectacular of all the denizens are the elephant seals, those lovably grotesque creatures who come here between December 15 and March 31 to breed. Back in 1800, elephant seals numbered in the hundreds of thousands; by the end of the century, they were practically extinct; it's only recently that they have achieved a comeback. When breeding, the bulls stage bloody battles and collect large harems, creating a spectacle that draws crowds every year. During breeding season, docents lead two-and-a-half-hour tours that must be booked eight weeks in advance by calling 800-444-4445. The tours cover seal-breeding areas, which otherwise are closed to the public throughout the breeding season; during the rest of the year the entire park and the seal rookery are open. Be forewarned that it's a three-mile roundtrip walk from the parking lot to the rookery. During the summer there are surf breaks off the end of beach, about ten minutes south of the rookery. Also be aware, the elephant seal population makes this beach attractive to sharks. The wildlife protection area is closed the first two weeks of December. The only facilities are toilets. Day-use fee, $6. ~ Off Route 1, about 26 miles south of Half Moon Bay; 650-879-2025, 650-879-0227 (recorded information), fax 650-879-2031; www.anonuevo.org.

GREYHOUND ROCK 🏊 One of the most secluded strands in the area, this beach is a beauty. There are startling cliffs in the background and a gigantic boulder—Greyhound Rock—in the foreground; the area is a favorite among those who love to fish. It is also, unfortunately, a favorite for thieves. Keep your valuables with you and lock your car. Although the beach has good conditions for swimming, it has been known to be "sharky." Restrooms and picnic areas are the only facilities. ~ Located along Route 1 about 30 miles south of Half Moon Bay. From the parking lot at the roadside follow the path down to the beach.

◀ *HIDDEN*

WADDELL BEACH 🏄 is known worldwide as one of *the* spots for windsurfing. With steady, strong northwest winds and good surf, the best windsurfers can launch from the tops of incoming waves, make a full loop and continue on their way. This is not the place for novice windsurfers. Dogs aren't allowed and there are no facilities. ~ Located along Route 1, seven miles north of Davenport; 831-427-2288.

BONNY DOON BEACH 🏊 This spot ranks among the most popular nude beaches in California. Known up and down the coast, the compact beach is protected on either flank by rugged cliffs. There are dunes at the south end of the beach, caves to the north, plus bevies of barebottomed bathers in between. Currents are strong; be careful when swimming. Keep a close eye on your valuables. This beach has no security nor facilities. ~ Off Route 1, about eight miles north of Santa Cruz. Watch for the parking lot near the junction with Bonny Doon Road; follow the path across the railroad tracks and down to the beach.

Santa Cruz

One of California's original missions, a University of California campus, a historic railroad, and some of the finest Victorian neighborhoods on the coast are just a few of the pluses in Santa Cruz. This town of more than 54,000 people is in many respects one big playground. It enjoys spectacular white sand beaches, entertaining nightlife, and an old-style boardwalk amusement park. The city faces south, providing the best weather along the Central Coast. Arts and crafts flourish here, and vintage houses adorn the area.

SIGHTS

Route 1, California's magnificent coastal highway, veers slightly inland upon reaching Santa Cruz, which means it's time to find a different waterfront drive. Not to worry, the best way to begin exploring the place is at the north end of town around **Natural Bridges State Beach**. A pretty spot for a picnic, this is the place to pick up West Cliff Drive, which sweeps the Santa Cruz waterfront. The shoreline is a honeycomb of tiny coves, sea arches, and pocket beaches. From **Lighthouse Point** on a clear day, the entire 40-mile curve of Monterey Bay silhouettes the skyline. Even in foggy weather, sea lions cavort on the rocks offshore, while surfers ride the challenging "Steamer Lane" breaks.

Testament to the surfers' talent is the tiny **Santa Cruz Surfing Museum** situated in the lighthouse at Lighthouse Point. Here vintage photos and antique boards re-create the history of the Hawaiian sport that landed on the shores of Santa Cruz early in the 20th century. Closed Tuesday and Wednesday. ~ 701 West Cliff Drive at Lighthouse Point, Santa Cruz; 831-420-6289; www.santacruzsurfingmuseum.org, e-mail jlthompson@ci.santa-cruz.ca.us.

Beach Street continues this coast-hugging route to **Santa Cruz Municipal Pier**, a half-mile-long wharf lined with bait shops, restaurants, and fishing charters. Those early-morning folks with the sun-furrowed faces are either fishing or crabbing. They are here everyday with lawn chairs and tackle boxes. When reality overcomes optimism, they have been known to duck into nearby fresh fish stores for the day's catch. The pier is a perfect place to promenade, soak up sun, and seek out local color. It also provides a peaceful counterpoint to the next attraction.

Santa Cruz Beach Boardwalk is Northern California's answer to Coney Island. Pride of the city, it dates back to 1907 and sports several old-fashioned rides. The penny arcade features vintage machines as well as modernistic video games. You'll find shooting galleries and candy stalls, coin-operated fortune tellers and do-it-yourself photo machines. Shops sell everything from baubles to bikinis. Then there are the ultimate entertainments: a slow-circling Ferris wheel with chairs suspended high above the beach; the antique merry-go-round, a whirl of mirrors and flashing color; a funicular whose brightly painted cars reflect the sun; rides with names that instantaneously evoke childhood memories—bumper cars, tilt-a-whirl, haunted castle; and that soaring symbol of amusement parks everywhere, the roller coaster. Closed December and most non-summer weekdays. ~ 400 Beach Street; 831-423-5590, fax 831-460-3336; www.beachboardwalk.com.

The Boardwalk's 1911 Loof carousel and the 1924 Giant Dipper roller coaster are both listed as National Historic Landmarks.

The playground for shoppers sits several blocks inland along Pacific Avenue. **Pacific Garden Mall** is a tree-lined promenade that stretches from Cathcart to Water streets. Beautifully executed, the entire mall is a study in urban landscaping and planning. On October 17, 1989, a 7.1 earthquake centered just a few miles from Santa Cruz sent most of the mall tumbling into the street, killing three people.

Within walking distance of the mall are several places that merit short visits. The **Museum of Art & History at the McPherson Center** features changing exhibits that focus primarily on California art. Permanent exhibits relate to the social history of the Santa Cruz area, using photographs and artifacts. Also here is the **Museum Store**, which houses a gift shop for the museum within its century-old, eight-sided structure. Closed Monday. Admission. ~ 705 Front Street; 831-429-1964, fax 831-429-1954; www.santacruzmah.org, e-mail vs@santacruzmah.org.

And the **Santa Cruz Mission**, a half-scale replica of the 1791 structure, pales by comparison with the missions in Carmel and San Juan Bautista. Closed Monday. ~ High Street at Emmet Street in Mission Plaza; 831-426-5686, fax 831-423-1043; e-mail bpedrazzi@sbcglobal.net.

A remarkable piece of restoration, **Santa Cruz Mission State Historic Park** provides a fascinating timeline on California's past. This 1791 adobe home was built for and by the Ohlone and Yocut Indians who sold the property to Californios (children of Spanish settlers). Later part of it was bought by Irish immigrants. Various rooms document each of these periods with artifacts excavated on the site. Reflecting the difficulties of early-19th-century interior design, the Californio Room is decorated with mismatched wallpaper that was sent at different times from the East Coast. Touring is self-guided, but guided tours are available by appointment. Special events including cooking demonstrations, candlemaking, and brick-making take place occasionally, as does American Indian storytelling (call for dates). Closed Monday through Wednesday. ~ 144 School Street near Mission Plaza; 831-425-5849, fax 831-429-2870.

The **Santa Cruz County Conference and Visitors Council** has information to help orient you with the area. ~ 1211 Ocean Street; 831-425-1234, 800-833-3494; www.santacruz.org, e-mail comments@santacruz.org.

Santa Cruz's rich history has left a legacy of elegant **Victorian houses**. Although there are no guided tours, if you set out on your own you won't be disappointed. In the Beach Hill area, not far from the Boardwalk, be sure to see the gem-like home at **1005 3rd Street**, counterpoint to the multilevel confection with Queen Anne turret at **311 Main Street**. Near Pacific Garden Mall is the Civil War–era **Calvary Episcopal Church**, with its clapboard siding and shingle roof. ~ 532 Center Street. The **200 block of Walnut Avenue** is practically wall-to-wall Victorians. Located near the Santa Cruz Mission is the white-painted brick **Holy Cross Roman Catholic Church**. The steeple of this 1889 Gothic Revival beauty is a landmark for miles around. ~ 126 High Street. Nearby **Francisco Alviza House**, vintage 1850s, is the oldest home in town. ~ 109 Sylvar Street. Around the corner, the **200 block of Mission Street** displays several houses built shortly afterwards. Nearby is **W. W. Reynolds House**, which was an Episcopal Church in 1850. ~ 123 Green Street.

From this last Victorian cluster, High Street leads to the **University of California–Santa Cruz** campus. Turn right at Glenn Coolidge Drive and you'll find an information booth dispensing maps, brochures, and words of wisdom. Those stone ruins and sunbleached buildings nearby are the remains of the old Cowell ranch and limestone quarry from which 2000 of the campus acres were drawn. ~ 1156 High Street; 831-459-0111; www.ucsc.edu.

No ivory tower ever enjoyed the view that UC Santa Cruz commands of Monterey Bay. Set on a hillside, with redwood forest and range land all around, the campus possesses incredible beauty. The university itself is divided into eight colleges, insular

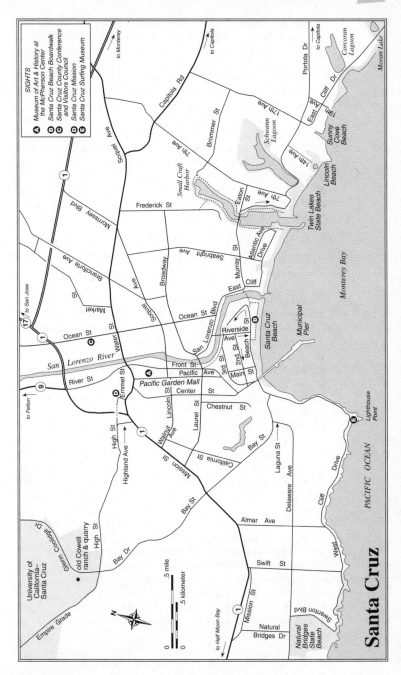

SIGHTS
- Ⓐ Museum of Art & History at the McPherson Center
- Ⓑ Santa Cruz Beach Boardwalk
- Ⓒ Santa Cruz County Conference and Visitors Council
- Ⓓ Santa Cruz Mission
- Ⓔ Santa Cruz Surfing Museum

Santa Cruz

PACIFIC OCEAN

Monterey Bay

University of California–Santa Cruz

old Cowell ranch & quarry

to Half Moon Bay

Natural Bridges State Beach

Lighthouse Point

Municipal Pier

Santa Cruz Beach

Pacific Garden Mall

San Lorenzo River

to Felton

to San Jose

to Monterey

to Capitola

Corcoran Lagoon

Moran Lake

Sunny Cove Beach

Lincoln Beach

Twin Lakes State Beach

Schwann Lagoon

Small Craft Harbor

.5 mile

.5 kilometer

and self-defined, each marked by a different architectural style. The best way to see this campus is simply to wander: Walk the fields, trek its redwood groves, and explore the different colleges that make it one of the West's most progressive institutions. Of particular interest at UC Santa Cruz are the organic farm as well as the arboretum, with its Mediterranean garden and outstanding collection of Australian and South African plants.

The **Seymour Marine Discovery Center** is located at the Joseph M. Long Marine Laboratory, a University of California research facility. Part museum, part working lab, the center is dedicated to teaching the public about the role of research in ocean conservation and features hands-on displays, working aquarium exhibits, and a family-friendly touch tank. The 87-foot blue whale skeleton (the largest on display in the world) is a highlight. There are several tours daily. Closed Monday. Admission. ~ End of Delaware Avenue; 831-459-3800; seymourcenter.ucsc.edu.

LODGING   When seeking overnight accommodations in Santa Cruz, the place to look is near the beach. That is where you'll want to be and, not surprisingly, where you'll find most hotels and motels. The problem during summer months is the cost. In winter you can have a room for a song, but come June the price tags climb.

An excellent facility is **Ocean Echo Motel and Cottages**, located near a quiet neighborhood beach. This 15-unit clapboard complex sits far from the madding Boardwalk crowd right on the beach. It represents a perfect choice for anyone seeking a studio or Cape Cod–style cottage. Some have kitchens and private patios. Weekly rentals are sometimes available. On weekends there's a two-night minimum. ~ 401 Johans Beach Drive; 831-462-4192, fax 831-462-0658; www.oceanecho.com, e-mail beach@ocean echo.com. MODERATE TO ULTRA-DELUXE.

It's big, brash, and blocky, but the **Coast Santa Cruz Hotel** is also right on the beach. With pool, jacuzzi, oceanfront restaurants, and lounge, this multitiered establishment extends from a hilltop

BEACH BARGAIN

The best bargain in town is **Surfside Apartments**. This seven-unit establishment contains several cottages and houses clustered around a flower garden and courtyard. They are truly efficiency units: no telephone, parking facilities, or housekeeping services. But they are comfortably furnished, possess a friendly "beach cottage" feel, feature kitchens. Located two blocks from the Boardwalk, there are one- and two-bedroom apartments. They are only available from late June through Labor Day. ~ 311 Cliff Street; 831-423-5302. MODERATE.

perch down to a sandy strand. Long on aesthetics it isn't, and it's sometimes noisy on weekends and in the summer, but for location it can't be topped. The boardwalk and fishing pier are a short stroll away. Each of the 163 guest rooms are trimly done with fabric walls and contemporary furnishings; each sports a private balcony and ocean view. The question is whether you'll endure the plastic atmosphere for the sake of proximity to the Pacific. It's your call. (Being lazy myself, I'd book reservations in a minute.) ~ 175 West Cliff Drive; 831-426-4330, 800-663-1144, fax 831-427-2025; www.coasthotels.com. DELUXE TO ULTRA-DELUXE.

Country inns are rare in Santa Cruz; this California custom is slowly catching on here. One exception is **Cliff Crest Bed & Breakfast Inn**, a five-bedroom establishment in a historic 1887 Victorian home with additional accommodations in an 1878 carriage house. Among the features of the house are a belvedere, a yard landscaped by the designer of San Francisco's Golden Gate Park, and a solarium illuminated through stained-glass windows. Rooms vary in cost from a small room with private bath to the spacious "Rose Room," which has a fireplace. In any case, the decor you're apt to find includes patterned wallpaper and four-poster beds in each room. ~ 407 Cliff Street; 831-427-2609, fax 831-427-2710; www.cliffcrestinn.com, e-mail info@cliffcrestinn. com. DELUXE.

There is also **Hostelling International—Santa Cruz**, located two blocks from the beach. Set in restored Victorian cottages on well-located Beach Hill, it offers 44 dorm-style beds, two private family rooms and one private couple's room. The cottages are two blocks from the beach and boardwalk. There are also hot showers, a kitchen, a dining area, internet access, and a common room; all linen provided free of charge. There is an 11 p.m. curfew and in summer a three-night maximum stay. Non-members pay $3 more. ~ 321 Main Street; 831-423-8304, 888-464-4872; www.hi-santacruz.org, e-mail info@hi-santacruz.org. BUDGET.

Less distinguished, but considerably cheaper, is **Harbor Inn** across town. The place sits in a two-story stucco house in a semi-residential neighborhood a couple blocks from the beach. It supports 19 bedrooms, all with refrigerators and microwaves. There are both private and shared baths. All are spacious, attractive, and inexpensively furnished. The staff is helpful and friendly, making this place a fortuitous addition to the local housing scene. ~ 645 7th Avenue; 831-479-9731, fax 831-479-1067; www.harborinn santacruz.com. BUDGET TO MODERATE.

Santa Cruz also has a string of neon motels within blocks of the Boardwalk. Count on them to provide small rooms with color television, wall-to-wall carpeting, nicked wooden tables, naugahyde chairs, stall showers, etc.; if they have any decorations at all you'll wish they didn't. But what the hell, for a night or two you can call them home. Their rates fluctuate wildly depending on the season and tourist flow. (Generally they charge budget prices in winter; summer prices escalate to the moderate range.) A solid choice is the **Beachview Inn**. Half a block from the Boardwalk and wharf, the motel has ocean views and a complimentary breakfast bar. ~ 50 Front Street, Santa Cruz; 831-426-3575, 800-946-0614; www.beach-viewinn.com, e-mail beachview inn@yahoo.com. BUDGET.

Located within walking distance of the beach is **Big 6 Motel**. It sits in a two-story stucco building and contains 21 rooms with private baths. ~ 335 Riverside Avenue; 831-423-1651. BUDGET TO MODERATE.

Right next door is the **Super 8 Motel**, which has 24 rooms decorated in a white and burgundy color scheme. Guests here enjoy lounging at the pool or soaking in the spa. Continental breakfast is included. ~ 338 Riverside Avenue; 831-426-3707, 800-800-8000, fax 831-426-0547. MODERATE.

DINING

Most Santa Cruz restaurants can be found near the Boardwalk or in the downtown area, with a few others scattered around town. Of course, along the Boardwalk the favorite dining style is to eat while you stroll. Stop at **Surf City Grill** for a corn dog, Italian sausage sandwich, or fried zucchini; sit down to a bowl of clam chowder or crab salad at the **Fisherman's Galley**; or pause at the **Barbary Coast** for cheeseburgers, baked potatoes, or "chicken nuggets." For dessert there are caramel apples, ice cream, cotton candy, popcorn, and saltwater taffy.

If all this proves a bit much, try one of the budget restaurants on Beach Street, across from the Boardwalk. Foremost is **Beach Street Café**, which houses the largest U.S. collection of Maxfield Parrish limited-edition prints. Breakfast begins with guacamole omelettes, bagels, croissants, or pancakes. Matter of fact, breakfast continues until late afternoon. Try the "Eggs Sardou" (artichoke bottoms with spinach, poached eggs, and hollandaise sauce) or the "Eggs Beach Street" (for which they replace the spinach with sautéed shrimp). The "mile-high" burgers are worth trying to get your teeth around. No dinner. ~ 399 Beach Street; 831-426-7621, fax 831-476-0654; www.beachstreetcafe.com. MODERATE.

Nearby **El Paisano Tamales** has the standard selection of tacos, tostadas, enchiladas, and burritos. Closed Monday and Tuesday and from January to mid-February. ~ 605 Beach Street; 831-426-2382. BUDGET.

Ideal Bar and Grill is a tourist trap with tradition. It's been one since 1917. It also has decent food (breakfast, lunch, and dinner), and a knockout view, especially from the outdoor deck right on the sand. The place is wedged in a corner between the beach and the pier, which means it looks out on everything, from boardwalk to bounding deep. The specialty is seafood—calamari, oysters, lobster, and salmon. Several pastas, plus a few meat and fowl dishes, round out the menu. ~ 106 Beach Street; 831-423-5271, fax 831-423-3827; www.idealbarandgrill.com, e-mail idealbar@aol.com. MODERATE.

Cozy **Casablanca Restaurant**, with its overhead fans and Moroccan flair, is an excellent dinner choice. The place has a wrap-around view of the ocean, not to mention a tony decor. The menu includes such gourmet selections as seared chicken with tarragon, sauteed prawns over capellini, and filet mignon with forest mushroom demi-glace. Casablanca boasts one of the largest selections of wines in Santa Cruz County. Dinner only. ~ 101 Main Street; 831-423-1570, fax 831-423-0235; www. casablanca-santacruz.com, e-mail casabeach@aol.com. DELUXE.

Among the many places in the Pacific Garden Mall area, my personal favorite is **The Catalyst**. I don't go there so much to eat   ◄ HIDDEN
as to watch. Not that the food is bad, it's just that The Catalyst is a scene. At night the place transmogrifies into a club with live music and unfathomable vibrations. By day, it's just itself, a cavernous structure with a glass roof and enough plants to make it an oversized greenhouse. Indeed, some of the clientele seem to have taken root. There are two bars if you're here to people watch. ~ 1011 Pacific Avenue; 831-423-1338, fax 831-429-4135; www.catalystclub.com. BUDGET.

For Japanese food there's **Benten**, a comfortable restaurant complete with a sushi bar. They serve an array of traditional dishes including sashimi, tempura, teriyaki, and a special plate called *kaki* fry (deep-fried breaded oysters). Understated and reliable. Closed Tuesday. ~ 1541 Pacific Avenue, Suite B; 831-425-7079. MODERATE TO DELUXE.

AUTHOR FAVORITE

I often join the locals at their favorite Mexican restaurant, **El Palomar**, named the best Mexican restaurant by the readers of *Good Times*, a local entertainment newspaper, for several years running. This leafy Mexican cantina is housed in a beautiful 1930s hotel and sports soaring ceilings and a giant mural of a Mexican woman cooking outdoors. El Palomar serves up such Mexican seafood dishes as prawn burritos and the Jose special—grilled skirt steak, snapper, and prawns. Homemade tortillas and specialty margaritas enhance the delicious fare. ~ 1336 Pacific Avenue; 831-425-7575, fax 831-423-3037; www.elpalomar restaurant.com, e-mail elpalomarrestaurant@msn.com. BUDGET TO DELUXE.

Aldo's Harbor Restaurant, a café with patio deck overlooking Santa Cruz Harbor, whips up seafood dishes, pastas, soups, salads, and sandwiches. Conveniently located near Seabright Beach, this unassuming little place serves fresh seafood and home-baked breads. No dinner on Sunday. ~ 616 Atlantic Avenue; 831-426-3736, fax 831-426-1362; www.aldos-cruz.com. BUDGET TO MODERATE.

Due to the lack of lodging facilities in the early 20th century, visitors to Santa Cruz stayed in Tent City, where the accommodations consisted of striped tents on wooden frames, with wood floors, lights, and running water.

Opa! For Greek food and fun hit up **Vasili's Greek Taverna.** It's a quirky place where the walls are chockablock with trinkets and the kebabs are great. Patrons like the flaming cheese appetizer, especially when the owner comes over and lights the dish up. Closed Monday. ~ 1501 Mission Street, Suite A; 831-458-9808. MODERATE.

SHOPPING   The central shopping district in Santa Cruz is along Pacific Garden Mall, a six-block strip of Pacific Avenue converted to a promenade. The section is neatly landscaped with flowering shrubs and potted trees and its sidewalks, widened for window browsers, overflow with people.

You can stop by **Artisans Gallery,** which deals in fine handcrafts and gift items by local artists. They feature outstanding pottery, woodwork, glassware, and jewelry. ~ 1368 Pacific Avenue; 831-423-8183. The **Bookshop Santa Cruz** is the finest among this college town's many wonderful bookstores. ~ 1520 Pacific Avenue; 831-423-0900; www.bookshopsantacruz.com.

Strolling along **Pacific Avenue,** you will find galleries, gift stores, plus arts-and-crafts shops run by local artists.

NIGHTLIFE   In Santa Cruz, **The Catalyst** is the common denominator. A popular restaurant and hangout by day, it becomes an entertainment spot at night. There's live music most weekday evenings in the Atrium, where local groups perform. But on weekends the heavyweights swing into town and The Catalyst lines up big rock performers. Some all-ages shows. Cover charge for live bands. ~ 1011 Pacific Avenue; 831-423-1336, fax 831-423-7853; www.catalystclub.com.

The unassuming **Kuumbwa Jazz Center** headlines top-name musicians Monday, Thursday, Friday, and Saturday nights. All ages are welcome here. Cover. ~ 320 Cedar Street; 831-427-2227; www.kuumbwajazz.org.

Coastline Brewery is a funky spot in an old repair shop. Relax on a couch and soak up the nightly local bands while sipping a pint of beer. Occasional cover. ~ 120 Union Street; 831-459-9876.

The **Crow's Nest** offers eclectic entertainment with an ocean view. On any given night they will be headlining jazz, reggae, salsa, rock, blues, or, on Sunday night, comedy. Cover. ~ 2218 East Cliff Drive; 831-476-4560; www.crowsnest-santacruz.com.

The crowd at **Blue Lagoon** dances to live hip-hop, house, and deejay music during the week, and watches go-go dancers on goth night (Friday) in summer. ~ 923 Pacific Avenue; 831-423-7117; www.thebluelagoon.com.

NATURAL BRIDGES STATE BEACH Northernmost of the Santa Cruz beaches, Natural Bridges is a small park with a halfmoon-shaped beach and tidepools. All but one of the sea arches here have collapsed, leading local wags to dub the spot "Fallen Arches." This is a popular windsurfing spot in the summer. It's quite pretty, though a row of houses flanks one side. In the winter, surfers gather on the reef break. This is also an excellent spot to watch monarch butterflies during their annual winter migration (from October to late February). During these months there are weekend guided tours of the eucalyptus groves. Facilities include picnic areas, a visitors center, a bookstore, restrooms, and wi-fi access. No dogs are allowed on the beach. The visitor center is closed Monday and Tuesday in summer. Day-use fee, $6. ~ Located at the end of West Cliff Drive near the western edge of Santa Cruz; 831-423-4609.

SANTA CRUZ BEACH Of the three major beaches extending along the Santa Cruz waterfront, this is the most popular, most crowded, and most famous. All for a very simple reason: the Santa Cruz Boardwalk, with its amusement park and restaurants, runs the length of the sand, and the Santa Cruz Municipal Pier anchors one end of the beach. This, then, is the place to come for crowds and excitement. "Steamer Lane" is the Santa Cruz surfing hotspot. A series of reef breaks are located along West Cliff Drive, extending west to Lighthouse Point. Facilities include restrooms, showers, seasonal lifeguard, volleyball, restaurants, and groceries. ~ Located along Beach Street; access from the Municipal Wharf and along the Boardwalk.

SEABRIGHT BEACH Also known as Castle Beach, Seabright is second in Santa Cruz's string of beaches. This beauty extends from the San Lorenzo River mouth to the jetty at Santa Cruz Harbor. It's long, wide, and backdropped by bluffs. The views are as magnificent as from other nearby beaches, and the crowds will be lighter than along the Boardwalk. There are restrooms, fire rings, and a lifeguard in summer. ~ Access to the beach is along East Cliff Drive at Mott Avenue, or at the end of 3rd Avenue; 831-429-2850, fax 831-475-8350.

TWIN LAKES STATE BEACH 🏃 🏊 🛶 🚣 ⚓ Just the other side of Santa Cruz Harbor is this odd-shaped beach. Smaller than the two beaches to the north, it is also less crowded. The park is 94 acres, with a lagoon behind the beach and a jetty flanking one side. A very pretty spot. Surfing is sometimes okay in winter or after a storm. There are restrooms and lifeguards during the summer. ~ At East Cliff Drive and 7th Avenue, south of Santa Cruz Harbor; 831-429-2850, fax 831-475-8350.

LINCOLN BEACH, SUNNY COVE, MORAN LAKE BEACH Located along the eastern end of Santa Cruz, these three sandy beaches are in residential areas. As a result, they draw local people, not tourists, and they're more difficult to get to. All are backdropped by bluffs. There are restrooms and picnic areas at Lincoln Beach and Moran Lake Beach; otherwise amenities are scarce. Parking is a problem throughout the area (though Moran Lake Beach has a parking lot where you can park all day for a fee during summer and weekends, otherwise free). ~ All three beaches are near East Cliff Drive. Blacks Beach (part of Twin Lakes State Beach) is at the end of 14th Avenue, Sunny Cove at the end of 17th Avenue, and Moran Lake Beach is near Lake Avenue.

▼▼▼▼▼▼▼▼▼▼▼▼▼▼▼
Santa Cruz to Monterey

From Santa Cruz, coastal Route 1 heads south through Capitola, known for its sparkling beach and September Begonia Festival, and through Aptos, another bedroom community with equally pretty beaches.

SIGHTS

Aptos' most popular place these days is a foreboding forest located at latitude 37° 2' and longitude 121° 53'. That precise spot, at the end of a two-mile trail in the Forest of Nisene Marks State Park, is the **1989 earthquake epicenter.** A stake now marks ground zero of the 7.1 shaker that devastated Northern California. To reach the trailhead, follow Aptos Creek Road north from Aptos to the Nisene Marks parking lot. Admission. ~ 831-763-7063.

HIDDEN ▶

In nearby Rio del Mar, there's a **rural side trip** that carries you past miles of farmland before rejoining Route 1 near Watsonville. To take this side trip follow San Andreas Road, which tunnels through forest, then opens into rich agricultural acres. Intricately tilled fields roll down to the sea and edge up to the foot of the mountains. At the end of San Andreas Road, follow Beach Street to the ocean. The entire stretch of coastline is flanked by high sand dunes, a wild and exotic counterpoint to the furrowed fields nearby.

Beach Street leads back into **Watsonville.** Central to the surrounding farm community, Watsonville is the world's strawberry-growing capital. It's also rich in **Victorian houses** and a population of birds so diverse that the **Chamber of Commerce** hosts an annual Birding Festival, in addition to offering maps and guides year-round. Closed weekends. ~ 449 Union Street, Watsonville; 831-724-3900, fax 831-728-5300; www.pajarovalleychamber. com, e-mail info@pajarovalleychamber.com.

Back on Route 1, you'll pass **Moss Landing**, a weather-beaten fishing harbor. With its antique stores, an old bridge, bright-painted boats, and unpainted fish market, the town has a warm personality. There is one eyesore, however, a huge power plant

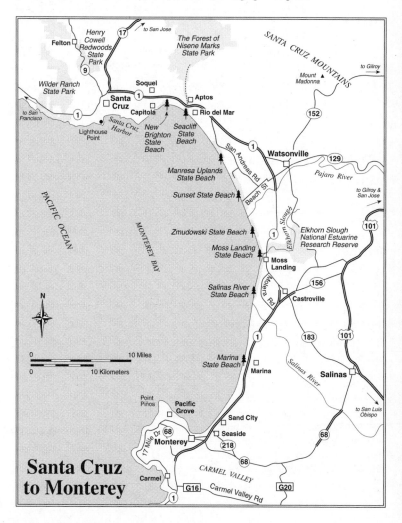

Santa Cruz to Monterey

with twin smokestacks that stand out like two sentinels of an occupying army. Otherwise the place is enchanting.

HIDDEN ▶   Nearby, **Elkhorn Slough National Estuarine Research
Reserve** is a 1400-acre world of salt marshes and tidal flats managed by a state and federal partnership between the California
Department of Fish and Game and the National Oceanic and
Atmospheric Administration. Within this delicate environment
live some 400 species of invertebrates, 80 species of fish, and 300
species of birds (among them great blue heron, great egret, and
acorn woodpeckers), as well as harbor seals. Guided tours on the
weekend. To get to the visitors center from Route 1, follow
Dolan Road for three miles, go left on Elkhorn Road, and then
proceed two more miles. Closed Monday and Tuesday. Admission. ~ 1700 Elkhorn Road, Watsonville; 831-728-2822; www.
elkhornslough.org, e-mail info@elkhornslough.org.

Next in this parade of small towns is **Castroville**, "Artichoke
Center of the World." Beyond it is a cluster of towns—Marina,
Sand City, and Seaside—that probably represent the sand capi-
tals of the world. The entire area rests on a sand dune that measures up to 300 feet in depth, and extends ten miles along the
coast and as much as eight miles inland. From here you can trace
a course into Monterey along wind-tilled rows of sand.

In Salinas, the **Steinbeck House** in which author John Stein-
beck grew up is located a few blocks from the National Steinbeck
Center. It now serves as a gift shop and restaurant, open for lunch
Tuesday through Saturday. Reservations are recommended. ~ 132
Central Avenue, Salinas; 831-424-2735, fax 831-757-5806;
www.steinbeckhouse.com, e-mail steinbeckhouse@sbcglobal.net.
MODERATE.

John Steinbeck's grave is in the Garden of Memories cemetery. ~ 768 Abbot Street, Salinas.

❖❖❖

FOR THE LOVE OF STEINBECK

The **National Steinbeck Center Museum**, located in the heart of
Oldtown Salinas (the historic downtown district), houses photographic, multimedia, and interactive exhibits about the life and work of Salinas-born author John Steinbeck, as well as a wing on the agricultural history of the region. It also contains a research archive of more than 45,000 manuscripts,
first editions, newspaper and magazine articles, photographs, and other
artifacts. The museum displays rotating art exhibits. There's also a store
offering books, artwork, and apparel. Admission. ~ 1 Main Street, Salinas
(eight miles southeast of Route 1 via Route 183); 831-775-4721, fax
831-796-3828; www.steinbeck.org, e-mail info@steinbeck.org.

Capitola Venetian Hotel is a mock Italian complex next to Capitola Beach. With its stucco and red tile veneer, ornamental molding, and carved wooden doors, it's a poor cousin to the grand villas of Venice. The 19 guest rooms come equipped with kitchens. There are few wall decorations and the furnishings lack character, but the atmosphere is pleasant. Two-night minimum on weekend. ~ 1500 Wharf Road, Capitola; 831-476-6471, 800-332-2780, fax 831-475-3897; www.capitolavenetian.com, e-mail information@capitolavenetian.com. MODERATE TO ULTRA-DELUXE.

Harbor Lights Motel, a few steps farther uphill from the beach, is similarly laid out but in a more modern fashion. This ten-unit stucco building has rooms with completely equipped kitchens and ocean views. The views of Monterey Bay are the real draw here. ~ 5000 Cliff Drive, Capitola; 831-476-0505, fax 831-476-0235; www.harborlightsmotel.net, e-mail info@harborlightsmotel.net. MODERATE TO ULTRA-DELUXE.

Does a trip around the world interest you? If so, the **Inn at Depot Hill** might save you time and money without sacrificing the feel of the trip. This 12-room bed and breakfast, fashioned from a former train station, features internationally decorated rooms with names like "Paris," "Côte d'Azur," and "Portofino." There is a fireplace in each room and some come with a patio and hot tub. Full breakfast, hors d'oeuvres with wine, and dessert are included with a night's stay. ~ 250 Monterey Avenue, Capitola; 831-462-3376, 800-572-2632, fax 831-462-3697; www.innsbythesea.com, e-mail depothill@innsbythesea.com. ULTRA-DELUXE.

Seascape Resort is the place to go for a complete indulgence. It has 285 suites and villas with full kitchens, fireplaces, wi-fi access, and HDTV. Amenities include in-room massage, a deluxe fitness center, a swim center with children's pool, sand volleyball, bocce ball and tennis courts, a golf course, and a pro shop. ~ Seascape Resort Drive, Aptos; 800-929-7727; www.seascaperesort.com, e-mail info@seascaperesort.com. ULTRA-DELUXE.

With two miles of beachfront, **Pajaro Dunes** is ideal for those who want to go down to the sea. Located midway between Santa Cruz and Monterey, this resort colony has 140 condominiums, townhouses, and beachhomes that range from one to five bedrooms. While decorating schemes vary from beach contemporary to brass and glass, all units offer kitchens, fireplaces, decks, and barbecues. There are 19 on-site tennis courts. The big units are a good bet for large family groups. Two-night minimum stay is required for houses. ~ 2661 Beach Road, Watsonville; 831-728-7400, 800-564-1771; www.pajarodunes.com, e-mail info@pajarodunes.com. ULTRA-DELUXE.

Built in 1906 for the Pacific Coast Steamship Company, **Captain's Inn** has done a wonderful job of retaining its heritage. The ten guest rooms—divided between the main Steamship Company building and the accompanying waterfront boathouse—are decorated with nautical antiques and include private baths, high-speed internet, and king- or queen-sized beds, complete with feather pillows. Nature lovers will also be thrilled: the surrounding area is populated with seals, coastal birds, and the occasional surfacing whale. ~ P.O. Box 570, Moss Landing Road, Moss Landing; 831-633-5550; www.captainsinn.com, e-mail res@captainsinn.com. MODERATE TO ULTRA-DELUXE.

DINING

The area's foremost dining room is actually outside Santa Cruz in a nearby suburb. True to its name, the multitiered **Shadowbrook Restaurant**, in operation since 1947, sits in a wooded spot through which a creek flows. Food is almost an afterthought at this elaborate affair; upon entering the grounds you descend either via a funicular or a sinuous, fern-draped path. Once inside, you'll encounter a labyrinth of dining levels and rooms, luxuriously decorated with potted plants, stone fireplaces, and candlelit tables. A mature tree grows through the floor and ceiling of one room here; in others, vines climb along the walls. When you finally chart the course to a table, you'll be offered a menu including prime rib, salmon, and other fresh seafood dishes. Definitely a dining experience. Live music on Saturday night. No lunch on Saturday. ~ 1750 Wharf Road, Capitola; 831-475-1511, 800-975-1511, fax 831-475-7764; www.shadowbrook-capitola.com, e-mail office@ shadowbrook-capitola.com. MODERATE TO DELUXE.

Capitola Beach is wall-to-wall with seafood restaurants. They line the strand, each with a different decorative theme but all seeming to merge into a collection of pit stops for hungry beachgoers. If you're expecting me to recommend one you are asking more than mortal man can do. I say when in doubt, guess.

Touted as the best Mexican restaurant in Monterey County is **The Whole Enchilada**, specializing in seafood dishes. The chef uses locally grown produce like Castroville artichokes and chiles, fresh fish, prawns, and oysters. Try the "whole enchilada" entrée—fillet of red snapper wrapped in corn tortillas topped with melted cheese and chile salsa. Save room for flan! ~ Route 1 at Moss Landing Road, Moss Landing; 831-633-3038, fax 831-633-5391; www.wenchilada.com, e-mail eat@wenchilada.com. BUDGET TO MODERATE.

Next door is the **Lighthouse Harbor and Grill**, offering early breakfast (they open at 5:30 a.m. on weekdays) and lunch. Mexican dishes are available, but more standard fare such as omelettes dominate the menu. There are even whole wheat hotcakes. ~ 7902 Route 1, Suite C, Moss Landing; 831-633-3858. BUDGET.

Located along Route 1 south of Santa Cruz, the coastal village **SHOPPING**
of Moss Landing is a must for antique hounds. More than 20
shops offer a wide array of treasures from the good old days.
Clustered around the intersection of Moss Landing Road and
Sandholdt Road are several shops that warrant a close look.

For furniture, nautical instruments, glass, and lamps, check
out **Waterfront Antiques**. ~ 7902 Sandholdt Road, Moss
Landing; 831-633-1112; www.waterfrontantiques.com. To peruse a bit of everything, stop by **The Little Red Barn**. ~ 8461
Moss Landing Road, Moss Landing; 831-578-2198.

For a relaxing evening, try **Shadowbrook Restaurant**. Its soft **NIGHTLIFE**
lighting and luxurious surroundings create a sense of well-being,
like brandy and a blazing fire. They present live music Saturday
nights in their Rockroom Lounge. ~ 1750 Wharf Road, Capitola; 831-475-1511; www.shadowbrook-capitola.com.

Several of the restaurant lounges lining Capitola's waterfront
have nightly entertainment. Over at **Zelda's** you can enjoy a
quick drink on the patio, and live music on Thursday, Friday,
and Saturday nights. ~ 203 Esplanade, Capitola; 831-475-4900.

CAPITOLA CITY BEACH 🐚 🎣 🏄 🚣 🚤 ⚓ Sedimentary **BEACHES**
cliffs flank a corner of this sand carpet but the rest is heavily de- **& PARKS**
veloped. Popular with visitors for decades, Capitola is a well-
known resort community. Seafood restaurants line its shore and
boutiques flourish within blocks of the beach. A great place for
families because of the adjacent facilities, it trades seclusion for
service. The ocean is well protected for water

sports and in winter, surfers enjoy the breaks near   Following a year of heavy
the jetty, pier, and river mouth. There are restrooms,   storms, the beach at
showers, lifeguards, a fishing pier, and volleyball. ~   Capitola City Beach
Located in the center of Capitola; 831-475-6522, fax   often disappears
831-475-6530.   under the high
                                                             tide.
NEW BRIGHTON STATE BEACH 🐚 🎣 ⚓ This sandy
crescent adjoins Seacliff Beach and enjoys a wide vista of
Monterey Bay. Headlands protect the beach for swimmers
and beginning surfers. Clamming is also popular. Within its mere
94 acres, the park contains a forested bluff. There are picnic
areas, fire pits, restrooms, and showers (for campers only).
Day-use fee, $6. ~ Off Route 1 in Capitola, four miles south of
Santa Cruz; 831-464-6330, 831-464-6329, fax 831-685-6443.

▲ There are 88 tent/RV sites (limited hookups) in a wooded
area inland from the beach; $25 to $35 per night. There are no
RV hookups. Reservations are required (people book up to seven
months in advance): 800-444-7275.

SEACLIFF STATE BEACH 🐚 🎣 🏄 ⚓ This two-mile strand is
very popular. *Too* popular: During summer, RVs park along its

entire length and crowds gather on the waterfront. That's because it provides the safest swimming along this section of coast. There are roving lifeguards on duty during the summer and a protective headland nearby. The visitors center offers guided walks year-round to look at fossils. The beach also sports a pier favored by anglers, but because of storm damage is closed. It's a pretty place, but oh so busy. There are picnic areas, restrooms, and showers. Day-use fee, $6. ~ Off Route 1 in Aptos, five miles south of Santa Cruz; 831-685-6442, fax 831-685-6443.

▲ There are 26 sites for RVs and self-contained vehicles (full hookups); $39 per night. There are also 2 overflow sites for self-contained vehicles (no picnic tables, fireplaces, or hookups); $30 per night. Reservations are required: 800-444-7275.

THE FOREST OF NISENE MARKS STATE PARK 🚶 🚲 This semi-wilderness expanse, several miles inland, encompasses over 10,000 acres. Within its domain are redwood groves, meandering streams, rolling countryside, and dense forest. About 30 miles of hiking trails wind through the preserve. Along them you can explore fossil beds, deserted logger cabins, old trestles, and railroad beds; you can also hike to the epicenter of the 1989 earthquake. The park is a welcome complement to the natural features along the coast. There are picnic tables and barbecues. Day-use fee, $6. ~ From Route 1 southbound take the Seacliff Beach exit in Aptos, five miles south of Santa Cruz. Take an immediate left on State Park Drive, pass over the highway, and then go right on Soquel Drive. Follow this for a half-mile; then head left on Aptos Creek Road. This paved road turns to gravel as it leads into the forest; 831-763-7063, fax 831-763-7120.

Remember the 1989 San Francisco quake? Well, it was actually centered in The Forest of Nisene Marks State Park; curious visitors can hike to the temblor's epicenter.

▲ There are 6 primitive sites; $5 per person per night. Reservations required: 831-763-7073.

MANRESA UPLANDS STATE BEACH 🏊 🚶 ⛵ Here you'll find a strip of white sand bookended by blufftop homes. Popular with surfers, it provides a sweeping view of Monterey Bay. A bit more removed than other nearby beaches, Manresa nevertheless can be quite popular on summer afternoons. Facilities include restrooms, lifeguards (in summer), picnic tables, and, for campers, fire pits and showers. Closed October through March. Day-use fee, $6. ~ Located 13 miles south of Santa Cruz; from Route 1, take the Larkin Valley Road and San Andreas Road exit, turn right onto San Andreas Road and follow it several miles to the park turnoff; 831-763-7064.

▲ There are 64 walk-in tent sites in Manresa Uplands Campground next to the beach; $25 per night. Reservations: 800-444-7275.

SUNSET STATE BEACH 🏊 🚶 🚣 Over three miles of beach and sand dunes create one of the area's prettiest parks. There are bluffs and meadows behind the beach as well as Monterey pines and cypress trees. This 324-acre park is a popular spot for fishing. Surfers also come here. But remember, there's more fog here and farther south than in the Santa Cruz area. There are picnic areas, restrooms, and showers. Day-use fee, $6. ~ Located 16 miles south of Santa Cruz; from Route 1, take the Larkin Valley and San Andreas Road exit, turn right onto San Andreas Road and follow it several miles to the park turnoff; 831-763-7063, fax 831-763-7120.

▲ Permitted in 91 sites (no RV hookups), $25 per night; hiker/biker camp available, $5 per person. Reservations: 800-444-7275.

ZMUDOWSKI, MOSS LANDING, AND SALINAS RIVER STATE BEACHES 🚶 🐎 🚶 🚴 🚣 🚣 🚣 These three state parks are part of a long stretch of sand dunes. They all contain broad beaches and vistas along Monterey Bay. Though relatively uncrowded, their proximity to Moss Landing's smoke-belching power plant is a severe drawback. Quite suitable anywhere else, they can't compete with their neighbors in this land of beautiful beaches. Surfing is good near the sandbar at Salinas River; great at Moss Landing, which draws locals from Santa Cruz. Each beach has portable toilets. ~ All three are located off Route 1 within a few miles of Moss Landing; 831-649-2836.

MARINA STATE BEACH 🚶 🏊 🚶 🚣 The tall, fluffy sand dunes at this 170-acre park are unreal. They're part of a giant dune covering 50 square miles throughout the area. A half-buried boardwalk takes you through the sand to the beach and gives you an up-close view of the unique vegetation. There are marvelous views of Monterey here, plus a chance to fish or sunbathe. It is also the perfect place to try out hang gliding. Swimming is allowed, though rip tides do occur. Regarding surfing, there's a great beach break in summer but it's dangerous in winter. There are restrooms and limited picnic areas. ~ Located along Route 1, nine miles north of Monterey; 831-384-7695.

Monterey

Over two million visitors visit the Monterey area every year. Little wonder. Its rocky coast fringed with cypress forests, its hills dotted with palatial homes—the area is unusually beautiful. The town of Monterey also serves as a gateway to the tumbling region of Big Sur.

For a tour of Monterey Peninsula, begin in Monterey itself. Here are historic homes, an old Spanish presidio, Fisherman's Wharf, and Cannery Row. Set in a natural amphitheater of forested hills, it is also home to one of the richest marine sanctuaries along the entire California coast. Little wonder that this town, with a population that numbers 30,000 people, has served as an inspiration for Robert Louis Stevenson and John Steinbeck. With a downtown district that reflects small town America and a waterfront that once supported a rich fishing and canning industry, Monterey remains one of the most vital spots on the Central Coast.

SIGHTS   History in Monterey is a precious commodity that in most cases has been carefully preserved. Ancient adobe houses and Spanish-style buildings are so commonplace that some have been converted into shops and restaurants.

For sightseeing tips and brochures, visit the **Monterey County Convention and Visitors Bureau**. Closed Saturday and Sunday. ~ 150 Olivier Street; 831-657-6400, 888-221-1010. If you need a little touring advice on the weekend, the **Monterey County Visitors Center** is open daily. ~ 401 Camino El Estero; 831-649-1770, 888-221-1010, fax 831-648-5373; www.montereyinfo.org, e-mail info@mccvb.org.

Argentine pirate Hipólito Bouchard sacked and burned the Monterey Presidio during his round-the-world rampage in 1818.

In the **Maritime Museum of Monterey** you'll find model ships, a World War II exhibit, and a two-story-tall rotating lighthouse lens. Closed Wednesday. Admission. ~ 5 Custom House Plaza; 831-375-2608, fax 831-655-3054; www.montereyhistory.org, e-mail info@montereyhistory.org.

Many of Monterey's historic buildings can be seen—and in most cases toured—along the two-mile **Path of History** (see "Walking Tour").

Two other places of historical note are located in Monterey but a significant distance from the Path of History. The **Royal Presidio Chapel** is a graceful expression of the 18th-century town. Decorative molding adorns the facade of the old adobe church while the towering belfry, rising along one side, makes the structure asymmetrical. Heavy wooden doors lead to a long, narrow chapel hung with dusty oil paintings. This was the mission that Father Junípero Serra founded in 1770, just before moving his congregation a few miles south to Carmel. ~ 550 Church Street; 831-373-4345.

The **Presidio of Monterey** sits on a hill near the northwest corner of town. Established as a fort by the Spanish in 1770, it currently serves as a foreign language institute for the military. There are cannons banked in a hillside, marking the site of Fort Mervine, built by the Americans in 1846. There's some evidence that the Presidio may also be the site of an ancient Costanoan Indian village and burial ground. And a granite monument at the corner of Pacific and Artillery streets marks the spot where in 1602 the Spanish celebrated the first Catholic mass in California. In addition to historic points, the Presidio grounds enjoy marvelous

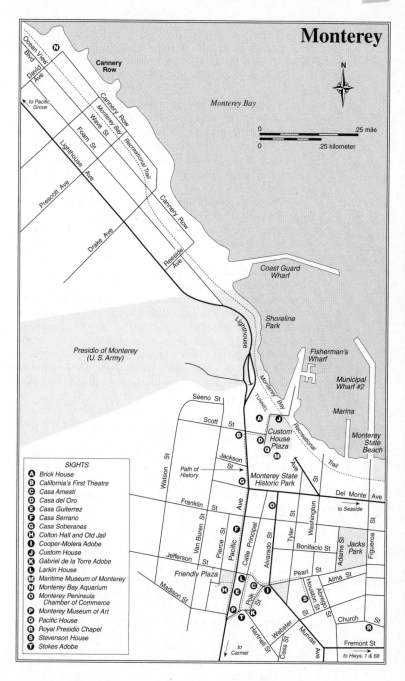

Monterey

Ocean View Blvd

David Ave

Cannery Row

to Pacific Grove

Monterey Bay

Wave St

Foam St

Cannery Row

Recreational Trail

Prescott Ave

Lighthouse Ave

Drake Ave

Reeside Ave

Cannery Row

Monterey Bay

.25 mile

.25 kilometer

Coast Guard Wharf

Shoreline Park

Lighthouse

Presidio of Monterey (U. S. Army)

Fisherman's Wharf

Municipal Wharf #2

Marina

Monterey State Beach

Monterey Bay

TUNNEL

Seeno St

Scott St

Watson St

Jackson St

Path of History

Monterey State Historic Park

Franklin St

Del Monte Ave

to Seaside

Madison St

Jefferson St

Friendly Plaza

Van Buren St

Pierce St

Pacific St

Calle Principal

Alvarado St

Washington St

Tyler St

Bonifacio St

Adams St

Jacks Park

Figueroa St

Pearl St

Alma St

Polk St

Hartnell St

Webster St

Cass St

Munras Ave

Houston St

Abrego St

Church St

Fremont St

to Carmel

to Hwys. 1 & 68

Recreational Trail

SIGHTS

- **A** Brick House
- **B** California's First Theatre
- **C** Casa Amesti
- **D** Casa del Oro
- **E** Casa Guiterrez
- **F** Casa Serrano
- **G** Casa Soberanes
- **H** Colton Hall and Old Jail
- **I** Cooper-Molera Adobe
- **J** Custom House
- **K** Gabriel de la Torre Adobe
- **L** Larkin House
- **M** Maritime Museum of Monterey
- **N** Monterey Bay Aquarium
- **O** Monterey Peninsula Chamber of Commerce
- **P** Monterey Museum of Art
- **Q** Pacific House
- **R** Royal Presidio Chapel
- **S** Stevenson House
- **T** Stokes Adobe

Custom House Plaza

views of Monterey. You can look down upon the town, then scan along the bay's curving horizon. Due to heightened security, the Presidio is not open to the public. ~ Pacific and Artillery streets; 831-242-5555, fax 831-242-5464; www.monterey.army.mil.

Strangely, Monterey, which elsewhere demonstrates special care in preserving its heritage, has let its wharves and piers fall prey to tinsel-minded developers. **Municipal Wharf #2** is a welcome exception. It's actually all that remains from the heyday of Monterey's fishing fleet. Here broad-hulled boats still beat at their moorings, while landlubbing anglers cast from pierside. Gulls perch along the handrails, sea lions bark from beneath the pilings, and pelicans work the waterfront. On one side is the dilapidated warehouse of a long-defunct freezer company. At the end of the dock, fish companies still operate. It's a primal place of cranes and pulleys, forklifts and conveyor belts. There are ice boxes and old packing crates scattered hither-thither, exuding the romance and stench of the industry. ~ Located at the foot of Figueroa Street.

Then there is the parody, much better known than the original. **Fisherman's Wharf**, like its San Francisco namesake, has been transmogrified into what the travel industry thinks tourists think a fishing pier should look like. Something was lost in the translation. Few fishing boats operate from the wharf these days; several charter companies sponsor glass-bottom boat tours and whale-watching expeditions. Otherwise the waterfront haven is just one more mall, a macadam corridor lined on either side with shops. There are ersatz art galleries, shops vending candy apples and personalized mugs, plus a school of seafood restaurants. A few outdoor fish markets still sell live crabs, lobsters, and squid, but the symbol of the place is the hurdy-gurdy man with performing monkey who greets you at the entrance.

Actually this is only the most recent in the wharf's long series of role changes. The dock was built in 1846 to serve cargo schooners dealing in hides. Within a decade the whaling industry took it over, followed finally by Italian fishermen catching salmon, cod,

AUTHOR FAVORITE

Monterey Bay features one of the world's biggest submarine canyons, deeper than the Grand Canyon. At the **Monterey Bay Aquarium** you'll encounter nearly 200 exhibits and display tanks representing the wealth of underwater life that inhabits this mineral-rich valley. Together the many displays and exhibitions make it one of the world's great aquariums. For more information, see page 227.

and mackerel. During the Cannery Row era of the '30s, the sardine industry played a vital part in the life of the wharf. Today all that has given way to a bizarre form of public nostalgia.

The same visionary appears responsible for the resurrection of **Cannery Row**. Made famous by John Steinbeck's feisty novels *Cannery Row* and *Sweet Thursday*, this oceanfront strip has been transformed into a neighborhood of wax museums and dainty antique shops. As Steinbeck remarked upon returning to the old sardine canning center, "They fish for tourists now."

Cannery Row of yore was an unappealing collection of corrugated warehouses, dilapidated stores, seedy hotels, and gaudy whorehouses. There were about 30 canneries, 100 fishing boats, and 4000 workers populating the place. The odor was horrible, but for several decades the sardine industry breathed life into the Monterey economy. The business died when the fish ran out just before *Cannery Row* was published in 1945.

Before the entire oceanfront strip was developed in the early 1980s, you could still capture a sense of the old Cannery Row. A few weather-beaten factories remained. Rust stained their ribbed sides, windows were punched, and roofs had settled to an inward curve. In places, the stone pilings of old loading docks still stood, haunted by sea gulls. Now only tourists and memories remain.

One of the modern additions to the historic street is the first **Bubba Gump Shrimp Co.** in the country, located in the 1916 building that was once the reduction plant for the Monterey Canning Company. ~ 720 Cannery Row; 831-373-1884, fax 831-373-0354; www.bubbagump.com, e-mail dtrombetta@bubba gump.com.

In the middle you'll encounter the scene of the malling of Cannery Row. Old warehouses were renovated into shopping centers, new buildings rose up, and the entire area experienced a face lift.

The most impressive feature is the **Monterey Bay Aquarium**, a state-of-the-art museum that re-creates the natural habitat of local sea life. For instance, the Monterey Bay Habitats, a 90-foot-long acrylic enclosure, portrays the local submarine world complete with sharks, schooling fish, and wharf pilings. The Outer Bay Galleries contain, among other delights, a million-gallon tank filled with all kinds of ocean species, including black sea turtles, ocean sunfish, hammerhead sharks, barracuda, and the only tuna in an American aquarium; the Vanishing Wildlife exhibit allows a ground-floor view into the galleries. Another aquarium contains a living kelp forest crowded with fish. Don't forget the hands-on exhibits where you can pet bat rays and touch crabs, starfish, and sea cucumbers. And don't miss the deep-sea video images beamed several times a day live from research vessels in undersea Monterey Canyon, two miles beneath

Text continued on page 230.

Monterey's Path of History

The Path of History, carrying through the center of Monterey, measures over two miles if walked in its entirety.

CUSTOM HOUSE The best place to begin is the Custom House (c. 1827) across from Fisherman's Wharf. In 1846, Commodore Sloat raised the American flag here, claiming California for the United States. Today the stone and adobe building houses displays from an 1830s-era cargo ship. ~ 1 Custom House Plaza.

PACIFIC HOUSE Across the plaza rises Pacific House (c. 1847), a two-story balconied adobe with a luxurious courtyard. The exhibits inside trace California's history from American Indian days to the advent of Spanish settlers and American pioneers. ~ 10 Custom House Plaza.

CASA DEL ORO Just behind Pacific House sits Casa del Oro, a tiny 1840s adobe that now houses the **Joseph Boston Store**, an old-fashioned mercantile shop selling Early American items. Closed Monday through Wednesday. ~ Olivier and Scott streets; 831-649-3364.

BRICK HOUSE Diagonally across the intersection on Olivier Street behind an office complex stands the oldest brick house, purportedly the first such house in California. Adjacent to this is the **Whaling Station**, an adobe with a balcony from which the early whalers spotted their migrating bounty.

CALIFORNIA'S FIRST THEATRE California's First Theatre, a block up the street, is still used to stage 19th-century melodramas that are performed by America's oldest continually operating theater troupe. The theater is partially closed for renovations. ~ Scott and Pacific streets.

CASA SOBERANES A left on Pacific Street leads to Casa Soberanes, a Monterey-style house with red tile roof and second-story balcony. Completed in the 1840s, this impressive structure is also called "the house with the blue gate" for its entrance. ~ 6 Pacific Street.

CASA SERRANO Casa Serrano (c. 1843) contains wrought-iron decorations over its narrow windows. Once home to a Spanish teacher who was Monterey's second *alcalde* (mayor), it is open for touring by appointment. For more information contact the Monterey History and Art Association. ~ 412 Pacific Street; 831-372-2608; www.montereyhistory.org.

FRIENDLY PLAZA Nearby spreads Friendly Plaza, a tree-shaded park that serves as a focus for several important places. The **Monterey Museum**

of Art exhibits works and artifacts by early and contemporary California artists. Closed Monday and Tuesday. Admission. ~ 559 Pacific Street; 831-372-5477; www.montereyart.org, e-mail info@monterey art.org. **La Mirada** is housed in an old adobe with period furnishings. Closed Monday and Tuesday. Admission. ~ 720 Via Mirada Avenue; 831-372-3689; www.montereyart.org, e-mail info@montereyart.org.

COLTON HALL   Pierce Street, running along the upper edge of the plaza, contains a string of historic 19th-century homes. Colton Hall, site of California's 1849 constitutional convention, displays memorabilia from that critical event. ~ Pacific Street between Jefferson and Madison streets. The squat granite **Old Jail** next door, with wrought-iron bars across the windows, dates back to the same era. **Casa Gutierrez**, across the street, was built in 1846 by a cavalryman with 15 children.

LARKIN HOUSE   After exploring the plaza, turn left into Madison Street from Pacific Street, then left again along Calle Principal to one of the town's most famous homes, the Larkin House. Designed in 1834 by Thomas Larkin, the antique home is now a house museum filled with period pieces. The only United States Consul to California lived here. Admission. ~ 510 Calle Principal.

HISTORIC HOMES   A right on Jefferson Street and another quick right on Polk takes you past a cluster of revered houses. **Casa Amesti** (c. 1824) is presently a private club. ~ 516 Polk Street. The **Cooper-Molera Adobe**, across the road, includes a 19th-century museum and a "historic garden" of herbs and vegetables of the Mexican era. Visit by guided tour (call Monterey State Historic Parks at 831-649-7118 for information). Admission. ~ 525 Polk Street. Facing each other on either side of Polk and Hartnell streets are the **Gabriel de la Torre Adobe** (c. 1836) and the **Stokes Adobe**, erected in the 1840s.

STEVENSON HOUSE   Backtrack along Polk Street one block to the five-way intersection, take a soft right onto Pearl Street, walk a few short blocks, then turn right on Houston Street to the Stevenson House, Robert Louis Stevenson's residence for several months in 1879. The house features personal belongings, original manuscripts, and first editions, all of which can be viewed on a guided tour (call 831-649-7118 for tour information). Admission. ~ 530 Houston Street.

GUIDED TOURS   You can see Casa Soberanes, Larkin House, and Cooper-Molera Adobe (from the outside) on a daily guided 45-minute walking tour. For information, contact Monterey State Historic Parks. Fee. ~ 831-649-7118; e-mail mshp@parks.ca.gov.

the surface of the bay. Definitely take the kids to the Splash Zone, where hands-on activities and animals like penguins, moray eels, and tropical sharks will keep them entertained for hours. Admission. ~ Cannery Row and David Avenue; 831-648-4888, 800-756-3737, fax 831-648-4810; www.montereybay aquarium.org.

LODGING
The problem with lodging on the Monterey Peninsula is the same dilemma plaguing much of the world—money. It takes a lot of it to stay here, especially when visiting one of the area's vaunted bed and breakfasts. These country inns are concentrated in Pacific Grove and Carmel, towns neighboring on Monterey. The town of Monterey features a few such inns as well as a string of moderately priced motels. Budget travelers will do well to check into the latter and also to consult several of the Carmel listings in the book. Monterey's motel row lies along Munras Avenue, a buzzing thoroughfare that leads from downtown to Route 1. Motels are also found along Fremont Street in the adjacent town of Seaside. These are cheaper, drabber, and not as conveniently situated as the Munras hostelries.

Since overnight facilities fill rapidly around Monterey, particularly on weekends and during summer, it's wise to reserve in advance. Contact **Resort 2 Me Lodging Reservations**, a free reservation agency for the Monterey Peninsula. ~ 831-642-6622, 800-757-5646, fax 831-642-6641; www.resort2me.com, e-mail info@resort2me.com.

One standard located five blocks from downtown, the **Days Inn Monterey** features 35 rooms with private baths. ~ 1288 Munras Avenue; 831-375-2168, 800-329-7466, fax 831-375-0368. MODERATE TO DELUXE.

For good cheer and elegance, the **Old Monterey Inn** provides a final word. Glorious rhododendrons and camellias in a lavish garden surround this ten-room Tudor-style bed and breakfast. The house rests on a quiet street yet is located within a few blocks of downtown Monterey. The trimly appointed rooms feature feather beds, tile fireplaces, woodwork, and delicate wallhangings; four have whirlpool tubs. There are spacious dining and drawing rooms downstairs and the landscaped grounds are studded with oak and redwood. An elaborate breakfast is included; they'll even serve you in bed. You'll find this friendly little inn a perfect spot for an evening fire and glass of port. Spa services also available. ~ 500 Martin Street; 831-375-8284, 800-350-2344, fax 831-375-6730; www.oldmontereyinn.com, e-mail omi @oldmontereyinn.com. ULTRA-DELUXE.

Located in the downtown district, **Merritt House Inn** is not only an overnight resting place but also a stopping point along Monterey's "Path of History." Part of this lovely inn rests in a vintage 1830 adobe home. Accommodations in the old house (three lavish suites) and the adjoining modern quarters (22 guest rooms) are furnished with hardwood period pieces and feature vaulted ceilings, fireplaces, and balconies. The garden abounds with magnolia, fig, pepper, and olive trees. Expanded continental breakfast is served. ~ 386 Pacific Street; 831-646-9686, 800-541-5599, fax 831-646-5392; www.merritthouseinn.com, e-mail merritthouse.@usa.net. ULTRA-DELUXE.

Oceanfront on Cannery Row stands the **Spindrift Inn**, an elegant 42-room hotel. The lobby is fashionably laid out with skylight and sculptures and there is a rooftop solarium overlooking the waterfront. Guest rooms carry out the award-winning architectural motif with bay windows, hardwood floors, woodburning fireplaces, and built-in armoires. ~ 652 Cannery Row; 831-646-8900, 800-841-1879, fax 831-646-5342; www.spindriftinn.com, e-mail reservations@innsofmonterey.com. ULTRA-DELUXE.

Catering to a mixed gay and straight clientele is the **Monterey Fireside Lodge**, a 27-room hostelry. In addition to comfortable accommodations, they have a jacuzzi and patio. Continental breakfast included. ~ 1131 10th Street; 831-373-4172, 800-722-2624, fax 831-655-5640; www.firesidemonterey.com, e-mail info@firesidemonterey.com. MODERATE TO DELUXE.

DINING

Few restaurants can compete with **Stokes Restaurant & Bar** for ambience. Housed in an 1833 California adobe with stucco walls, artwork by local artists, and European antiques, this restaurant serves California-Mediterranean cuisine including delicious pizzas and tapas. Featuring flavors from northern Italy, southern France, and Spain and an extensive wine list with French, Italian, Australian, and California vintages. No lunch on weekends. Closed the first week of January. ~ 500 Hartnell Street; 831-373-1110, fax 831-373-1202; www.stokesrestaurant.com, e-mail stokes@stokesrestaurant.com. MODERATE TO DELUXE.

Tasty *kalbi* and *bi bim bap* are among the traditional favorites at **Won Ju Korean Restaurant**. You'll find meat dishes as well as

AUTHOR IN LOVE

Robert Louis Stevenson, the vivacious but sickly Scottish writer, sailed the Atlantic and traveled overland across the continent to visit his wife-to-be Fanny Osbourne in Monterey. Writing for local newspapers, depending in part upon the kindness of strangers for sustenance, the fragile wanderer fell in love with Fanny and Monterey both. From the surrounding countryside he drew inspiration for some of his most famous books, including *Treasure Island*.

seafood and vegetarian options. Dinner comes with a Korean potato pancake, rice, and a wide variety of side dishes such as sesame-flavored spinach and spicy *kim chee* (pickled cabbage). ~ 570 Lighthouse Avenue; 831-656-0672. MODERATE TO DELUXE.

Eating at **Gianni's Pizza** is a guaranteed good time. You can feel it when you walk in the door of this casual restaurant. The tables sport red-and-white-checked tablecloths, there are bottles of wine and pictures of Italy on the walls, and on weekends banjo and accordion players serenade diners with lively tunes. You can order fresh pastas, hand-tossed, thick-crusted pizza, or oven-baked sandwiches from various stations, and they are prepared and delivered to your table. There's also a bar and wonderful gelato for dessert. No lunch Monday through Thursday. ~ 725 Lighthouse Avenue; 831-649-1500. BUDGET TO MODERATE.

One of Monterey Bay's most abundant seafood products is squid, the inky creature that often turns up on local restaurant menus as the more palatable-sounding calamari. Under any name, the best place to enjoy it is **Abalonetti**, a casual wharfside restaurant overlooking the bay. The menu presents calamari in an array of guises, including deep-fried, sautéed with wine and garlic, and baked with eggplant. Seven or more fresh fish specials round out the menu. ~ 57 Fisherman's Wharf; 831-373-1851, fax 831-373-2058; www.abalonettimonterey.com. MODERATE TO DELUXE.

Enjoy a cuppa java in a coffee shop quite unlike any you've ever visited before. At **Plumes Coffee** they grind the beans for each cup and brew it individually. So that your own special cup of coffee is not mistakenly served to someone else, you pick up your order under a picture of, say, a waterfall or sunset. Plumes also serves cheesecake, fruit tarts, custard eclairs, and other sweet treats from the best bakeries in the area. It's a free wi-fi hotspot, too. ~ 400 Alvarado Street; 831-373-4526, fax 831-655-1621. BUDGET.

AUTHOR FAVORITE

Small and personalized with an understated elegance is the most fitting way to describe **Fresh Cream**. Its light green and gray walls are decorated with French prints and leaded glass. One wall is floor-to-ceiling windows that provide a great view of the bay. Service is excellent and the menu, printed daily, numbers among the finest on the Central Coast. On a given night you might choose from filet mignon in Madeira sauce, sautéed veal loin, blackened ahi tuna, duckling in black currant sauce, and rack of lamb. That's not even mentioning the appetizers, which are outstanding, or the desserts, which should be outlawed. Four stars. Dinner only. ~ Heritage Harbor, 99 Pacific Street; 831-375-9798; www.fresh cream.com, e-mail dining@freshcream.com. ULTRA-DELUXE.

In Monterey, there are stores throughout the downtown area and **SHOPPING** malls galore over on **Cannery Row**. Every year another shopping complex seems to rise along the Row. Already the area features cheese and wine stores, clothiers, a fudge factory, and a gourmet supply store. There's also a collector's comic book store, the inevitable T-shirt shop, knickknack stores, and galleries selling artworks that are like Muzak on canvas.

Stepping into **Book Haven** is like discovering a private library filled with antiquarian treasures. Bibliophiles and casual browsers will surely find what they are looking for in the store's collection of new, used, rare, paperback, hardcover, and antique books. Closed Sunday. ~ 559 Tyler Street; 831-333-0383.

The classiest spot around is **Club Octane**. Entertainment changes **NIGHTLIFE** nightly, with four different rooms featuring deejays spinning dance tunes plus an outdoor patio and go-go cages. "Upscale" dress code enforced on weekends. Closed Tuesday and Wednesday. ~ 321 Alvarado Street; 831-646-9244, www.cluboctane.com.

Monterey Live is a performing arts venue featuring live music from every continent. You can get your groove on to West African harp, Australian folk, or Czech bluegrass. ~ 414 Alvarado Street; 831-646-1415.

The only gay establishment in Monterey, the **Lighthouse Bar & Grill** serves American pub food. Patrons also shoot pool, play pinball, or relax with a drink on the patio. Closed Sunday and Monday. ~ 281 Lighthouse Avenue; 831-373-4488.

Pacific Grove

Projecting out from the northern tip of Monterey Peninsula is the diminutive town of Pacific Grove. Covering just 1700 acres, it is reached from Monterey along Lighthouse Avenue. Better yet, pick up Ocean View Boulevard near Cannery Row and follow as it winds along Pacific Grove's surf-washed shores. A quiet town with a lightly developed waterfront, Pacific Grove offers paths that lead for miles along a rock-crusted shore.

Costanoan Indians once dove for abalone in these waters. By the 19th century, Pacific Grove had become a religious retreat. Methodist Episcopal ministers pitched a tent city and decreed that "bathing suits shall be provided with double crotches or with skirts of ample size to cover the buttocks." The town was dry until 1969. Given the fish canneries in Monterey and teetotalers in this nearby town, local folks called the area "Carmel-by-the-Sea, Monterey-by-the-Smell, and Pacific Grove-by-God."

Today Pacific Grove is a sleepy residential area decorated with **SIGHTS** Victorians, brown-shingle houses, and clapboard ocean cottages. The waterfront drive goes past rocky beaches to **Point Pinos Lighthouse**. When this beacon first flashed in 1855, it burned sperm whale oil. Little has changed except the introduction of electricity; this is the only early lighthouse along the entire California coast to be preserved in its original condition. The U.S. Coast Guard still uses it to guide ships; it is the oldest continually operating lighthouse on the West Coast. Two rooms have been restored to look as they did in Victorian times, and there's a short history of Emily Fish, the woman who ran the lighthouse in the 19th century. The lighthouse is open for self-guided tours. Call for winter hours. ~ North of Lighthouse Avenue; 831-648-5716; www.pgmuseum.org.

Sunset Drive continues along the sea to **Asilomar State Beach**. Here sand dunes mantled with ice plant front a wave-lashed shore. There are tidepools galore, plus beaches for picnics, and trails leading through the rolling dunes.

Pacific Grove's major claim to fame lies in an area several blocks inland: around George Washington Park on Melrose Street and in a grove at 1073 Lighthouse Avenue. This otherwise unassuming municipality is known as "Butterfly Town, U.S.A." Every mid-October, brilliant orange-and-black **monarch butterflies** migrate here, remaining until mid-March. Some arrive from several hundred miles away to breed amid the cypress and oak trees. At night they cling to one another, curtaining the branches in clusters that sometimes number over a thousand. Then, at first light, they come to life, fluttering around the groves in a frenzy of wings and color.

Also of interest are the **Pacific Grove Museum of Natural History**, an excellent small museum with exhibits on native animals and early peoples, and a touch gallery for kids. Closed Sunday and Monday. ~ Central and Forest avenues; 831-648-5716, fax 831-372-3256; www.pgmuseum.org, e-mail pgmuseum@mbay.net.

Gosby House Inn is a century-old Victorian mansion decorated in period antiques. ~ 643 Lighthouse Avenue. Next door, the **Hart Mansion** (now a full-service restaurant) is another elaborate old Victorian house. ~ 649 Lighthouse Avenue.

17 MILE DRIVE From Pacific Grove, 17 Mile Drive leads to Pebble Beach, one of America's most lavish communities. This place is so exclusive that the rich charge a fee to anyone wishing to drive around admiring their homes. No wonder they're rich.

Galling as the gate fee might be, this is an extraordinary region that must not be missed. The road winds through pine groves down to a wind-combed beach. There are miles of rolling dunes tufted with sea vegetation. (The oceanfront can be as cool and damp as it is beautiful, so carry a sweater or jacket, or better yet, both.)

Among the first spots you'll encounter is **Spanish Bay**, where Juan Gaspar de Portolá camped during his 1769 expedition up the California coast. (The picnic area here is a choice place to spread a feast.) At **Point Joe**, converging ocean currents create a wild frothing sea that has drawn several ships to their doom.

Seal Rock and **Bird Rock**, true to their nomenclature, are carpeted with sea lions, harbor and leopard seals, cormorants, brown pelicans, and gulls. Throughout this thriving 17 Mile Drive area are black-tail deer, sooty shearwaters, sea otters, and, during migration periods, California gray whales.

There are crescent beaches and granite headlands as well as vista points for scanning the coast. You'll also pass the **Lone Cypress**, the solitary tree on a rocky point that has become as symbolic of Northern California as perhaps the Golden Gate Bridge.

The **private homes** en route are mansions, exquisite affairs fashioned from marble and fine hardwoods. Some appear like stone fortresses, others seem made solely of glass. They range from American Colonial to futuristic and were designed by noted architects like Bernard Maybeck, Julia Morgan, and Willis Polk.

This is also home to several of the world's most renowned **golf courses**—Pebble Beach, Spyglass Hill, and Cypress Point—where the AT&T National Pro-Am Championship takes place each year. More than the designer homes and their celebrity residents, these courses have made Pebble Beach a place fabled for wealth and beauty.

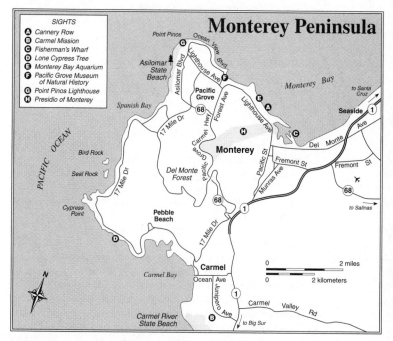

Monterey Peninsula

SIGHTS
- Ⓐ Cannery Row
- Ⓑ Carmel Mission
- Ⓒ Fisherman's Wharf
- Ⓓ Lone Cypress Tree
- Ⓔ Monterey Bay Aquarium
- Ⓕ Pacific Grove Museum of Natural History
- Ⓖ Point Pinos Lighthouse
- Ⓗ Presidio of Monterey

The best part of the drive lies along the coast between the Pacific Grove and Carmel gates. Along the backside of 17 Mile Drive, where it loops up into Del Monte Forest, there are marvelous views of Monterey Bay and the San Gabilan Mountains. Here also is **Huckleberry Hill**, a forest of Monterey and Bishop pine freckled with bushes.

LODGING **Asilomar Conference Center** provides one of the area's best housing arrangements. Set in a state beach, it's surrounded by more than 100 acres of sand dunes and pine forests. The beach is a stroll away from any of the center's 313 rooms divided among 30 hotel lodges. There's a dining hall on the premises as well as meeting rooms and recreational facilities (pool and volleyball court). Breakfast is included in the price. Catering primarily to groups, Asilomar does provide accommodations (depending on availability) for independent travelers. Rooms in the "rustic buildings" are small and spartan but adequate (*and* designed by Julia Morgan). They lack carpeting on the hardwood floors and include little decoration. The "deluxe building" rooms are nicely appointed with wallhangings, study desks, and comfortable furnishings. Fireplaces are also available in some rooms, and every lodge includes a spacious lounge area with stone fireplace. In keeping with the restful atmosphere, the rooms have neither telephones nor televisions. No doubt about it, Asilomar is a splendid place at a relaxing price. ~ 800 Asilomar Boulevard; 831-372-8016, 866-654-2878, fax 831-372-7227; www.visitasilomar.com, e-mail asilomarsales@dncinc.com. MODERATE TO DELUXE.

> The ivy-cloaked cottage at 147 11th Street is where John Steinbeck lived and wrote *In Dubious Battle* and *Of Mice and Men*. Unfortunately, it's not open to the public.

One of Monterey Peninsula's less expensive B&Bs is nearby. **Gosby House Inn**, a century-old Victorian mansion, includes 22 refurbished rooms. Each is different, and all have been decorated with special attention to detail. In any one you are liable to discover an antique armoire, brass lighting fixtures, stained glass, or a Tiffany lamp. The two rooms in the carriage house have jacuzzi tubs. They are all small after the Victorian fashion, which sacrifices space for coziness. The full breakfast, afternoon wine and hors d'oeuvres, and nightly turn-down service add to the homey feeling. ~ 643 Lighthouse Avenue; 831-375-1287, 800-527-8828, fax 831-655-9621; www.foursisters.com. DELUXE.

Green Gables Inn represents one of the region's most impressive bed and breakfasts. The house, a Queen Anne–style Victorian, dates from 1888. Adorned with step-gables, stained glass, and bay windows, it rests in a storybook setting overlooking Monterey Bay. Five bedrooms upstairs and a suite below have been fastidiously decorated with lavish antiques. Three of these share a bathroom, but offer the best ocean views. Set in a town filled with old Victorian homes, this oceanside residence is an ideal representation of Pacific Grove. There are also five separate units in a building adjacent to the main house. These are suites with private bath and fireplace. All rooms have king or queen beds; full breakfast, afternoon wine and cheese, and access to the main house are included. ~ 301 Ocean View Boulevard; 831-375-2095, 800-722-1774, fax 831-375-5437; www.foursisters.com, e-mail info@foursisters.com. MODERATE TO ULTRA-DELUXE.

Commanding a front and center view of the spectacular waterfront is the **Martine Inn**, a pastel stucco Mediterranean-style villa with 24 individually decorated rooms, many with fireplaces. Among the accommodations is the Edith Head Room, which has 1920s furnishings from the Hollywood costume designer's estate. A full sit-down breakfast and afternoon wine and hors d'oeuvres are included. There is a two-night minimum stay on high-season weekends. ~ 255 Ocean View Boulevard; 831-373-3388, 800-852-5588, fax 831-373-3896; www.martineinn.com, e-mail don@martineinn.com. DELUXE TO ULTRA-DELUXE.

DINING

Or take a little stroll into town to **Fandango Restaurant** and ask for the Cellar or Alcove rooms for the most romantic seating. Exquisitely prepared entrées such as abalone, paella, and rack of lamb, and an extensive wine list make this is a highly popular dining destination. Reservations strongly recommended. ~ 223 17th Street; 831-372-3456, fax 831-372-2673; www.fandangorestaurant.com. DELUXE.

The quaint, shingled **Red House Café** is a cozy place to join the locals for breakfast, lunch, or dinner. Morning brings Belgian waffles, frittatas, and croissant sandwiches, while the later meals feature oven-roasted chicken sandwiches and warm eggplant with fontina cheese. Breakfast on weekends only. No dinner on Sunday. Closed Monday. ~ 662 Lighthouse Avenue; 831-643-1060; www.redhousecafe.com, e-mail info@redhousecafe.com. MODERATE.

Peppers Mexicali Cafe pays homage to the red chile and has attracted an incredible number of devotees, as witnessed by the sometimes lengthy wait for a table. Chile posters and pepper prints by local artists decorate the walls, and the food is Mexican and Central American seafood. Among the offerings are grilled prawns with fresh lime and cilantro dressing, grilled seafood tacos, grilled halibut, snapper Veracruz, and more mundane dishes such as tacos, burritos, and enchiladas. A full bar offers blue agave tequilas for some of the best margaritas in town. No lunch on Sunday. Closed Tuesday. ~ 170 Forest Avenue; 831-373-6892, fax 831-373-5467; www.peppersmexicalicafe.com. BUDGET TO MODERATE.

SHOPPING The main area for window browsing in town can be found along Lighthouse Avenue. Just above this busy thoroughfare, on 17th Street, artisans have renovated a row of small beach cottages. In each is a creatively named shop. There's **Reincarnation Vintage Clothing**, which sells vintage and vintage-inspired contemporary clothing, jewelry, and accessories. Closed Sunday. ~ 214 17th Street; 831-649-0689. At **Mum's Place**, there's high-quality oak, maple, cherry, and pine furniture. ~ 246 Forest Avenue; 831-372-6250; www.mumsfurniture.com.

For inexpensive snacks, try the hot dog stand at the bottom of the steps in Lovers Point Park. It's a local institution. ~ Ocean View Boulevard at the foot of 16th Street.

From designer fashions to gourmet cookware, the shops at **American Tin Cannery Outlets** are a shopper's paradise. A good place to look for luggage, books, shoes, housewares, and linens, this renovated two-story complex has a variety of outlet stores. If you're looking for bargains in the Monterey area, don't miss this gem. ~ 125 Ocean View Boulevard; 831-372-1442, fax 831-372-5707; www.americantincannery.com.

NIGHTLIFE The **Terrace Lounge** at Pebble Beach Resort is a thoroughly elegant, clubby place where pianists and small jazz groups play each night. The service is superb, and the view overlooking the 18th green of the Pebble Beach golf course is well worth the drive and the dressing up—be sure to wear a jacket. ~ 1700 17-Mile Drive, Pebble Beach; 831-647-7500.

BEACHES & PARKS **ASILOMAR STATE BEACH** 🏊 🚶 🏖 ⛵ This oceanfront facility features over 100 acres of pine forest, snowy white sand dunes, tidepools, and beach. It's a perfect place for daytripping and exploring. The best surfing here is just off the main sandy beach. Since northern and southern currents run together here, the waters are teeming with marine life. Swimming is not recommended. The conference grounds feature historic buildings and enchanting grounds (overnight accommodations are described in "Lodging" above). ~ Located along Sunset Drive in Pacific Grove; 831-646-6440 (ranger office), fax 831-372-3759; www.visitasilomar.com.

Carmel

The first law of real estate should be this: The best land is always occupied by the military, bohemians, or the rich. Think about it. The principle holds for many of the world's prettiest spots. Generally the military arrives first, on an exploratory mission or as an occupying force. It takes strategic ground, which happens to be the beaches, headlands, and mountaintops. The bohemians select beautiful locales because they possess good taste. When the rich discover where the artists have settled, they start moving in, driving up the rents, and forcing the displaced bohemians to discover new homes, which will then be taken by another wave of the wealthy.

The Monterey Peninsula is no exception. In Carmel the military established an early beachhead when Spanish soldiers occupied a barracks in the old Catholic mission. Later the bohemians arrived in numbers. Poet George Sterling came in 1905, followed by Mary Austin, the novelist. Eventually such luminaries as Upton Sinclair, Lincoln Steffens, and Sinclair Lewis, writers all, settled for varying periods. Jack London and Ambrose Bierce visited. Later, photographers Ansel Adams and Edward Weston relocated here.

The figure most closely associated with this "seacoast of Bohemia" was Robinson Jeffers, a poet who came seeking solitude in 1914. Quarrying rock from the shoreline, he built the Tor House and Hawk Tower, where he lived and wrote haunting poems and epics about the coast.

Then like death and tax collectors, the rich inevitably moved in. As John Steinbeck noted when he later returned to this artists' colony, "If Carmel's founders should return, they could not afford to live there. . . . They would instantly be picked up as suspicious characters and deported over the city line."

It's doubtful many would want to remain anyway. Today Carmel is so cute it cloys. The tiny town is cluttered with over four dozen inns, about six dozen restaurants, and more than 300 shops. Ocean Avenue, the main street, is wall-to-wall with merchants. Shopping malls have replaced artists' garrets, and there are traffic jams where there was once solitude.

Typifying the town is the **Tuck Box**, a gingerbread-style building on Dolores Street between Ocean and 7th avenues (there are no street numbers in Carmel), or the fairy tale–like **Hansel-and-Gretel cottages** on Torres Street between 5th and 6th avenues.

SIGHTS

Still, reasons remain to visit Carmel, which is reached from Monterey via Route 1 or from the Carmel gate along 17 Mile Drive. The window shopping is good and several galleries are outstanding. Some of the town's quaint characteristics have appeal. There are no traffic lights or parking meters, and at night few street lights. Drive around the side streets and you will encounter an architectural mixture of log cabins, adobe structures, board-and-batten cottages, and Spanish villas.

A secret that local residents have long withheld from visitors is **Mission Trails Park**. No signs will direct you here, so watch for an entrance at the corner of Mountain View and Crespi avenues. Within this forest preserve are miles of hiking trails. They wind across footbridges, through redwood groves, and past meadows of wildflowers en route to Carmel Mission. There are

◄ HIDDEN

ocean vistas, deer grazing the hillsides, and an arboretum seeded with native California plants.

Carmel's most alluring feature is the one that early drew the bohemians—the Pacific. At the foot of Ocean Avenue rests **Carmel Beach**, a snowy strand shadowed by cypress trees. From here, Scenic Road hugs the coast, winding above rocky outcroppings.

Just beyond stretches **Carmel River State Beach**, a sandy corridor at the foot of Carmel Bay. For additional information, see the "Beaches & Parks" section below.

Even for the non-religious, a visit to **Carmel Mission Basilica** becomes a pilgrimage. If the holiness holds no appeal, there's the aesthetic sense of the place. Dating back to 1770, its Old World beauty captivates and confounds. The courtyards are alive with flowers and birds. The adobe buildings have been dusted with time—their eaves are hunchbacked, the tile roofs coated in moss. Admission. ~ Located on Rio Road just off Route 1; 831-624-1271.

Established by Father Junípero Serra, this mission is one of California's most remarkable. The basilica is a vaulted-ceiling affair adorned with old oil paintings and wooden statues of Christ; its walls are lime plaster made from burnt seashells. The exterior is topped with a Moorish tower and 11 bells.

Junípero Serra lies buried in the sanctuary, his grave marked with a stone plaque. There are also museum rooms demonstrating early California life—a kitchen with stone hearth and rudimentary tools, the state's first library (complete with water-stained bibles), and the cell where Father Serra died, its bed a slab of wood with a single blanket and no mattress. Close by, in the cemetery beside the basilica, several thousand American Indians are also buried.

Just two miles south of Carmel lies **Point Lobos State Reserve**, an incomparable natural area of rocky headlands and placid coves. The park features hillside crow's nests from which to gaze out along Carmel Bay. Before Westerners arrived, the American Indians gathered mussels and abalone here. Later Point Lobos was a whaling station and an abalone cannery. Today it's a park intended primarily for nature hikers. You can explore pine forests and cypress groves, a jagged shoreline of granite promontories, and wave-lapped coves. Every tidepool is a miniature aquarium pulsing with color and sea life. The water is clear as sky. Offshore rise sea stacks, their rocky bases ringed with mussels, their domes crowned by sea birds. This region, also rich in wildlife and underwater life, should not be bypassed; for complete information, see the "Beaches & Parks" section below.

As if its shoreline was not enough, Carmel also boasts an extraordinary interior. Carmel Valley Road leads from Route 1 into the distant hills, paralleling the Carmel River in its circuitous course. The lower end of the **Carmel Valley** promises fruit orchards and fields of grazing horses before the road ascends into the wooded heights that separate Carmel from the farmlands of Salinas. Along the way you can stop by **Château Julien Winery** for a tasting and tour (reservations recommended for tour). ~ 8940 Carmel Valley Road, five miles from Route 1; 831-624-2600; www.chateaujulien.com.

You may want to follow the trails that lead from the visitors center near the Carmel River through woodlands and meadows to Snively's Ridge, a 2000-foot peak in 3700-acre **Garland Ranch Regional Park**. Pick up a map at the visitors center for information about hiking and horseback riding. ~ 700 West Carmel Valley Road, nine miles from Route 1; 831-659-4488; www.mprpd.org, e-mail info@mprpd.org.

LODGING

Carmel River Inn, located on the southern outskirts of town, is a 43-unit establishment with both a motel and woodframe cottages (the latter have greater appeal). The less expensive guest units are studio-size structures with wall-to-wall carpeting, televisions, refrigerators, and telephones; their interior designer was obviously a capable, if uninspired, individual. The pricier cottages vary in size and facilities, but all have DVD players, while some may contain extra rooms, a fireplace, or a kitchen. There's a heated pool and several patios. ~ Route 1 at Carmel River

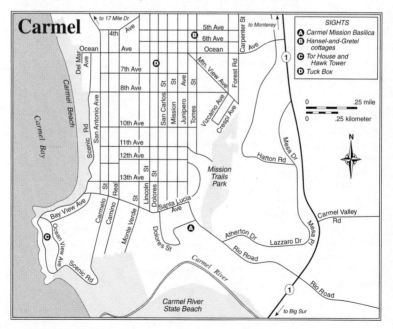

Carmel

to 17 Mile Dr

SIGHTS
Ⓐ Carmel Mission Basilica
Ⓑ Hansel-and-Gretel cottages
Ⓒ Tor House and Hawk Tower
Ⓓ Tuck Box

0   .25 mile
0   .25 kilometer

N

Carmel Beach
Carmel Bay

Del Mar Ave
Ocean Ave
Scenic Rd
San Antonio Ave
7th Ave
8th Ave
10th Ave
11th Ave
12th Ave
13th Ave
Carmelo St
Camino Real
Monte Verde St
Lincoln St
Dolores St
Santa Lucia Ave
Bay View Ave
Ocean View Ave
Scenic Rd

San Carlos St
Mission St
Junipero Ave
Torres St
Vizcaino Ave
Crespi Ave
Mtn. View Ave

4th Ave
Ocean Ave
5th Ave
6th Ave
Ocean Ave

Carpenter St
Forest Rd

to Monterey

Mission Trails Park

Hatton Rd

Mesa Dr

Carmel Valley Rd

Atherton Dr
Lazzaro Dr
Rio Road

Mesa Pl
Rio Road

Carmel River

Carmel River State Beach

to Big Sur

Bridge; 831-624-1575, 800-882-8142, fax 831-624-0290; www.
carmelriverinn.com, e-mail info@carmelriverinn.com. DELUXE TO
ULTRA-DELUXE.

HIDDEN ►

Carmel's most closely kept secret is a hideaway resort set on
22 acres and overlooking the ocean at a distance. Scattered about
the tree-shaded grounds at the **Mission Ranch** are triplex cottages and a quadraplex unit, 31 rooms in all, in addition to the
older white clapboard farmhouse. There are tennis courts, trim
lawns, and ancient cypress trees. With mountains in the background, the views extend across a broad lagoon and out along
sandy beachfront. The ranch dining room is favored by local
people. A rare find indeed with continental breakfast included.
On-site restaurant. ~ 26270 Dolores Street; 831-624-6436,
800-538-8221, fax 831-626-4163; www.missionranchcarmel.
com. MODERATE TO ULTRA-DELUXE.

The Pine Inn is not only Carmel's oldest hostelry, but also another of the town's more reasonably priced places. This 49-room
hotel dates back to 1889 and still possesses the charm that has
drawn visitors for decades. The lobby is a fashionable affair with
black lacquered furniture, dark, warm woods, and a brick fireplace. The less expensive accommodations are smaller but do
have canopied beds, private baths, TVs, and phones common to
all the rooms. Each room has touches of both Europe and the
Far East. Rather than a country inn, this is a full-service hotel
with restaurant and bar downstairs as well as room service for
the guests. ~ Ocean Avenue between Lincoln and Monte Verde
streets; 831-624-3851, 800-228-3851, fax 831-624-3030;
www.pineinn.com. DELUXE TO ULTRA-DELUXE.

Highlands Inn, Park Hyatt Carmel is one of those raw-wood-
and-polished-stone places that evoke the muted elegance of the

STONE POEM

Just before the intersection with Stewart Way, gaze uphill toward those two
stone edifices. Poet Robinson Jeffers' **Tor House and Hawk Tower** seem
drawn from another place and time, perhaps a Scottish headland in the 19th
century. In fact, the poet modeled the house after an English-style barn and
built the 40-foot-high garret with walls six feet thick in the fashion of an
Irish tower. Completed during the 1920s, the structures are granite and
include porthole windows that Jeffers salvaged from a shipwreck. One-
hour tours of the house and tower are conducted on Friday and Saturday by reservation. No children under 12 years allowed. Admission. ~
26304 Ocean View Avenue; for information and reservations, call 831-
624-1813, fax 831-624-3696; www.torhouse.org, e-mail thf@tor
house.org.

California coast. Ultramodern in execution, it features a stone lodge surrounded by wood-shingle buildings. The lodge houses two restaurants and an oceanview lounge while the neighboring structures contain 48 guest rooms, each a warren of blond woods. Most have patios or balconies, and wood-burning fireplaces; several have double spa tub. Parked on a hillside overlooking an awesome sweep of ocean, the inn is the ultimate in Carmel chic. ~ Route 1 about four miles south of Carmel; 831-620-1234, 800-682-4811, fax 831-626-1574; www.high landsinn.hyatt.com. ULTRA-DELUXE.

DINING

In Carmel, the thing to do is drop by the **Tuck Box** for afternoon tea. The establishment sits in a dollhouselike creation with a swirl roof and curved chimney. The prim and tiny dining room also serves breakfast and lunch. During the noon meal there are omelettes, sandwiches, shrimp salad, and Welsh rarebit. Tea includes scones, muffins, or homemade pie. Jams and scone mix are available for purchase. ~ Dolores Street between Ocean and 7th avenues; 831-624-6365, fax 831-626-3939; www.tuckbox.com. BUDGET TO MODERATE.

Crispy coconut prawns, crab mango bisque, and macadamia nut-crusted halibut are just a few of the reasons **Bahama Billy's,** an upbeat local favorite, recommends reservations. Though the menu concentrates on Caribbean-style seafood, you'll also find a selection of prime steaks and several vegetarian options. The upscale tropical ambiance is complemented by a heated patio, full bar, and frequent live music. ~ Barnyard Shopping Center, 3690 The Barnyard; 831-626-0430; www.bahamabillys.com. MODERATE TO DELUXE.

Join the line in front of **Tutto Mondo Trattoria** for good times and a great meal. As you step through the door you might think you're in Italy: Wine bottles, cooking utensils, and strings of garlic adorn the walls, and the staff is very friendly, often breaking into song for impromptu celebrations. If that isn't enough, the food is *molto delizioso*. You can't go wrong with a fresh pasta dish such as the San Remo (sun-dried tomatoes and goat cheese in cream sauce) or *la mafiosa* (calamari, prawns, and scallops in a spicy tomato sauce). Dinner specials include veal, seafood, fish, and chicken entrées, and at lunch sandwiches are added to the menu. Save room for the desserts, especially the tiramisu! ~ Dolores Street between Ocean and 7th avenues; 831-624-8977, fax 831-624-4102; www.mondos.com, e-mail info@mondos.com. MODERATE TO DELUXE.

Reasonably priced, casual, and contemporary. Who could ask for more than what they're offering at critically acclaimed **Rio Grill**? The cuisine at this popular dining room is American grill

Text continued on page 246.

The Old Spanish Mission Town

Time permitting, there's one overland excursion that must be added to your itinerary—a visit to the **Old Mission San Juan Bautista**. While this graceful mission town, located 90 miles south of San Francisco, is easily reached from Route 101, the most inspiring route is via Route 156 from the Monterey Peninsula.

Anyone who has read Frank Norris' muckraking novel about the railroads, *The Octopus*, will recognize this placid village and its thick, cool adobe church. And anyone who remembers the climax to Hitchcock's *Vertigo* will instantly picture the mission, even though the bell tower that Jimmy Stewart struggled to climb was a Hollywood addition that you won't see at the real San Juan Bautista. Founded in 1797, the mission was completed in 1812. Today it numbers among California's most enchanting locales. With its colonnade and sagging crossbeams, the mission has the musty scent of history. The old monastery and church consist of a low-slung building roofed in Spanish tile and topped with a belfry. ~ 831-623-4528; www.oldmissionsjb.org.

My favorite spot in this most favored town is **Mission Cemetery**, a small plot bounded by a stone fence and overlooking valley and mountains. It's difficult to believe that over 4300 American Indians are buried here in unmarked graves. The few recognizable resting places are memorialized with wooden crosses and circling enclosures of stone. Shade trees cool the yard. Just below the cemetery, symbolic perhaps of change and mortality, are the old Spanish Road (*El Camino Real*) and the San Andreas Fault.

The mission rests on a grassy square facing **Plaza Hall**. Originally a dormitory for unwed American Indian women, this structure was rebuilt in 1868 and used as a meeting place and private residence. Peek inside its shuttered windows or tour the building and encounter a child's room cluttered with old dolls, a sitting room dominated by a baby grand piano, and other rooms containing period furniture.

Behind the hall sits a **blacksmith shop**, filled now with wagon wheels, oxen yokes, and the "San Juan Eagle," a hook-and-ladder wagon drawn by a ten-man firefighting crew back in 1869. Nearby **Plaza Stable** houses an impressive collection of buggies and carriages.

The **Plaza Hotel** lines another side of the square. Consisting of several adobe structures, the earliest built in 1814, the place once served as a stagecoach stop. Today its myriad rooms contain historic exhibits and 1860s-era furnishings. Similarly, the **Castro-Breen Adobe** next door is decorated with Spanish-style pieces. Owned by a Mexican general and later by Donner Party survivors, it is a window into California frontier life.

Nearby are **San Juan Jail**, an oversized outhouse constructed in 1870, and the **settler's cabin**, a rough log cabin built by East Coast pioneers in the 1830s or 1840s.

All are part of the **state historic park** that comprises San Juan Bautista. Like the plaza, 3rd Street is lined with 19th-century stores and houses. Here, amid porticoed haciendas and crumbling adobe, are antique stores, a bakery, restaurants, and other shops. Admission. ~ 831-623-4526, fax 831-623-4612.

A block away is **El Teatro Campesino**, an excellent resident theater group. This Latino company originated *Zoot Suit*, an important and provocative play that was eventually filmed as a movie. With a penetrating sense of Mexican-American history and an unsettling awareness of contemporary Latino social roles, it is a modern expression of the vigor and spirit of this old Spanish town. From May to September summer productions are held in its theater; the Christmas show is staged in Mission San Juan Bautista. ~ 705 4th Street; 831-623-2444, fax 831-623-4127; www.elteatrocampesino.com, e-mail info@elteatrocampesino.com.

Accommodations are scarce in San Juan Bautista, but **Posada de San Juan** offers comfortable, unassuming rooms within walking distance of the mission and 3rd Street's shops and restaurants. The 33 rooms are equipped with wetbars, whirlpool bathtubs, and gas fireplaces. Decorated in a hacienda style, this inn reflects the distinctly Mexican flavor of San Juan Bautista. ~ 310 4th Street; 831-623-4030, fax 831-623-2378. MODERATE.

Your other lodging option is the **San Juan Inn**, a reliable resting spot to call home for the night. The Inn has an outdoor pool and hot tub, and each of its 42 room comes with a coffeemaker, microwave, and cable TV. Or for $10 more, you can chose a slightly larger suite, which includes a subdivided livingroom. Note: The Inn is also the only place in town that allows pets. ~ 410 The Alameda; 831-623-4380; MODERATE.

As for restaurants, **La Casa Rosa** sits in an 1858 house. Open for lunch only, this family-run eatery features an "old California casserole," a "new California casserole," a chicken soufflé, and a seafood soufflé. The first entrée is made with cheese, meat sauce, and a corn base; the second dish features green chiles. La Casa Rosa is charming and intimate. Closed Tuesday. ~ 107 3rd Street; 831-623-4563, fax 831-623-1031. MODERATE.

In the same block, **Jardines de San Juan** is recommended as much for its garden as its food. In addition to the usual tacos, burritos, and flautas, weekend specials get fancy: Veracruz-style red snapper served with *crema* on a bed of rice, or *pollos borrachos* cooked in sherry with ham and sausage. ~ 115 3rd Street; 831-623-4466, fax 831-623-4340; www.jardinesrestaurant. com, e-mail info@jardinesrestaurant.com. BUDGET TO MODERATE.

with a Southwestern touch. Smoked chicken and artichokes and baby-back ribs with cayenne-sprinkled yam are among the entrées. ~ Crossroads Shopping Center, Route 1 and Rio Road; 831-625-5436, fax 831-625-2950; www.riogrill.com, e-mail chris@riogrill.com. MODERATE TO DELUXE.

Patisserie Boissière belongs to that endangered species—the moderately priced French restaurant. The simple French country dining room adjoins a small bakery. In addition to outrageous pastries for breakfast, they offer brunch on the weekend. Entrées include coquilles St. Jacques, salmon in parchment paper, and braised lamb shank. Baked brie and French onion soup are also on the bill of fare. A bargain-hunter's delight in dear Carmel. No dinner on Monday and Tuesday. ~ Mission Street between Ocean and 7th avenues; 831-624-5008, fax 831-626-9155; www.patisserieboissiere.com. MODERATE.

Of course the ultimate dining place is **The Covey at Quail Lodge** in Carmel Valley. Set in one of the region's most prestigious hotels, The Covey is a contemporary European restaurant with a California influence, serving, for example, rack of lamb with ratatouille tart and grilled porcini mushrooms. Richly decorated, it overlooks the lodge's lake and grounds. Reservations, please. Breakfast and dinner. Closed Sunday and Monday. ~ 8205 Valley Greens Drive; 831-620-8860, 888-828-8787; www.quaillodge.com. DELUXE TO ULTRA-DELUXE.

SHOPPING   In Carmel, shopping seems to be the raison d'être. If ever an entire town was dressed to look like a boutique, this is the one. Its shops are stylish and expensive.

The major shopping strip is located along Ocean Avenue between Mission and Monte Verde streets, but the best stores generally are situated on the side streets. The **Doud Arcade** is a mall featuring artisan shops. Here you'll find leather merchants, pot-

AUTHOR FAVORITE

Old-time Carmel residents will tell you about **The Restaurant at Mission Ranch**, how it dates back over a century to the days when it was a creamery. Today it's just a warm, homey old building with a stone fireplace plus a view of a sheep pasture and the neighboring ocean. The menu is a combo of fresh seafood and all-American fare: steak, prime rib, chicken, and pasta. Dinner served nightly, as well as Sunday jazz champagne brunch. ~ 26270 Dolores Street; 831-625-9040, 800-538-8221, fax 831-625-5502; www.missionranchcarmel.com. MODERATE TO ULTRA-DELUXE.

ters, and jewelers. ~ Ocean Avenue between San Carlos and Dolores streets.

Most of the artists who made Carmel famous have long since departed, but the city still maintains a wealth of art galleries. While many are not even worth browsing, others are outstanding. The **Carmel Bay Company** features unique home furnishings, as well as art and crafts by local artisans, potters, and woodworkers. ~ Lincoln Street and Ocean Avenue; 831-624-3868. The **Carmel Art Association Gallery**, owned and operated by artists, offers paintings and sculpture by local figures. ~ Dolores Street between 5th and 6th avenues; 831-624-6176; www.carmelart. org. Also of note is the **Chapman Gallery**, which features local artists as well. Closed Sunday and Monday, except by appointment. ~ 7th Avenue between Mission and San Carlos streets; 831-626-1766; www.chapmangallery.com.

Carmel is recognized as an international center for photographers. Two of the nation's most famous—Ansel Adams and Edward Weston—lived here. **The Weston Gallery** displays photographs by both men, as well as works by other 19th- and 20th-century photographers. ~ 6th Avenue between Dolores and Lincoln streets; 831-624-4453; www.westongallery.com. At **Photography West Gallery** Weston and Adams are represented, as are Imogen Cunningham, Brett Weston, and Christopher Burkett. Closed Tuesday and Wednesday in January and sometimes in June. ~ Dolores Street between Ocean and 7th avenues; 831-625-1587.

Carmel, Big Sur, and the Central Coast are the home of a potpourri of metaphysical movements, so it's fitting that one of the coast's best bookstores, **The Pilgrim's Way**, is here. From animal health to Wicca, there are books and gifts for every category. ~ On Dolores Street between 5th and 6th streets; 800-549-9922; 831-624-4955; www.pilgrimsway.com.

The Barnyard Shopping Village is an innovative mall housing about 50 shops and restaurants. Set amid flowering gardens is a series of raw wood structures reminiscent of old farm buildings. For the man with impeccable taste, visit **J. Lawrence Khaki's Men's Clothier** (831-625-8106, 800-664-8106). **Mountain and Sea Gallery** (831-626-7788) captures the area's rugged beauty in photographs. ~ Route 1 and Carmel Valley Road; 831-624-8886; www.thebarnyard.com.

NIGHTLIFE

The Forge in the Forest is a restaurant-cum-bar with its copper walls, hand-carved bar, and open fire. ~ Junipero Street and 5th Avenue; 831-624-2233.

Possibly the prettiest place you'll ever indulge the spirits in is the **Lobos Lounge** at Highlands Inn. An entire wall of this leather-armchair-and-marble-table establishment is plate glass. And the picture on the other side of those panes is classic Carmel—rocky shoreline fringed with cypress trees and lashed by passionate waves. If that's not entertainment enough, there's jazz on weekends. ~ Route 1, about four miles south of Carmel; 831-620-1234, fax 831-626-1574; www.highlandsinn.hyatt.com.

BEACHES & PARKS

CARMEL RIVER STATE BEACH 🧍 This beach would be more attractive were it not upstaged by Point Lobos, its remarkable neighbor to the south. Nevertheless, there's a sandy beach here as well as a view of the surrounding hills. The chief feature is the bird refuge along the river. The marshes offer willets, sandpipers, pelicans, hawks, and kingfishers, plus an occasional Canadian snow goose (and lots of gulls). The beach has restrooms. ~ Located at the end of Carmelo Road in Carmel (take Rio Road exit off Route 1); 831-624-2836, fax 831-624-9265.

POINT LOBOS STATE RESERVE 🧍 🚲 🛶 🤿 In a region packed with uncommonly beautiful scenery, this park stands out as something special. A 1225-acre reserve, only 456 acres of which are above water, it contains over 300 species of plants and more than 250 species of animals and birds. This is a perfect place to study sea otters, harbor seals, and sea lions. During migrating season in mid-winter and mid-spring, gray whales cruise the coast. Along with Pebble Beach, Point Lobos is the only spot in the world where Monterey cypresses, those ghostly, wind-gnarled coastal trees, still survive in the wild. There are 80-foot-high kelp forests offshore, popular with scuba divers who know the reserve as one of the most fascinating places on the coast. Reservations to dive are necessary and can be made up to two months in advance by phone or e-mail. There are picnic areas and restrooms. Dogs aren't allowed. Parking fee, $8. ~ Route 1, about three miles south of Carmel; 831-624-4909; pt-lobos.parks.state.ca.us, e-mail pointlobos@parks.ca.gov.

PINNACLES NATIONAL MONUMENT 🧍 Set far inland amid the softly rolling Gabilan Mountains are the sharp, dramatic volcanic peaks that centerpiece this unusual park. Sheer spires and solitary minarets vault 1200 feet from the canyon floor. Comprising the weathered remains of a 23-million-year-old volcano, these towering peaks challenge day hikers and technical rock climbers alike. Rockclimbing is a major activity here in spring and fall (it's too hot in summer). There are caves to explore, and more than 30 miles of trails leading through the remnants of the volcano. Prairie falcons, coyote, gray fox, and bobcat roam the region, while golden eagles work the skies above. Since the cliffs are accessible only by trail, visitors should be prepared to hike. Bring water, durable shoes, loose clothing, and a flashlight for cave exploring. (Caves are subject to seasonal closures due to flooding and "bat protection.") The best time to visit is spring, when the wildflowers bloom, or autumn; summer brings stifling heat to the area and winter carries rain. The east side of the park has an information center, picnic areas, and restrooms. The west side offers a ranger station, picnic areas, and restrooms. There are no concession services in the park. Day-use fee, $5. ~ No road traverses the park. You must enter either on the east side by following Route 25 south from Hollister for 32 miles, then proceeding four miles west on Route 146; or on the west side along Route 146, about 13 miles east from Soledad (which is just off Route 101); 831-389-4485, fax 831-389-4489; www.nps.gov/pinn, e-mail pinn_visitor_information@nps.gov. The lengthy drive to the east entrance makes for a long day trip. If you plan to hike, start early in the day.

▲ **Pinnacles Campground Inc.**, a private facility with 139 sites (some with partial RV hookups), sits astride the park's east side. Hot shower, a pool, and campground activities are perks. Two-night stay may be required. Fees range from $10 for one person to $75 for groups of ten. There is also a $7 reservation fee. A small grocery store with limited hours is also on-site. ~ 2400 Route 146, Paicines; 831-389-4462; www.pinncamp.com.

From Point Lobos, the highway hugs the coastline as it snakes south toward Big Sur. Like Route 1 north of San Francisco, this is one of America's great stretches of roadway. Situated between the Santa Lucia Mountains and the Pacific, Route 1 courses about 30 miles from Carmel to Big Sur, then spirals farther south along the coast toward San Luis Obispo and Los Angeles.

Big Sur

The Big Sur district is where the Santa Lucia Mountains encounter the Pacific. Backed by the challenging Ventana Wilderness, the region is marked by sharp coastal cliffs and unbelievable scenery. Though it's hard to conceive, Big Sur may be even more beautiful than the other sections of the Central Coast.

HENRY MILLER LITE

There's not much to the **Henry Miller Library**, but somehow the unassuming nature of the place befits its candid subject. Occupying a small woodframe house donated by Miller's friend Emil White, the museum contains volumes from the novelist's library as well as his evocative artworks. There's also local artwork and a great bookstore that hosts periodic concerts, readings, and workshops. Closed Tuesday. ~ Route 1 about a mile south of Ventana Inn; 831-667-2574; www.henrymiller.org, e-mail magnus@henrymiller.org.

Along Route 1, each turnout provides another glimpse into a magic-lantern world. Here the glass pictures a beach crusted with rocks, there a wave-wracked cliff or pocket of tidepools. The canyons are narrow and precipitous, while the headlands are so close to the surf they seem like beached whales. Trees are broken and blasted before the wind. The houses, though millionaire affairs, appear inconsequential against the backdrop of ocean and stone.

SIGHTS   At **Soberanes Point**, eight miles south of Carmel, hiking trails lead out along the headlands. Here you can stand on a rock shelf directly above the ocean and gaze back at the encroaching hills.

HIDDEN ▶   For an intriguing excursion into those hills, head about six miles up **Palo Colorado Road**, which intersects with Route 1 a couple of miles south of Garrapata Creek. Though paved, this country road is one lane. The corridor tunnels through an arcade of redwoods past log cabins and rustic homes. If you're feeling adventurous, follow the twisting eight-mile road to its terminus at Los Padres National Forest.

Back on Route 1 you'll traverse **Bixby Creek Bridge**, which stretches from one cliff to another across an infernal chasm. Local legend cites it incorrectly as the world's longest concrete arch span. With fluted hills in the background and a fluffy beach below, it may, however, be the world's prettiest.

HIDDEN ▶   For another incredible side trip, you can follow **Coast Road** for about 11 miles up into the Santa Lucia Mountains. Climbing along narrow ledges, then corkscrewing deep into overgrown canyons, the road carries you past exquisite views of forests and mountain ridges. There are hawk's-eye vistas of the Pacific, the rolling Big Sur countryside, and Pico Blanco, a 3709-foot lime-rich peak. This is the old coast road, the principal thoroughfare before Route 1 was completed in the 1930s. Take heed: It is so curvy it makes Route 1 seem a desert straightaway; it is also entirely unpaved, narrow, rutted, and impassable in wet weather. But oh those views!

Coast Road begins at Bixby Bridge and rejoins Route 1 at Andrew Molera State Park. If instead of detouring you stay on Route 1, it will climb along **Hurricane Point**, a promontory blessed with sweeping views and cursed by lashing winds, and descend toward **Little Sur Beach**. This sandy crescent is bounded by a shallow lagoon. There are dunes and lofty hills all around, as well as shore birds. Another lengthy beach leads to **Point Sur Light Station**, set on a volcanic headland. This solitary sentinel dates back to 1889. The only way to visit this lighthouse is by a three-hour guided tour. Tours run Saturday at 10 a.m. and 2 p.m., and Sunday at 10 a.m. There are additional tours added in

summer, including a moonlight tour. Call for details. Admission.
~ 831-625-4419.

Then the road enters the six-mile-long Big Sur River Valley.
Big Sur, a rural community of under 2000 people, stretches the
length of the valley. Lacking a town center, it consists of houses
and a few stores dotted along the Big Sur River. The place received its name from early Spanish settlers, who called the wilderness south of Carmel *El País Grande del Sur*, "the big country to the south."

Later it became a rural retreat and an artists' colony. Henry
Miller lived here from 1947 until 1964, writing *Big Sur and the
Oranges of Hieronymus Bosch*, *Plexus*, and *Nexus* during his
residence. Today the artists are being displaced by soaring land
values, while the region is gaining increased popularity among
visitors. It's not difficult to understand why as you cruise along
its knife-edge cliffs and timbered mountainsides. You can drive
for miles past eye-boggling vistas, then turn back on Route 1 to

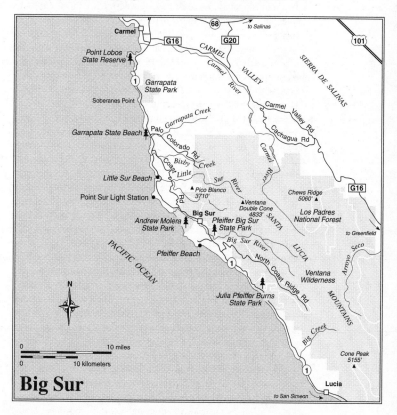

Big Sur

the Monterey Peninsula, or continue on to a strange and exotic land called Southern California.

LODGING For a variety of accommodations, consider **Big Sur Campground and Cabins**. Set in a redwood grove along the Big Sur River, this 13-acre facility has campsites, tent cabins, and A-frames. Camping out on the grounds includes access to hot showers, a laundry, a store, a basketball court, and a playground. The tent cabins consist of woodframe skeletons with canvas sides and transparent roofs. They come with beds, bedding, and towels, and share a bath house. The "cabins" along the river are actually mobile homes, neatly furnished but rather sterile. More intimate are the A-frame cabins with Franklin stoves, kitchens, and sleeping lofts. The newer modular units include pine floors with bedrooms as well as a kitchen and a private bath. ~ Route 1; 831-667-2322; www.bigsurcamp.com. BUDGET TO DELUXE.

Ripplewood Resort has 16 cabins and a café. The least expensive cabin is a small, basic duplex unit with redwood walls, a gas heater, and carpeting. It has a bath but lacks a kitchen. The more expensive units are larger, with kitchens, sitting rooms, and decks, and are located above the river. My advice? Compromise with one of the riverfront cabins. They feature kitchens, decks, and spacious bedrooms. (No extra charge for the river tumbling past your doorstep.) ~ Route 1; 831-667-2242, 800-575-1935, fax 831-667-2108; www.ripplewoodresort.com. MODERATE TO DELUXE.

Located within Pfeiffer Big Sur State Park is **Big Sur Lodge**, a complex containing 20 cottages with two to six units per cottage. The "lodge" represents a full-facility establishment complete with conference center, restaurant, gift shop, grocery, laundromat, and heated pool in the summer. It's very convenient, if undistinguished. The cottages are frame houses with wood-shingle roofs. They are simple in design, yet some have a kitchen and a fireplace. The interiors are pine and feature wall-to-wall carpeting and high beam ceilings; each cottage features a porch or a deck. ~ 47225 Route 1; 831-667-3100, 800-424-4787, fax 831-667-3110; www.bigsurlodge.com, e-mail info@bigsurlodge.com. DELUXE.

Big Sur has long been associated with bohemian values and an easy lifestyle. Today landed gentry and wealthy speculators have taken over many of the old haunts, but a few still remain. One such is **Deetjen's Big Sur Inn**, a 20-unit slapdash affair where formality is an inconvenience. The place consists of a hodgepodge collection of buildings. The outer walls are unpainted and the doors have no locks, lending the residence a tumbledown charm. Rooms are roughhewn, poorly insulated, and rustic, but some have woodburning stoves. Throw rugs are scattered about, the furniture is traditional, and local art pieces along the wall serve as decoration. No in-room phones or TVs. If all this is beginning to discourage you, you're getting older than you think; after all, this offbeat hideaway does possess an enchanting quality. ~ 48665 South Route 1; 831-667-2377, fax 831-667-0466; www. deetjens.com. DELUXE TO ULTRA-DELUXE.

When I'm ready to spend *beaucoup* bucks, I book lodging at the **Ventana Inn and Spa.** Set along 243 mountainside acres overlooking the Pacific Ocean, this fabled resort is the *ne plus ultra* of refined rusticity. Buildings are fashioned from raw wood and most guest rooms and suites are equipped with tile fireplaces. There are cedar walls and quilt beds. With Japanese hot baths, saunas, two pools, a spa, a fitness room, a library, and a clothing-optional sun deck, the place exudes an air of languor. Guests enjoy a continental breakfast and afternoon wine and cheese, hike nearby trails, partake in activities like mushroom hunting and photography, and congratulate themselves for having discovered a secluded resort where doing nothing is a way of life. Leaving the kids at home is suggested. ~ Route 1; 831-667-2331, 800-628-6500, fax 831-667-0573; www.ventanainn.com. ULTRA-DELUXE.

If, on the other hand, you spell Big Sur with a capital $, consider **The Post Ranch Inn**, located just across the highway from the Ventana Inn. Defying description, this cliff-edge hotel is a testimony to rustic perfection. Consisting of 30 separate units and designed to fit the surrounding landscape, some rooms are built into the hillside and covered by grass; others are perched on stilts high above the forest floor. Each room is decorated by wood and stone, has a king-size bed, and, best of all, offers an open view of the Pacific Ocean or tree-covered hillside. ~ Route 1; 831-667-2200, 800-527-2200, fax 831-667-2512; www.postranchinn. com, e-mail reservations@postranchinn.com. ULTRA-DELUXE.

The ultimate resting place in this corner of the world is the **Tassajara Zen Mountain Center.** Set deep in the Santa Lucia Mountains along a meandering country road, Tassajara has been a hot springs resort since the 1860s. Before that its salubrious waters were known to American Indians and the Spanish. When the Zen Center purchased the place in 1966, they converted it into a meditation center. There are only a few telephones and electrical outlets in the entire complex, making it ideal for people seeking serenity. Every year from May until September, the Zen Center welcomes day-visitors and overnight guests to use the Japanese-style bath houses and natural steam showers. The hosts provide three vegetarian meals daily plus lodging in the private rooms and cabins dotted about the grounds. Day-visitors are also welcome; shuttle service into the resort is available from Jamesburg, south of the Carmel Valley. In summer, Tassajara hosts a number of special workshops and retreats, including tea ceremonies and calligraphy writing. For day and overnight visits be sure to make your reservations far in advance, since this unique

◄ HIDDEN

place is very popular. Closed September through April. ~ For information, contact the Zen Center, 300 Page Street, San Francisco, CA 94102; 415-865-1895; for reservations, call 415-865-1899; www.sfzc.org/tassajara, e-mail tassrez@sfzc.org. DELUXE.

DINING

The Big Sur Roadhouse Restaurant has a prime location along Big Sur. The menu highlights fresh local seafoods and California fare with a Latin flair. The wine list features central California vintages. This small restaurant is a local favorite; reservations are recommended. Dinner only. Closed Tuesday. ~ Route 1; 831-667-2264, fax 831-667-2865. MODERATE TO DELUXE.

Fernwood Resort, a combination restaurant-bar-store with motel-like accommodations and RV hookups, has a changing menu that usually includes hamburgers, salads, and the like. This local gathering spot is your best bet for an inexpensive lunch or dinner. ~ Route 1; 831-667-2422, fax 831-667-2663; www.fernwoodbigsur.com. BUDGET TO MODERATE.

Cielo, part of the extraordinary complex that includes a prestigious inn, is one of the region's most elegant dining places. Resting on a hillside overlooking the mountains and sea, it's a perfect spot for a special meal. At lunch you'll be served salad, steak sandwiches, or fresh pasta, either inside the wood-paneled dining room, or alfresco on a sweeping veranda. For dinner you can start with oysters on the half shell or roasted red and golden beet salad, then proceed to such entrées as glazed duck breast, sauteed venison, or fresh fish grilled over oak. ~ Route 1; 831-667-4242, 800-628-6500; www.ventanainn.com. ULTRA-DELUXE.

Whether or not you're staying at the Post Ranch Inn, you will hardly want to miss dinner at the resort's signature restaurant, **Sierra Mar**. The magnificent views of the ocean and surf 1100 feet below become tenfold more dramatic at dinnertime when the sun drops behind the Pacific. The menu features health-conscious California cuisine and changes daily. Among the flexible prix-fixe menu selections are lean beef, seafood, poultry and vegetarian dishes. The bar serves a light luncheon all afternoon. Reservations required. ~ Route 1; 831-667-2800, fax 831-667-2824; www.postranchinn.com. ULTRA-DELUXE.

The beach scenes from *Basic Instinct*, starring Sharon Stone and Michael Douglas, were filmed at Garrapata State Beach.

Another bird's-eye view is offered at **Nepenthe**. Perched on a cliff 800 feet above the Pacific, this fabled dining spot has plenty of personality. People come across the continent to line its curving bar or dine along the open-air patio. It's a gathering place for locals, tourists, and everyone in between. There are sandwiches, quiches, and salads for lunch. At dinner the menu includes fresh fish, broiled chicken, and steak. If you're not hungry, stop in for a drink—the scene is a must. ~ Route 1; 831-667-2345, fax 831-

667-2394; www.nepenthebigsur.com, e-mail lpotter@nepenthe bigsur.com. MODERATE TO ULTRA-DELUXE.

For breakfast or lunch, try the outdoor **Café Kevah**, downstairs. Personally, I think it's a much better deal than Nepenthe. They serve yummy breakfast fare, like eggs benedict and french toast, and lunch dishes with a Mediterranean focus. Their homemade pastries are the perfect companions for an afternoon gazing out at the ocean. Closed January to mid-February and when it rains. ~ 831-667-2344, fax 831-667-2394; www.nepenthebig sur.com. BUDGET TO MODERATE.

Set in a circular wooden structure resembling an oversized wine cask (and made from old water tanks) is one of Big Sur's best-known art centers. The **Coast Gallery** is justifiably famous for its displays of arts and crafts by local artists. There are lithographs by novelist Henry Miller as well as paintings, sculptures, ceramics, woodwork, handmade candles, and blown glass by Northern California craftspeople. An adjoining shop features a wide selection of Miller's books. ~ 49901 Route 1, 33 miles south of Carmel; 831-667-2301, 800-797-6869, fax 831-667-2303; www. coastgalleries.com.

SHOPPING

Down in Big Sur the lights go out early. There is one place, **Big Sur River Inn**, that has a wood-paneled bar overlooking the Big Sur River and keeps a candle burning. Live music on Sunday afternoon in the summer. ~ Route 1; 831-667-2700, 800-548-3610; www.bigsurriverinn.com.

NIGHTLIFE

GARRAPATA STATE PARK This broad swath of white sand is particularly favored by local people, some of whom use it as a nude beach (which remains illegal). Easily accessible, it's nevertheless off the beaten tourist path, making an ideal hideaway for picnicking and skinny dipping. There are no facilities. A rough current and lack of lifeguards make swimming inadvisable. ~ It's along Route 1 about 7 miles south of Carmel. Watch for the curving beach from the highway; stop at the long turnout just north of the Garrapata Creek bridge. From here a path leads down to the beach; 831-649-2866.

BEACHES & PARKS

ANDREW MOLERA STATE PARK An adventurer's hideaway, this 4800-acre park rises from the sea to a 3455-foot elevation. It features three miles of beach and over 15 miles of hiking trails. The forests range from cottonwood to oak to redwood, while the wildlife includes mule deer, bobcat, harbor seals, and gray whales. Big Sur River rumbles through the landscape and surfers try the breaks on the beach. The only thing missing is a road: this is a hiker's oasis, its natural areas accessible only by heel and toe. The wilderness rewards are well worth the shoe leather. This is the only place in Big Sur where you can ride a horse; you can hire a horse from a concessionaire and check out Captain Cooper's Cabin, a late-19th-century pioneer log cabin. Toilets are the only facilities. Day-use fee, $8. ~ Located along Route 1 about three miles north of Big Sur; 831-667-2315, fax 831-667-2886.

▲ There are 24 hike-in sites (tents only); $9 per night. Primitive facilities, but water and flush toilets are available.

PFEIFFER BIG SUR STATE PARK 🏃 🛶 🏊 One of California's southernmost redwood parks, this 1000-acre facility is very popular, particularly in summer. With cottages, a restaurant, a grocery, a gift shop, picnic areas, restrooms, showers, and a laundromat on the premises, it's quite developed. However, nature still retains a toehold in these parts: the Big Sur River overflows with trout and salmon (fishing is prohibited, however), Pfeiffer Falls tumbles through a fern-banked canyon. Day-use fee, $8. ~ Located along Route 1 in Big Sur; 831-667-2315, fax 831-667-2886.

▲ There are 204 sites for both tents and RVs (no hookups); $20 to $35 per night. Reservations: 800-444-7275.

PFEIFFER BEACH 🏃 🛶 ⛵ 🎣 🚴 Of Big Sur's many wonders, this may be the most exotic. It's a sandy beach littered with boulders and bisected by a meandering stream. Behind the strand rise high bluffs that mark the terminus of a narrow gorge. Just offshore loom rock formations into which the sea has carved tunnels and arches. Little wonder poet Robinson Jeffers chose this haunting spot for his primal poem "Give Your Heart to the Hawks." The only facilities are toilets. Day-use fee, $5. ~ Follow Route 1 for about a mile south past the entrance to Pfeiffer Big Sur State Park. Turn right onto Sycamore Canyon Road (unmarked), which leads downhill two miles to the beach; 831-667-2315, fax 831-667-2886.

JULIA PFEIFFER BURNS STATE PARK 🏃 This 3700-acre extravaganza extends from the ocean to about 1500 feet elevation and is bisected by Route 1. The central park area sits in a redwood canyon with a stream that feeds through a steep defile into the ocean. Backdropped by sharp hills in a kind of natural amphitheater, it's an enchanting glade. A path leads beneath the highway to a spectacular vista point where 80-foot-high McWay Waterfall plunges into the ocean. Another path, one-and-eight-tenths miles north of the park entrance, descends from the highway to an isolated beach near Partington Cove that has been declared an underwater park (permit required). There are restrooms. ~ Route 1, about 11 miles south of Pfeiffer Big Sur State Park; 831-667-2315, fax 831-667-2886.

▲ There are two hike-in environmental campsites for tents only; $13 to $20 per night with an eight-person maximum. Reservations are required; call 800-444-7275.

VENTANA WILDERNESS 🏃🐎🦌🛶 Part of Los Padres National Forest, this magnificent 216,500-acre preserve parallels Route 1 a few miles inland. It covers a broad swath of the Santa Lucia Mountains with elevations ranging from 600 feet to 5800 feet. Within its rugged confines are 237 miles of hiking trails. Wild boars and turkeys, mountain lions, and deer roam its slopes. Bald eagles soar the skies. The only facilities are ranger stations. Parking fee, $4. ~ From Route 1 in the Big Sur area, there are two entry points. The ranger station, where maps and fire permits can be acquired, is just south of Pfeiffer Big Sur State Park. For information and permits, contact the U.S. Forest Service (Monterey District, 406 South Mildred Avenue, King City, CA 93930; 831-385-5434), or 831-667-2315, fax 831-667-2886.

🔺 There are hike-in sites only, which are free.

Outdoor Adventures

The North Central Coast is renowned for its open-sea fishing. Charter boats comb the waters for rock cod, salmon, and albacore. Most trips leave the dock by 6 a.m. and return by 3 p.m.

SPORT-FISHING

SOUTH OF SAN FRANCISCO If you want to test your skill, or luck, contact **Half Moon Bay Sportsfishing**. They operate three boats, ranging from 55 to 65 feet. You can go deep-sea fishing for rock cod or ling cod any day of the week. April through November there's salmon fishing and December through March there's whale watching. Bait and tackle available. ~ 111 Johnson Pier, Princeton-by-the-Sea; 650-726-2913.

> The summer whale-watching season typically runs from mid-June through September while the winter migration is viewable from mid-December to mid-March.

SANTA CRUZ To take a charter from Santa Cruz in search of tuna, salmon, or rock cod, call **Leo's Marine Supply and Sportfishing**. Bait included, rods and tackle available. They run a 44-footer. ~ 2210 East Cliff Drive at the Santa Cruz Yacht Harbor; 831-476-2648; www.mtmcharters.com. For do-it-yourself adventures, **Santa Cruz Boat Rentals** has 18 boats to rent and a 16-foot wood skiff that seats up to four adults. Fishing gear is provided. There is also bait, tackle, and a gift shop. ~ Santa Cruz Municipal Pier; 831-423-1739; www.santacruzboatrentals.net.

MONTEREY Spend the day on one of two boats with **Randy's Fishing Trips**. Advance reservations recommended. ~ 66 Old Fisherman's Wharf; 831-372-7440. **Sam's Fishing Fleet** also offers charters and day-long fishing trips for albacore, salmon, and deep-sea catches. ~ 48 Old Fisherman's Wharf; 831-372-0577.

WHALE WATCHING

To see the whales during their annual migration, head for whale-watching lookouts at Pillar Point in Half Moon Bay, the coast around Davenport, Point Pinos in Pacific Grove, or Cypress Point in Point Lobos State Reserve. (See the "Whale Watching" section in Chapter Five.)

SOUTH OF SAN FRANCISCO November through March, **Half Moon Bay Sportfishing** offers two whale-watching excursions daily. The party boat plies the coast in search of cetaceans, pinnipeds, and other marine life. ~ 21 Johnson Pier, Princeton-by-the-Sea; 650-726-2913.

MONTEREY If you'd prefer a close look at these migrating mammals and other marine life—sea lions, seals, otters, sea birds—catch a cruise with **Randy's Fishing Trips**. They can accommodate up to 48 people, and the two- or three-hour trip is fully narrated by a marine biologist. ~ 66 Old Fisherman's Wharf; 831-372-7440. To catch glimpses of blue whales, humpbacks, and dolphins, hop on board a 75- or 100-foot vessel with **Monterey Whalewatching**. Trips last about three hours and feature a naturalist; sonar equipment is used to help locate whales. ~ 96 Old Fisherman's Wharf #1; 831-372-2203. **Sam's Fishing Fleet** offers cruises that last anywhere from two to six hours. Their three boats are fully equipped with fish finders and radar. ~ 48 Old Fisherman's Wharf; 831-372-0577.

KAYAKING Whether you are young or old, experienced or a novice, the Central Coast awaits discovery by sea kayak.

MONTEREY Explore Monterey Bay and Elkhorn Slough, or paddle your way along the coastal waters with **Monterey Bay Kayaks**. They also offer naturalist-led trips around the Monterey National Marine Sanctuary, where you'll see a wide variety of marine life. The tour to Elkhorn Slough goes through an inland saltwater marsh to view seals, otters, and birds. Reservations recommended. ~ 693 Del Monte Avenue, Monterey; 831-373-5357, 800-649-5357; www.montereybaykayaks.com. **Adventures by the Sea** has double and single kayaks for rent. The twice-daily tours are led by a local naturalist who describes the history of Cannery Row, local geology, natural history, and native lore. ~ 299 Cannery Row; 831-372-1807; www.adventuresbythesea.com, e-mail sales@ adventuresbythesea.com.

AUTHOR FAVORITE

Of all the adventures in nature that await along the Central Coast, the one I remember most vividly is kayaking among the playful sea otters and boisterous sea lions on Monterey Bay. Guided excursions of the bay or Elkhorn Slough afford an up-close and personal look at the region's greatest treasures. See above for kayaking tour outfitters.

The Central Coast offers premiere diving in Northern California. Although coastal waters are quite frigid, the unique kelp forests, wide array of fish, spotted harbor seals, and other fascinating marine life make for unforgettable diving.

DIVING

SANTA CRUZ   Adventure Sports offers everything from one- or two-week-long dive trips taking you to hotspots to brunch dives leaving from Monastery Beach. They rent and sell gear, and give classes ranging from beginning to assistant instructor. Closed Sunday. ~ 303 Potrero Street #15, Santa Cruz; 831-458-3648, 888-839-4286; www.asudoit.com, e-mail dennis@asudoit.com.

MONTEREY   Aquarius Dive Shop offers beach dives unless otherwise requested. One- and two-tank dives are available, as are night dives. They rent and sell all the gear. Classes are offered for open water, advanced rescue, dive master, and nitrox. Reservations required. ~ 2040 Del Monte Avenue, Monterey; 831-375-1933; www.aquariusdivers.com. For morning or afternoon dives, contact **Monterey Bay Dive Company**. All equipment is available to rent. ~ 225 Cannery Row; 831-656-0454; www.monterey scubadiving.com.

CARMEL   Point Lobos State Reserve has some of the finest shore diving opportunities on the Pacific Coast. You'll spot sea otters, sea lions, and schools of fish. The numbers of divers per day is limited so reservations are a must (up to two months in advance to the day). ~ Route 1; 831-624-8413; www.pt-lobos. parks.state.ca.us, e-mail pointlobos@parks.ca.gov.

Catching a wave when the surf's up near Lighthouse Point north of Santa Cruz is a surfer's dream. Known as "Steamer Lane," this stretch of coastline hosts many international surfing competitions. On the east side, Pleasure Point is a popular surf spot with several reef breaks. Mavericks Break, located north of Half Moon Bay, is world-renowned among surfers for its huge— sometimes deadly—waves. Even experienced wave riders need to be careful here. Avoid surfing too far north near Año Nuevo— the waters are popular with great white sharks. On the east side, long and short fiberglass boards, boogieboards, and wet suits can be rented or purchased from **Freeline Design**. ~ 821 41st Avenue, Santa Cruz; 831-476-2950. **O'Neill's Surf Shop**, a one-stop surf mecca, rents surfboards, boogieboards, and wetsuits, and sells all the accessories. ~ 1115 41st Avenue, Capitola; 831-475-4151; www.oneill.com.

SURFING & WIND-SURFING

Or catch the wind on a windsurfing board. Rentals and lessons are available at **Club Ed**, as are regular surfing lessons and equipment. Besides surfboards they also rent body boards and wetsuits. ~ Look for the trailer on Cowell Beach next to the Santa Cruz wharf; 831-464-0177; www.club-ed.com.

RIDING STABLES   Exploring the coast and inland trails astride a galloping horse is one way to enjoy a visit to the Central Coast.

SOUTH OF SAN FRANCISCO   With its four-mile white-sand beach and surrounding farm country, Half Moon Bay is a choice region for riding. **Seahorse and Friendly Acres Ranch**, located on the coast, rents more than 150 horses. They also have pony rides for kids. No reservations are necessary. ~ 2150 Route 1, Half Moon Bay; 650-726-9903.

PACIFIC GROVE   There are escorted tours at the **Pebble Beach Equestrian Center**. A one-and-a-half-hour ride takes you through the forest and down to the beach. Call ahead to reserve a horse. ~ Portola Road and Alva Lane, Pebble Beach; 831-624-2756; www.ridepebblebeach.com, e-mail info@ridepebblebeach.com.

GOLF   For golfers, visiting the Monterey Peninsula is tantamount to arriving in heaven. Pebble Beach is home to the annual AT&T National Pro-Am Golf Championship. Several courses rank among the top in the nation.

With stunning views of the rugged coastline, **Pebble Beach Golf Course** is the most noted. Four U.S. Open Tournaments have been held here. The 7th, 8th, 17th, and 18th holes are world-renowned as highly difficult ocean holes. Reservations are required a day in advance for non-hotel guests. ~ 17 Mile Drive, Pebble Beach; 831-625-8518, 800-654-9300. **Spyglass Hill Golf Course**, known as one of the toughest courses in the nation, has six of the holes with ocean views while the rest are set in the forest. Reservations are required. ~ Stevenson Drive, Pebble Beach; 831-625-8563, 800-654-9300. Set on a century-old property, **Del Monte Golf Course** is a relatively flat course studded with ancient trees. ~ 1300 Sylvan Road, Monterey; 831-373-2700. **Pacific Grove Golf Course** overlooks Monterey Bay and the Pacific Ocean. It has a pro shop and driving range. ~ 77 Asilomar Avenue, Pacific Grove; 831-648-5777.

BIKING   The **Pacific Coast Route** follows Route 1 through the entire Central Coast area to Big Sur and beyond. There are camping sites along the way. The ocean views and rolling pastures make this an ideal course to peddle, if you are experienced and careful.

Both Santa Cruz and Monterey have bike paths for beginners and skilled riders alike. Especially good for touring are **17 Mile Drive**, the bike trail along the bayshore from **Seaside to Marina**, the trail from **Seaside to Lover's Point** (via Cannery Row), and the roads in **Point Lobos State Reserve**.

Bike Rentals   **Bay Bike Rentals** carries hybrids, mountain bikes, tandems, and surreys (four-wheeled, pedal-powered vehicles). ~ 585 Cannery Row, Monterey; 831-655-2453.

To fully capture the beauty and serenity of the region's woodlands, chaparral country, and beaches, explore its hiking trails. The Santa Cruz and Santa Lucia mountains offer several hundred miles of trails through fir, madrone, and redwood forests. Getting lost, so to speak, among these stands of ancient trees is a splendid way to vacation. Or hike the inland hills with their caves and rock spires. Down at the sea's edge you'll discover more caves, as well as tidepools, sand dunes, and a world of marine life.

HIKING

All distances listed for hiking trails are one way unless otherwise noted.

SOUTH OF SAN FRANCISCO   If you've an urge to see elephant seals breeding, take the three-mile guided walk led by docents at Año Nuevo State Reserve. To protect these mammoth mammals, the preserve is open during breeding season only to those on the guided tours. Tours are scheduled from December through March. The tours are popular and space is limited so make reservations well in advance; call 800-444-4445. To explore this area after mating season, you can hike on your own past sand dunes, tidepools, and sea caves. Follow Año Nuevo Trail (2.5 miles), beginning at the west end of the parking lot, to Año Nuevo Point.

> Be careful when driving along the coast in the summer—thick fogs occasionally creep in, making for dangerous driving conditions.

MONTEREY AREA   One of California's most beautiful spots is the six-mile shoreline at Point Lobos State Reserve. The park is laced with trails leading to tidepools, sandy coves, and whale-watching vistas.

Cypress Grove Trail (.8 mile), one of the most popular (and populated) in the park, leads through a stand of Monterey cypress trees and offers cliff-top views of the ocean.

Bird Island Trail (.8 mile) takes you through coastal shrubbery to two exquisite white-sand beaches—China Cove and Gibson Beach. The path also overlooks Bird Island, a refuge for cormorants and brown pelicans.

Pine Ridge Trail (.7 mile), beginning near Piney Woods, goes inland through forests of Monterey pines and Coast live oak. Deer, squirrel, and such birds as pygmy nuthatches and chestnut-backed chickadees make this a tranquil nature hike.

South Shore Trail (1 mile), an oceanside walk between Sea Lion Point and the Bird Rock parking area, allows close looks at tidepool life and shore birds. You can also play amateur geologist, examining multicolored patterns in sedimentary rocks.

For rock climbers and hikers alike, Pinnacles National Monument offers great sport. Because of the summer heat and winter weather, it's recommended that you come in spring or fall to explore the park's rock spires, talus caves, and covered canyons. At any time of year, bring plenty of water and a flashlight.

Hiking along the narrow ledges of **High Peaks Trail** (5.4 miles), you'll find splendid views of the entire park. The steep trail begins across from the Chalone Creek picnic area, travels up through the High Peaks and ends up at the Moses Spring parking lot. Allow at least three to four hours.

Old Pinnacles Trail (2.3 miles) begins at Chalone Creek picnic area and goes along relatively level terrain near the west fork of the creek to Balconies Caves.

Juniper Canyon Trail (1.8 miles) starts near the west end of the park at the Chaparral ranger station and climbs 760 feet to connect with the park's east side High Peaks Trail. It's the steepest trail in the monument.

BIG SUR Over 240,000 acres of rugged mountain terrain comprise the **Ventana Wilderness** of Los Padres National Forest. About 200 miles of hiking trails make it easy to explore the Santa Lucia Mountains while escaping the trappings of civilization. Several roads off Route 1 will take you onto the preserve. Big Sur Station is the only staffed coastal entrance.

Bottchers Gap–Devils Peak Trail (4 miles) is a steep hike through coniferous forests to spectacular vistas overlooking the northern section of the Ventana Wilderness.

Kirk Creek–Vicente Flat Trail (5.1 miles) winds along ridgelines that afford mountain views.

Pine Ridge Trail (27 miles) begins at Big Sur Station and carries two miles to the park boundary before heading into the Ventana Wilderness. First stop is Ventana Camp, near the Big Sur River. Then the trail leads past several campgrounds and ends at China Camp.

Transportation

CAR

From San Francisco, coastal highway **Route 1** is the most scenic way to explore the Central Coast. In the Santa Cruz Mountains, **Routes 35** and **9** lead through redwood forests and rural towns. **Route 101**, which runs inland parallel to the coast is the fastest route. Numerous side roads lead from this highway to points along the Central Coast.

AIR

Several airlines fly regular schedules to the **Monterey Peninsula Airport**. American Eagle Airlines, Delta Air Lines, ExpressJet, United, United Express, and US Airways, service this area from San Francisco and other departure points. ~ Route 68 and Olmstead Road; 831-648-7000; www.montereyairport.com.

BUS

Greyhound Bus Lines has continual service to Santa Cruz (425 Front Street; 831-423-1800) from San Francisco and Los Angeles. ~ 800-231-2222; www.greyhound.com.

For railroad buffs, **Amtrak** offers daily service on the "Coast
Starlight." The train runs from Seattle to Los Angeles with stops
in Oakland, San Jose, and Salinas (11 Station Place). Once in Salinas, passengers can transfer to a Greyhound or Monterey–
Salinas Transit bus. ~ 800-872-7245.

If flying directly into Monterey, you can rent a car at the airport
from **Alamo** (800-327-9633), **Avis Rent A Car** (800-331-1212),
Budget Rent A Car (800-527-0700), **Enterprise** (800-736-8222),
Hertz Rent A Car (800-654-3131), or **National Car Rental** (800-
227-7368). Additional rental agencies are located in town. Try
American International Rent A Car (800-392-8724).

San Mateo County Transit, or **SamTrans**, departing from the Daly
City and Colma BART stations, has local bus service to Pacifica,
Moss Beach, and Half Moon Bay. Bus service is also available
between Año Nuevo and San Mateo and Half Moon Bay during
seal season (January through March). Reservations are required
(through SamTrans). ~ 800-660-4287; www.samtrans.com.
    From Waddell Creek in northern Santa Cruz County, the
Santa Cruz Metropolitan Transit District covers Route 1 as far
south as Watsonville. ~ 831-425-8600.
    From Watsonville, connections can be made to Monterey and
Big Sur via the **Monterey–Salinas Transit Company**. These buses
carry passengers to many points of interest including Cannery
Row, Point Lobos, and Andrew Molera and Pfeiffer Big Sur State
Parks (seasonal). Buses from Monterey to Big Sur run twice daily
from Memorial Day to Labor Day, and on weekends year-round.
~ 831-899-2555; www.mst.org.

FIVE

South Central Coast

To call any one section of the California Coast the most alluring is to embark upon uncertain waters. Surely the Central Coast, that 200-mile swath from Ventura to San Simeon, is a region of rare beauty. Stretching across Ventura, Santa Barbara, and San Luis Obispo counties, it embraces many of the West's finest beaches.

Five of California's 21 missions—in Ventura, Santa Barbara, Lompoc, San Luis Obispo, and farther inland in Solvang—lie along this stretch. Chosen by the Spanish in the 1780s for their fertile pastures, natural harbors, and placid surroundings, they are a historic testimonial to the varied richness of the landscape.

The towns that grew up around these missions, evocative of old Spanish traditions, are emblems of California's singular culture. Santa Barbara, perhaps the state's prettiest town, is a warren of whitewashed buildings and red tile roofs, backdropped by rocky peaks and bounded by a five-mile palm-fringed beach.

Ventura and San Luis Obispo represent two of California's most underrated towns. In addition to a wealthy heritage, Ventura has beautiful beaches and San Luis Obispo is set amid velvet hills and rich agricultural areas. Both are less expensive than elsewhere and offer many of the same features without the pretensions.

Offshore are the Channel Islands, a 25-million-year-old chain and vital wildlife preserve. Sandblasted by fierce storms, pristine in their magnificence, they are a china shop of endangered species and unique life forms. While the nearby reefs are headstones for the many ships that have crashed here, the surrounding waters are crowded with sea life.

Together with the rest of the coast, the islands were discovered by Juan Rodríguez Cabrillo in 1542. The noted explorer found them inhabited by Chumash Indians, a collection of tribes occupying the coast from Malibu to Morro Bay. Hunters and gatherers, the Chumash were master mariners who built woodplank canoes called *tomols*, capable of carrying ten people across treacherous waters to the Channel Islands. They in turn were preceded by the Oak Grove Tribes, which inhabited the region from 7000 to 3000 B.C.

Once Gaspar de Portolá opened the coast to Spanish colonialists with his 1769 explorations, few Indians from any California tribes survived. Forced into servitude and religious conversion by the padres, the Chumash revolted at Santa Barbara Mission and Mission de la Purísima Concepción in 1824. They held Purísima for a month before troops from Monterey overwhelmed them. By 1910 the Westerners who had come to save them had so decimated the Indians that their 30,000 population dwindled to 1250.

By the mid-1800s these lately arrived white men set out in pursuit of any sea mammal whose pelt would fetch a price. The Central Coast was a prime whale-hunting ground. Harpooners by the hundreds speared leviathans, seals, and sea lions, hunting them practically to extinction. Earlier in the century American merchants, immortalized in Richard Henry Dana's *Two Years Before the Mast*, had combed the coast trading for cattle hides.

The land that bore witness to this colonial carnage endured. Today the South Central Coast and its offshore islands abound in sea lions, harbor seals, Northern fur seals, and elephant seals. Whales inhabit the deeper waters and gamefish are plentiful. The only threats remaining are those from developers and the oil industry, whose offshore drilling resulted in the disastrous 1969 Santa Barbara spill.

The South Central Coast traveler finds a Mediterranean climate, dry and hot in the summer, tempered by morning fog and winds off the ocean, then cool and rainy during winter months. Two highways, Routes 1 and 101, lead through this salubrious environment. The former hugs the coast much of the way, traveling inland to Lompoc and San Luis Obispo, and the latter, at times joining with Route 1 to form a single roadway, eventually diverges into the interior valleys.

Almost as much as the ocean, mountains play a vital part in the life of the coast. Along the southern stretches are the Santa Monica Mountains, which give way farther north to the Santa Ynez Mountains. Below them, stretching along the coastal plain, are the towns of Oxnard, Ventura, Santa Barbara, and Goleta.

Both mountain systems are part of the unique Transverse Range, which, unlike most North American mountains, travels from east to west rather than north and south. They are California's Great Divide, a point of demarcation between the chic, polished regions near Santa Barbara and the rough, wild territory around San Luis Obispo.

Arriving at the ocean around Point Conception, the Transverse Range separates the curving pocket beaches of the south and the endless sand dunes to the north. Here the continent takes a sharp right turn as the beaches, facing south in Santa Barbara, wheel about to look west across the Pacific.

Amid this geologic turmoil lies Lompoc, the top flower seed–producing area in the world, a region of agricultural beauty and color beyond belief, home to 40 percent of the United States' flower crop. To the north are the Nipomo Sand Dunes, extending 18 miles from Point Sal to Pismo Beach, one of the nation's largest dune systems. A habitat for the endangered California brown pelican and the California least tern, these are tremendous piles of sand, towering to 450 feet, held in place against the sea wind by a lacework of ice plant, grasses, verbena, and silver lupine. They are also the site of an Egyptian city, complete with walls 110 feet high and a grand boulevard lined with sphinxes and pharaohs. Today, like other glorious cities of yesteryear, it lies buried beneath the sand.

In San Luis Obispo oceanfront rolls into ranch land as the landscape reveals a Western visage. Unlike Spanish-style Santa Barbara to the south and Monterey to the north, San Luis Obispo has defined its own culture, a blend of hard-riding ranch hand and easygoing college student. Its roots nonetheless are similar, deriving from the Spanish, who founded their mission here in 1772, and the 19th-century Americans who built the town's gracious Victorian homes.

Rich too in natural history, the region between San Luis Obispo and Morro Bay is dominated by nine mountain peaks, each an extinct volcano dating back 20 million years. Last in the line is Morro Rock, an imposing monolith that's surrounded by a fertile wetlands that represents one of the country's ten most vital bird habitats.

Farther north civilization gives way to coastal quietude. There are untracked beaches and wind-honed sea cliffs, a prelude to Big Sur farther up the coast. Among the few signs of the modern world are the artist colony of Cambria and that big house on the hill, Hearst Castle, California's own eighth wonder of the world. Symbol of boundless artistry and unbridled egotism, it is also one of the Central Coast's many wonders.

Ventura–Oxnard Area

Situated 60 miles northwest of Los Angeles and 30 miles to the southeast of Santa Barbara, the 18th-century mission town of Ventura has generally been overlooked by travelers. History has not been so remiss. Long known to the Chumash Indians, who inhabited a nearby village named Shisholop, the place was revealed to Europeans in 1542 by the Portuguese explorer Juan Rodríguez Cabrillo. Father Junípero Serra founded a mission here in 1782 and the region soon became renowned for its fruit orchards. Oxnard is known chiefly as an agricultural community, contributing a large share of the area's produce.

SIGHTS Today Ventura preserves its heritage in a number of historic sites. Stop by the **Ventura Visitors & Convention Bureau** for brochures and maps. ~ 89 South California Street, Suite C, Ventura; 805-648-2075, 800-483-6214; www.ventura-usa.com, e-mail tourism@ventura-usa.com.

Downtown Ventura is compact and walkable, and the highlight of a stroll through Ventura is **San Buenaventura Mission**, a whitewash and red-tile church flanked by a flowering garden. The dark, deep chapel is lined with Stations of the Cross paintings and features a Romanesque altar adorned with statues and pilasters. My favorite spot is the adjacent garden with its tile fountain and stately Norfolk pines. Entrance to the mission is actually through a small gift shop a few steps to the east. Admission. ~ 211 East Main Street, Ventura; 805-643-4318, fax 805-643-7831; www.sanbuenaventuramission.org, e-mail mission@sanbuenaventuramission.org.

Then cross Main Street to the **Ventura County Museum of History & Art,** which traces the region's secular history with displays of Chumash Indian artifacts and a farm implement collection. The art gallery features revolving exhibits of local painters and photographers. There's a collection of 40,000 photos depicting Ventura County from its origin to the present. One gallery features a permanent display of George Stuart's historical figures. The artist is exacting in his detail, right down to eyelashes and fingernails, when crafting a Martin Luther King, Jr., or Abraham Lincoln. A research library and archive houses maps, manuscripts, and photographs pertaining to Ventura County. Closed Monday. Admission. ~ 100 East Main Street, Ventura; 805-653-0323, fax 805-653-5267; www.venturamuseum.org.

Just west of the mission, the **Albinger Archaeological Museum** sits at the site of an archaeological dig that dates back 3500 years, representing five different cultures. The small museum displays

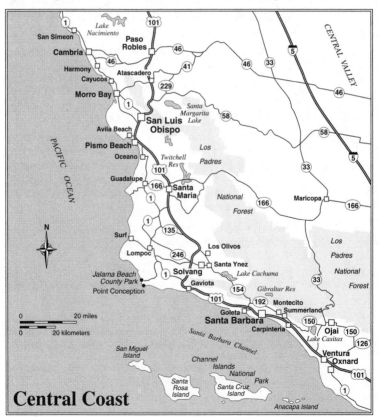

Central Coast

Text continued on page 270.

South Central Coast

This excursion takes you up the coast, avoiding the freeway wherever possible, for a visit to Hearst Castle, the area's biggest "must-see" attraction. The only trick is to book your reservations for the Hearst Castle tour(s) well in advance—in most cases, *months* ahead. The return trip takes you on a journey through California's wild Sierra Madre.

Day 1
- Head north from the Los Angeles area on Route 101, leaving early enough to arrive in Santa Barbara by around 10 a.m.

- Explore Santa Barbara's historic district on the self-guided **Red Tile Tour** (pages 280–81).

- Visit the restored **Mission Santa Barbara** (page 276), the most beautiful of Padre Junipero Serra's California missions.

- Before leaving Santa Barbara, stop by **Brophy Brothers Restaurant & Clam Bar** (page 289) for a fresh seafood lunch and enjoy the spectacular harbor views from their patio.

- Follow legendary Route 1 north as it changes back and forth between fast divided highway and pastoral two-lane road, all the while playing hide-and-seek with the ocean. If you have extra time along the way, explore **San Luis Obispo**'s pretty downtown (page 300), or stop for a hike or a swim at one of the beaches and parks around **Morro Bay** (page 302).

- Arrive in **Cambria** (page 314) and check into your choice of bed-and-breakfast inns for a two-night stay.

Day 2
- The high point of the day is a visit to the opulent **Hearst Castle** (page 314). Take Tour 1 and one of the other three tours.

- Spend the remainder of the day in blissful relaxation, exploring the art galleries of cute little Cambria or enjoying Moonstone Beach and San Simeon Creek in **San Simeon State Park** (page 318).

- Have dinner in town and return to your B&B or check out the music at **Camozzi's Saloon** (page 318).

Day 3 • After breakfast, take Route 1 south for 52 miles to the little town of Guadalupe, and turn east (left) on Route 166.

• Drive through Santa Maria and up into the Sierra Madre, a distance of 74 miles to the junction with Route 33. Turn south (right) and continue for another 57 miles. Allow at least half a day for this drive. There are no notable sightseeing highlights along the way, just the solitude and dramatic mountain landscapes of **Los Padres National Forest** (page 313) rising from the sea to over 9000 feet elevation.

Route 101 will take you back to central Los Angeles in about an hour—depending on traffic conditions.

arrowheads, shell beads, crucifixes, and pottery uncovered here. At the dig site itself you'll see the foundation of an 18th-century mission church, an ancient earth oven, and a remnant of the Spanish padres' elaborate aqueduct system. Closed Monday and Tuesday. ~ 113 East Main Street, Ventura; 805-648-5823, fax 805-653-5267.

About four blocks west of the mission sits the **Ortega Adobe Historic Residence**, a small, squat home built in 1857 that eventually gave birth to Ortega Chile. With its woodplank furniture and bare interior it provides a strong example of how hard and rudimentary life was in that early era. Grounds open daily, house open by appointment. ~ 215 West Main Street, Ventura; 805-658-4726, fax 805-648-1030.

Backtrack to San Buenaventura Mission and wander down **Figueroa Plaza**, a broad promenade decorated with tile fountains and flowerbeds. This is the site of the town's old Chinatown section, long since passed into myth and memory. Be sure to contemplate the colorful mural depicting the history and contributions of Ventura's Chinese population.

Figueroa Street continues to the waterfront, where a **promenade** parallels the beach. This is a prime area for water sports, and countless surfers, with their blond hair and black wetsuits, will be waiting offshore, poised for the perfect wave. Along the far end of the esplanade, at the **Ventura Pier**, you'll encounter one more Southern California species, the surf fisherman.

If it's not too hazy, the outline of Anacapa, one of the **Channel Islands**, should be visible from the pier and other high spots in Ventura. Day trips to Anacapa, which lies about 14 miles offshore, can be arranged through **Island Packers**. Tours are limited in winter; call ahead. ~ 1691 Spinnaker Drive, Ventura Harbor; 805-642-1393; www.islandpackers.com. For an orientation to the special habitat of the Channel Islands, visit the **Channel Islands Visitors Center** at Ventura Harbor. ~ 1901 Spinnaker Drive, Ventura Harbor; 805-658-5730. (For more information about the islands and excursions to visit them, see "The Channel Islands" in this chapter.)

Another local wonder is the **Ventura County Courthouse**, a sprawling neoclassical-style structure. Now serving as the town's city hall, the place is a mélange of Doric columns, bronze fixtures, and Roman flourishes. But forget the marble entranceway and grand staircase—what makes it memorable is the row of friars' heads adorning the facade. Where else but in Southern California would a dozen baroque priests stare out at you from the hall of justice? ~ 501 Poli Street, Ventura.

The **Olivas Adobe** is a spacious hacienda surrounded by flowering gardens. This two-story gem, with balconies running the full length of the upper floor, is a study in the Monterey-style architecture of 19th-century California. The rooms are furnished in period pieces and there is a museum adjacent to the house, providing a window on the world of California's prosperous Spanish settlers. Special events such as summer concerts, a Western-style fair, and a Christmas candlelight tour are staged. Call for information. Grounds open daily, museum closed week-days. Tours are available on the weekends. ~ 4200 Olivas Park Drive, Ventura; 805-658-4728, fax 805-648-1030; www.olivas adobe.org, e-mail mail@olivasadobe.org.

It's mostly the agricultural fields of strawberries and the bustle of suburbia that you'll notice as you drive through the Oxnard area. But the city also has a seven-mile stretch of shoreline and the **Channel Islands Harbor,** a busy commercial port providing a de-parture point for trips to the Channel Islands.

A fun way to see the harbor is via the **Channel Islands Harbor Water Taxi,** which makes a roundtrip of the harbor in about 35 minutes ($8). The water taxi stops at six different lo-cations around the harbor, but operates on a limited schedule: Thursday through Sunday, from noon to 6 p.m. ~ 805-985-4677; www.channelislandsharbor.org.

Several of Ventura County's late-19th-century homes were relocated to an area called **Heritage Square** in downtown Ox-

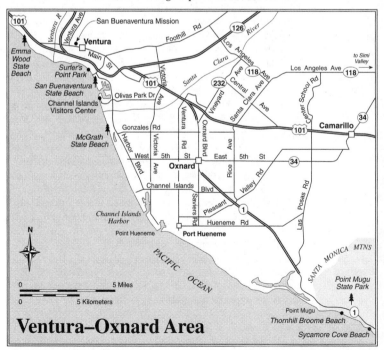

Ventura–Oxnard Area

nard. Most of the houses are given over to small professional offices, but there are historic exhibits, a restaurant, and a community theater as well. Tours are available on Saturday or by appointment. Free concerts on Fridays in summer. ~ 715 South A Street, Oxnard; 805-483-7960; e-mail heritagesquare@aol.com.

East of Ventura and Oxnard in the suburban town of Simi Valley lies the **Ronald Reagan Presidential Library**. Here you'll find a visual history of Reagan's 1980s-era presidency in the form of film clips, videos, artifacts, and photos. There's a piece of the Berlin Wall, a re-creation of the White House cabinet room, a replica of the Oval Office, and, re-creating Reagan's earlier years, memorabilia from his boyhood and Hollywood career. A separate building houses a Reagan-era Air Force One plane and other presidential transports. Admission. ~ 40 Presidential Drive, Simi Valley; 805-577-4000, 800-410-8354, fax 805-577-4074; www.reaganlibrary.com, e-mail reagan.library@nara.gov.

LODGING

HIDDEN ▶

For something spacious, plush, and formal consider the **Bella Maggiore Inn**. Set in downtown Ventura, this 28-room hostelry follows the tradition of a provincial Italian inn. There are European appointments and antique chandeliers in the lobby and a Roman-style fountain in the courtyard. The accommodations I saw were painted in soft hues and decorated with pastel prints. The furniture was a mixture of cane, washed pine, and antiques. A full breakfast is included. ~ 67 South California Street, Ventura; 805-652-0277, 800-523-8479, fax 805-648-5670. MODERATE TO DELUXE.

HIDDEN ▶

Get into the nautical theme of the area by staying aboard a 35-foot Chinese junk that's securely docked in Ventura Harbor. **Boatel Bunk and Breakfast** offers accommodations for two on restored wooden boats. Breakfast is included, but you'll have to go topside for the shower. ~ 1567 Spinnaker Drive, Slip D-8, Ventura Harbor; 805-598-2628. DELUXE.

Besides being an all-suite property, the **Embassy Suites Mandalay Beach Resort** is the only full-service hotel on the beach in this area. As you might expect, the oceanfront suites are almost always sold out on weekends, so plan ahead and reserve early. A full, complimentary breakfast is included in the price. ~ 2101 Mandalay Beach Road, Oxnard; 805-984-2500, 800-362-2779, fax 805-984-8339; www.embassymandalay.com, e-mail info@embassymandalay.com. ULTRA-DELUXE.

DINING

Landmark No. 78 is exactly what its name states: a beautifully restored 1912 Victorian residence listed on the historic register. Today it's home to fine dining, featuring pasta, steak, and seafood dishes. There is much to recommend it. For one thing, it's not on the main drag, and, for another, the house claims to have its own ghost, Rosa, whose story is a sad one. No lunch on weekends. Closed Monday. ~ 211 East Santa Clara Street, Ventura; 805-643-3264 or 805-643-6267, fax 805-643-3267; www. landmark78.com. MODERATE.

The brick-walled, flower-filled **Nona's Courtyard Café** pro-   ◀ HIDDEN
vides a cool and charming indoor spot for breakfast or lunch. Salads and sandwiches are tasty and generous, as are the pastas, risottos, chicken, and other entrées. ~ Bella Maggiore Inn, 67 South California Street, Ventura; 805-641-2783. MODERATE.

Try **Eric Ericsson's On the Pier**, a small snuggery done in ca-
sual California style with indoor/outdoor seating. At lunch they could be serving fish chowder, seafood pasta, poached shrimp, or fresh fish tacos. Then for dinner they might charbroil mahi-mahi, salmon, swordfish, or sea bass, depending on the season. Tapas are served in the upstairs bar and they also have a walk-up snack shack where you can grab a smoothie, burger, or break-fast sandwich for your stroll along the beach. ~ 668 Harbor Boulevard, Ventura; 805-643-4783, fax 805-643-2904; www. ericericssons.com, e-mail ericericssons@sbcglobal.net. DELUXE TO ULTRA-DELUXE.

Bombay Bar & Grill, known for a 140-foot bar, offers live enter-   **NIGHTLIFE**
tainment nightly with a musical medley that varies from rock to disco and R&B. The room in back hosts live deejays on select weekends. Cover on weekends. ~ 143 South California Street, Ventura; 805-643-4404; www.bombaybarandgrill.com.

If a little high-energy entertainment is what you're looking for, try **Nicholby's**. Upstairs above the antique store, they dish out a mix of live music and deejay-spun tunes. It's a young scene, funky and hip. Closed Sunday and Tuesday. Occasional cover. ~

WATERFRONT DINING

Even if you're not a seafood lover, it's hard to resist the allure of waterfront dining. The Channel Islands Harbor offers several options. **The Whale's Tail** is a casual, nautically themed spot (don't miss the tugboat salad bar) offering both Boston and Manhattan clam chowder, fresh local fish, pasta, and prime rib. ~ 3900 Bluefin Circle; 805-985-2511; www.thewhalestail.com. DELUXE. Just as casual, with captains' chairs and a lively bar, is **Lobster Trap**. Dinner features seafood, steak, and prime rib; the lunch menu includes fish tacos; and there's a champagne brunch on Sunday. ~ 3605 Peninsula Road; 805-985-6363. DELUXE. White linen and fine tableware set **Port Royal** apart as the fanciest of the harbor restaurants, with a menu that's a bit more sophisticated and cozy booths and a fireplace that create a more romantic mood. ~ 3900 Bluefine Circle; 805-382-7678. ULTRA-DELUXE.

410 East Main Street, Ventura; 805-653-2320; www.nicholbys nightclub.com.

There is an improvisational comedy crew working out of the **Livery Theatre**, which, until a few years ago, was actually a working stable with some ramshackle attached buildings. Now it's a stylish complex of offices, shops, and the theater, which hosts a variety of events on weekends—from live music to comedy improv to interactive theater performances. ~ 34 North Palm Street, Ventura; 805-643-5701; www.liverytheatre.org.

BEACHES & PARKS

POINT MUGU STATE PARK 🚶 🚲 🐎 🏊 🏃 ⚓ This outstanding facility extends along five miles of beachfront and reaches back six miles into the Santa Monica Mountains. Much of the landscape is characterized by hilly, chaparral-cloaked terrain. Vegetation is plentiful, and the campgrounds are very open. The beaches—which include **Sycamore Cove Beach, Thornhill Broome**, and **Point Mugu Beach**—are wide and sandy, with rocky outcroppings and a spectacular sand dune. To the interior, the park rises to 1266-foot Mugu Peak and to Tri-Peaks, 3010 feet in elevation. There are two large canyons as well as wide, forested valleys. More than 70 miles of hiking trails lace this diverse park. Facilities include picnic areas, restrooms, and lifeguards. Swimming and bodysurfing are popular but watch for rip currents. There is good surf a few miles south of the park at **County Line Beach**. Day-use fees vary by area. ~ 9000 West Pacific Coast Highway, 15 miles south of Oxnard. Information: 818-880-0363, fax 818-880-6165.

▲ There are two separate park campgrounds. At Sycamore Canyon there are 45 tent/RV sites (no hookups); $25 per night. Thornhill Broome Beach has 63 primitive tent/RV sites (no hookups) right on the beach; $15 per night. Reservations are recommended for Sycamore Canyon and Thornhill Broome Beach campgrounds; call 800-444-7275.

MCGRATH STATE BEACH 🚲 🏊 🏃 ⚓ This long, narrow park extends for two miles along the water. The beach is broad and bounded by dunes. A lake and wildlife area attract over 200 bird species. The Santa Clara River, on the northern boundary, is home to bobcats, squirrels, possums, weasels, and other wildlife. Together the lake and preserve make it a great spot for camping or daytripping at the beach. There are restrooms, showers, and lifeguards. Swimming and surfing is recommended for strong swimmers only; watch for rip currents. Day-use fee, $8 per vehicle. ~ 2211 Harbor Boulevard, Oxnard; 805-968-1033.

▲ There are 174 tent/RV sites (no hookups); $25 per night. Reservations strongly recommended: 800-444-7275.

SAN BUENAVENTURA STATE BEACH 🚲 ⛵ 🎣 ⚓ In the world of urban parks this 114-acre facility ranks high. The broad sandy beach, bordered by dunes, extends for two miles to the Ventura pier. Since the pier is a short stroll from the city center, the beach provides a perfect escape hatch after you have toured the town. Facilities include picnic areas, restrooms, outdoor showers, food vendors, and lifeguards. The breakwaters here provide excellent swimming. Surfing is popular at **Surfer's Point Park**, foot of Figueroa Street; and at **Peninsula Beach**, at the north end of Spinnaker Drive. Fishing from the 1700-foot pier is good, and anglers may catch bass, shark, surf perch, corbina, and halibut. The nearby rock jetties are a haven for crabs and mussels. Day-use fee, $8. ~ Located along Harbor Boulevard southeast of the Ventura Pier in Ventura; 805-968-1033.

> The lush riverbanks of the Santa Clara River in McGrath State Beach make for some of the best birdwatching in the state.

EMMA WOOD STATE BEACH 🏃 🚲 ⛵ 🎣 ⚓ Sandwiched between the ocean and the Union Pacific railroad tracks, this slender park measures only 109 acres. Because of tide fluctuations, the beach can become extremely rocky, making it undesirable for swimmers and sunbathers. There is a marsh at one end inhabited by songbirds and small mammals. Considering the fabulous beaches hereabouts, I rank this one pretty low. Restrooms are available. Cabezon, perch, bass, and corbina are caught here. Day-use fee, $8. ~ Located on the northwest boundary of Ventura just off Route 101; 805-968-1033.

▲ There's camping nearby along the small, rocky beaches north of Emma Wood State Beach at three different campgrounds. **Emma Wood–North Beach** has 90 first-come, first-serve tent/RV sites (no hookups); $20 per night; for information, call 805-968-1033. **Faria County Park** is a bit smaller with 42 tent/RV sites (some hookups); $30 per night. **Hobson County Park** is smaller still with 31 tent/RV sites (some hookups); $30 per night. Information: 805-654-3951.

From Ventura, Route 101 speeds north and west to Santa Barbara. For a slow-paced tour of the shoreline, take the Old Pacific Coast Highway

Santa Barbara Area

instead. Paralleling the freeway and the Southern Pacific Railroad tracks, it rests on a narrow shelf between sharply rising hills and the ocean. The road glides for miles along sandy beaches and rocky shoreline, passing the woodframe communities of Solimar Beach and Seacliff Beach.

Past this last enclave the old road ends as you join Route 101 once more. With the Santa Ynez Mountains looming on one side and the Pacific extending along the other, you'll pass the resort town of Carpinteria. The temperature might be 80° with a blazing sun overhead and a soft breeze off the ocean. Certainly the furthest thing from your mind is the North Pole, but there it is, just past Carpinteria—the turnoff for Santa Claus Lane.

SIGHTS   Tucked between a curving bay and the Santa Ynez Mountains lies one of the prettiest places in all California. It's little wonder that the Spanish who settled **Santa Barbara**, establishing a presidio in 1782 and a mission several years later, called it *la tierra adorada*, the beloved land.

Discovered by a Portuguese navigator in 1542, it was an important center of Spanish culture until the Americans seized California in the 19th century. The town these Anglo interlopers built was an early-20th-century community. But a monstrous earthquake leveled the downtown area in 1925 and created a *tabula rasa* for architects and city planners.

Faced with rebuilding Santa Barbara, they returned the place to its historic roots, combining Spanish and Mission architecture to create a Mediterranean metropolis. The result is modern-day Santa Barbara with its adobe walls, red tile roofs, rounded archways, and palm-lined boulevards.

Sightseeing Santa Barbara is as simple as it is rewarding. First, stop at the **Santa Barbara Visitors Center**. The myriad materials here include more pamphlets, books, and booklets than you ever want to see. The most important piece is a map entitled "Welcome to Santa Barbara" that outlines a "Red Tile Tour" for walkers as well as a lengthier "Scenic Drive." Together they form two concentric circles along the perimeters of which lie nearly all the city's points of interest. ~ 1 Garden Street, Santa Barbara; 805-965-3021 or 805-568-1811; www.sbchamber.org.

SCENIC DRIVE   The **Scenic Drive** around Santa Barbara, a 21-mile circular tour, incorporates several of the sites covered along the Red Tile Tour. To avoid repetition, begin at the **Santa Barbara Museum of Art** with its collection of American and European paintings and photography, Asian art, and classical sculpture. Closed Monday. Admission. ~ 1130 State Street; 805-963-4364, fax 805-966-6840; www.sbma.net.

Then head up to **Mission Santa Barbara**, which sits on a knoll overlooking the city. Founded in 1786 and restored in 1820, this twin-towered beauty, known as the "Queen of the Missions," follows a design from an ancient Roman architecture book. The interior courtyard is a colonnaded affair with a central fountain and graceful flower garden. The chapel itself is quite impressive with a row of wrought-iron chandeliers leading to a multicolored altar. There are also museum displays representing the original Indian population and early-19th-century mission artifacts. Also visit the Mission Cemetery, a placid and pretty spot where frontier families and about 4000 Chumash Indians are buried in the shade of a Moreton Bay fig tree. Mission Santa Barbara is the only California mission that has been continuously used by Franciscan fathers throughout its 200-year history. Admission. ~ 2201 Laguna Street; 805-682-4713, fax 805-682-6067; www.santabarbaramission.org.

Farther uphill at the **Santa Barbara Museum of Natural History** are successive rooms devoted to marine, plant, vertebrate, and insect life. Excellent for kids, it also features an extensive collection of artifacts from the local Chumash tribe. You'll recognize the museum by the 72-foot skeleton of a blue whale out front. There is also a lizard lounge and a planetarium with a space lab. Admission. ~ 2559 Puesta del Sol Road; 805-682-4711, fax 805-569-3170; www.sbnature.org, e-mail info@sbnature2.org.

Nearby Mission Canyon Road continues into the hills for close-up views of the rocky Santa Ynez Mountains and a tour of **Santa Barbara Botanic Garden**. Trails here wind past eight different habitats, including a desert section carpeted with cactus and a meadow filled with wildflowers. In the spring, near the top of the garden, beyond the ancient Indian step, where the forest edges down from the mountains, is a stand of cool, lofty red-

◄ HIDDEN

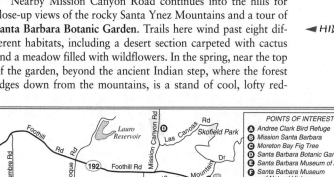

POINTS OF INTEREST

A Andree Clark Bird Refuge
B Mission Santa Barbara
C Moreton Bay Fig Tree
D Santa Barbara Botanic Garden
E Santa Barbara Museum of Art
F Santa Barbara Museum of Natural History
G Santa Barbara Visitors Center
H Santa Barbara Zoological Gardens
I Sea Center

0   1 mile
0   1 kilometer

Santa Barbara

wood trees. Be sure to visit the traditional Japanese teahouse and tea garden exhibit. Guided tours daily. Admission. ~ 1212 Mission Canyon Road; 805-682-4726, fax 805-563-0352; www. sbbg.org, e-mail info@sbbg.org.

Backtrack to Alameda Padre Serra and cruise this elite roadway past million-dollar homes with million-dollar views. From this thoroughfare a series of side roads leads through the exclusive bedroom community of **Montecito**. Here a variety of architectural styles combine to create a luxurious neighborhood.

Montecito is where the real money is in the Santa Barbara area. A drive through this community, which flanks Santa Barbara on the south, will give you only a glimpse of the well-tended natural beauty of the place because homes for the most part are secluded behind walls and lavish landscaping. One former resident, Madame Ganna Walska, turned her hillside estate into what is now one of the most famous private gardens in the country: **Lotusland**. By the time she arrived in Santa Barbara in 1941, Madame, a Polish-born opera singer, was on her sixth husband. He persuaded her to buy a Montecito estate in order to establish a spiritual center for Tibetan scholar-monks. When that idea, along with the marriage, failed, Madame turned to horticulture. The result was a magnificent private garden that visitors may tour on a reservations-only basis. The gardens are closed Sunday through Tuesday and mid-November to mid-February. Admission. ~ 805-969-9990, fax 805-969-4423; www.lotusland.org, e-mail info@lotusland.org.

After exploring the town's shady groves and manicured lawns, you can pick up **Channel Drive**, a spectacular street that skirts beaches and bluffs as it loops back toward Santa Barbara. From this curving roadway you'll spy oddly shaped structures offshore. Looking like a line of battleships ready to attack Santa Barbara, they are in fact **oil derricks**. Despite protests from environmentalists and a disastrous 1969 oil spill, these coastal waters have been the site of drilling operations for decades. Those hazy humps farther out past the wells are the Channel Islands.

MERRY KITSCH-MAS

Santa Claus Lane? It's a block-long stretch of trinket shops and toy stores with a single theme. It's one of those places that's so tacky you feel like you've missed something if you pass it by. If nothing else, you can mail an early Christmas card. Just drop it in the mailbox at **The Candy Kitchen** and it will be postmarked (ready for this?) "Santa Claus, California." ~ 3821 Santa Claus Lane, Carpinteria; 805-684-3515.

The **Andree Clark Bird Refuge** is a placid lagoon filled with geese and other freshwater fowl. There are three tree-tufted islands in the center and a trail around the park. ~ 1400 East Cabrillo Boulevard.

Upstaging all this is the adjacent **Santa Barbara Zoological Gardens** with its miniature train ride and population of monkeys, lions, elephants, giraffes, and exotic birds. Admission. ~ 500 Niños Drive; 805-962-6310; www.sbzoo.org, e-mail zooinfo @sbzoo.org.

Cabrillo Boulevard hugs the shore as it tracks past **East Beach**, Santa Barbara's longest, prettiest strand. With its rows of palm trees, grassy acres, and sunbathing crowds, it's an enchanting spot.

Every Sunday morning, the greenbelt at East Beach next to Stearns Wharf turns into an **outdoor art show**. Dozens of local and regional artists exhibit their artwork, photography, jewelry, and crafts. Quality varies, of course, but the setting is unbeatable. ~ Cabrillo Boulevard at State Street.

For a taste of sea air and salt spray, walk out along **Stearns Wharf**. From the end of this wooden pier you can gaze back at Santa Barbara, realizing how aptly author Richard Henry Dana described the place: "The town is finely situated, with a bay in front, and an amphitheater of hills behind." Favored by local anglers, the wharf is also noted for the **Sea Center**, a working marine laboratory where visitors can engage in the work of scientist who study, monitor, and determine how best to protect the ocean. Admission. ~ At the foot of State Street, 211 Stearns Wharf; 805-962-2526, fax 805-569-3170; www.sbnature.org/seacenter.

If you tire of walking, remember that Stearns Wharf is the departure point for the **Santa Barbara Old Town Trolley**, an old-fashioned vehicle that carries visitors on a narrated tour along the waterfront, through the downtown area, and out to the mission. Fee. ~ 805-965-0353, fax 805-965-1075; www.sbtrolley.com, e-mail sbtrolley@aol.com.

The **Moreton Bay Fig Tree** is a century-old giant with branches ◄ HIDDEN that spread 160 feet. This magnificent specimen stands as the largest tree of its kind in the United States. ~ Chapala and Montecito streets.

Back along the waterfront, Cabrillo Boulevard continues to the **Yacht Harbor,** where 1200 pleasure boats, some worth more than homes, lie moored. The walkway leads past yawls, ketches, sloops, and fishing boats to a breakwater. From here you can survey the fleet and take in the surrounding mountains and ocean. ~ West Cabrillo Boulevard and Castillo Street.

To continue this seafront excursion, follow Shoreline, Cliff, and Marina drives as they parallel the Pacific, past headlands and beaches, en route to **Hope Ranch**. Santa Barbara is flanked by

Text continued on page 282.

Santa Barbara's Red Tile Tour

For a lesson in Santa Barbara's colorful history, embark on the 14-block Red Tile Tour, which introduces visitors to many of the town's landmarks.

SANTA BARBARA COUNTY COURTHOUSE   The Red Tile loop begins at the Santa Barbara County Courthouse, the city's grandest building. This U-shaped Spanish–Moorish "palace" covers almost three sides of a city block. The interior is a masterwork of beamed ceilings, arched corridors, and palacio tile floors. On the second floor of this 1929 courthouse are murals depicting California history. The highlight of every visit is the sweeping view of Santa Barbara at the top of the clock tower. From the Santa Ynez Mountains down to the ocean, all that meets the eye are palm trees and red tile roofs. No tours on Sunday. ~ 1100 block of Anacapa Street; 805-962-6464, fax 805-967-4104.

HILL–CARRILLO ADOBE   Two blocks down, the Hill–Carrillo Adobe is an 1826-vintage home built by a Massachusetts settler for his Spanish bride. The house is closed to the public but can be viewed from the street. ~ 11 East Carrillo Street.

ANTIQUE BUILDINGS   Along State Street, the heart of Santa Barbara's shopping district, many stores occupy antique buildings. **El Paseo** represented one of the most original malls in the entire country. It was a labyrinthine shopping arcade consisting of several complexes. Today, it is composed mostly of offices. ~ 814 State Street. Incorporated into the architectural motif is **Casa de la Guerra**, a splendid house built in 1818 for the commander of the Santa Barbara presidio and described by Richard Henry Dana in his classic book *Two Years Before the Mast*. Closed Monday through Wednesday. Admission. ~ 15 East de la Guerra Street; 805-965-0093; www.sbthp.org, e-mail info@sbthp.org.

PLAZA DE LA GUERRA   Across the street rests Plaza de la Guerra, a palm-fringed park where the first city hall stood in 1875. Nearby, another series of historic structures has been converted into a warren of shops and offices. In the center of the mall is **Presidio Gardens**, a tranquil park with a carp pond and elephant-shaped fountains that spray water through their trunks. ~ On de la Guerra Street between Anacapa and Garden streets. The **Santiago de la Guerra Adobe** and the **Lugo Adobe**, set in a charming courtyard, are other 19th-century homes that have been converted to private use. ~ 114 East de la Guerra Street.

SANTA BARBARA HISTORICAL MUSEUM   The Santa Barbara Historical Museum certainly looks its part. Set in an adobe building with tile roof and wrought-iron window bars, the facility sits behind heavy wooden doors. Within are fine art displays and a series depicting the Spanish, Mexican, Chinese, and early American periods of Santa Barbara's history. Closed Monday. ~ 136 East de la Guerra Street; 805-966-1601, fax 805-966-1603; www.santabarbaramuseum.com.

CASA DE COVARRUBIAS   A right turn on Garden Street carries you to Casa de Covarrubias. Most places in town are a little too neatly refurbished to provide a dusty sense of history. But this L-shaped house, and the adjacent **Historic Fremont Adobe**, are sufficiently wind-blasted to evoke the early 19th century. The former structure, dating to 1817, is said to be the site of the last Mexican assembly in 1846; the latter became headquarters for Colonel John C. Fremont after Americans captured the town later that year. ~ 715 Garden Street. Turn back along Garden Street and pass the **Rochin Adobe**. This 1856 adobe, now covered with clapboard siding, is a private home. ~ 820 Garden Street.

EL PRESIDIO DE SANTA BARBARA STATE HISTORIC PARK   It's a few steps over to El Presidio de Santa Barbara State Historic Park, which occupies both sides of the street and incorporates some of the city's earliest buildings. Founded in 1782, the Presidio was one of four military fortresses built by the Spanish in California. Protecting settlers and missionaries from Indians, it also served as a seat of government and center of Western culture. Today only two original buildings survive. **El Cuartel**, the guards' house, served as the soldiers' quarters. The **Cañedo Adobe**, also built as a military residence, is now the offices of the Santa Barbara Trust for Historic Preservation. Most interesting of all is the **Santa Barbara Presidio Chapel**, which re-creates an early Spanish church in its full array of colors. Compared to the plain exterior, the interior is a shock to the eye. Everything is done in red and yellow ochre and dark blue. The altar is painted to simulate a great cathedral. Drapes and columns, difficult to obtain during Spanish days, have been drawn onto the walls. Even the altar railing is painted to imitate colored marble. Admission. ~ 123 East Cañon Perdido Street; 805-966-9719; www.sbthp.org, e-mail info@sbthp.org.

LOBERO THEATRE   The last stop on this walking tour will carry you a step closer to the present. The Lobero Theatre was constructed in 1924. It is a three-tiered design that ascends to a 70-foot-high stage house. The original Lobero dates back to 1873, Santa Barbara's first theater. The Lobero presents a variety of performing arts. Call Monday through Friday for tickets. ~ 33 East Cañon Perdido Street; 805-963-0761, fax 805-963-8752; www.lobero.com.

two posh communities: Montecito in the east and this elite enclave to the west. It's a world of country clubs and cocktail parties, where money and nature meet to create forested estates.

NORTH OF SANTA BARBARA   Route 101 streams northwest past a series of suburban communities, including Goleta and Isla Vista, where the **University of California–Santa Barbara** is located. Stop by the visitors center to pick up a campus map and brochures for one of the state's most beautiful universities, or join a guided tour. Closed weekends. ~ 805-893-8175, fax 805-893-8160; www.admissions.ucsb.edu.

Cutting a swath between mountains and ocean, the road passes a series of attractive beach parks, then turns inland toward the mountains and interior valleys.

About 35 miles from Santa Barbara Routes 101 and 1 diverge. For a rural drive past white barns and meandering creeks, follow **Route 1**. En route to Lompoc it passes farmlands, pastures, and rolling hills. About five miles south of Lompoc, you can follow **Jalama Road**, a country lane that cuts through sharp canyons and graceful valleys on a winding 15-mile course to the ocean, ending at a beach park.

HIDDEN ►

This journey becomes a pilgrimage when Route 1 approaches **La Purísima Mission**. The best restored of all 21 California missions, this historic site has an eerie way of projecting you back to Spanish days. There's the mayordomo's abode with the table set and a pan on the stove, or the mission store, its barrels overflowing with corn and beans. The entire mission complex, from the church to the tallow vats where the fat from slaughtered cattle was rendered into soap, was re-created in the 1930s by the Civilian Conservation Corps. Founded nearby in 1787, the mission was re-established at this site in 1813. Today you can tour the living quarters of priests, soldiers, and Indians, the workshops where weaving, leathermaking, and carpentry were practiced, and the mission's original water system. You can also see animals such as burros and goats in their period mission setting. Living-history events occur here periodically; call ahead for details. Admission. ~ 2295 Purisima Road, Lompoc; 805-733-3713, fax 805-733-2497; www.lapurisimamission.org, e-mail lpinfo@parks.ca.gov.

In spring and summer, the hills around **Lompoc** dazzle with thousands of acres of cultivated flowers. The countryside is a rainbow of color throughout the season. Then, in fall, fields of poppies, nasturtiums, and larkspurs bloom.

LODGING   Two centralized reservation agencies provide an idea of the full range of accommodations available in the Santa Barbara area. One is **Coastal Escapes Accommodations**. ~ 5320 Carpinteria Avenue, Carpinteria; 800-292-2222; www.coastalescapes.com,

e-mail info@coastalescapes.com. **Santa Barbara Hotspots** can
also give information on prices and availability. Closed Sunday.
~ 805-564-1637, 800-793-7666, fax 805-564-1633; www.hot
spotusa.com. Since room rates in Santa Barbara fluctuate by season and day of the week, it's advisable to check.

South of Santa Barbara in Carpinteria, the **Eugenia Motel** has
ten rooms (four with kitchens). Each is small, carpeted, and clean.
The furniture is comfortable though nicked. The baths have stall
showers. ~ 5277 Carpinteria Avenue, Carpinteria; 805-684-4416.
BUDGET TO MODERATE.

Because of its excellent beach, many families spend their entire vacation in Carpinteria, so most facilities rent by the week
or month. Among the less expensive spots is **La Casa del Sol
Motel**. This multi-unit complex has 23 units, including some suites
with jacuzzis. The one I saw was paneled in knotty pine and trimly
furnished. Small pool and laundry facilities are found on-site. ~
5585 Carpinteria Avenue, Carpinteria; 805-684-4307, fax 805-
745-1027. MODERATE.

For modest-priced accommodations within a block or two of
the beach, check out **Cabrillo Boulevard**. This artery skirts the
shoreline for several miles. Establishments lining the boulevard
are usually a little higher in price. But along the side streets leading from Cabrillo are numerous generic motels. From these you
can generally expect rooms that are small but tidy and clean. The

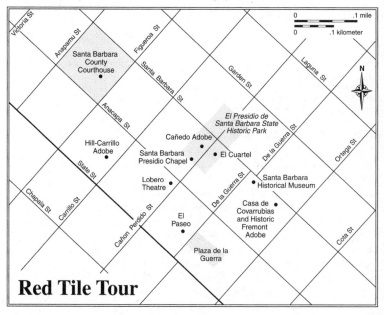

Red Tile Tour

wall-to-wall carpeting is industrial grade, the furniture consists of naugahyde chairs and formica tables, and the artworks make you appreciate minimalism. There's usually a swimming pool and surrounding terrace, plus a wall of ice machines and soda dispensers.

There are two such places located a block from Santa Barbara's best all-around beach. **Pacific Crest Motel** has 25 units renting at affordable prices. ~ 433 Corona del Mar Drive, Santa Barbara; 805-966-3103, fax 805-568-0673; www.pacificcrestinn. com, e-mail info@pacificcrestinn.com. DELUXE TO ULTRA-DELUXE. Next door, that generic facility, **Motel 6**, has 51 guest rooms. ~ 443 Corona del Mar Drive, Santa Barbara; 805-564-1392, 800-466-8356. MODERATE.

The **Old Yacht Club Inn** is two inns in one. The main facility is a 1912 California Craftsman–style house with five rooms. There is a cozy parlor downstairs where wine and cheese are served in the evening. Next door, in a 1927 vintage stucco, there are seven guest rooms with private baths. Some have been decorated by different families and feature personal photographs and other heirlooms, other rooms feature elegant European decor. The inn is just one block from East Beach, serves a full gourmet breakfast and provides bikes, beach chairs, and towels to guests. Owner Nancy Donaldson usually offers an elegantly prepared five-course gourmet Saturday dinner to guests. The inn books far in advance on these nights and there is a two-night minimum, but it's well worth the wait. ~ 431 Corona del Mar Drive, Santa Barbara; 805-962-1277, 800-676-1676, fax 805-962-3989; www.oldyachtclubinn.com, e-mail info@oldyachtclubinn.com. DELUXE TO ULTRA-DELUXE.

Over in the West Beach area, **Beach House Inn & Apartments** has 12 quiet units located two blocks from the beach and har-

AUTHOR FAVORITE

Upham Hotel is "the oldest cosmopolitan hotel in continuous operation in Southern California." Established in 1871, it shares a sense of history with the country inns, but enjoys the lobby and restaurant amenities of a hotel. Victorian in style, the two-story clapboard is marked by sweeping verandas and a cupola; the accommodations here are nicely appointed with hardwood and period furnishings. Around the landscaped grounds are garden cottages, some with private patios and fireplaces, and a carriage house with five Victorian-style rooms. Continental breakfast, afternoon wine and cheese, and cookies at bedtime are included. ~ 1404 de la Vina Street, Santa Barbara; 805-962-0058, 800-727-0876, fax 805-963-2825; www. uphamhotel.com, e-mail innkeeper@uphamhotel.com. ULTRA-DELUXE.

bor. Rooms here are larger than usual, most have fully equipped kitchens, but there's no pool. Small pets are allowed. ~ 320 West Yanonali Street, Santa Barbara; 805-966-1126, fax 805-969-6058; www.thebeachhouseinn.com, e-mail beachhouseinn@hot mail.com. DELUXE TO ULTRA-DELUXE.

For chic surroundings there is **The Villa Rosa Inn**. Built during the 1930s in Spanish palazzo fashion, it was originally an apartment house. Today it is an 18-room inn with raw wood furnishings and private baths. There's a pool and spa in the courtyard. Guests co-mingle over continental breakfast and afternoon wine and cheese, then settle into plump armchairs around a tile fireplace with port and sherry in the evening. The spacious rooms, some with fireplaces, are pleasantly understated and located half a block from the beach. ~ 15 Chapala Street, Santa Barbara; 805-966-0851, fax 805-962-7159; www.villarosainnsb.com, e-mail info@villarosainnsb.com. DELUXE TO ULTRA-DELUXE.

The Eagle Inn is an attractive Mediterranean-style apartment house converted into a 29-room hotel. Just two blocks from the beach, most of the rooms have king beds with jacuzzi tubs. ~ 232 Natoma Avenue, Santa Barbara; 805-965-3586, 800-767-0030, fax 805-966-1218; www.theeagleinn.com, e-mail stay@theeagle inn.com. DELUXE TO ULTRA-DELUXE.

Small and intimate as bed and breakfasts tend to be, the **Simpson House Inn** is even more so. Close to downtown, it resides along a quiet tree-lined block secluded in an acre of English gardens complete with fountains and intimate sitting areas. The century-old Victorian inn features 15 guest rooms, restored-barn suites, and garden cottages—all decorated with antiques and fine art. Some feature private decks or patios, fireplaces, and jacuzzis. A gourmet breakfast is served on the veranda or to private patios or rooms; beverages are served in the afternoon, and hors d'oeuvres and wine are provided in the evening. Bikes and croquet complete the package. ~ 121 East Arrellaga Street, Santa Barbara; 805-963-7067, 800-676-1280, fax 805-564-4811; www. simpsonhouseinn.com, e-mail info@simpsonhouseinn.com. ULTRA-DELUXE.

The **Tiffany Country House** is a beautifully restored 1898 mansion. The front entry sets the tone with its antique furnishings, dark woods, and massive fireplace. Wine and snacks are served there nightly. The six rooms and lavish third-floor penthouse all feature period art and antiques, queen beds, and private baths. The private yard and gardens in back offer a genteel setting for morning coffee in nice china rather than paper cups. ~ 1323 De La Vina Street, Santa Barbara; 805-963-2283, 800-999-567, fax 805-962-0994; www.tiffanycountryhouse.com, e-mail frontdesk@tiffanycountryhouse.com. DELUXE.

Text continued on page 288.

The Channel Islands

Gaze out from the Ventura or Santa Barbara shoreline and you will spy a fleet of islands moored offshore. At times fringed with mist, on other occasions standing a hand's reach away in the crystal air, they are the Channel Islands, a group of eight volcanic islands.

Situated in the Santa Barbara Channel 11 to 60 miles from the coast, they are a place apart, a wild and storm-blown region of sharp cliffs, rocky coves, and curving grasslands. Five of the islands—Anacapa, Santa Cruz, Santa Rosa, San Miguel, and Santa Barbara—comprise Channel Islands National Park while the surrounding waters are a marine sanctuary.

Nicknamed "North America's Galápagos," the chain teems with every imaginable form of life. Sea lions and harbor seals frequent the caves, blowholes, and offshore pillars. Brown pelicans and black oystercatchers roost on the sea arches and sandy beaches. There are tidepools crowded with brilliant purple hydrocorals and white-plumed sea anemones. Like the Galápagos, this isolated archipelago has given rise to many unique life forms, including over 40 endemic plant species and the island fox, which grows only to the size of a house cat.

The northern islands were created about 30 million years ago by volcanic activity. Archaeological discoveries indicate that they could be among the oldest sites of human habitation in the Americas. When explorer Juan Cabrillo revealed them to Europe in 1542 they were populated with thousands of Chumash Indians.

Today, long since the Chumash were removed to the mainland and the islands given over to hunters, ranchers, and settlers, the Channel Islands are largely uninhabited. All five, however, are open to hikers and campers. At the mainland-based **Channel Islands National Park Visitors Center** there are contemporary museum displays, an observation deck, an indoor tidepool, and an excellent 25-minute movie to familiarize you with the park. Also on display is a skeleton of a pygmy mammoth found on Santa Rosa Island in 1994. ~ 1901 Spinnaker Drive, Ventura; 805-658-5730, fax 805-658-5799; www.nps.gov/chis.

Nearby at **Island Packers** you can arrange transportation to the islands. This outfit schedules regular daytrips by boat to Anacapa, Santa

Barbara, Santa Cruz, Santa Rosa, and San Miguel islands. ~ 1691 Spin-naker Drive, Ventura; 805-642-1393; www.islandpackers.com. **Channel Islands Aviation** will fly you to Santa Rosa Island for a day of fishing or hiking or overnight camping. Flights leave at 9 a.m. and return around 3:30 p.m. ~ 805-987-1301; www.flycia.com, e-mail cia@flycia.com.

Island Packers leads seasonal tours of **Santa Cruz**, the largest and most diverse of the islands. Here you will find an island just 24 miles long that supports 600 species of plants, 130 types of land birds, and several unique plant species. There are Indian middens, earthquake faults, and two mountain ranges to explore. To the center lies a pastoral valley while the shoreline is a rugged region of cliffs, tidepools, and offshore rocks. Note: Camping is not allowed on Nature Conservancy property but *is* permitted on the eastern part on national park land. Call ahead to make reservations. ~ 1691 Spinnaker Drive, Ventura; 805-642-1393; www.islandpackers.com.

Anacapa Island, the island closest to shore, is a series of three islets parked 11 miles southwest of Oxnard. There is a nature trail here. Like the other islands, it is a prime whale-watching spot and is surrounded by the giant kelp forests that make the Channel Islands one of the nation's richest marine environments.

The varied landscape of **Santa Rosa Island** includes grasslands, volcanic formations, and marshes. You may spot harbor and elephant seals as you stroll the island's beaches. Nature and history draw visitors to **San Miguel**, where you can hike to the caliche forest or visit a monument to Juan Cabrillo, the first European to discover California. **Santa Barbara Island** is a good spot for birdwatching. Hikers can traverse the five and a half miles of trails here.

Outdoor aficionados will be glad to hear that camping is allowed in the national park. However, you must obtain a permit by calling 800-365-2267. All campgrounds have picnic tables and pit toilets, but generally, water must be carried in—and trash must be carried out. Fires are not permitted.

Whether you are a sailor, swimmer, daytripper, hiker, archaeologist, birdwatcher, camper, tidepooler, scuba diver, seal lover, or simply an interested observer, you'll find this amazing island chain a place of singular beauty and serenity.

The White Jasmine Inn is laid out in similar fashion. The main house is a 1906 California Craftsman design with extensive wood detailing and a combination of contemporary and period furniture. A suite in the main house is decorated in turn-of-the-20th-century nouveau style with a fireplace, private entrance, garden, and jacuzzi tub. The second house is an 1880s-era cottage with rooms and suites that have fireplaces and private baths. The theme in both abodes is romance. The individually decorated rooms include the Victorian Suite, with furniture and decor from that era, and the Castaway Suite, with seashells and other maritime accents; several have jacuzzi tubs. Guests enjoy a gourmet breakfast brought to their door, and nightly tea and cookies; they also share a cozy living room that has a tile fireplace. ~ 1327 Bath Street, Santa Barbara; 805-966-0589, fax 805-564-8610; www.whitejasmineinnsantabarbara.com, e-mail stay@whitejasm ineinnsantabarbara.com. DELUXE TO ULTRA-DELUXE.

Down the road at the Bath Street Inn you'll encounter a Queen Anne Victorian constructed in 1890. Enter along a garden walkway into a warm living room with a marble-trimmed fireplace. The patio in back is set in another garden. Some of the guest rooms on the second floor feature the hardwood floors and patterned wallpaper that are the hallmarks of California bed and breakfasts. The third floor has a cozy sloped roof and a television lounge. Rooms include private baths, televisions, breakfast, and evening refreshments. ~ 1720 Bath Street, Santa Barbara; 805-682-9680, 800-341-2284; www.bathstreetinn.com, e-mail innkeepers@bathstreetinn.com. DELUXE TO ULTRA-DELUXE.

Santa Barbara's two finest hotels dominate the town's two geographic locales, the ocean and the mountains. Four Seasons Resort Biltmore Santa Barbara is a grand old Spanish-style hotel set on 20 acres beside the beach. It's the kind of place where guests play croquet or practice putting on manicured lawns, then meander over to Butterfly Beach. There is an ocean-view dining room as well as tennis courts, swimming pools, and a complete spa. The refurbished rooms are quite large and have an airy feel, with light wood furnishings and full marble baths. Many are located in multiplex cottages and are spotted around the magnificent grounds that have made this one of California's most famous hotels since it opened back in 1927. ~ 1260 Channel Drive, Santa Barbara; 805-969-2261, 800-819-5053, fax 805-565-8323; www.fourseasons.com/santabarbara. ULTRA-DELUXE.

In the Santa Ynez foothills above Montecito sits another retreat where the rich and powerful mix with the merely talented. San Ysidro Ranch sprawls across 500 acres, most of which is wilderness traversed by hiking trails. The grounds vie with the Santa Barbara Botanic Garden in the variety of plant life: there are meadows, mountain forests, and an orange grove. The Stonehouse Restaurant serves gourmet dishes and the complex also features sitting rooms and lounges. Privacy is the password: all these features are shared by guests occupying just 40 units. The accommodations are dotted around the property in cottages and small multiplexes. Pets are welcome. Rooms vary in decor, but even the simplest are trimly appointed and spacious with hardwood furnishings, wood-burning fireplaces, king-sized beds, and a mountain, ocean, or garden view. Many have hot tubs. ~ 900 San Ysidro Lane, Montecito; 805-565-1700, 800-368-6788, fax 805-565-1995; www. sanysidroranch.com. ULTRA-DELUXE.

John and Jackie Kennedy spent part of their honeymoon at San Ysidro Ranch.

About 20 miles north of Santa Barbara, there is a private campground, **El Capitan Canyon,** about one-half mile inland from El Capitan State Beach. You can choose from a variety of cabins and tent cabins, or stay in the traditional campground that has 80 RV and 20 tent sites. This sprawling 100-acre complex features picnic areas, restrooms, showers, a store, a pool, a playground, game areas, and an outdoor theater that has live music on Saturday ~ 11560 Calle Real, Goleta; 805-685-3887, 866-352-2729, fax 805-968-6772; www.elcapitancanyon.com, e-mail terri@elcapitancanyon.com. MODERATE TO ULTRA-DELUXE.

DINING

At **The Palms** you cook your own steak or halibut dinner, or have them prepare a shrimp, scallop, crab, lobster, lamb, or chicken meal. A family-style restaurant with oak chairs and pseudo-Tiffany lamps, it hosts a salad bar and adjoining lounge. Dinner only. ~ 701 Linden Avenue, Carpinteria; 805-684-3811, fax 805-684-2149. MODERATE TO ULTRA-DELUXE.

A step upscale at **Clementine's Steak House** they feature filet mignon, fresh fish dishes, vegetarian casserole, steak teriyaki, fried chicken, and Danish-style liver. It's dinner only here, but the meal—which includes soup, salad, vegetable, starch dish, homemade bread, and pie—could hold you well into the next day. The interior has a beamed ceiling and patterned wallpaper. Lean back in a captain's chair and enjoy some home-style cooking. Closed Monday and Tuesday. ~ 4631 Carpinteria Avenue, Carpinteria; 805-684-5119. MODERATE TO DELUXE.

For a scent of Santa Barbara salt air with your lunch or dinner, **Brophy Brothers Restaurant & Clam Bar** is the spot. Located out on the Breakwater, overlooking the marina, mountains, and open sea, it features a small dining room and patio. If you love seafood, it's heaven; if not, then fate has cast you in the wrong direction. The clam bar serves all manner of clam and oyster concoctions, and the restaurant is so committed to fresh fish they print a new menu daily to tell you what the boats brought in. When I was there the daily fare included fresh snapper, shark, scampi, salmon, sea bass, halibut, and mahimahi. ~ 119 Harbor Way, Santa Barbara; 805-966-4418, fax 805-966-6298; www.brophy bros.com. DELUXE.

One of the more romantic restaurants in Santa Barbara is the **Wine Cask**, where you can dine outside in a lovely courtyard or indoors under the colorful hand-painted ceiling mural that dates from the 1920s. Among the innovative entrées are braised beef short ribs with green chile tamales, miso-broiled black cod, and truffled potato gnocchi. Appetizers are equally creative and tempting. Don't forget to check out the wine list with more than 3500 vintages. ~ 813 Anacapa Street, Santa Barbara; 805-966-9463; www.winecask.com, e-mail winecask@winecask.com. ULTRA-DELUXE.

A south-of-the-border favorite is **La Super Rica**. The menu includes *alambre de pechuga* (marinated chicken strips fried with peppers and onions on a warm tortilla), and chiles rellenos. The homemade salsa is recommended. ~ 622 North Milpas Street, Santa Barbara; 805-963-4940. BUDGET.

HIDDEN ►

Santa Barbara natives have been eating at **Joe's Café** since 1928. Crowds line the coal-black bar, pile into the booths, and fill the tables. They come for a meat-and-potatoes lunch and dinner menu that stars prime rib. This is where you go for pork chops, steak, and French dip. The walls are loaded with mementos and faded photographs; softball trophies and deer antlers decorate the place; and the noise level is the same as the Indy 500. Paradise for slummers. ~ 536 State Street, Santa Barbara; 805-966-4638, fax 805-962-7489. MODERATE TO DELUXE.

Downey's, a small, understated dining room, numbers among Santa Barbara's premier restaurants. The dozen tables here are set amid sage-colored walls lined with local artwork. The food is renowned: specializing in California cuisine, Downey's has a menu that changes daily. A typical evening's entrées might include ragout of local lobster with wild mushrooms, lamb loin with grilled eggplant and chiles, duck with cabernet sauce, and Hawaiian ahi tuna with fresh mango salsa. There is a good wine list featuring California vintages. Very highly recommended. Dinner only. Closed Monday. ~ 1305 State Street, Santa Barbara; 805-966-5006, fax 805-966-5000; www.downeyssb.com. ULTRA-DELUXE.

HIDDEN ►

For truly prodigious breakfasts, locals know that nondescript **Esau's** is *the* place. Pancakes, omelettes, scrambles and homemade hash are nicely prepared and served in generous portions. If there's a queue (usually the case on weekends), look for a stool at the counter. Breakfast and lunch only. ~ 403 State Street, Santa Barbara; 805-965-4416. BUDGET.

Bouchon, opened in 1982, is a warm and classy little bistro tucked away on a quiet alley off State Street. Braised lamb shank and fresh terrines, maple, and bourbon-glazed duck, locally caught ahi tuna, and vegetarian dishes with produce fresh from the farmer's market are some of the favorites. There are more than 40 wines on the by-the-glass list. ~ 9 West Victoria Street, Santa Barbara; 805-730-1160; www.bouchonsantabarbara.com, e-mail info@bouchonsantabarbara.com. MODERATE TO ULTRA-DELUXE.

Hanging out in coffeehouses is my favorite avocation. There's no better spot in Santa Barbara than **Sojourner Coffeehouse**. Not only do they serve espresso and cappuccino, but lunch, dinner, and weekend brunch as well. Everyone seems to know everyone else in this easygoing café. They come to kibitz and enjoy the tostadas, rice-and-vegetable plates, and gourmet salads. The accent is vegetarian so expect daily specials like polenta cake royale, sweet tomato linguini, or garden Indian dhal. ~ 134 East Cañon Perdido, Santa Barbara; 805-965-7922; www.sojournercafe.com, e-mail sojo@sojournercafe.com. BUDGET TO MODERATE.

Cafe del Sol is the rarest of creatures, an upscale "Santa Barbara–style" eatery, where you'll find a tortilla deli/bar. Here you can sample tapas, Mexican appetizers, and margaritas. A large bank of windows allows dining room guests a view of the Andree Clark Bird Refuge while they dine on a menu varying from lamb shanks and fish to pasta and enchiladas. Closed Sunday. ~ 30 Los Patos Way, Santa Barbara; 805-969-0448, fax 805-969-5347. MODERATE TO DELUXE.

On the beach at Arroyo Burro Beach Park is the **Brown Pelican**. It's a decent restaurant with great ocean views—what more need be said? Sandwiches, salads, hamburgers, and several fresh seafood and pasta dinners are served. Breakfast is available daily until 11 a.m. or later. Trimly appointed and fitted with a wall of plate glass, it looks out upon a sandy beach and tawny bluffs. ~ 2981½ Cliff Drive, Santa Barbara; 805-687-4550, fax 805-569-0188; e-mail thepelican@aol.com. MODERATE TO ULTRA-DELUXE.

AUTHOR FAVORITE

The graphics on the wall tell a story about the cuisine at **The Palace Grill**. Portrayed are jazz musicians, catfish, redfish, and scenes from New Orleans. The message is Cajun, Creole, and Italian, and this lively, informal bistro is very good at delivering it. This restaurant prepares soft-shelled crab, blackened filet mignon, crawfish étouffée, jambalaya, pastas, and grilled steak. For dessert, Honey, we have Key lime pie and bread pudding soufflé. ~ 8 East Cota Street, Santa Barbara; 805-963-5000, fax 805-962-3200; www.thepalacegrill.com, e-mail michael@thepalace grill.com. MODERATE TO DELUXE.

The **Stonehouse Restaurant**, located at the legendary San Ysidro Ranch, serves new California cuisine with an international flavor. You can begin with fresh oysters or lobster, then indulge in the spring rolls with a ginger glaze for dipping, skillet-roasted rack of lamb, salmon garlic brulée, or charred yellowfin tuna with a mango garnish. Top off the meal with something scrumptious from the ever-changing dessert selection. Dinner only. ~ 900 San Ysidro Lane, Montecito; 805-565-1700, 800-368-6788, fax 805-565-1995; www.sanysidroranch.com. ULTRA-DELUXE.

SHOPPING   Since Santa Barbara's shops are clustered together, you can easily uncover the town's hottest items and best bargains by concentrating on a few key areas. The prime shopping center lies along State Street, particularly between the 600 and 1300 blocks.

Paseo Nuevo is, literally, a new *paseo*—a mall, really, with department stores, chain shops, and a few homegrown merchants lining a tastefully designed Spanish-style pedestrian promenade. ~ 651 Paseo Nuevo, Santa Barbara; 805-963-2202; www.sbmall.com.

Located on upper State Street, **La Cumbre Plaza** is a large, open-air shopping complex that features over 60 restaurants and retail stores. Don't miss the farmer's market held every Wednesday from 1 p.m. to 5 p.m. ~ 121 South Hope Street, Santa Barbara; 805-687-6458 or 805-687-3500; www.shoplacumbre.com.

La Arcada Court is another spiffy mall done in Spanish style. The shops, along the upper lengths of State Street, are more chic and contemporary than they are elsewhere. **Blue Bee** features fun clothing and accessories by exclusive designers. Closed Sunday. ~ 1114 State Street, Santa Barbara; 805-966-6634.

Near the corner of State and Cota streets is the center for vintage clothing. **Yellowstone Vintage Clothing** features Hawaiian shirts, used Levi's, and other old-time favorites. ~ 527 State Street, Santa Barbara; 805-963-9609.

SMALL CRAFT WARNING

For over 20 years Santa Barbara County artists and craftspeople have turned out for the **Arts & Crafts Show**. Every Sunday and holiday from 10 a.m. until dusk they line East Cabrillo Boulevard. The original artwork for sale includes paintings, graphics, sculptures, and drawings. Among the crafts are macrame, stained glass, woodwork, textiles, weaving, and jewelry. If you are in town on a Sunday make it a point to stop by.

The **Palms** features local rock-and-roll bands Friday and Saturday
nights. There's a small dancefloor here for footloose revelers. ~
701 Linden Avenue, Carpinteria; 805-684-3811.

The State Street strip in downtown Santa Barbara offers several party places. **Zelo** has dancing to a variety of deejay music
including hip-hop, disco, funk, and salsa. Live bands often perform outside. Occasional cover. ~ 630 State Street, Santa Barbara; 805-966-5792; www.zelo.net.

Up at **Acapulco Restaurant**, in La Arcada Court, you can sip
a margarita next to an antique wooden bar or out on the patio.
~ 1114 State Street, Santa Barbara; 805-963-3469.

If for no other reason than the view, **Harbor Restaurant** is a
prime place for the evening. A plate-glass establishment, it sits
out on a pier with the city skyline on one side and open ocean
on the other. The bar upstairs, **Longboards**, features sports television and surf videos. ~ 210 Stearns Wharf, Santa Barbara; 805-963-3311.

You can also consider the **Lobero Theatre**, which presents
dance, drama, concerts, and lectures. ~ 33 East Cañon Perdido
Street, Santa Barbara; 805-963-0761; www.lobero.com.

The **Four Seasons Resort Biltmore Santa Barbara** has an elegant lobby lounge where live music and dancing—the kind in
which couples actually hold each other in their arms—have become very popular on Friday and Saturday nights. The music
varies nightly. ~ 1260 Channel Drive, Santa Barbara; 805-969-2261, 800-819-5053; www.fourseasons.com/santabarbara.

Or head into the mountains about 27 miles outside Santa
Barbara and catch a show at the **Circle Bar B Dinner Theatre**.
This well-known facility offers a menu of comedies and musicals.
Open weekends only from April through October. ~ 1800 Refugio Road, 27 miles north of Santa Barbara; 805-967-1962;
www.circlebarbtheatre.com.

RINCON BEACH COUNTY PARK 🏊 🎣 ⛵ Wildly popular   **BEACHES**
with nudists and surfers, this is a pretty white-sand beach backed   **& PARKS**
by bluffs. At the bottom of the wooden stairway leading down
to the beach, take a right along the strand and head over to the
seawall. There will often be a bevy of nude sunbathers snuggled
here between the hillside and the ocean in an area known as
Bates Beach, or **Backside Rincon**. Be warned: Nude sunbathing
is illegal. Occasionally the sheriff *will* crack down on nudists.
Surfers, on the other hand, turn left and paddle out to Rincon
Point, one of the most popular surfing spots along the entire
California coast. There are picnic areas and restrooms. ~ Located
three miles southeast of Carpinteria; from Route 101 take the

Bates Road exit; 805-568-2461, fax 805-568-2459; e-mail ad
ministration@sbparks.org.

CARPINTERIA STATE BEACH 🚲 🚶 🎣 🏊 🛶 This
ribbon-shaped park extends for nearly a mile along the coast. Bordered to the east by dunes and along the west by a bluff, the beach
has an offshore shelf that shelters it from the surf. As a result, Carpinteria provides exceptionally good swimming and is nicknamed
"the world's safest beach." Wildlife here consists of small mammals and reptiles as well as seals and many seabirds. Don't bring
your pets; dogs are not allowed on the beach. It's a good spot for
tidepooling; there is also a lagoon here. The Santa Ynez Mountains rise in the background. Facilities include picnic areas, restrooms, dressing rooms, showers, and lifeguards (during summer
only). Swimming is excellent, and skindiving is good along the
breakwater reef, a habitat for abalone and lobsters. Surfing is very
good in the "tar pits" area near the east end of the park. If you
are into fishing, cabezon, corbina, and barred perch are caught
here. Day-use fee, $8. ~ Located at the end of Palm Avenue in
Carpinteria; 805-684-2811.

▲ There are 216 tent/RV sites, about half with hookups,
from $21 to $45 per night. Reservations: 800-444-7275.

SUMMERLAND BEACH 🚶 🐎 🚶 🏄 🛶 🚤 Part of this
narrow strip of white sand used to be a popular nude beach. It's
backed by low-lying hills, which afford privacy from the nearby
freeway and railroad tracks. The favored skinny-dipping spot is
on the east end between two protective rock piles. Gay men
sometimes congregate farther down the beach at Loon Point, but
families are rapidly taking over. Nudists beware: law enforcement
at the beach has been stepped up in response to public demand.
There are no facilities here, but nearby **Lookout Park** (805-568-
2461) has picnic areas, restrooms, and a playground. Swimming
is popular, and there is good bodysurfing here. ~ Located in Summerland six miles east of Santa Barbara. Take the Summerland
exit off Route 101 and get on Wallace Avenue, the frontage road
between the freeway and ocean. Follow it east for three-tenths of
a mile to Finney Road and the beach.

EAST BEACH 🚲 🚶 Everyone's favorite Santa Barbara
beach, this broad beauty stretches more than a mile from Montecito to Stearns Wharf. In addition to a fluffy sand corridor there
are grassy areas, palm trees, and a wealth of service facilities. Beyond the wharf the strand continues as **West Beach**. The area
known as "Butterfly Beach" at the far east end is frequented by
nude sunbathers. Facilities include restrooms, showers, lifeguards,
a playground, a weight room, and volleyball courts. Fishing and
swimming are recommended. **Cabrillo Pavilion Bathhouse** (1118
East Cabrillo Boulevard, Santa Barbara; 805-564-5421) pro-

vides lockers, showers, and a weight room for a small daily fee. There's a restaurant next door. Other facilities are at Stearns Wharf. ~ In Santa Barbara along East Cabrillo Boulevard between the Andree Clark Bird Refuge and Stearns Wharf. Butterfly Beach can be reached by following East Cabrillo Boulevard east past the Cabrillo Pavilion Bathhouse until the road turns inland. From this juncture continue along the beach on foot. Although sunbathers use the beach as a clothing-optional area, this spot, just beyond the Clark Mansion, is sometimes patrolled by the sheriff to discourage nudity; 805-564-5418.

LEDBETTER BEACH A crescent of white sand, this beach rests along a shallow cove. While it's quite pretty here, with a headland bordering one end of the strand, it simply doesn't compare to nearby East Beach. There are picnic areas, restrooms, lifeguards (summer only), and a restaurant. Surfing is good, particularly for beginners, west of the breakwater. ~ Located along the 800 block of Shoreline Drive in Santa Barbara; 805-564-5418.

SHORELINE PARK The attraction here is not the park but the beach that lies below it. The park rests at the edge of a high bluff; at the bottom, secluded from view, is a narrow, curving length of white sand. It's a great spot to escape the Santa Barbara crowds while enjoying a pretty beach. Stairs from the park lead down to the shore, though the beach is inaccessible at high tide. Topside in the park are picnic areas, restrooms, and a playground. ~ Located in Santa Barbara along Shoreline Drive; 805-564-5418.

MESA LANE BEACH This is the spot Santa Barbarans head ◄ *HIDDEN* when they want to escape the crowds at the better-known beaches. It's a meandering ribbon of sand backed by steep bluffs. You can walk long distances along this secluded beach during low tide, but be careful not to get stranded when the tide comes in. There are

THE WRITING ON THE WALL

Rare and intricate cave paintings by Chumash Indians decorate the sandstone walls at **Chumash Painted Cave State Historic Park**. Strange animal and human figures, as well as various abstract shapes, appear in vivid red, white, and black colors. The oldest paintings here are thought to be 1000 years old, but some of them are quite recent. The Chumash still consider their art sacred—these paintings are one of the only examples on view to the public. ~ On Painted Caves Road, three miles south of San Marcos Pass. Take Route 154 out of Santa Barbara and turn right on Painted Caves Road. The cave is on the left, up a narrow, steep road. Warning: Trailers and RVs should not attempt this road.

no facilities so be sure to pack a snack. ~ There's a stairway to the beach at the end of Mesa Lane, off Cliff Drive in Santa Barbara.

ARROYO BURRO BEACH PARK 🏇 ⚓ 🎣 🚣 This 13-acre facility is a little gem on summer days. The sandy beach and surrounding hills are packed with locals, who often refer to it as "Hendry's Beach." If you can arrive at an uncrowded time you'll find beautiful scenery along this lengthy strand. There are picnic areas, restrooms, lifeguards (during the summer), a restaurant, a bar, and a snack bar. Swimming and fishing is good and surfing is excellent west of the breakwater. ~ 2981 Cliff Drive, Santa Barbara; 805-568-2461, fax 805-568-2459.

HIDDEN ►   **MORE MESA** ⚓ According to nude-beach aficionado Dave Patrick, this is the region's favorite bare-buns rendezvous. Thousands of sunbathers gather at this remote site on a single afternoon. "On a hot day," Patrick reports, "the beach almost takes on a carnival atmosphere, with jugglers, surfers, world-class frisbee experts, musicians, dancers, joggers, and volleyball champs." A scene that should not be missed. No facilities. ~ Located between Hope Ranch and Goleta, three miles from Route 101. Take the Turnpike Road exit from Route 101; follow it south to Hollister Avenue, then go left; from Hollister turn right on Puente Drive, right again on Vieja Drive, then left on Mockingbird Lane. At the end of Mockingbird Lane a path leads about three-quarters of a mile to the beach.

EL CAPITAN STATE BEACH 🏃 ⚓ 🎣 🚴 🚣 Another one of Southern California's sparkling beaches, El Capitan stretches along three miles of oceanfront. The park is 168 acres and features a nature trail, tidepools, and wonderful opportunities for hiking along the beach. El Capitan Creek, fringed by oak and sycamore trees, traverses the area. Seals and sea lions often romp offshore and in winter gray whales cruise by. Swimming is good; surfing is good off El Capitan Point. This beach is also a good place to catch grunion. Facilities include picnic areas, restrooms, showers, a store, and seasonal lifeguards. Day-use fee, $8. ~ Located in Goleta off Route 101 about 20 miles north of Santa Barbara; 805-968-1033.

▲ There are 131 tent/RV sites (no hookups) in the park near the beach; $25 per night. Reservations: 800-444-7275.

REFUGIO STATE BEACH 🏃 🚲 ⚓ 🎣 🚴 🚣 This is a 39-acre park with over a mile of ocean frontage. You can bask on a sandy beach, lie under palm trees on the greensward, and hike or bicycle along the two-and-a-half-mile path that connects this park with El Capitan. There are also interesting tidepools. Facilities include picnic areas, restrooms, showers, seasonal lifeguard, and a store. Fishing, swimming, and surfing are good. Day-use fee, $8. ~ 10 Refugio Road, off Route 101 about 20 miles north of Santa Barbara; 805-968-1033.

▲ There are 82 tent/RV sites (no hookups); $25 per night. Reservations: 800-444-7275.

SAN ONOFRE BEACH 🏃 ⚓ This nude beach is a rare find indeed. Frequented by few people, it is a pretty white-sand beach that winds along rocky headlands. There's not much here except beautiful views, shore plant life, and savvy sunbathers. Wander for miles past cliffs and coves. ~ Located off Route 101 about 30 miles north of Santa Barbara and two miles south of Gaviota. Driving north on Route 101 make a U-turn on Vista del Mar Road; drive south on Route 101 for seven-tenths of a mile to a dirt parking area. Cross the railroad tracks; a path next to the railroad light signal leads to the beach.

GAVIOTA STATE PARK 🏃 ⚓ 🎣 🚣 🏄 ⚓ 🚤 This mammoth 2776-acre facility stretches along both sides of Route 101. The beach rests in a sandy cove guarded on either side by dramatic sedimentary rock formations. A railroad trestle traverses the beach and a fishing pier extends offshore. Facilities include picnic areas, restrooms, showers, and lifeguards. Day-use fee, $8. ~ The beach is located off Route 101 about 30 miles northwest of Santa Barbara; 805-968-1033.

> On the inland side of Gaviota State Park a hiking trail leads up to Gaviota Hot Springs and into Los Padres National Forest.

▲ There are 39 tent/RV sites (no hookups); $25 per night. The vegetation is sparse from the forest fires a few years ago, and there is no drinking water, so bring your own. Sites are first-come, first-served.

JALAMA BEACH COUNTY PARK 🎣 🚣 🚤 This remote park sits at the far end of a 14-mile-long country road. Nevertheless, in summer the campground is likely to be full. They come because the broad sandy beach is fringed by coastal bluffs and undulating hills. Jalama Creek cuts through the park, creating a wetland frequented by many species of birds. Point Conception lies a few miles to the south, and the area all around is undeveloped and quite pretty (though Vandenberg Air Force Base is situated north of the beach). This is a good area for beachcombing as well as rock-hounding for chert, agate, travertine, and fossils. Facilities include picnic areas, restrooms, hot showers, a store, a snack bar, and a playground. Swim with caution because of dangerous rip currents. Lifeguard on duty during the summer only. Surfing is good at Tarantula Point about one-half mile south of the park. You can surf-fish for perch or fish from the rocky points for cabezon and rock fish. Day-use fee, $6. ~ From Lompoc take Route 1 south for five miles; turn onto Jalama Beach Road and follow it 15 miles to the end; 805-736-3504, fax 805-735-8020.

▲ There are 110 tent/RV sites (28 with electrical hookups); $18 to $25 per night.

▼ ▼ ▼ ▼ ▼ ▼ ▼ ▼ ▼ ▼ ▼ ▼ ▼ ▼

San Luis Obispo Area

Craggy volcanic peaks and rolling hills dramatically punctuate this stretch of coastline lying about halfway between Los Angeles and San Francisco. The towns of San Luis Obispo, Morro Bay, and Pismo Beach are popular stopovers on the long scenic drive between northern and southern California. The county's growing wine industry also draws visitors to tasting rooms and winery tours. San Luis Obispo (don't say "San Louie"—pronounce the "s") is the region's commercial center, as well as the site of California Polytechnic State University (Cal Poly). Home of an old Spanish mission, pretty San Luis has enough small-city sophistication and cultural offerings to impress even big-city cosmopolites, while Pismo Beach and Morro Bay retain their earthier California beach town character.

SIGHTS   **PISMO BEACH**   An unattractive congeries of mobile homes and beach rental stands, Pismo Beach and its immediate neighbor Oceano are nondescript towns that have a single saving grace— the dunes of Oceano, several miles south of town. Wave after wave after wave of these ever-changing hills of sand parallel the beach, like a crystalline continuation of the ocean.

Otherwise, Pismo Beach, with its population of 8500 people, is a tacky tourist enclave known for an annual clam festival and for the migrating monarch butterflies that land just south of the town pier every year from late November to March. Traveling north, you reach Pismo Beach after Route 1 completes its lengthy inland course through Lompoc and Guadalupe, then rejoins Route 101 and returns to the coast.

Those vaunted sand piles comprise the most extensive coastal dunes in California. From Pismo Beach the sand hills run six miles south where they meet the 450-foot-high **Guadalupe dunes** (see "Beaches & Parks" section), forming a unique habitat for wildflowers and shorebirds.

Back in the 1930s and 1940s a group of bohemians, the "Dunites," occupied this wild terrain. Comprised of nudists, artists, and mystics, the movement believed that the dunes were a center of cosmic energy. Today the area is filled with beachcombers, sunbathers, and off-highway vehicles.

At the **Oceano Dunes State Vehicular Recreation Area** (see "Beaches & Parks" section below), you may drive your car onto the beach and operate off-highway and all-terrain vehicles in a specified area of the park.

Aside from exploring the dunes and studying the monarchs, Pismo Beach has a large jazz festival in October, as well as tidepools teeming with sea life just west of the pier. Stop by the **Pismo Beach Visitor Information Center** for brochures and maps of the San Luis Bay region. ~ 581 Dolliver Street, Pismo Beach;

805-773-4382, 800-443-7778, fax 805-773-6772; www.classic
california.com.

An ironic twist of fate that has led to the decline of adjacent
Avila Beach may turn out to be the town's salvation. In 1989, it
was discovered that an oil pipeline leak was contaminating the
ground underneath the tiny beachside enclave. As a result, property values plunged, and the town took on an increasingly run-
down look. Recently, it was decided that the town's commercial
core—a two-block stretch overlooking a white-sand beach and
three fishing piers—would be torn down to remove tons of con-
taminated soil below. After the cleanup, the business district was
completely rebuilt, and now refurbished shops and restaurants
are slowly bringing the town back to life.

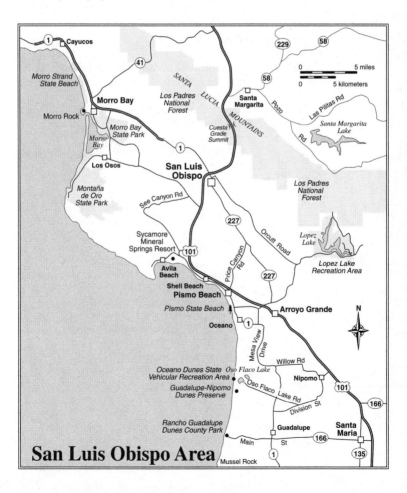

San Luis Obispo Area

There are hot springs in the hills around Avila Beach. **Sycamore Mineral Springs Resort** has tapped these local waters and created a lovely spa with hotel units, a gift shop, and a swimming pool. The real attractions here, however, are the redwood hot tubs. Very private, they are dotted about on a hillside and shaded by oak and sycamore. Admission. ~ 1215 Avila Beach Drive, Avila Beach; 805-595-7302, 800-234-5831, fax 805-595-4007; www. sycamoresprings.com, e-mail info@smsr.com.

HIDDEN ▶

From Pismo Beach, you can buzz into San Luis Obispo on Route 101 or take a quiet country drive into town via **See Canyon Road**. The latter begins in Avila Beach and corkscrews up into the hills past apple orchards and horse farms. Along its 13-mile length, half unpaved, you'll encounter mountain meadows and ridgetop vistas. During the fall harvest season you can pick apples at farms along the way.

SAN LUIS OBISPO   San Luis Obispo, a pretty jewel of a town, lies 12 miles from the ocean in the center of an expansive agricultural region. Backdropped by the Santa Lucia Mountains, the town focuses around an old Spanish mission. Cowboys from outlying ranches and students from the campuses of Cal Poly and Cuesta College add to the cultural mix, creating a vital atmosphere that has energized San Luis Obispo's rapid growth.

Parking on weekends and during the summer can be a nightmare, but don't let that deter you. The town is completely walkable, so once you've found a spot in one of the numerous small public lots, two parking garages, or on the street (bring quarters), leave the car there and set out on foot. Your first stop should be the **San Luis Obispo Chamber of Commerce**. Here you can pick up brochures about the area's attractions, including a map for a self-guided walking tour. ~ 1039 Chorro Street, San Luis Obispo; 805-781-2777, fax 805-543-1255; www.visitslo.com, e-mail slo chamber@slochamber.org.

A self-guided tour of this historic town logically begins at **Mission San Luis Obispo de Tolosa**. Dating to 1772, the old Spanish outpost has been nicely reconstructed, though the complex is not as extensive as La Purísima Mission in Lompoc. There's a museum re-creating the American Indian, Spanish, and Mexican eras as well as a pretty church and a gift shop. Mission Plaza, fronting the chapel, is a well-landscaped park. ~ Chorro and Monterey streets, San Luis Obispo; 805-781-8220, fax 805-781-8214; www. missionsanluisobispo.org, e-mail office@oldmissionslo.org.

The **San Luis Obispo Art Center** exhibits works by the area's artists. Closed Tuesday from Labor Day to July 4. ~ 1010 Broad Street at Monterey Street, San Luis Obispo; 805-543-8562, fax 805-543-4518; www.sloartcenter.org, e-mail info@sloartcenter.org.

St. Stephen's Episcopal Church is a narrow, lofty, and strikingly attractive chapel. Built in 1867, it was one of California's first Protestant churches. ~ Nipomo and Pismo streets, San Luis Obispo.

The **Dallidet Adobe,** constructed by a French vintner in 1859, is another local architectural landmark. ~ On Pacific Street between Santa Rosa and Toro streets, San Luis Obispo. A block away and about a century later Frank Lloyd Wright designed the **Kundert Medical Building.** ~ Pacific and Santa Rosa streets, San Luis Obispo.

The **Ah Louis Store** symbolizes the Chinese presence here. A sturdy brick building with wrought-iron shutters and balcony, it dates to 1874 and once served the 2000 Chinese coolies who worked on nearby railroad tunnels. ~ 800 Palm Street, San Luis Obispo.

Around the corner, the **Sauer-Adams Adobe,** covered in clapboard, is an 1800s-era house with a second-story balcony. By the turn of the century, Victorian-style homes had become the vogue. Many of San Luis Obispo's finest Victorians are located in the blocks adjacent to where Broad Street intersects with Pismo and Buchon streets. ~ 964 Chorro Street, San Luis Obispo.

Those with young ones in tow can stop by the **San Luis Obispo Children's Museum.** In this imaginative environment kids can

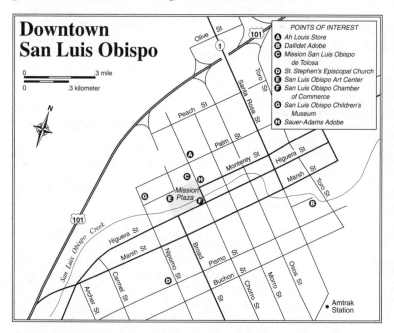

Downtown San Luis Obispo

0 _____ .3 mile
0 _____ .3 kilometer

N

POINTS OF INTEREST
- **A** Ah Louis Store
- **B** Dallidet Adobe
- **C** Mission San Luis Obispo de Tolosa
- **D** St. Stephen's Episcopal Church
- **E** San Luis Obispo Art Center
- **F** San Luis Obispo Chamber of Commerce
- **G** San Luis Obispo Children's Museum
- **H** Sauer-Adams Adobe

Olive St
Toro St
Santa Rosa St
Peach St
Palm St
Monterey St
Higuera St
Marsh St
Toro St
Mission Plaza
San Luis Obispo Creek
Higuera St
Marsh St
Nipomo St
Broad St
Pismo St
Buchon St
Carmel St
Archer St
Chorro St
Morro St
Osos St
• Amtrak Station

race to a fire engine, vote in a voting booth, learn the principles of photography, and discover a Chumash Indian cave. Closed for renovations until December 2007. ~ 1010 Nipomo Street, San Luis Obispo; 805-544-5437; www.slokids.org, e-mail rmueller@slokids.org.

MORRO BAY   As Route 1 angles north and west from San Luis Obispo toward the ocean, separating again from Route 101, you will encounter a procession of nine volcanic peaks. Last in this geologic parade is a 576-foot plug dome called **Morro Rock**. The pride of Morro Bay, it stands like a little Gibraltar, connected to the mainland by a sand isthmus. You can drive out and inspect the brute. Years ago, before conservationists and common sense prevailed, the site was a rock quarry. Today it's a nesting area for peregrine falcons.

Morro Bay is one of those places with obscure natural treasures that are often overlooked at first glance. That's because Morro Bay is largely a working fishing town, not a pretty recreational harbor with a gleaming fleet of expensive, handsome vessels, like Newport Harbor in Orange County. Morro Bay comes with a gritty legacy, first as a busy 19th-century port for the region's cattle and dairy industry, then as a naval training base during World War II. In the 1950s, a power plant was built on the site, providing a tax base that led to the town's incorporation.

The real working waterfront of Morro Bay lies to the north of Harbor Street, in the shadow of the three giant smokestacks of the power plant. A walk along the touristy waterfront stretch called the Embarcadero, which is south of Harbor Street, reveals a predictable mix of tacky tourist shops and so-called galleries, along with plenty of restaurants offering fish and chips and "harbor views." The **Morro Bay Chamber of Commerce** offers plenty of brochures and information about the area. Closed Sunday. ~ 845 Embarcadero Road, Suite D, Morro Bay; 805-772-4467, 800-231-0592; www.morrobay.org.

Young children might enjoy playing on the whale's tail or just watching the boats in the Morro Bay marina at Tidelands Children's Park, at the south end of Embarcadero.

But the real pleasures of Morro Bay lie hidden behind its ugly manmade features.

The best place to learn something of the local natural environment is at the small **Morro Bay State Park Museum of Natural History**. It's located at White Point, a rocky outcropping (Indian mortar holes are still visible) in Morro Bay State Park, with fine views of the surrounding estuary, which is a protected habitat for 250 migratory and resident bird species and one of the largest salt marshes in California. From this height there are also views of the sandspit, Morro Bay, and Morro Rock. "Rocky," the museum's mascot, helps out with the museum's educational displays of local history and wildlife. Lots of hands-on interactive exhibits make it enjoyable for restless children. And a docent is always on hand to answer questions. Admission. ~ Morro Bay State Park Road (from Morro Bay, follow Main Street into the state park), Morro Bay; 805-772-2694, fax 805-772-7129; www.morrobaymuseum.org.

The Morro Bay Estuary is one of the largest unspoiled coastal marshes in California. This unique environment, where salty sea meets fresh water, is a stopover for hundreds of migratory birds, including blue heron, who nest and rear their young at the **Morro Bay Heron Rookery**. When this eucalyptus grove was threatened some years ago with development, the people of California purchased it to retain it as a permanent nesting site. It is now the only remaining large rookery of great blue heron on the California coast between San Francisco and Mexico. Nesting begins in January, when the birds choose mates and build nests. Eggs are laid in February and hatch in late March. The nestlings are fed by both parents until they're able to fly away a few months later, sometime in late June or early July. ~ Morro Bay State Park Road, just south of Park View Drive, Morro Bay.

◄ *HIDDEN*

The Los Osos/Morro Bay chapter of the Small Wilderness Area Preservation offers monthly walks through **El Morro Elfin Forest**, an ecological preserve of pygmy oaks and other unusual flora. ~ Santa Ysabel Avenue at 15th Street, Los Osos; 805-528-0392.

◄ *HIDDEN*

At the mouth of Morro Bay, Morro Rock competes for attention, sadly, with the three concrete smokestacks of the power plant across the harbor, something that seems even to embarrass the locals. But turn your back on the travesty as they do, and gaze across the bay instead to the **sandspit** that holds back the Pacific and extends in a narrow sliver for four miles and teems with bird and other wildlife.

For a bit of underwater exploration, take a dive, so to speak, in a semi-submersible vessel with **Sub-Sea Tours** for a look at Morro Bay's giant kelp forest and the marine life that inhabits it. Otters are occasionally spotted on the tours. ~ Marina Square, 699 Embarcadero; 805-772-9463; www.subseatours.com.

◄ *HIDDEN*

Lodging in the Pismo Beach–Shell Beach area generally means finding a motel. None of these seaside towns has expanded more than a few blocks from the waterfront, so wherever you book a room will be walking distance from the beach.

LODGING

Located on the beach, the 77-unit **Sea Gypsy Motel** offers a comfortable option with standard motel rooms with no view or studios with kitchens and balconies, some with oceanfront views. Laundry facilities, a heated pool, and a spa round out the amenities. ~ 1020 Cypress Street, Pismo Beach; 805-773-1801,

800-592-5923, fax 805-773-9286; www.seagypsymotel.com, e-mail info@seagypsymotel.com. BUDGET TO DELUXE.

If it's panoramic Pacific Coast views you are after, try the **Best Western Shore Cliff Lodge**. Perched on the cliffs just off Route 101, the hotel offers spacious, although conventional, rooms with private balconies, microwaves, and refrigerators. There is a restaurant, pool, spa, sauna, and access to tennis courts. Guest rooms aren't cheap, but what a view! ~ 2555 Price Street, Pismo Beach; 805-773-4671, 800-441-8885, fax 805-773-2341; www.shorecliff.com. ULTRA-DELUXE.

The small, seven-room **Beachcomber Inn** is neat and clean and just a block from the beach. Quaintly furnished with wicker furniture and floral prints, rooms also come equipped with microwaves and coffee makers. None of the rooms, however, have a full-on ocean view. Two-night minimum. ~ 541 Cypress Street, Pismo Beach; 805-773-5505, fax 805-773-0880; www.pismobeach.com/beachcomberinn, e-mail bcomberinn@ aol.com. BUDGET TO DELUXE.

San Luis Obispo also offers several distinctive accommodations, including the **Petit Soleil**, a classic motel that's been transformed into a B&B with a French flavor. Here the 16 non-smoking rooms are simple but comfortable. The view is of the surrounding hills, and a night's stay includes a trip to the inn's bounteous breakfast buffet, and afternoon hors d'oeuvres and wine. ~ 1473 Monterey Street, San Luis Obispo; 805-549-0321, 800-676-1588, fax 805-549-0383; www.psslo.com, e-mail petitsoleil@ charter.net. DELUXE TO ULTRA-DELUXE.

Sycamore Mineral Springs Resort reposes on a hillside one mile inland from Avila Beach. Situated in a stand of oak and sycamore trees are 74 rooms and suites. Each has a private patio spa; there are also redwood hot tubs scattered about in the surrounding forest and a swimming pool. The rooms are decorated in contemporary style. An on-site yoga institute and restaurant round out the amenities. ~ 1215 Avila Beach Drive, San Luis Obispo; 805-595-7302, 800-234-5831; www.sycamoresprings. com, e-mail info@smsr.com. ULTRA-DELUXE.

Heritage Inn Bed & Breakfast is a San Luis Obispo anomaly. There aren't many country inns in town and this one is not even representative of the species. It sits in a neighborhood surrounded by motels and a nearby freeway, though it is in walking distance of historic downtown. What's more, the house was moved—lock, stock, and bay windows—to this odd location. Once inside, you'll be quite pleased. There's a warm, comfortable sitting parlor and seven guest rooms, all furnished with antiques, reflecting the house's 1905 birthdate; some accommodations include window seats and terraces that look out to a lovely creekside garden. Three rooms have private baths; the other four share two baths, and four rooms have fireplaces. There's a cat in residence—allergics beware. Full breakfast is included. ~ 978 Olive Street, San Luis Obispo; 805-544-7440, fax 805-544-2819; www.heritageinnslo.com. BUDGET TO MODERATE.

The **Garden Street Inn**, located in the beautiful downtown district, is a beautifully restored 1887 Victorian that has 13 rooms and suites. Each is individually decorated in such themes as "Walden," "Amadeus," and "Emerald Isle." Some accommodations honor local history; others are filled with family mementoes. A full breakfast is served in the bay-windowed morning room and the innkeeper's reception in the afternoon features hors d'oeuvres and local wines. ~ 1212 Garden Street, San Luis Obispo; 805-545-9802, 800-488-2045, fax 805-545-9403; www.gardenstreetinn. com, e-mail innkeeper@gardenstreetinn.com. DELUXE TO ULTRA-DELUXE.

For your pick of typical motels in San Luis Obispo, head for the stretch of Monterey Street north of California Boulevard known as Motel Row.

The **Apple Farm** is two lodgings in one. The ultra-deluxe-priced inn represents another example of a classic country inn set in a neighborhood of drive-in motels. Its carefully landscaped property, including a stream that runs by the old Victorian-style buildings, takes you away from the hubbub of Monterey Street and into Old America complete with apple pies fresh from the Inn's bakery and a working, water-powered mill. Two new suites in the mill building each have a private deck and hot tub. The adjoining Trellis Court has all the advantages of the inn but its 34 smaller rooms are more affordably priced. While no two rooms are the same in either accommodation, they all have working gas fireplaces. ~ 2015 Monterey Street, San Luis Obispo; 805-544-2040, 800-374-3705, fax 805-544-2452; www.applefarm.com, e-mail info@applefarm.com. MODERATE TO ULTRA-DELUXE.

The most outlandish place in town is a roadside confection called the **Madonna Inn**. Architecturally it's a cross between a castle and a gingerbread house, culturally it's somewhere between light opera and heavy metal. The lampposts are painted pink, and the gift shop contains the biggest, gaudiest chandeliers you've ever seen. Personally, I wouldn't be caught dead staying in the place, but I would never miss an opportunity to visit. If you prove more daring than I, there are 108 rooms on the 2000-acre ranch, each decorated in a different flamboyant style ranging from an African Safari to something out of the Flintstones. Rooms offer a wide variety of amenities including waterfall showers and seven-foot bathtubs. There is a café, a formal dining room with live music, a fabulous bakery, and a gourmet shop offering picnic lunches and winetasting. ~ 100 Madonna Road, San Luis Obispo; 805-543-3000, 800-543-9666, fax 805-543-1800; www.madonna inn.com, e-mail info@madonnainn.com. ULTRA-DELUXE.

There are countless motels to choose from in Morro Bay, ranging across the entire spectrum in price and amenities. For information on availability contact the **Morro Bay Chamber of Commerce.** Closed Sunday. ~ 845 Embarcadero Road, Suite D, Morro Bay; 805-772-4467, 800-231-0592; www.morrobay.org.

Located next to Tidelands Park at the quieter southern portion of Embarcadero is the 33-room **Embarcadero Inn.** All rooms, which are spacious, very clean, and comfortable, face the bay; several come with gas fireplaces and balconies. Other amenities include VCRs with free movie rentals, refrigerators, and coffee makers, as well as a continental breakfast each morning. One room is set up for guests with mobility disabilities. ~ 456 Embarcadero, Morro Bay; 805-772-2700, 800-292-7625, fax 805-772-1060; www.embarcaderoinn.com, e-mail info@embarcaderoinn.com. DELUXE.

HIDDEN ▶   A flower-filled garden surrounds the **Marina Street Bed and Breakfast,** a yellow New England–style home with bay windows located two blocks from the bay and Morro Rock. Operated by Vern and Claudia Foster, retired teachers from Colorado, the inn has four separately themed rooms: the Bordeaux Room, with a tiger oak sleigh bed and bay view; the green-and-apricot-hued Garden Room, with a willow four-poster canopy bed and bay view; the nautically themed Dockside Room; and the romantic Rambling Rose Room, with delicate touches of lace throughout. The morning's full gourmet breakfast is served in the dining room and might include an apple-pecan panache or a spicy sausage casserole. ~ 305 Marina Street, Morro Bay; 805-772-4016, 888-683-9389, fax 805-772-0667; www.marinastreetinn.com, e-mail vfoster105@aol.com. DELUXE.

Fashionable but casual, **The Inn at Morro Bay** is a waterfront complex with the amenities of a small resort: a restaurant, a lounge, a swimming pool, and an adjacent golf course. It sits on ten acres overlooking Morro Bay and contains 98 guest rooms. Many rooms have feather beds, fireplaces, hot tubs, shuttered windows, and oak armoires. ~ 60 State Park Road, Morro Bay; 805-772-5651,

FARMERS' FEAST

If you're in San Luis Obispo on a Thursday evening, be sure to stop by the **Farmers Market**. Farmers from the surrounding area turn out to sell fresh fruits and vegetables. They barbecue ribs, cook sweet corn and fresh fish, then serve them on paper plates to the throngs that turn out weekly. Puppeteers and street dancers perform as the celebration assumes a carnival atmosphere. ~ At Higuera Street between Osos and Nipomo streets, San Luis Obispo.

800-321-9566, fax 805-772-4779; www.innatmorrobay.com, e-mail info@innatmorrobay.com. DELUXE TO ULTRA-DELUXE.

DINING

◄ *HIDDEN*

Fish-and-chip joints are everywhere on the Central Coast, but **Pismo Fish & Chips** is special—mainly because it's good, but also because it's a local institution. The fish is fresh, the portions generous, and the service friendly. Closed Monday. ~ 505 Cypress Street, Pismo Beach; 805-773-2853. MODERATE TO DELUXE.

If you missed the swinging doors in the saloon you'll get the idea from the moose head trophies and branding irons. "Taste the Great American West" is the motto for **F. McLintocks Saloon & Dining House**. Every evening, when the oak pit barbecue really gets going, there are a dozen kinds of steak, ribs, and seafood. If popularity means anything, this place is tops. It's always mobbed. So dust off the Stetson and prepare to chow down. Dinner only. ~ 750 Mattie Road, Shell Beach; 805-773-1892, 800-866-6372, fax 805-773-5183; www.mclintocks.com, e-mail fmc@mclintocks.com. MODERATE TO DELUXE.

Sick of seafood by now? Tired of saloons serving cowboy-sized steaks? Happily, San Luis Obispo has several ethnic restaurants. Two are located in The Creamery, a turn-of-the-20th-century dairy plant that has been transformed into a shopping mall. **Tsurugi Japanese Restaurant** features a sushi bar and dining area decorated with oriental screens and wallhangings. At lunch and dinner there are shrimp tempura, chicken teriyaki, *nigiri*, and other Asian specialties. The atmosphere is placid and the food quite good. ~ 570 Higuera Street, San Luis Obispo; phone/fax 805-543-8942. MODERATE.

An unassuming little trattoria just north of Higuera Street, **Buona Tavola** offers a garden patio setting away from any tourist bustle. Northern Italian cuisine includes lots of antipasti, pastas such as agnolotti stuffed with scampi in saffron sauce, steaks, chicken, over-the-top tiramisu, and fine gelatos. The wine list is long and varied. ~ 1037 Monterey Street, San Luis Obispo; 805-545-8000; www.btslo.com, e-mail slo@btslo.com. MODERATE TO DELUXE.

Italy enters the picture with **Cafe Roma**, a delightful restaurant decorated in country Tuscan style. Copper pots as well as portraits from the old country decorate the walls. Lunch and dinner feature several prix-fixe choices, each with an appetizer, entrée, and dessert. Run by an Italian family, it serves excellent food; highly recommended. No lunch on Saturday. Closed Sunday. ~ 1020 Railroad Avenue, San Luis Obispo; 805-541-6800, fax 805-786-2522; www.caferomaslo.com, e-mail info@caferomaslo.com. MODERATE TO DELUXE.

For a low-priced meal in a white-tablecloth restaurant with views of the surrounding hills, beat a path to the California Poly-

HIDDEN ▶ technic campus. **Vista Grande Restaurant** serves Cal Poly students as well as the public in a comfortable plate-glass dining room. Open for lunch and Sunday brunch, it features salad, pasta, fish, and vegetarian dishes. No lunch on Saturday, and dinner only during performances at the arts center across the street. Hours vary in summer, so call ahead. ~ On the Cal Poly campus, off Grand Avenue, San Luis Obispo; 805-756-1204, fax 805-756-6457. BUDGET TO MODERATE.

The **Corner View Restaurant & Bar** is a friendly neighborhood bar with better-than-average fare—entrées range from warm spinach salad, to stroganoff to fish and chips. No breakfast on weekdays. ~ 1141 Chorro Street, San Luis Obispo; 805-546-8444, fax 805-546-9185; www.cornerviewrestaurant.com, e-mail info@cornerviewrestaurant.com. MODERATE TO DELUXE.

You needn't cast far in Morro Bay to find a seafood restaurant. Sometimes they seem as ubiquitous as fishing boats. One of the most venerable is **Dorn's Original Breakers Café**. It's a bright, airy place with a postcard view of the waterfront from indoor and patio tables. While they serve all three meals, in the evening you better want seafood because there are about two dozen fish dishes and only a couple of steak, chicken, pasta, and veal platters. For breakfast try their out-of-this-world blueberry pancakes with a healthy dollop of whipped cream. ~ 801 Market Street, Morro Bay; 805-772-4415, fax 805-772-4695. MODERATE TO DELUXE.

The name says it all at **Windows on the Water**, a big airy place with water views from every table. Menu favorites include bouillabaisse and steaks done with Tuscan touches and crab cakes with jalapeño aioli. Live dangerously and try the prawn martini or the cocktail sauce sorbet—more delicious than you may assume. There's a large wine list showcasing California wines. Arrive in early evening to get the best sunset-watching tables. ~ 699 Embarcadero, Morro Bay; 805-772-0677; www.windows onthewater.net. MODERATE.

The picturesque setting—a grove of eucalyptus trees beside a small marina in Morro Bay State Park—is enough to recommend HIDDEN ▶ the small, rustic **Bayside Café**, where you can sit outside on the heated deck and take in the scenery. Locals come here for fresh fish, of course, and California/Mexican-inspired dishes like chicken pasta Veracruz, and chile verde. Desserts, like *tres leches* cake, are all homemade. No dinner Monday through Wednesday. ~ Morro Bay State Park Road (from Morro Bay, follow Main Street into the park), Morro Bay; 805-772-1465. MODERATE.

Fine California cuisine is the order of the day at **The Orchard Inn**. Situated in a waterfront resort, the dining room looks out over Morro Bay. In addition to great views and commodious surroundings, it features an enticing list of California cuisine with a

Mediterranean influence. All three meals are served, but the highlight is dinner. The menu might include ahi with couscous, seared duck with chipotle cream, or a medley of seafood. There's a Sunday champagne brunch. ~ The Inn at Morro Bay, 60 State Park Road, Morro Bay; 805-772-5651, 800-321-9566, fax 805-772-4779; www.innatmorrobay.com. MODERATE TO DELUXE.

In the old Spanish town of San Luis Obispo, the best stores are located along the blocks surrounding Mission Plaza. Stroll the two blocks along Monterey Street between Osos and Chorro streets, then browse the five-block stretch on Higuera Street from Osos Street to Nipomo Street. These two arteries and the side streets between form the heart of downtown. **SHOPPING**

The Creamery is an old dairy plant converted into an ingenious shopping center with several small artists' galleries, restaurants, and shops. ~ 570 Higuera Street, San Luis Obispo.

In Morro Bay, the waterfront Embarcadero offers the ubiquitous souvenir/T-shirt emporiums that predominate in such touristy enclaves.

Up the hill, along Morro Bay Boulevard and Main Street, there are several antique and vintage stores that for collectors might offer an enjoyable afternoon of browsing. The Chamber of Commerce puts out a brochure and map pinpointing these shops.

The **Frog and Peach Pub** is your standard sports bar. More than 40 beers and a TV in every corner make it the perfect place to watch the game. The interior is dark and calm, while the back patio gets a bit more rowdy. When they host live rock or blues music (which is most nights), there is sometimes a cover. ~ 728 Higuera Street, San Luis Obispo; 805-595-3764. **NIGHTLIFE**

Across the street at **Mother's Tavern** the mood is a little more mellow. With live big-band music on Sunday, karaoke on Monday, and deejays the other evenings, this bar serves a college-aged clientele out for a good time. There's often a line at the door and the generous dancefloor fills quickly, but it is usually possible to

DOWN WHERE THE LIGHTS ARE BRIGHT

San Luis Obispo's quaint downtown is home to a lively bar scene where college students and cowboys mix it up. From intimate coffeehouses and restaurants with live music to bars featuring 25-cent beers, you're likely to find something entertaining—walk around Monterey, Higuera, and Marsh streets and the paths that connect them, until you find what you want. Or just head over to the 700 block of Higuera Street, where a triangle of bars offers something for everyone.

grab an intimate table upstairs. Occasional cover. ~ 725 Higuera Street, San Luis Obispo; 805-541-8733, fax 805-541-1641; www.motherstavern.com, e-mail events@motherstavern.com.

The mood is definitely not mellow at **The Library Lounge** next door. Despite its name's quiet, studious connotations, this is the seen-and-be-seen scene for local college students. In fact, every Cal Poly mother should be a little suspicious when her student starts spending inordinate amounts of time at "the library." The deejay music is loud, the dancefloor is packed, and nightly drink specials keep the crowd going. ~ 723 Higuera Street, San Luis Obispo; 805-542-0199.

There's live entertainment in the lounge every Friday and Saturday night, as well as Sunday mornings during the summer at **The Inn at Morro Bay**. Appointed with bentwood furniture and pastel paneling, it's a beautiful bar. The most striking feature of all is the view, which extends out across the water to Morro Rock; an ideal location for watching the sunset. ~ 60 State Park Road, Morro Bay; 805-772-5651; www.innatmorrobay.com.

The **Performing Arts Center of San Luis Obispo County** is located on the Cal Poly campus. Seating 1298, it gives the region a year-round professional performance venue. ~ 805-756-2787 or 888-233-2787 for schedule and tickets; www.pacslo.org.

GAY SCENE There's no particular neighborhood in San Luis that's become the preferred turf for gay men and lesbians or that has a concentration of gay-oriented business. In fact, although there are a fair number of gays and lesbians living in the SLO area, their profile is generally conservative, quiet, and "pretty closeted," as one gay business owner put it.

But the area is not without committed resources: the **Gay and Lesbian Alliance of the Central Coast** (GALA) operates a community center and provides a meeting place for various groups. Closed Saturday and Sunday. ~ 11573 Los Osos Valley Road, San Luis Obispo; 805-541-4252; www.ccgala.org, e-mail email@ccgala.org.

HIDDEN ► The gay-friendly atmosphere at **Linnaea's Café**, a "hipster hangout" downtown, attracts the city's young gays and lesbians, as well as artists and other creative types. It's usually open until 11 p.m., late for this neck of the woods. ~ 1110 Garden Street, San Luis Obispo; 805-541-5888; www.linnaeas.com.

The **Big Sky Café** is another popular and gay-friendly spot and can be recommended for its modern American-style cooking. ~ 1121 Broad Street, San Luis Obispo; 805-545-5401; www.big skycafe.com.

BEACHES & PARKS   **RANCHO GUADALUPE DUNES COUNTY PARK** 🚶 🚲 ⚓ ↵
The Sahara Desert has nothing on this place. The sand dunes throughout the area are spectacular; they provide a habitat for

California brown pelicans, Western snowy plovers, and other endangered birds and plants. The Santa Maria River, which empties here, forms a pretty wetland area. Fishing is ◆◆◆◆◆◆◆◆◆◆◆◆◆◆◆◆◆◆◆◆◆◆◆◆◆
very popular here. Primitive restrooms are on   The 450-foot Mussel
site. Be sure to visit the **Dunes Center** (closed   Rock in Rancho
Monday) for exhibits on mammals, dune formation,   Guadalupe Dunes
birds, reptiles, orientation videos and maps, and visi-   County Park is the
tor information. ~ From Route 1 in Guadalupe, follow   highest dune on
Main Street (Route 166) west for three miles to the   the West Coast.
beach. Windblown sand sometimes closes the road, so
call beforehand; 805-343-2455 (Dunes Center), fax 805-
343-0442; www.dunescenter.org, e-mail info@dunescenter.org.

OCEANO DUNES STATE VEHICULAR RECREATION AREA This
is the only spot in California where standard and four-wheel-
drive vehicles may still be driven right on the beach. A five-and-
half-mile-long section of dunes is open year-round to four-wheelers
and all-terrain vehicles. OHVs can be driven only in designated
areas and must be registered and display flags. Day-use fee, $5
per vehicle. ~ Off Route 1, south of downtown Pismo Beach.
Enter on Pier Avenue or Grand Avenue; 805-473-7223
(recorded) or 805-473-7220; www.ohv.parks.ca.gov.

▲ There are primitive campsites, with only chemical toilets;
$10 per vehicle. Reservations are recommended: 800-444-7275.
To access the campsite, you must drive across two miles of sand
and cross a creek, which can be treacherous during high tide.

PISMO STATE BEACH 🏃 🏊 🎣 🚶 This spectacular
beach runs for six miles from Pismo Beach north to the Santa
Maria River. Along its oceanfront are some of the finest sand
dunes in California, fluffy hills inhabited by shorebirds and tenacious plants. A freshwater lagoon abuts the campgrounds. Also
home to the pismo clam, it's a wonderful place to hike and explore. Surfing is popular here, but exercise caution in the water—
rip tides occur here occasionally. Lifeguards on duty in the summer. There are picnic areas here, and restrooms with hot showers
at both campgrounds. Fishing for cod and red snapper is good
from the Pismo Pier (at the end of Hinds Avenue, Pismo Beach).
You can also dig for pismo clams along the beach (check for local
restrictions). Day-use fee, $6. ~ The park parallels Route 1 in
Pismo Beach; 805-489-1869, fax 805-489-6004.

▲ There are limited tent sites; $25 per night. Call 800-444-
7275 for reservations. There is also camping at **Oceano
Memorial Campground** (near Mendel Drive and Pier Avenue,
Oceano; 805-781-5930) at 24 tent/RV sites (full hookups); $25
to $34 per night. Sites are first-come, first-served.

PIRATE'S COVE OR MALLAGH LANDING 🏊 This crescent-   ◀ *HIDDEN*
shaped nude beach is a beauty. Protected by 100-foot cliffs, it

curves for a half mile along a placid cove. At one end is a rocky headland pockmarked by caves. Restaurants and groceries are in Avila Beach. Swimming and skindiving are very good because the beach is in a sheltered area. ~ Located ten miles south of San Luis Obispo in Avila Beach. From Route 101 take Avila Beach Drive west for two miles, turn left on Cave Landing Road (the road travels immediately uphill), and go six-tenths of a mile to a dirt parking lot; crude stairs lead down to the beach.

MONTAÑA DE ORO STATE PARK This 13,000-acre facility is one of the finest parks along the entire Central Coast. It stretches more than seven miles along the shore, past a sandspit, tidepools, and sharp cliffs. There are remote coves for viewing seals, sea otters, and migrating whales and for sunbathing on hidden beaches. Monarch butterflies roost in the eucalyptus-filled canyons and a hiking trail leads to Valencia Peak, with views scanning almost 100 miles of coastline. Wildlife is abundant along 50 miles of hiking trails. Chaparral, Bishop pine, and coast live oak cover the hills; in spring wildflowers riot, giving the park its name, "Mountain of Gold." You can go fishing, but swimming is not recommended because of the lack of lifeguards, occasional rip tides, and chilly water. Surfing is good around Hazard Canyon. There are picnic areas and primitive restrooms. ~ Located on Pecho Valley Road about ten miles south of Morro Bay; 805-528-0513, fax 805-528-6857.

▲ There are 50 tent/RV sites (no hookups); $15 per night. Reservations strongly recommended for this busy campground from mid-May through Labor Day: 800-444-7275.

MORRO BAY STATE PARK Located amid one of the biggest marshlands along the California coast, this 2435-acre domain is like an outdoor museum. The tidal basin attracts over 250 species of sea, land, and shore birds. Great blue herons roost in the eucalyptus trees. There's a marina where you can rent canoes or kayaks to explore the salt marsh and nearby sandspit, a natural-history museum with environmental displays, and an incredible golf course. Day-use fee, $6. ~ On State Park Road in Morro Bay; 805-772-7434, fax 805-772-5760.

▲ There are 122 tent/RV sites (27 with hook-ups); $25 to $34 per night.

MORRO STRAND STATE BEACH Another of the Central Coast's long, skinny parks, this sandy beach stretches almost two miles along Morro Bay. Private homes border one side, but in the other direction there are great views of Morro Rock. It's a good place for beachcombing, fishing, and surfing. This beach is subject to rip currents and there are no lifeguards on duty. There are restrooms and cold showers. ~ Located parallel to

Route 1 north of Morro Bay; park entrance is along Yerba Buena Street; 805-772-2560, fax 805-772-5760.

▲ There are 76 tent/RV sites; $20 per night. Reservations recommended Memorial Day through Labor Day: 800-444-7275.

LOS PADRES NATIONAL FOREST 🚶 🚲 🐎 ⛵ The southern section of this mammoth forest parallels the coast from Ventura to Carmel. Rising from sea level to almost 9000 feet, it contains the Sierra Madre, San Rafael, Santa Ynez, Santa Lucia, and La Panza mountains. Characterized by sharp slopes and a dry climate, most of the region is covered with chaparral and oak. But there are coast redwoods, piñon pines, and an amazing diversity of other plant life. Animals you might see include golden eagles, quail, owls, woodpeckers, wild pig, mule deer, and black bear. The northern and southern sectors of the national forest contain over 1500 miles of hiking trails, almost 500 miles of streams, and a cross-country ski trail on Mt. Pinos. For information and permits contact forest headquarters at 6755 Hollister Avenue, Suite 150, Goleta, CA 93117. Day-use permit, $5, is required in some areas; call ahead for purchase instructions. ~ Route 33 cuts through the heart of Los Padres. Route 101 provides numerous access points; 805-968-6640, fax 805-961-5729; www.fs.fed.us/r5/lospadres.

The endangered California condor, which with its nine-foot wingspan is the largest land bird in North America, has recently been reintroduced to Los Padres National Forest.

▲ There are 83 tent/RV sites (no hookups) and 250 trail camps; prices vary from free to $22 per night.

Cambria and San Simeon Area

Cambria itself is a seaside town that was originally settled in the 1860s and later expanded into a major seaport and whaling center. As the railroad replaced coastal shipping, Cambria declined, only to be resurrected during the past few decades as an artist colony and tourist center.

SIGHTS

If your approach to Cambria is along Route 1 from the south, you'll first pass the privately owned village of **Harmony**, which was a dairy cooperative in the early part of the century. Since the 1970s, however, it's been an artisans' colony of sorts, with the old dairy buildings converted to gift shops and glassmaking and pottery studios. In recent years, Harmony has been purchased by a new owner and the restaurant has been mostly closed, and the creative energy seems less vibrant than in the past. The post office is still in operation, however, and on a hill overlooking the town, you'll find **Harmony Cellars**, a winery offering daily tastings. Tasting fee. ~ Harmony Valley Road and Route 1; phone/fax 800-432-9239 (winetasting information); www.harmonycellars.net.

A few miles north of Harmony is the turnoff for **Cambria**. The town is divided into two separate sections: the East Village and West Village. Galleries, gift shops, and antique stores abound in both villages, so it really doesn't matter where you start exploring the town. The **Chamber of Commerce** is located in the West Village. ~ 767 Main Street, Cambria; 805-927-3624; www.cambria chamber.org, e-mail info@cambriachamber.org.

Start wandering around and you'll find that it's a pretty place, with ridgetop homes, sandy beaches, and rocky coves. But like many of California's small creative communities, Cambria has begun peering too long in the mirror. The architecture along Main Street has assumed a cutesy mock-Tudor look and the place is taking on an air of unreality.

Still, there are many fine artists and several exceptional galleries here. It's a choice place to shop and seek out gourmet food. While you're at it, head up to **Nit Wit Ridge**. That hodgepodge house on the left, the one decorated with every type of bric-a-brac, was the home of Art Beal, a.k.a. Captain Nit Wit, who died in 1992. He worked on this folk-art estate, listed in the National Register of Historic Landmarks, from 1928 until his death. ~ Hillcrest Drive just above Cornwall Street.

Then take a ride along **Moonstone Beach Drive**, a lovely oceanfront corridor with vista points and tidepools. It's a marvelous place for beachcombers and daydreamers.

Funny thing about travel, you often end up visiting places in spite of themselves. You realize that as soon as you get back home friends are going to ask if you saw this or that, so your itinerary becomes a combination of the locales you've always longed to experience and the places everyone else says you "must see."

The world-renowned **Hearst Castle** is one of the latter. Built by newspaper magnate William Randolph Hearst and designed by architect Julia Morgan, the Hearst San Simeon State Historical Monument includes a main house that sports 38 bedrooms, three guesthouses, and part of the old Hearst ranch, which once stretched 40 miles along the coast.

The entire complex took 27 years to build. In the 1930s and 1940s, when Hearst resided here and film stars like Charlie Chaplin, Mary Pickford, Clark Gable, and Cary Grant frequented the place, the grounds contained the largest private zoo in the world.

An insatiable art collector, Hearst stuffed every building with priceless works. Casa Grande, the main house, is fronted by two cathedral towers and filled with Renaissance and Gothic art. To see it is overwhelming. There is no place for the eye to rest. The main sitting room is covered everywhere with tapestries, bas-relief works, 16th-century paintings, Roman columns, and a carved wood ceiling. The walls are fashioned from 500-year-old choir pews, the French fireplace dates back 400 years; there are hand-carved tables and silver candelabra (I am still describing the same room), overstuffed furniture, and antique statuary. It is the most lavish mismatch in history.

Hearst Castle crosses the line from visual art to visual assault. The parts are exquisite, the whole a travesty. And yet, as I said, you must see the place. It's so huge that four different two-hour tours are scheduled daily to various parts of the property.

A fifth tour of "The Ranch," as Hearst called the castle, is conducted at night, on most Fridays and Saturdays only from March through May and September through December. It begins at sunset and takes in the gardens that are illuminated by 100 historic light fixtures. Docents dressed in 1930s fashions appear as Hearst's domestic staff and celebrated guests.

In the visitors center, which is just off Route 1, there's a National Geographic Theater that shows the film *Hearst Castle—Building the Dream* on a huge five-story-tall movie screen. Admission. ~ 805-927-6811, fax 805-927-6710; www.hearstcastle.com.

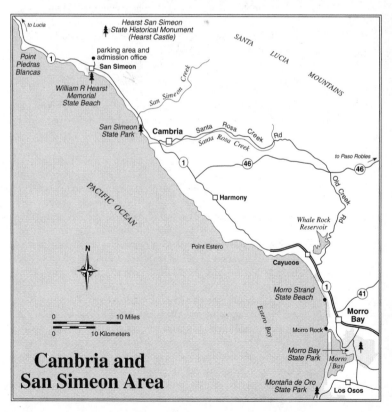

All tours of the castle, which is on the hilltop above, depart from the center. The five-mile bus ride up takes several minutes; a tour guide will greet you upon your arrival at the top. The tours involve considerable walking and include many stairs.

Since over one million people a year visit, the guided tours are often booked solid. I recommend that you reserve as much as two months in advance and plan on taking Tour 1, which covers the ground floor of Casa Grande, a guesthouse, the pools, and the gardens. Call 800-444-4445 for reservations.

Ultimately you'll find that in spite of the pomp and grandiosity, there is a magic about the place. In the early morning, when tour shuttles begin climbing from sea level to the 1600-foot-elevation residence, fog feathers through the surrounding valleys, obscuring everything but the spiked peaks of the Santa Lucia Mountains and the lofty towers of the castle. The entire complex, overbearing as it is, evokes a simpler, more glamorous era, before the Depression and World War II turned the nation's thoughts inward, when without blinking a man could build an outlandish testimonial to himself. Admission. ~ Route 1, San Simeon; 805-927-2020, 800-444-4445 (tour reservations), fax 805-927-2041; www.hearstcastle.org.

Ninety species of wild animals—including lions, tigers, yaks, and camels—roamed about Hearst Castle.

Beyond Hearst Castle, Route 1 winds north past tidepools and pocket beaches. There are pretty coves and surf-washed rocks offshore. To leeward the hills give way to mountains as the highway ascends toward the dramatic Big Sur coastline. Two hundred miles farther north sits the city that Hearst made the center of his publishing empire, an oceanfront metropolis called San Francisco.

LODGING   In the coastal art colony of Cambria is an 1873 bed and breakfast called the **Olallieberry Inn**. The Greek Revival clapboard house contains nine guest rooms, done in Victorian style with 19th-century antiques. All rooms have fireplaces and private baths; some have balconies. The sitting room is attractively furnished with oak wood. A full breakfast is included in the rate, and wine and hors d'eouvres are served every evening. Closed the first two weeks of January. ~ 2476 Main Street, Cambria; 805-927-3222, 888-927-3222, fax 805-927-0202; www.olallieberry.com, e-mail info@olallieberry.com. DELUXE TO ULTRA-DELUXE.

If you would prefer a more rustic atmosphere, head up to **Cambria Pines Lodge**. Set one and a half miles from the beach, amid 25 acres of Monterey pines, are rambling split-rail lodges with additional cabins dotted about the property. The main building offers a spacious lobby plus a restaurant and lounge with a stone fireplace and nightly entertainment; other amenities include a swimming pool, jacuzzi, and a day spa. For a more luxurious stay, hotel-style suites are available. All prices include breakfast.

~ 2905 Burton Drive, Cambria; 805-927-4200, 800-445-6868, fax 805-927-4016; www.cambriapineslodge.com, e-mail info@ cambriapineslodge.com. DELUXE TO ULTRA-DELUXE.

About four miles from Hearst Castle, the San Simeon Lodge is a typical roadside motel. The 62 rooms, some with ocean views, are located on two levels around a garden courtyard. It has a heated pool and the beach is across the street. A bar and grill adjoins the property. ~ 9520 Castillo Drive, San Simeon; 805-827-4601. BUDGET TO ULTRA-DELUXE.

Farther along, on a ridge poised between the highway and ocean, sits the more appealing Ragged Point Inn. This 30-unit facility has attractive rooms furnished with contemporary hardwood furniture. Some of the rooms have gas fireplaces and jacuzzi tubs. Another compelling reason to stay is the beautiful ocean view from this clifftop abode. Despite the inn's proximity to the road, it's peaceful and quiet here; a variety of wildlife wanders and flutters through the grounds and sea sounds fill the air. ~ Route 1, 15 miles north of Hearst Castle; 805-927-4502, fax 805-927-8862; www.raggedpointinn.net, e-mail info@ragged pointinn.net. MODERATE TO ULTRA-DELUXE.

DINING

In a small town like this, when a restaurant has managed to stay in business since 1986, you know they're doing something right. Mustache Pete's stirs up fine Italian cooking seven days a week. Along with gourmet pizza they offer slow-roasted prime rib. ~ 4090 Burton Drive, Cambria; 805-927-8589, fax 805-927-0976; www.mustachepetes.com. MODERATE TO DELUXE.

Ethnic and vegetarian food lovers will fare well at Robin's. Set in a 1930s Mexican-style house, it serves homemade lunches and dinners. Selections range from burritos to tandoori prawns to stir-fried tofu. It's an eclectic blend with the accent on European and Asian cuisine. Patio seating is available. ~ 4095 Burton Drive, Cambria; 805-927-5007, fax 805-927-1320; www.robins restaurant.com, e-mail robins@robinsrestaurant.com. MODERATE TO DELUXE.

SHOPPING

Located a few miles south of Hearst Castle, the seaside enclave of Cambria has developed into an artist colony and become an important arts-and-crafts center, with numerous galleries and specialty shops. Several antique shops are also here; like the crafts stores, they cluster along Main Street and Burton Drive.

Among the foremost galleries in here is Seekers Collection & Gallery. It's a glass menagerie inhabited by contemporary, one-of-a-kind vases, goblets, and sculptures. ~ 4090 Burton Drive, Cambria; 805-927-4352, 800-841-5250; www.seekersglass.com.

The Soldier Gallery is a journey back to childhood. Part toy store and part aviation gallery, it serves as headquarters for thousands of hand-painted toy soldiers from around the world. Some of these are deployed in battle formation, re-enacting a clash from the Civil War. This unique shop has been featured in the *Wall Street Journal*. ~ 789 Main Street, Cambria; 805-927-3804; www.soldiergallery.com.

NIGHTLIFE   **Camozzi's Saloon** is a century-old bar with longhorns over the bar, wagon wheels on the wall, and a floor that leans worse than a midnight drunk. The place is famous. Besides that, it has a rock band on Saturday. ~ 2262 Main Street, Cambria; 805-927-8941; www.sbstateparks.com/san_simeon.

BEACHES & PARKS   **SAN SIMEON STATE PARK** This wide sand corridor reaches for about two miles from San Simeon Creek to Santa Rosa Creek. It's a wonderful place to wander, and the streams, with their abundant wildlife, add to the enjoyment. Unfortunately, Route 1 divides the beach from the camping area and disturbs the quietude. Other parts of the park are very peaceful, especially the **Moonstone Beach** section in Cambria, known for its moonstone agates and otters. There are picnic areas, restrooms, and showers. ~ Route 1, Cambria; 805-927-2020, fax 805-927-2041.

▲ There are two campgrounds in the park with a total of 204 campsites. The larger San Simeon Creek has tent/RV spots (no hookups); $20 to $25 per night. At Washburn there are 70 tent/RV sites (no hookups); $11 to $15 per night. Reservations: 800-444-7275.

WILLIAM R. HEARST MEMORIAL STATE BEACH Located directly below Hearst Castle, this is a placid crescent-shaped beach. The facility measures only two acres, including a grassy area on a rise above the beach; there is a 1000-foot-long fishing pier. Scenic San Simeon Point curves out from the shoreline, creating a pretty cove and protecting the beach from surf. Swimming and fishing are very good. Facilities include picnic areas and restrooms. ~ On Route 1 opposite Hearst Castle; 805-927-2020, fax 805-927-2041; www.hearstcastle.com.

Outdoor Adventures

SPORT-FISHING   Interested in hooking calico bass or yellowtail? Then book a half-day or overnight charter to the Channel Islands, a few of the more popular trips at **Channel Island Sportfishing**. There's also a full tackle shop here that rents equipment, too. ~ 4151 South Victoria Avenue, Oxnard; 805-985-8511; www.sportfishingreport.com. **Sea Landing** offers half-, three-quarter-, and full-day cruises. Look to catch calico bass, red snapper, barracuda, and an occasional tuna. ~ 301 West Cabrillo Boulevard, Santa Barbara; 805-963-3564; www.stardustsportfishing.com. **Patriot Sportfishing** specializes in deep-sea and rock fishing and targets salmon and albacore seasonally. ~ Pier 3, Avila Beach; 805-595-7200; www.patriotsportfishing.com. **Virg's Sportfishing** books three-quarter-day charters for rock cod (in the fall) and overnight charters for albacore (from July to December). They also offer multiday trips from November to June. ~ 1215 Embarcadero, Morro Bay; 805-772-1222; www.virgs.com.

If you're in the mood for a whale-watching excursion, take your pick from numerous companies. You can also opt for either of two whale-watching seasons. From January through May, you'll see California gray whales on their northern migration. The second season, from June to September, brings blue and humpback whales to the Channel Islands.

WHALE WATCHING

Contact **Channel Island Sportfishing** for tours from January through March. ~ 4151 South Victoria Avenue, Oxnard; 805-985-8511; www.sportfishingreport.com. For excursions in both seasons, call **Captain Don's**. From February through May, Captain Don's sails along the Santa Barbara coast on a 90-foot boat looking for gray whales around the Channel Islands. You're bound to see a sea lion, otter, or dolphin on the harbor cruise. ~ Stearns Wharf, Santa Barbara; 805-969-5217; www.captdon.com. **Sea Landing** will take you whale watching from December through October on the 75-foot *Condor Express*. ~ 301 West Cabrillo Boulevard, Santa Barbara; 805-963-3564; www.condorcruises.com. **Patriot Sportfishing** operates whale-watching tours from the end of December through April. The three-hour trips go in search of the California gray whale. ~ Pier 3, Avila Beach; 805-595-7200; www.patriotsportfishing.com. **Virg's Sportfishing** offers day trips to see gray whales from the end of December through April. ~ 1215 Embarcadero, Morro Bay; 805-772-1222; www.virgs.com.

Sea kayaking is excellent along the Central Coast and out to the Channel Islands. Many outfits offer tours, rentals, and lessons.

KAYAKING

GO FISH

The waters off the South Central Coast and the Channel Islands provide excellent fishing. In the summer, you can fish the surface for barracuda, calico bass, and yellowtail, or the shallow waters for ling cod. Due to the relatively shallow water in the South Central Coast area, winter bottom fishing is some of the best in the world. Common catches are rock cod, cabazon, red snapper, and blue bass. Most charter companies in the area sell bait and rent tackle.

You can rent a kayak or arrange instructional paddling trips to the sea caves of Santa Cruz Island with **Aquasports**. ~ 111 Verona Avenue, Goleta; 805-968-7231, 800-773-2309; www.island kayaking.com. **Adventours Outdoor Excursions, Inc**. can arrange trips combining kayaking with other outdoor activities such as camping, hiking, biking, and backpacking. ~ P.O. Box 215, Santa Barbara, CA 93102; 805-898-9569; www.adventours.com. **Good Clean Fun** offers rentals, instructional guided tours north along the coast, and lessons. ~ 136 Ocean Front, Cayucos; 805-995-1993; www.gcfsurf.com. **Kayak Horizons** provides you the means to hobnob with seals and local birds. ~ 551 Embarcadero, Morro Bay; 805-772-6444; www.kayakhorizons.com. Paddle around the bay in a rented canoe or sit-on-top kayak from **Subsea Tours & Kayaks**. ~ Marina Square, 699 Embarcadero; 805-772-3349; www.subseatours.com.

DIVING

For those more interested in watching fish, several companies charter dive boats and also offer scuba diving rentals and lessons. The waters around the Channel Islands provide some of the world's best diving spots.

Ventura Dive and Sport, a five-star PADI facility, has one-, two-, or three-day diving excursions to the northern Channel Islands, where you will see a wide array of sea life, including harbor seals and bat rays. ~ 1559 Spinnaker Drive #108, Ventura; 805-650-6500; www.venturadive.com. In Santa Barbara, call **Anacapa Dive Center** for scuba instruction, rentals, and trips to the Channel Islands. ~ 22 Anacapa Street, Santa Barbara; 805-963-8917; www.anacapadivecenter.com. Dive charters to local waters and the Channel Islands are arranged by **Sea Landing**. They offer one-day open-water trips as well as two-, three-, and five-day charters. ~ 301 West Cabrillo Boulevard, Santa Barbara; 805-963-3564; www.truth aquatics.com.

In the Santa Barbara area, surfers head to Rincon, Ledbetter, Santa Claus Lane, and La Conchita.

SURFING

There's good surfing all along the Central Coast. Catch a wave with surfboard rentals from the following enterprises.

The **Santa Barbara Adventure Company** will not only teach you how to surf, they will take you kayaking along the coast and over to the Channel Islands, or guide you on a mountain biking adventure. They have professional guides for every activity. ~ P.O. Box 208, Santa Barbara, CA 93102; 805-898-0671, 888-773-3239; www.sbadventureco.com.

In Cayucos **Good Clean Fun** rents and sells wetsuits, surfboards, and boogieboards. ~ 136 Ocean Front, Cayucos; 805-995-1993; www.gcfsurf.com. **Wavelengths Surf Shop** offers wetsuits and surfboards to surfers ready to take on the waves. For a good location, try The Rock right down the street from the shop. ~ 998 Embarcadero, Morro Bay; 805-772-3904; www.wave lengthssurfshop.com.

The South Central Coast and the Channel Islands are prime areas for boating. You can rent your own boat or go on one of the various cruises and charters offered.

To sail the Pacific, visit the Channel Islands, watch whales, or take a romantic sunset champagne cruise, contact **Santa Barbara Sailing Center** for boat rentals and charters. They also offer a variety of lessons. ~ The Breakwater, Santa Barbara; 805-962-2826, 800-350-9090; www.sbsail.com. **Sea Landing** offers cruises and charters. Sunset dinner trips are a specialty. ~ 301 West Cabrillo Boulevard, Santa Barbara; 805-963-3564. In the summer **Captain Don's** has sunset and dinner cruises as well as sightseeing tours. ~ Stearns Wharf, Santa Barbara; 805-969-5217; www.captdon.com. **Pacific Sailing** provides sailboat charters and instruction. ~ 1567 Spinnaker Drive, Suite 203–131, Ventura Harbor; 805-658-6508; www.pacsail.com.

Golf enthusiasts will enjoy the weather as well as the courses along the Central Coast. Courses have 18 holes unless otherwise stated.

VENTURA–OXNARD AREA   The **River Ridge Golf Club** is a links-style course with an island green on the 14th hole. ~ 2401 West Vineyard Avenue, Oxnard; 805-983-4653; www.riverridge-golfclub.com. **Olivas Park** comes complete with driving range and putting green. ~ 3750 Olivas Park Drive, Ventura; 805-642-4303; www.olivasparkgolf.com.

SANTA BARBARA AREA   Santa Barbara Golf Club's course is dotted with oaks, pines, and sycamores. ~ Las Positas Road and McCaw Avenue, Santa Barbara; 805-687-7087. The executive nine-hole **Twin Lakes Golf Course** meanders around two lakes. ~ 6034 Hollister Avenue, Goleta; 805-964-1414; www.twinlakes golf.org. Two miles north of Twin Lakes is **Sandpiper Golf Course**, a championship course right on the ocean. ~ 7925 Hollister Avenue, Goleta; 805-968-1541; www. sandpipergolf. com. A creek winds through the nine-hole **Ocean Meadows Golf Course**, which is a relatively flat playing field. ~ 6925 Whittier Drive, Goleta; 805-968-6814; www.oceanmeadowsgolf.com.

SAN LUIS OBISPO AREA   A creek runs through the par-3, nine-hole **Pismo State Beach Golf Course**. ~ 25 Grand Avenue, Grover City; 805-481-5215; www.pismoweddings.com. The nine-hole **Laguna Lake Golf Course** is a hilly green surrounded by mountains. They also have a putting green and chipping area. ~ 11175 Los Osos Valley Road, San Luis Obispo; 805-781-7309. **Avila Beach Resort Golf Course** is dotted with trees and water hazards. The driving range overlooks the beach. ~ Anabay Drive, Avila Beach; 805-595-4000; www.avilabeachresort.com. Lined with lofty pine trees, part of **Morro Bay Golf Course** overlooks the ocean. ~ 201 State Park Road, Morro Bay; 805-782-8060; www.centralcoastgolf.com. **Sea Pines Golf Course** offers a nine-hole green whose gently rolling hills are speckled with mature pines. ~ 1945 Solano, Los Osos; 805-528-1788; www.seapines golfresort.com.

TENNIS

Tennis, anyone? This area offers a number of opportunities for tennis fiends. **Moranda Park Tennis Complex** has eight lighted courts situated in a beautiful park setting. Equipment rentals available. ~ 200 Moranda Parkway, Port Hueneme; 805-986-3587. **Santa Barbara Municipal Courts** features four facilities with a total of 28 courts; 17 are lighted. Bring your own equipment. Fee. ~ 1414 Park Place; 805-564-5573. **Cuesta College** has eight courts that open to the public on the weekend. ~ Route 1, San Luis Obispo; 805-546-3207. **Sinsheimer Park** has six courts. ~ 900 Southwood Drive, San Luis Obispo; 805-781-7300. Additional courts are located at **French Park**, off Poinsettia Street. For night games, try the lighted courts at the high school, on the corner of San Luis Drive and California Street. There are four more courts at **Shell Beach and Florin roads**.

RIDING STABLES

Circle Bar B Stables takes riders on a one-and-a-half-hour trip through a canyon, past waterfalls, and then up to a vista point overlooking the Channel Islands. A half-day lunch ride is also available. Reservations are required. ~ 1800 Refugio Road, Goleta; 805-968-3901; www.circlebarb.com. To ride right on the beach, you can go on one of **Pacific Dunes Ranch Riding Stables** guided tours or rent a horse from them to explore the area on your own in the off-season. Closed Thursday and on rainy days. ~ 1205 Silverspur Place, Oceano; 805-489-8100.

BIKING

Biking the South Central Coast can be a rewarding experience. The coastal route, however, presents problems in populated areas during rush hour.

The town of **Ventura** offers an interesting bicycle tour through the historical section of town with a visit to the county historical museum and mission. Another bike tour of note, off of Harbor Boulevard, leads to the Channel Islands National Park Visitors Center. The **Ventura River Trail** (6 miles) is an asphalt trail featuring locally designed sculptures and links to coastal, mountain, and downtown trails. A bike map of Ventura County is available at the **Ventura Visitors Bureau**. ~ 89 South California Street #C, Ventura; 805-648-2075, 800-333-2989; www.goventura.org.

Santa Barbara is chock full of beautiful bike paths and trails. Two notable beach excursions are the **Atascadero Recreation Trail**, which starts at the corner of Encore Drive and Modoc Road and ends over seven miles later at Goleta Beach, and **Cabrillo bikeway**, which takes you from Andree Clark Bird Refuge to Leadbetter Beach. Also, the **University of California–Santa Barbara** has many bike paths through the campus grounds and into Isla Vista.

> The Goleta Valley bikeway travels from Santa Barbara to Goleta along Cathedral Oaks Road.

Up the coast, a stunning, three-mile bike path links **El Capitan** and **Refugio** state beaches.

Exploring the shores of Morro Bay is popular with cyclists. For the hardy biker a ride up **Black Mountain** leads to sweeping views of the Pacific Ocean.

Bike Rentals and Tours   **Adventours Outdoor Excursions, Inc.** offers bike tours to the Santa Ynez Mountains, the Santa Ynez Valley wine country, and the Santa Barbara coast. ~ P.O. Box 215, Santa Barbara, CA 93102; 805-898-9569, 877-467-2148; www. adventours.com. In the summer **Beach Rentals** rents tandems, three-wheelers, mountain bikes, and inline skates. ~ Embassy Suites Mandalay Beach Resort Inn, 2101 Mandalay Beach Road, Oxnard, 805-984-2500; and 23 East Cabrillo Boulevard, Santa Barbara, 805-966-2282.

With its endless beaches and mountain backdrop, the Central Coast is wide open for exploration. Shoreline paths and mountain trails crisscross the entire region. All distances listed for hiking trails are one way unless otherwise noted.

HIKING

First among equals in this hiker's dreamland is the **California Coastal Trail**, the 1200-mile route that runs the entire length of the state. Here it begins at Point Mugu and travels along state beaches from Ventura County to Santa Barbara. In Santa Barbara the trail turns inland toward the Santa Ynez Mountains and Los Padres National Forest. It returns to the coast at Point Sal, then parallels sand dunes, passes the hot springs at Avila Beach, and continues up the coast to San Simeon.

VENTURA–OXNARD AREA   Bounded by the Santa Monica and Santa Ynez mountains and bordered by 43 miles of shoreline, Ventura County offers a variety of hiking opportunities. (Note, however, that some trails were damaged in recent Southern California fires.) For more information on local hiking trails and guided trail walks in the area, contact the City of Ventura Community Services Department at 805-658-4733.

Ocean's Edge Trail (.6 mile) is a lovely shore hike from the Emma Wood State Beach to Seaside Wilderness Park; popular with birders.

River's Edge Trail (6.3 mile) is a great hike for exploring the riparian woodlands along the Ventura River.

SANTA BARBARA AREA What distinguishes Santa Barbara from most of California's coastal communities is the magnificent Santa Ynez mountain range, which forms a backdrop to the city and provides excellent hiking terrain.

A red steel gate marks the beginning of **Romero Canyon Trail** (6 miles) on Bella Vista Road in Santa Barbara. After joining a fire road at the 2350-foot elevation, the trail follows a stream shaded by oak, sycamore, and bay trees. From here you can keep climbing or return via the right fork, a fire road that offers an easier but longer return trip.

San Ysidro Trail (4.5 miles) begins at Park Lane and East Mountain Drive in Santa Barbara, follows a stream dotted with pools and waterfalls, then climbs to the top of Camino Cielo ridge. For a different loop back, it's only a short walk to Cold Springs Trail.

Also located in the Santa Ynez Mountains is **Rattlesnake Canyon Trail** (2.5 miles). Beginning near Skofield Park, the trail follows Mission Creek, along which an aqueduct was built in the early 19th century. Portions of the waterway can still be seen. This pleasant trail offers shaded pools and meadows.

Cold Springs Trail, East Fork (4.5 miles) heads east from Mountain Drive in Santa Barbara. The trail takes you through a canyon covered with alder and along a creek punctuated by pools and waterfalls. It continues up into Hot Springs Canyon and crosses the flank of Montecito Peak.

Cold Springs Trail, West Fork (5 miles) leads off the better known East Fork. It climbs and descends along the left side of a lushly vegetated canyon before arriving at an open valley.

Tunnel Trail (2.9 miles) is named for the turn-of-the-20th-century tunnel through the mountains that brought fresh water to Santa Barbara. The trail begins at the end of Tunnel Road in Santa Barbara and passes through various sandstone formations and crosses a creek before arriving at Mission Falls.

San Antonio Creek Trail (1.7 miles), an easy hike along a creek bed, starts from the far end of Tucker's Grove County Park in Goleta. In the morning or late afternoon you'll often catch glimpses of deer foraging in the woods.

Thirty-five miles of coastline stretches from Stearns Wharf in Santa Barbara to Gaviota State Beach. There are hiking opportunities galore along the entire span.

The **Gaviota Hot Springs and Peak Trail** (3 miles) begins in Gaviota State Park, with a delicious first stop at the mineral pools at Gaviota Hot Springs (located about a half mile from the trailhead). After a leisurely dip you can continue on a somewhat strenuous route into Los Padres National Forest, climbing to Gaviota Peak for a marvelous view of ranch land and the Pacific Ocean.

Summerland Trail (1-mile loop), starting at Lookout Park in Summerland, takes you along Summerland Beach, past tiny coves, then along Montecito's coastline to the beach fronting the Biltmore Hotel.

Goleta Beach Trail (2 miles) begins at Goleta Beach County Park in Goleta and curves past tidepools and sand dunes en route to Goleta Point. Beyond the dunes is Devereux Slough, a reserve populated by egrets, herons, plovers, and sandpipers. The hike also passes the Ellwood Oil Field where a Japanese submarine fired shots at the mainland United States during World War II.

SAN LUIS OBISPO AREA   The San Luis Obispo area, rich in wild-life, offers hikers everything from seaside strolls to mountain treks. Many of the trails in this area are in the Los Padres National Forest (for information, call 805-925-9538).

Guadalupe-Nipomo Dunes Preserve (2.5 miles) is especially rewarding for dune lovers. This wetland area is a habitat for many endangered birds. The boardwalk trail passes a freshwater lake, a willow community, and many dunes, ending at the Oceano Dunes. At Oso Flaco Lake there's an entrance kiosk with trail and hiking information. ~ 805-343-2455; www.dunescenter.org.

The golden mustard plants and poppies along the way give **Montaña de Oro Bluffs Trail** (2 miles) its name ("Mountain of Gold"). This coastal trail takes you past Spooner's Cove (a mooring place for bootleggers during Prohibition). You'll pass clear tidepools, sea caves, basking seals, otters, and ocean bluffs.

For an interesting hike along the sandspit that separates Morro Bay from Estero Bay, try the **Morro Bay Sandspit Trail** (5 miles). The trail passes sand dunes and ancient Chumash shell mounds. Stay on the ocean side of the sandspit to avoid the muck.

Several trails in the vicinity of **Lopez Lake Recreational Area** offer opportunities to see the region's flora and fauna. Deer, raccoon, fox, and wood-rats predominate, along with a variety of birds species (not to mention rattlesnakes and poison oak). ~ 805-788-2381; www.slocountyparks.com.

AUTHOR FAVORITE

The **Point Sal Trail** (6 miles) offers an excellent opportunity to hike in a forgotten spot along the coast. (But beware, it's not for inexperienced hikers or those afraid of heights.) Alternating between cliffs and seashore, the trail takes you past tidepools, pelicans, cormorants, and basking seals. An excellent whale-watching area, the trail ends near the mouth of the Santa Maria River.

At the entrance to the park, **Turkey Ridge Trail** (.8 mile) is a strenuous climb through oak and chaparral and offers splendid views of the lake and the Santa Lucia Mountains.

Two Waters Trail (1.3 miles) connects the Lopez and Wittenberg arms of Lopez Lake. It is a moderate hike that offers marvelous views. The trailheads are at Encinal or Miller's Cove.

Blackberry Spring Trail (.8 mile) commences at upper Squirrel campground and passes many plant species used by the Chumash Indians. This is a moderate hike with a 260-foot climb that connects with High Ridge Trail.

Little Falls Creek Trail (2.75 miles) begins along Lopez Canyon Road (High Mountain Road) and ascends 1350 feet up the canyon past a spectacular waterfall. Views of the Santa Lucia wilderness await you at the top of the mountain.

Transportation

CAR

As it proceeds north from the Los Angeles area, coastal highway **Route 1** weaves in and out from **Route 101**. The two highways join in Oxnard and continue as a single roadway until a point 30 miles north of Santa Barbara. Here they diverge, Route 1 heading toward the coast while Route 101 takes an inland route. The highways merge again near Pismo Beach and continue north to San Luis Obispo. Here Route 1 leaves Route 101 and begins its long, beautiful course up the coast past Morro Bay and San Simeon.

AIR

Santa Barbara and San Luis Obispo have small airports serving the Central Coast. Airlines that stop at the **Santa Barbara Municipal Airport** include America West Express, American Eagle, Delta Connection, Horizon Air, SkyWest, and United Express. ~ 805-967-7111; www.flysba.com.

The **Santa Barbara Airbus** can be scheduled to meet arrivals at the airport; it otherwise goes to Carpinteria, Goleta, and downtown Santa Barbara, as well as Los Angeles International Airport. ~ 805-964-7759, 800-423-1618; www.sbairbus.com. There are also a number of taxi companies available. For the disabled, call **Easy Lift Transportation**. ~ 805-681-1181.

San Luis Obispo Municipal Airport is serviced by America West Express, American Eagle Airlines, SkyWest, and United Express. ~ 805-781-5205; www.sloairport.com.

Ground transportation from San Luis Obispo Municipal Airport is provided by **Big City Cab**. ~ 805-543-1234.

BUS

Greyhound Bus Lines (800-231-2222; www.greyhound.com) has continual service along the Central Coast from both Los Angeles and San Francisco. The Ventura bus terminal is located at 291 East Thompson Boulevard (805-653-0164). Santa Barbara has one at 34 West Carrillo Street (805-965-7551). The terminal in San Luis Obispo is at 150 South Street (805-543-2121).

TRAIN

For those who want spectacular views of the coastline, try **Amtrak's** "Coast Starlight." This train hugs the shoreline, providing rare views of the Central Coast's cliffs, headlands, and untracked beaches. Amtrak stops in Oxnard, Santa Barbara, and San Luis Obispo on its way north to Oakland and Seattle. ~ 800-872-7245; www.amtrak.com.

CAR RENTALS

The larger towns in the Central Coast have car rental agencies; check the Yellow Pages to find the best bargains.

To pick up a car in the Oxnard–Ventura area, try **Avis Rent A Car** (800-331-1212), **Budget Rent A Car** (800-527-0700), or **Hertz Rent A Car** (800-654-3131).

At the airport in Santa Barbara try **Avis Rent A Car** (800-331-1212), **Budget Rent A Car** (800-527-0700), **Hertz Rent A Car** (800-654-3131), **National Car Rental** (800-227-7368), or **Thrifty Car Rental** (800-367-2277). Agencies located outside the airport with free pick-up include **Enterprise Rent A Car** (800-325-8007).

In San Luis Obispo, car-rental agencies at the airport include **Avis Rent A Car** (800-331-1212), **Budget Rent A Car** (800-527-0700 or **Hertz Rent A Car** (800-654-3131). Among those with free pickup service, try **Enterprise Rent A Car** (800-325-8007).

PUBLIC TRANSIT

Public transportation in the Central Coast is fairly limited. In the Ventura area you'll find **South Coast Area Transit**, or SCAT, which serves Oxnard, Port Hueneme, Ojai, and Ventura. ~ 805-487-4222; www.scat.org.

In the Santa Barbara area, the **Santa Barbara Metropolitan Transit** stops in Summerland, Carpinteria, Santa Barbara, Goleta, and Isla Vista. ~ Carrillo and Chapala streets; 805-683-3702; www.sbmtd.gov.

The San Luis Obispo area has **San Luis Obispo Transit,** or SLO, which operates on weekdays during daylight hours and even less frequently on weekends. ~ 805-541-2877; www.slocity.org.

SIX

Los Angeles Coast

L.A., according to a popular song, is a great big freeway. Actually, this sprawling metropolis by the sea is a great big beach. From Long Beach north to Malibu is a 74-mile stretch of sand that attracts visitors in the tens of millions every year. Life here reflects the culture of the beach, a freewheeling, hedonist philosophy that combines pleasure-seeking with healthfulness. Perfectly fitted to this philosophy is the weather. The coastal climatic zone, called a maritime fringe, is characterized by cooler summers, warmer winters, and higher humidity than elsewhere in California. Sea breezes and salt air keep the beaches relatively free from smog. During summer months the thermometer hovers around 75° or 80° and water temperatures average 67°. Winter carries intermittent rain and brings the ocean down to a chilly 55°.

Add a broadly ranging coastal topography and Los Angeles has an urban escape valve less than an hour from downtown. The shoreline lies along the lip of the Los Angeles basin, a flat expanse interrupted by the sharp cliffs of the Palos Verdes Peninsula and the rocky heights of the Santa Monica Mountains. There are broad strands lapped by gentle waves and pocket beaches exploding with surf. Though most of the coast is built up, some sections remain raw and undeveloped.

Route 1, the Pacific Coast Highway, parallels the coast the entire length of Los Angeles County, tying its beach communities together. To the south lie Long Beach and San Pedro, industrial enclaves which form the port of Los Angeles, a world center for commerce and shipping. Embodying 35 miles of heavily developed waterfront, the port is a maze of inlets, islets, and channels protected by a six-mile breakwater. It is one of the world's largest manmade harbors; over $79 billion in cargo crosses its docks every year. Despite all this hubbub, the harbor supports over 125 fish species and over 90 types of birds, including several endangered species.

The great port dates to 1835 when a small landing was built on the shore. Following the Civil War an imaginative entrepreneur named Phineas Banning developed the area, brought in the railroad, and launched Los Angeles into the 20th century. Now Long Beach wears several hats. In addition to being a major port and manufacturing center, it is the site of a naval base and a revitalized tourist center.

Home to the retired ocean liner *Queen Mary* and the Aquarium of the Pacific, Long Beach also contains the neighborhood of Naples, a system of islands, canals, and footbridges reminiscent of Italy's gondola cities.

Once an amusement center complete with airship, carousel, and sword swallowers, the city became one big oil field during the 1920s. That's when wildcat wells struck rich deposits and the region was transformed into a two-square-mile maze of derricks. Even today the offshore "islands" hide hundreds of oil wells.

Commercial fishing, another vital industry in Long Beach and San Pedro, supports an international collection of sailors. Mariners from Portugal, Greece, and elsewhere work the waterfront and add to the ethnic ambience.

Just a few miles north, along the Palos Verdes Peninsula, blue collar gives way to white collar and the urban surrenders to the exotic. A region of exclusive neighborhoods and striking geologic contrasts, Palos Verdes possesses Los Angeles' prettiest seascapes. A series of 13 marine terraces, interrupted by sheer cliffs, descend to a rocky shoreline. For 15 miles the roadway rides high above the surf past tidepools, rocky points, a lighthouse, and secluded coves.

This wealthy suburban environment is replaced in turn by another type of culture, typified by blond-haired surfers. Santa Monica Bay, the predominant feature of the Los Angeles Coast, is a single broad crescent of sand extending 30 miles from Redondo Beach through Venice and Santa Monica to Point Dume. South Bay— comprising the towns of Redondo Beach, Hermosa Beach, and Manhattan Beach— is the surfing center of Southern California, where the sport was first imported from Hawaii. This strip of coast is also home to Los Angeles International Airport.

Like most of the coastal communities, the South Bay didn't take off as a beach resort until the turn of the 20th century, after railroad lines were extended from the city center to the shore and several decades after downtown Los Angeles experienced its 1880s population boom.

It was well into the 20th century, 1962 to be exact, that neighboring Marina del Rey, the largest manmade small boat harbor in the world, was developed. Nearby Venice, on the other hand, was an early 1900s attempt to re-create its Italian namesake. Built around plazas and grand canals, Venice originally was a fashionable resort town with oceanfront hotels and an amusement park. Today studios and galleries have replaced canals and gondolas in this seaside artist colony. The place has become a center for thinkers at the cutting edge and street people who have stepped over it. Zany and unchartable, modern-day Venice is an open ward for artists, the place where bohemians go to the beach, where roller-skating is an art form and weightlifting a way of life.

The town of Santa Monica next door was originally developed as a beachside resort in 1875. Back in 1769 explorer Gaspar de Portolá had claimed the surrounding area for the Spanish crown. Over the years this royal domain has served as a major port, retirement community, and location for silent movies; today it is a bastion of brown-shingle houses, flower-covered trellises, and left-wing politics.

Bordering it to the north are the Santa Monica Mountains, a succession of rugged peaks that are part of the Transverse Range, the only mountains in California running east and west. Extending to the very edge of the sea, the Santa Monicas create Los Angeles' most varied terrain. White-sand beaches are framed by bald peaks, crystal waters and flourishing kelp beds attract abundant sea life and make for excellent fishing and skindiving, while the mountains provide a getaway for hikers and campers.

Lying along a narrow corridor between the Santa Monicas and the sea is Malibu, that quintessential symbol of California, a rich, glamorous community known for its movie stars and surfers. Once inhabited by Chumash Indians, whose skeletal remains are still occasionally uncovered, Malibu escaped Los Angeles' coastal development until 1928, when the aging widow who controlled the region like a personal fiefdom finally succumbed to the pressures of progress and profit. Within a few years it became a haven for Hollywood. Stars like Ronald Colman and John Gilbert found their paradise on the sands of Malibu. Like figures out of *The Great Gatsby*, they lived insouciant lives in movie-set houses.

By the 1960s artists and counterculturalists, seeking to flee a town that in turn had become too commercial and crowded, left Malibu for the outlying mountains. In Topanga Canyon they established freeform communities, undermined in recent years by breathtaking real-estate prices, but still retaining vestiges of their days as a flower children's retreat.

The most romantic locale along the Los Angeles Coast lies 22 miles offshore. Santa Catalina, highlighted by Avalon, a resort town tucked between mountains and ocean, is a 21-mile-long island almost entirely undeveloped, given over to cactus and grazing buffalo. Through the centuries this solitary island has undergone many incarnations—habitat for Stone Age Indians; base for Russian fur hunters; center for pirates, smugglers, and gold prospectors; gathering place for the big bands of the 1930s; and strategic military base during World War II. Today it's a singular spot where visitors enjoy the amenities of Avalon and the seclusion of the island's outback. If Avalon, with its art-deco waterfront, provides a picture of Los Angeles circa 1933, the rest of the island is a window on Los Angeles in its natural state, wild and alluring, long before freighters embarked from Long Beach, surfers worked the South Bay, and movie moguls uncovered Malibu.

Long Beach

Anchoring the southern end of Los Angeles County is Long Beach, one of California's largest cities (the fifth-largest, in fact). Back in the Roaring Twenties, after oil was discovered and the area experienced a tremendous building boom, Long Beach became known as "The Coney Island of the West." Boasting five and a half miles of beachfront and a grand amusement park, it was a favorite spot for daytripping Angelenos.

Several decades of decline followed, but in more recent years the metropolis launched a redevelopment plan dubbed the Queensway Bay Development. The star of this facelift is the Aquarium of the Pacific. Together with the *Queen Mary* and Shoreline Village, the aquarium rounded out an oceanfront triumvirate of family-oriented attractions, each of which is accessible to the others by a water taxi called the AquaBus.

Today Long Beach ranks together with neighboring San Pedro as one of the largest manmade harbors in the world and is a popular tourist destination. It's a revealing place, a kind of social

studies lesson in modern American life. Travel Ocean Boulevard
as it parallels the sea and you'll pass from quaint homes to downtown skyscrapers to fire-breathing smokestacks.

For a dynamic example of what I mean, visit the enclave of
Naples near the south end of town. Conceived early in the 20th
century, modeled on Italy's fabled canal towns, it's a tiny community of three islands separated by canals and linked with
walkways. Waterfront greenswards gaze out on Alamitos Bay
and its fleet of sloops and motorboats. You can wander along
bayside paths past comfortable homes, contemporary condos,
and humble cottages. Fountains and miniature traffic circles,
alleyways and boulevards, all form an incredible labyrinth along
which you undoubtedly will become lost.

SIGHTS

Adding to the sense of old Italia is the **Gondola Getaway**, a
romantic hour-long cruise through the canals of Naples. For a
hefty price (less, however, than a ticket to Italy), you can climb
aboard a gondola, dine on hors d'oeuvres, and occasionally be

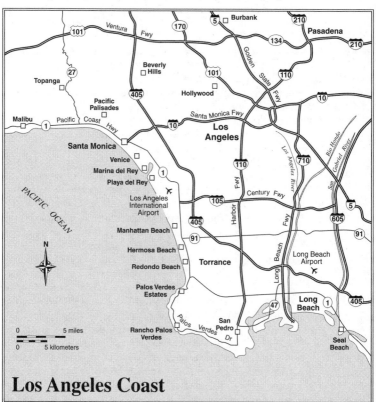

Los Angeles Coast

serenaded with Italian music. Reservations of up to three weeks in advance are strongly suggested. ~ 5437 East Ocean Boulevard, Naples; 562-433-9595; www.gondola.getawayinc.com.

Housed in a converted skating rink, the **Museum of Latin American Art** is the only museum in the western United States to exclusively exhibit contemporary art from Latin America. The museum store also features the works of Latin American artists, as does the 15,000-square-foot sculpture garden. For children there are hands-on art-making workshops on Sunday. Closed Monday. Admission. ~ 628 Alamitos Avenue; 562-437-1689, fax 562-437-7043; www.molaa.org, e-mail info@molaa.org.

For a touch of early Spanish/Mexican culture, plan on visiting the region's old adobes. Built around 1800 with walls more than two feet thick, the adobe core of **Rancho Los Alamitos** is one of Southern California's oldest remaining houses. In its gardens, which cover more than three acres, are brick walkways and a variety of majestic trees. You can tour old barns (housing draft horses, sheep, and chickens), a blacksmith shop, and a feed shed. There's also a chuck wagon with a coffeepot still resting on the wood-burning stove. Closed Monday and Tuesday. ~ 6400 Bixby Hill Road (enter at guard gate at Palo Verde and Anaheim); 562-431-3541, fax 562-430-9694; rancholosalamitos.com, e-mail info@rancholosalamitos.com.

Rancho Los Cerritos, a two-story Monterey Colonial home built in 1844, once served as headquarters for a 27,000-acre ranch. Now the adobe is filled with Victorian furniture and reflects the families and workers who lived and worked on the ranch in the 19th century. The site includes historic gardens, a California history research library and an orientation exhibit. Closed Monday and Tuesday. ~ 4600 North Virginia Road; 562-570-1755, fax 562-570-1893; www.rancholoscerritos.org.

The Pacific Ocean may be Long Beach's biggest natural attraction, but many birds in the area prefer the **El Dorado Nature Center**. Part of the 450-acre El Dorado East Regional Park, this 102-acre wildlife sanctuary offers one- and two-mile hikes past two lakes and a stream. About 150 bird species as well as numerous land animals can be sighted. Though located in a heavily urbanized area, the facility encompasses several ecological zones. There's also a quarter-mile paved, handicapped-accessible nature trail. Closed Monday. Parking fee, $4 to $6. ~ 7550 East Spring Street; 562-570-1745, fax 562-570-8530; www.lbparks.org.

Another side of Long Beach is the steel-and-glass downtown area, where highrise hotels vie for dominance. The best way to tour this crowded commercial district is to stroll **The Promenade**, a six-block brick walkway leading from 3rd Street to the waterfront. There's a **tile mosaic** (Promenade and 3rd Street) at the near end portraying an idyllic day at the beach complete with sailboats, sunbathers, and lifeguards. Visit the **Long Beach Area Convention & Visitors Bureau,** home to maps, brochures, and other bits of information. Open daily in summer; closed Saturday and Sunday at other times. ~ 1 World Trade Center, Suite 300; 562-436-3645, 800-452-7829, fax 562-435-5653; www.visitlong beach.com, e-mail info@longbeachcvb.org.

Cross Ocean Boulevard and you'll arrive at a park shaded with palm trees and adjacent to **Shoreline Village,** a shopping center and marina disguised as a 19th-century fishing village. ~ 407 Shoreline Village Drive.

Another aspect of Long Beach rises in the form of oil derricks and industrial complexes just across the water. To view the freighters, tankers, and warships lining the city's piers, gaze out from the northern fringes of Shoreline Village.

Fittingly, the climax of a Long Beach tour comes at the very end, after you have experienced the three phases of urban existence. Just across the Los Angeles River, along Harbor Scenic Drive ("scenic" in this case meaning construction cranes and cargo containers), lies one of the strangest sights I've ever encountered. The first time I saw it, peering through the steel filigree of a suspension bridge, with harbor lights emblazoning the scene, I thought something had gone colossally wrong with the world. An old-style ocean liner, gleaming eerily in the false light, appeared to be parked on the ground. Next to it an overgrown geodesic dome, a kind of giant aluminum breast, was swelling up out of the earth.

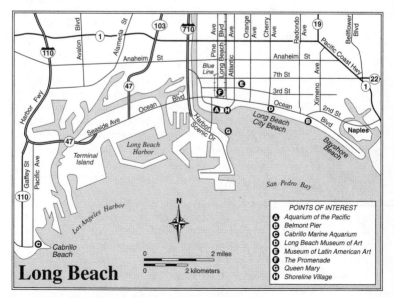

POINTS OF INTEREST
- Ⓐ Aquarium of the Pacific
- Ⓑ Belmont Pier
- Ⓒ Cabrillo Marine Aquarium
- Ⓓ Long Beach Museum of Art
- Ⓔ Museum of Latin American Art
- Ⓕ The Promenade
- Ⓖ Queen Mary
- Ⓗ Shoreline Village

Long Beach

Unwittingly I had happened upon Long Beach's top tourist attraction, the *Queen Mary*, once the world's largest ocean liner. Making her maiden voyage in 1936, the **Queen Mary** was the pride of Great Britain. Winston Churchill, the Duke and Duchess of Windsor, Greta Garbo, and Fred Astaire sailed on her, and during World War II, she was converted to military service. The *Queen Mary* carried so many troops across the Atlantic Ocean that Adolf Hitler offered $250,000 and the Iron Cross to the U-boat captain who sank her.

Today she is the pride of Long Beach, a 1000-foot-long "city at sea" transformed into a floating museum and hotel that brilliantly re-create shipboard life. An elaborate walking tour carries you down into the engine room (a world of pumps and propellers), out along the decks, and up to each level of this multistage behemoth. There's a parking fee and admission to the ship (the admission fee is waived for hotel guests).

The *Queen Mary* is expertly refurbished and wonderfully laid out, an important addition to the Long Beach seafront and the anchor attraction for Queen Mary Seaport, which also includes the **Queen Mary Seawalk** shopping and dining area. Her neighbor is the world's largest clear-span geodesic dome. The dome once housed Howard Hughes' *Spruce Goose*, the largest plane ever built. Admission. ~ 1126 Queen's Highway; 562-435-3511, 800-437-2934, fax 562-437-4531; www.queenmary.com.

Docked alongside the *Queen Mary* is the Soviet-built submarine **Scorpion**. Visitors enter through the forward hatch of the 300-foot Foxtrot-class Russian sub, then squeeze their way along corridors for a look through the periscope and a self-guided tour of the torpedo room, crew quarters, and communications center. Admission. ~ 1126 Queen's Highway; 562-435-3511.

The **Aquarium of the Pacific**, located at the waterfront Rainbow Harbor in downtown Long Beach, has three major permanent galleries designed to lead visitors on a "journey of discovery" through the waters of the Pacific Ocean. The journey begins in the temperate waters of Southern California and Baja, and includes touchpools. The Bering Sea is the focus of the exhibit representing the icy waters of the northern Pacific, which are in-

sights

AUTHOR FAVORITE

The **Long Beach Museum of Art** is a must. Dedicated to the past 300 years of design and decorative arts, this museum has ever-changing exhibits, bluff-top gardens, a historic mansion and carriage house, and an oceanview café. Closed Monday. Admission, except on Friday. ~ 2300 East Ocean Boulevard; 562-439-2119, fax 562-439-3587; www.lbma.org, e-mail tours@lbma.org.

habited by sea otters, a giant octopus, and spider crabs. The coral reefs and lagoons of Palau in Micronesia are spotlighted in the Tropical Pacific Gallery, which also features the huge Tropical Reef exhibit, where microphone-equipped scuba divers swim along with schools of brilliant fish and sharks, answering questions for visitors. There's also an outdoor lagoon where visitors can touch sharks and a lorikeet forest where visitors can hand-feed colorful birds. Admission. ~ 100 Aquarium Way; 562-590-3100, fax 562-951-1733; www.aquariumofpacific.org, e-mail aquariumofpacific@lbaop.org.

The latest addition to Long Beach's popular waterfront attractions is **The Pike at Rainbow Harbor.** Located on 18 acres beside the Aquarium of the Pacific, The Pike features a slew of restaurants and places to play, including a pedestrian bridge over Shoreline Village Drive, a carousel, Ferris wheel and movie theater and video arcade. ~ 95 South Pine Avenue; 562-432-8325, fax 562-432-8374; www.thepikeatlongbeach.com.

The **AquaBus**, a water taxi service, links the city's main waterfront attractions—the aquarium, Shoreline Village, the *Queen Mary*, Catalina Express, and the convention center—with seasonal daily service. Reservations recommended. ~ 562-591-2301.

Long Beach is also a departure point for the **Catalina Express** shuttle boats to Catalina Island. Reservations recommended. ~ 310-519-1212, 800-897-7154; www.catalinaexpress.com.

Beyond all the shoreline hubbub, the venerable Pacific gray whales migrate along the "Whale Freeway" between late December and mid-April, and several enterprises in Long Beach offer whale-watching opportunities. The **Long Beach Area Convention & Visitors Bureau** can put you in touch with a whale-watching operator. ~ 1 World Trade Center, Suite 300; 800-452-7829; www.visitlongbeach.com, e-mail info@longbeachcvb.org.

The **Beach Plaza Hotel** has 40 units, some with ocean views, many offering kitchens and all with private access to the beach. Each room is furnished in contemporary fashion. There's a pool, private jacuzzi, and gym. ~ 2010 East Ocean Boulevard; 562-437-0771, 800-485-8758, fax 562-437-0900. MODERATE TO ULTRA-DELUXE.

LODGING

Granted I'm a fool for gimmicks, but somehow the opportunity to stay aboard a historic ocean liner seems overwhelming. Where else but at the **Hotel Queen Mary** can you recapture the magic of British gentility before World War II? What other hotel offers guests a "sunning deck"? Staying in the original staterooms of this grand old ship, permanently docked on the Long Beach waterfront, you are surrounded by the art-deco designs for which the *Queen Mary* is famous. Some of the 365 guest rooms are small (this *is* a ship!) and dimly illuminated through portholes, but the decor is classic. There are also restaurants, lounges, and shops on board. ~ 1126 Queen's Highway; 562-435-3511, 800-437-2934, fax 562-437-4531; www.queenmary.com, e-mail reservations@queenmary.com. DELUXE.

DINING

One of the first small brewery/restaurants in the Long Beach area, the **Belmont Brewing Company** brews pale and amber ales, seasonal beers, and a dark, rich porter—Long Beach Crude—that closely resembles the real stuff pumped from nearby coastal oil derricks. Gourmet pizzas, fresh seafood, steaks, and pastas are served in the dining area, at the bar, and outside on the patio. I'd opt for the patio where you can enjoy watching the sun set over the water. Breakfast is served on the weekends. ~ 25 39th Place; 562-433-3891, fax 562-434-0604; www.belmontbrewing.com, e-mail mail@belmontbrewing.com. MODERATE.

HIDDEN ►

Southern cooking at the **Shenandoah at the Arbor** is becoming a tradition among savvy shore residents. The quilts decorating this understated establishment lend a country air to the place. Add waitresses dishing out hot apple fritters and it gets downright homey. Diners enjoy "riverwalk steak" (filet topped with mustard caper sauce), prime rib, gumbo, "granny's fried chicken," and Texas-style beef brisket. Try it! No lunch on Sunday. ~ 10631 Los Alamitos Boulevard, Los Alamitos; 562-431-1990, fax 562-431-1910. MODERATE TO ULTRA-DELUXE.

In downtown Long Beach the **King's Pine Avenue Fish House** is a prime spot for seafood. The private booths and dark wood trim lend an antique atmosphere to this open-kitchen establishment. The seafood platters are too numerous to recite (besides, the menu changes daily); suffice it to say that you can have them baked, broiled, sautéed, or grilled. For those not keen on seafood, there are also pasta and chicken dishes. ~ 100 West Broadway; 562-432-7463, fax 562-435-6143; www.kingsfishhouse.com. MODERATE.

Good eats and frugal budgets meet at **Acapulco Mexican Restaurant & Cantina**, which offers standard as well as innovative dishes. Tacos, burritos, and enchiladas are only the beginning; this comfortable eatery also serves several Mexican-style seafood dishes. ~ 6270 East Pacific Coast Highway; 562-596-3371, fax 562-430-7031. MODERATE TO DELUXE.

A haven for locals and a bastion of warm, speedy service, the **Long Beach Café** serves breakfast all day plus lunch and dinner. Portions are enormous. Go for fluffy pancakes, giant omelettes, and the longshoreman's breakfast of three eggs, four sausages, four pieces of bacon, hash browns, and toast. It's always busy on the weekends and in the wee hours when the bars start closing. ~ 615 East Ocean Boulevard; 562-436-6037; www.thelongbeach cafe.com. MODERATE.

The Reef on the Water is rambling, ramshackle, and wonderful. Built of rough-sawn cedar, it sits along the waterfront on a dizzying series of levels. The Continental American cuisine includes such contemporary choices as seafood collage and jumbo shrimp scampi. For the traditionalists, there are steaks, pasta, and swordfish. There's also Sunday brunch. ~ 880 Harbor Scenic Drive; 562-435-8013, fax 562-432-6823; www.reefrestaurant. com, e-mail gmunit41@srcmail.com. MODERATE TO DELUXE.

What more elegant a setting in which to dine than aboard the *Queen Mary*. There you will find everything from snack kiosks to coffee shops to first-class dining rooms. The **Promenade Café** offers a reasonably priced menu of chicken, steak, and seafood dishes. They also have salads and sandwiches. The café is a lovely art-deco restaurant featuring period lamps and stunning views. Breakfast, lunch and dinner served. ~ 1126 Queen's Highway; 562-435-3511, fax 562-432-7674; www.queenmary.com. MODERATE.

For a true taste of regal life aboard the old ship, cast anchor at **Sir Winston's**, the *Queen Mary*'s most elegant restaurant. The Continental and California cuisine in this dining emporium includes rack of lamb, veal medallion, muscovy duck, venison, châteaubriand, broiled swordfish, and Australian lobster. Sir Winston's is a wood-paneled dining room with copper-rimmed mirrors, white tablecloths, and upholstered armchairs. The walls are adorned with photos of the great prime minister and every window opens onto a full view of Long Beach. A semiformal dress code is enforced and jackets are requested. Reservations required. Dinner only. ~ 1126 Queen's Highway; 562-499-1657, fax 562-499-1789; www.queen mary.com, e-mail sirwinstons@queenmary.com. ULTRA-DELUXE.

Look for a copy of the *Long Beach Antique and Vintage Shopping Guide* to help you map out your itinerary.

SHOPPING

The best street shopping in Long Beach is in Belmont Shore along **East 2nd Street**. This 15-block strip between Livingston Drive and Bayshore Avenue is a gentrified row. Either side is lined with art galleries, book shops, boutiques, jewelers, and import stores.

For **vintage-store and antiques** shoppers, Redondo Avenue, East Broadway, and East 4th Street in downtown Long Beach have nearly two dozen stores where you can find everything from Bauer pottery to antique furniture to Depression glass to beaded sweaters. Look for a copy of the Long Beach Antique and Vintage Shopping Guide to help you map out your itinerary.

Shoreline Village is one of those waterfront malls Southern California specializes in. With a marina on both sides, the buildings are New England–style shingle and clapboard structures designed to re-create an Atlantic Coast port town. ~ 429 Shoreline Village Drive; 562-435-2668; www.shorelinevillage.com.

There are more than half a dozen stores onboard the **Queen Mary**. There is a fee charged to board the ship. Concentrated in the Piccadilly Circus section of the old ship are several souvenir shops as well as stores specializing in artifacts and old-fashioned items. Perhaps the prettiest shopping arcade you'll ever enter, it is an art-deco masterpiece with etched glass, dentil molding, and brass appointments. ~ 1126 Queen's Highway; 562-435-3511; www.queenmary.com.

Adjacent to the *Queen Mary*, the **Queen Mary Seawalk** is a shopping plaza styled after a 19th-century British village and offering a variety of speciality and souvenir shops.

NIGHTLIFE   **Panama Joe's Grill & Cantina** cooks Thursday through Sunday night. The bands are R&B ensembles, rock groups, and assorted others, which create an eclectic blend of music. Your average Tiffany-lamp-and-hanging-plant nightspot, the place is lined with sports photos and proudly displays an old oak bar. ~ 5100 East 2nd Street; 562-434-7417, fax 562-434-7810; www.panamajoes.com.

E. J. Malloy's is a small sports bar with a comfortable pub-style interior including a long wood bar, brick walls, and plenty of televisions for watching a Lakers game with the locals. There's a fireplace, bar, and patio seating. The sports fans can get loud and rambunctious on game nights. ~ 3411 East Broadway; 562-433-3769, fax 562-987-3580.

The Queen Mary carried so many troops across the Atlantic Ocean that Adolf Hitler offered $250,000 and the Iron Cross to the U-boat captain who sank her.

Located right along the promenade in downtown is **The Blue Café**. This tavern serves up live blues, swing, and alternative music nightly and tasty dishes from the deli and grill. Hip hustlers hang out upstairs where there are billiard tables and a karaoke lounge on Friday nights. Closed Monday. Cover. ~ 210 Promenade North; 562-983-7111, fax 562-901-3057; www.thebluecafe.com.

No matter how grand, regardless of how much money went into its design, despite the care taken to assure quality, any Long Beach nightspot is hard pressed to match the elegance of the **Observation Bar** aboard the *Queen Mary*. Once the first-class bar for this grand old ship, the room commands a 180° view across the bow and out to the Long Beach skyline. The walls are lined with fine woods, a mural decorates the bar, and art-deco appointments appear everywhere. The bar features live jazz as well as rock-and-roll on the weekends.

If live music is not your thing, you can always adjourn aft to **Sir Winston's Piano Bar**, a cozy and elegant setting decorated with memorabilia of the WWII British leader. ~ 1126 Queen's Highway; 562-499-1657.

GAY SCENE   A long-time favorite is **Ripples**, which has a dance-club upstairs and a bar downstairs. There's also a pool table and patio. Cover. ~ 5101 East Ocean Boulevard; 562-433-0357; www.clubripples.com. **Mineshaft** has pool tables, pinball machines, and a jukebox. ~ 1720 East Broadway; 562-436-2433.

The Falcon is a gay bar complete with a digital jukebox, dart boards, and deejays on the weekend. ~ 1435 East Broadway; 562-432-4146.

ALAMITOS PENINSULA The ocean side of this slender salient offers a pretty sand beach looking out on a tiny island. Paralleling the beach is an endless string of woodframe houses. The sand corridor extends all the way to the entrance of Alamitos Bay where a stone jetty provides recreation for anglers, occasional surfers, swimmers, and climbers with sturdy hiking shoes. Facilities include restrooms, summer lifeguards, and volleyball courts; the paved bike path leading to Aquarium of the Pacific begins here. ~ Along Ocean Boulevard between 54th and 72nd places; park at the end of the road; 562-570-3100, fax 562-570-3109.

BAYSHORE BEACH This hook-shaped strand curves along the eastern and southern shores of a narrow inlet. Houses line the beach along most of its length. Protected from surf and tide, this is a safe, outstanding spot for swimming, and conditions are perfect for windsurfing. At the corner of Bayshore and Ocean there are basketball and handball courts as well as kayak and sailboat rentals. Restrooms are available at the beach; lifeguards in summer only. ~ Located along Bayshore Avenue and Ocean Boulevard; 562-570-3215, fax 562-570-3247.

LONG BEACH CITY BEACH They don't call it Long Beach for nothing. This strand is broad and boundless, a silvery swath traveling much of the length of town. There are several islets parked offshore. Along the miles of beachfront you'll find numerous facilities and good size crowds. **Belmont Veterans Memorial Pier**, a 1300-foot-long, hammerhead-shaped walkway, bisects the beach and offers fishing services. Fishing is good from the pier, where halibut and sea bass are common catches, and the beach is protected by the harbor breakwater, making for safe swimming. Along the beach you'll find restrooms, lifeguards, a snack bar, a playground, and volleyball courts. A paved bike path along Long Beach City Beach leads to the Aquarium of the Pacific. ~ Located along Ocean Boulevard between 1st and 72nd places. Belmont Pier is at Ocean Boulevard and 39th Place; 562-570-3100, fax 562-570-3109.

BEACHES & PARKS

San Pedro

Overlooking the busy Port of Los Angeles, one of the largest deep-water ports in the nation, San Pedro lies at the eastern end of the rocky Palos Verdes Peninsula. In 1542, Portuguese explorer Juan Cabrillo named it "Bay of Smokes," inspired by the hillside fires of the Gabrieleño Indians;

San Pedro was given its current name by Spanish navigator Sebastian Vizcaino in 1602. The city began to develop its reputation as a major port in the mid-19th century, when the railroad came to town. Almost 100 years later, during World War II, Fort MacArthur was built on the bluff to protect the bustling harbor from invasion. Now the fort houses a small museum and a youth hostel, and all manner of boats—from tankers to fishing vessels to cruise ships—steam in and out of the bay in peace.

SIGHTS

The Los Angeles Harbor, a region of creosote and rust, is marked by 28 miles of busy waterfront. This landscape of oil tanks and cargo containers services thousands of ships every year.

HIDDEN ►

Head over to the **22nd Street Landing** and watch sportfishing boats embark on high-sea adventures. Then wander the waterfront and survey this frontier of steel and oil. Here awkward, unattractive ships glide as gracefully as figure skaters and the machinery of civilization goes about the world's work with a clatter and boom. The most common shorebirds are cargo cranes. ~ At the foot of 22nd Street.

Ports O' Call Village, a shopping mall in the form of a 19th-century port town, is home to an outfit conducting harbor cruises. ~ The entrance is at the foot of 6th Street. The boats sail around the San Pedro waterfront and venture out for glimpses of the surrounding shoreline; for information, call **Spirit Cruises**. ~ Ports O' Call Village; 310-548-8080; www.spiritdinnercruises.com.

San Pedro is a departure point for the Catalina Express Shuttleboats to Santa Catalina Island. ~ 800-897-7154.

Extending along 6th Street between Mesa Street and Harbor Boulevard is the **Sportswalk**, featuring plaques dedicated to Olympic medalists as well as great collegiate and professional athletes.

Moored serenely between two bustling docks is the **S.S. Lane Victory**. This World War II cargo ship, a 455-foot-long National Historic Landmark, offers weekend cruises from mid-July to mid-September as well as daily tours. Reservations required. Admission. ~ Berth 94; 310-519-9545, fax 310-519-0265; www.lanevictory.org, e-mail sslanevictory@juno.com.

For more of our history on the sea, stop by the **Los Angeles Maritime Museum**. This dockside showplace displays models of ships ranging from fully rigged brigs to 19th-century steam schooners to World War II battleships. Exhibits include a comprehensive display on the history of commercial (hard-hat) diving in Los Angeles Harbor and a history of San Pedro's fishing and canning industry. Closed Monday. Admission. ~ Berth 84; 310-548-7618, fax 310-832-6537; www.lamaritimemuseum.org, e-mail museum@lamaritimemuseum.org.

HIDDEN ►

Another piece in the port's historic puzzle is placed several miles inland at the **Phineas Banning Residence Museum**. This imposing Greek Revival house, built in 1864, was home to the man who dreamed, dredged, and developed Los Angeles Harbor. Today Phineas Banning's Mansion, complete with a cupola from which he watched ships navigate his port, is furnished in period pieces and open for guided tours (except on Monday and Friday). ~ 401 East M Street, Wilmington; 310-548-7777; www. banningmuseum.org, e-mail visit@banningmuseum.org.

By definition any shipping center is of strategic importance. Head up to **Fort MacArthur** and discover the gun batteries with which World War II generals planned to protect Los Angeles Harbor. From this cement-and-steel compound you can inspect the bunkers and a small military museum, then survey the coast. Once a site of gun turrets and grisly prospects, today it is a testimonial to the invasion that never came. Museum closed Monday, Wednesday, and Friday. ~ Angel's Gate Park, 3601 South Gaffey Street; 310-548-2631; www.ftmac.org, e-mail director@ftmac.org.

Nearby, you can visit the **Bell of Friendship**, which the people of South Korea presented to the United States during its 1976 bicentennial. Housed in a multicolor pagoda and cast with floral and symbolic images, it rests on a hilltop looking out on Los Angeles Harbor and the region's sharply profiled coastline.

Down the hill at the **Cabrillo Marine Aquarium**, there is a modest collection of display cases with samples of shells, coral, and shorebirds. Several dozen aquariums exhibit local fish and marine plants, and there's a large outdoor touch tank. Closed Monday. ~ 3720 Stephen M. White Drive; 310-548-7562, fax 310-548-2649; www.cabrilloaq.org, e-mail info@cabrilloaq.org.

Of greater interest is **Point Fermin Park**, a 37-acre blufftop facility resting above spectacular tidepools and a marine preserve. The tidepools are accessible from the Cabrillo Marine Aquarium, which sponsors exploratory tours, and via steep trails from the park. Also of note, and open to the public during regularly scheduled tours, is the **Point Fermin Lighthouse** (closed Monday; 310-241-0684), a unique 19th-century clapboard house with a beacon set in a rooftop crow's nest. From the park plateau, like lighthouse keepers of old, you'll have open vistas of the cliff-fringed coastline and a perfect perch for sighting whales during their winter migration. ~ 805 Paseo del Mar; 310-548-7705.

Then drive along Paseo del Mar, through arcades of stately palm trees and along sharp sea cliffs, until it meets 25th Street. The sedimentary rocks throughout this region have been twisted and contorted into grotesque shapes by tremendous geologic pressures.

Hostelling International—Los Angeles South Bay is located in the Army barracks of old Fort MacArthur. Set in Angel's Gate Park on a hilltop overlooking the ocean, it's a pretty site with easy ac-

LODGING

cess to beaches. Men and women are housed separately in dorms but couples can be accommodated. Kitchen facilities are provided. Reservations are highly recommended from June through August; only large groups allowed October through May. ~ 3601 South Gaffey Street, Building 613; 310-831-8109, fax 310-831-4635; www.lahostels.org, e-mail southbay@lahostels.org. BUDGET.

San Pedro also has several chain hotels designed to serve the needs of departing or returning cruise ship passengers. Perhaps the most distinctive among them is the **Holiday Inn San Pedro**, which captures the flavor of a traditional European hotel. Behind the columned facade with its faux mansard roof are 60 individually decorated Victorian-style rooms; some have kitchenettes. Two-room suites with harbor views and fireplaces are available. ~ 111 South Gaffey Street; 310-514-1414, 800-465-4329, fax 310-514-1367; www.holidayinnsanpedro.com, e-mail holiday innsanpedro@yahoo.com. MODERATE.

DINING

The vintage shopping mall at **Ports O' Call Village** is Los Angeles Harbor's prime tourist center. It's situated right on the San Pedro waterfront and houses numerous restaurants. Try to avoid the high-ticket dining rooms, as they are overpriced and serve mediocre food to out-of-town hordes. But there are a number of takeout stands and ethnic eateries, priced in the budget and moderate ranges, which provide an opportunity to dine inexpensively on the water. ~ The entrance is at the foot of 6th Street and Harbor Boulevard; 310-548-8080.

HIDDEN ▶

Of course local anglers rarely frequent Ports O' Call. The old salts are over at **Canetti's Seafood Grotto**. It ain't on the waterfront, but it is within casting distance of the fishing fleet. Which means it's the right spot for fresh fish platters at good prices. Dinner Friday and Saturday; breakfast and lunch all week. ~ 309 East 22nd Street; 310-831-4036. MODERATE TO DELUXE.

Trade the Pacific for the Aegean and set anchor at **Papadakis Taverna**. The menu features moussaka, Greek-style cheese dishes, lamb baked in pastry, grilled contessa shrimp in tomato and feta and occasional specials like stuffed eggplant, fresh seafood, and regional delicacies. Dinner only. ~ 301 West 6th Street; 310-548-1186; www.papadakistaverna.com. DELUXE.

A longtime local favorite is the **Whale & Ale**, a charming two-tiered British pub that is at once casual and elegant. A large oak whale is sculpted into the wall above the full bar and candles accent the Victorian ambiance at night. The menu ranges from traditional fare, such as shepherd's pie, to more decadent items like beef Wellington and dijon-crusted rack of lamb. Live music Friday and Saturday. ~ 327 West 7th Street, San Pedro; 310-832-0363; www.whaleandale.com, e-mail info@whaleand ale.com. MODERATE TO DELUXE.

Los Angeles Harbor's answer to the theme shopping mall craze is **Ports O' Call Village**, a mock 19th-century fishing village. There are clapboard stores with shuttered windows, New England–style structures with gabled roofs, and storehouses of corrugated metal. Dozens of shops here are located right on the water, giving you a chance to view the harbor while browsing the stores. It's one of those hokey but inevitable places that I swear to avoid but always seem to end up visiting. ~ The entrance is at the foot of 6th Street; 310-548-8080.

SHOPPING

Landlubbers can enjoy a quiet drink on the waterfront at **Ports O' Call Restaurant**. In addition to a spiffy oak bar, they have a dockside patio. In summer there's live blues and jazz. ~ Ports O' Call Village; 310-833-3553.

NIGHTLIFE

CABRILLO BEACH 🐚 ⛵ 🎣 🏄 🏖 🚤 🛥 The edge of Los Angeles harbor is an unappealing locale for a beach, but here it is, a two-part strand, covered with heavy-grain sand and bisected by a fishing pier. One half faces the shipping facility; the other half looks out on the glorious Pacific and abuts on the Point Fermin Marine Life Refuge, a rocky corridor filled with outstanding tidepools and backdropped by dramatic cliffs. You'll also find restrooms, showers, picnic areas, lifeguards, an aquarium, a playground, and volleyball courts. Fires are permitted. Fishing can be done from the pier, and for surfing try the beachfront and near the jetty; this area is a windsurfing mecca. People do swim here, but I saw a lot of refuse from the nearby shipping harbor. After heavy rains, storm drainage increases the bacteria count; stick to the oceanside during these times. If you like tidepooling, beeline to Cabrillo—if not, there are hundreds of other beaches in the Golden State. Parking fee, $1 per hour. ~ 3720 Stephen M. White Drive; 310-372-2166, fax 310-372-6902.

BEACHES & PARKS

The 1200-foot Cabrillo Fishing Pier stretches into the Pacific from Cabrillo Beach, where on a clear day you can see Santa Catalina.

ROYAL PALMS COUNTY BEACH 🏃 ⛵ 🎣 🛥 Situated at the base of a sedimentary cliff, this boulder-strewn beach gains its name from a grove of elegant palm trees. This was an erstwhile hub of elegant activity in the 1920s; the Royal Palms country club and a Japanese-owned resort presided here until a violent storm destroyed them in 1939. Today the guests of honor are surfers and tidepoolers. While the location is quite extraordinary, I prefer another beach, Point Fermin Park's **Wilder Annex**, located to the east. This little gem also lacks sand, but is built on three tiers of a cliff. The upper level is decorated with palm trees, the middle tier has a grassy plot studded with shady magnolias, and the bottom floor is a rocky beach with promising tidepools and camera-eye views of Point Fermin. Fishing is good at both parks, but swimming is not recommended. Surfing is popular at Royal Palms, where there are lifeguards, and off White Point, a peninsula separating the two parks. Snorkelers and divers take advantage of Diver's Cove, at the far east end of the parking lot. Facilities are limited to restrooms. ~ Both parks are located along Paseo del Mar in San Pedro. Royal Palms is near the intersection with Western Avenue and Wilder Annex is around the intersection with Meyler Street; 310-372-2166, fax 310-372-6902.

Palos Verdes Peninsula Though Portuguese explorer Juan Cabrillo first described the area in 1542, the peninsula was home to the Gabrieleño Indians until 1827, when Don Dolores Sepulveda received 75,000 acres in an original land grant. By 1913, a consortium of New York investors owned most of the property, which it planned to divide into large estates. However, the first homes didn't start appearing here until the mid-20th century. Today it is an upscale residential neighborhood overlooking one of Southern California's loveliest stretches of coastline. Residents embrace an active lifestyle: Equestrian and hiking trails wind through lovely tree-shaded areas past pristine homes on large lots, and golfers try their luck on Los Angeles' only oceanfront golf course.

SIGHTS The forces of nature seem to dominate as you proceed out along the Palos Verdes Peninsula from San Pedro. Follow 25th Street, then Palos Verdes Drive South and encounter a tumbling region where terraced hills fall away to sharp coastal bluffs.

As you turn **Portuguese Bend**, the geology of this tumultuous area becomes startlingly evident when the road begins undulating through landslide zones. The earthquake faults that underlie the Los Angeles basin periodically fold and collapse the ground here. To one side you'll see the old road, fractured and useless. Even the present highway, with more patches than your favorite dungarees, is in a state of constant repair.

Of course the terrible power of nature has not dissuaded people from building here. Along the ridgetops and curving hills below are colonies of stately homes. With its rocky headlands, tidepool beaches and sun-spangled views, the place is simply so magnificent no one can resist.

Most lordly of all these structures is the **Wayfarers Chapel**, a simple but extraordinary center designed by the son of Frank Lloyd Wright. Nestled neatly into the surrounding landscape, the sunlit chapel is built entirely of glass and commands broad views of the terrain and ocean. With its stone altar and easy repose the chapel was built to honor Emanuel Swedenborg, the 18th-century Swedish philosopher and mystic. A visitors center designed by Wrights's son, Eric Lloyd Wright, also graces the grounds. ~

5755 Palos Verdes Drive South, Rancho Palos Verdes; 310-377-1650, fax 310-377-8589; www.wayfarerschapel.org, e-mail har veyt@wayfarerschapel.org.

The **Point Vicente Lighthouse** rises farther down the coast, casting an antique aura upon the area. The beacon is open to the public on the second Saturday of every month (except in March, when it's the first Saturday). The nearby **Point Vicente Interpretive Center** offers a small regional museum. This is a prime whale-watching spot from December through April when onlookers gather in the adjacent park to catch glimpses of migrating gray whales. ~ 31501 Palos Verdes Drive West, Rancho Palos Verdes; 310-377-5370, fax 310-544-5294; www.palosverdes.com/rpv.

For a vision of how truly beautiful this region is, turn off Palos Verdes Drive West in Palos Verdes Estates and follow Paseo Lunado until it meets the sea at **Lunada Bay**. This half-moon inlet, backdropped by the jagged face of a rocky cliff, looks out upon an unending expanse of ocean. Steep paths lead down to a rocky shoreline rich in tidepools.   ◄ HIDDEN

The road changes names to Paseo del Mar but continues past equally extraordinary coastline. There is a series of open fields and vista points along this shoreline preserve where you can gaze down from the blufftop to beaches and tidepools. Below, surfers

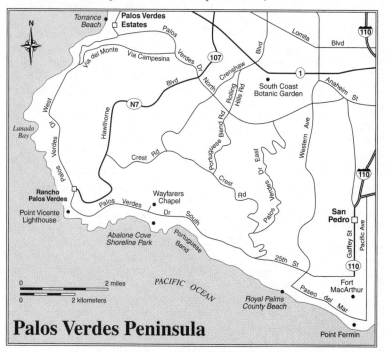

Palos Verdes Peninsula

ride the curl of frothing breaks and a few hardy hikers pick their way goat-like along precipitous slopes.

The setting is decidedly more demure at the **South Coast Botanic Garden**. This 87-acre garden is planted with exotic vegetation from Africa and New Zealand as well as species from other parts of the world. Admission. ~ 26300 South Crenshaw Boulevard, Palos Verdes; 310-544-6815, fax 310-544-6820; www. southcoastbotanicgarden.org.

DINING

Restaurants are a rare commodity along the Palos Verdes Peninsula. You'll find a cluster of them, however, in the Golden Cove Shopping Center. Granted, a mall is not the most appetizing spot to dine, but in this case who's complaining?

The Admiral Risty is one of those nautical cliché restaurants decorated along the outside with ropes and pilings and on the interior with brass fixtures. Know the type? Normally I wouldn't mention it, but the place has a full bar, a knockout view of the ocean, and happens to be the only member of its species in the entire area. My advice is to play it safe and order fresh fish (or never leave the bar). The menu is a surf-and-turf inventory of fish (prepared four ways), steak, chicken, and so on. Dinner and Sunday brunch. ~ 31250 Palos Verdes Drive West, Rancho Palos Verdes; 310-377-0050; www.admiral-risty.com, e-mail tim@admiral-risty.com. DELUXE.

For genuine elegance, make lunch or dinner reservations at **La Rive Gauche**, an attractively appointed French restaurant. With its upholstered chairs, brass wall sconces, and vintage travel posters, this cozy candlelit dining room is unique to the peninsula. The three-course dinner menu is a study in classic French cooking including veal chop with *foie gras* and truffles, duck *à l'orange*, and a selection of fresh seafood like Norway salmon and John Dory. A pianist adds to the romance. The lunch offerings, while more modest, follow a similar theme. In sum, gourmet cuisine, warm ambience, and a world-class wine list. No lunch on Monday. ~ 320 Tejon Place, Palos Verdes Estates; 310-378-0267, fax 310-373-5837. MODERATE TO ULTRA-DELUXE

BEACHES & PARKS

ABALONE COVE SHORELINE PARK 🏃 🏊 🎣 ⚓ The Palos Verdes Peninsula is so rugged and inaccessible that any beach by definition will be secluded. This gray-sand hideaway is no exception. It sits in a natural amphitheater guarded by sedimentary rock formations and looks out on Catalina Island. There are tidepools to ponder and a marine ecological reserve to explore, and the fishing and swimming are good. For surfing, try the east end of the cove. There are also picnic areas, restrooms, and lifeguards on weekends, holidays, and in summer. Parking fee, $5. ~ Located off of Palos Verdes Drive South in Rancho Palos

Verdes. From the parking lot a path leads down to the beach; 310-377-1222.

TORRANCE BEACH 🚴 🏊 🏄 🏃 ⛵ This beach is a lengthy stretch of bleach-blond sand guarded on one flank by the stately Palos Verdes Peninsula and on the other by an industrial complex and colony of smokestacks. Just your average middle-class beach; it's not one of my favorites, but it has the only white sand hereabouts. Also consider adjacent **Malaga Cove**, noted for tidepools, shells, and rock-hounding. Prettier than its pedestrian partner, Malaga Cove is framed by rocky bluffs. At Torrance there are restrooms, a seasonal concession stand, and lifeguards; around Malaga Cove you're on your own. Fishing for corbina is good at both beaches, and surfing is generally good (but better in winter) at Malaga Cove with steady, rolling waves ideal for beginners. For swimming I recommend Torrance, where life-guards are on duty year-round. Parking fee, $6. ~ Paseo de la Playa in Torrance parallels the beach. To reach Malaga Cove, walk south from Torrance toward the cliffs; 310-372-2166, fax 310-372-6902.

South Bay

The birthplace of California's beach culture lies in a string of towns on the southern skirt of Santa Monica Bay—Manhattan Beach, Hermosa Beach, and Redondo Beach. It all began here in the South Bay with George Freeth, "the man who can walk on water." It seems that while growing up in Hawaii, Freeth resurrected the ancient Polynesian sport of surf-ing and transplanted it to California. Equipped with a 200-pound, solid wood board, he intro-duced surfing to fascinated onlookers at a 1907 event in Redondo Beach.

> The South Bay is *the* place for surfing, sun-ning, swimming, and soaking up the laid-back atmosphere.

It wasn't until the 1950s that the surfing wave crested. The surrounding towns became synonymous with the sport and a new culture was born, symbolized by blond-haired, blue-eyed surfers committed to sun, sand, and the personal freedom to ride the last wave. By the 1960s, a group of local kids called The Beach Boys were recording classic beach songs.

Sightseeing spots are rather scarce in these beach towns. As you can imagine, the interesting places are inevitably along the waterfront. Each town sports a municipal pier, with rows of knickknack shops, cafés, and oceanview lounges, either along the pier or on the nearby waterfront.

SIGHTS

In Redondo Beach, **Fisherman's Wharf** is home to surfcasters and hungry seagulls. Walk out past the shops, salt breeze in your face, and you can gaze along the waterfront to open ocean. Waves wash against the pilings. Beneath the wood plank walkway, sea birds dive for fish. These sights and sounds are repeated again and again on the countless piers that line the California coast.

In fact you'll find them recurring right up in Hermosa Beach at the **Municipal Pier**. Less grandiose than its neighbor, this 1320-foot concrete corridor is simply equipped with a snack bar and bait shop. From the end you'll have a sweeping view back along Hermosa Beach's low skyline. ~ Located at the foot of Pier Avenue, Hermosa Beach.

The **Manhattan Beach Pier**, which extends extends 900 feet from the beach, is the site of the **Roundhouse Marine Studies Lab and Aquarium**, a community marine science center full of local sea creatures. A mini-reef tank, shark tank, and touch tank make this a great place to take kids. ~ At the west end of Manhattan Beach Boulevard, Manhattan Beach; 310-379-8117, fax 310-937-9366; www.roundhouseaquarium.org, e-mail roundhouse. aquarium@verizon.net.

The other sightseeing diversion in these parts is the stroll. The stroll, that is, along the beach. **Esplanade** in Redondo Beach is a wide boulevard paralleling the waterfront. Wander its length and take in the surfers, sunbathers, and swimmers who keep this resort town on the map. Or walk down to the waterline and let the cool Pacific bathe your feet.

In Hermosa Beach you can saunter along **The Strand**. This pedestrian thoroughfare borders a broad beach and passes an endless row of bungalows, cottages, and condominiums. It's a pleasant walk with shops and restaurants along the way.

The Strand continues along Manhattan Beach but lacks the commercial storefronts of Hermosa Beach. Wide and wonderful, the beach is lined by beautiful homes with plate-glass windows that reflect the blue hues of sea and sky. Together, these ocean-front walkways link the South Bay towns in a course that bicyclists can follow for miles.

LODGING   Route 1 barrels through Los Angeles' beach towns and serves as the commercial strip for generic motels. As elsewhere, these facilities are characterized by clean, sterile rooms and comfortable, if unimaginative surroundings. Right on the edge of the marina, the **Best Western Sunrise Hotel** offers 111 standard, motel-style rooms. ~ 400 North Harbor Drive, Redondo Beach; 310-376-0746; 800-334-7384; www.bestwestern-sunrise.com, e-mail res ervations326@bestwestern-sunrise.com. BUDGET TO MODERATE.

The **Ramada Ltd.** features 40 rooms with refrigerators, microwaves, and TVs. One of the rooms has a jacuzzi. This establishment rests two blocks from the beach. Continental breakfast is included. ~ 435 South Pacific Coast Highway, Redondo Beach; 310-540-5998, fax 310-543-9828. BUDGET TO MODERATE.

Fresh from an $11-million overhaul, **The Portofino Hotel and Yacht Club** seeks to impress with a two-story lobby displaying views of King Harbor. The 163 units are decorated in contemporary fashion and look out either on the ocean or the adjoining marina. There is a lounge as well as a waterside swimming pool and a restaurant; other facilities are nearby in the marina. ~ 260 Portofino Way, Redondo Beach; 310-379-8481, 800-468-4292, fax 310-372-7329; www.hotelportofino.com. ULTRA-DELUXE.

The best lodging bargain in South Bay is found at **Sea Sprite Motel & Apartments**. Located right on Hermosa Beach, this multibuilding complex offers oceanview rooms with kitchenettes at moderate to deluxe prices. The accommodations are tidy, well furnished, and fairly attractive. There is a swimming pool and sundeck overlooking the beach. The central shopping district is just two blocks away, making the location hard to match. You can also rent suites at deluxe prices or a two-bedroom beach cottage at an ultra-deluxe price. Be sure to ask for an oceanview room in one of the beachfront buildings. ~ 1016 The Strand, Hermosa Beach; 310-376-6933, fax 310-376-4107; www.seaspritemotel.com, e-mail questions@seaspritemotel.com. MODERATE TO ULTRA-DELUXE.

At the **Hi View Motel**, you're only a step away from the beach, shopping malls, and restaurants. There are 21 standard guest rooms and 4 studio apartments (these are ultra-deluxe in price and rent by the week) for rent. ~ 100 South Sepulveda Boulevard, Manhattan Beach; 310-374-4608, fax 310-937-9542; e-mail reservations@hiviewmotel.com. MODERATE.

The **Sea View Inn at the Beach** is a compound of five buildings a block up from the beach. Accommodations range from single and double rooms to suites to apartment-style units with kitchens. You'll find comfortable furniture, refrigerators, microwaves, and air conditioning in every room; many have ocean views and balconies. In addition, it is close to the surf and lodging is rare in these parts. The inn offers complimentary bikes, boogieboards, wi-fi, towels, beach umbrellas, and chairs, which you can use at the outdoor heated pool. ~ 3400 Highland Ave-

SLEEP ON THE SHARE

One of the few Southern California beach hotels that is actually on the beach, the **Beach House at Hermosa** is a beautifully appointed, elegant three-story affair that offers 96 loft suites complete with fireplace, CD player, television, and continental breakfast. ~ 1300 The Strand, Hermosa Beach; 310-374-3001, 888-895-4559, fax 310-372-2115; www.beach-house.com, e-mail info@beach-house.com. ULTRA-DELUXE.

nue, Manhattan Beach; 310-545-1504, fax 310-545-4052; www.seaview-inn.com, e-mail info@seaview-inn.com. MODERATE TO ULTRA-DELUXE.

DINING
In downtown Redondo Beach, just a couple blocks from the water, are several small restaurants serving a diversity of cuisines.

Petit Casino, a French bakery, serves quiche, soups, salads, and sandwiches (including the French standard, *croque monsieur*). ~ 1767 South Elena Avenue, Redondo Beach; 310-543-5585. BUDGET.

A family-run, longtime Redondo Beach favorite, **Captain Kidd's Fish Market and Restaurant** has live crabs and lobsters, fresh shrimp and clams, and at least 18 kinds of fresh fish. Pick what you want and they'll cook it to order, whether charbroiled, panfried, deep-fried, or simmered into a chowder, gumbo, jambalaya, or Italian-style cioppino stew. There's indoor and outdoor seating at the harbor's edge. ~ 209 North Harbor Drive, Redondo Beach; 310-372-7703, fax 310-379-1531; www.captainkidds.com. BUDGET TO MODERATE.

In addition to serving good Asian food, **Thai Thani** is an extremely attractive restaurant. Black trim and pastel shades set off the blond wood furniture and etched glass. There are fresh flowers all around plus a few well-placed wall prints. Lunch and dinner include dozens of pork, beef, vegetable, poultry, and seafood dishes. Unusual choices like spicy shrimp coconut soup, whole pompano smothered in pork, and whole baby hen make this a dining adventure. No lunch on the weekend. ~ 1109 South Pacific Coast Highway, Redondo Beach; 310-316-1580. BUDGET TO MODERATE.

A wider than usual selection of healthy dishes—not to mention the surfboard decor—sets the **GoodStuff Restaurant** at the entrance to Riviera Village apart from other chain restaurants in the area (there are also branches in El Segundo and Hermosa Beach). The menu features a full range of meat, fish, and vegan dishes for breakfast, lunch, and dinner. There's even heart-healthy options, such as ground turkey enchiladas, for the not *quite* vegetarian. ~ 1617 Pacific Coast Highway, Redondo Beach; 310-316-0262, fax 310-316-3182; www.eatgoodstuff.com. MODERATE.

The capital of "in" dining around the South Bay is **Chez Melange**. As the name suggests, and as current trends demand, the cuisine is eclectic, thanks to its on-site cooking school and daily-changing menu. You'll find a hip crowd ordering everything from English bangers for breakfast to Cajun meatloaf for dinner. ~ 1716 Pacific Coast Highway, Redondo Beach; 310-540-1222, fax 310-316-9283; www.chezmelange.com, e-mail info@chezmelange.com. MODERATE TO ULTRA-DELUXE.

HIDDEN ▶
There is excellent thin-crust pizza at **Pedone's**. Popular with the beach crowd, it's a good spot for a quick meal in a convenient

locale. ~ 1332 Hermosa Avenue, Hermosa Beach; 310-376-0949;
www.pedonespizza.com. BUDGET TO MODERATE.

No restaurants line the Strand in Manhattan Beach, so you'll
have to make do with the pier's snack shop or hike up the hill
into town, where you'll find **Mama D's Original Italian Kitchen**
just around the corner. It has the feel of a genuine neighborhood
eatery. There's usually a wait for supper, but the occasional tray
of warm garlic bread, fresh from the oven, passed among the pro-
spective diners reminds you why you're in line. Entrées include
homemade ravioli, lasagna with *diablo* sauce, and cioppino with
linguine. The thin New York–style pizza is a perennial favorite.
~ 1125-A Manhattan Avenue, Manhattan Beach; 310-546-1492.
MODERATE TO DELUXE.

Café Pierre is an excellent choice for adventurous gourmets.
Black chairs and cherry wood furnishings create a contemporary
but warm atmosphere. You can feast on flamed filet mignon
Roquefort, striped bass filet niçoise, and homemade pasta. Daily
specials may include stuffed swordfish or venison. No lunch on
Saturday and Sunday. ~ 317 Manhattan Beach Boulevard,
Manhattan Beach; 310-545-5252, fax 310-546-6072; www.cafe
pierre.com, e-mail business@cafepierre.com. MODERATE TO DELUXE.

SHOPPING

If they weren't famous Pacific beach communities, the South Bay
enclaves of Manhattan, Hermosa, and Redondo beaches would
seem like small-town America. Their central shopping districts
are filled with pharmacies, supply shops, and shoe stores. There
are a few places of interest to folks from out of town.

In Manhattan Beach, Manhattan Beach Boulevard and
Manhattan Avenue are the best options.

Shops in Hermosa Beach concentrate along Pier and Hermosa
avenues, especially where they intersect.

In Redondo Beach, scout out Catalina Avenue, particularly
along its southern stretches.

AUTHOR FAVORITE

The Comedy & Magic Club features name acts nightly. Many
of the comedians are television personalities with a regional, if not national,
following. Jay Leno, for instance, frequently tests his new *Tonight Show* material on the club's Sunday-night crowd. The supper club atmosphere is
upscale and appealing. There's a showroom that features star memorabilia. Reservations are required. Closed Monday. Cover. ~ 1018
Hermosa Avenue, Hermosa Beach; 310-372-1193, fax 310-379-2806;
www.comedyandmagicclub.com.

NIGHTLIFE   The **Lighthouse Café** spotlights blues, reggae, rock-and-roll, and funk bands; the different styles draw vastly different crowds. Cover on Friday and Saturday. ~ 30 Pier Avenue, Hermosa Beach; 310-372-9833; www.thelighthousecafe.net.

HIDDEN ▶   Locals still bemoan the passing of Manhattan Beach's funky old La Paz Bar, a victim of urban gentrification that was turned into a parking lot. Since then, the surfer and beach-bum crowd from the La Paz has gravitated to the **Shellback Tavern** to carry on the endless beach party with tacos and burgers, loud music, cheap beer, and elbow-to-elbow tanned bodies. ~ 116 Manhattan Beach Boulevard, Manhattan Beach; 310-376-7857.

BEACHES & PARKS   **REDONDO BEACH** 🚲 🏊 🏃 🚶 🎣 ⛵ Surfers know this strand and so should you. Together with neighboring Hermosa and Manhattan beaches, it symbolizes the Southern California beach scene. You'll find a long strip of white sand bordered by a hillside carpeted with ice plants. In addition to surfers, the area is populated by bicyclists and joggers, while anglers cast from the nearby piers. Not surprisingly, fishing is particularly good from nearby Fisherman's Wharf. The swimming at Redondo is good, and surfing is even better. Facilities include restrooms, lifeguards, and volleyball courts. ~ Along the Esplanade, Redondo Beach; 310-372-2166, fax 310-372-6902.

HERMOSA BEACH 🚲 🏊 🏃 ⛵ One of the great beaches of Southern California, this is a very, very wide (and very, very white) sand beach extending the entire length of Hermosa Beach. Two miles of pearly sand are only part of the attraction. There's also The Strand, a pedestrian lane that runs the length of the beach; Pier Avenue, an adjacent street lined with interesting shops; a quarter-mile fishing pier; and a local community known for its artistic creativity. Personally, if I were headed to the beach, I would head in this direction. The swimming is good and the surfing is very good around the pier and all along the beach. Lifeguards are on duty, and facilities include restrooms, volleyball courts, and a playground. Parking fee, varies seasonally, up to $3 an hour. ~ At the foot of Pier Avenue, Hermosa Beach; 310-372-2166, fax 310-372-6902; www.hermosawave.net.

MANHATTAN COUNTY BEACH 🚲 🏊 🏃 🎣 ⛵ Back in those halcyon days when their first songs were climbing the charts, the Beach Boys were regular fixtures at this silvery strand. They came to swim and check out the scene along The Strand, the walkway that extends the length of Manhattan Beach. What can you say, the gentlemen had good taste—the surfing here is some of the best in Southern California; the prime spot hereabouts is perhaps El Porto, located at the northern end of the beach. This sand corridor is wide as a desert, fronted by an aquamarine ocean and backed by the beautiful homes of the very lucky. If that's not enough, there's a fishing pier, an adjacent commercial area door-to-door with excellent restaurants, and a small aquarium at the end of the pier. The swimming here is good, and the surfing is tops. Other facilities include restrooms, lifeguards, and volleyball courts. ~ At the foot of Manhattan Beach Boulevard, Manhattan Beach; 310-372-2166.

DOCKWEILER STATE BEACH It's long, wide, and has fluffy white sand—what more could you ask? Rather, it's what less can you request. Dockweiler suffers a minor problem. It's right next to Los Angeles International Airport, one of the world's busiest terminals. Every minute planes are taking off, thundering, reverberating, right over the beach. To add insult to infamy, there is a sewage treatment plant nearby. Nevertheless, swimming and surfing are good, fires are permitted, and fishing is good from the jetties. You'll also find picnic areas and restrooms. Parking fee, $5. ~ At the foot of Imperial Highway, along Vista del Mar Boulevard, Playa del Rey; 310-322-4951, fax 310-726-0371.

▲ There is an RV park with 83 sites with full hookups and 35 without; $20 to $28 per night. Reservations are recommended and are accepted 7 to 90 days in advance: 800-950-7275.

Venice

Venice, California, was the dream of one man, a tobacco magnate named Abbot Kinney. He envisioned a "Venice of America," a Renaissance town of gondoliers and single-lane bridges, connected by 16 miles of canals. After convincing railroad barons and city fathers, Kinney dredged swampland along Santa Monica Bay, carved a network of canals, and founded this dream city in 1905. The place was an early-20th-century answer to Disneyland with gondola rides and amusement parks. The canals were lined with vaulted arches and rococo-style hotels.

Oil spelled the doom of Kinney's dream. Once black gold was discovered beneath the sands of Venice, the region became a landscape of drilling rigs and oil derricks. Spills polluted the canals and blackened the beaches. In 1929, the city of Los Angeles filled in most of the canals, and during the subsequent decades Venice more resembled a tar pit than a cultural center.

But by the 1950s, latter-day visionaries—artists and bohemians—rediscovered "Kinney's Folly" and transformed it into an avant-garde community. It became a magnet for Beats in the 1950s and hippies during the next decade. Musician Jim Morrison of The Doors lived here and Venice developed a reputation as a center for the cultural renaissance that Abbot Kinney once envisioned. Today the creative energy of Venice is hard to stifle.

> Venice, to quote Bob Dylan, represents "life and life only," but a rarefied form of life, slightly, beautifully askew.

The town is filled with galleries and covered by murals, making it one of the region's most important art centers.

Today Venice seems to represent some sort of socially ideal community where there's room for everyone—aging hippies, retirees, world-class artists, and millionaire movie stars—to call Venice home. The reality, of course, is that gentrification of beachfront districts sent housing costs soaring. Still, the creative energy of Venice is hard to stifle. The town is filled with galleries and covered by murals, making it one of the region's most important art centers.

SIGHTS   The revolution might have sputtered elsewhere, but in Venice artists seized control. City Hall has become the **Beyond Baroque Literary Arts Center,** housing a library (open Friday through Sunday) and a bookstore (open Friday only) devoted to small presses and chapbooks. ~ 681 Venice Boulevard; 310-822-3006, fax 310-827-7432; www.beyondbaroque.org.

Next door, the former **Venice Police Station** is home to SPARC, or the Social and Public Art Resource Center. Some of the jail cells of this imposing 1929 art deco–style building have been converted into an art gallery. The holding pen is intact and you'll walk through an iron door to view contemporary artwork by mostly local alternative, cutting-edge artists. The center also houses a gift shop and the UCLA/SPARC Cesar Chavez Digital Mural Lab. Closed most weekends. ~ 685 Venice Boulevard; 310-822-9560, fax 310-827-8717; www.sparcmurals.org, e-mail sparc@sparcmurals.org.

Both the Venice City Hall and Police Station are great places to learn about what's going on in the community. Also consider the **Venice Chamber of Commerce.** If you can find someone there (which is not always easy), you can obtain maps, brochures, and answers. ~ 583¾ North Venice Boulevard, Suite C; 310-822-5425, fax 310-314-7641; www.venicechamber.net, e-mail info@venicechamber.net.

The commercial center of Venice rests at the intersection of Windward Avenue and Main Street. Windward was the central boulevard of Kinney's dream city, and the Traffic Circle was to be an equally grand lagoon. Continue along Windward Avenue to the arcades, a series of Italian-style colonnades that represent one of the few surviving elements of old Venice.

What's left of **Kinney's canals** can be found a few blocks south of Windward between Venice and Washington boulevards. Here three small canals flanked by two larger ones comprise an enclave of charming bungalows and showy mini-mansion remodels. Strains of opera or jazz float out of open windows as resident ducks, squawking loudly, paddle along the canals and joggers run along the narrow walkways and over small arched wooden bridges.

The heart of modern-day Venice pulses along the **boardwalk**, a two-mile strip that follows Ocean Front Walk from Washington Street to Rose Avenue. **Venice Pier**, an 1100-foot fishing pier, anchors one end. The pier is renovated with excellent lighting and coin-operated telescopes for lovely views of the Strand. Between Washington Street and Windward Avenue, the promenade is bordered by a palisade of beachfront homes, two- and three-story houses with plate-glass facades. ~ Ocean Front Walk and Washington Boulevard.

Walking north, the real action begins around 18th Avenue, at **Muscle Beach,** where rope-armed heavies work out in the world-class weight pen, smacking punching bags and flexing their pecs, while gawking onlookers dream of oiling their bodies and walking with a muscle-bound strut.

The rest of the boardwalk is a grand open-air carnival that you should try to visit on the weekend. It is a world of artists and anarchists, derelicts and dreamers, a vision of what life would be if heaven were an insane asylum. Guitarists, jugglers, conga drummers, and clowns perform for the crowds. Kids on roller skates and bicycles whiz past rickshaws and unicycles. Street

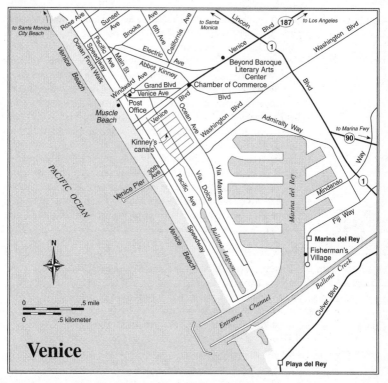

Venice

hawkers and panhandlers work the unwary while singers with scratchy voices pass the hat. Vendors dispense everything from corn dogs to cotton candy, T-shirts to wind-up toys.

South of Venice and Washington Boulevard is **Marina del Rey**, the largest manmade small-boat harbor in the world. Over 6000 pleasure boats and yachts dock at the manmade small-boat harbor here, the largest in the world. Private charters, dinner, sunset, dance, and Sunday champagne brunch cruises are provided by **Hornblower Cruises & Events**. ~ 13755 Fiji Way; 310-301-9900, 800-668-4322; www.hornblower.com, e-mail md@ hornblower.com.

The entire region was once a marsh inhabited by a variety of waterfowl. Personally, I think they should have left it to the birds. Marina del Rey is an ersatz community, a completely fabricated place where the main shopping area, **Fisherman's Village**, resembles a New England whaling town, and everything else attempts to portray something it's not. ~ 13755 Fiji Way; 310-823-5411.

With its endless condominiums, pretentious homes, and overpriced restaurants, Marina del Rey is an artificial limb appended to the coast of Los Angeles.

LODGING   There's nothing quite like **The Venice Beach House**. That may well be because there are so few bed-and-breakfast inns in the Los Angeles area. But it's also that this is such a charming house, an elegant and spacious California craftsman–style home built in 1911 by Warren Wilson. The living room, with its beam ceiling, dark wood paneling, and brick fireplace, is a masterwork. Guests also enjoy a sunny alcove, patio, and garden. The stroll to the Venice boardwalk and beach is only one-half block. The nine guest rooms are beautifully appointed and furnished with antiques; each features patterned wallpaper and period artwork. I can't recommend the place highly enough. ~ 15 30th Avenue; 310-823-1966, fax 310-823-1842; www.venicebeachhouse.com, e-mail info@venicebeachhouse.com. DELUXE TO ULTRA-DELUXE.

Also consider the **Best Western Marina Pacific Hotel & Suites**. Located in the recreational center of Venice only 200 feet from

AUTHOR FAVORITE

Shutters on the Beach, perched directly on Santa Monica Beach, is cozy and sedate. The lobby has two large fireplaces and the 198 gray-and-white rooms are well appointed with dark walnut furniture. Most rooms have coastal views; all feature, yes, shutters, as well as marble baths with jacuzzis. The hotel has a lovely pool terrace, two restaurants, and an oceanview bar. ~ 1 Pico Boulevard; 310-458-0030, 800-334-9000; www.shuttersonthebeach. ULTRA-DELUXE.

the sand, this three-story, 88-unit hostelry has a small lobby and café downstairs. The guest rooms are spacious, nicely furnished, and well maintained; all have refrigerators, hairdryers, coffee-makers, and irons. Very large one-bedroom suites, complete with kitchen and fireplace, are also available. All rooms have small balconies. Amenities include a coin laundry. ~ 1697 Pacific Avenue; 310-452-1111, 800-786-7789, fax 310-452-5479; www.mp hotel.com, e-mail info@mphotel.com. DELUXE TO ULTRA-DELUXE.

For the international hostel-hopper, Venice Beach is a veritable heaven by the ocean. The **Venice Beach Cotel,** located right on the beach, offers both private and shared rooms. Passports are required at check-in. ~ 25 Windward Avenue; 310-399-7649, 888-718-8287, fax 310-399-1930; www.venicebeachcotel.com, e-mail reservations@venicebeachcotel.com. BUDGET TO MODERATE.

Hostel California features ten units with shared baths: six dorm-style rooms hold six beds, four rooms are available for couples. Other amenities include kitchen and laundry facilities. Reservations are not taken for private rooms. ~ 2221 Lincoln Boulevard; 310-305-0250; www.hostelcalifornia.us, e-mail hoca90291@aol.com. BUDGET.

Situated a few blocks from a broad, pleasant beach, the **Inn at Playa del Rey** abuts the Ballona Wetlands, one of the last wetlands habitats in Southern California. With 21 rooms and suites, about half with fireplaces and whirlpool tubs, the gray-and-white clapboard inn looks more like a New England beach house than a California B&B. Bicycles are available for guests' use, and the outdoor jacuzzi is a popular feature. In addition to a full breakfast, owner Susan Zolla provides afternoon wine and cheese. ~ 435 Culver Boulevard, Playa del Rey; 310-574-1920, fax 310-574-9920; www.innatplayadelrey.com, e-mail info@innatplaya delrey.com. DELUXE TO ULTRA-DELUXE.

DINING

The best place for finger food and junk food in all Southern California might well be the **boardwalk** in Venice. Along Ocean Front Walk are vendor stands galore serving pizza, frozen yogurt, hamburgers, falafel, submarine sandwiches, corn dogs, etc.

Regardless, there's really only one spot in Venice to consider for dining. It simply *is* Venice, an oceanfront café right on the boardwalk, **The Sidewalk Café.** Skaters whiz past, drummers ◄ *HIDDEN* beat rhythms in the distance, and the sun stands like a big orange wafer above the ocean. Food is really a second thought here, but eventually they're going to want you to spend some money. So, on to the menu . . . breakfast, lunch, and dinner are what you'd expect—omelettes, sandwiches, hamburgers, pizza, and pasta. There are also fresh fish dishes plus specialty salads, steak, spicy chicken, and fried shrimp. Validated parking is a block away in the lot at Market and Speedway. ~ 1401 Ocean Front Walk at

Horizon Avenue; 310-399-5547, fax 310-399-4512; www.the sidewalkcafe.com. MODERATE.

Take a walk down the boardwalk to **Venice Bistro**. This beachfront establishment is a casual dining room with a tile floor and brick walls. Cozy and comfortable, it features a menu that includes hamburgers, salads, pasta, and some Mexican dishes. There's a full bar. ~ 323 Ocean Front Walk; 310-392-7472. BUDGET TO MODERATE.

Check out **Jody Maroni's Sausage Kingdom**, a beach stand with over a dozen types of sausage, all natural. There's sweet Italian, Yucatán chicken, Louisiana hotlinks, and, of course, Polish. Breakfast served daily. Open until sunset; closed on rainy days. ~ 2011 Ocean Front Walk; 310-822-5639, 800-428-8364, fax 310-348-1510; www.jodymaroni.com, e-mail info@jodymaroni.com. BUDGET.

A great bargain with its imaginative dishes and lovely patio, **Joe's Restaurant** offers a four-course prix-fixe menu highlighting seasonal specials like beet risotto with grilled asparagus and bacon-wrapped fallow deer in black currant sauce. For dessert, try the apricot or Key lime tarts. ~ 1023 Abbot Kinney Boulevard; 310-399-5811, fax 310-392-5655; www.joesrestaurant.com, e-mail joe@joesrestaurant.com. MODERATE.

HIDDEN ► The landing ground for Venetians is a warehouse dining place called **The Rose Café**. There's a full-scale deli, bakery counter, and a restaurant offering indoor seating and outdoor patio service. The last serves lunch and dinner daily from a reasonably priced menu that may include entrées like linguine with smoked salmon, sautéed chicken, and a good selection of vegetarian dishes. A good spot for pasta and salad, The Rose Café, with its wall murals and paintings, is also a place to appreciate the vital culture of Venice. Call for hours. ~ 220 Rose Avenue; 310-399-0711, fax 310-396-2660; www.rosecafe.com. MODERATE.

In the mood for Asian cuisine? **Hama Sushi Restaurant** is a well-respected Japanese restaurant in the center of Venice. The place features an angular sushi bar, a long, narrow dining room, and a patio out back. The crowd is young and the place is decorated to reflect Venice's vibrant culture. There are paintings on display representing many of the area's artists. In addition to scrumptious sushi, Hama offers a complete selection of Japanese dishes including tempura, teriyaki, and sashimi. Dinner only. ~ 213 Windward Avenue; 310-396-8783; www.hamasushi.com. ULTRA-DELUXE.

"American comfort cooking"—braised short rib with polenta and kale; roast chicken with a side of madeira gravy; fried calamari served with chipotle-pepper dipping sauce; calf's liver with pancetta; and roasted beet and squash salad, for example—that's what **James' Beach** is all about. Frequented by the Venice

Murals of Venice & Santa Monica

Nowhere is the spirit of Venice and Santa Monica more evident than in the murals adorning their walls. Both seaside cities house major art colonies, and numerous galleries and studios make them important centers for contemporary art.

Over the years, as more and more artists made their homes here, they began decorating the twin towns with their art. The product of this creative energy lives along street corners and alleyways, on storefronts and roadways. Crowded with contemporary and historic images, these murals express the inner life of the city.

Murals adorn nooks and crannies all over Venice. You'll find a cluster of them around Windward Avenue between Main Street and Ocean Front Walk. The interior of the **Post Office** is adorned with public art. There's a trompe l'oeil mural nearby on the old St. Marks Hotel that beautifully reflects the street along which you are gazing. Don't miss the woman in the upper floor window. ~ Windward Avenue and Main Street. On the other side of the building, facing the ocean, **Venice Reconstituted** depicts the unique culture of Venice Beach. ~ Windward Avenue and Speedway.

At last count Santa Monica boasted about two dozen outdoor murals. Route 1, or Lincoln Boulevard, is a corridor decorated with local artworks. **John Muir Woods** portrays a redwood forest. ~ Lincoln and Ocean Park boulevards. **Early Ocean Park and Venice Scenes** captures the seaside at the turn of the 20th century. ~ Located two blocks west of Lincoln Boulevard along Kensington Road in Joslyn Park.

Ocean Park Boulevard is another locus of creativity. At its intersection with the 4th Street underpass you'll encounter **Whale of a Mural**, illustrating whales and underwater life common to California waters, and **Unbridled**, depicting a herd of horses fleeing from the Santa Monica Pier carousel. One of the area's famous murals awaits you at Ocean Park Boulevard and Main street, where **Early Ocean Park** vividly re-creates scenes from the past.

For more information or a tour of these and other murals, contact the **Social and Public Art Resource Center**. ~ 685 Venice Boulevard; 310-822-9560; www.sparcmurals.org. Less expensive tours are available from the **Santa Monica Cultural Affairs Division**. ~ 310-458-8350; www.arts.santa-monica.org. Los Angeles has earned a reputation as the mural capital of the United States, making this tour a highpoint for admirers of public art.

arts-and-letters crowd, this art-filled restaurant (Billy Al Bengston designed the interior) offers daily dinner specials that are well conceived and reasonably priced. Dinner and weekend brunch; lunch Wednesday through Friday. ~ 60 North Venice Boulevard; 310-823-5396, fax 310-823-5397; www.jamesbeach. com. MODERATE.

SHOPPING　To combine slumming with shopping, be sure to wander the **boardwalk** in Venice. Ocean Front Walk between Windward and Ozone avenues is lined with low-rent stalls selling beach hats, cheap jewelry, sunglasses, beach bags, and souvenirs. You'll also encounter **Small World Books**, a marvelous beachside shop crammed with fiction, mysteries (novels, that is), poetry, and other books. ~ 1407 Ocean Front Walk; 310-399-2360; www.small worldbooks.com, e-mail info@smallworldbooks.com.

L.A. Louver is one of Venice's many vital and original galleries. It represents David Hockney, Ken Price, Gajin Fujita, and other contemporary American and European artists. Closed Sunday and Monday. ~ 45 North Venice Boulevard; 310-822-4955, fax 310-821-7529; www.lalouver.com, e-mail info@lalouver.com.

HIDDEN ►　**Philip Garaway Native American Art** specializes in museum-quality antique American Indian art, 19th-century Navajo blankets, antique rugs, vintage kachina dolls, Western American Indian basketry, late-19th-century and early-20th-century Western and California plein air paintings, and Pueblo pottery dating from A.D. 700 to the 20th century. By appointment only. ~ Venice; 310-577-8555, fax 310-577-8557; www.losangeles tribal.com, e-mail philipgaraway@earthlink.net.

In addition, a covey of art galleries and antique shops lines the 1200 to 1500 blocks of West Washington Boulevard.

The **Beyond Baroque Literary Arts Center**, a clearinghouse for local talent, has a bookstore and sponsors poetry readings, dramatic revues, lectures, and concerts. It's located in the old Venice City Hall. Closed Monday through Thursday. ~ 681 Venice Boulevard; 310-822-3006; www.beyondbaroque.org.

PARKING POINTERS

Parking in Venice, especially on hot summer weekends, can be a pain, and an expensive one at that. Street parking close to the beach cannot be found after 10 or 11 in the morning; lots closest to the beach will charge between $9 and $12 per car. If you don't mind a bit of walking, try your luck in the public lots at Venice Boulevard and Pacific Avenue; a day of parking here should cost between $7 and $10. The best advice: come early and be patient.

The town's erstwhile jail, the **Social and Public Art Resource Center**, or SPARC, has a store offering Latin American and Southwestern folk art as well as a selection of art books, prints, and cards. ~ 685 Venice Boulevard; 310-822-9560; www.sparcmurals.org.

NIGHTLIFE

The Townhouse, set in a '20s-era speakeasy, has live music occasionally. Otherwise, you can stop by for a drink or a game of darts or pool. ~ 52 Windward Avenue; 310-392-4040.

The Venice Bistro features a different style of live music every night—bluegrass, blues, rock, acoustic, folk—and there's never a cover charge. Call ahead for the schedule. ~ 323 Ocean Front Walk; 310-392-7472.

The Sidewalk Café is also a popular nightspot and gathering place, more for its central location than anything else. ~ 1401 Ocean Front Walk; 310-399-5547.

For an unusual way to spend the evening in the summer months, ask **Malibu Ocean Sports** about their moonlight kayak tours around Marina del Rey. The evening can include dinner at one of the marina's restaurants. ~ 310-456-6302.

BEACHES & PARKS

VENICE BEACH This broad white-sand corridor runs the entire length of Venice and features Venice Pier. But the real attraction—and the reason you'll find the beach described in the "Dining," "Sights," and "Shopping" sections—is the boardwalk. A center of culture, street artistry, and excitement, the boardwalk parallels Venice Beach for two miles. As far as beach facilities, you'll find restrooms, showers, lifeguards, playgrounds, basketball courts, weightlifting facilities ($10 per day), a bike path, and handball and paddle ball courts. If you can tear yourself away from the action on the boardwalk, the swimming and surfing are good here, too. Closed on rainy days. ~ Ocean Front Walk in Venice parallels the beach; 310-399-2775, fax 310-577-1046.

Santa Monica

Pass from Venice into Santa Monica and you'll trade the boardwalk for a promenade. It's possible to walk for miles along Santa Monica's fluffy beach, past pastel-colored condominiums and funky woodframe houses. Roller skaters and bicyclists galore crowd the byways and chess players congregate at the picnic tables.

A middle-class answer to mod Malibu, Santa Monica started as a seaside resort in the 1870s when visitors bumped over long, dusty roads by stagecoach from Los Angeles. After flirting with the film industry in the age of silent movies, Santa Monica reverted in the 1930s to a quiet beach town that nevertheless was notorious for the gambling ships moored offshore. It was during this period that detective writer Raymond Chandler immortalized the place as "Bay City" in his brilliant Philip Marlowe novels.

Today Santa Monica is *in*. Its clean air, pretty beaches, and attractive homes have made it one of the most popular places to live in Los Angeles. As real-estate prices skyrocketed, liberal politics ascended. Santa Monica is, in a manner of speaking, Southern California's answer to Berkeley.

SIGHTS   Highlight of the beach promenade (and perhaps all Santa Monica) is the **Santa Monica Pier**. No doubt about it, the place is a scene. Acrobats work out on the playground below, surfers catch waves offshore, and street musicians strum guitars. And I haven't even mentioned the official attractions. There's a late-19th-century carousel with hand-painted horses that was featured in that cinematic classic, *The Sting*. There are video parlors, pinball machines, skee ball, bumper cars, and a restaurant. ~ Located at the foot of Colorado Avenue.

At the Santa Monica Pier is **Pacific Park**, a family amusement park featuring 12 rides, 21 amusement games and an oceanfront food plaza. Reaching up to 55 feet in height, the Santa Monica West Coaster cruises around the park at 35 miles per hour and makes two 360-degree turns. The nine-story-high Ferris wheel offers a bird's-eye view of the beach and coastline. Other attractions include adult and kid bumper cars and a slew of kiddie rides. ~ 380 Santa Monica Pier; 310-260-8744, fax 310-260-8748; www.pacpark.com.

From here it's a jaunt up to the **Santa Monica Visitor Information Kiosk**, which has maps, brochures, and helpful workers. ~ 1400 Ocean Avenue; 310-393-7593, 800-544-5319, fax 310-394-0750; www.santamonica.com, e-mail info@santamonica.com.

The booth is located in **Palisades Park**, a pretty, palm-lined greensward that extends north from Colorado Avenue more than a mile along the sandstone cliffs fronting Santa Monica beach. One of the park's stranger attractions here is the **Camera Obscura**, a periscope of sorts through which you can view the pier, beach, and surrounding streets. ~ In the Senior Recreation Center, 1450 Ocean Avenue.

For 25 cents, the **Tide Shuttle** takes you through the heart of Santa Monica's tourist zone, from Main Street to the Santa Monica Pier and the Third Street Promenade. It also stops at many beachfront hotels. Running every 15 minutes starting at noon, the shuttle is a great way to visit the city's central attractions. Maps and schedules are available at the visitor center and most central hotels.

For a glimpse into Santa Monica's past, take in the **California Heritage Museum**. Heirlooms and antiques are housed in a grand American Colonial Revival home. The mansion dates to 1894 and is furnished entirely in period California pieces. There are photo archives, historic artifacts galore, and rotating exhibits of decorative and fine arts. Closed Monday and Tuesday. Admission. ~

2612 Main Street; 310-392-8537, fax 310-396-0547; www.cali
forniaheritagemuseum.org.

Sympathetic as it is to liberal politics, Santa Monica is nonetheless an extremely wealthy town. In fact, it's a fusion of two
very different neighbors, mixing the bohemian strains of Venice
with the monied elements of Malibu. For a look at the latter influence, take a drive from Ocean Avenue out along **San Vicente
Boulevard**. This fashionable avenue, with its arcade of magnolias, is lined on either side with lovely homes. But they pale by
comparison with the estates you will see by turning left on **La
Mesa Drive**. This quiet suburban street boasts a series of marvelous Spanish Colonial, Tudor, and contemporary-style houses.

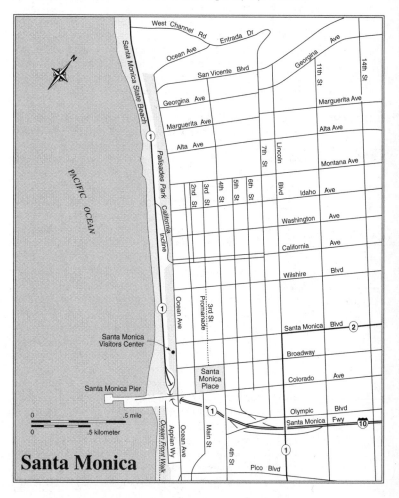

Santa Monica

HIDDEN ▶   At first glance, the **Self Realization Fellowship Lake Shrine** in nearby Pacific Palisades is an odd amalgam of pretty things. Gathered along the shore of a placid pond are a Dutch windmill, a houseboat, and a shrine topped with something resembling a giant artichoke. In fact, the windmill is a chapel, the houseboat is a former stopping place of yogi and Self Realization Fellowship founder Paramahansa Yogananda, and the oversized artichoke is a golden lotus archway near which some of Indian leader Mahatma Gandhi's ashes are enshrined. A strange but potent collection of icons in an evocative setting, the Fellowship is a meditation garden open to people of any religion. Closed Monday. ~ 17190 Sunset Boulevard, Pacific Palisades; 310-454-4114, fax 310-459-7461; www. yogananda-srf.org.

Several miles inland at **Will Rogers State Historic Park**, on a hillside overlooking the Pacific, you can tour the ranch and home of America's greatest cowboy philosopher. Will Rogers, who started as a trick roper in traveling rodeos, hit the big time in Hollywood during the 1920s as a kind of cerebral comedian whose humorous wisdom plucked a chord in the American psyche.

LODGING   Ocean Avenue, which runs the length of Santa Monica, paralleling the ocean one block above the beach, boasts the most hotels and the best location in town. Among its varied facilities are several generic motels. These are all-American-type places furnished in veneer, carpeted wall-to-wall, and equipped with telephones and color televisions.

A reasonably good bargain is the **Bayside Hotel**. Laid out in motel fashion, this two-story complex offers plusher carpets and plumper furniture than motels hereabouts. More important, it's just 50 yards from the beach across a palm-studded park. Some rooms have ocean views and fully equipped kitchens. ~ 2001 Ocean Avenue; 310-396-6000, 800-525-4447, fax 310-396-1000; www.baysidehotel.com, e-mail info@baysidehotel. com. MODERATE TO DELUXE.

If you book a room in one of the motels, ask for quiet accommodations since Ocean Avenue is a busy, noisy street.

Just off Ocean Avenue and a little quieter than most, the **Sea Shore Motel** has 19 guest rooms and nine suites located two blocks from the beach and within walking distance of all Santa Monica sights. The rooms have terra-cotta tile floors, granite counter tops, and refrigerators. There's a sundeck and off-street parking. ~ 2637 Main Street; 310-392-2787, fax 310-392-5167; www.seashoremotel.com, e-mail reservations@sea shoremotel.com. MODERATE.

Of course the ultimate bargain is found at **Hostelling International—Santa Monica**. This four-story, dorm-like structure boasts 30,000 square feet, room for 260 beds. There are several common rooms, internet kiosks, a central courtyard, and a kitchen. In addition to facilities for independent travelers, the hostel has set aside nine private rooms for couples. ~ 1436 2nd Street; 310-393-9913, 888-464-4872, fax 310-393-1769; www. losangeleshi.org. MODERATE.

Despite its location on a busy street, **Channel Road Inn** conveys a cozy sense of home. Colonial Revival in style, built in 1910, this sprawling 14-room bed and breakfast offers guests a living room, library, and dining room as well as a jacuzzi and hillside garden. The guest rooms vary widely in decor—some traditional, others contemporary; some florid, others demure. ~ 219 West Channel Road; 310-459-1920, fax 310-454-9920; www.channelroadinn.com, e-mail info@channelroadinn.com. DELUXE TO ULTRA-DELUXE.

The **Viceroy Hotel** looks the part of a contemporary Southern California hotel. Across the street from the beach, this sprawling 163-room facility boasts a pool, exercise room, and patio. There's a restaurant off the lobby as well as a lounge. ~ 1819 Ocean Avenue; 310-260-7500, 800-670-6185, fax 310-260-7515; www.viceroysantamonica.com, e-mail reservations@viceroysantamonica.com. ULTRA-DELUXE.

Think of sunflowers backdropped by a deep blue Mediterranean sky. That's what the **Hotel Oceana Santa Monica** evokes. From its magnificent oceanfront setting to its lush courtyard planted with fragrant flowers, this exquisite hotel—reminiscent of the beauty of the Côte d'Azur—is a lesson in understated elegance. Each guest suite comes with a fully equipped kitchen and is individually decorated. The amenities include room service from Rosti's, a fitness center, and a pool. ~ 849 Ocean Avenue; 310-393-0486, 800-777-0758, fax 310-458-1182; www.hotel oceana.com, e-mail info_sm@hoteloceana.com. ULTRA-DELUXE.

The **Loews Santa Monica Beach Hotel**, a creamy yellow structure, features a mock turn-of-the-20th-century design. Its spectacular five-story glass atrium lobby and most of the 342 guest rooms provide views of the famed Santa Monica Pier. Room decor is modern and low-key. Non-beachies love the oceanview outdoor pool. ~ 1700 Ocean Avenue; 310-458-6700, 800-235-6397, fax 310-458-6761; www.loewshotels.com. ULTRA-DELUXE.

It looks like a typical upscale beachfront hotel from the outside, but inside **Le Merigot** distinguishes itself with a high level of luxury and service. The 175 rooms and suites are spacious, with large desks and ergonomic desk chairs, and down duvets and pillows. The "Club Meg" pet program caters to dogs with special food and beds, while the spa pampers human guests with a large menu of body and skin services. ~ 1740 Ocean Avenue; 310-395-9700, fax 310-395-9200; www.lemerigothotel.com, e-mail info@lemerigothotel.com. DELUXE TO ULTRA-DELUXE.

DINING

Santa Monica is a restaurant town. Its long tradition of seafood establishments has been expanded in recent years by a wave of ethnic and California cuisine restaurants. While some of the most fashionable and expensive dining rooms in L.A. are right here, there are also many excellent, inexpensive cafés. Generally you'll find everything from the sublime to the reasonable located within several commercial clusters—near the beach along Ocean Avenue, downtown on Wilshire and Santa Monica boulevards, and in the chic, gentrified corridors of Main Street and Montana Avenue.

One of the best places in Southern California for stuffing yourself with junk food while soaking up sun and having a whale of a good time is the **Santa Monica Pier**. There are taco stands, fish-and-chips shops, hot dog vendors, oyster bars, snack shops, pizzerias, and all those good things guaranteed to leave you clutching your stomach. The prices are low to modest and the food is amusement park quality. ~ At the foot of Colorado Avenue.

There's a sense of the Mediterranean at the sidewalk cafés lining Santa Monica's Ocean Avenue: palm trees along the boulevard, ocean views in the distance, and (usually) a warm breeze blowing. Any of these bistros will do (since it's atmosphere we're seeking), so try **Ivy at the Shore**. It features a full bar, serves espresso, and, if you want to get serious about it, has a full lunch and dinner menu with pizza, pasta, steaks, and Cajun dishes. ~ 1535 Ocean Avenue; 310-393-3113, fax 310-458-9259. ULTRA-DELUXE.

In business since the 1950s, **Chez Jays** is a Santa Monica institution. It's a sort of chic dive where aging surfers rub elbows with high-profile Hollywood stars. To say that the decor is unpretentious is an understatement, but the no-nonsense steaks are always tender and tasty and the seafood unfailingly fresh. Owner Jay Fiondella, a legend in his own right, still seats customers and just may regale you with tales of his colorful life if asked. The bar is always jam-packed with an eclectic array of locals. No lunch on Monday. ~ 1657 Ocean Avenue; 310-395-1741; www.chezjays.com. DELUXE.

A number of excellent eateries line Santa Monica's vaunted Third Street Promenade. This three-block-long walkway, filled with movie theaters and located in the downtown district, boasts some of the best coffeehouses and restaurants in the area.

If steak-and-kidney pie, bangers and mash, or shepherds' pie sound appetizing, head over to **Ye Olde King's Head**. You won't see a king's head on the wall of this British pub, but you will find British memorabilia alongside photographs of the celebrities who inhabit the pub. Like you, they are drawn here by the cozy ambience and the lively crowd. ~ 116 Santa Monica Boulevard; 310-451-1402, fax 310-393-6869; www.yeoldekingshead.com, e-mail lisa88@earthlink.net. MODERATE.

In the world of high chic, **Chinois on Main** stands taller than most. Owned by famous restaurateur Wolfgang Puck, the fashionable dining room is done in nouveau art deco–style with track lights, pastel colors, and a central skylight. The curved bar is hand-painted; contemporary artwork adorn the walls. Once you drink in the glamorous surroundings, move on to the menu, which includes Shanghai lobster with curry sauce, whole sizzling catfish, and grilled Szechuan beef. The appetizers and other entrées are equal in originality, a medley of French, Chinese, and California cuisine. This is an excellent restaurant with high standards of quality. No lunch Saturday through Tuesday. ~ 2709 Main Street; 310-392-9025, fax 310-396-5102; www.wolfgangpuck.com. DELUXE TO ULTRA-DELUXE.

The spot for breakfast in Santa Monica is **Rae's Restaurant**, ◄ *HIDDEN*
a diner on the edge of town several miles from the beach. With its formica counter and naugahyde booths, Rae's is a local institution, always packed. The breakfasts are hearty American-style feasts complete with biscuits and gravy. At lunch they serve the usual selection of sandwiches and side orders. Come dinner time they have fried shrimp, liver, fried chicken, steaks, and other platters at prices that seem like they haven't changed since the place opened in 1958. ~ 2901 Pico Boulevard; 310-828-7937. BUDGET.

Hailed by several critics as the best Italian restaurant in America, **Valentino's** showcases cheese from Puglia, white truffles from Piedmont, fish from the Mediterranean and Adriatic seas, Napa quail and meats from a small East Coast farm. The wine list has over 4000 selections. Ask for the "extravaganza menu" of multiple small courses from the day's specialties and plan on a lengthy, expensive, memorable evening. Dinner only. ~ 3115 Pico Boulevard; 310-829-4313; www.welovewine.com. DELUXE.

The word's spread about **Louise's**. A friendly trattoria atmosphere, creative Italian fare, and reasonable prices account for its popularity. ~ 1008 Montana Avenue; 310-394-8888. MODERATE.

There's no denying that the tariff at quietly elegant **Melisse** is ◄ *HIDDEN*
steep, but the exquisite service and food make it one of the Westside's finest eateries. A gracious and ever-present, but un-hovering, waitstaff serves up perfectly cooked, French-inspired

GOURMET GHETTO

Every type of cuisine imaginable is found on the bottom level of **Santa Monica Place**. This multitiered shopping mall has an entire floor of take-out food stands. It's like the United Nations of dining, where everything is affordably priced. ~ On Broadway between 2nd and 4th streets. BUDGET.

dishes such as rotisserie chicken stuffed with truffles, roasted Dover sole with potato gnocchi, and bluefin tuna tartare with avocado mousseline. Dinner only. Closed Sunday and Monday. ~ 1104 Wilshire Boulevard; 310-395-0881, fax 310-395-3810; www.melisse.com, e-mail mail@melisse.com. ULTRA-DELUXE.

There are many who believe the dining experience at **Michael's** to be the finest in all Los Angeles. Set in a restored stucco structure and decorated with original artworks by David Hockney and Jasper Johns, it is certainly one of the region's prettiest dining rooms. The menu is Californian, with original entrées such as lemon-thyme roasted halibut with garbanzo bean purée, and crispy duck breast and leg confit with blood-orange Grand Marnier sauce. At lunch there is goat cheese and bermuda onion ravioli, a filet mignon sandwich with mustard aioli, and several delicious sides. Haute cuisine is the order of the evening here. The artistry that has gone into the restaurant's cuisine and design have permanently established Michael's reputation. There is a cozy lounge and a garden terrace. No lunch Saturday. Closed Sunday. ~ 1147 3rd Street; 310-451-0843, fax 310-394-1830; www.michaelssantamonica.com. ULTRA-DELUXE.

SHOPPING   **Montana Avenue** is Santa Monica's version of designer heaven, making it an interesting, if inflationary, strip to shop. From 7th to 17th Street, chic shops and upscale establishments line either side of the thoroughfare.

Brenda Himmel, an elegant stationary and gift store, just oozes refinement and good taste. While they sell buttery-leather journals, photo albums, and engagement books, and sterling silver picture frames, their forte is custom invitations and stationary. Almost nothing is impossible (provided you can afford it). Closed Sunday. ~ 1126 Montana Avenue; 310-395-2437.

A SIDE ORDER OF ENLIGHTENMENT, PLEASE

Up in the Santa Monica Mountains, high above the clamor of Los Angeles, rests the **Inn of the Seventh Ray**. A throwback to the days when Topanga Canyon was a hippie enclave, this mellow dining spot serves organic "energized" foods to "raise your body's light vibrations." Vegan, raw, organic, and range-fed entrées include roasted squab with pomegranate gremolata and chestnut polenta with porcini mushrooms. There is also a selection of fresh seafood, duckling, and lamb dishes. Open for lunch and dinner, the restaurant features dining indoors or outside on a pretty, tree-shaded patio, where coyotes can often be seen from your table. Far out. ~ 128 Old Topanga Canyon Road, Topanga; 310-455-1311, fax 310-455-0033; www.innoftheseventhray.com. DELUXE TO ULTRA-DELUXE.

For men's and women's fashion sportswear, try **Weathervane For Men.** ~ 1132 Montana Avenue; 310-395-0397.

Across the street, but no relation, is another **Weathervane**, this one featuring high-end designer clothing for women. Owner Jan Brilliot opened her shop in 1974, long before Montana Avenue had all the buzz. She journeys twice yearly to Paris and Italy looking for clothing that makes a statement. And her store certainly does with its architectural features and provocative art. You feel the thought and care that's gone into every detail. Closed Sunday. ~ 1209 Montana Avenue, Santa Monica; 310-393-5344.

Though they carry elegant traditional styles as well, **A. Mason** will offer you a look at worldwide cutting-edge fashion with their presentation of creations for women by emerging international talent. The emphasis in this special store is on originality. ~ 1511 Montana Avenue, Santa Monica; 310-394-7179.

Room with a View is a sort of Bed, Bath & Beyond for the rich. Exuding class, with its wooden floors, thick carpets, and potpourri aroma, the shop sells all sorts of high-end household accessories. The linens are nothing but the best; sheets have lofty thread counts, and towels are luxuriously fluffy. Combined with to-die-for table settings and gleaming silver accent pieces, this is a place that makes credit card max-out a definite possibility. ~ 1600 Montana Avenue; 310-998-5858.

Browse **Main Street** and you'll realize that Montana Avenue is only a practice round. Block after block of this thoroughfare is filled with trendy fashion and stylish shops.

The shopper's parade stretches most of the length of Main Street, but the center of action resides around the 2700 block. **Galleria Di Maio** is an art-deco mall with several spiffy shops including **Suji**, which carries fun, romantic women's clothing. ~ 2525 Main Street; 310-396-7614.

For designer labels at a fraction of their original cost, **The ◄ HIDDEN Address Boutique** is the place to go. The rich and famous from the nearby communities of Brentwood and Bel Air bring their hardly worn couturier clothes and accessories here to be resold. Why buy new when you can get a $1494 Vera Wang knit dress and jacket for $395 or a $2500 ivory satin Valentino gown for a mere $350? ~ 1116 Wilshire Boulevard; 310-394-1406; www.theaddressboutique.com, e-mail addressboutique@earthlink.net.

The last of Santa Monica's several shopping enclaves is in the center of town. Here you'll find **Santa Monica Place**, a mammoth triple-tiered complex with about 100 shops. This flashy atrium mall has everything from clothes to books to luggage to leather work, jewelry, toys, hats, and shoes. ~ On Broadway between 2nd and 4th streets; 310-394-1049; www.santamonicaplace.com.

Step out from this glittery gathering place and you'll immediately encounter the **Third Street Promenade**, a three-block walkway lined on either side with shops, upscale cafés, and movie theaters. ~ Located between Broadway and Wilshire Boulevard.

An anomaly among the mainstream stores on Third Street Promenade, **Arcana: Books on the Arts** has more than 100,000 books devoted to art, architecture, design, and photography, including hundreds of rare and out-of-print tomes. Some of the most remarkable books and gift items are hidden away in the back rooms so ask a staffer to help search. ~ 1229 Third Street Promenade; 310-458-1499; www.arcanabooks.com.

NIGHTLIFE **Ye Olde King's Head** might be the most popular British pub this side of the Thames. From dart boards to dark wood walls, trophy heads to draft beer, it's a classic English watering hole. Known throughout the area, it draws crowds of locals and expatriate Brits. ~ 116 Santa Monica Boulevard; 310-451-1402; www.yeoldekingshead.com, e-mail lisa88@earthlink.net.

McCabe's Guitar Shop is a folksy spot with live entertainment on weekends. The sounds are almost all acoustic and range from Scottish folk bands to jazz to blues to country. The concert hall is a room in back lined with guitars; performances run Friday through Sunday. Cover. ~ 3101 Pico Boulevard; 310-828-4497; www.mccabes.com.

For a raucous good time, try **O'Briens**. This bar is a loud, brash place that draws hearty crowds. There are live bands nightly, ranging from Irish rock to Texas blues. The decor is what you'd expect from an Irish pub, with old pictures and beer signs hanging from the walls. Cover on Friday and Saturday. ~ 2941 Main Street; 310-396-4725; www.obriensonmain.com.

For blues, R&B, soul, and jazz, try **Harvelle's**, which hosts local acts nightly. Cover. ~ 1432 4th Street; 310-395-1676; www.harvelles.com.

BEACHES & PARKS **SANTA MONICA CITY BEACH** 🐚 🏊 🎣 If the pop song is right and "L.A. is a great big freeway," then truly Santa Monica is a great big beach. Face it, the sand is very white, the water is very blue, the beach is very broad, and they all continue for miles. From Venice to Pacific Palisades, it's a sandbox gone wild. Skaters, strollers, and bicyclists pass along the promenade, sunbathers lie moribund in the sand, and volleyball players perform acrobatic shots. At the center of all this stands the Santa Monica Pier with its amusement park atmosphere. If it wasn't right next door to Venice this would be the hottest beach around. Lifeguards are on duty; facilities include picnic areas, restrooms, and snack bars. Swimming and surfing are good, and anglers usually opt for the pier. Parking fee, $7. ~ Route 1, at the foot of Colorado Avenue; 310-394-3261.

WILL ROGERS STATE BEACH 🚲 🏄 ⛵ Simple and home-spun he might have been, but Will Rogers was also a canny busi-nessman with a passion for real estate. He bought up three miles of beachfront property that eventually became his namesake park. It's a sandy strand with an expansive parking lot running the length of the beach. Route 1 parallels the parking area and beyond that rise the sharp cliffs that lend Pacific Palisades its name. The South Bay Bike Trail makes its northernmost appear-ance here. You'll find good swimming, and surfing is best in the area where Sunset Boulevard meets the ocean. Lifeguards are on duty. Facilities include restrooms, showers, and volleyball courts. Parking fees vary from $5 to $10, depending on season. ~ Located south along Route 1 from Sunset Boulevard in Pacific Palisades; 310-305-9546.

WILL ROGERS STATE HISTORIC PARK 🚶 🚲 🐎 The former ranch of humorist Will Rogers, this 186-acre spread sits in the hills of Pacific Palisades. The late cowboy's home is open for tours Tuesday through Sunday. There are hiking trails leading around the property and out into adjacent Topanga Canyon State Park. Horse fans can cheer on the Will Rogers Polo Club each week-end from April to October, or take horseback-riding lessons. Facilities include picnic areas, a museum, and restrooms. Day-use fee, $7 per vehicle. ~ 1501 Will Rogers State Park Road, Pacific Palisades; 310-454-8212, fax 310-459-2031.

SANTA MONICA MOUNTAINS NATIONAL RECREATION AREA 🚶 🚲 🐎 One of the few mountain ranges in the United States to run transversely (from east to west), the Santa Monicas reach for 50 miles to form the northwestern boundary of the Los Angeles basin. This federal preserve, which covers part of the mountain range, encompasses about 153,000 acres between Routes 1 and 101, much of which is laced with hiking trails (about 500 miles); in addition to high country, it includes a coastal stretch from Santa Monica to Point Mugu. Mountain lions, golden eagles, and many of California's early ani-mal species still survive here. ~ Several access roads lead into the area; Mulholland Drive and Mulholland Highway follow the crest of the Santa Monica Mountains for about 50 miles from Hollywood to Malibu. The National Park Service visitor center is at 401 West Hillcrest Drive, Thousand Oaks; 805-370-2301, fax 805-370-1850; www.nps.gov/samo.

> Considered a "botanical island," the Santa Monica Mountains sup-port chaparral, coastal sage, and oak forests; mountain lions, golden eagles, and many of California's early animal species still survive here.

▲ There is a group campground that accommodates 10 to 50 people; $2 per person, 10 person minimum. Reservations are required.

▼ ▼ ▼ ▼ ▼ ▼ ▼ ▼ ▼ ▼
Malibu

Malibu is a 27-mile-long ribbon lined on one side with pearly beaches and on the other by the Santa Monica Mountains. Famed as a movie star retreat and surfer's heaven, it is one of America's mythic communities. It has been a favored spot among Hollywood celebrities since the 1920s, when a new highway opened the region and film stars like Clara Bow and John Gilbert publicized the idyllic community. By the 1950s, Malibu was rapidly developing and becoming nationally known for its rolling surf and freewheeling lifestyle. The 1959 movie *Gidget* cast Sandra Dee and James Darren as Malibu beach bums and the seaside community was on its way to surfing immortality.

Today surfers by the dozens hang ten near the pier, just south of where movie and television greats live behind locked gates in lavish mansions on stretches of sand that normal folk have limited access to. That lack of access may change, however, as there's a movement afoot to make these hitherto "private" beaches public.

SIGHTS

Today blond-mopped surfers still line the shore and celebrities continue to congregate in beachfront bungalows. Matter of fact, the most popular sightseeing in Malibu consists of ogling the homes of the very rich. **Malibu Road**, which parallels the waterfront, is a prime strip. To make it as difficult as possible for common riffraff to reach the beach, the homes are built townhouse-style with no space between them. It's possible to drive for miles along the water without seeing the beach, only the backs of baronial estates. Happily there are a few accessways to the beach, so it's possible to wander along the sand enjoying views of both the ocean and the picture-window palaces. Among the Malibu beach accessways is one that local wags named after the "Doonesbury" character Zonker Harris.

What's amazing about these beachfront colonies is not the houses, but the fact that people insist on building them so close to the ocean that every few years several are demolished by high surf while others sink into the sand.

One of Malibu's loveliest houses is open to the public. The **Adamson House**, located at Malibu Lagoon State Beach, is a stately Spanish Colonial Revival–style structure adorned with ceramic tiles. With its bare-beam ceilings and inlaid floors, the house is a study in early-20th-century elegance. The building is surrounded by landscaped grounds, which border the beach at Malibu, overlook a lagoon alive with waterfowl, and are open to the public. Though there is an admission for the house, there is no fee to stroll the gardens. Closed Sunday through Tuesday. Admission. ~ 23200 Pacific Coast Highway; 310-456-8432; www.adamsonhouse.org.

After a prolonged closure due to storm damage, the **Malibu Pier** is once again open to the public. Saltwater fishing is popular at this seafront attraction, but you can also take a leisurely stroll down the breezy expanse. ~ 23000 Pacific Coast Highway.

At **Casa Malibu Inn on the Beach,** you'll be in a 21-room smoke-free facility with two suites that actually overhangs the sand. Located smack in the center of Malibu, the building features a central courtyard with lawn furniture and ocean view, oceanfront red-brick patio plus a balcony dripping with flowering plants. The rooms are decorated in an attractive but casual fashion; some have private balconies, fireplaces, kitchens, and/or ocean or garden views. Continental breakfast and wi-fi access are complimentary. ~ 22752 Pacific Coast Highway; 310-456-2219, 800-831-0858, fax 310-456-5418; www.casamalibu.com, e-mail casamalibu@earthlink.net. MODERATE TO ULTRA-DELUXE.

LODGING

The **Malibu Beach Inn** is posh and each of its 47 guest rooms offers spectacular ocean views from private balconies. Minibars round out the amenities. Some rooms feature jacuzzis and fireplaces. The location on the beach, one block from the Malibu Pier, makes this an ideal getaway. Two-night minimum stay on weekends. ~ 22878 Pacific Coast Highway; 310-456-6444, 800-462-5428, fax 310-456-1499; www.malibubeachinn.com, e-mail reservations@malibubeachinn.com. ULTRA-DELUXE.

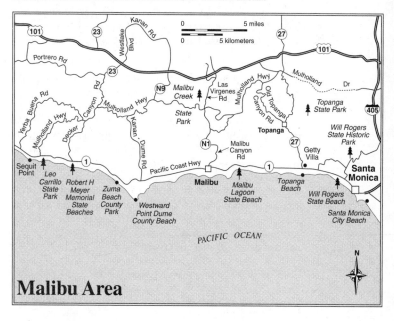

Malibu Area

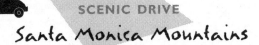

Santa Monica Mountains

When you've had your fill of Malibu's sand and surf, take a detour from Route 1 up into the Santa Monica Mountains. This chaparral country filled with oak and sycamore forests offers sweeping views back along the coast. As long as you remember which direction the water is (south), it's hard to get lost no matter how crazily the roads wind and twist. But if you descend on the wrong side of the mountains—that is, the north side—into the vast suburban sprawl of the San Fernando Valley, it can be an all-day challenge to find your way back around the mountains to Los Angeles. You'll find a fair amount of solitude if you take this drive on a weekday; on weekends you can expect traffic and full parking lots.

TOPANGA CANYON   Topanga Canyon Boulevard (Route 27), perhaps the best known of these mountain roads, turns off Route 1 five miles west of Santa Monica, or eight miles east of the village of Malibu, near the temporarily closed J. Paul Getty Villa. It curves gradually up the rocky canyon to the rustic town of **Topanga**. Back in the '60s this was a fabled retreat for flower children. Even today vestiges of the hippie era remain in the form of health food stores, New Age shops, and organic restaurants. Many of the woodframe houses are handcrafted, and the community still vibrates to a slower rhythm than coastal Malibu and cosmopolitan Los Angeles. Turn right in town on Entrada Road to go for a walk in **Topanga State Park** (page 377), the world's largest wilder-

At the northern Zuma Beach end of Malibu, you'll find the 16-room **Malibu Country Inn** perched atop a hillside above Pacific Coast Highway. Draped in bougainvillea, this property also has four suites and a restaurant. Since the inn isn't directly on the beach, only some of the rooms have partial ocean views; but all have unobstructed mountain views, private decks, coffee makers, and a floral-wicker decor scheme. The suites include fireplace and spa tub. There's a small pool surrounded by a garden of roses and other flowers and herbs. Continental breakfast at the restaurant is included. ~ 6506 Westward Beach Road at Pacific Coast Highway; 310-457-9622, 800-386-6787, fax 310-457-1349; www.malibucountryinn.com, e-mail info@malibucountry inn.com. DELUXE TO ULTRA-DELUXE.

DINING   The **Reel Inn Restaurant** is my idea of heaven—a reasonably priced seafood restaurant. Located across the highway from the beach, it's an oilcloth restaurant with an outdoor patio and a

ness located entirely within the boundaries of a major city. The gentlest and prettiest trails for a short hike start at Trippet Ranch near the park entrance. There's a parking fee.

MULHOLLAND HIGHWAY   To reach the top of the world, retrace your route from Entrada a short distance back down Topanga Boulevard to where Old Topanga Canyon Road forks off to the northwest. Turn right, follow this road for about five miles to the intersection with Mulholland Highway, and turn left. With its panoramic views of the Los Angeles Basin and San Fernando Valley, Mulholland is justifiably famous. On weekend nights, Mulholland Drive (as it's known in town) is a rendezvous for lovers and a drag strip for daredevil drivers, but the rest of the time you'll find it a sinuous country road far from the madding mobs. If you have time and don't mind paying another parking fee, **Malibu Creek State Park** (page 378), near the junction of Mulholland and Las Virgenes/Malibu Canyon Road, has a creek, a lake, lava rock formations, and miles of hiking trails.

KANAN DUME ROAD   Depending on how far you want to drive, any of the several roads that turn off Mulholland to the left will bring you out of the mountains at a nice beach; staying on Mulholland all the way to the end will, too. Our favorite is Kanan Dume Road, which comes out at **Westward Point Dume County Beach** (page 378). A great spot to while away the remainder of the afternoon, it's just 19 miles from Santa Monica on Route 1.

flair for serving good, healthful food at low prices. Among the fresh fish lunches and dinners are salmon, snapper, lobster, and swordfish. ~ 18661 Pacific Coast Highway; 310-456-8221, fax 310-456-3568. MODERATE.

For a possible celebrity sighting over your whole-wheat pancakes with strawberries and bananas or eggs Benedict, try Coogie's Beach Cafe. ~ 23755 Malibu Road; 310-317-1444, fax 310-317-1446. MODERATE.

Chef Nobu Matshisa has a string of popular Japanese eateries in hip cities (Tokyo, Milan, and New York, to name a few). The Malibu incarnation, **Nobu**, sits in a shopping mall, but still attracts its share of celebrities and loyal customers. The menu is decidedly Japanese with some Latin touches such as Peruvian-style chicken skewers, but its strength is the fresh fish highlighted in dishes such as *toro* (fatty tuna) tartare with caviar, yellowtail sashimi with jalapeños, black cod with miso, and Chilean sea bass with black bean sauce. Dinner only. ~ Malibu Country Mart,

3835 Cross Creek Road; 310-317-9140, fax 310-317-9136. ULTRA-DELUXE.

There's nothing fancy about **Malibu Fish & Seafood.** It's just a fish-and-chips stand across the highway from the beach with picnic tables under a covered patio outside, but the menu includes such tantalizing specialties as ahi tuna burgers and steamed lobster. The price is hard to beat when you add the ocean view. ~ 25653 Pacific Coast Highway; 310-456-3430, fax 310-456-8017; www.malibuseafood.com. BUDGET TO DELUXE.

Among the Malibu beach accessways is one that local wags named after the "Doonesbury" character Zonker Harris.

BeauRivage Mediterranean Restaurant, another gourmet gathering place, located across the highway from the ocean, boasts a cozy dining room and ocean-view terrace. With exposed-beam ceiling, brick trim, and copper pots along the wall, it has the feel of a French country inn. The dinner menu, however, is strictly Mediterranean. In addition to several pasta dishes, including gnocchi al pesto and linguine with clams, tomatoes, and garlic, there is New Zealand rack of lamb, Long Island duckling, Norwegian salmon, and grilled Italian bass. Dinner and Sunday brunch served. ~ 26025 Pacific Coast Highway; 310-456-5733, fax 310-317-1589; www.beaurivagerestaurant.com, e-mail beaurivagemalibu@aol.com. MODERATE TO ULTRA-DELUXE.

The quintessential Malibu dining experience is **Geoffrey's**, a clifftop restaurant overlooking the ocean. The marble bar, stucco walls, stone pebble tiles, and flowering plants exude wealth and elegance. The entire hillside has been landscaped and beautifully terraced, creating a Mediterranean atmosphere. The menu, a variation on California cuisine, includes filet mignon, day-boat scallops, tuna tartare, and prosciutto-wrapped salmon. The lunch and dinner menus are almost identical, and on Saturday and Sunday they also serve brunch. The setting, cuisine, and high prices make Geoffrey's a prime place for celebrity gazing. ~ 27400 Pacific Coast Highway; 310-457-1519, 800-927-4197, fax 310-457-7885; www.geoffreysmalibu.com, e-mail gmalibu@earthlink.net. DELUXE TO ULTRA-DELUXE.

When you're out at the beaches around Point Dume or elsewhere in northern Malibu, there are two adjacent roadside restaurants worth checking out. The cozy **Coral Beach Cantina** is a simple Mexican restaurant with a small patio. The menu contains standard south-of-the-border fare. ~ 29350 Pacific Coast Highway; 310-457-5503; www.coralbeachcantinamalibu.com. BUDGET TO MODERATE.

HIDDEN ►

HIDDEN ►

Over at **Zuma Sushi** they have a sushi bar and table service. In addition to the house specialty there are tempura and teriyaki dishes. Like its neighbor, this is a small, unassuming café. Dinner only. ~ 29350 Pacific Coast Highway; 310-457-4131. BUDGET TO MODERATE.

For a good meal near the beach there's **Neptune's Net Seafood.** ◄ HIDDEN Located across the highway from County Line Beach (at the Los Angeles–Ventura county border), it's a breezy café frequented by surfers. Fresh seafood, live lobster, sandwiches, burgers, and clam chowder, as well as oyster, shrimp, clam, and scallop baskets fill the bellies here. Ocean views at beach-bum prices. Closed one week before Christmas. ~ 42505 Route 1; 310-457-3095; www.neptunesnet.com. MODERATE.

Zuma Canyon Orchids offers elegant, exquisite prize-winning or- **SHOPPING** chids that can be shipped anywhere in the world. Or, since you're there, take a tour of the greenhouses. Closed Sunday. ~ 5949 Bonsall Drive; 310-457-9771; www.zumacanyonorchids.com.

Up in the secluded reaches of Topanga Canyon there are numerous artists and craftspeople who have traded the chaos of the city for the serenity of the Santa Monica Mountains. Craft shops come and go with frustrating regularity here, but it's worth a drive into the hills to see who is currently selling their wares.

For some easy listening, check out **BeauRivage Mediterranean** **NIGHTLIFE** **Restaurant.** There's a piano player Monday through Friday. A cozy bar and fireplace add charm to the scene. ~ 26025 Pacific Coast Highway; 310-456-5733; www.beaurivagerestaurant.com.

Malibu is largely a bedroom community; it's not known for wild nightlife, unless it's a private party at one of the beachfront homes in the colony. For music, theater, dance, and art, Pepperdine University's Center for the Arts offers performances and exhibitions by visiting artists in the **Smothers Theatre.** ~ 24255 Pacific Coast Highway; 310-506-4522; www.pepperdine.edu.

TOPANGA STATE PARK 🚶 🚲 🐎 Not much sand here, but you **BEACHES** will find forests of oak and fields of rye. This 10,000-plus-acre **& PARKS** hideaway nestles in the Santa Monica Mountains above Pacific Palisades. Along the 36 miles of hiking trails and fire roads are views of the ocean, San Gabriel Mountains, and San Fernando Valley. There are meadows and a stream to explore. The park climbs from 200 to 2100 feet in elevation, providing an introduction to one of Los Angeles' few remaining natural areas. Biking is restricted to the fire roads. Facilities include trails, picnic areas, and restrooms. Parking fee, $5 to $6. ~ From Route 1 in Malibu take Topanga Canyon Road up to Entrada Road. The park is at 20825 Entrada Road; 310-455-2465, fax 310-455-7085.

▲ There are eight hike-in sites, tents only; $2 per person per night.

TOPANGA BEACH 🏄 🚶 🚻 ⚓ This narrow sand corridor extends for over a mile. The adjacent highway breaks the quietude, but the strand is still popular with surfers and those wanting to be close to Malibu services. The swimming is good; surfing and windsurfing are excellent around Topanga Creek. Lifeguards are on duty; facilities include restrooms, showers, picnic tables, and barbecues. Parking fee, $5. ~ Route 1, near Topanga Canyon Road in Malibu; 310-451-2906, fax 310-458-6445.

MALIBU CREEK STATE PARK 🚶 🚴 🐎 🏄 ⚓ Once the location site for *M*A*S*H* and the original *Planet of the Apes*, this 7000-acre facility spreads through rugged, virgin country in the Santa Monica Mountains. Among its features are over 80 miles of hiking trails, four-acre Century Lake, and Malibu Creek, which is lined with willow and cottonwood. In spring the meadows explode with wildflowers; at other times of the year you'll encounter squirrels, rabbits, mule deer, coyotes, and bobcats. The bird life ranges from aquatic species such as ducks and great blue herons along the lake to hawks, woodpeckers, quail, and golden eagles. The lava hills, sloping grasslands, and twisted sedimentary rock formations make it an intriguing escape from the city. Facilities here include picnic areas, restrooms, and showers. Parking fee, $8. ~ Located off Mulholland Highway at 1925 Las Virgenes Road, Calabasas; 818-880-0367, fax 818-706-3869.

▲ There are 60 sites for tents and trailers or RVs (no hookups); $25 per night. Reservations: 800-444-7275.

MALIBU LAGOON STATE BEACH 🚶 🏄 🚻 ⚓ Not only is there a pretty beach here but an estuary and wetlands area as well. You can stroll the white sands past an unending succession of lavish beachfront homes, or study a different species entirely in the park's salt marsh. Here Malibu Creek feeds into the ocean, creating a rich tidal area busy with marine life and shorebirds. The surfing is world-renowned. This is also a very popular spot for swimming; lifeguards are on duty most of the year. Facilities include picnic areas and restrooms. Parking fee, $10. ~ Pacific Coast Highway at Cross Creek Road in Malibu; 818-880-0350.

HIDDEN ▶ **WESTWARD POINT DUME COUNTY BEACH** 🚶 🚴 🏄 🎣 🚻 ⚓ This long narrow stretch is really a southerly continuation of Zuma Beach. Unlike its neighbor, it is conveniently located away from the highway and bordered by lofty sandstone cliffs. For white sand serenity this is a choice spot. Matter of fact, on the far side of Point Dume you'll encounter what was once a popular nude beach in **Pirate's Cove**. Swimming is good, but beware of dangerous currents. Surfing is good along Westward Beach and off Point Dume. Lifeguards are on duty and restrooms are available. Parking fee, $7. ~ The park entrance is located near the southern entrance to Zuma Beach County Park; take Westward Beach Road off of Route 1 about six miles west of Malibu. To reach the beach at Pirate's Cove, take the trail over the Point Dume Headlands; 310-457-2525, fax 310-457-1632.

ZUMA BEACH COUNTY PARK This long, broad beach is a study in the territorial instincts of the species. Los Angeles County's largest beach park, it is frequented in one area by Latinos; "Vals," young residents of the San Fernando Valley, have staked claim to another section, while families and students inhabit another stretch (Zuma 3 and 4). Not as pretty as other Malibu beaches, Zuma offers more space and better facilities, such as restrooms, lifeguards, playgrounds, volleyball courts, and proximity to restaurants and stores. Swimming and surfing are good; for information on surf conditions, call 310-457-9701. Parking fee, $7. ~ Route 1, approximately six miles west of Malibu; 310-457-2525, fax 310-457-1632.

ROBERT H. MEYER MEMORIAL STATE BEACHES This unusual facility consists of three separate pocket beaches—**El Pescador, La Piedra,** and **El Matador.** Each is a pretty strand with sandy beach and eroded bluffs. Together they are among the nicest beaches in Malibu. My favorite is El Matador with its rock formations, sea stacks, and adjacent Malibu mansions. Use caution swimming at these beaches; there are unstationed lifeguards Memorial Day to Labor Day. Facilities include toilets. Access to the beaches is by stairs and short, steep trails. Parking for all beaches is $4. ~ Route 1, about 11 miles west of Malibu; 818-880-0350 (recorded information).

LEO CARRILLO STATE PARK Extending more than a mile, this white-sand corridor rests directly below Route 1. Named after Leo Carrillo, the TV actor who played sidekick Pancho in "The Cisco Kid," the beach offers tidepools and interesting rock formations. Nicer still is **Leo Carrillo North Beach**, a sandy swath located just beyond Sequit Point and backdropped by a sharp bluff. This entire area is a prime whale-watching site from February through April. At the south end of this 1600-acre park people have been known to bathe in the buff—but beware, if caught you will be cited. Facilities here include limited picnic areas, restrooms, showers, and lifeguards. Swimming and surfing are good; the best waves break around Sequit Point, and there's also excellent surfing a few miles north at **County Line Beach**. Day-use fee, $10. ~ On Route 1 about 14 miles west of Malibu. There's access to Leo Carrillo Beach North from the parking lot at 35000 Pacific Coast Highway; 818-880-0350 (recorded information).

Look for the natural tunnel under lifeguard tower #3 at Leo Carrillo State Park.

▲ There are 136 sites for tents and trailers or RVs (no hookups); $25 per night. Reservations: 800-444-7275.

Santa Catalina Island

There's something surprising about finding a little slice of the Mediterranean sitting in the middle of the sea just a short ferry ride from the urban sprawl of L.A. Along its 54 miles of shoreline, Santa Catalina Island offers sheer cliffs, pocket beaches, hidden coves, and some of the finest skin diving anywhere. To the interior, mountains rise sharply to over 2000 feet in elevation. Island fox and 150-200 bison range the island while its waters teem with marlin, swordfish, and barracuda. Happily, this unique habitat is preserved for posterity and adventurous travelers by an arrangement under which 86 percent of the island lies undeveloped, protected by the Santa Catalina Conservancy. Avalon, the famous coastal resort enclave, is the only town on the island. The rest is given over to mountain wilderness and pristine shoreline.

As romantic as its setting is the history of the island. Originally part of the Baja coastline, it broke off from the mainland eons ago and drifted 100 miles to the northwest. Its earliest inhabitants arrived perhaps 4000 or 5000 years ago, leaving scattered evidence of their presence before being supplanted by the Gabrieleño Indians around 500 B.C. A society of sun worshippers, the Gabrieleños constructed a sacrificial temple, fished island waters, and traded ceramics and soapstone carvings with mainland tribes, crossing the channel in canoes.

Juan Rodríguez Cabrillo discovered Catalina in 1542, but the place proved of such little interest to the Spanish that, other than Sebastian Vizcaíno's exploration in 1602, they virtually ignored it. By the 19th century, Russian fur traders, attracted by the rich colonies of sea otters, succeeded in exterminating both the otters and the indigenous people. Cattle and sheep herders took over the Gabrieleños' land while pirates and smugglers, hiding in Catalina's secluded coves, menaced the coast. Later in the century, Chinese laborers were secretly landed on the island before being illegally carried to the mainland.

Other visionaries, seeing in Catalina a major resort area, also took control. After changing hands several times, the island was purchased in 1919 by William Wrigley, Jr. The Wrigley family—better known for their ownership of a chewing gum company and the Chicago Cubs baseball team—developed Avalon for tourism and left the rest of the island to nature. Attracting big-name entertainers and providing an escape from urban Los Angeles, Avalon soon captured the fancy of movie stars and wealthy Californians. Today the island is popular with Angelenos who are looking for a nearby getaway, be it a day or a week, while tourists enjoy the novelty of visiting a laidback and rural island just a short ferry ride away from the hustle and bustle of the rest of L.A.

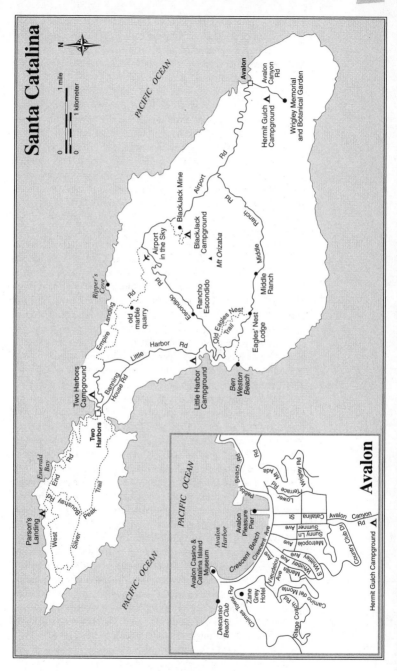

Santa Catalina

N

1 mile
1 kilometer
0

PACIFIC OCEAN

Avalon
Avalon Canyon Rd
Hermit Gulch Campground
Wrigley Memorial and Botanical Garden

Airport Rd
Blackjack Mine
Airport in the Sky
Blackjack Campground
Mt Orizaba
Rancho Escondido
Ranch Rd
Middle Ranch
Middle
Ripper's Cove
old marble quarry
Empire Landing Rd
Escondido Rd
Old Eagles Nest Trail
Eagles' Nest Lodge
Harbor Rd
Little Harbor Rd
Banning House Rd
Little Harbor Campground
Ben Weston Beach
Two Harbors Campground
Two Harbors
Emerald Bay
West End Rd
Boushay Rd
Silver Peak
Peak Trail
Parson's Landing

PACIFIC OCEAN
PACIFIC OCEAN

Avalon

PACIFIC OCEAN

Pebbly Beach Rd
Lower Terrace Rd
Wrigley Rd
Ada Av
Avalon Pleasure Pier
Avalon Harbor
Sunny Ln
Summer Ave
Metropole Ave
St
Catalina
Avalon Canyon Rd
Country Club Dr
Avalon Casino & Catalina Island Museum
Crescent Beach
Crescent Ave
E Whitley Ave
Whitley Ave
Marilla Ave
Beaudelou Ave
Camino del Monte
Chimes Tower Rd
Zane Grey Hotel
Descanso Beach Club
Stage Coast
Hermit Gulch Campground

SIGHTS   Set in a luxurious amphitheater of green mountains, **Avalon** is like a time warp of Southern California early in the 20th century. The architecture is a blend of Mediterranean and Victorian homes as well as vernacular structures designed by creative locals who captured both the beautiful and whimsical.

From the ferry dock you can wander **Crescent Avenue**, Avalon's oceanfront promenade. Stroll out along the **Avalon Pleasure Pier**, located at Crescent Avenue and Catalina Street, for a view of the entire town and its surrounding crescent of mountains. Located along this wood plank promenade are food stands, the harbormaster's office, and bait-and-tackle shops. The **Catalina Island Visitors Bureau and Chamber of Commerce** has an information center here that will help orient you to Avalon and the island. ~ #1 Green Pier; 310-510-1520, fax 310-510-7606; www.catalinachamber.com, e-mail info@catalinachamber.com.

Among the pier kiosks is a ticket booth offering guided tours in a **semi-submersible vessel** out to a nearby cove filled with colorful fish and marine plant life. Known as Catalina's "undersea gardens," the area is crowded with rich kelp beds and is a favorite haunt of spotted and calico bass, golden adult Garibaldi, and leopard sharks. **Santa Catalina Island Company** has tours in the day and also at night when huge floodlights are used to attract sea life. In the summer they seek out the spectacular flying fish that seasonally inhabit these waters. They also offer coastal cruises and inland motor tours. Drop by their visitor information center. ~ 423 Crescent Avenue; 310-510-2000, 800-626-1496, fax 310-510-2300; www.visitcatalinaisland.com, e-mail sales@scico.com.

Farther along the waterfront, dominating the skyline, sits the **Catalina Casino**. A massive circular building painted white and capped with a red tile roof, it was built in 1929 after a Spanish Moorish design. What can you say other than that the place is famous: it has appeared on countless postcards and travel posters. The ballroom has heard the big band sounds of Count Basie and Tommy Dorsey and the entire complex is a study in art deco with fabulous murals and tile paintings. ~ On Casino Way at the end of Crescent Avenue; 310-510-2000, 800-626-1496; www.visitcatalinaisland.com.

Downstairs is the **Catalina Island Museum**, which holds a varied collection of local artifacts. Of particular interest is the contour relief map of the island, which provides an excellent perspective for anyone venturing into the interior. The museum also features an award-winning interactive exhibit chronicling the history of steamship transportation and other exhibits relating to elements of local culture. Closed Thursday from January through March. Admission. ~ Catalina Casino; 310-510-2414, fax 310-510-2780; www.catalinamuseum.org, e-mail info@catalinamuseum.org.

Another point of particular interest, located one and a half miles inland in Avalon Canyon, is the **Wrigley Memorial and Botanical Garden**, a tribute to William Wrigley, Jr. The monument, an imposing 130-foot structure fashioned with glazed tiles and Georgia marble, features a spiral staircase in a solitary tower. The gardens, a showplace for native island plants, display an array of succulents and cactus. Admission. ~ 1400 Avalon Canyon Road; 310-510-2897.

The most exhilarating sightseeing excursion in Avalon lies in the hills around town. Head out Pebbly Beach Road along the water, turn right on **Wrigley Terrace Road**, and you'll be on one of the many terraces that rise above Avalon. The old **Wrigley Mansion** (currently The Inn on Mt. Ada, Wrigley Road), an elegant estate with sweeping views, was once the (ho hum) summer residence of the Wrigley family.

During Prohibition Catalina proved a favorite place among rumrunners and bootleggers.

Other scenic drives on the opposite side of town lie along Stage and Chimes Tower roads. Here you'll pass the **Zane Grey Hotel**, a 1926 pueblo adobe that was formerly the Western novel writer's home. ~ 199 Chimes Tower Road; 310-510-0966, fax 310-510-1340; www.zanegreypueblo hotel.com, e-mail zanegrey@catalinaisp.com.

Both routes snake into the hills past rocky outcroppings and patches of cactus. The slopes are steep and unrelenting. Below you blocks of houses run in rows out to a fringe of palm trees and undergrowth. Gaze around from this precarious perch and you'll see that Avalon rests in a green bowl surrounded by mountains.

Regardless of how you journey into Catalina's outback, there's only one way to get there, **Airport Road**. This paved thoroughfare climbs steadily from Avalon, offering views of the rugged coast and surrounding hills. Oak, pine, and eucalyptus dot the hillsides as the road follows a ridgetop with steep canyons falling away on either side. **Mt. Orizaba**, a flat-topped peak which represents the highest point on the island, rises in the distance.

A side road out to BlackJack Campground leads past **BlackJack Mine**, a silver mine closed since early in the century. Today little remains except tailing piles and a 520-foot shaft. Then the main road climbs to Catalina's **Airport in the Sky** (310-510-0143), a small landing facility located at 1600-foot elevation.

From the airport you might want to follow a figure eight course in your route around the island, covering most of the island's roads and taking in as much of the landscape as possible (beyond the airport all the roads are dirt). Just follow Empire Landing Road, a curving, bumping track with side roads that lead down past an **old marble quarry** to **Ripper's Cove**. Characteristic of the many inlets dotting the island, the cove is framed by sharply rising hills. There's a boulder-and-sand beach here and a coastline bordered by interesting rock formations.

Two Harbors, at the intersection of the figure-eight's loops, is a half-mile wide isthmus connecting the two sections of Catalina Island. A small fishing pier, several tourist facilities, and a boat harbor make this modest enclave the only developed area outside Avalon.

Gold fever swept Santa Catalina in 1863 as miners swept onto the island, but the rush never panned out.

From here **West End Road** curves and climbs, bends and descends along a rocky coast pocked with cactus and covered by scrub growth. There are Catalina cherry trees along the route and numerous coves at the bottom of steep cliffs. Not for the faint-hearted, West End Road is a narrow, bumpy course that winds high above the shore.

Anchored off **Emerald Bay** are several rock islets crowded with sea birds. From **Parson's Landing**, a small inlet with a brown-gray sand beach, dirt roads continue in a long loop out to the west end of the island, then back to Two Harbors.

Catalina possesses about 400 species of flora, some unique to the island, and is rich in wildlife. Anywhere along its slopes you are likely to spy quail, island fox, and mule deer. Bison, placed on the island by a movie company filming a Western way back in the 1920s, graze seemingly everywhere. En route back toward Avalon, Little Harbor Road climbs into the mountains. From the hilltops around **Little Harbor** you can see a series of ridges that drop along sheer rockfaces to the frothing surf below.

Discovery Tours (through the Santa Catalina Island Company) can take you up to **Rancho Escondido**, a working ranch that boards champion Arabian horses. There's an arena here where trainers work these exquisite animals through their paces, and a "saddle and trophy room" filled with handcrafted riding gear as well as prizes from major horse shows. ~ 800-322-3434.

Back at Little Harbor, Middle Ranch Road cuts through a mountain canyon past **Middle Ranch**, a small spread with livestock and oat fields. En route lies **Eagles' Nest Lodge**, a stagecoach stop dating to 1890. Numbered among the antique effects of this simple woodframe house are wagon wheels and a split-rail fence. Carry on to Airport Road then back to Avalon, completing this easy-eight route around an extraordinary island.

LODGING   One fact about lodging in Catalina everyone seems to agree upon is that it is overpriced. Particularly in the summer, when Avalon's population swells from about 3200 to over 10,000, hotels charge stiff rates for rooms. But what's a traveler to do? The island is both pretty and popular, so you have no recourse but to pay the piper.

It's also a fact that rates jump seasonally more than on the mainland. Summer is the most expensive period, winter the cheapest, with spring and fall somewhere in between. Weekend rates are also sometimes higher than weekday room tabs and usually require a two-night minimum stay. So make sure you book lodging before you arrive on the island; package deals that include ferry and accommodations are available.

The last fact of life for lodgers to remember is that since most of the island is a nature preserve, most hotels are located in Avalon.

Low-price lodgings are as rare as snow in Avalon. But at the **Hotel Atwater** you'll find accommodations to suit all budgets. The newer wing offers 26 country-style rooms in the deluxe-to-ultra-deluxe range. The older part of the hotel has wicker chairs and blond wood furniture. Besides, it has a friendly lobby with oak trim and tasteful blue furniture, plus dozens of rooms to choose from. Closed mid-November to April. ~ 125 Sumner Avenue; 310-510-1788, 800-322-3434, fax 310-510-1673; www.visit catalinaisland.com. MODERATE TO ULTRA-DELUXE.

One of Santa Catalina's most popular hotels is the **Pavilion Lodge,** a 73-room facility on Avalon's waterfront street. Designed around a central courtyard, it offers guests a lawn and patio for sunbathing. The rooms contain modern furniture, ceramic tile flooring, and Italian bedding. If you want to be at the heart of downtown in a comfortable if undistinguished establishment, this is the place. ~ 513 Crescent Avenue; 310-510-1788, 800-322-3434, fax 310-510-2073; www.scico.com. ULTRA-DELUXE.

Plainly put, the **Hotel Vista del Mar** is a gem. Each of the 13 spacious Mediterranean-style rooms is decorated in soft pastels and features a wet bar, fireplace, and full tiled bath. All surround an open-air atrium courtyard lobby, where guests enjoy ocean breezes and views from comfortable wicker rockers. One smaller room is priced deluxe, while courtyard rooms command ultra-deluxe rates. ~ 417 Crescent Avenue; 310-510-1452, 800-601-3836; www.hotel-vistadelmar.com, e-mail vista@catalinas.net. ULTRA-DELUXE.

Farther along the same street is **Hotel Villa Portofino** with 35 rooms situated around a split-level brick patio. The accommodations are small but have been stylishly decorated with modern furniture, dressing tables, and wallpaper in pastel shades. There are tile baths with stall showers; a few have tubs. The oceanview suites have marble tubs. A small lobby downstairs has been finished with potted plants and marble. ~ 111 Crescent Avenue; 310-510-0555, 888-510-0555, fax 310-510-0839; www.hotel villaportofino.com, e-mail vpstaff@catalinaisp.com. DELUXE TO ULTRA-DELUXE.

It's a big, bold, blue and white structure rising for five levels above the hillside. **Hotel Catalina** has been a fixture on the Avalon skyline since 1892. The 32-unit, completely non-smoking facility features a comfortable lobby complete with overhead fans, plus a sundeck and jacuzzi. The sleeping rooms are small but comfy with standard furnishings; many offer ocean views and all the rooms have ceiling fans, small fridges, and VCRs. There are also four trim little cottages that are warmly decorated. A bright, summer atmosphere pervades the place. ~ 129 Whittley Avenue; 310-510-0027, 800-540-0184, fax 310-510-1495; www.hotelcata lina.com, e-mail info@hotelcatalina.com. MODERATE TO DELUXE.

La Paloma Cottages, a rambling complex consisting of several buildings, features a string of eight contiguous cottages. These are cozy units with original decor and comfortable furnishings. There are also six larger family units (with kitchens) available in a nearby building. Set on a terraced street in a quiet part of town, La Paloma is attractively landscaped. There are no phones or daily maid service in the rooms. However, at **Las Flores,** an addition to the original hotel, you can get pricier rooms with maid service and a whirlpool bath to boot. ~ 326 Sunny Lane; 310-510-0737, 800-310-1505, fax 310-510-2424; www.catalina.com/lapaloma. html, e-mail lapaloma@catalinaisp.com. BUDGET TO DELUXE.

Best Western Catalina Canyon Resort and Spa is a chic, modern 72-room complex complete with pool, jacuzzi, sauna, restaurant, and bar. This Mediterranean-style hotel sits on a hillside in Avalon Canyon. The grounds are nicely landscaped with banana plants and palm trees. Each guest room is furnished in an upscale beach style with wrought iron and granite, adorned with art prints, and decorated in a motif of natural colors. ~ 888 Country Club Drive; 310-510-0325, 800-253-9361, fax 310-510-0900; www.catalina.com/canyon. ULTRA-DELUXE.

The romantic **Hotel St. Lauren** rises with a pink blush a block from the sand above Catalina's famed harbor. The Victorian-style hotel is a honeymoon paradise, with 42 spacious rooms and jacuzzi tubs in minisuites. ~ 231 Beacon Street; 310-510-2299, 800-645-2496, fax 310-510-1369; www.stlauren.com. DELUXE TO ULTRA-DELUXE.

AUTHOR FAVORITE

Banning House Lodge, is an early-20th-century hunting lodge. Set in the isthmus that connects the two sections of Santa Catalina, it's a low-slung shingle building with a dining room and a mountain-lodge atmosphere. The living room boasts a brick fireplace. The guest rooms are trimly and individually decorated with throw rugs and wood furniture. The lodge provides an excellent opportunity to experience the island's outback. Continental breakfast is served in the lodge's breakfast room. ~ Two Harbors; 310-510-4228, 800-626-1496, fax 310-510-1303; www.visit catalinaisland.com. DELUXE TO ULTRA-DELUXE.

Rare and incredible is the only way to describe **The Inn on Mt. Ada**. Nothing on the island, and few places along the California coast, compare. Perched on a hillside overlooking Avalon and its emerald shoreline, this stately hostelry resides in the old Wrigley mansion, a 7000-square-foot Georgian Colonial home built by the chewing gum baron in 1921. A masterwork of French doors and elegant columns, curved ceilings, and ornamental molding, the grande dame is beautifully appointed with antiques and plush furnishings. The entire ground floor—with rattan-furnished sitting room, oceanfront veranda, formal dining room, and spacious living room—is for the benefit of visitors. Wine and hors d'oeuvres are served in the evening and there's a full breakfast and lunch served to guests and a limited number of visitors. The wonder of the place is that all this luxury is for just six guest rooms, two of which have semiprivate terraces, guaranteeing personal service and an atmosphere of intimacy. The private rooms are stylishly furnished in period pieces and adorned with a creative selection of artwork. The room fee includes a golf cart for transportation. Reserve at least two months in advance. Closed Christmas Eve and Christmas Day. ~ 398 Wrigley Road, Avalon; 310-510-2030, 800-608-7669, fax 310-510-2237; www.innonmtada.com. ULTRA-DELUXE.

DINING

As with Catalina hotels, there are a few points to remember when shopping for a restaurant. Prices are higher than on the mainland. With very few exceptions the dining spots are concentrated in Avalon; services around the rest of the island are minimal. Also, business is seasonal, so restaurants may vary their schedules, serving three meals daily during summer and weekends but only dinner during winter. The wisest course is to check beforehand.

Original Antonio's Pizzeria & Deli is a hole-in-the-wall, but a hole-in-the-wall with panache. It's chockablock with junk—old pin-up pictures, record covers, dolls, and trophies. There's sawdust on the floor and a vague '50s theme to the place. The food— pizza, pasta, and hot sandwiches—is good, filling, and served daily at lunch and dinner. "Come on in," as the sign suggests, "and bask in the ambience of the decaying 1950s." ~ 114 Sumner Avenue; 310-510-0060; e-mail antonios@catalinaisp.com. BUDGET TO MODERATE.

Up the hill less than a half-mile from the harbor, the mission-style **Catalina Country Club Restaurant** was once the spring training clubhouse for the Chicago Cubs. The fresh salmon BLT with organic red wine and a crispy apple dumpling stand out from typical American steak and seafood dishes. The only spot with a good ocean view is the private balcony, so ask ahead. The adjacent bar is great for an after-dinner drink; it connects to the old Cubs locker room. Reservations are essential. ~ One Country Club Drive; 310-510-7404. MODERATE TO DELUXE.

HIDDEN ► The Busy Bee is a local gathering place located right on the beach. It's hard to match the views from the patio of this simple café. This is one place in Catalina that's open for breakfast, lunch, and dinner year-round. For lunch you can dine on vegetable platters, tacos, tostadas, salads, and sandwiches while gazing out at the pier and harbor. The dinner menu offers buffalo burgers, fried shrimp, teriyaki chicken, and steak. ~ 306-B Crescent Avenue; 310-510-1983, fax 310-510-1205. MODERATE TO DELUXE.

The other half of the vintage stucco-and-red-tile building housing the Busy Bee is the site of **Armstrong's Seafood Restaurant and Fish Market**. The interior is trimly finished in knotty pine and white tile with mounted gamefish on the walls. Since the establishment doubles as a fish market you can count on fresh seafood. The menu is the same at lunch and dinner with only the portions and prices changing. Mesquite-grilled dishes include mahimahi, scallops, swordfish, skewered shrimp, and steak. They also feature lobster, ahi, and orange roughy. You can dine indoors or on the patio right along the waterfront, making Armstrong's reasonable prices a bargain. ~ 306-A Crescent Avenue; 310-510-0113, fax 310-510-0266; www.armstrongseafood.com, e-mail info@armstrongseafood.com. MODERATE TO DELUXE.

On the beachfront, **El Galleon** is a local favorite for juicy steaks, local and live Maine lobster, barbecue ribs, and fresh abalone. While the food is excellent, be forewarned that karaoke starts after lunch and continues until closing. For a quieter dinner and fresh-air views, ask for a table on the patio. ~ 411 Crescent Avenue; 310-510-1188, fax 310-510-2949; e-mail elgalleon@catalinaisp.com. MODERATE TO ULTRA-DELUXE.

No one sails to Santa Catalina Island searching for bargains. Everything here has been shipped from the mainland and is that much more expensive as a result.

For a step upscale head down the street to **Ristorante Villa Portofino**, where you'll find pink stucco walls and candlelit tables set off by flowers. With art-deco curves and colorful art prints the place has a Mediterranean feel. The Continental cuisine includes several veal dishes, scampi, grilled rack of lamb, lobster, and a selection of pasta dishes. This is the place for a romantic meal. Dinner only. Closed in January; closed Wednesday in winter. ~ 101 Crescent Avenue; 310-510-2009, fax 310-510-1780; www.ristorantevillaportofino.com. MODERATE TO ULTRA-DELUXE.

Buffalo Springs Station, situated up in the mountains at 1600 feet, is part of Catalina's Airport in the Sky complex. This facility serves egg dishes, hot cakes, buffalo burgers, and a variety of sandwiches. There's not much to the self-service restaurant itself, but it adjoins a lobby with stone fireplace and a tile patio that overlooks the surrounding mountains. Breakfast, lunch, and early dinner are served. ~ 310-510-2196, fax 310-510-2140; www.buffalospringsstation.com. BUDGET.

Catalina's remotest dining place is the **Harbor Reef Restaurant**, located way out in the Two Harbors area. This rambling establishment has a dining room done in nautical motif with fish nets and shell lamps. There's also an adjoining patio for enjoying the soft breezes that blow through this isthmus area. Fresh seafood and fresh fish are to be expected, of course, as are steak and pasta dishes. Reservations are recommended. ~ Two Harbors; 310-510-4215. MODERATE TO ULTRA-DELUXE.   ◀ *HIDDEN*

Next to the Harbor Reef Restaurant there's an adjoining **snack bar** serving three meals daily; breakfast and lunch in winter months. It offers egg dishes, sandwiches, burgers, pizza, and burritos. ~ Two Harbors. BUDGET.

The town of Avalon has a row of shops lining its main thoroughfare, Crescent Avenue, and other stores along the streets running up from the waterfront. Within this commercial checkerboard are also several mini-malls, one of which, **Metropole Market Place**, is a nicely designed complex. ~ Crescent and Whitney avenues.   **SHOPPING**

Half the stores in town are souvenir or curio shops. I'd wait 'til you return to that shopping metropolis 26 miles across the sea.

Like all other Catalina amenities, nightspots are concentrated in Avalon. The **Chi Chi Club**, renovated to its original '50s tiki panache, is the hottest danceclub on the island with live and deejay music (ranging from Top-40 and hip-hop to retro) and an enthusiastic crowd. Live entertainment, including comedy shows, female impersonators, and bands, are offered on summer weekends. Occasional cover. ~ 105 Sumner Avenue; 310-510-2828.   **NIGHTLIFE**

Also check the schedule for **Catalina Casino**. This fabulous vintage ballroom still hosts big bands and most of the island's major events. The Avalon also shows films at night in its restored golden-era motion picture theater. ~ Located at the end of Crescent Avenue; 310-510-2000, 800-322-3434.

If you are planning to camp on Catalina, there are a few things to know. First, there is a fee for camping and reservations are a must (reservation numbers are listed under the particular park).   **BEACHES & PARKS**

In addition to designated beaches, camping is permitted in many of the island's coves. These are undeveloped sites with no facilities; most are readily accessible by boat. Patrolling rangers collect the fees here.

For information on hiking permits, camping, and transportation to campgrounds, contact the **Santa Catalina Island Conservancy** (125 Claressa Avenue, Avalon; 310-510-1421; www.cata

linaconservancy.org), **Two Harbors Enterprises** (P.O. Box 5086, Two Harbors; 310-510-4202; www.visittwoharbors.com),or the agent at **Two Harbors Campground** (310-510-8368) who seems to know just about everything relating to camping in the area.

DESCANSO BEACH About as relaxing as Coney Island, this beach is at the center of the action. Avalon's main drag parallels the beach and a pier divides it into two separate strips of sand. Facing Avalon Harbor, the strand is flanked on one side with a ferry dock and along the other by the famous Catalina Casino. Full service facilities (including restrooms and beach rentals) are available on the street adjacent to the beach; lifeguards are also on duty in summer. Fishing is good from the pier, and the harbor provides protection from the surf, making it an excellent swimming area. ~ Along Crescent Avenue in Avalon; 310-510-7408.

DESCANSO BEACH CLUB Somehow the appeal of this private enclave escapes me. A rock-strewn beach on the far side of the Catalina Casino, it seconds as a mooring facility for sailboats. Granted, there is a rolling lawn dotted with palm trees and the complex is nicely surrounded by hills. But with all the commotion at the snack bar and volleyball courts it's more like being on an amusement pier than a beach. Besides that, you have to pay to get onto the beach. Once there, you'll find good swimming, a seasonal restaurant, restrooms, and showers. ~ Located off Crescent Avenue past Casino Way; 310-510-7410.

HERMIT GULCH CAMPGROUND This grassy field, dotted with palm and pine trees, is the only campground serving the Avalon area. Located up in Avalon Canyon inland from the beach, it provides a convenient and inexpensive way to visit Avalon and utilize its many services. There are pretty views of the surrounding hills and hiking trails are nearby. Facilities include picnic areas, restrooms, and showers. ~ Located on Avalon Canyon Road a mile from downtown Avalon; 310-510-8368, fax 310-510-7254; www.scico.com/camping.

▲ There are extensive camping facilities, ranging from tent cabins to basic camping to equipment rentals. There are 43 tent sites, $12 per adult per night. Ten-day maximum stay. Reservations are recommended in July and August.

HIDDEN ▶ **BLACKJACK CAMPGROUND** Situated at 1600 feet elevation, this facility sits on a plateau below Mt. BlackJack, the island's second-highest peak. It's a lovely spot shaded by pine and eucalyptus trees and affording views across the rolling hills and out along the ocean. Among backcountry facilities this is about the least popular on the island. The campground has picnic areas, toilets, and showers. ~ Located south of The Airport in the

Touring Catalina
Sans Rental Car

When it comes time to venture further afield, you'll find that traveling around Santa Catalina Island is more complicated than it first seems. Preserving nature is probably what the island's caretakers had in mind when they made driving cars illegal on Catalina for non-residents. While golf carts are allowed in Avalon, visitors must navigate the remainder of the island's roads by two wheels, two feet, or a shuttle.

You can hike or bicycle to most places on the island, although permits are required outside Avalon. They can be obtained from the **Santa Catalina Island Conservancy**. ~ 125 Claressa Avenue; 310-510-2595; www.catalinaconservancy.org. Permits are also available at **The Airport in the Sky**. ~ 310-510-0143. You can also call **Two Harbors Visitors Services**. ~ P.O. Box 5086, Two Harbors, CA 90704; 310-510-0303.

Brown's Bikes rents bicycles, tandems, mountain bikes, and kids' bikes. Maps and helmets are included. ~ 107 Pebbly Beach Road; 310-510-0986; www.catalinabiking.com. In Avalon proper, rent golf carts from outfits like **Island Rentals**. ~ 125 Pebbly Beach Road; 310-510-1456. You can also try **Catalina Auto Rental**, which rents golf carts as well as mountain bikes. Bike rentals include helmets. ~ 309 Crescent Avenue; 310-510-0111. There are also taxis in town.

Catalina Safari Bus provides a shuttle service to Two Harbors. ~ 310-510-2800, 800-785-8425. Santa Catalina Island Conservancy, the agency charged with overseeing the island, shuttles visitors to the airport and provides jeep tours.

Sky off Airport Road. Seasonal shuttle available from Avalon to BlackJack Trail Junction; 310-510-2800, fax 310-510-7254; www.scico.com/camping.

▲ There is a hike-in campground with 10 sites; $12 per person per night. Ten-day maximum stay. Reservations are required.

BEN WESTON BEACH 🏃 🏊 🏄 ⚓ A favorite among locals, this pewter-colored beach is surrounded by rocky hills. Located at the end of a long canyon road, it is serene and secluded. Avalon residents come here to flee the tourists, so you might consider making it your hideaway. This is a day-use beach only. Fishing and swimming are good, and it is one of the island's best spots for surfing. Facilities are limited to toilets. ~ Located about two miles south of Little Harbor off Middle Ranch Road; 310-510-1421.

LITTLE HARBOR CAMPGROUND 🏊 🎣 🏄 ⚓ On the southwest shore of the island, this camp sits near a sandy beach between rocky headlands. It's studded with palm trees and occasionally filled with grazing bison, making it one of the island's prettiest facilities. In addition, Shark Harbor, a section of Little Harbor, is excellent for shell collecting and bodysurfing. Fishing, swimming, and skindiving are good here; facilities include picnic areas, toilets, and cold showers. ~ Located about seven miles east of Two Harbors along Little Harbor Road; 310-510-2800, fax 310-510-7254; www. scico.com/camping.

The Santa Catalina Island Conservancy runs Jeep eco-tours of the interior, where you may catch sight of foxes, bald eagles, and even American bison.

▲ The campground has a 150-person maximum (tents only). $12 per person per night. Ten-day maximum stay.

TWO HARBORS CAMPGROUND 🏃 🚲 🏊 🎣 🚿 ⚓ Set along a series of terraces above a brown sand beach, this facility is adjacent to the services at Two Harbors. It's also a convenient base camp from which to hike out along the island's west end. Facilities include picnic areas, restrooms, and showers. The fishing and swimming are good, and the colorful waters here make skindiving especially rewarding. ~ Located next to Two Harbors in Little Fisherman's Cove; 310-510-2800, fax 310-510-7254; www.scico.com.

▲ The facilities here are extensive and include 42 tent sites and 13 tent cabins with added amenities, a 24-hour-a-day ranger, and more. Prices vary; call for information. Ten-day maximum stay.

PARSON'S LANDING 🏃 🚲 🏊 🎣 ⚓ The most remote of Catalina's campgrounds, this isolated facility sits along a small brown-gray sand beach with grass-covered hills in the background. Fishing, swimming, and skindiving are all good; facilities include picnic areas and toilets. The beach is ideal for shell combing, amethyst and beach glass. Accessible only by hike or kayak.

~ Located seven miles west of Two Harbors along West End Road; 310-510-2800, fax 310-510-7254; www.scico.com/camping.

▲ The campground holds a maximum of 45 people; there are 8 tent-only sites; $12 per person per night. Ten-day maximum stay.

Outdoor Adventures

Fish the waters around Los Angeles and you can try your hand at landing a barracuda, calico bass, halibut, white sea bass, white croaker, or maybe even a relative of Jaws.

SPORT-FISHING

L.A. Harbor Sportfishing offers scheduled and chartered trips for yellowtail, bass, tuna, barracuda, and bonito. ~ 1150 Nagoya Way, Berth 79, San Pedro; 310-547-9916; www.laharborsport fishing.com. **Pierpoint Landing** has six charter boats offering half-day to overnight fishing charters. ~ 200 Aquarium Way, Long Beach; 562-983-9300; www.pierpoint.net.

Redondo Sportfishing offers half- and three-quarter-day trips in and around the Santa Monica Bay on six boats. ~ 233 North Harbor Drive, Redondo Beach; 310-372-2111; www.redon dosportfishing.com.

For half- and three-quarter-day trips seeking yellowtail and white sea bass, contact **Marina del Rey Sportfishing**. ~ Dock 52, Fiji Way, Marina del Rey; 310-822-3625.

In Catalina you can contact the **Santa Catalina Island Visitors Bureau and Chamber of Commerce** for listings of private boat owners who outfit sportfishing expeditions. ~ 310-510-1520; www.catalinachamber.com.

DIVING

If you'd rather search for starfish than stars along L.A.'s coastline, you'll find an active diving scene.

To explore L.A.'s submerged depths, contact **Pacific Sporting Goods**, which provides lessons and equipment and organizes boat trips. ~ 11 39th Place, Long Beach; 562-434-1604.

Pacific Wilderness is a PADI training center that sells and rents equipment. ~ 1719 South Pacific Avenue, San Pedro; 310-833-2422.

Lessons at **Dive 'n Surf** are also PADI-certified; dive trips to Catalina and Santa Barbara are available. ~ 504 North Broadway, Redondo Beach; 310-372-8423; www.divensurf.com. For full-day trips around local islands call **Sea D Sea**. ~ 1911 South Catalina Avenue, Redondo Beach; 310-373-6355.

Blue Cheer Ocean Dive & Surf runs trips from Ventura to Anacapa and Santa Cruz islands. ~ 1112 Wilshire Boulevard, Santa Monica; 310-319-1370. For NAUI and SSI certification classes and dive trips near the islands contact **Scuba Haus**. ~ 2501 Wilshire Boulevard, Santa Monica; 310-828-2916.

Malibu Divers rents and sells gear and periodically runs full-day trips to Catalina and other locations. Private lessons are available. ~ 21231 Pacific Coast Highway, Malibu; 310-456-2396; www.malibudivers.com.

If you're visiting Los Angeles from winter to early spring, hop aboard a whale-watching vessel and keep your eyes peeled for plumes and tails.

Without doubt Santa Catalina offers some of the finest scuba diving anywhere in the world. Perfectly positioned to attract fish from both the northern and southern Pacific, it teems with sea life. Large fish ascend from the deep waters surrounding the island while small colorful species inhabit rich kelp forests along the coast. There are caves and caverns to explore as well as the wrecks of rusting ships.

Several outfits rent skindiving and scuba equipment and sponsor dive trips, including **Catalina Divers Supply**. ~ 310-510-0330. **Island Charters, Inc.** offers similar services. ~ 310-510-2616. For guided or unguided full-day chartered trips try **Argo Diving Service**. ~ 310-510-2208.

WHALE WATCHING

During the annual migration (January through March) several outfits offer local whale-watching trips. This is a fun thing to do on a clear day, whether you see any whales or not.

Pierpoint Landing will take you out on the briny deep for a three-hour cruise. ~ 200 Aquarium Way, Long Beach; 562-983-9300. Harbor Breeze Corporation takes two-and-a-half-hour trips along the coast. ~ Dock #2, 100 Aquarium Way, Long Beach; 562-983-6880; www.longbeachcruises.com.

Spirit Cruises gives you a guarantee with your trip. You see a whale or you get a gift certificate for a later trip. ~ Berth 77, San Pedro; 310-548-8080; www.spiritmarine.com. **L.A. Harbor Sportfishing** offers two-and-a-half-hour trips. ~ Berth 79, San Pedro; 310-547-9916; www.laharborsportfishing.com.

SURFING & WIND-SURFING

"Surfing is the only life," so when in the Southland, sample a bit of Los Angeles' seminal subculture. Redondo, Hermosa, and Manhattan beaches have come to represent the L.A. scene. Other popular spots include Royal Palms State Beach and Torrance County Beach's Malaga Cove. If you're in Malibu, check out the waves at Topanga Beach, Malibu Surfrider Beach, and Leo Carrillo State Beach. Santa Catalina also has its share of waves: Ben Weston Beach for surfing and Shark Harbor for bodysurfing. Remember, it's more fun to hang ten than just hang out.

Rent a surfboard, bodyboard, or wetsuit from **Manhattan Beach Bike and Skate Rentals**. Closed Monday; also closed Tuesday in winter. ~ 1116 Manhattan Avenue, Manhattan Beach; 310-372-8500. **Jeffers** offers surfboards and boogieboards. ~ 39 14th Street, Hermosa Beach; 310-372-9492.

You'll find surfboard, boogieboard, and wetsuit rentals in Malibu at **Zuma Jay Surfboards**. ~ 22775 Pacific Coast Highway, Malibu; 310-456-8044; www.zumajays.com.

For kayak rentals, contact **Malibu Ocean Sports**. Closed Monday and Tuesday in winter. ~ 16910 Pacific Coast Highway, Sunset Beach; 562-592-0800; www.malibuoceansports.com. **KAYAKING**

On Santa Catalina Island, **Descanso Beach Ocean Sports** offers rentals and several different guided expeditions in the waters around Catalina, among them a two-hour trip to Frog Rock and a full-day excursion that includes hiking and picnicking. ~ Descanso Beach, Avalon; 310-510-1226, fax 310-510-3577; www.kayakcatalinaisland.com.

Los Angeles may well be the skating capital of California, and skateboarding, of course, is the closest thing to surfing without waves. Between the two of them, you can't get much more L.A., so find a way to put yourself on wheels. **SKATING & SKATE-BOARDING**

Manhattan Beach Bike and Skate Rentals rents skates. ~ 1116 Manhattan Avenue, Manhattan Beach; 310-372-8500. **Rentals on the Beach** offers inline skates, bikes, tandems, and other gear at three beach locations. ~ Near the parking lots at Washington Boulevard, Venice Boulevard, and Rose Avenue. **Spokes 'n Stuff** has two convenient locations and rents both inline skates and rollerskates. ~ At the parking lot on Admiralty Way at Jamaica Bay Inn Hotel, Marina del Rey, 310-306-3332; and near the Santa Monica Pier in Loews Santa Monica, 310-395-4748. Along the Santa Monica Pier, **Sea Mist Skate Rentals** has inline skates, mountain bikes, and everything else needed for a day on the South Bay Trail. ~ 1619 Ocean Front Walk, Santa Monica; 310-395-7076.

Tee off in the gentle sea breeze—L.A.'s coastal climate is ideal for spending a day on the greens. Just don't swing too hard, because those golf balls don't float! Most courses have 18 holes and rent clubs and carts. **GOLF**

The beautiful **El Dorado Park Municipal Golf Course**, home of the Long Beach Open, has two putting greens and a driving range. ~ 2400 Studebaker Road, Long Beach; 562-430-5411. The 18-hole **Skylink Golf Course** is a duffer's delight with club and cart rentals, a driving range, night lighting, and an on-site sports bar. ~ 4800 East Wardlow Road, Long Beach; 562-421-3388. The hilly **Recreation Park** offers both an 18-hole and a 9-hole course. ~ 5001 Deukmeijian Drive, Long Beach; 562-494-5000.

The coastal **Los Verdes Golf Course** is one of the finest public facilities in Southern California; along with spectacular views you'll find a driving range and two putting greens. ~ 7000 West Los Verdes Drive, Rancho Palos Verdes; 310-377-7370; www. americangolf.com.

If you can take a break from the action in Venice, head to the nine-hole **Penmar Golf Course**. ~ 1233 Rose Avenue, Venice; 310-396-6228.

Catalina Visitors Golf Club is a par-32 nine-hole course with plenty of sand traps. ~ 1 Country Club Drive, Avalon; 310-510-0530; www.visitcatalinaisland.com.

TENNIS

A visit to the Los Angeles coast is reason enough to re-string your racquet and start enjoying the weather. These waterfront communities sport an abundance of hardtop courts, though there's usually a fee to play; call ahead to check.

There are 15 lighted courts available at **El Dorado Park**. ~ 2800 Studebaker Road, Long Beach; 562-425-0553. The **Billie Jean King Tennis Center** offers eight lighted courts. ~ 1040 Park Avenue, Long Beach; 562-438-8509.

The **Alta Vista Tennis Courts** have eight lighted courts as well. ~ 715 Julia Avenue, Redondo Beach; 310-318-0670. Two lighted courts are available at **Spectrum Redondo Beach**. ~ 819 North Harbor Drive, Redondo Beach; 310-372-8868.

In Santa Monica, it's a good idea to call for reservations at public tennis courts during the summer. **Reed Park** has six lighted courts. ~ 1133 7th Street, Santa Monica; 310-394-6011. **Memorial Park** offers four lighted courts. ~ Olympic Boulevard at 14th Street, Santa Monica; 310-394-6011. Also try one of the six courts at **Ocean View Park**. ~ Barnard Way south of Ocean Park Boulevard, Santa Monica; 310-394-6011.

BIKING

Along the coast, there are scores of shoreline bike trails and routes for scenic excursions. Whether you're up for a leisurely and level beachfront loop, or a more strenuous trek through coastal cliffside communities, the weather and scenery make this area a beautiful place for a bike ride.

The **South Bay Bike Trail**, with over 22 miles of coastal vistas, is an easy ride and extremely popular. It runs from RAT Beach in Torrance to Will Rogers State Beach in Pacific Palisades. The path intersects the Ballona Creek Bikeway in Marina Del Rey, which extends seven miles east and passes the Venice Boardwalk, as well as piers and marinas along the way.

Naples, a Venice-like neighborhood in Long Beach, provides a charming area for freeform bike rides. There are no designated paths but you can cycle with ease past beautiful homes, parks, and canals.

Of moderate difficulty is the **Palos Verdes Peninsula** coastline trail. Offering wonderful scenery, the 14-mile roundtrip ride goes from Malaga Cove Plaza in Palos Verdes Estates to the Wayfarers Chapel. (Part of the trail is a bike path, the rest follows city streets.)

The **Venice Boardwalk** is a casual, two-mile bike ride where a host of kooky characters and performers line the promenade, vying for your attention.

A strenuous but worthwhile excursion is a bike ride along **Mulholland Drive**. Not recommended during commuter hours, this route traverses the spine of the Santa Monica Mountains and offers fabulous views of the city and ocean.

The **Santa Monica Loop** is an easy ride starting at San Vicente Boulevard and going up Ocean Avenue, past Palisades Park and the Santa Monica Pier. Most of the trail is on bike lanes and paths; five miles roundtrip.

In **Catalina**, free use of bikes is allowed only in Avalon. Elsewhere permits are required: they may be obtained from the **Santa Catalina Island Conservancy**. Closed Sunday. ~ 125 Claressa Avenue, Avalon; 310-510-2595; www.catalinaconservancy.org. Cross-channel carriers have special requirements for transporting bicycles and must be contacted in advance for complete details.

Bike Rentals To rent mountain bikes, cruisers, or tandems, try **Manhattan Beach Bike and Skate Rentals**. ~ 1116 Manhattan Avenue, Manhattan Beach; 310-372-8500. In Hermosa Beach, **Jeffers** rents beach cruisers. ~ 39 14th Street, Hermosa Beach; 310-372-9492. **Spokes 'n Stuff** offers mountain bikes, tandems, and cruisers. ~ Near the pier in Loews Santa Monica; 310-395-4748. Also in Santa Monica, **Sea Mist Skate Rentals** has mountain bikes and helmets. ~ 1619 Ocean Front Walk, Santa Monica; 310-395-7076. In Catalina try **Brown's Bikes**. ~ 107 Pebbly Beach Road, Avalon; 310-510-0986.

HIKING

The terrain of this region offers a wide array of pedestrian options, from beaches and tidepools to busy boardwalks to the trails of the rugged coast range. Depending on where you go for your hike, you may want your boots, spiffy street shoes, or Tevas. For a unique foray, try exploring a beached shipwreck or hiking in to the familiar-looking filming location of *M*A*S*H*. The only

AUTHOR FAVORITE

For a nostalgic visit to the location of many movie and television shows, including *M*A*S*H* and *Love Is a Many Splendored Thing*, check out the **Craggs-Century Ranch Trail** (3.8 miles) in Malibu Creek State Park. The moderate trail travels along Malibu Creek to Rock Pool, the Gorge, and Century Lake. Continue over a rocky trail to view the *M*A*S*H* site.

common denominators for hiking around here are the fine weather and sweeping vistas.

All distances listed for hiking trails are one way unless otherwise noted.

The Los Angeles portion of the **California Coastal Trail** begins on Naples Island in Long Beach. From here the trail is a varied journey across open bluffs, boat basins, rocky outcroppings accessible only at low tide, along beachwalks filled with rollerskaters, jugglers, and skate boarders, and up goat trails with stunning views of the Pacific Ocean.

PALOS VERDES PENINSULA Set beneath wave-carved bluffs, the moderate **Palos Verdes Peninsula Trail** (5 miles) takes you along a rocky beachside past coves and teeming tidepools. The trail begins at Malaga Cove and ends at Point Vicente Lighthouse.

If you're interested in exploring a shipwreck, head to Palos Verdes Estate Shoreline Preserve, near Malaga Cove, and hike the **Seashore–Shipwreck Trail** (2.25 miles). The moderate-to-difficult trail hugs the shoreline (and requires an ability to jump boulders), skirting tidepools and coves, until it arrives at what is left of an old Greek ship, the *Dominator*. Wear sturdy hiking shoes and bring water.

SANTA MONICA MOUNTAINS It's difficult to imagine, but Los Angeles does have undeveloped mountain wilderness areas prime for hiking. The Santa Monica Mountains offer chaparral-covered landscapes, grassy knolls, mountain streams, and dark canyons.

Topanga State Park has over 36 miles of trails. The **Musch Ranch Loop Trail** (5-mile loop) passes through five different types of plant communities. Or try the moderate **Santa Ynez Fire Road Trail** (7 miles), which guides you along the Palisades Highlands with views of the ocean and Santa Ynez Canyon. In spring wildflowers add to the already spectacular scenery.

Several trails trace the "backbone" of the Santa Monica Mountains. In fact, the **Backbone Trail** roughly follows the crest of these mountains, from Will Rogers State Historic Park to Point Mugu State Park—a 70-mile stretch. If you're not up for the long haul, you can pick up pieces of the trail at several points along the way, including the Circle X Ranch, Malibu Creek State Park, and Topanga State Park.

The moderate **Eagle Rock to Eagle Springs Loop Trail** (6 miles), for instance, begins in Topanga State Park and traverses oak and chaparral countryside on its way to Eagle Spring. Another section of the "Backbone Trail," **Malibu Creek State Park Loop** (15.5 miles roundtrip) begins near the crossroads of Piuma Road and Malibu Canyon Road. The difficult trail follows fire roads and offers choice views of the ocean and Channel Islands before it climbs up to Kanan-Dume Road. **Charmlee Park** is a little-visited wildflower paradise in the hills overlooking the ocean.

HIDDEN ▶

A 1.75-mile trail offers great coastal views. Take Encinal Canyon Road four miles into the mountains from Pacific Coast Highway. **Solstice Canyon Park** is another hidden beauty with trails offering hikes of up to six miles. The moderate three-mile roundtrip to the Roberts Ranch House ruins follows a perennial stream and ends at the burned-out remains of a terraced dream house that retains a palm-shaded charm. Take Corral Canyon Road a quarter-mile north from Pacific Coast Highway.

◄ *HIDDEN*

An easy (though in spots difficult) climb up **Zuma Ridge Trail** (6 miles) brings you to the center of the Santa Monica Mountains and affords otherworldly views of the Pacific. The trail begins off Encinal Canyon Road, one and a half miles from Mulholland Highway.

MALIBU   **Zuma-Dume Trail** (3 miles) in Malibu takes you on an easy walk from Zuma Beach County Park, along Pirate's Cove (which used to be a nude beach) to the Point Dume headlands and Paradise Cove, a popular diving spot.

For a pleasant, easy hike along part of the Malibu coast dotted with coves and caves and providing terrific swimming, surfing, and skindiving, head out the **Leo Carrillo Trail** (1.5 miles), located at Leo Carrillo State Beach. Or to hike up a gently sloping hill for a view of the coastline, take the easy, nearby **Yellow Hill Trail** (2 miles).

SANTA CATALINA ISLAND   For a true adventure in hiking, gather your gear and head for Santa Catalina. A network of spectacular trails crisscrosses this largely undeveloped island. Bring plenty of water and beware of rattlesnakes and poison oak. You'll also need a hiking permit, free from the Santa Catalina Island Conservancy. ~ 125 Claressa Avenue, Avalon; 310-510-2595.

Empire Landing Road Trail (11.5 miles) begins at BlackJack Junction and ends up at Two Harbors. The path passes a lot of interesting terrain and provides glimpses of island wildlife, especially buffalo. (You can arrange with the ferry service to ride back to the mainland from Two Harbors.)

Other routes to consider are **Sheep Chute Trail** (3.3 miles), a moderate hike between Little Harbor and Empire Landing; and **Parson's Landing to Starlight Trail** (4 miles), a strenuous trek between Silver Peak Trail and Parsons Landing.

Route 1, which parallels the coast throughout Los Angeles County, undergoing several name changes during its course, is the main coastal route. **Route 101** shadows the coast further inland, while **Route 405** provides access to the Los Angeles basin from San Diego and **Route 10** arrives from the east.

▼ ▼ ▼ ▼ ▼ ▼ ▼ ▼ ▼ ▼
Transportation

CAR

Two airports bring visitors to the L.A. coast area: the small **Long Beach Airport** and the very big, very busy **Los Angeles Interna-**

AIR

tional Airport (LAX). LAX is served by many domestic and foreign carriers. Currently (and this seems to change daily) the following airlines fly into LAX: Alaska Airlines, America West Airlines, American Airlines, Continental Airlines, Delta Air Lines, Hawaiian Airlines, Northwest Airlines, Southwest Airlines, and United Airlines.

International carriers are also numerous: Air Canada, Air France, Air New Zealand, All Nippon Airways, British Airways, China Airlines, Japan Airlines, KLM, Lufthansa German Airlines, Mexicana Airlines, Philippine Airlines, QANTAS Airways, Singapore Airlines, and TACA International Airlines. ~ 310-646-5252; www.lawa.org/lax.

The **Airport in the Sky** (the Catalina Airport), set at 1600-foot elevation in the mountains of Santa Catalina, may be the prettiest landing strip anywhere. The small terminal building conveys a mountain lodge atmosphere with a stone fireplace adorned by a trophy bison head. ~ 310-510-0143. **National Air**, also called **Catalina Vegas Airlines**, services the airport from the mainland. ~ 800-339-0359.

Another way to Catalina is **Island Express**, a helicopter service from Long Beach and San Pedro. They also offer around-the-island tours. ~ 310-510-2525; www.islandexpress.com.

TRAIN

Amtrak will carry you into Los Angeles via the "Coast Starlight" from the North, the "Pacific Surfliner" from San Diego, the "Southwest Chief" from Chicago, and the "Sunset Limited" from New Orleans. The downtown L.A. station, Union Station, is at 800 North Alameda Street. To get to coastal destinations, taxis and buslines are available. ~ 800-872-7245; www.amtrak.com.

BOAT

Several companies provide regular transportation to Catalina by boat. The island is just 22 miles across the sea, but it's still necessary to make advance reservations. **Catalina Express** has service to Avalon and Two Harbors from the Catalina Terminal in San Pedro; service to Avalon leaves from Long Beach next to the *Queen Mary*. ~ 310-519-1212. **Catalina Passenger Service** makes daily trips to Catalina from Orange County. ~ 400 Main Street, Newport Beach; 949-673-5245.

BUS

Greyhound Bus Lines has service to the Los Angeles area from around the country. The Long Beach terminal is at 1498 Long Beach Boulevard (562-218-3011), and the Los Angeles terminal is at 1716 East 7th Street (213-629-8400).

CAR RENTALS

Avis Rent A Car (800-331-1212), **Budget Rent A Car** (800-221-1203), **Enterprise Rent A Car** (800-736-8222), **Hertz Rent A Car** (800-654-3131), and **National Car Rental** (800-227-7368) are located at, or within shuttle distance of, the Long Beach Airport.

To save even more money, try agencies that rent used cars. In the Long Beach area this includes **Robin Hood Rent A Car**. ~ 310-518-2292, 800-743-2992.

In Catalina, golf carts are the only vehicles permitted for sightseeing in Avalon. Check with **Catalina Auto and Bike Rental**. ~ 301 Crescent Avenue; 310-510-0111. **Island Rentals** is another option. ~ 125 Pebbly Beach Road; 310-510-1456. For further information on vehicle rentals on Catalina see the "Santa Catalina Island" section in this chapter.

Long Beach Transit transports riders throughout the Long Beach area. Among the services is the Tour of the Art bus, which carries visitors between major points of interest. ~ 1963 East Anaheim, Long Beach; 562-591-2301; www.lbtransit.com.

PUBLIC TRANSIT

MTA **Bus Line** serves all of Los Angeles County; disabled riders can call a hotline for information, 800-621-7828 (this number is functional only within the designated area). ~ 213-626-4455, 800-266-6883; www.mta.net.

In Santa Monica, call the **Big Blue Bus**, which hits such destinations as LAX and downtown L.A. ~ Santa Monica Municipal Bus Lines, 612 Colorado Avenue; 310-451-5444; www.bigbluebus.com.

In Catalina, **Catalina Safari Bus** provides daily buses from Avalon to Two Harbors and all campgrounds. This shuttle service also takes passengers from Avalon to the Airport in the Sky. ~ 310-510-2800, 800-785-8425.

In Santa Monica, call **Taxi Taxi**. ~ 310-828-2233. **Long Beach Yellow Cab** provides taxi service in Long Beach. ~ 562-435-6111. In Catalina you'll find the **Catalina Cab Company**. ~ 310-510-0025.

TAXIS

SEVEN

Orange Coast

Places are known through their nicknames. More than official titles or proper names, sobriquets reveal the real identity of a region. "Orange Coast" can never describe the 42 miles of cobalt blue ocean and whitewashed sand from Seal Beach to San Clemente. That moniker derives from the days when Orange County was row on row with orchards of plump citrus. Today prestigious homes and marinas sprout from the shoreline. This is the "Gold Coast," habitat of beachboys, yachtsmen, and tennis buffs, the "American Riviera."

The theme that ties the territory together and gives rise to these nicknames is money. Money and the trappings that attend it—glamour, celebrity, elegance, power. The image of Orange County is of a sun-blessed realm of beautiful people, where politics are right-wing and real estate prices are astronomical.

Some half-dozen freeways crisscross the broad coastal plane where Spain's Gaspar de Portolá led the first overland expedition into present-day Orange County in 1769. Today, nearly three million people live, work, and play where, during the mid-19th century, a few hundred Mexican ranchers tended herds of livestock on a handful of extensive land grants.

Ever since Walt Disney founded his fantasy empire here in the 1950s, Orange County has exploded with population and profits. In Disney's wake came the crowds, and as they arrived they developed housing projects and condominium complexes, mini-malls and business centers.

Along the coast progress also levied a tremendous toll but has left intact some of the natural beauty, the deep canyons and curving hills, soft sand beaches and sharp escarpments. The towns too have retained their separate styles, each projecting its own identifying image.

Seal Beach, Orange County's answer to small-town America, is a pretty community with a sense of serenity. To the south lies Huntington Beach, a place that claims the nickname "Surfing Capital of the World." The social capital of this beach-side society is Newport Beach, a fashion-conscious center for celebrities, business executives, and those to whom God granted little patience and a lot of money.

Corona del Mar is a model community with quiet streets and a placid waterfront. Laguna Beach is an artist colony so *in* that real estate prices have driven the artists *out*. Dana Point represents a marina development in search of a soul. San Juan Capistrano, a small town surrounding an old mission, is closer to its roots than any place in this futuristic area. San Clemente, which served as President Nixon's Western White House, is a trim, strait-laced residential community. Linking this string of beach towns together is Route 1, the Pacific Coast Highway, which runs south from Los Angeles to Capistrano Beach.

The geography throughout Orange County is varied and unpredictable. Around Newport Beach and Huntington Beach, rugged heights give way to low-lying terrain cut by rivers and opening into estuaries. These northerly towns, together with Dana Point, are manmade harbors carved from swamps and surrounded by landfill islands and peninsulas. Huntington Harbor, the first of its kind, consists of eight islands weighted down with luxury homes and bordered by a mazework of marinas. To the south, particularly around Laguna Beach, a series of uplifted marine terraces create bold headlands, coastal bluffs, and pocket coves.

Land here is so highly prized that it's not surprising the city fathers chose to create more by dredging it from river bottoms. The Gabrieleño and Juañero Indians who originally inhabited the area considered the ground sacred, while the Spanish who conquered them divided it into two immense land grants, the San Joaquin and Niguel ranchos.

Establishing themselves at the San Juan Capistrano mission in 1776, the Spanish padres held sway until the 19th century. By the 1830s American merchants from the East Coast were sending tall-masted trading ships up from Cape Horn. Richard Henry Dana, who sailed the shoreline, giving his name to Dana Point, described the area in *Two Years Before the Mast* as "the most romantic spot along the coast."

By the 1860s, after California became a state, the Spanish ranchos were joined into the Irvine Ranch, a land parcel extending ten miles along the coast and 22 miles inland, and controlled with a steel fist by a single family.

They held in their sway all but Laguna Beach, which was settled in the 1870s by pioneers developing 160-acre government land grants. A freestyle community, Laguna developed into an artist colony filled with galleries and renowned for its cliff-rimmed beaches. Over the years artists and individualists—including the late LSD guru Timothy Leary and a retinue of hippies, who arrived during the 1960s—have been lured by the simple beauty of the place.

Laguna Beach has always relied on natural beauty, but Newport Beach has worked for its reputation. During the 1870s the harbor was built; channels were dredged, marshes filled, and stone jetties constructed as stern-wheelers began frequenting the "new port" between San Diego and Los Angeles. Newport Pier followed in 1888, allowing cattle hides and grain from Irvine Ranch to be loaded onto waiting ships.

While Laguna Beach developed as a resort community during the 1880s, it wasn't until 1904 that Newport Beach became a noted pleasure stop. That was the year the red trolley arrived and the town became the terminus for the Pacific Electric, Los Angeles' early streetcar line.

Within two years the population jumped sixfold and land values went into orbit. Balboa Pavilion was built in 1905 and soon became the center for Max Sennett–type bathing beauty contests. Years later it would be a dancehall and gambling casino, and finally a showroom for the Big Bands.

By the 1960s those brassy sounds had surrendered to the twanging strains of electric guitars as the Orange Coast earned its final nickname, "Surfer Heaven." Dick Dale, the "King of the Surf Guitar," hit the top of the charts with "Pipeline," setting off a wave that the Beach Boys and Jan and Dean rode to the crest. Down in Dana Point local boy Bruce Brown contributed to the coast culture in 1964 with a surf flick called *The Endless Summer*, which achieved cult status and earned for its director a reputation as "the Fellini of foam."

As the Orange Coast, particularly Huntington Beach, earned its surfing reputation in the 1960s, the entire county broke from the power of the Irvine Ranch. The suicide of a third-generation scion resulted in the land passing from a conservative family to an aggressive foundation. Within a few years it built Newport Center, the area's highrise district, and crowned it with the chic Fashion Island enclave. Orange County rapidly entered the modern age of multimillion-dollar development, adding a certain luster to its image (tarnished in the 1990s when risky investments forced the county temporarily into bankruptcy) and granting to its shoreline, for better or worse, an everlasting reputation as California's "Gold Coast."

▼▼▼▼▼▼▼▼▼

Seal Beach

Rare find indeed, this is a small town with a small-town beach tucked between Huntington Beach and Long Beach. In addition to a swath of fine-grain sand, there is a fishing pier from which you can engage in sportfishing. Oil derricks loom offshore and Long Beach rises in the misty distance. The beach, located along Ocean Avenue, features a pier and is popular with swimmers and surfers alike.

LODGING
Ayres Hotel is emblematic of the changes happening in many of Southern California's small beach towns, where old-fashioned B&Bs are being replaced with more upscale small hotels. Close to the Seal Beach Pier and convenient to Route 405 and the Long Beach Convention Center, the Ayers has a European boutique feel, with sophisticated wallpaper, high ceilings, and clean, modern furnishings in all 112 spacious rooms. The staff is exceptionally warm and knowledgeable. A full American breakfast is served. ~ 12850 Seal Beach Boulevard; 562-596-8330, 800-706-4890; www.ayreshotel.com. MODERATE.

DINING
You've probably discovered that Southern California is a land of extremes. One of the great examples of that is **Bonadonna's Shore House Cafe**. The decor, the atmosphere, and the menu all bring to mind the word "exaggeration." They describe their portions as "huge"—and that's *not* an exaggeration. Italian, Mexican, Chinese, Texas chili, prime rib—they offer them all abun-

dantly 24/7/365! ~ 941 East Pacific Coast Highway; 562-430-0116, fax 562-430-2298. MODERATE.

Walt's Wharf restaurant specializes in creative seafood dishes but there's also Walt's oyster bar with a premium well, more than 40 imported beers, and more than 400 wines. Start off with appetizers such as the blackened ahi sashimi. Entrées vary with the catch of the day but may include oak-grilled swordfish, sea bass with roasted macadamia nut sauce, or blackened Louisiana catfish with cilantro cream and fried polenta. ~ 201 Main Street;

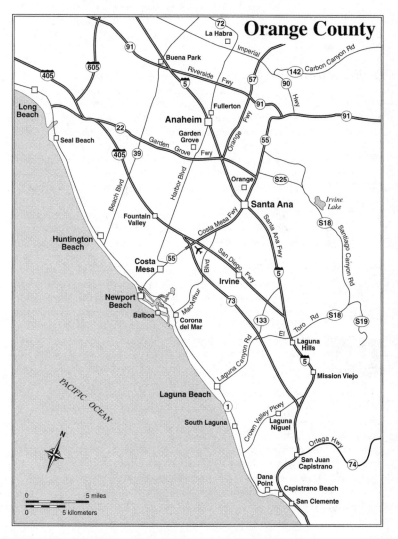

562-598-4433, fax 562-598-8554; www.waltswharf.com, e-mail info@waltswharf.com. MODERATE TO ULTRA-DELUXE.

For something different in a Mexican restaurant, try the **Yucatan Grill**, specializing in dishes from the Mexican Caribbean such as *cochinita pibil* (pork barbecued in banana leaves with a tangy sauce) and Mayan *dorado* (mahimahi with a pungent orange sauce). There are also offerings from other parts of the Caribbean, such as Jamaican jerk chicken and steak *cubano*. With seating both indoors and out, the atmosphere is supercasual. Weekend breakfast offers complimentary bloody marys and mimosas. ~ 550 Pacific Coast Highway; 562-430-4422, fax 562-430-0305; www.yucatangrill.com. MODERATE.

Huntington Beach

In most of Orange County, a reference to "Duke" will conjure images of John Wayne, former resident and namesake of the airport here; in Huntington Beach, however, natives are more likely to assume you're talking about Duke Kahanamoku, the Hawaiian Olympic swimmer who brought the sport of surfing to the mainland in 1911. His bust stands at the foot of the Huntington Beach Pier, and his legacy continues through the international surfing competitions held here. At the surfing museum, located a few blocks from the beach, you can learn anything else you want to know about the history and culture of the sport.

There are, of course, many other ways to enjoy the beautiful coastline here: you can pedal the bike paths, dig for Pismo clams, hike in a wetlands preserve, and warm up at beach bonfires in the evening. But no matter what you do, you'll encounter surfing in some shape or form, even if it's only to admire a wave rider in the distance or watch a "woody," loaded with boards, driving through the streets. While the official story is that the discovery of offshore oil made Huntington Beach the largest city in Orange County, beach bums will argue that it was the discovery of how to ride the onshore breaks.

sights

AUTHOR FAVORITE

When Disneyland was young and I was a child, the Beach Boys' anthems gave me surfing daydreams, thwarted by the fact that I lived hundreds of miles from the nearest beach. So today I treasure the nostalgic **International Surfing Museum**. The showplace sits two blocks from the beach and features boards, boards, and more boards as well as an array of surfing paraphernalia and historical exhibits. Hours vary; call for schedule. Admission. ~ 411 Olive Avenue, Huntington Beach; 714-960-3483, fax 714-960-1434; www.surfingmuseum.org, e-mail intsurf ing@earthlink.net.

As Route 1 buzzes south from Los Angeles it is bordered on one side by broad beaches and on the other by **Bolsa Chica Ecological Reserve**. An important wetlands area dotted with islands and overgrown in cord grass and pickleweed, this 1250-acre preserve features a three-mile-long loop trail. Among the hundreds of animal species inhabiting or visiting the marsh are egrets, herons, and five endangered species. There are raucous seagulls as well as rare Belding's savannah sparrows and California least terns. There is an interpretive center (closed Monday) with scientific displays, educational material, and trail guides. ~ The accessways are across from the entrance to Bolsa Chica State Beach and at 3842 Warner Avenue; 714-846-1114, fax 714-846-4065; www. bolsachica.org, e-mail info@bolsachica.org.

Leave this natural world behind and you will enter the surf capital of California. In the mythology of surfing, Huntington Beach rides with Hawaii's Waimea Bay and the great breaks of Australia. Since the 1920s boys with boards have been as much a part of the seascape as blue skies and billowing clouds.

Synonymous with Huntington Beach is the **Huntington Beach Pier**. First built in 1904 for oil drilling purposes, it has been damaged by storms and extensively repaired four times. The pier's current incarnation, which opened in July 1992, is 1856 feet long, 38 feet above the water, and has a life expectancy of 100 years. But, as anyone who has lived by the ocean will agree, that century-long life span could be shortened dramatically by the next winter storm. ~ At the end of Main Street.

At the **Newland House Museum** visitors can see what life in 19th-century Huntington Beach was all about. Listed on the National Register of Historic Places and built in 1898, the grand dame is filled with furnishings and antiques from the town's early days. Open weekends, weather permitting. ~ 19820 Beach Boulevard; 714-962-5777.

About four miles from the beach and 15 minutes from Disneyland, **The Comfort Suites** caters to leisure travelers and corporate clients. The large orange three-story building surrounded by palm trees features stylish theme suites. Full breakfast included. ~ 16301 Beach Boulevard; 714-841-1812, 800-714-4040, fax 714-841-0241; www.huntingtonbeachcomfortsuites.com. MODERATE TO DELUXE.

The adventurous curiosity seeker might want to try staying at the **Edelweiss Inn**. Frankly, this 30-room hostelry has seen better days. In fact, it's very difficult to get the innkeeper to answer the phone. But it's located in the Bavarian Old World Village, a delightful replica of a Bavarian community built some 30 years ago by the same German builder who created the Alpine Village in Torrance. Shops and restaurants line the street. Bring your *liederhosen*: It's Oktoberfest year-round. ~ 7561 Center Avenue; 714-373-4999. BUDGET.

DINING

At **Spark Woodfire Grill** you can dine on fine Italian cuisine for reasonable prices. Try one of their fresh pasta dishes, such as rigatoni with grilled vegetables tossed in olive oil, or a California-style pizza with one of their inventive salads. Daily "chef's creations" guarantee you'll never tire of the menu. The restaurant is open and airy with modern decor, plenty of windows, and a heated patio overlooking the ocean. Dinner only. ~ 300 Pacific Coast Highway; 714-960-0996, fax 714-960-7332; www.sparkwoodfiregrill.com. MODERATE TO ULTRA-DELUXE.

HIDDEN ►

Harbor House Café is one of those hole-in-the-wall places packed with local folks. In this case it's "open 24 hours, 365 days a year" and has been around since 1939. Add knotty-pine walls covered with black-and-whites of your favorite movies stars and you've got a coastal classic. The menu, as you have surmised, includes burgers and sandwiches. Actually, it's pretty varied—in addition to croissant sandwiches there are Mexican dishes, seafood platters, chicken entrées, and omelettes. ~ 16341 Pacific Coast Highway; 562-592-5404. BUDGET TO MODERATE.

Chimayo at the Beach's location at the base of the Huntington Beach Pier can't be beat, and the rustic South Seas atmosphere adds to the enjoyment. Start with a mango martini at the oceanview bar, then graduate to selections from the raw bar, lobster tacos, or other seafood from the grill, wok, or wood-burning oven. Sunday brunch. ~ 315 Pacific Coast Highway; 714-374-7273; www.culinaryadventures.com, ggaytan@culinaryadventures.com. MODERATE TO DELUXE.

Housed in a cozy red barn lakeside in Central Park, **Alice's Breakfast in the Park** serves generous breakfasts that could very well hold you until dinner. Omelettes, scrambles, and huevos rancheros share the menu with breakfast burritos, pancakes, and french toast. At lunch you can opt for a BLT, an ABC (avocado, bacon, and cheese), a fresh salad, or burger. All the pastries and breads are baked onsite, including the decadent cinnamon rolls draped in icing. No dinner. ~ 6622 Lakeview Drive; 714-848-0690; www.breakfastinthepark.com. BUDGET.

NIGHTLIFE

Located at the Waterfront Hilton Beach Resort, **The West Coast Club** is a bar and lounge. Featuring seasonal live entertainment, a fireplace, floor-to-ceiling windows, and a patio for cigar lovers, it's a perfect spot for unwinding. ~ 21100 Pacific Coast Highway; 714-960-7873, 714-845-8000.

BEACHES & PARKS

SURFSIDE BEACH 🐾 🦆 🎣 🛶 **AND SUNSET BEACH** 🐾 🎣 🛶 These contiguous strands extend over three miles along the ocean side of Huntington Harbor. Broad carpets of cushioning sand, they are lined with beach houses and lifeguard stands. Both are popular with local people. But Surfside, which fronts a private community and lacks facilities, is still a great beach to get away from the crowds. Sunset Beach has restrooms and lifeguards. Swimming and surfing are good at both beaches, although spectacular winter breaks near the jetty at the end of Surfside Beach make it the better choice during that season. For fishing, Sunset is the best bet. ~ Surfside runs north from Anderson Street, which provides the only public access to the beach; Sunset is off the Pacific Coast Highway, extending from Warner Avenue to Anderson Street in Sunset Beach.

BOLSA CHICA STATE BEACH With three miles of fluffy sand, this is another in a series of broad, beautiful beaches. There are rich clam beds here; the beach is backdropped by the **Bolsa Chica Conservancy**, an important wetlands area. Since the summer surf is gentler here than at Huntington Beach, Bolsa Chica is ideal for swimmers and families. You'll find picnic areas, restrooms, lifeguards, outdoor showers, snack bars, fire pits, basketball courts, and beach rentals. The fishing is good year-round at Bolsa Chica; swimming is better in the summer. For surfing, there are small summer waves and big winter breaks. Parking fee, $10. ~ Located along Pacific Coast

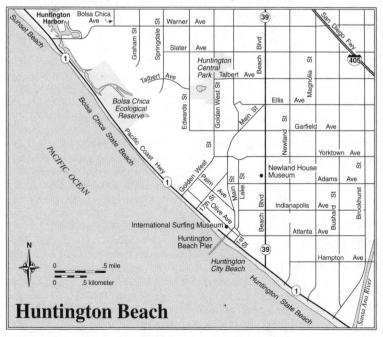

Huntington Beach

Highway between Warner Avenue and Huntington Pier in Huntington Beach; 714-846-3460 or 714-377-5691.

▲ There are 57 sites with water and electric hookups; $34 to $44 per night. Reservations required: 800-444-7275.

HUNTINGTON CITY BEACH 🚲 🏊 🚶 ⛵ An urban continuation of the state beach to the south, this strand runs for several miles. This is one of the most famous surfing spots in the world, hosting an international surf tournament each July. The Huntington Pier is the pride of the city. The surrounding waters are crowded with surfers in wet suits. The beach is a great place for water sports and people-watching. This surfer heaven gives way to a field of offshore oil derricks north of the pier, so stay south of the pier and make use of the fire pits, restrooms and outdoor showers, volleyball courts, snack bars, and beach rentals. Swimming is good if you can find a time when the swells aren't too big, but the surf pumps year-round here (lifeguards are on duty year-round, too). Fishing tackle shops are nearby in Huntington Beach; if you're aiming to angle, try the pier. Parking south of the pier is $10 a day; hourly parking is available on either side. ~ Located along Pacific Coast Highway in Huntington Beach with numerous accesses; 714-536-5281, fax 714-374-1500.

International surfing competitions are held throughout the summer months and in September at Huntington City Beach.

▲ Camping is available October through May for $45, with a $5 discount for seniors, people with disabilities, and Huntington Beach residents.

HUNTINGTON STATE BEACH 🚶 🚲 🏊 🚶 ⛵ One of Southern California's broadest beaches, this strand extends for three miles. In addition to a desert of soft sand, it has those curling waves that surfer dreams (and movies) are made of. A bike path parallels the water, and there is a five-acre preserve for endangered least terns. Before you decide to move here permanently, take heed: these natural wonders are sandwiched between industrial plants and offshore oil derricks. Nonetheless, your visit will be made more comfortable by the restrooms, fire rings, lifeguards, outdoor showers, dressing rooms, snack bars, volleyball, and beach rentals. The fishing is good here, and the surfing is excellent. Swimming is prime when the surf is low. Day-use fee, $10. ~ Located along Pacific Coast Highway in Huntington Beach; entrances are at Beach Boulevard, Magnolia Street, and Brookhurst Street; 714-536-1454, fax 714-536-0074.

Newport Beach

Newport Beach is a mélange of manmade islands and a peninsula surrounding a harbor, and as a result, boating is the order of the day here. One of the largest pleasure harbors in the world, Newport Harbor is the starting point for the famous Tommy Bahama Ensenada Race, a 125-mile sailboat race to Baja held every April.

In addition to recreational boats, fishing boats are a common sight; Newport Pier, the oldest in Southern California, is where the fishing boats return every morning to sell the day's catch. If you don't buy from them directly, you can still sample local seafood at the myriad waterfront area restaurants.

Although virtually the entire shoreline of the lower bay is developed, the upper bay, a narrow channel carved by a Pleistocene river, is a protected wetlands, and it offers perhaps the only escape from the constant flow of boat traffic and manmade vistas of the lower bay.

SIGHTS

For help finding your bearings around this labyrinth of waterways, contact the **Newport Harbor Area Chamber of Commerce**. Closed Saturday and Sunday. ~ 1470 Jamboree Road; 949-729-4400, fax 949-729-4417; www.newportbeach.com, e-mail info@newportbeach.com. The **Newport Beach Conference & Visitors Bureau** can also provide information. Closed Saturday and Sunday. ~ 110 Newport Center Drive, Suite 120; 949-719-6100, 800-942-6278, fax 949-719-6101; www.visitnewportbeach.com, e-mail frontdesk@nbcvb.com.

The **Orange County Museum of Art** is a fine little museum, presenting a permanent collection of some 6500 works of contemporary and modern art. Though the museum is international in scope, its collection of California-based works is one of the finest anywhere and is especially rich in California impressionism and scene painting, pop art, and minimalism. Closed Monday and Tuesday. Admission (free on Thursday). ~ 850 San Clemente Drive; 949-759-1122, fax 949-759-5623; www.ocma.net.

Further evidence of Newport's creativity can be found at the **Lovell Beach House**. This private residence, set on the beach, is a modern masterpiece. Designed by Rudolf Schindler in 1926, it features a Bauhaus-like design with columns and cantilevers of poured concrete creating a series of striking geometric forms. ~ 13th Street and West Ocean Front.

One of Newport Beach's prettiest neighborhoods is **Balboa Island**, composed of two manmade islets in the middle of Newport Harbor. It can be reached by bridge along Marine Avenue or via a short ferry ride from Balboa Peninsula. Walk the pathways that circumnavigate both islands and you will pass clapboard cottages, Cape Cod homes, and modern block-design houses that seem made entirely of glass. While sailboats sit moored along the waterfront, streets that are little more than alleys lead into the center of the island.

Another dredged island, **Lido Isle**, sits just off Balboa Peninsula. Surrounded by Newport Harbor, lined with sprawling homes and pocket beaches, it is another of Newport Beach's wealthy residential enclaves.

Nearby **Lido Peninsula** seems like yet one more upscale neighborhood. But wait a minute, doesn't that house have a corrugated roofline? And the one next to it is made entirely of metal. Far from an ordinary suburban neighborhood, Lido Peninsula is a trailer park. In Newport Beach? Granted they call them "mobile homes" here, and many are hardly mobile with their brick foundations, flower boxes, and shrubs. But a trailer park it is, probably one of the fanciest in the country, with tin homes disguised by elaborate landscape designs, awnings, and wooden additions. Surreal to say the least.

The central piece in this jigsaw puzzle of manmade plots is **Balboa Peninsula**, a long, narrow finger of land bounded by Newport Harbor and the open ocean. High point of the peninsula is **Balboa Pavilion** located at the end of Main Street, a Victorian landmark that dates back to 1905, when it was a bathhouse for swimmers in ankle-length outfits. Marked by its well-known cupola, the bayfront building hosted the nation's first surfing tournament in 1932 and gave birth to its own dance sensation, the "Balboa." Today it's a mini-amusement park with carousel, Ferris wheel, photograph booths, skee ball, video games, and pinball machines.

Finding a parking space is one of the biggest challenges facing visitors to Balboa Peninsula. Be prepared to pump plenty of quarters into the metered spaces around Newport Pier, at the northern end of the peninsula, or pay $7 or more at an attendant lot near Balboa Pier, at the southern end.

Cruise ships to Catalina Island embark daily from the dock here and there are harbor cruises offered by **Catalina Passenger Service** aboard the *Pavilion Paddy*. The boat motors around the mazeway that is Newport Harbor. Fee. ~ 400 Main Street; 949-673-5245; www.catalinainfo.com, e-mail kurt@catalinainfo.com.

This is also home to the **Balboa Island Ferry**, a kind of floating landmark that has shuttled between Balboa Peninsula and Balboa Island since 1919. A simple, single-deck ferry that carries three cars (for a fee) and sports a pilot house the size of a phone booth, it crosses the narrow waterway every few minutes. ~ www.balboaislandferry.com.

For those who'd like to paddle around Newport Bay, **kayaks** can be rented at the Balboa Fun Pavilion, next to the ferry launch on Balboa Peninsula (see "Outdoor Adventures"). A more romantic way to see Newport Bay is as a passenger aboard a gondola cruise, sipping champagne and nibbling chocolate. **Gondola Adventures** offers one- and two-hour gondola cruises, including an all-out three-course catered dinner cruise. ~ 3101 West Coast Highway, Suite 110, Newport Beach; 888-446-6365, fax 949-642-4760; www.gondola.com.

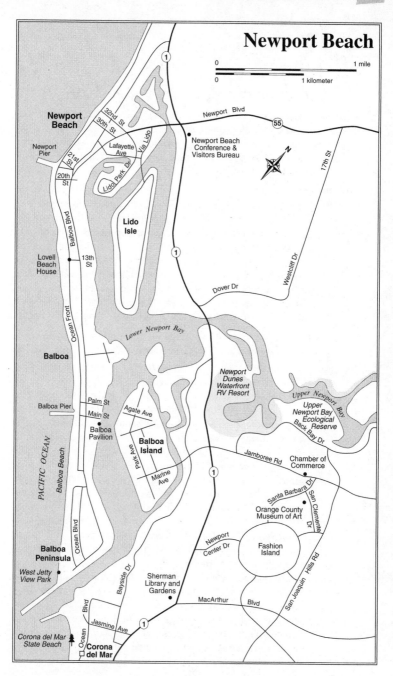

Newport Beach

0 _____ 1 mile
0 _____ 1 kilometer

Newport Blvd

55

17th St

Newport
Beach

32nd St

30th St

Lafayette
Ave

Via Lido

● Newport Beach
Conference &
Visitors Bureau

N

Newport
Pier

21st St

20th
St

Lido Park Dr

Balboa Blvd

Ocean Front

Lido
Isle

Lovell
Beach
House

13th
St

Westcliff Dr

Dover Dr

Lower Newport Bay

Balboa

Newport
Dunes
Waterfront
RV Resort

Upper Newport Bay

Upper
Newport Bay
Ecological
Reserve

Back Bay Dr

Balboa Pier

Palm St

Main St

Agate Ave

●
Balboa
Pavilion

Park Ave

**Balboa
Island**

Marine
Ave

Jamboree Rd

Chamber of
Commerce

Santa Barbara Dr

San Clemente Dr

Orange County
Museum of Art

PACIFIC OCEAN

Balboa Beach

Ocean Blvd

**Balboa
Peninsula**

West Jetty
View Park ●

Bayside Dr

Newport
Center Dr

Fashion
Island

San Joaquin Hills Rd

Sherman
Library and
Gardens ●

MacArthur   Blvd

Ocean Blvd

Jasmine Ave

1

Corona del Mar
State Beach

□ **Corona
del Mar**

Adventures in Imagination

Sure, the Southern California Coast has sun, sand, and surf. But when your kids look like they need something a little different (you'll know it's time by the sun-burnt expressions on their little faces), you're in luck: Orange County has that, too. No less than four kid-friendly museums dot the inland landscape, and each one is just a short drive from Newport Beach.

THE BOWERS KIDSEUM   The Bowers Kidseum gives a new twist to the children's museum genre, adding a dash of multicultural flair through ac-tivities, play things, and performances. Despite its diminutive size, the place ignites the imagination with dress-up, puppets, and scads of crafts and activities. Visit on a Saturday and you might just happen upon one of the family festivals (one Saturday each month). And there's always the interesting (albeit decidedly more grown-up) Bowers Museum next door with art and artifacts from around the world. Closed for renovations; call ahead for status. ~ 1802 North Main Street, Santa Ana; 714-480-1522, fax 714-480-0053; www.bowers.org, e-mail info@bowers.org.

DISCOVERY SCIENCE CENTER   Budding scientists can experiment with the physical world at the Discovery Science Center in Santa Ana. This

---

The beach scene in this seaside city extends for nine miles along the Pacific side of Balboa Peninsula. Here a broad white-sand beach, lined with lifeguard stands and houses, reaches along the entire length. The centers of attention and amenities are **Newport Pier**, located at Balboa Boulevard and McFadden Place, and **Balboa Pier** found at Balboa Boulevard and Main Street. At Newport Pier, also known as McFadden's Pier, the skiffs of the **Newport Dory Fishing Fleet** are beached every day while local fishermen sell their catches. This flotilla of small wooden boats has been here so long it has achieved historic land-mark status. At dawn the fishermen sail ten miles offshore, set trawl lines, and haul in the mackerel, flounder, rock fish, and hal-ibut sold at the afternoon market.

To capture a sense of the beauty that still inheres in Newport Beach, take a walk out to **West Jetty View Park** at the tip of Balboa Peninsula. Here civilization meets the sea. To the left ex-tend the rock jetties forming the mouth of Newport Harbor. Behind you are the plate-glass houses of the city. A wide beach, tufted with ice plants and occasional palm trees, forms another border. Before you, changing its hue with the phases of the sun

science playground is gizmo and gadget heaven; 59,000 square feet of space with activities from a bed of nails (illustrating the principles of weight dispersion) to electronic finger painting. Admission. ~ 2500 North Main Street, Santa Ana; 714-542-2823, fax 714-542-2828; www. discoverycube.org.

CENTENNIAL HERITAGE MUSEUM If newfangled science isn't your thing, go back in time at the Centennial Heritage Museum. The museum has household items and knickknacks from a bygone era: old-fashioned games, a Victrola, and even a washboard you can try. Outside the main structure, a 12-acre spread has a nature center and blacksmith shop. Closed Sunday and Monday. Admission. ~ 3101 West Harvard Street, Santa Ana; 714-540-0404; www.centennialmuseum.org.

CHILDREN'S MUSEUM For plain-old modern thrills, you can't beat the Children's Museum in La Habra. Housed in a renovated train depot, this cozy spot is kid heaven, where little ones can get in the driver's seat of an actual city bus (don't worry, it doesn't go anywhere!) or play operator on an old-time switchboard. There's lots more. The highlight: a well-stocked stage (complete with lighting, props, and microphone) where pint-sized thespians can get ready for their closeups. An extra perk for moms and dads: such imagination-fueled activities let beleaguered parents sit back and watch for a while. Admission. ~ 301 South Euclid Street, La Habra; 562-905-9693, fax 562-905-9698; www.lhcm.org.

and clouds, is the Pacific, a single sweep of water that makes those million-dollar homes seem fragile and tenuous. ~ Ocean Boulevard at Channel Road.

Not all the wealth of Newport Beach is measured in finances. The richness of the natural environment is evident as well when you venture through **Upper Newport Bay Ecological Reserve.**   ◄ *HIDDEN* Whether you bike (see "Outdoor Adventures") or drive part way through the 752-acre reserve, you'll have the chance to glimpse what's left of an ancient landscape that was first carved out by glaciers some 300,000 years ago. Development has reduced the marshes to a fraction of what they used to be, but what's left is one of the last remaining coastal wetlands in California. The road passes limestone bluffs and sandstone hills. Reeds and cattails line the shore. Over 200 species of birds can be seen here; and six endangered species, including Belding's savannah sparrow, the brown pelican, and the light-footed clapper rail, live along the bay. Be sure to visit the interpretive center (949-923-6833). Closed Monday. Guided walking, electric pontoon boat, canoeing, and kayaking tours are available. ~ 600 Shellmaker; 949-640-6746; www.newportbay.org, e-mail info@newportbay.org.

Located at the far northwest end of Newport Bay, the unusual **Upper Newport Bay–Peter and Mary Muth Interpretive Center** isn't visible from the road. The rooftop is planted with native grasses that blend into the landscape, while the center itself is built underground. Hands-on interactive exhibits reveal the intricate workings of this complex ecosystem. Closed Monday. ~ 2301 University Drive; 949-923-2290, fax 949-642-3189; www.ocparks.com/unbic.

> Southern California's largest estuary, Upper Newport Bay is a vital stopping place for thousands of migrating birds on the Pacific Flyway.

Back on Route 1, head south through **Corona del Mar** en route to Laguna Beach. A wealthy enclave with trim lawns and spacious homes, Corona del Mar offers a pretty coastal drive along residential Ocean Boulevard.

In Corona del Mar, drop by the **Sherman Library and Gardens**. Devoted to the culture and recent history of the "Pacific Southwest," this complex features a specialized library set in Early California–style buildings. Also inviting are the koi pond, botanical garden, and the tropical conservatory. Admission; free on Monday. ~ 2647 East Coast Highway, Corona del Mar; 949-673-2261, fax 949-675-5458; www.slgardens.org, e-mail info@slgardens.org.

LODGING   You'd have a hell of a time docking your boat at the **Little Inn by the Bay**. Actually it's on an island, but the island is a median strip dividing the two busiest streets on the Balboa Peninsula. Offering 18 standard motel rooms, the inn is a block from the beach and walking distance from many restaurants. ~ 2627 Newport Boulevard; 949-673-8800, 800-438-4466, fax 949-673-4943; www.littleinnbythebay.com, e-mail reservations@littleinnbythebay.com. DELUXE.

A Spanish-style hotel with cream-colored walls and a tile-roofed tower, the **Balboa Inn** is ideally situated right next to the beach at Balboa Pier. Adding to the ambience are two jacuzzi tubs that look out on the water. The 45 rooms and suites, some of which have ocean views, are furnished in knotty pine, decorated with colorful prints, and supplied with jacuzzi tubs, brass fixtures, and fireplaces. ~ 105 Main Street; 949-675-3412, 877-225-2629, fax 949-673-4587; www.balboainn.com, e-mail info@balboainn.com. DELUXE TO ULTRA-DELUXE.

The **Newport Beach Hotel**, a 15-room B&B inn, rests on the beach in a newly renovated early-20th-century building. Each room has hardwood floors and Cape Cod–esque furnishings and is equipped with a private bath; many have jacuzzis, skylights, fireplaces, and ocean views. ~ 2306 West Ocean Front; 949-673-7030, 800-571-8749, fax 949-723-4370; www.thenewportbeachhotel.com, e-mail info@thenewportbeachhotel.com. DELUXE.

On tiny Balboa Island you'll find the **Balboa Island Hotel**, a family-operated, three-bedroom, bed-and-breakfast affair. Set in a 1925 building, it's about one block from the water (of course, on Balboa Island everything is one block from the water). Each room of this B&B inn has been decorated in period and furnished with antiques. The place has a small, intimate, homey feel. Guests share bathrooms and there are two porches that serve as sitting rooms. ~ 127 Agate Avenue; 949-675-3613. MODERATE.

By way of full-facility destinations, Southern California–style, few places match the **Hyatt Regency Newport Beach**. Situated on a hillside above Upper Newport Bay, it sprawls across 26 acres and sports three swimming pools, three jacuzzis, a nine-hole pitch-and-putt course, and a tennis club. There are restaurants, a lounge, a lavishly decorated lobby, and a series of terraced patios. Guest rooms are modern in design, comfortably furnished, and tastefully appointed. An inviting combination of elegance and amenities. ~ 1107 Jamboree Road; 949-729-1234, 800-233-1234, fax 949-644-1552; www.newportbeach.hyatt.com, e-mail info@hyattnewportbeach.com. ULTRA-DELUXE.

DINING

Believed by many to be the finest dining in Newport Beach, **Pascal** provides a taste of Provence and contemporary France. The menu includes their popular rendition of sea bass, as well as rabbit, duck, and free-range chicken with a French accent. No dinner on Monday and no lunch on Saturday. ~ 1000 North Bristol Street; 949-263-9400, fax 949-261-5279; www.pascalnewportbeach.com, e-mail info@pascalnpb.com. DELUXE TO ULTRA-DELUXE.

21 Ocean Front is a gourmet seafood dining place known for fine cuisine. Located on the beach overlooking Newport Pier, the interior is done (or rather, overdone) in a kind of shiny Victorian style with black trim and brass chandeliers. The secret is to close your eyes and surrender to the senses of taste and smell. At dinner the chef prepares carp and Hawaiian fish specials as well as abalone, Maine lobster, and cioppino. For those who miss the point there's rack of lamb, pork tenderloin, filet mignon, and Kobe beef (when available). Live entertainment and a wine cellar contribute to the extravagant atmosphere. Dinner only. ~ 2100 West Ocean Front; 949-673-2100, fax 949-673-2101; www.21oceanfront.com, e-mail info@21oceanfront.com. ULTRA-DELUXE.

Around **Balboa Pavilion** you'll find snack bars and amusement park food stands.

A place nearby that's worth recommending is **Newport Landing**, a double-decker affair where you can have an intimate supper downstairs in a wood-paneled dining room or a casual meal upstairs on a deck overlooking the harbor. The upper deck features live music on the weekend. Serving lunch, dinner, and Sunday brunch, Newport Landing specializes in fresh fish selections (including swordfish, salmon, and halibut) but also serves pasta, hickory-smoked prime rib, and chicken with artichokes. ~ 503 East Edgewater Avenue; 949-675-2373, 877-526-3464, fax 949-675-0682; www.newport-landing.com, e-mail info@newport-landing.com. MODERATE TO DELUXE.

Who could imagine that at the end of Balboa Pier there would be a vintage 1940s-era diner complete with art-deco curves and red plastic booths. **Ruby's Diner** is a classic. Besides that it provides 270-degree views of the ocean. Of course the menu, whether breakfast, lunch, or dinner, contains little more than omelettes, hamburgers, sandwiches, chili, and salads. But who's hungry anyway with all that history and scenery to savor? ~ 1 Balboa Pier; 949-675-7829, fax 949-673-3237; www.rubys.com. BUDGET TO MODERATE.

HIDDEN ► **Amelia's**, a family-run restaurant serving Italian dishes and seafood, is a local institution. At lunch you'll find them serving a multitude of pasta dishes, fresh fish entrées, sandwiches, and salads. Then in the evening the chef prepares filet mignon with scampi, fresh fish with linguini and clams, cioppino, bouillabaisse, veal piccata, and another round of pasta platters. Dinner is served daily; lunch on Friday and Saturday. Sunday brunch. ~ 311 Marine Avenue; 949-673-6580, fax 949-673-5395; www.ameliasbalboaisland.com. MODERATE TO DELUXE.

If you were hoping to spend a little less money, **Wilma's Patio** is just down the street. It's casual family dining at its best—open morning, noon, and night—with multicourse American, Chinese, and Mexican meals. ~ 203 Marine Avenue; 949-675-5542, fax 949-675-7243; www.wilmaspatio.com, e-mail wilmas patio@menusunlimited.com. BUDGET TO MODERATE.

With a bakery on the premises, you know that the pastries at **Haute Cakes** must be fresh. Enjoy the daily breakfast or lunch special in a cozy, simple setting, or have a hot scrambler out in the courtyard. The grilled vegetable sandwich with a salad also

AUTHOR FAVORITE

You won't miss **The Crab Cooker**. First, it's painted bright red; second, it's located at a busy intersection near Newport Pier; last, the place has been a local institution since the 1950s. Actually, you don't *want* to miss The Crab Cooker. This informal eatery, where lunch and dinner are served on paper plates, has fish, scallops, shrimp, crab, and oysters. There's a fish market attached to the restaurant, so freshness and quality are assured. ~ 2200 Newport Boulevard; 949-673-0100, fax 949-675-8445; www.crabcooker.com. MODERATE TO DELUXE.

hits the spot. Breakfast and lunch served. ~ 1807 Westcliff Drive; 949-642-4114; www.hautecakescaffe.net. BUDGET TO MODERATE.

If it's people watching you're after, **Baja Sharkeez** will deliver. This chain eatery serves lunch and dinner, as well as breakfast all day. It specializes in Mexi-California food—gourmet burritos, mesquite-grilled platters, tacos, and fajitas. The atmosphere is nothing to write home about, but the service is friendly and it's a good place to go for an inexpensive meal before a day of sight-seeing or hitting the beach. ~ 114 McFadden Place; 949-673-0292, fax 949-673-0294; www.sharkeez.net. BUDGET.

Ironically enough, one of Newport Beach's top dining bargains lies at the heart of the region's priciest shopping malls. Encircling the lower level of **Fashion Island** is a collection of stands dispensing sushi, soup and sandwiches, Mexican food, pasta salads, hamburgers, and other light fare. ~ 401 Newport Center Drive; 949-721-2000, fax 949-719-1421; www.shop fashionisland.com. BUDGET TO MODERATE.

A local favorite in Corona del Mar, the small town adjacent to Newport Beach, is **The Quiet Woman**, a small, dark, friendly   ◄ HIDDEN
place serving mesquite-grilled food. The lunch and dinner menus both feature steak and seafood. Over 4000 bottles are offered on the wine list. Live entertainment accompanies evening meals Tuesday through Saturday. No lunch on weekends. ~ 3224 East Coast Highway, Corona del Mar; 949-640-7440, fax 949-640-5869; www.quietwoman.com. DELUXE TO ULTRA-DELUXE.

The streets radiating out from **Balboa Pavilion** (end of Main   **SHOPPING**
Street) are lined with beachwear stores, sundries shops, and souvenir stands. While there's little of value here, it is a good place to shop for knickknacks. The scene is much the same around **Newport Pier**, located at Balboa Avenue and McFadden Place.

Another Newport Beach shopping enclave lies along Marine Avenue on Balboa Island. This consumer strip is door-to-door with card shops, gift shops, and sundries stores. Without exaggerating, I would estimate that more than half the outlets here sell beachwear.

After all is said and done, but hopefully before the money is all spent, the center for Newport Beach shopping is **Fashion Island**. Situated at the heart of Newport Center, the town's highrise financial district, it is also the best place for beautiful-people watching. Every self-respecting department store is here. Neiman Marcus, Macy's, and Bloomingdale's are all represented. ~ 401 Newport Center Drive; 949-721-2000; www.shopfashionisland.com.

There's an outdoor plaza filled with fashion outlets and an atrium displaying one floor of designer dreams. If you don't believe Newport Beach is a match for Beverly Hills in flash and cash, take a tour of the parking lot. It's a showplace for Rolls

Royces, Jaguars, and Mercedes, as well as more plebeian Volvos and Audis.

For contemporary paintings, I particularly recommend **Southern California Art Projects and Exhibitions (SCAPE)**, which displays the work of R. Kenton Nelson, Michael Eastman, Sharon Loper, and other artists. Closed Sunday and Monday. ~ 2859 East Coast Highway, Corona del Mar; 949-723-3406, fax 949-723-3407; www.scapesite.com, e-mail info@scapesite.com.

NIGHTLIFE For a lively happy hour, televised sports, and pool games, check out **Cabo Cantina**, a watering hole near Balboa Pier. ~ 100 Main Street; 949-675-7760.

There's music, food, and drink specials Thursday through Saturday nights at **Baja Sharkeez**. Thursday night attracts a raucous college crowd fond of imbibing huge frozen drink concoctions. ~ 114 McFadden Place; 949-673-0292; www.sharkeez.net.

The **Entertainer** cruises around the bay on Friday and Saturday evenings and Sunday afternoons year-round. In addition to a delicious supper prepared fresh on board there is dancing on the upper deck to live music. The Sunday brunch cruise offers free flowing champagne. ~ 2431 West Pacific Coast Highway; 949-646-0155, 800-668-4322, fax 949-646-5924; www.horn blower.com, e-mail nb@hornblower.com.

BEACHES & PARKS **NEWPORT BEACH** 🚴 🏄 🎣 ⚓ Narrow at the northern end and widening to the south, this sandy strip extends for several miles along the base of the Balboa Peninsula. Newport Pier (also known as McFadden's Pier) and the surrounding facilities serve as the center of the strand. A wonderful beach, with entrances along its entire length, this is an important gathering place for the crowds that pour into town. There are restrooms, lifeguards, and beach rentals; at the foot of the pier you will find restaurants, groceries, and all amenities imaginable. The pier is also the place for fishing. Swimming and surfing are both good. If you want to ride the waves, try in the morning around Newport Pier and then in the afternoon at the 30th Street section of the beach. There are year-round breaks near the Santa Ana River mouth at the far north end of the beach. ~ The beach parallels Balboa Boulevard in Newport Beach. Newport Pier is between 20th and 21st streets; 949-719-6100.

BALBOA BEACH 🚴 🏄 🎣 ⚓ This broad sandy strip forms the ocean side of Balboa Peninsula and extends along its entire length. There are entrances to the beach from numerous side streets, but the center of the facility is around Balboa Pier, a concrete fishing pier. With a palm-shaded lawn and many nearby amenities, this beach, together with neighboring Newport Beach, is the most popular spot in town. Facilities include restrooms, showers, lifeguards, a playground, and beach rentals. Fishing is good from the pier. ~ The beach parallels Balboa Boulevard; Balboa Pier is at the end of Main Street; 949-644-3000.

L.A. Laker superstar Kobe Bryant and colorful ex-NBA player Dennis Rodman both own homes in Newport Beach.

WEST JETTY VIEW PARK 🏃 Set at the very end of the Balboa Peninsula, this triangle of sand is perfectly placed. From the tip extends a rock jetty that borders Newport Harbor. You can climb the rocks and watch boats in the bay, or turn your back on these trifles and wander across the broad sand carpet that rolls down to the ocean. There are wonderful views of Newport Beach and the coast. If you're daring enough, you can challenge the waves at **The Wedge**. Known to bodysurfers around the world, the area between the jetty and beach is one of the finest and most dangerous shore breaks anywhere, the "Mount Everest of bodysurfing." If it's any comfort, there are lifeguards. Swimming is very dangerous; the shore break here is fierce. Bodysurfing is the main sport; surfing is permitted further down the beach and only in the winter. But take heed, these breaks are only for veteran bodysurfers. ~ At the end of Balboa and Ocean boulevards at the tip of the Balboa Peninsula; 949-644-3151.

NEWPORT DUNES WATERFRONT RV RESORT 🏃 🚲 ⛵ 🍴 🚣 🏄 🚤 This resort has a broad, horseshoe-shaped beach about a half-mile in length. It curves around the lake-like waters of Upper Newport Bay, one mile inland from the ocean. Very popular with families and campers, it offers a wide range of possibilities, including playground activities, volleyball, a swimming pool, jacuzzi, and boat and watersport rentals. Lifeguards are on duty in the summer. Other facilities include restrooms, a café, groceries, picnic areas, and laundry. The park is very popular, so plan to come for the attractions, not peace and quiet. Parking fee, $10. ~ 1131 Back Bay Drive, Newport Beach; 949-729-3863, 800-765-7661, fax 949-729-1133; www.newportdunes.com, e-mail info@newportdunes.com.

▲ There are 382 sites for freestanding tents and RVs (all with hookups, some with cable TV and phone access); $55 to $185 per night. There are also 24 cottages; $65 to $365 per night.

CORONA DEL MAR STATE BEACH ⛵ 🏄 Located at the mouth of Newport Harbor, this park offers an opportunity to watch sailboats tacking in and out from the bay. Bounded on one side by a jetty, on the other by homes, with a huge parking lot behind, it is less than idyllic, yet it is also inevitably crowded. Throngs congregate because of its easy access, landscaped lawn, and excellent facilities, which include restrooms, picnic areas, lifeguards, showers, concession stands, and volleyball courts.

(You will find one possible escape valve: there are a pair of pocket beaches on the other side of the rocks next to the jetty.) It's well protected for swimming and also popular for fishing—cast from the jetty bordering Newport Harbor. Skindiving is also good around the jetty. Parking fee, $8 to $10. ~ Located at Jasmine Avenue and Ocean Boulevard in Corona del Mar; 949-644-3000.

LITTLE CORONA DEL MAR STATE BEACH Another in the proud line of pocket beaches along the Orange Coast, this preserve features the **Corona del Mar Tidepool Reserve**. These are endangered and protected, and may be closed at times. The bluff to the north consists of sandstone that has been contorted into a myriad of magnificent lines. There's a marsh behind the beach thick with reeds and cattails. Unfortunately you won't be the first explorer to hit the sand; Little Corona is known to a big group of local people. The beach is also popular with swimmers, snorkelers, and skindivers; for anglers, try casting from the rocks. ~ There is an entrance to the beach at Poppy Avenue and Ocean Boulevard in Corona del Mar; 949-644-3000.

Laguna Beach

Next stop on this cavalcade of coastal cities is Laguna Beach. Framed by the San Joaquin hills, the place is an intaglio of coves and bluffs, sand beaches and rock outcroppings. It conjures images of the Mediterranean with deep bays and greenery running to the sea's edge.

Little wonder that Laguna, with its wealthy residents and leisurely beachfront, has become synonymous with the chic but informal style of Southern California. Its long tradition as an artist colony adds to this sense of beauty and bounty, aesthetics and aggrandizement.

Laguna's traditional tranquility has weathered natural disasters quite well. Although hillside fires remain a threat, and winter storms sometimes leave debris on beaches, Laguna always recovers.

SIGHTS   Part of Laguna Beach's artistic tradition is the **Festival of Arts and Pageant of the Masters**, staged every year during July and August. While the festival displays the work of approximately 140 local artists and craftspeople, the Pageant of the Masters is the high point, an event you *absolutely must not miss*. It presents a series of *tableaux vivants* in which local residents, dressed to resemble figures from famous paintings, remain motionless against a frieze that re-creates the painting. Elaborate make-up and lighting techniques flatten the figures and create a sense of two-dimensionality. If you attend, be sure to arrange lodging, transportation, and dining reservations ahead of time; check out the package deals offered by local hotels. Admission. ~ Irvine

Bowl, 650 Laguna Canyon Road; 949-494-1145, 800-487-3378, fax 949-494-9387; www.lagunafestivalofarts.com.

During the 1960s freelance artists, excluded from the more formal Festival of the Arts, founded the **Sawdust Festival** across the street. Over the years this fair has become pretty established, but it still provides an opportunity from late June to early September to wander along sawdust-covered paths past hundreds of arts and crafts displays accompanied by musicians and jugglers. Admission. ~ 935 Laguna Canyon Road; 949-494-3030, fax 949-494-7390; www.sawdustartfestival.org, e-mail info@saw dustartfestival.org.

Laguna Beach's artistic heritage is evident in the many studios around town. The **Laguna Beach Visitors Center**, with its maps and brochures, can help direct you. They can also assist with hotel and restaurant reservations. Closed Sunday, except in July and August. ~ 252 Broadway; 949-497-9229, 800-877-1115, fax 949-376-0558; www.lagunabeachinfo.org, e-mail laguna@ lagunabeachinfo.com.

The **Laguna Art Museum** has a wonderfully chosen collection of historic and contemporary paintings and photographs, with an emphasis on the art of California. Descended from the oldest cultural institution in Orange County, it will help you find your way

Laguna Beach

through the local art world. Admission. ~ 307 Cliff Drive; 949-494-8971, fax 949-494-1530; www.lagunaartmuseum.org.

Beauty in Laguna is not only found on canvases. The coastline too is particularly pretty and well worth exploring (see the "Beaches & Parks" section below). One of the most enchanting areas is along **Heisler Park**, a winding promenade set on the cliffs above the ocean. Here you can relax on the lawn, sit beneath a palm tree, and gaze out on the horizon. There are broad vistas out along the coast and down to the wave-whitened shoreline. Paths from the park descend to a series of coves with tidepools and sandy beaches. The surrounding rocks, twisted by geologic pressure into curving designs, rise in a series of protective bluffs. ~ Located on Cliff Drive.

> Drive by the Bette Davis House, an English Tudor–style home where the silver screen diva lived in the early 1940s. ~ 1991 Ocean Way, Laguna Beach.

Cliff Drive streams along Heisler Park and then past a series of entranceways to sparkling coves and pocket beaches. At the north end of this shoreline street take a left onto Coast Highway, then another quick left onto Crescent Bay Drive, which leads to **Crescent Bay Point Park**. Seated high upon a coastal cliff, this landscaped facility offers magnificent views for miles along the Laguna shore.

When you're ready to leave the beach behind and head for the hills, take Park Avenue up from the center of Laguna Beach, turn right at the end onto Alta Laguna Boulevard, and right again to head back down on Temple Hills Drive and Thalia Street. This climbing course will carry you high into the **Laguna Hills** with spectacular vistas along the coastline and into the interior valleys.

HIDDEN ►

In town, in the Laguna-North section, you'll find a charming historical link with Laguna's past in this neighborhood of **1920s bungalows**. Built by year-round residents who worked or owned businesses in town to serve the seasonal visitors, the bungalows were humble interpretations of the Craftsman style popularized by Pasadena architects Charles and Henry Greene. The homeowners over the years individualized their dwellings by adding columns, changing roof styles, rebuilding entries, and making other modifications. Pick up a map at the Laguna Beach Visitors Bureau to follow a self-guided tour. ~ East of Coast Highway and north of Broadway.

South on Route 1, called the Pacific Coast Highway in these parts, you will pass through **Dana Point**. This ultramodern enclave, with its manmade port and 2500-boat marina, has a history dating back to the 1830s when Richard Henry Dana immortalized the place. Writing in *Two Years Before the Mast*, the Boston gentleman-turned-sailor described the surrounding countryside: "There was a grandeur in everything around."

Today much of the grandeur has been replaced with condominiums, leaving little for the sightseer. There is the **Ocean**

Institute with sealife aquariums, learning labs, a modern research vessel named the *R/V Sea Explorer*, and a 130-foot replica of Dana's brig, *The Pilgrim*. The Institute also offers cruises, for a fee, on weekends. The Institute is closed on most major holidays, the aquarium, labs and ships are open only on weekends. ~ 24200 Dana Point Harbor Drive, Dana Point; 949-496-2274, fax 949-496-4296; www.ocean-institute.org, e-mail oi@ocean-institute.org.

LODGING

Boasting 70 guest rooms, a pool, spa, and sundeck overlooking the sea, the **Inn at Laguna Beach** offers great ocean views from its blufftop perch. Rooms are small, the construction uneven, and the furnishings modern at this coastside property. But continental breakfast and a local paper are brought to your room, gratis. ~ 211 North Coast Highway; 949-497-9722, 800-544-4479, fax 949-497-9972; www.innatlagunabeach.com, e-mail info@innat lagunabeach.com. ULTRA-DELUXE.

The premier resting place in Laguna Beach is a sprawling 165-room establishment overhanging the sand. The **Surf & Sand Resort** is a blocky 1950s-era complex, an architectural mélange of five buildings and a shopping mall. The accent here is on the ocean: nearly every room has a sea view and private balcony, the pool sits just above the sand, and the beach is a short step away. A full-service hotel, the Surf & Sand has an oceanfront restaurant and lounge, as well as a full-service spa. Guest rooms are understated but attractive with blond woods and sand-hued walls. ~ 1555 South Coast Highway; 949-497-4477, 888-869-7569, fax 949-494-2897; www.surfandsandresort.com, e-mail surfand sandresort@jcresorts.com. ULTRA-DELUXE.

Casa Laguna Inn & Spa, a hillside hacienda, has a dreamlike quality about it. The cottages and rooms are nestled in a garden setting complete with stone terraces and winding paths. Built in the 1930s, the Spanish-style complex features a courtyard, bell tower, and a heated swimming pool with an ocean view. The rooms are small, equipped with overhead fans and air conditioning, and furnished in antiques; many offer ocean views and double-jetted tubs. Full gourmet breakfast and afternoon wine and cheese are served in a restored landmark Mission house. ~ 2510 South Coast Highway; 949-494-2996, 800-233-0449, fax 949-494-5009; www.casalaguna.com, e-mail info@casalaguna.com. ULTRA-DELUXE.

It's not just the residential neighborhood that makes **The Carriage House** unique. The colonial architecture of the "New Orleans style" B&B inn also sets it apart. Within this historic landmark structure are six suites, each with a sitting room, a private bath, and separate bedroom; some have dining rooms and kitchenettes. All face a verdant brick courtyard filled with flowering plants and adorned with a tiered fountain—in case you get tired of the ocean views. Certainly the Carriage House is one of the prettiest and most peaceful inns along the entire Orange Coast. ~ 1322 Catalina Street; 949-494-8945, 888-335-8945, fax 949-494-6829; www.carriagehouse.com, e-mail crgehsebb@aol.com. DELUXE.

Accommodations with kitchen facilities are hard to come by in Laguna Beach. You'll find them in most of the units at **Capri Laguna**, a multilevel motel situated on the beach. This 49-unit resting place provides contemporary motel-style furnishings, plus a pool, sauna, and sundeck with barbecue facilities. Continental breakfast is included. ~ 1441 South Coast Highway; 949-494-6533, 800-225-4551, fax 949-497-6962; www.caprilaguna.com, e-mail caprilagun@aol.com. DELUXE TO ULTRA-DELUXE.

Holiday Inn Laguna Beach is fashioned in the luxurious style of the French Caribbean: the lobby is a breezy affair with provincial furnishings; the 54 guest rooms surround a lushly landscaped courtyard complete with swimming pool and patio. For a touch of the tropics right here in Laguna Beach, you can't go astray at this hotel. ~ 696 South Coast Highway; 949-494-1001, 800-228-5691, fax 949-497-7107; www.hilagunabeach.com. ULTRA-DELUXE.

Tucked into a secluded canyon is **Aliso Creek Inn and Golf Resort**, an appealing 83-acre resort complete with swimming pools, jacuzzi, restaurant, lounge, and nine-hole golf course. Particularly attractive for families, every unit includes a sitting area, patio, and kitchen. Removed from the highway but within 400 yards of a beach, the resort is surrounded by steep hillsides that are populated by deer, rabbits and raccoon. Tying this easy rusticity together is a small creek that tumbles through the resort. ~ 31106 South Coast Highway; 949-499-2271, 800-223-3309, fax 949-499-4601; www.alisocreekinn.com, e-mail sales@aliso creekinn.com. ULTRA-DELUXE.

AUTHOR FAVORITE

Even if you never stay there, you won't miss the **Hotel Laguna**. With its octagonal bell tower and Spanish motif, this huge whitewashed building dominates downtown Laguna Beach. The oldest hotel in Laguna, it sits in the center of town, adjacent to Main Beach. In addition to 65 guest rooms there is a restaurant, lounge, and lobby terrace. For a place on the water *and* at the center of the action, it cannot be matched. ~ 425 South Coast Highway; 949-494-1151, 800-524-2927, fax 949-497-2163; www.hotella guna.com, e-mail hotelinfo@hotellaguna.com. DELUXE TO ULTRA-DELUXE.

The **Ritz-Carlton Laguna Niguel**, set on a 150-foot-high cliff above the Pacific, is simply the finest resort hotel along the California coast. Built in the fashion of a Mediterranean villa, it dominates a broad sweep of coastline, a 393-room mansion replete with gourmet restaurants and dark wood lounges. The grounds are landscaped with willows, sycamores, and a spectrum of flowering plants. Tile courtyards lead to two swimming pools, a pair of jacuzzis, tennis courts, and a fitness and massage center. The rooms are equal in luxury to the rest of the resort. ~ 1 Ritz-Carlton Drive, Dana Point; 949-240-2000, 800-241-3333, fax 949-240-1061. ULTRA-DELUXE.

Most motels have a stream of traffic whizzing past outside, but the **Dana Marina Inn Motel**, situated on an island where the highway divides, manages to have traffic on both sides! The reason I'm mentioning it is not because I'm sadistic but because rooms in this 24-unit facility are inexpensive. The accommodations are roadside-motel style. ~ 34111 Pacific Coast Highway, Dana Point; 949-496-1300, fax 949-496-3710; www.danamarina inn.com. BUDGET.

Four Sisters Inns, a bed-and-breakfast "chain" with several properties along the coast, has a 29-room property, **Blue Lantern Inn**, situated on an oceanside bluff in Dana Point. A contemporary building designed in classic Cape Cod–style, this bed and breakfast, offers lovely views. Each room features a fireplace and jacuzzi as well as a sitting area; most have decks overlooking the ocean. The tower rooms offer spectacular ocean views and telescopes for stargazing. The sitting rooms are spacious and comfortable and the inn provides a well-done, though self-conscious, re-creation of a classic era. Full breakfast and afternoon wine and hors d'oeuvres are served. Be sure to book rooms in advance. ~ 34343 Street of the Blue Lantern, Dana Point; 949-661-1304, 800-950-1236, fax 949-496-1483; www.foursisters.com, e-mail bluelanterninn@foursisters.com. DELUXE TO ULTRA-DELUXE.

DINING

Laguna Beach is never at a loss for oceanfront restaurants. But somehow the sea seems closer and more intimate at **The Cliff Restaurant**, probably because this informal eatery was once entirely outdoors, with tables placed at the very edge of the coastal bluff (now they've added indoor seating warmed by a fireplace). The menu is simple: Egg dishes at breakfast, while fresh seafood, steaks, salads, and sandwiches make up lunch and dinner offerings. Among the more popular choices: crab blended with several cheeses and artichoke for a savory dip, fresh fish tacos, hand-cut steaks, wraps, and a Louie salad with crab or shrimp. Music on weekends. ~ 577 South Coast Highway; 949-494-1956; e-mail thecliffrestaurant@hotmail.com. MODERATE.

The **Penguin Malt Shop** is from another era entirely. The 1950s to be exact. A tiny café featuring counter jukeboxes and swivel stools, as well as penguin memorabilia brought in by customers, it's a time capsule with a kitchen. Breakfast and lunch are all-American affairs from ham and eggs to hamburgers to roast beef. It's cheap, so what have you got to lose? Step on in and order a chocolate malt with a side of fries. No dinner. ~ 981 South Coast Highway; 949-494-1353. BUDGET.

The **White House Tavern and Restaurant** seems nearly as permanent a Laguna Beach fixture as the ocean. Dating to early in the 20th century this simple wooden structure serves as bar, restaurant, and local landmark. The White House is lined with historic photos of Laguna Beach and works by local artists. You can drop by from early morning until late evening to partake of a menu that includes pasta, steak, chicken, and seafood dishes. ~ 340 South Coast Highway; 949-494-8088, fax 949-494-0986; www.whitehouserestaurant.com. MODERATE TO DELUXE.

Don't get sidetracked by the extensive martini menu at **230 Forest Avenue**, because what really shines here is the inventive food. The Maui onion soup or the salmon salad pave the way for the entrées: spicy lemon caper shrimp scampi, applejack brandy–smoked barbecued ribs, and Pacific Northwest cioppino, or the restaurant's signature hazelnut-crusted halibut. Then top the savory with sweet specialties such as bread pudding. ~ 230 Forest Avenue; 949-494-2545, fax 949-376-1644; www.230for estavenue.com. MODERATE TO ULTRA-DELUXE.

Choose one place to symbolize the easy elegance of Laguna and it inevitably will be **Las Brisas**. Something about this white-washed Spanish building with arched windows captures the natural-living-but-class-conscious style of the Southland. Its cliff-side locale on the water is part of this ambience. Then there are the beautiful people who frequent the place. Plus there is a dual kitchen arrangement that permits formal dining in a white-tablecloth room or bistro dining on an outdoor patio. The menu consists of Continental-Mexican seafood dishes and other specialties from south of the border. Out on the patio there are sandwiches, salads, and appetizers. ~ 361 Cliff Drive; 949-497-5434, fax 949-376-1644; www.lasbrisaslagunabeach.com. DELUXE TO ULTRA-DELUXE.

For people watching and swimming pool–sized lattes, try **Zinc Café and Market**. Here you'll find sidewalk seating complete with the obligatory umbrellas. They serve vegetarian fare that attracts a casual-intellectual crowd. No dinner. ~ 350 Ocean Avenue; 949-494-6302, fax 949-497-8294; www.zinccafe.com. BUDGET TO MODERATE.

Five Feet Restaurant prepares a succulent interpretation of "modern Chinese cuisine" that carries you from catfish to lamb chinoise. Often on the ever-changing and always unique bill of fare are Hawaiian swordfish with garlic-parmesan crust and New York steak with shallot-hoisin sauce. Applying the principles of California cuisine to Chinese cooking and adding a few French flourishes, Five Feet has gained an impressive reputation. The decor is as avant-garde as the food. Dinner only. ~ 328 Glenneyre Street; 949-497-4955, fax 949-497-4186; www.five feetrestaurants.com. DELUXE TO ULTRA-DELUXE.

Dizz's Restaurant represents one of those singular dining spots that should not be overlooked. Funk is elevated to an art form in this woodframe house. The tiny dining room is decorated with art-deco pieces and 1930s-era tunes play throughout dinner. This studied informality ends at the kitchen, where talented chefs prepare international cuisine that includes veal piccata, Cornish game hen, chicken stuffed with cheese and shallots, pasta with prawns, and cioppino. Dinner only. ~ 2794 South Coast Highway; 949-494-5250. DELUXE TO ULTRA-DELUXE.

The most remarkable aspect of the **Cottage Restaurant** is the cottage itself, an early-20th-century California bungalow. The place has been neatly decorated with turn-of-the-20th-century antiques, oil paintings, and stained glass. Meal time in this historic house is a traditional American affair. They serve eggs-and-bacon breakfasts starting at 7 a.m. Lunch consists of salads and sandwiches plus specials like top sirloin, fresh fish, and steamed vegetables. For dinner there is chicken fettuccine, top sirloin, broiled lamb, fresh shrimp, and swordfish as well as daily fresh fish specials. ~ 308 North Coast Highway; 949-494-3023, fax 949-497-5183; www. thecottagerestaurant.com. MODERATE TO DELUXE.

> John Steinbeck wrote *Tortilla Flats* while living at 504 Park Avenue in Laguna Beach.

Ti Amo is a little jewel set on a coastal bluff. Situated in a former home, it offers intimate dining indoors or outside on the patio. The restaurant has Renaissance decor with Italian-style murals and heavy draperies. In addition to ocean views, it offers daily specials. On a typical evening you can expect such entrées as paella, fresh seafood, homemade pastas, and a variety of beef and poultry dishes. Desserts here—ranging from a light berry ice cream to a decadent chocolate cake—are not to be skipped. Dinner only. ~ 31727 South Coast Highway; 949-499-5350, fax 949-499-9760; www.tiamolagunabeach.com, e-mail jim@tiamo lagunabeach.com. MODERATE.

The **Harbor Grill**, located in Dana Point Harbor, lacks the view and polish of its splashy neighbors. But this understated restaurant serves excellent seafood dishes. The menu includes fresh swordfish and salmon with pesto sauce, but the real attraction is the list of daily specials. This might include sea bass with black-bean sauce, gumbo, and other fresh fish dishes. Lunch, dinner, and Sunday brunch are served in a light, bright dining room with contemporary artwork. Patio dining and a full bar are also options here. ~ 34499 Golden Lantern Street, Dana Point; 949-240-1416, fax 949-240-2013; www.harborgrill.com, e-mail john@harborgrill.com. MODERATE TO DELUXE.

If you'd prefer to dine alfresco overlooking the harbor, there's **Proud Mary's**, a little hole in the wall where you can order sandwiches, salads, hamburgers, and a few chicken and steak platters, then dine on picnic tables outside. Breakfast is served all day. No dinner. ~ 34689 Golden Lantern Street, Dana Point; 949-493-5853, fax 949-493-3911. BUDGET.

SHOPPING   Laguna Beach claims to support more goldsmiths and jewelers than any place in the country. Add a few designer clothing shops plus antique stores and you have one very promising shopping spot. The center of this action lies along Route 1 (Coast Highway) between Bluebird Canyon Drive and Laguna Canyon Road.

Fine fashion is taken for granted at **Shebue**. This plush shop houses beautiful designer clothing for women. *Très chic* (and *très cher*). Closed Sunday and Monday. ~ 31678 South Coast Highway; 949-494-3148.

Since you're likely to be spending a good bit of time tooling around town wearing sandals, **Shelby's Foot Jewelry** will allow you to do so in style with its wide selection of beaded, sterling silver, and gold anklets and toe rings. Closed Wednesday from mid-October to mid-February. ~ 577 South Coast Highway; 949-494-7992; www.shelbyslaguna.com.

Tippecanoes is a vintage clothing store with a collection of antique knickknacks. ~ 648 South Coast Highway; 949-494-1200.

For a huge selection of pre-1940s American Indian art, I particularly recommend **Len Wood's Indian Territory, Inc.** The gallery carries everything: Navajo rugs and blankets, Pueblo pottery, Hopi kachinas, and Hopi, Navajo, and Zuni jewelry. Closed Sunday. ~ 305 North Coast Highway #D; 949-497-5747; www.indianterritory.com.

Laguna Beach's other shopping strip is Forest Avenue, a three-block promenade with specialty stores. **Laura Downing** is here, a clothing store specializing in upscale clothing and jewelry. ~ 241 Forest Avenue; 949-494-4300; www.lauradowningboutique.com.

The Foxes Trot has an unpredictable inventory, a kind of cultural hodgepodge ranging from ethnic jewelry and clothing to African art. ~ 260 Forest Avenue; 949-494-4997.

NIGHTLIFE   **The White House Tavern and Restaurant** is a landmark 1917 building downtown. A wide-open dancefloor turns tradition upside down every night with live rock, reggae, Motown, blues, and funk. Cover. ~ 340 South Coast Highway; 949-494-8088, fax 949-494-0986; www.whitehouserestaurant.com.

Laguna Beach Art Galleries

Given its long tradition as an artist colony, it's little wonder that Laguna Beach is crowded with galleries and studios. The historic Gallery Row area, located along the 300 and 400 blocks of North Coast Highway around the Laguna Beach Art Museum, has more than 20 galleries. **Marion Meyer Contemporary Art** represents both emerging local artists and well-established international figures. Closed Wednesday. ~ 354 North Coast Highway; 949-497-5442; www.marionmeyergallery.com. Impressionist local landscapes and seascapes at affordable prices are the stock in trade at **Studio 7 Gallery**. ~ 384-B North Coast Highway; 949-497-1080.

The downtown Village, along the quaint streets of Forest, Ocean, Coast Highway, Peppertree Lane, and Laguna Avenue, offers another assortment of galleries. The eclectic **Sherwood Gallery** has a reputation for its unconventional approach to art and its strong commitment to progressive artists. ~ 460 South Coast Highway; 949-497-2668; www.sherwoodgallery.com. At the three **Wyland Galleries** you'll find paintings from the world's leading environmental marine life artist. ~ 509 South Coast Highway, 218 Forest Avenue, and 2171 Laguna Canyon; 949-376-8000; www.wyland.com. The **Diane DeBilzan Gallery** features the colorful, contemporary work of William DeBilzan. ~ 224 Forest Avenue; 949-494-5757; www.dianedebilzan gallery.com.

South Village, located along South Coast Highway between the 900 and 1800 blocks, is lined with a multitude of galleries. Foremost among them is the **Redfern Gallery**, specializing in museum-quality paintings of the California impressionist school (1890–1940s). ~ 1540 South Coast Highway; 949-497-3356; www.redferngallery.com. Early California impressionism is also the focus of **De Ru's Fine Arts**. Closed Monday and Tuesday. ~ 1590 South Coast Highway; 949-376-3785; www.derusfinearts.com. **Bluebird Gallery** carries contemporary artists. Closed Monday and Tuesday. ~ 1540 South Coast Highway; 949-497-5377; www.bluebirdgallery.net.

Russian impressionist paintings from the 1940s through the 1980s are exhibited at **J. Kamin Fine Art**, along with contemporary impressionism by artist Jacqueline Kamin. Closed Monday and Tuesday. ~ 353 North Pacific Coast Highway; 949-494-5076; www.jkaminfineart.com. Another artist-owned gallery, the **Vladimir Sokolov Studio Gallery** presents works, including mixed media collages, by Mr. Sokolov. ~ 1540 South Coast Highway; 949-494-3633; www.vladimirsokolovgallery.com. The **Esther Wells Collection** features contemporary oil paintings, watercolors, and sculptures. ~ 1390 South Coast Highway; 949-494-2497; www.estherwellscollection.com.

One of Laguna Beach's hottest nightspots is also its most funky. **The Sandpiper** is a run-down club filled with dart boards, a pool table, and pinball machines. Often it is also filled with some of the finest sounds around. Rock, reggae, blues, and other music is live nightly, sometimes preformed by well-known groups. There's a deejay on Monday. Cover. ~ 1185 South Coast Highway; 949-494-4694.

Las Brisas, a sleek, clifftop restaurant overlooking the ocean, is a gathering place for the fast and fashionable. A wonderful place to enjoy a quiet cocktail, it features a tile bar as well as an open-air patio. Mariachis play one night each week in summer. ~ 361 Cliff Drive; 949-497-5434, fax 949-497-9210.

Cozy neighborhood-bar-by-day, the **Marine Room Tavern** morphs into the area's hottest venue for live rock and blues at night. Although rough around the edges, the Marine Room has a dancefloor that's always teeming with locals and visitors of all ages, a full bar, and several beers on tap. The staff tends to be surly, even though they provide excellent, speedy service. All the patrons are friendly, though, and (unless you're wearing ear plugs) you'll leave with a nice ringing in your ears from the groups that crank up the sound each night and on Sunday afternoons. ~ 214 Ocean Avenue; 949-494-3027.

The **Wind & Sea Restaurant**, on the waterfront in Dana Point Harbor, features sparkling views, an open-air patio, and live musical entertainment nightly. ~ 34699 Golden Lantern Street, Dana Point; 949-496-6500; www.windandsearestaurant.com.

GAY SCENE   For two decades, Laguna Beach enjoyed a reputation as one of the most popular gay vacation destinations in California. But recently, Laguna's gay scene has quieted down a bit, as flocks of gay men and lesbians, most driven out by the extraordinarily high real estate prices in Laguna Beach, have decamped to Palm Springs and other locales. Two of Laguna Beaches long-time gay establishments, the Coast Inn and the legendary Boom Boom Room, were sold in 2006, and the new owner planned on closing them, leaving the town without a gay hotel and a much-diminished nightlife scene.

The gay-owned **Woodys at the Beach** is an attractive contemporary restaurant with ocean views from its art-filled dining room and outdoor patio. The menu features a variety of meat and seafood dishes along with pastas, soups, and salads. Full bar. Dinner only. ~ 1305 South Coast Highway; 949-376-8809; www.woodysatthebeach.com.

Club Bounce is really two clubs. Downstairs, the friendly bar attracts a mostly gay male clientele and features live entertainment most nights; Monday and Tuesday karaoke nights draw a large mixed crowd. Upstairs on weekends is a danceclub. ~ 1460 South Coast Highway; 949-494-0056.

CRYSTAL COVE STATE PARK 🧍 🚲 🏖 🎣 🏊 ⚓ This outstanding facility has a long, winding sand beach that is sometimes sectioned into a series of coves by high tides. The park stretches for over three miles along the coast and extends up into the hills. Grassy terraces grace the sea cliffs and the offshore area is designated an underwater preserve. Providing long walks along an undeveloped coastline and on upland trails in El Moro Canyon, it's the perfect park when you're seeking solitude. Facilities are limited to lifeguards (summer only) and restrooms. Onshore fishing is permitted (with a fishing license), and swimming is good. For surfing, try the breaks north of Reef Point in Scotchman's Cove, or head south to Abalone Point. Day-use fee, $10. ~ Located along the Coast Highway between Corona del Mar and Laguna Beach. There are entrances at Pelican Point, Los Trancos, Reef Point, and El Moro Canyon; 949-494-3539, fax 949-494-6911; www.crystalcovestatepark.com.

▲ Environmental camping is permitted at three campgrounds, a three- to four-mile hike inland from the parking lot; $11 to $15 per night. No open campfires allowed. There are also cabins available; $30 to $325 per night.

CRESCENT BAY 🏖 🎣 ⚓ This half-moon inlet is flanked by a curving cliff upon which the fortunate few have parked their palatial homes. Down on the beach, the sand is as soft and thick as the carpets in those houses. Offshore stands Seal Rock, with barking denizens whose cries echo off the surrounding cliffs. This, to say the least, is a pretty place. You can swim, skindive, sunbathe, explore the rocks and tidepools, or venture up to the vista point that overlooks this natural setting. The beach has restrooms, and lifeguards in summer. Fishing and swimming are good, and there's also very good bodysurfing and excellent skindiving. ~ Entrances to the beach are located near the intersection of Cliff Drive and Circle Way.

> Visit seals and sea lions at the Marine Mammal Rescue Center, open daily from 10 a.m. to 4 p.m. ~ 20612 Laguna Canyon Road; 949-494-3050; www.pacific mmc.org.

SHAW'S COVE, FISHERMAN'S COVE, AND DIVER'S COVE 🏖 🎣 ⚓ These three miniature inlets sit adjacent to one another, creating one of Laguna Beach's most scenic and popular sections of shoreline. Each features a white sand beach backdropped by a sharp bluff. Rock formations at either end are covered in spuming surf and honeycombed with tidepool pockets (particularly at the south end of Shaw's Cove). Well-known to local residents, the beaches are sometimes crowded. There are lifeguards, but no facilities. Fishing is not permitted at Diver's Cove, and swimming, while generally good, can be hazardous at Fisherman's Cove because of rocks. Diver's Cove, in keeping with its name, is often awash with scuba divers, but skindiving is excellent along this entire shoreline. ~ All three coves rest along Cliff Drive. The walkway to Shaw's Cove is at the end of Fairview Street; the entrances to Fisherman's and Diver's are within 50 feet of each other in the 600 block of Cliff Drive.

HEISLER PARK, PICNIC BEACH, AND ROCK PILE BEACH One of Laguna's prettiest stretches of shoreline lies along the clifftop in Heisler Park and below on the boulder-strewn sands of Picnic and Rock Pile beaches. The park provides a promenade with grassy areas and shade trees. You can scan the coastline from Laguna Beach south for miles, then meander down to the beach where sedimentary formations shatter the wave patterns and create marvelous tidepools. Picnic and Rock Pile form adjacent coves, both worthy of exploration. In addition to the tidepools, you'll find picnic areas, restrooms, lifeguards, and—get ready—shuffleboard. Fishing is excellent here and along most of the Laguna coast: perch, cod, bass, and halibut inhabit these waters. Swimming is permitted at Picnic Beach but not at Rock Pile Beach. For surfing, the south end of Rock Pile has some of the biggest waves in Laguna Beach. However, skindiving is also good at Picnic Beach, as the rocks offer great places to explore. ~ Heisler Park is located along Cliff Drive. Picnic Beach lies to the north at the end of Myrtle Street; Rock Pile Beach is at the end of Jasmine Street.

> For a lighthouse keeper's view of the harbor and coast, visit the lookout points at the end of Old Golden Lantern or Blue Lantern streets in Dana Point.

MAIN BEACH You'll have to venture north to Muscle Beach in Venice to find a scene equal to this one. It's located at the very center of Laguna Beach, with shopping streets radiating in several directions. A sinuous boardwalk winds along the waterfront, past basketball players, sunbathers, volleyball aficionados, little kids on swings, and aging kids on roller skates. Here and there an adventuresome soul has even dipped a toe in the wa-wa-water. In the midst of this humanity on holiday stands the lifeguard tower, an imposing glass-encased structure that looks more like a conning tower and has become a Laguna Beach icon. There are also restrooms, showers, picnic areas, a playground, and a grassy area. Fishing is good, and swimming is very good, as the beach is well-guarded. And because the Laguna Beach Marine Life Refuge lies just offshore, this a popular place for diving and snorkeling. ~ Located at Coast Highway and Broadway.

STREET BEACHES Paralleling downtown Laguna for nearly a mile is a single slender strand known to locals by the streets that intersect it. Lined with luxury homes, it provides little privacy but affords easy access to the town's amenities. There are lifeguards, and everything you want, need, or couldn't care less about is within a couple blocks. Swimming is good, and excellent peaks are created by a submerged reef off Brooks Street, making it a prime surfing and bodysurfing locale. The surf is also usually up around Thalia Street. ~ Off Coast Highway there are beach entrances at the ends of Sleepy Hollow Lane, and Cleo, St. Ann's, Thalia, Anita, Oak, and Brooks streets.

ARCH COVE Stretching for more than a half mile, ◀ *HIDDEN* bordered by a palisade of luxury homes and resort hotels, this sandy swath is ideal for sunbathers. A sea arch and blowhole rise along the south end of the beach; the northern stretch is more populated and not as pretty. Lifeguards are on duty, and swimming, although not as protected as the pocket beaches, is still okay. For surfing, there are sizeable breaks around Agate Street. ~ Entrances to the beach are at the ends of Cress Street, Mountain Road, Bluebird Canyon Drive, Agate Street, and Pearl Street. As a result, you will hear sections of the strand referred to as "Agate Beach," "Pearl Beach," etc.

WOOD'S COVE An S-shaped strand backed by ◀ *HIDDEN* Laguna's ever-loving shore bluff, this is another in the town's string of hidden wonders. Three rock peninsulas give the area its topography, creating a pair of sandy pocket beaches. The sea works in, around, and over the rocks, creating a tumultuous presence in an otherwise placid scene. Swimming is well protected by rock outcroppings, and skindiving is good off the rocks; lifeguards are on duty. ~ Steps from Diamond Street and Ocean Way lead down to the water.

MOSS POINT This tiny gem is little more than 50 ◀ *HIDDEN* yards long, but for serenity and simple beauty it challenges the giant strands. Rocky points border both sides and sharp hills overlook the entire scene. The sea streams in through the mouth of a cove and debouches onto a fan-shaped beach. The cove is well protected for swimming, and there is a lifeguard; the surrounding rocks also provide interesting areas for skindiving. ~ Located at the end of Moss Street.

VICTORIA BEACH Known primarily to locals, this ◀ *HIDDEN* quarter-mile sand corridor is flanked by homes and hills. The rocks on either side of the beach make for good exploring and provide excellent tidepooling opportunities. Amenities are few, but that's the price to pay for getting away from Laguna's crowds. At least there's a lifeguard, and even volleyball. Swimming is okay, but watch for the strong shore break and off-shore rocks. Skindiving here is good. ~ From Coast Highway take Victoria Drive, then turn right on Dumond Street.

ALISO CREEK BEACH PARK Set in a wide ◀ *HIDDEN* cove and bounded by low coastal bluffs, this park is popular with local folks. The nearby highway buzzes past and the surrounding hills are adorned with houses. A sand scimitar with rocks guarding both ends, the beach is bisected by a fishing pier. To escape the crowds head over to the park's **southern cove**, a pretty beach with fluffy sand, or check out the tidepools. Facilities include picnic areas, restrooms, showers, lifeguards, volleyball, and a snack bar. Fishing is good from the pier. When swimming, beware of strong shore breaks. Bodysurfing is a better bet than board surfing at Aliso. ~ Along the Coast Highway in South Laguna; there's a public accessway to the southern cove along the 31300 block of Coast Highway.

HIDDEN ➤

HIDDEN ➤

SOUTH LAGUNA COVES 🚴 🏊 🎣 🚣 Hidden by the hillsides that flank South Laguna's waterfront are a series of pocket beaches. Each is a crescent of white sand bounded by sharp cliffs of conglomerate rock. These in turn are crowned with plate-glass homes. Two particularly pretty inlets can be reached via accessways called **1000 Steps** and **West Street**. Both beaches have seasonal lifeguards and restrooms. Swimming is good, and the bodysurfing is excellent in both coves. Parking fee. ~ Both accessways are on Coast Highway in South Laguna—1000 Steps is at 9th Avenue; West Street is (surprise!) at West Street.

SALT CREEK BEACH PARK 🚴 🏊 🎣 🚣 ⛵ This marvelous locale consists of two half-mile sections of beach divided by a lofty point on which the Ritz-Carlton Laguna Niguel Hotel stands. Each beach is a broad strip of white sand, backdropped by bluffs and looking out on Santa Catalina Island. The hotel above dominates the region like a palatial fortress on the Mediterranean. Though both beaches are part of Salt Creek, the strand to the south is also known as **Dana Strand**. It's possible to walk from one beach to the other. Both beaches have restrooms and seasonal lifeguards; at Salt Creek (north) there is also a snack bar. The swimming is good at either beach, but for fishing you're better off at Dana Strand. It's also a good spot if you're hoping to hang ten. Salt Creek has two well-known breaks, "The Gravels," just north of the outcropping separating the two beaches, and at "The Point" itself. Parking fee. ~ Dana Strand is reached via a long stairway at the end of Selva Road. The staircase to Salt Creek is on Ritz-Carlton Drive. Both lie off Coast Highway in Laguna Niguel; 949-923-2280, fax 949-661-2641.

DOHENY STATE BEACH 🚴 🚣 ⛵ This park wrote the book on oceanside facilities. In addition to a broad swath of sandy beach there is a five-acre lawn complete with private picnic areas, beach rentals, restrooms with changing areas, lifeguards, horseshoe pits, volleyball courts, and food concessions. The grassy area offers plenty of shade trees. Surfers work the north end of the beach, leaving plenty of room for swimmers to the south.

Dana Point Harbor, with complete marina facilities, borders the beach. For fishing, try the jetty in Dana Point Harbor. Swimming is not particularly good here, as the ocean bottom is rocky, but surfing is comfortable for beginners, particularly on a south swell. Day-use fee, $10 per vehicle. ~ Located off Dana Point Harbor Drive in Dana Point; 949-496-6171, fax 949-496-9469; www.dohenystatebeach.org.

▲ There are 121 tent/RV sites (no hookups), including 32 beach sites, $25 to $35 per night. Reservations: 800-444-7275.

San Juan Capistrano

When you're ready to flee Southern California's ultramodern coastline, Camino Capistrano is the perfect escape valve. Perhaps you've heard the 1939 tune "When the Swallows Return to Capistrano." The lyrics, just to refresh your memory, describe the return of flocks of swallows every March 19. And return they still do, though in ever-decreasing numbers and not always on March 19. When you're ready to follow the swallows, head up Camino Capistrano to the mission and get out your telephoto lens—swallows are small and fast. They remain in the area until October, when winter's approach prompts them to depart for Argentina, where, blissfully, they are welcomed by no similar ditties. While you're here, take time to explore the beautiful mission and local architectural gems.

SIGHTS

Seventh in the state's chain of 21 missions, the **Mission San Juan Capistrano** was founded in 1776 by Father Junípero Serra. Considered "the jewel of the missions," it is a hauntingly beautiful site, placid and magical.

There are ponds and gardens here, ten acres of standing adobe buildings, and the ruins of the original 1797 stone church, which was destroyed by an earthquake in 1812. The museum displays American Indian crafts, an assortment of artifacts, and Spanish weaponry, while an Indian cemetery memorializes the

AUTHOR FAVORITE

sights The **Capistrano Depot** is a vital part of the town's history. Today it houses a restaurant and a saloon, but the beautifully preserved 1894 depot is still operating as a train station. Built of brick in a series of Spanish-style arches, the old structure also features railroad memorabilia. An antique Pullman, a brightly colored freight car, and other vintage cars line the tracks. ~ 26701 Verdugo Street; 949-487-2322, fax 949-493-4243; www.capistranodepot.com, e-mail dining@capistranodepot.com.

enslaved people who built this magnificent structure. There is a living-history program on the second Saturday of every month, with costumed "characters" playing the role of Father Serra and others, and craftspeople showing how old-time crafts were made. On select Saturday nights during the summer, you can hear live music under the stars. In addition, a variety of festivals, folk-art exhibits, and cultural programs are held throughout the year; call or visit the website for details. The highlight of the mission is the Serra chapel, the oldest continually used building in California; it is the only remaining church that was once used by Father Serra. Admission. ~ 26801 Ortega Highway; 949-234-1300, fax 949-481-9895; www.missionsjc.com.

> The chapel at San Juan Capistrano—the oldest continually used building in California—is the only remaining church used by Father Serra.

In the surrounding blocks are a dozen or so 19th-century structures. The **O'Neill Museum** is housed in a tiny 1870s Victorian and furnished with Victorian decor. Closed Monday. ~ 31831 Los Rios Street; 949-493-8444, fax 949-493-0061; www.sjchistoricalsociety.com, e-mail sjchs1979@sbcglobal.net.

Jolting you back to contemporary times are two buildings near the Capistrano Depot, both constructed in the 1980s. The **New Church of Mission San Juan Capistrano**, a towering edifice next to the town's historic chapel, is a replica of the original structure. Spanish Renaissance in design, the new church even re-creates the brilliantly painted interior of the old mission. ~ 31522 Camino Capistrano; 949-234-1360.

Across the street is the **San Juan Capistrano Regional Library**, an oddly eclectic building. Drawing heavily from the Moorish-style Alhambra in Spain, the architect, Michael Graves, also incorporated ideas from ancient Egypt and classical Greece. Closed Friday. ~ 31495 El Camino Real; 949-493-1752; www.ocpl.org.

DINING   One of San Juan Capistrano's many historic points, a 19th-century building, **El Adobe de Capistrano** has been converted into a Mexican steakhouse. The interior is a warren of white-washed rooms, supported by *vigas* and displaying the flourishes of Spanish California. Stop by for a drink next to the old jail (today a wine cellar) or tour the building. (Counterpoint to all this dusty history is a display of Nixon memorabilia.) If you decide to dine, the menu includes lunch, dinner, and Sunday brunch, featuring many Mexican-California specialties, fresh steaks, and seafood from the mesquite grill. ~ 31891 Camino Capistrano; 949-493-1163, fax 949-493-4565; www.eladobedecapistrano.com, e-mail info@eladobecapistrano.com. MODERATE TO DELUXE.

Who can match the combination of intimacy and French and Belgian cuisine at **L'Hirondelle**? It's quite small, and conveys a

French-country atmosphere. The restaurant offers a varied menu beginning with escargots, crab-stuffed mushrooms, and crab crêpes. Entrées include roast duck, rabbit in wine sauce, rack of lamb, bouillabaisse, sautéed sweetbreads, and fresh fish specials. Brunch only on Sunday. Closed Monday. ~ 31631 Camino Capistrano; 949-661-0425, fax 949-661-3405; www.sjc.net/din ing/l'hirondelle. DELUXE TO ULTRA-DELUXE.

Situated in a beautifully restored train depot, **Sarducci's Capistrano Depot** offers creative American cuisine at reasonable prices. Picture windows overlooking the depot add flourish, and guests can dine on lovely oak tables. Be sure to try the blackened ahi tuna with mustard-soy sauce. Lovers of veggies should definitely not miss the chef's eggplant parmesan and asparagus and sun-dried tomato pasta. ~ 26701 Verdugo Street; 949-487-2322, fax 949-493-4243; www.capistranodepot.com, e-mail dining@ capistranodepot.com. MODERATE TO DELUXE.

SHOPPING

The mission town of San Juan Capistrano has many shops clustered along its main thoroughfare, Camino Capistrano. Not surprisingly, the most common establishment in this centuries-old town is the antique store. In line with contemporary times, there are also pocket malls featuring boutiques, jewelers, and other outlets.

Particularly noteworthy is **The Old Barn**, a warehouse-size store filled to the rafters with antiques. ~ 31792 Camino Capistrano; 949-493-9144.

NIGHTLIFE

Swallows Inn is a hellbent Western bar with ranch tools tacked to the walls. Wednesday through Sunday nights, you can kick up your heels to live country-and-western, except when the music takes on a rock-and-roll, jazz, or blues feel. ~ 31786 Camino Capistrano; 949-493-3188; www.swallowsinn.com.

BEACHES & PARKS

CAPISTRANO BEACH PARK This is a big rectangular sandbox facing the open ocean. Like many beaches in the area it offers ample facilities and is often quite crowded. Bounded by sedimentary cliffs and offering views of Dana Point Harbor, the beach is landscaped with palm and deciduous trees. The park is particularly popular with families and surfers, who all take advantage of the picnic areas, bonfire pits, restrooms, showers, lifeguards, volleyball and basketball courts, and rollerblade rentals. Swimming is good here, but it's the surfing that's the big draw. "Killer Capo" breaks are about 400 yards offshore along the northern fringes of the beach (near Doheny State Park), and "Dody's Reef" breaks are about one-half mile to the south, but are not predictable. Parking fee. ~ Located along Coast Highway in Capistrano Beach.

▼▼▼▼▼▼▼▼▼▼▼
San Clemente

If any place is the capital of Republican politics, it is San Clemente, a seaside town that sets the standard for Southern California's notorious conservatism because of one man. Richard Milhous Nixon, President of the United States from 1969 until his ignominious resignation during the Watergate scandal in 1974, established the Western White House on a 25-acre site overlooking the ocean.

SIGHTS

La Casa Pacífica, a magnificent Spanish-style home, was famous not only during Nixon's presidency, but afterwards when he retreated to San Clemente to lick his wounds. There are stories of Nixon, ever the brooding, socially awkward man, pacing the beach in a business suit and leather shoes.

The Nixon house is located off Avenida del Presidente in a private enclave called Cypress Shore. You can see it, a grand white stucco home with red tile roof, on the cliffs above San Clemente State Beach. Just walk south from the beach entrance about one-half mile toward a point of land obscured by palms; the house is set back in the trees.

Another point of interest (quite literally) is **San Clemente Municipal Pier**, a popular fishing spot and centerpiece of the city beach. There are food concessions, bait and tackle shops, and local crowds galore. ~ Foot of Avenida del Mar.

For more information on the area, call the **San Clemente Chamber of Commerce**. ~ 1100 North El Camino Real; 949-492-1131, fax 949-492-3764; www.scchamber.com.

LODGING

Algodon Motel is a standard 20-unit facility several blocks from the beach. Some units have kitchens. Not much to write home about, but it is clean and affordable. ~ 135 Avenida Algodon; 949-492-3382, fax 949-492-3972. BUDGET TO MODERATE.

For families and extended stays, a stint at the **Seahorse Resort** is a sure bet. Located right on the beach, accommodations vary from studios to one- and two-bedroom suites. All boast modern conveniences as well as uncluttered views of the ocean and pier, full kitchens, and private patios and balconies. Complimentary beach chairs and umbrellas are available. ~ 602 Avenida Victoria; 949-492-1720, fax 949-498-8857; www.seahorsesanclemente.com, e-mail info@seahorsesanclemente.com. ULTRA-DELUXE.

DINING

Center of the casual dining scene in San Clemente is along the beach at the foot of the municipal pier (end of Avenida del Mar). Several takeout stands and cafés are here. The **Fisherman's Restaurant and Bar**, a knotty-pine-and-plate-glass establishment, sits right on the pier, affording views all along the beach. With a waterfront patio it's a good spot for seafood dishes at lunch or dinner. There is also breakfast on Saturday, and Sunday brunch. ~ 611 Avenida Victoria; 949-498-6390, fax 949-498-8681, www.fisher mansrestaurant.com. MODERATE TO ULTRA-DELUXE.

Though it sounds forbidding, **The Mole Hole Unique Gift Gallery** is a colorful and inviting shop specializing in limited-edition collectibles from around the world. Wee Forest Folk, hand-painted Limoges boxes, Franz porcelain, and bronze from "The Frogman" are part of the unusual selection. You'll also find art glass and sculpture from internationally known artists. ~ Ocean View Plaza, 638 Camino de los Mares, Suite G140; 949-443-1670, 800-863-5395, fax 949-443-1681; www.themolehole.net, e-mail moleweb@ themolehole.net.

SHOPPING

SAN CLEMENTE CITY BEACH 🏊 🏄 🎣 Running nearly the length of town, this silver strand is the pride of San Clemente. Landlubbers congregate near the municipal pier, anglers work its waters, and surfers blanket the beachfront. There are railroad tracks and coastal bluffs paralleling the entire beach. Eden this ain't: San Clemente is heavily developed, but the beach is a pleasant place to spend a day. There are restaurants and other amenities at the municipal pier including picnic areas, restrooms, lifeguards, and a playground. The **Ole Hanson Beach Club** (105 Avenida Pico; 949-361-8207; admission) at the north end of the beach is a public pool with dressing rooms. Fishing is best from the pier, and surfing is good alongside of the pier. The beach is also good for swimming. ~ The pier is located at the foot of Avenida del Mar in San Clemente.

BEACHES & PARKS

San Clemente boasts an average temperature of 70 degrees and 342 days of sunshine per year.

SAN CLEMENTE STATE BEACH 🚶 🏊 🏄 🎣 Walk down the deeply eroded cliffs guarding this coastline, and you'll discover a long narrow strip of sand that curves north from San Diego County up to San Clemente City Beach. There are camping areas and picnic plots on top of the bluff. Down below a railroad track parallels the beach and surfers paddle offshore. You can stroll north toward downtown San Clemente or south to President Nixon's old home. Beach facilities include lifeguards, picnic areas, and restrooms. Surf fishing is best in spring, and surfers will find year-round breaks at the south end of the beach. Swimmers should beware of rip currents. Day-use fee, $10. ~ Located off Avenida Calafia in San Clemente; 949-492-0802.

▲ There are 160 tent/RV sites (71 with hookups); $25 for tents, $30 for hookups.

Outdoor Adventures

Whether you want to snatch a tuna or watch a spouting whale, the Orange County coast offers plenty of possibilities.

SPORT-FISHING & WHALE WATCHING FISHING

Davey's Locker offers half- and full-day sportfishing charters for yellowtail, bass, and barracuda. ~ 400 Main Street, Balboa; 949-673-1434; www.daveyslocker.com. For trips to Catalina and Clemente islands for bass, dorado, and tuna, contact **Dana Wharf Sportfishing**. ~ 34675 Golden Lantern Street, Dana Point; 949-496-5794; www.danawharfsportfishing.com. Dana Wharf Sportfishing and Davey's Locker also sponsor two-hour whale-watching cruises during migratory season (December to late March).

DIVING

The coastal waters abound in interesting kelp beds rich with sea life; several companies are available to help you through the kelp.

For weekly lessons and rentals on Catalina, contact **Beach Cities Scuba Center**. ~ 4537 West Coast Highway, Newport Beach; 949-650-5440; www.beachcitiesscuba.com. **Laguna Sea Sports** rents equipment and provides lessons. ~ 925 North Coast Highway, Laguna Beach; 949-494-6965; www.scuba-superstore.com.

SURFING

Orange County is surfer heaven, so when you're in the area, don't miss out on Orange County's wild waves.

Practically all the beaches here are surfable; these are just a few spots to get you started. Early risers head to Newport Pier at Newport Beach. If you're in town during the winter, try the jetty at the end of Surfside Beach. World-renowned Huntington City Beach hosts international surfing competitions in the summer. The south end of San Clemente State Beach offers great breaks any time of the year. Large waves can be found at Salt Creek Beach Park and the south end of Rock Pile Beach; Capistrano Beach Park is known for its "Killer Capo" breaks. Beginners choose to learn at Doheny State Beach. For surf reports call 949-492-1011.

If bodysurfing is your thing, the Wedge at West Jetty View Park is the place to do it.

For surfboards, boogieboards, wetsuit rentals, sales, and repairs, contact **Huntington Surf and Sport**. ~ 300 Pacific Coast Highway, Huntington Beach; 714-841-4000; www.hsssurf.com. **Hobie Sports** also rents boards. ~ 24825 Del Prado, Dana Point; 949-496-2366; www.hobie.com. **Stewart's Surf Boards** sells and rents surfboards and boogieboards. Inquire about lessons—some of the employees have information regarding private instruction. ~ 2102 South El Camino Real, San Clemente; 949-492-1085; www.stewartsurfboards.com.

KAYAKING & BOATING

With elaborate marina complexes at Huntington Beach, Newport Beach, and Dana Point, this is a spectacular area for boating. If you yearn to make some waves, call one of the outfits listed below.

Fishing skiffs are available for rent at **Davey's Locker**. ~ 400 Main Street, Balboa; 949-673-1434; www.daveyslocker.com. In Newport Beach, try **Marina Sailing** for lessons or six-passenger charters. ~ 300 Pacific Coast Highway, Suite F, Newport Beach; 949-548-8900; www.marinasailing.com. Electric boats, motorboats, sailboats, kayaks, and offshore runabouts can be rented at **Balboa Boat Rentals**. ~ 510 East Edgewater, Balboa; 949-673-7200; www.boats4rent.com.

GOLF

The climate and terrain of Orange County make for excellent golfing. Take a break from Southern California freeways, and do some driving on the greens instead.

Tee up at the 18-hole executive **Newport Beach Golf Course**, but expect to carry your own clubs: this course has no electric carts. ~ 3100 Irvine Avenue, Newport Beach; 949-852-8681. The enchanting nine-hole **Aliso Creek Golf Course** is set in the middle of a steep canyon with a creek winding through it. ~ 31106 Coast Highway, Laguna Beach; 949-499-1919; www.aliso creekinn.com. The coastal course at **The Golf Links at Monarch Beach** is designed by Robert Trent Jones, Jr., and has a beautiful view of the water. ~ 22 Monarch Beach Resort North, Dana Point; 949-240-8247; www.monarch beachgolf.com. If you're looking for a dry course with ocean views, visit the **San Clemente Municipal Golf Course**. ~ 150 East Avenida Magdalena, San Clemente; 949-361-8384. Situated in a narrow canyon, the public, par-72 **Shorecliffs Golf Course** has a driving range and putting green. The greens are small and the course is fast and in good condition. Carts are mandatory. ~ 501 Avenida Vaquero, San Clemente; 949-492-1177.

> Richard Nixon used to play the greens at Shorecliffs Golf Course in San Clemente.

TENNIS

Even though public courts are hard to find in this area, who says Orange County is elitist? There are still many private clubs, and given the wonderful climate and the way you'll fit in wearing those white shorts and tennis sweaters, it's probably worth the club fee after all.

In Newport Beach, you can try one of the eight lighted, plexipaved courts at **Hotel Tennis Club**. A pro is available for lessons. Fee. ~ Marriott Hotel, 900 Newport Center Drive, Newport Beach; 949-729-3566. Laguna Beach's **Moulton Meadows Park** has two courts. ~ Del Mar and Balboa avenues, Laguna Beach; 949-497-0716. **Laguna Niguel Regional Park** features four lighted tennis courts. ~ 28241 La Paz Road, Laguna Niguel; 949-923-2240. There are eight lighted courts at **Dana Hills Tennis Center**. Fee. ~ 24911 Calle de Tenis, Dana Point; 949-240-2104.

Strangely enough, San Clemente is the one Orange County town that does seem to have an abundance of public courts.

Bonito Canyon Park offers two lighted courts. ~ 1304 Calle Valle, San Clemente; 949-361-8264. There are three lighted courts at San Luis Rey Park. ~ 109 Avenida San Luis Rey, San Clemente; 949-361-8264. San Gorgonio Park has two unlit courts. ~ 2916 Via San Gorgonio, San Clemente; 949-361-8264. Verde Park also has one court for day-use only. ~ 301 Calle Escuela; 949-361-8264.

BIKING

Wind and wheels are a perfect blend with Southern California's weather, and you can avoid adding to the smog and sitting in traffic by tooling around on a bike rather than in a car. Whether you like road riding or mountain biking, you'll find a suitable place to cycle in Orange County. Route 1, the Pacific Coast Highway, offers cyclists an opportunity to explore the Orange County coastline. The problem, of course, is the traffic. Along Bolsa Chica State Beach, however, a special pathway runs the length of the beach. Another way to avoid traffic is to mountain-bike; Moro Canyon in Crystal Cove State Park is a favorite off-road riding area.

Skirting the Upper Newport Bay Ecological Reserve are about ten miles of bikeway; there are some hills, but nothing too strenuous. You can park for about $10 at Newport Dunes (an RV resort) or try for one of the spots in the small Big Canyon lot in the reserve. Back Bay Drive, a multi-use paved roadway, has a double-wide bike route; it links up with a dedicated bike route around the northern perimeter of the reserve. Eventually, along the western flank, the bike route gives way to a bike lane on city-streets to complete the loop around the reserve. ~ Back Bay Drive at Jamboree Road.

Other interesting areas to explore are Balboa Island and the Balboa Peninsula in Newport Beach. Both offer quiet residential streets and are connected by a ferry that permits bicycles. A pop-

ROAD RUNNING

If you'd rather shake up the cellulite than the water, you can do it on Orange County's miles of beaches and running trails. Mecca for Orange County runners is the Santa Ana Riverbed Trail, a smooth asphalt ribbon stretching 20.6 miles from Anaheim to Huntington Beach State Park. There are par courses and excellent running trails at both Laguna Niguel Regional Park (La Paz and Aliso Creek Road) and Mile Square Regional Park (16801 Euclid Avenue in Fountain Valley). In Mission Viejo there's a beautiful two-and-a-half-mile trail around Lake Mission Viejo. And then there are the miles and miles of beaches for which Orange County is renowned.

ular inland ride is along **Santiago Canyon Road**; leaving from Orange the route skirts Irvine Lake and Cleveland National Forest.

Call the **Newport Beach Department of Public Works** and ask for a copy of the "Bikeways" map; it shows all the trails in Newport Beach. ~ City Hall, 3300 Newport Boulevard; 949-644-3311; www.city.newport-beach.ca.us.

Bike Rentals **Rainbow Bicycle Company** rents, repairs, and sells mountain bikes. ~ 485 North Coast Highway, Laguna Beach; 949-494-5806; www.teamrain.com.

Though heavily developed, the Orange Coast still provides several outstanding trails. All are located near the beaches and offer views of private homes and open ocean.

HIKING

The **California Coastal Trail** extends over 40 miles from the San Gabriel River in Seal Beach to San Mateo Point in San Clemente. Much of the route follows sandy beachfront and sedimentary bluffs. There are lagoons and tidepools, fishing piers, and marinas en route.

At the **Bolsa Chica Ecological Reserve Trail** (1.5 miles) you can say hello to birds traveling along the Pacific Flyway. A migratory rest stop, this lagoon features a loop trail that runs atop a levee past fields of cord grass and pickleweed.

Huntington Beach Paved Bike and Hike Trail (8.5 miles) parallels the Pacific from Bolsa Chica Lagoon to Beach Boulevard in Huntington Beach. Along the way it takes in Huntington Pier, a haven for surfers, and passes an army of unspeakably ugly oil derricks.

Newport Trail (2.5 miles) traces the ocean side of Balboa Peninsula from Newport Pier south to Balboa Pier, then proceeds to the peninsula's end at Jetty View Park. Private homes run the length of this pretty beach walk.

Back Bay Trail (3.5 miles) follows Back Bay Drive in Newport Beach along the shores of Upper Newport Bay. This fragile wetland, an important stop on the Pacific Flyway, is an ideal birdwatching area.

Crystal Cove Trail (3 miles) provides a pleasant seaside stroll. Starting from Pelican Point at the western boundary of Crystal Cove State Park, the paved path leads to the beach. The trail continues another mile to a cluster of cottages at Crystal Cove, then follows an undeveloped beach to Reef Point.

Aliso Creek Canyon Hiking Trail (1 mile) begins near the fishing pier at Aliso Beach County Park in South Laguna, leads north through a natural arch, and passes the ruins of an old boat landing.

Transportation

CAR

Several major highways crisscross Orange County. Route 1, known in this area as the **Pacific Coast Highway**, ends its long journey down the California Coast in Capistrano Beach. A few miles farther inland, **Route 405** runs from Long Beach to Irvine, with feeder roads leading to the main coastal towns.

AIR

John Wayne International Airport, located in Santa Ana, is the main terminal in these parts. Major carriers presently serving it include Alaska Airlines, Aloha Airlines, America West, American Airlines, Continental Airlines, Delta Air Lines, Frontier Airlines, Northwest Airlines, Southwest Airlines, and United Airlines. ~ 18601 Airport Way, Santa Ana; 949-252-5200; www.ocair.com.

BUS

Greyhound Bus Lines (800-231-2222; www.greyhound.com) serves Orange County, stopping in Anaheim and Santa Ana.

TRAIN

Amtrak's "San Diegan" travels between Los Angeles and San Diego, with Orange County stops at Fullerton, Anaheim Stadium, Santa Ana, San Juan Capistrano, and San Clemente. ~ 800-872-7245; www.amtrak.com.

CAR RENTALS

Arriving at John Wayne International Airport, you'll find the following car rental agencies: **Alamo Rent A Car** (800-327-9633), **Avis Rent A Car** (800-230-4898), **Budget Rent A Car** (800-527-0700), **Hertz Rent A Car** (800-654-3131), and **National Car Rental** (800-227-7368). For less expensive (and less convenient) service, try **Enterprise Rent A Car** (800-736-8222).

PUBLIC TRANSIT

Orange County Transportation Authority, or RIDE from southern Orange County, has bus service throughout Orange County, including most inland areas. Along the coast it stops at beach fronts including Seal Beach, Huntington Beach, Newport Beach, Corona del Mar, Laguna Beach, San Juan Capistrano, and San Clemente. ~ 714-636-7433; www.octa.net.

EIGHT

San Diego Coast

San Diego County's 4200 square miles occupy a Connecticut-sized chunk of real estate that forms the southwestern corner of the continental United States. Geographically, it is as varied a parcel of landscape as any in the world. Surely this spot is one of the few places on the planet where, in a matter of hours, you can journey from bluff-lined beaches up and over craggy mountain peaks and down again to sun-scorched desert sands.

Moving east from the Pacific to the county's interior, travelers discover lush valleys and irrigated hillsides. Planted with citrus orchards, vineyards, and rows of vegetables, this curving countryside eventually gives way to the Palomar and Laguna mountains—cool, pine-crested ranges that rise over 6500 feet.

But it is the coast—some 76 sparkling miles stretching from San Mateo Point near San Clemente to the Mexican border—that always has held the fascination of residents and visitors alike.

When Portuguese explorer Juan Rodríguez Cabrillo laid eyes on these shores in 1542, he discovered a prospering settlement of Kumeyaay Indians. For hundreds of years, these native peoples had been living in quiet contentment on lands overlooking the Pacific; they had harvested the rich estuaries and ventured only occasionally into the scrubby hills and canyons for firewood and game.

Sixty years passed before the next visitor, Spanish explorer Sebastian Vizcaíno, came seeking a hideout for royal galleons beset by pirates. It was Vizcaíno who named the bay for San Diego de Alcala.

In 1769, the Spanish came to stay. The doughty Franciscan missionary Junípero Serra marched north from Mexico with a company of other priests and soldiers and built Mission San Diego de Alcala. It was the first of a chain of 21 missions and the earliest site in California to be settled by Europeans. Father Serra's mission, relocated a few miles inland in 1774, now sits incongruously amid the shopping centers and housing developments of Mission Valley.

California's earliest civilian settlement evolved in the 1820s on a dusty mesa beneath the hilltop presidio that protected the original mission. Pueblo San Diego quickly developed into a thriving trade and cattle ranching center after the ruling Spanish colonial regime was overthrown and replaced by the Republic of Mexico.

By the end of the century, new residents, spurred partly by land speculators, had taken root and developed the harbor and downtown business district. After the rails finally reached San Diego in 1885, the city flourished. Grand Victorian buildings lined 5th Avenue all the way from the harbor to Broadway and 1400 barren acres were set aside uptown for a city park.

After its turn-of-the-20th-century spurt of activity, the city languished until World War II, when the U.S. Navy invaded the town en masse to establish the 11th Naval District headquarters and one of the world's largest Navy bases. San Diego's reputation as "Navytown USA" persisted well after the war-weary sailors went home. Despite the closure of the San Diego Naval Training Center, some 103,000 Navy and Marine personnel are still based in San Diego and at Camp Pendleton to the north. With 101,000 family members, 26,000 civilian Navy employees, and 59,000 Navy retirees, the military presence remains a major influence, but this is changing as high-tech industries locate in San Diego, bringing "new economy" diversity and a spirit of renewal.

The military has not been the only force to foster San Diego's growth. In the early 1960s, construction began on an important university that was to spawn a completely new industry. Many peg the emergence of the "new" San Diego to the opening of the University of California's La Jolla campus. Not only did the influx of 15,000 students help revive a floundering economy, it tended to liberalize an otherwise insular and conservative city.

Truth is, San Diego is no longer the sleepy, semitransparent little resort city it once was. Nowhere is the fact more evident than in the downtown district, where a building boom brought new offices, condominiums, and hotels.

But for all the city's manmade appeal, it is nature's handiwork and an ideal Mediterranean climate that most delights San Diego visitors. With bays and beaches bathed in sunshine 75 percent of the time, less than ten inches of rainfall per year and average temperatures that mirror a proverbial day in June, San Diego offers the casual outdoor lifestyle that fulfills vacation dreams. There's a beach for every taste, ranging from broad sweeps of white sand to slender scimitars beneath eroded sandstone bluffs.

Situated 120 miles south of Los Angeles on Route 5, San Diego is not so much a city as a collection of communities hiding in canyons and gathered on small shoulders of land that shrug down to the sea. As a result, it hardly seems big enough (a bit under 1.3 million) to rank as America's seventh largest city. Total county population is 3 million, and nine of ten residents live within 30 miles of the coast.

The city of San Diego is divided into several geographic sections. To the south lies Coronado, nestled on a peninsula jutting into San Diego Bay and connected to the mainland by a narrow sandbar known as the Silver Strand.

Although they are within the boundaries of the city of San Diego, the seaside communities of Ocean Beach, Mission Beach, Pacific Beach, and La Jolla have developed their own identities, moods, and styles.

"OB," as the first of these is known, along with Mission and Pacific beaches, exults in the sunny, sporty Southern California lifestyle fostered by nearby

Mission Bay Park. These neighboring communities are fronted by broad beaches and an almost continuous boardwalk that is jammed with joggers, skaters, and cyclists. The beaches are saturated in the summer by local sun-seekers, but they have much to offer visitors.

Like a beautiful but slightly spoiled child, La Jolla is an enclave of wealth and stubborn independence that calls itself "The Village" and insists on having its own post office, although it's actually just another part of the extended San Diego family. Mediterranean-style mansions and small cottages shrouded by jasmine and hibiscus share multimillion-dollar views of beaches, coves, and wild, eroded sea cliffs. Swank shops and galleries, trendy restaurants and classy little hotels combine in a Riviera-like setting that rivals even Carmel for chicness.

North County is a string of beach towns stretching from Oceanside south to Del Mar, where outdoor enthusiasts can find their fill of white-sand beaches, world-class golf courses, and state parks. Shops and restaurants dot Route 101, the coastal highway that threads through the towns of Oceanside, Carlsbad, Leucadia, Encinitas, Cardiff-by-the-Sea, and Del Mar. A varied area, these towns boast residents from every walk of life—from the ultra-wealthy (as found in La Costa and Del Mar), to the Southern Californian artisans (as found in Leucadia), to the short-haired Marines of Oceanside.

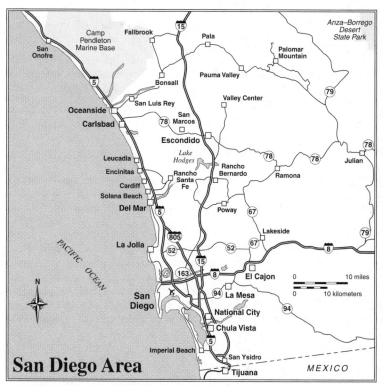

San Diego Area

Text continued on page 452.

History, Culture, and Wildlife

This tour will introduce you to the many facets of San Diego in a brief visit. Conspicuously absent here are **SeaWorld San Diego** (page 475), an all-day theme park that's a must-see if you have kids, and the **San Diego Zoo** (page 496), which is compelling whether or not you have kids in tow. Another all-day adventure for those who have extra time is a visit to **Tijuana** (page 516).

Day 1
- Start your day in **Old Town** (page 486) with a tour on the Old Town Trolley, then stroll through the lively **Bazaar del Mundo** (page 486) marketplace.

- Visit the **Junipero Serra Museum** (page 486) for an account of San Diego's birth.

- In the mood for Mexican food? Stop by **El Indio** (page 489) and pick up some savory items for an alfresco lunch.

- If you wish, round out the historical segment of your tour with a drive out to **Mission San Diego de Alcala** (page 487), the first California mission church, now surrounded by suburban sprawl.

- Head down to the waterfront for a **San Diego Harbor Excursion** (page 506) to see the commercial shipping and U.S. Navy activity that drives the city's economy.

- Enjoy a seafood feast at **Anthony's Fish Grotto** (page 508).

- If you're still bursting with energy after this busy day, why not drive out to Coronado island for cocktails at the classy **Babcock & Story Bar** (page 512) in the Hotel del Coronado?

Day 2
- Pack a picnic lunch and plan your day around a visit to **Balboa Park** (page 494), where you can choose among world-class museums devoted to fine art, folk art, photography, astronomy, natural history, aerospace technology, anthropology, sports, and model railroads. Between museums, take plenty of time to stroll this magnificently landscaped 1400-acre park with its Spanish colonial revival architecture.

- Dine in Downtown San Diego's Gaslamp Quarter at **Ida Bailey's Restaurant** (page 504), an elegant Victorian-style restaurant named for the madam who used to run a house of ill-repute there. Later, stick around the Quarter and hop your way among the many nightclubs of San Diego's premier entertainment zone.

Day 3
- Drive up north to the **San Diego Zoo's Wild Animal Park** (page 454) to spend the morning watching the free-roaming wildlife from the monorail and walkways.

- Returning from the animal park, stop for lunch in Del Mar at **The Fish Market** (page 461).

- Follow the coast highway down to **La Jolla** (page 466). Round out your wildlife-watching day with a stop at the **Birch Aquarium at Scripps** (page 468).

- Head up to the top of the bluffs in **Torrey Pines State Reserve and Beach** (page 468) for a great sunset view.

- Return to La Jolla for dinner at one of the village's many great restaurants, such as **George's at the Cove** (page 471).

It is safe to say that the San Diego area is not as eccentric and sophisticated as San Francisco, nor as glamorous and fast-paced as Los Angeles. But those who still perceive it as a laid-back mecca for beach bums—or as a lunch stop en route to Mexico—are in for a huge surprise.

▼▼▼▼▼▼▼▼▼▼▼▼▼
North San Diego County

Stretching along the coast above San Diego is a string of towns with a host of personalities and populations. Residents here range from the county's wealthiest folks in Rancho Santa Fe to Marine privates at Oceanside's Camp Pendleton to yogis in retreat at Encinitas. This part of the county really shines, however, in its many sparkling beaches.

The best way to see North County's fine beaches is to cruise along Old Route 101, which preceded Route 5 as the north–south coastal route. It changes names in each beach town along the way, but once you're on it you won't be easily sidetracked.

SIGHTS
Your first sightseeing opportunity in San Diego County is at **San Onofre State Beach**, about 16 miles north of Oceanside. Unique in that it's actually two beaches, North and South, this certainly is one of the county's most scenic beach parks. Its eroded sandstone bluffs hide a variety of secluded sandy coves and pocket beaches. But all this beauty is broken by an eerie and ungainly structure rising from the shoreline. Dividing the park's twin beaches is a mammoth facility, potent and ominous, the **San Onofre nuclear power plant**. Admission. ~ 949-492-0802, fax 949-492-8412.

Old Route 101 leads next into **Oceanside**, gateway to Camp Pendleton Marine Base. San Diego County's third-largest city is busy renovating its beachfront and image. The refurbished fishing pier is a lengthy one, stretching almost 2000 feet into the Pacific.

If you'd like to learn more about California's "cultural" side, stop by the **California Surf Museum**, which features exhibits on the history of the sport and its early pioneers. On display is the very first surfing trophy, named after Tom Blake, one of the first waterproof cameras that was used to capture up-close footage, wooden boards from the early 1900s, and changing special exhibits. A museum shop offers vintage books and videos. ~ 223 North Coast Highway, Oceanside; 760-721-6876; www.surfmuseum.org, e-mail csm@surfmuseum.org.

From Oceanside, Mission Avenue, which merges with Route 76, will carry you to **Mission San Luis Rey**. Known as the "King of the Missions" (and named originally after a king of France), this beautifully restored complex was originally constructed in 1798 and represents the largest California mission. Today you can visit the museum chapel and cemetery while walking these historic grounds. Admission. ~ 4050 Mission Avenue, Oceanside; 760-757-3651, fax 760-757-4613; www.sanluisrey.org.

Back on coastal Route 5 and farther south of Oceanside is **Carlsbad**, a friendly, sunny beachfront town that has been entirely redeveloped, complete with cobblestone streets and quaint shops. Originally the place established its reputation around the similarity of its mineral waters to the springs of the original Karlsbad in the Czech Republic. But don't waste your time looking for the fountain of youth, the spring has long since dried up. Go to the beach instead.

Added to Southern California's theme park lineup is LEGO-LAND, patterned after the park in Denmark where Legos are made. Designed with kids ages two to twelve in mind, attractions include cruises, rides (such as roller coasters), and walkways that take visitors past huge, elaborate constructions made from the colorful plastic snap-together bricks, including models of the Golden Gate Bridge, the New York skyline, the Taj Mahal, 18-foot giraffes, a larger-than-life Albert Einstein, a buffalo herd, and much more. Even grown-ups are likely to be amazed. Closed Tuesday and Wednesday except in summer. Admission. ~ LEGOLAND Drive, Carlsbad; 760-918-5346, fax 760-918-5375; www.legoland.com.

Get a quick and fascinating tour of 100 years of American popular music at **The Museum of Making Music**. The galleries

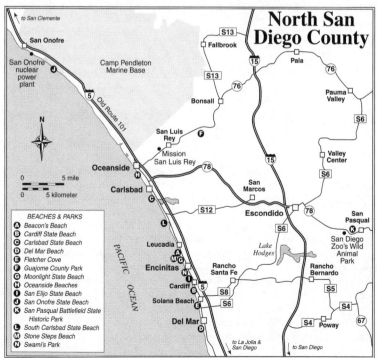

North San Diego County

to San Clemente

San Onofre

San Onofre nuclear power plant

Camp Pendleton Marine Base

S13
Fallbrook

15   Pala

76

S13

76

Bonsall

Pauma Valley

S6

Old Route 101

N

San Luis Rey   **F**

Mission San Luis Rey

Oceanside   **H**

78

15

Valley Center

S6

0   5 mile

0   5 kilometer

Carlsbad   **G**

San Marcos

S12

Escondido

S6

78

San Pasqual

BEACHES & PARKS
A Beacon's Beach
B Cardiff State Beach
C Carlsbad State Beach
D Del Mar Beach
E Fletcher Cove
F Guajome County Park
G Moonlight State Beach
H Oceanside Beaches
I San Elijo State Beach
J San Onofre State Beach
K San Pasqual Battlefield State Historic Park
L South Carlsbad State Beach
M Stone Steps Beach
N Swami's Park

L

Leucadia

Encinitas   **M** **N** **G**

Lake Hodges

Rancho Santa Fe

San Diego Zoo's Wild Animal Park   **K**

San Pasqual

San Diego Zoo's Wild Animal Park

Rancho Bernardo

Cardiff   5
S8

Solana Beach   **E**
S6

S5

Del Mar   **D**

S4

S4   Poway

67

PACIFIC OCEAN

to La Jolla & San Diego

to San Diego

display more than 450 vintage instruments and artifacts, and offer hundreds of audio samples. Kids will love the "performance" area where they can play real instruments. Closed Monday. Admission. ~ 5790 Armada Drive, Carlsbad; 760-438-5996, fax 760-438-8964; www.museumofmakingmusic.org.

Encinitas is popularly known as the "Flower Capital of the World" and the hillsides east of the beach are a riot of colors. A quick call to the friendly folks at the local **Chamber of Commerce and Visitor Center** will net you information concerning the area. Closed Sunday. ~ 138 Encinitas Boulevard, Encinitas; 760-753-6041, 800-953-6041, fax 760-753-6270; www.encinitas chamber.com, e-mail info@encinitaschamber.com.

A self-guided walking tour at **Quail Botanical Gardens** treats visitors to 30 acres of colorful plants and flowers, including the area's natural chaparral, and gardens that display rainforest vegetation, orchids and bamboo. A lookout tower provides a 360-degree view of the grounds. Admission. ~ 230 Quail Gardens Drive at Encinitas Boulevard, Encinitas; 760-436-3036, fax 760-632-0917; www.qbgardens.com, e-mail info@qbgardens.org.

Yogis, as well as those of us still residing on terra firma, might want to make a stop at Paramahansa Yogananda's **Self-Realization Fellowship Retreat**. The gold-domed towers of this retreat and ashram center were built in the 1920s and are still used today. Although the gardens inside the compound are beautifully maintained and open to the public daily, Yogananda's hermitage is only open on Sunday. The views, overlooking the famous "Swami's" surfing beach, are spectacular. Closed Monday. ~ 215 K Street, Encinitas; 760-753-2888, fax 760-753-8156; www.yoga nanda-srf.org.

Although **Del Mar** is inundated every summer by "beautiful people" who flock here for the horse racing, the town itself has retained a casual, small-town identity. Its trim, Tudor-style village center and luxurious oceanfront homes reflect the town's subtle efforts to "keep up with the Joneses" next door (i.e., La Jolla).

WHERE THE WILD THINGS ARE

There's no finer wildlife sanctuary in the country than the remarkable **San Diego Zoo's Wild Animal Park**. This 1800-acre spread, skillfully landscaped to resemble Asian and African habitats, houses over 3500 animals. Among them are several endangered species not found in zoos elsewhere. Many of the animals roam free while you view them from a monorail. After visiting the fearsome lions and gorillas, you can follow that line of children to the "Discovery Station," where kids can learn about Africa through hands-on exhibits. Admission. ~ 15500 San Pasqual Valley Road, Escondido; 619-234-6541; www.sandiegozoo.org/wap.

While seasonal, **Del Mar Race Track** and companion **Fairgrounds** are the main attractions in Del Mar. The track was financed in the 1930s by such stars as Bing Crosby and Pat O'Brien to bring thoroughbred racing to the fairgrounds. It was no coincidence that this town, "where the turf meets the surf," became a second home for these and many other top Hollywood stars. Track season is from the end of July to mid-September. The rest of the year you can bet on races televised via satellite. Admission. ~ 2260 Jimmy Durante Boulevard, Del Mar; 858-755-1141 (race track), 858-755-1161 (fairgrounds); www.delmarracing.com, e-mail tickets@dmtc.com.

On the east side of Route 5, about five miles inland on either Via de la Valle or Lomas Santa Fe Drive, is **Rancho Santa Fe**. If La Jolla is a jewel, then this stylish enclave is the crown itself. Residing in hillside mansions and horse ranches parceled out from an old Spanish land grant are some of America's wealthiest folks. Rancho Santa Fe is like Beverly Hills gone country. The area became popular as a retreat for rich industrialists and movie stars in the 1920s when Douglas Fairbanks and Mary Pickford built their sprawling **Fairbanks Ranch**. To make a looping tour of this affluent community, drive in on Via de la Valle, then return to Route 5 via Linea del Cielo and Lomas Santa Fe Drive.

LODGING

Many of San Diego's best beaches lie to the north, between Oceanside and Del Mar. Sadly, most of the good hotels do not. But don't worry, among those listed below all but a handful are either oceanfront or oceanview properties.

The Mediterranean-style **Southern California Beach Club** is a 43-suite, time-share facility situated on the beach near Oceanside Pier. Each suite is graciously appointed with quality furnishings in contemporary hues of yellow, green, and blue. Kitchens are standard; other extras include a rooftop jacuzzi and laundry facilities. ~ 121 South Pacific Highway, Oceanside; 760-722-6666, fax 760-722-8950. ULTRA-DELUXE.

Carlsbad offers several nice oceanview facilities, including **Tamarack Beach Resort**, a Mediterranean contemporary-style hotel. Finished in peach and aqua hues, the Tamarack rents standard rooms as well as one- and two-bedroom suites. Most are smashingly decorated in upbeat tones and textures and incorporate such touches as potted plants and photographic prints. Suites, though ultra-deluxe-priced, may be the best value on the North Coast. They have private balconies with panoramic views. Guests can make use of the oceanview restaurant, clubhouse, fitness center, jacuzzis, DVD library, and activities program as well as enjoying the adjacent beach. Complimentary continental breakfast is included. ~ 3200 Carlsbad Boulevard, Carlsbad; 760-729-

3500, 800-334-2199, fax 760-434-5942; www.tamarackresort. com, e-mail sarah@tamarackresort.com. ULTRA-DELUXE.

Advertised as "a very special bed and breakfast," the **Pelican Cove Inn** is a lovely Cape Cod–style house with ten guest rooms. Each features a fireplace and is well-furnished with antique pieces, including feather beds; some rooms have spa tubs. Visitors share a sundeck and patio with gazebo. The inn is located just two blocks from the beach. ~ 320 Walnut Avenue, Carlsbad; 760-434-5995, 888-735-2683, fax 760-434-7649; www.pelican-cove. com, e-mail pelicancoveinn@pelican-cove.com. MODERATE TO ULTRA-DELUXE.

The **Beach Terrace Inn** is a 49-unit establishment with stucco facade and the feel of a motel. There's a pool and jacuzzi, plus a single feature that differentiates the Beach Terrace from most other places hereabouts—it is located right on the beach. A broad swath of white sand borders the property, making the price for a room with kitchen a worthwhile investment. ~ 2775 Ocean Street, Carlsbad; 760-729-5951, 800-433-5415, fax 760-729-1078; www.beachterraceinn.com. DELUXE.

Sporting a fresh look, the fabled **La Costa Resort & Spa** can justly claim to be one of the world's great "total" resorts. This luxurious 400-acre complex boasts 595 guest rooms, two 18-hole championship golf courses and a golf practice facility, 21 tennis courts (hard, clay, *and* grass), activity centers for kids and teens, 10 shops, 2 restaurants, and one of the country's largest and most respected spa and fitness centers. Simply put, the place is awesome. With rooms *starting* well up in the ethereal range, La Costa's appeal to the well-monied few is apparent. ~ 2100 Costa del Mar Road, Carlsbad; 760-438-9111, 800-854-5000, fax 760-438-3758; www.lacosta.com, e-mail info@lacosta.com. ULTRA-DELUXE.

Located on a lofty knoll above the Pacific, **Best Western Encinitas Inn and Suites** is built on three levels and looks like a condominium. With a pool and jacuzzi, it has many of the same features. The 93 rooms include private balconies overlooking the ocean. Deluxe continental breakfast is served at the poolside cabaña. ~ 85 Encinitas Boulevard, Encinitas; 760-942-7455, 866-362-4648, fax 760-632-9481; www.bwencinitas.com. DELUXE.

HIDDEN ► The best reasonably priced lodging near the beach in Encinitas is **Moonlight Beach Motel**. This three-story, 24-unit family-run motel is tucked away in a residential neighborhood overlooking Moonlight Beach State Park. Guest rooms are modern as well as clean, and contain everything you'll need, including full kitchens. Most of the accommodations command ocean views. ~ 233 2nd Street, Encinitas; 760-753-0623, 800-323-1259, fax 760-944-9827; www.moonlightbeachmotel.com. MODERATE TO DELUXE.

Every room is individually decorated at **Cardiff-by-the-Sea Lodge** with themes such as Victorian, Southwest, and Mediterranean, and many rooms have ocean views, fireplaces and in-room whirlpools. It's a bed and breakfast, but not of the converted-home variety; everyone has a private entrance and bath. Breakfast is served buffet-style in a center courtyard, but you can take it to your room or up to the rooftop garden and savor a panoramic view of the Pacific. ~ 142 Chesterfield Avenue, Cardiff; 760-944-6474, fax 760-944-6841; www.cardifflodge.com, e-mail innkeeper @cardifflodge.com. DELUXE TO ULTRA-DELUXE.

It's all in the name when it comes to locating **Del Mar Motel on the Beach**, the only motel between Carlsbad and La Jolla on the beach. All 67 rooms in this plain stucco building are steps from the sand. That's undoubtedly where you'll spend your time because there is little about the rooms to enchant you. They are basic in design, equipped with refrigerators, color TVs, and air conditioning. Because the hotel is at a right angle to the beach, only two rooms have full views of the water. ~ 1702 Coast Boulevard, Del Mar; 858-755-1534, 800-223-8449, fax 858-259-5403; www. delmarmotelonthebeach.com, e-mail info@delmarmotelonthe beach.com. DELUXE TO ULTRA-DELUXE.

A two-story Spanish Mediterranean inn conveniently situated a few blocks from downtown Del Mar, **Les Artistes** honors several of the world's favorite artists: Diego Rivera, Georgia O'Keeffe, Erté, Claude Monet, and Paul Gauguin. The owner, who is an architect from Thailand, designed each room in the style and spirit of the artist. Other architectural delights include a pond filled with water lilies and koi, and a classic Spanish-style courtyard with a fountain. ~ 944 Camino del Mar, Del Mar; 858-755-4646; www.lesartistesinn.com. MODERATE TO DELUXE.

AUTHOR FAVORITE

Affordability and quiet are the order of the day at **Ocean Palms Beach Resort.** This tidy, 57-room mom-and-pop complex is so near the sea you can hear it, but a row of expensive beach houses blocks the view from all but one beachfront building. Some sections of the rambling ocean manor date back to 1939, and "new" additions have a tropical feel to them, so the general decor could best be described as "beach bungalow." An oldie but goodie in this case, however. The place is clean and lovingly maintained and features a landscaped patio and pool area, complete with two jacuzzis. All rooms have fully equipped kitchens. ~ 2950 Ocean Street, Carlsbad; 760-729-2493, 888-802-3224, fax 760-729-0579; www. opbr.com, e-mail info@ocean-palms.net. DELUXE TO ULTRA-DELUXE.

Built on the site of a once-famous Del Mar Beach getaway, **L'Auberge Del Mar Resort and Spa** replicates the old hotel's nostalgic past of the '20s, '30s, and '40s. The original Tudor/Craftsman inn's rich lobby is dominated by a replica of the huge original brick fireplace. Along with 120 guest rooms and suites, the inn features a restaurant with patio dining, bar, full-service European spa, tennis courts, leisure and lap pools, shops, a park amphitheater, and partial ocean views. Most rooms have their own patios. ~ 1540 Camino del Mar, Del Mar; 858-259-1515, 800-245-9757, fax 858-755-4940; www.laubergedelmar.com, e-mail laubergereservations@destinationhotels.com. ULTRA-DELUXE.

L'Auberge Del Mar was frequented by Hollywood greats such as Bing Crosby, Jimmy Durante, and Rudolph Valentino.

For an elegant country inn consider **The Inn at Rancho Santa Fe**. Widely known among the world's genteel, it's a country inn comprised of Early California–style *casitas* on a 23-acre site. Situated five miles inland from Solana Beach, the inn offers individually decorated guest rooms as well as one-, two-, and three-bedroom cottages. Many rooms and all cottages feature private sun terraces, fireplaces, and kitchenettes. Displayed in the homespun lobby is a priceless collection of antique hand-carved model ships. There are tennis courts, a swimming pool, a jacuzzi, an exercise room, croquet, a spa, wi-fi access, a bistro, and a restaurant. ~ 5951 Linea del Cielo, Rancho Santa Fe; 858-756-1131, 800-843-4661, fax 858-759-1604; www.theinnatrsf.com, e-mail reservations@theinnatrsf.com. ULTRA-DELUXE.

DINING

The **Harbor House Café** is a great place for breakfast. Decorated with brightly colored murals, this eatery serves up innovative omelettes, buckwheat pancakes, and delicious home fries. For lunch, try the mushroom burger with sautéed onions, mushrooms, and jack cheese. Patio dining is also available. Dinner also served Friday through Sunday. ~ 714 North Coast Highway, Oceanside; 760-722-2254. BUDGET.

HIDDEN ►

For a downright homey café, try **Robin's Nest**, a country-style establishment with good eats and a gregarious chef. The menu features omelettes, soups, and burgers. With a decor of soft blues and artwork by local artists, this place is quite popular with locals and has an outdoor patio that faces the harbor. Breakfast, lunch, and dinner served daily. ~ 280-A Harbor Drive South, Oceanside; 760-722-7837, fax 760-967-9076; www.robinsnestcafe.com. MODERATE.

Legends California Bistro at La Costa Resort & Spa incorporates Ayurveda guidelines from the Chopra Center into its menu. Breakfast offerings may include a power smoothie, fresh melon and berries, or a tofu scramble. Lunch is a variety of health-conscious bites such as ahi tuna tartare, crisp salads, sandwiches, and veggie stirfries. Dinner is a more upscale affair with seafood, lamb, and steak dishes. No dinner on Tuesday. ~ 2100 Costa del Mar Road, Carlsbad; 760-438-9111, 800-854-5000; www.lacosta.com, e-mail info@lacosta.com. DELUXE.

Ocean House at Carlsbad Village, an eye-catching Victorian landmark, houses both a dining room and café/bar. My favorite for lunch or dinner is the café, where the menu includes trendy dishes such as coconut shrimp, Caribbean chicken, and macadamia-crusted salmon. They also serve burgers, pasta, and salads. The Sunday brunch in the sprawling early 1900s dining room is a definite "must," featuring a tremendous buffet assortment of breakfast and lunch items. ~ 300 Carlsbad Village Drive, Carlsbad; 760-729-4131, fax 760-729-6131; www.oceanhousecarlsbad.com, e-mail info@oceanhousecarlsbad.com. MODERATE TO DELUXE.

For light, inexpensive fare there's the **Daily News Café.** Breakfast features eggs, pancakes, French toast, and their "world famous" sticky buns and cinnamon rolls, while the heartier lunch fare includes an array of soups, salads, sandwiches, and burgers. Breakfast and lunch only. ~ 3001 Carlsbad Boulevard, Carlsbad; 760-729-1023. BUDGET.

Pasta lovers should be sure to try the penne or fusilli in vodka-tomato sauce at **When In Rome.** The art-filled Roman decor provides the proper atmosphere, and the Italian owners certainly know their trade. All the breads and pastas are made fresh daily. Entrées include a variety of veal and seafood items. Dinner only. Open for traditional Italian breakfast on Saturday and Sunday. Closed Monday. ~ 1108 South Coast Highway, Encinitas; 760-944-1771, fax 760-944-3849; www.wheninrome.signonsandiego.com. MODERATE TO ULTRA-DELUXE.

Most visitors to Encinitas never lay eyes on the **Potato Shack** ◀ HIDDEN **Café,** hidden away on a side street. But locals start packing its pine-paneled walls at dawn to tackle North County's best and biggest breakfast for the buck. There are three-egg omelettes and manhole-size pancakes, but best of all are the home-style taters and the old-fashioned biscuits and gravy. Lunch is also served, but the Potato Shack is really a breakfast institution, and as such serves breakfast until 2 p.m. ('til 2:30 p.m. on weekends). No dinner. ~ 120 West I Street, Encinitas; phone/fax 760-436-1282; www.potatoshackcafe.com. BUDGET.

Another popular feeding spot is **Sakura Bana Sushi Bar.** The sushi here is heavenly, especially the *sakura* roll, crafted by Japanese masters from shrimp, crab, scallop, smelt egg, and avocado. The bar serves only sushi and sashimi, but table service will bring you such treats as teriyaki, tempura, and shrimp *shumai.* No lunch Saturday or Sunday; closed Monday. ~ 1031 South Coast Highway, Encinitas; 760-942-6414. DELUXE.

Encinitas' contribution to the Thai food craze is an intimate café called **Siamese Basil,** set along the town's main drag. At lunch and dinner this white-washed eatery serves up about six dozen dishes. You can start with the spicy shrimp soup and satay, then graduate to an entrée menu that includes noodle, curry, seafood, and vegetable selections. House specialties include roast duck with soy bean and ginger sauce, honey-marinated spare ribs, and barbecued chicken. ~ 527 South Coast Highway, Encinitas; 760-753-3940. MODERATE.

Best of the beachfront dining spots in Cardiff is **Charlie's by the Sea**, where the surf rolls right up to the glass. Here you can choose from an innovative selection of fresh seafood items or an all-American menu of grilled chicken, steak, and lamb chops. Charlie's has a smartly decorated contemporary setting with a full bar, but still creates an easy, informal atmosphere. Sunday brunch. ~ 2526 South Coast Highway, Cardiff; 760-942-1300, fax 760-942-1228; www.charliesbythesea.com. MODERATE TO DELUXE.

HIDDEN ▶ Mention the words "Mexican food" in Solana Beach and the reply is sure to be **Fidel's**. This favored spot has as many rooms and patios as a rambling hacienda. Given the good food and cheap prices, all of them are inevitably crowded. Fidel's serves the best *tostada suprema* anywhere and the burritos, enchiladas, and *chimichangas* are always good. ~ 607 Valley Avenue, Solana Beach; 858-755-5292, fax 858-755-2392. MODERATE.

Il Fornaio, an Italian restaurant/bakery, boasts magnificent ocean views, outside dining terraces, elegant Italian marble floors and bar, trompe l'oeil murals, and an enormous exhibition kitchen. The place is packed with eager patrons ready to sample the pastas, pizzas, rotisserie, meats, and *dolci* (desserts). There's also weekend brunch. ~ 1555 Camino del Mar, Del Mar Plaza, Del Mar; 858-755-8876, fax 858-755-8906; www.ilfornaio.com, e-mail delmar@ilfo.com. MODERATE TO DELUXE.

Since life is lived outdoors in Southern California, **Pacifica Del Mar**, part of a local restaurant mini-chain, features a terrace overlooking the ocean as well as a white-tablecloth dining room.

AUTHOR FAVORITE

Whatever you do during your North County visit, don't pass up the chance to dine at **El Bizcocho**. Tucked away in the upscale Rancho Bernardo Inn, an Early California–style resort, this award-winning restaurant rates among greater San Diego's best. The traditional French haute cuisine menu includes a nice balance of beef, veal, fish, and fowl dishes. Each item has a unique wine pairing. Dinner and Sunday brunch only. No dinner on Sunday. ~ 17550 Bernardo Oaks Drive; 858-675-8550, fax 858-675-8443; www.ranchobernardoinn.com/bizcocho. ULTRA-DELUXE.

The Pacific Rim accent here is on seafood, as in barbecued sugar-spiced salmon, pepper and coriander ahi, and green curry sea bass. ~ 1555 Camino del Mar, Del Mar Plaza, Del Mar; 858-792-0476, fax 858-792-0848; www.pacificadelmar.com. DELUXE TO ULTRA-DELUXE.

The place is mobbed all summer long, but **The Fish Market** remains one of my favorite Del Mar restaurants. I like the noise, nautical atmosphere, oyster bar, on-the-run service, and the dozen or so fresh fish items. Among the best dishes are the sea bass, yellowtail, orange roughy, and salmon, either sautéed or mesquite charbroiled. ~ 640 Via de la Valle, Del Mar; 858-755-2277, fax 858-755-3912; www.thefishmarket.com. MODERATE.

Scalini, housed in a classy contemporary-style building with arched windows overlooking a polo field, is strictly star-quality northern Italian fare. The place has been decorated in a mix of modern and antique furnishings and wrapped in all the latest Southern California colors. But the brightest star of all is the menu. The veal chops parmigiana and breaded swordfish are exceptional. There are many good homemade pasta dishes including fettuccine, linguine, and tortellini. Dinner only. ~ 3790 Via de la Valle, Del Mar; 858-259-9944, fax 858-259-2270; www.scalinisandiego.com, e-mail eat@scalinisandiego.com. DELUXE TO ULTRA-DELUXE.

Mille Fleurs tops everyone's list as San Diego's best French restaurant. The à la carte menu, which changes daily, provides exquisite appetizers, soup, and such entrées as rack of lamb with black-olive crust, grilled Alaskan halibut with saffron sauce, and loin of antelope. A sophisticated interior features fireside dining, Portuguese tiles, and stunning trompe l'oeil paintings. There is also a Spanish courtyard for dining as well as a piano bar. No lunch on the weekend. ~ 6009 Paseo Delicias, Rancho Santa Fe; 858-756-3085; www.millefleurs.com, e-mail milfleurs@aol.com. ULTRA-DELUXE.

Delicias, a comfortable and spacious restaurant with an adjoining bar, is decorated with French decor and fresh flowers. The chefs in the open-view kitchen whip up contemporary California cuisine. Delicious food, personable service. No lunch on Monday. ~ 6106 Paseo Delicias, Rancho Santa Fe; 858-756-8000, fax 858-759-1739; www.deliciasrestaurant.com. MODERATE TO ULTRA-DELUXE.

SHOPPING

There are two malls in Carlsbad. The **Westfield Plaza Camino Real** features 175 stores and is anchored by JC Penney, Macy's, and Sears. ~ 2525 El Camino Real; 760-729-7927; www.westfield.com/plazacaminoreal. **The Forum** is much smaller, with a good variety of specialty shops and restaurants. 1923 Calle Barcelona; 760-479-0166.

If little else, Solana Beach harbors an enclave of good antique stores. One of the best is the **Antique Warehouse**, with its collection of 101 small shops. Closed Tuesday. ~ 212 South Cedros Avenue, Solana Beach; 858-755-5156.

A seacoast village atmosphere prevails along Del Mar's half-mile-long strip of shops. Tudor-style **Stratford Square**, the focal point, houses a number of shops in what is the area's first commercial building. **Earth Song Bookstore** offers traditional books as well as an eclectic selection of titles focusing on health, spirituality, and psychology. ~ 1440 Camino del Mar, Del Mar; 858-755-4254.

Carolyn's is a consignment shop with designer fashions from the closets of the community's best-dressed women. ~ 1310 Camino Del Mar, Del Mar; 858-481-4133.

The stylized **Del Mar Plaza** is a welcome addition. Home to over 30 retail shops, this tri-level mall sells everything from fashion accessories to upscale home furnishings and has a host of eateries. ~ 1555 Camino del Mar, Del Mar; 858-792-1555; www.del marplaza.com.

Flower Hill Promenade, a rustic mall, has the usual fashion and specialty shops. But the real draw here is **Bookworks** (858-755-3735; www.book-works.com) and an adjoining coffeehouse called **Pannikin Coffee and Tea** (858-481-8007). Together they're perfect for a relaxed bit of book browsing and a spot of tea. ~ 2670 Via de la Valle, Del Mar; 858-481-7131.

Detouring, as every sophisticated shopper must, to Rancho Santa Fe, you'll find an assortment of chic shops and galleries along Paseo Delicias. One of my favorites is **Marilyn Mulloy Estate & Fine Jewelers**, with its collection of old and new pieces. Closed Sunday. ~ 6024 Paseo Delicias, Rancho Santa Fe; 858-756-4010. There are lots of millionaires per acre here, but bargains can still be found: **Country Friends** is a charity-operated repository of antique furniture, silver, glass, and china priced well below local antique shops. Closed Sunday. ~ 6030 El Tordo, Rancho Santa Fe; 858-756-1192.

NIGHTLIFE For a harbor view and daily entertainment, cast an eye toward **Monterey Bay Canners**. ~ 1325 Harbor Drive North, Oceanside; 760-722-3474.

HIDDEN ► **First Street Bar** is a neighborhood bar with three pool tables. It is consistently on the best neighborhood bar list, voted on by locals. ~ 656 South Coast Highway, Encinitas; 760-944-0233.

Solana Beach's low-profile daytime image shifts gears in the evening when the-little-town-that-could spotlights one of North County's hottest clubs. The **Belly Up Tavern** is a converted quonset hut that now houses a concert club and often draws big-name rock, reggae, jazz, and blues stars. Cover. ~ 143 South Cedros

Avenue, Solana Beach; 858-481-9022, 858-481-8140 (box office); www.bellyup.com.

Tucked away in the Flower Hill Promenade, **Pannikin Coffee and Tea** brings a true taste of culture in the form of live jazz, classical guitarists, and poetry readings on Friday nights. ~ 2670 Via de la Valle, Del Mar; 858-481-8007.

SAN ONOFRE STATE BEACH 🏃 🚲 🤿 🎣 ⛵ San Diego County's northernmost beach is about 16 miles north of Oceanside, uneasily sandwiched between Camp Pendleton and the San Onofre nuclear power plant. It's well worth a visit if you're not put off by the nearby presence of atomic energy. San Onofre has a number of sections separated by the power plant and connected via a public walkway along the seawall. On the north side of the power plant, off Cristianitos Road, is San Mateo Campground, with developed sites. Eroded bluffs rumple down to the beach creating a variety of sandy coves and pockets. South of Bluffs and not far from famous Trestles Beach is Surf Beach, a favorite with surfers and kayakers. The southern side of the plant is Bluffs Campground, a superb campground with trailer spaces and primitive tent sites, the only primitive campsite anywhere on San Diego County beaches. Gentle surf, which picks up considerably to the north, makes this a good swimming and bodysurfing spot. You'll find restrooms, lifeguards, and trails. Parking fee, $12. ~ From Route 5, take Basilone Road exit and follow the signs to the beach; 949-492-0802, fax 949-492-8412.

BEACHES & PARKS

It is more than a rumor that some discreet nude sunbathing takes place at the end of beach path #6 at San Onofre.

▲ There are 221 tent/RV sites (no hookups) at Bluffs Campground (949-492-4872) open from May to September, $29 per night; and 157 tent and RV sites (hookups and showers) at San Mateo Campground, $29 per night. Reservations: 800-444-7275.

OCEANSIDE BEACHES 🚲 🤿 🎣 ⛵ 🚤 Over three miles of clean, rock-free beaches front North County's largest city, stretching from Buena Vista Lagoon in the south to Oceanside Harbor in the north. Along the entire length the water can get rough in the summer and fall, and it's important to be wary of riptides here. Lots of Marines from nearby Camp Pendleton favor this beach. The nicest section of all is around Oceanside Pier, a 1900-foot-long fishing pier. Nearby, palm trees line a grassy promenade dotted with picnickers; the sand is as clean as a whistle. Added to the attractions is **Buena Vista Lagoon**, a bird sanctuary and nature reserve. Facilities include picnic areas, restrooms, lifeguards, basketball courts, and volleyball courts. There are kayak rentals at the harbor; the only boat ramp for miles around is located here. Restaurants are at the end of the pier and harbor. Try fishing from the pier, rocks, or beach. Swimming is good and surf-

◄ *HIDDEN*

ing is reliable year-round. ~ Located along The Strand in Oceanside; 760-435-4018, fax 760-435-4022.

▲ Limited to a few RV sites in a parking lot with no hookups; $15 per night.

CARLSBAD STATE BEACH ⚓ 🏄 🏃 🚣 🎣 Conditions here are about the same as at South Carlsbad (see below), a sand and rock beach bordered by bluffs. Rock and surf fishing are quite good at this beach and even better at the adjoining Encinas Fishing Area (at the San Diego Gas and Electric power plant), where Agua Hedionda Lagoon opens to the sea. The beach extends another mile or so to the mouth of the Buena Vista Lagoon. Facilities include restrooms and lifeguards. The beach offers swimming, surfing, and skindiving. ~ The park entrance is at Tamarack Avenue, west of Carlsbad Boulevard, Carlsbad; 760-438-3143, fax 760-438-2762.

The 2002 film *Antwone Fisher*, about a young man whose life was changed for the better when he enlisted in the Navy, was filmed at Camp Pendleton.

SOUTH CARLSBAD STATE BEACH ⚓ 🏄 🏃 🚣 🎣 This is a big, bustling beachfront rimmed by bluffs. The pebbles strewn everywhere put towel space at a premium, but the water is gentle and super for swimming. The beach has restrooms, lifeguards, showers, groceries, and beach rentals. Swimming, fishing, surfing, and skindiving are popular activities. ~ Located west of Carlsbad Boulevard south of Palomar Airport Road, Carlsbad; 760-438-3143, fax 760-438-2762.

▲ There are 196 blufftop tent/RV sites (no hookups), $25 to $35 per night. Reservations: 800-444-7275.

BEACON'S BEACH ⚓ 🏄 🏃 🎣 A broad sand corridor backdropped by coastal bluffs, this beach has appeal, though it's certainly not North County's finest. The strand is widest at the north end, but the breakers are bigger at the south end, a favorite with local surfers. Swimming, surfing, and skindiving are good. ~ There is a trail off the parking lot at Leucadia Boulevard and Neptune Avenue, Encinitas; 760-633-2740, fax 760-633-2626; www.ci.encinitas.ca.us.

HIDDEN ► **STONE STEPS BEACH** ⚓ 🏃 🎣 Locals come here to hide away from the tourists. It is indeed stony and narrow to boot, but secluded and hard to find. Much like Moonlight to the south, its surf conditions are good for several types of water sports. There are no facilities; a lifeguard is stationed here in summer. ~ The staircase to the beach is located at South El Portal Street, off Neptune Avenue, Leucadia.

MOONLIGHT STATE BEACH ⚓ 🏄 🏃 🚴 🚣 🛶 🎣 A very popular beach, Moonlight boasts a big sandy cove flanked by sandstone bluffs. Surf is relatively tame at the center, entertaining swimmers and bodysurfers. Volleyball courts, a playground and fire circles are added attractions. Surfers like the wave action to the south, particularly at the foot of D Street. There are picnic areas, firepits, restrooms, showers, lifeguards, a snack bar, equipment (surfboards, boogieboards, beach gear) rentals, and places to fish. ~ 400 B Street, Encinitas; 760-633-2740, fax 760-633-2626; www.ci.encinitas.ca.us.

SWAMI'S PARK North County's most famous surfing beach derives its name from an Indian guru who founded the Self Realization Fellowship Temple here in the 1920s. The gold-domed compound is located on the cliff-top just to the north of the park. A small, grassy picnic area gives way to stairs leading to a narrow, rocky beach favored almost exclusively by surfers, though divers and anglers like the spot as well. The reef point break here makes for spectacular waves. The stretch between this beach and D Street is a marine refuge, so don't get any ideas about taking an invertebrate home with you. Facilities include restrooms, picnic areas, lifeguards, and a funky outdoor shower. ~ 1298 South Route 101 about one mile south of Encinitas Boulevard, Encinitas; 760-633-2740, fax 760-633-2626; www.ci.encinitas.ca.us.

SAN ELIJO STATE BEACH Although the beach is wide and sandy, low tide reveals a mantle of rocks just offshore and there are reefs, too, making this another of North County's most popular surf fishing and skindiving spots. Lifeguards are stationed here during summer. There is a campground atop the bluff overlooking the beach. Most amenities are located at the campground and include restrooms, showers, beach rentals, and groceries. Day-use fee, $8. ~ Off South Route 101 north of Chesterfield Drive, Cardiff; 760-753-5091.

▲ There are 171 tent/RV sites (some hookups), $25 to $44 per night. Reservations: 800-444-7275.

CARDIFF STATE BEACH This strand begins where the cliffs of Solana Beach end and where the town's most intriguing feature, a network of tidepools, begins. Popular with surfers because of the interesting pitches off its reef break, this wide, sandy beach is part of a two-mile swath of state beaches. At the beach there are restrooms, cold showers, and lifeguards (summer only). Fishing, swimming, and surfing are popular activities here. Day-use fee, $6. ~ Off South Route 101 directly west of San Elijo Lagoon, Cardiff; 760-753-5091.

FLETCHER COVE Lined by cliffs and carpeted with sand, this is a popular spot for water sports. There's a natural break in the cliffs where the beach widens and the surf eases up to allow comfortable swimming. Surfers gather to the north and south of Plaza Street where the beach is narrow and the surf much bigger. It's also a prime area for grunion runs. Facilities include restrooms, outdoor showers, lifeguards, and basketball courts. ~ Located at the end of Plaza Street, Solana Beach; 858-755-1560, fax 858-793-7734.

DEL MAR BEACH Though rather narrow from Torrey Pines to about 15th Street, the beach widens further north. The part around 15th Street is action central, with teens playing sand volleyball and frisbee while the elders read magazines beneath their umbrellas. Surfers congregate at the foot of 13th Street. Quintessential North County! There are picnic tables, a snack bar, restrooms, showers, and lifeguards. Fishing is good, and there are regular grunion runs. There is typical beach surf with smooth peaks, year-round. ~ Easiest beach access is at street ends from 15th to 29th streets off Coast Boulevard, one block below South Route 101, Del Mar; 858-755-1556, fax 858-259-3264; www.delmar.ca.us.

La Jolla

A certain fascination centers around the origins of the name La Jolla. It means "jewel" in Spanish, but according to Indian legend it means "hole" or "caves." Both are fairly apt interpretations: this Mediterranean-style enclave perched on a bluff above the Pacific is indeed a jewel; and its dramatic coves and cliffs are pocked with sea caves. Choose your favorite interpretation but for goodness sake don't pronounce the name phonetically—it's "La Hoya."

La Jolla is a community within the city of San Diego, though it considers itself something more on the order of a principality—like Monaco. Locals call it "The Village" and boast that it's an ideal walking town, which is another way of saying La Jolla is a frustrating place to drive around. Narrow, curvy 1930s-era streets are jammed with traffic and hard to follow. A parking place in The Village is truly a jewel within the jewel.

The beauty of its seven miles of cliff-lined sea coast is La Jolla's *raison d'être*. Spectacular homes, posh hotels, chic boutiques, and gourmet restaurants crowd shoulder to shoulder for a better view of the ocean. Each of the area's many beaches has its own particular character and flock of local devotees. Though most beaches are narrow, rocky, and not really suitable for swimming or sunbathing, they are the best in the county for surfing and skindiving.

SIGHTS

To get the lay of the land, wind your way up **Mount Soledad** (east on Nautilus Street from La Jolla Boulevard), where the view extends across the city skyline and out over the ocean. That large white cross at the summit is a memorial to the war dead and the setting for sunrise services every Easter Sunday.

Ah, but exploring The Village is the reason you're here, so head back down Nautilus Street, go right on La Jolla Boulevard, and continue until it leads into **Prospect Street**. This is La Jolla's hottest thoroughfare and the intersection with **Girard Avenue**, the town's traditional "main street," is the town epicenter. Here, in the heart of La Jolla, you are surrounded by the elite and elegant.

Although Girard Avenue features as wide a selection of shops as anyplace in San Diego, Prospect Street is much more interesting and stylish. By all means, walk Prospect's curving mile from the cottage shops and galleries on the north to the **Museum of Contemporary Art San Diego** on the south. The museum, by the way, is a piece of art in itself, one of many striking contemporary structures in La Jolla, originally designed by noted architect Irving Gill. The museum's highly regarded collection focuses on Minimalist, California, Pop, and other avant-garde developments in painting, sculpture, and photography. Closed Wednesday. Admission. ~ 700 Prospect Street; 858-454-3541, fax 858-454-6985; www.mcasd.org, e-mail info@mcasd.org.

The Museum of Contemporary Art San Diego's modern lines belie the fact that it was designed as a private villa back in 1915.

During this stroll along Prospect Street, also visit the lovely **La Valencia Hotel**, a very pink, very prominent resting place nicknamed "La V." This pink lady is a La Jolla landmark and a local institution, serving as both village pub and town meeting hall. You can feel the charm and sense the rich tradition of the place the moment you enter. While "La V" has always been a haven for the gods and goddesses of Hollywood, the Gregory Peck and Olivia de Haviland gang of old has been replaced by a client roster of current stars like Will Smith and Jada Pinkett. ~ 1132 Prospect Street; 858-454-0771, 800-451-0772, fax 858-456-3921; www.lavalencia.com, e-mail info@lavalencia.com.

Another center of interest lies at the northern end of La Jolla. The best beaches are here, stretching from the ritzy La Jolla Shores to the scientific sands at Scripps Beach.

Driving along North Torrey Pines Road you will undoubtedly cross the **University of California–San Diego** (858-534-2230) campus, a sprawling 1200 acres set on a mesa above the Pacific Ocean. Home to over 22,000 undergraduate and graduate students, the university boasts natural chaparral canyons, green lawns, and eucalyptus groves, contrasted with urban student plazas and buildings. Spread throughout this expansive campus is the **Stuart Collection of sculpture**, featuring permanent outdoor sculptures by leading contemporary artists. Maps are available at the information kiosk. ~ 858-534-2117, fax 858-534-9713; stuartcollection.ucsd.edu.

Part of the university is the **Scripps Institution of Oceanography**, the oldest institution in the nation devoted to oceanography and the home of the **Birch Aquarium at Scripps**. Here you'll find 60 marine life tanks, manmade tidepools, breathtaking exhibits of coastal underwater habitats, interactive displays for children and adults, and displays illustrating recent advances in oceanographic research. Admission. ~ 2300 Expedition Way; 858-534-3474, fax 858-534-7114; www.aquarium.ucsd.edu, e-mail aquariuminfo@ucsd.edu.

Another research center, the **Salk Institute**, created by the man whose vaccine helped vanquish polio, is renowned not only for its research but its architecture as well. The surrealistic concrete structure was designed by Louis Kahn in 1960 to be an environment that would stimulate original thinking. It is a stunning site, perched on the lip of a high canyon overlooking the Pacific. Tours by appointment. ~ 10010 North Torrey Pines Road, just north of the University of California–San Diego campus; tour information, 858-453-4100, fax 858-625-2404; www.salk.edu.

Next to the institute is the **Torrey Pines Glider Port**, where you can watch hang-gliding and paragliding masters soar over the waves from atop a 360-foot cliff. ~ 2800 Torrey Pines Scenic Drive; 858-452-9858, 877-359-8326, fax 858-452-9983; www.flytorrey.com, e-mail info@flytorrey.com.

HIDDEN ► Trails leading down to the notorious **Black's Beach** begin here. Black's is San Diego's unofficial, illegal, ever-loving nude beach. And a beautiful strip of natural landscape it is.

Bordering Black's on the north is **Torrey Pines State Reserve and Beach**, whose 1750-acre preserve was established to protect one of the world's rarest pine trees, the Torrey Pine. The tree itself is a gnarled and twisted specimen. Centuries ago these pines covered the southern coast of California; today they are indigenous only to Santa Rosa Island, off the coast of Santa Barbara, and to the reserve. A network of trails through this blufftop reserve makes hiking sheer pleasure. Among the rewards are the views, extending along the cliffs and ocean, and the chance to walk quietly among La Jolla's rare treasures. Parking fee. ~ Located west of North Torrey Pines Road, two miles north of Genessee Avenue; 858-755-2063; www.torreypines.org.

LODGING Like a Monopoly master, La Jolla possesses the lion's share of "Park Place" accommodations in the San Diego area. Understandably, there are no budget hotels in this fashionable village by the sea.

Sands of La Jolla is a small, 39-room motel on a busy thoroughfare just a quick drive away from the bustle of Girard Avenue and Prospect Street. Rooms (kitchenettes are available) are not exactly designer showcases, but they are tastefully appointed and neatly maintained. Amenities include a heated pool and minifridges. ~ 5417 La Jolla Boulevard; 858-459-3336, 800-643-0530, fax 858-454-0922; www.sandsoflajolla.com, e-mail mail@sands oflajolla.com. BUDGET TO MODERATE.

Small, European-style hotels have always been popular in La Jolla, and the granddaddy of them all is the **The Grande Colonial**. Established in 1913, the 93-room establishment features rooms lavishly decorated with historically inspired furnishings. Ocean-front rooms provide matchless views. There's a restaurant on site. ~ 910 Prospect Street; 858-454-2181, 800-826-1278, fax 858-454-5679; www.thegrandecolonial.com, e-mail info@thegrande colonial.com. ULTRA-DELUXE.

Nestled into the triangular corner in the heart of the village, **La Jolla Inn** is a small, friendly European-style hostelry with 23 rooms. Ask for a view room, which will give you an ocean view from a flower-bedecked balcony. This is a nonsmoking hotel that provides such touches as handmade quilts, wi-fi access, coffee-makers, continental breakfast, and complimentary beverages and cookies in the afternoon. ~ 1110 Prospect Street, La Jolla; 858-454-0133, 888-855-7829, fax 858-454-2056; www.lajollainn. com, e-mail lajolla6@san.rr.com. DELUXE TO ULTRA-DELUXE.

More than just a hotel, **La Valencia** is a La Jolla institution and one of the loveliest hotels in San Diego. Resplendent in pink stucco and Spanish tile, it is perched on a breezy promontory overlooking the coves and sea cliffs of La Jolla. From the moment guests enter via a trellis-covered tile loggia into a lobby that

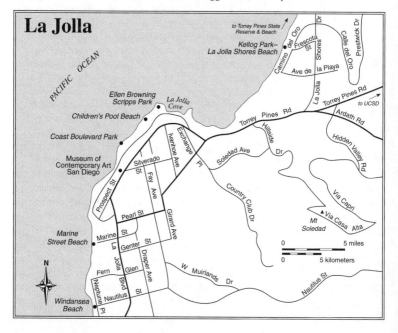

could pass for King Juan Carlos' living room, they are enveloped in elegance. The 116 private accommodations reflect the European feel—that is, they tend to run on the small side and are furnished in reproduction antiques. Ah, but out back there's a beautiful garden terrace opening onto the sea and tumbling down to a free-form swimming pool edged with lawn. Facilities include a gym, whirlpool, and three distinctive restaurants. ~ 1132 Prospect Street; 858-454-0771, 800-451-0772, fax 858-456-3921; www.lavalencia.com, e-mail info@lavalencia.com. ULTRA-DELUXE.

Also smack dab in the Village is the **Empress Hotel,** a five-story L-shaped building set on a quiet street just a stone's throw from both the beach and the bustle of Prospect Street. A contemporary establishment blending Victorian and European boutique styles, its 73 spacious rooms and suites offer amenities such as mini-fridges, bathrobes, coffeemakers, and high-speed internet. If you're looking to splash out, you probably can't get any fancier than one of the two jacuzzi suites outfitted with a baby grand piano. There are also fitness facilities, a sauna, a spa, and a restaurant. Enjoy complimentary continental breakfast on the flower-lined patio. ~ 7766 Fay Avenue; 858-454-3001, 888-369-9900, fax 858-454-6387; www.empress-hotel.com, e-mail reservations411@empress-hotel.com. ULTRA-DELUXE.

Just as the village boasts San Diego's finest selection of small hotels, it can also claim a well-known bed and breakfast. **The Bed and Breakfast Inn at La Jolla,** listed as a historical site, was designed as a private home in 1913 by the architect Irving Gill. The John Phillip Sousa family resided here in 1921. Faithfully restored by its present owners as a 15-room inn, it stands today as Gill's finest example of Cubist-style architecture. Ideally situated a block and a half from the ocean, this inn is the essence of La Jolla. Each guest room features an individual decorative theme carried out in period furnishings. Some have fireplaces and ocean views. All have private baths. Bicycles are available for guests' use. ~ 7753 Draper Avenue; 858-456-2066, 800-582-2466, fax 858-456-1510; www.innlajolla.com, e-mail bedandbreakfast@innlajolla.com. ULTRA-DELUXE.

La Jolla's only true beachfront hotel is **La Jolla Shores Hotel.** Designed and landscaped to resemble an old California hacienda, this 128-room retreat overlooks the Pacific on a mile-long beach. With its stuccoed arches, terra-cotta roofs, ceramic tilework, fountains, and flowers, Sea Lodge offers a relaxing south-of-the-border setting. Guest rooms are large; most feature balconies, some have kitchens, and all have access to the usual amenities: fitness room, sauna, jacuzzi, pool, and tennis courts. Five-night minimum stay during summer. ~ 8110 Camino del Oro; 858-459-8271, 800-237-5211, fax 858-456-9346; www.ljshoreshotel.com, e-mail reservations@ljshoreshotel.com. ULTRA-DELUXE.

Just north of UCSD, the **Hilton La Jolla Torrey Pines**, adorned with marble and polished wood, is an outstanding white-glove establishment. Here, art deco visits the 21st century in a series of terraces that lead past plush dining rooms, multitiered fountains, a luxurious swimming pool, and a fitness center. Avid golfers will appreciate its location—the 18th fairway of the Torrey Pines Golf Course, and the site of the 2008 U.S. Open. ~ 10950 North Torrey Pines Road; 858-558-1500, 800-762-6160, fax 858-450-4584; www.hilton.com. ULTRA-DELUXE.

DINING

Just as it is blessed with many fine hotels, La Jolla is a restaurant paradise. **George's at the Cove** based its climb to success on its knockout view of the water, a casual, contemporary environment, fine service, and a trendsetting regional menu. Daily menus incorporate the freshest seafood, beef, lamb, poultry, and pasta available. Downstairs in the fine-dining room are selections such as sesame-crusted tuna with eggplant-citrus broth, and roasted lamb chops with curried carrots. The food presentation alone is a work of art. ~ 1250 Prospect Place; 858-454-4244, fax 858-454-5458; www.georgesatthecove.com, e-mail info@georges atthecove.com. MODERATE TO ULTRA-DELUXE.

Jose's Court Room, a noisy, down-to-earth Mexican pub, is the best place in town for quick, casual snacks. They offer all the typical taco, tostada, and enchilada plates plus tasty sautéed shrimp and chicken *ranchero* dinners. ~ 1037 Prospect Street; 858-454-7655. BUDGET TO DELUXE.

A great stop for picnic supplies is the La Jolla Farmers Market, held Sunday at the La Jolla Elementary School. ~ Center and Girard streets.

Illuminated only by the flickering of candles and the incandescent glow of fish tanks, the **Manhattan** at the Empress Hotel features cozy booths, boisterous patrons, and a singing maître d', successfully replicating a New York City family-style Italian restaurant. Popular dishes include cannelloni, veal marsala, and chicken piccata; in addition there are wonderful caesar salads and tiramisu. No lunch Saturday, Sunday, or Monday. ~ Empress Hotel, 7766 Fay Avenue; 858-459-0700, fax 858-454-4741. MODERATE TO ULTRA-DELUXE.

◀ HIDDEN

If, during your shopping foray down Girard Avenue, you come across a line of locals snaking out of a small, unassuming eatery, you've no doubt reached **Girard Gourmet**. You may have to wait to partake of the deli goods (salads, quiches, sandwiches, pastries), but it's worth it. Take it to go, or dine out on the sidewalk or inside in an alpine-like setting. ~ 7837 Girard Avenue; 858-454-3325, fax 858-454-2325; www.girardgourmet.com, e-mail info@girardgourmet.com. BUDGET.

SHOPPING

Once a secluded seaside village, La Jolla has emerged as a world-famous resort community that offers style and substance. The shopping focuses on Girard Avenue (from Torrey Pines Road to Prospect Street) and along Prospect Street. Both are lined with designer boutiques, specialty shops, and art galleries.

In La Jolla's numerous galleries, traditional art blends with contemporary paintings, and rare Oriental antiques complement 20th-century bronze sculpture. The **Tasende Gallery** has a large display area and patio garden that pack in contemporary art by big names like Henry Moore and Roberto Matta. The gallery showcases sculpture, paintings, and drawings as well. Closed Sunday and Monday. ~ 820 Prospect Street; 858-454-3691; www.tasendegallery.com.

NIGHTLIFE   The dark red **Whaling Bar** attracts lots of La Jolla's big fish. A fine place to relax and nibble gourmet hors d'oeuvres. ~ La Valencia Hotel, 1132 Prospect Street; 858-454-0771.

The Comedy Store features comedians exclusively, many with national reputations. Closed Monday and Tuesday. Cover. ~ 916 Pearl Street; 858-454-9176; www.thecomedystore.com.

HIDDEN ▶   **D. G. Wills Books** is a tiny literary haven featuring lectures and poetry readings. ~ 7461 Girard Avenue; 858-456-1800; www.dgwillsbooks.com.

Jack's La Jolla just might be the "all-things-for-all-people" place in town, with four bars, one on each of the four levels. A crowd of young professionals fills the Wall Street Bar, where there's deejay dance music Thursday through Sunday. The Beach Bar is more varied; live music plays here every night and on weekend afternoons. ~ 7863 Girard Avenue; 858-456-8111; www.jackslajolla.com. MODERATE.

The **La Jolla Music Society** hosts year-round performances by such notables as Anne Sophie Von Otter, the Mark Morris Dance Group, and the Royal Philharmonic Orchestra. ~ 858-459-3728; www.ljms.org.

The prestigious **La Jolla Playhouse**, located on the University of California's San Diego campus, produces innovative dramas and musicals and spotlights famous actors during the summer and fall. ~ 858-550-1010; www.lajollaplayhouse.org.

BEACHES & PARKS   **TORREY PINES STATE RESERVE AND BEACH** 🧍 🏊 🎣 ⛵ A long, wide, sandy stretch adjacent to Los Peñasquitos Lagoon and Torrey Pines State Reserve, this beach is highly visible from the highway and therefore heavily used. It is popular for sunning, swimming, surf fishing, and volleyball. Nearby trails lead through the reserves with their lagoons, rare trees, and abundant birdlife. Keep in mind that food is prohibited in the reserve but allowed on the beach. The beach is patrolled year-round, but lifeguards are on duty only in summer. Restrooms are available. Day-use fee, $8 per vehicle. ~ Located just south of Carmel Valley Road,

Del Mar; 858-755-2063, fax 858-509-0981; www.torreypine. org, e-mail contact@torreypine.org.

BLACK'S BEACH 🏄 ⚐ ⚑ One of the world's most famous ◄HIDDEN nude beaches, on hot summer days it attracts bathers by the thousands, many in the buff. The sand is lovely and soft and the 300-foot cliffs rising up behind make for a spectacular setting. Hanggliders and paragliders soar from the glider port above to add even more enchantment. Swimming is dangerous; beware of the currents and exercise caution as the beach is infrequently patrolled. Surfing is excellent; one of the most awesome beach breaks in California. Lifeguards are here in summer. ~ From Route 5 in La Jolla follow Genesee Avenue west; turn left on North Torrey Pines Road, then right at Torrey Pines Scenic Drive. There's a parking lot at the Torrey Pines Glider Port, but trails to the beach from here are very steep and often dangerous. If you're in doubt just park at the Torrey Pines State Reserve lot one mile north and walk back along the shore to Black's during low tide.

SCRIPPS BEACH 🏃 ⚐ 🏄 With coastal bluffs above, narrow sand beach below, and rich tidepools offshore, this is a great strand for beachcombers. Two **underwater reserves** as well as museum displays at the Scripps Institution of Oceanography are among the attractions. There are museum facilities at Scripps Institution. ~ Scripps Institution is located at the 8600 block of La Jolla Shores Drive in La Jolla. You can park at Kellogg Park–La Jolla Shores Beach and walk north to Scripps.

The spectacular natural beauty of La Jolla Cove makes it one of the most photographed beaches of Southern California.

KELLOGG PARK–LA JOLLA SHORES BEACH 🏄 🏄 The sand is wide and the swimming is easy at La Jolla Shores; so, naturally, the beach is covered with bodies whenever the sun appears. Just to the east is Kellogg Park, an ideal place for a picnic, swimming, and surfing. There are restrooms, a playground, and lifeguards. ~ Off Camino del Oro and Costa Boulevard.

ELLEN BROWNING SCRIPPS PARK AND LA JOLLA COVE 🏄 ⚑ This grassy park sits on a bluff overlooking the cove and is the scenic focal point of La Jolla. The naturally formed cove is almost always free of breakers, has a small but sandy beach, and is a popular spot for swimmers and divers. It's also the site of the **La Jolla Ecological Reserve**, an underwater park and diving reserve. There are picnic areas, restrooms, shuffleboard, and lifeguards. ~ 1100 Coast Boulevard at Girard Avenue.

CHILDREN'S POOL BEACH 🏊 ⚐ ⚑ At the north end of Coast Boulevard Beach (see below) a concrete breakwater loops around a small lagoon. Harbor seals like to sun themselves on the rock promontories here. Despite its name, the beach's strong rip currents and seasonal rip tides can make swimming hazardous, so check with lifeguards. There are lifeguards and restrooms. Fishing is good from the surf. ~ Located off of Coast Boulevard in La Jolla.

HIDDEN ▶ **COAST BOULEVARD PARK** After about a half-mile of wide sandy beach, the bluffs and tiny pocket beaches that characterize Windansea (see below) reappear at what locals call "Coast Beach." The pounding waves make watersports unsafe, but savvy locals find the smooth sandstone boulders and sandy coves perfect for reading, sunbathing, and picnicking. ~ Paths lead to the beach at several points along Coast Boulevard.

MARINE STREET BEACH Separated from Windansea to the south by towering sandstone bluffs, this is a much wider and more sandy strand, favored by sunbathers, swimmers, skindivers, and frisbee-tossing youths. The rock-free shoreline is ideal for walking or jogging. The beach is good for board and bodysurfing; watch for rip currents and high surf. ~ Turn west off La Jolla Boulevard on Marine Street.

WINDANSEA BEACH This is surely one of the most picturesque beaches in the country. It has been portrayed in the movies and was immortalized in Tom Wolfe's 1968 nonfiction classic, *The Pumphouse Gang*, about the surfers who still hang around the old pumphouse (part of the city's sewer system), zealously protecting their famous surf from outsiders. Windansea is rated by experts as one of the best surfing locales on the West Coast. In the evenings, crowds line the Neptune Place sidewalk, which runs along the top of the cliffs, to watch the sunset. North of the pumphouse are several sandy nooks sandwiched between sandstone outcroppings. Romantic spot! There are lifeguards in the summer. ~ At the end of Nautilus Street.

HERMOSA TERRACE PARK This beach is said to be "seasonally sandy," which is another way of saying it's rocky at times. Best chance for sand is in the summer when this is a pretty good sunning beach. The surfing is good. There are no facilities. ~ Off Winamar Avenue; a paved path leads to the beach.

BIRD ROCK Named for a large sandstone boulder about 50 yards off the coast, this beach is rocky and thus favored by divers. The surf rarely breaks here, but when it does this spot is primo for surfing; exercise caution. Fishing is also good. Facilities are nonexistent. ~ At the end of Bird Rock Avenue.

SOUTH BIRD ROCK Tidepools are the attractions along this rocky, cliff-lined beach. Surfing is best in summer. ~ From Midway or Forward streets in La Jolla follow paths down to the beach.

TOURMALINE SURFING PARK A year-round reef break and consistently big waves make La Jolla one of the best surfing areas on the West Coast. Tourmaline is popular with surfers. Skindiving is permitted, as is swimming. You'll find picnic areas and restrooms. ~ At the end of Tourmaline Street.

Mission Bay Park Area

Dredged from a shallow, mosquito-infested tidal bay, 4600-acre Mission Bay Park is the largest municipal aquatic park in the world. For San Diego's athletic set it is Mecca, a recreational paradise dotted with islands and lagoons and ringed by 27 miles of sandy beaches.

Here, visitors join with residents to enjoy swimming, sailing, windsurfing, waterskiing, fishing, jogging, cycling, golf, and tennis. Or perhaps a relaxing day of kite flying and sunbathing.

SIGHTS

More than just a playground, Mission Bay Park features a shopping complex, resort hotels, restaurants, and the popular marine park, **SeaWorld San Diego**. This 189-acre park-within-a-park is one of the world's largest oceanarium. Admission. ~ SeaWorld Drive; 619-226-3901, 800-257-4268, fax 619-226-3996; www.seaworld.com.

Among the attractions are killer whales; one of the largest penguin colonies north of Antarctica; a "Forbidden Reef" inhabited by bat rays and over 100 moray eels; and "Rocky Point Preserve," an exhibit boasting a wave pool, pettable dolphins, and a colony of California sea otters. "Manatee Rescue," only one of three U.S. manatee exhibits outside of Florida, is a venture designed to relieve the Florida SeaWorld of its overflowing supply of rehabilitating manatees. The exhibit provides over 800 feet of underwater viewing. The park also includes "Journey to Atlantis," a wet and wild ride that takes thrill seekers on a tour of Poseidon's island nation; a Sky Tower that lifts visitors nearly 300 feet above Mission Bay; a helicopter simulator dubbed the "Wild Arctic" that takes visitors to an Arctic research station to explore two capsized sailing ships from a century-old wreck and see native Arctic mammals; and "Shipwreck Rapids," a wet and winding ride in a raft-like innertube.

SEE SEAWORLD

One of the best bargains at SeaWorld is the guided tour of the park (fee). It's expert guides take the guests on adventures that may include the Shark Laboratory, the animal care area, and killer whale facility. I prefer simply to watch the penguins waddling about on a simulated iceberg and zipping around after fish in their glass-contained ocean, or to peer in at the fearsome makos at "Shark Encounter." The park's magnificent marine creatures are all the entertainment I need.

Down along the oceanfront, **Mission Beach** is strung out along a narrow jetty of sand protecting Mission Bay from the sea. Mission Boulevard threads its way through this eclectic, wall-to-wall mix of shingled beach shanties, condominiums, and luxury homes.

The historic 1925 "Giant Dipper" has come back to life after years of neglect at **Belmont Park**. One of only two original West Coast seaside coasters, this beauty is not all the park has to offer. There's also a carousel, a video arcade, a large indoor swimming pool, and a host of shops and eateries along the beach and boardwalk. ~ 3146 Mission Boulevard or on the beach at Mission Boulevard and West Mission Bay Drive; 858-228-9283; www.belmontpark.com, e-mail info@giantdipper.com.

Pacific Beach, which picks up at the northern edge of the bay, is the liveliest of the city beaches, an area packed with high school and college students. Designer shorts, a garish Hawaiian shirt, strapped-on sunglasses, and a skateboard are all you need to fit in perfectly along the frenetic boardwalk at "PB." If you're missing any or all of these accoutrements, Garnet Avenue is the city's core, lined with skate and surf shops and funky boutiques, as well as colorful bars and taco eateries.

LODGING   Pacific Beach boasts the San Diego County lodging with the most character of all. **Crystal Pier Hotel** is a throwback to the late 1920s. Fittingly so, because that's when this quaint-looking assemblage of 29 cottages on Crystal Pier was built. This blue-and-white woodframe complex, perched over the waves, features tiny little cottages. Each comes with a kitchen and patio-over-the-sea, not to mention your own parking place on the pier. A unique discovery indeed. ~ 4500 Ocean Boulevard, Pacific Beach; 858-483-6983, 800-748-5894, fax 858-483-6811; www.crystalpier.com. ULTRA-DELUXE.

Most of the hotels within sprawling Mission Bay Park are upscale resorts in the deluxe to ultra-deluxe price range. But there's budget-priced relief at the **Western Shores**, located just across the street from Mission Bay Golf Course. This is a quiet 40-unit court that simply can't be matched for value anywhere in the area. ~ 4345 Mission Bay Drive, Pacific Beach; 858-273-1121, fax 858-273-2944. BUDGET.

A real bargain is **Banana Bungalow**, a privately run hostel right on Pacific Beach. The accommodations are of the co-ed bunk-bed variety for the backpacking set who don't mind sharing rooms with strangers. (There are a few private rooms with their own baths available.) You must be a traveler with an out-of-state license or passport. A complimentary breakfast is served every morning. ~ 707 Reed Avenue, Pacific Beach; 858-273-3060, 800-546-7835, fax 858-273-1440; www.bananabungalowsandiego.com. BUDGET.

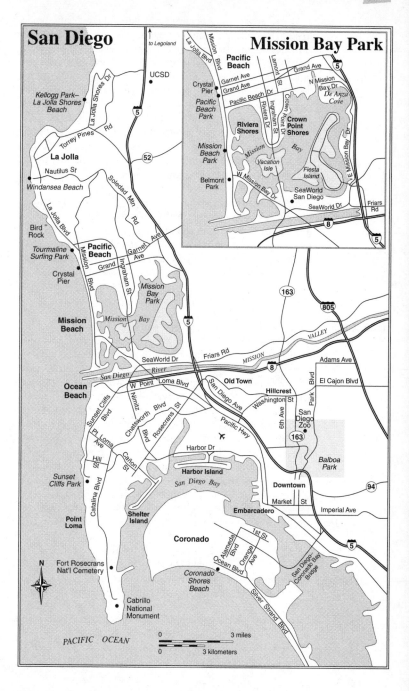

There aren't many beachfront facilities along Pacific Beach, Mission Beach, and Ocean Beach, except for condominiums. One particularly pretty four-unit condominium, **Ventanas al Mar**, overlooks the ocean in Mission Beach. Its contemporary two- and three-bedroom units feature fireplaces, jacuzzis, kitchens, and washer-dryers. They sleep as many as eight people. In the summer, these rent by week only. ~ 3631 Ocean Front Walk, Mission Beach; 858-488-1580, 800-869-7858, fax 858-539-0904; www.billluther.com, e-mail vacation@billluther.com. ULTRA-DELUXE.

Only one Mission Bay resort stands out as unique—the **San Diego Paradise Point Resort & Spa**. Over 40 acres of lush gardens, lagoons, and white-sand beach surround the bungalows of this 462-room resort. Except for some fancy suites, room decor is basic and pleasant, with quality furnishings. But guests don't spend much time in their rooms anyway. At Paradise Point there's more than a mile of beach, catamaran and bike rentals, a spa, a fitness center, five tennis courts, five pools, a basketball court, sand volleyball, two restaurants, and an 18-hole putting course. A self-contained island paradise. ~ 1404 Vacation Road, Mission Beach; 858-274-4630, 800-344-2626, fax 858-581-5929; www.paradisepoint.com, e-mail reservations@paradisepoint.com. ULTRA-DELUXE.

DINING

Critic's choice for the area's best omelettes is **Broken Yolk Café**. Choose from nearly 30 of these eggy creations or invent your own. If you can eat it all within an hour, the ironman/woman special—including a dozen eggs, mushrooms, onions, cheese, etc.—comes free! Faint or fail and you pay much more. They make soups, sandwiches, and salads, too. Outdoor patio seating is available. Breakfast and lunch only. ~ 1851 Garnet Avenue, Pacific Beach; 858-270-9645, fax 858-270-4745; www.thebrokenyolkcafe.com. BUDGET.

The most creative restaurant in Pacific Beach is **Château Orleans**, one of the city's finest Cajun-Creole restaurants. Everything, including the sauces, is homemade here. Tasty appetizers fresh from the bayous include Louisiana crabcakes and Southern-fried 'gator bites. Yes, indeed, they eat alligators down in Cajun country, and you should be brave enough to find out why. Mardi Gras gumbo chocked with crawfish, Uncle Bubba's rib-eye steak, Creole salmon stuffed with blue crab and Provençale sauce, and colorful jambalaya are typical menu choices. Everything is authentic except the decor, which thankfully shuns board floors and bare bulbs in favor of carpets, original New Orleans artwork, and patio seating in a New Orleans–style garden. Dinner only. Closed Sunday and Monday. ~ 926 Turquoise Street, Pacific Beach; 858-488-6744, fax 858-488-6745; www.chateauorleans.com, e-mail ljonaitis@cox.net. MODERATE TO DELUXE.

The Château Orleans features live jazz and blues Thursday through Saturday.

The Mission Cafe is a casual neighborhood restaurant where folks are likely to chat with whoever is dining next to them. The ambience is funky, the furniture eclectic, and the walls are enlivened with local art. Blending Asian and Latin influences, the cuisine emphasizes food that is healthy, tasty, and original. There are breakfast standards with a twist—the French toast is served with berries and blueberry purée. If you're in the mood for something more Mexican, order the *plata verde con huevos* (slightly sweet tamales with eggs, roasted chile verde and cheese). For lunchtime there are such creations as ginger-sesame chicken roll-up or Baja shrimp wrap. You can also choose from several soups, salads, and sandwiches. No dinner. ~ 3795 Mission Boulevard, Mission Beach; 858-488-9060; www.themission1.signonsan diego.com. BUDGET.

SHOPPING

Commercial enterprises in the beach communities cater primarily to sun worshipers. Beachie boutiques and rental shops are everywhere. A shopping center on the beach, **Belmont Park** has a host of shops and restaurants. ~ 3146 Mission Boulevard, Mission Bay Park.

The Promenade Mall at Pacific Beach, a modern, Mediterranean-style shopping complex, houses 25 or so smartly decorated specialty shops and restaurants. A farmer's market is held here on Saturday. ~ Located on Mission Boulevard between Pacific Beach Drive and Reed Street, Pacific Beach; 858-490-9097.

NIGHTLIFE

Blind Melons, beside the Crystal Pier, is best described as a Chicago beach bar featuring local acts every night of the week. Cover. ~ 710 Garnet Avenue, Pacific Beach; 858-483-7844; www. blindmelonspb.com.

Moray's Lounge features piano jazz nightly. ~ Catamaran Resort Hotel, 3999 Mission Boulevard, Pacific Beach; 858-488-1081; www.catamaranresort.com.

◄ *HIDDEN*

Javanican Coffee House is hard to miss since it's painted deep purple and has a flowering bright-pink bougainvillea crawling up the side. Inside, the place is strictly a retro 1950s coffee house. They serve up organic coffees and light snacks, as well as serendipitous live entertainment. There's no schedule, but the owner is a musician, so no telling who will show up to jam. ~ 4338 Cass Street, Pacific Beach; 858-483-8035; www.sluka.com.

The Pennant is a Mission Beach landmark where local beachies congregate en masse on the deck to get rowdy and watch the sunset. The entertainment here is the clientele. ~ 2893 Mission Boulevard, Mission Beach; 858-488-1671.

PACIFIC BEACH PARK 🚲 🏄 🏊 At its south end, "PB" is a major gathering place, its boardwalk crowded with teens and

BEACHES & PARKS

assorted rowdies, but a few blocks north, just before Crystal Pier, the boardwalk becomes a quieter concrete promenade that follows scenic, sloping cliffs. The beach widens here and the crowd becomes more family oriented. The surf is moderate and fine for swimming and bodysurfing. Pier and surf fishing are great for corbina and surf perch. South of the pier Ocean Boulevard becomes a pedestrian-only mall with a bike path, benches, and picnic tables. Amenities include restrooms, lifeguards, and restaurants. ~ Located near Grand Avenue and Pacific Beach Drive.

MISSION BAY PARK One of the nation's largest and most diverse city-owned aquatic parks, Mission Bay has something to suit just about everyone's recreational interest. Key areas and facilities are as follows: **Dana Landing** and **Quivira Basin** make up the southwest portion of this 4200-acre park. Most boating activities begin here, where a large marina is located. Adjacent is **Bonita Cove**, used for swimming, picnicking and volleyball. Mission Boulevard shops, restaurants, and recreational equipment rentals are within easy walking distance. **Ventura Cove** houses a large hotel complex but its sandy beach is open to the public. Calm waters make it a popular swimming spot for small children.

> Mission Bay Park was a vast tidal marsh until 1944, when the city converted the land into an aquatic park.

Vacation Isle and **Ski Beach** are easily reached via the bridge on Ingraham Street, which bisects the island. The west side contains public swimming areas, boat rentals, and a model yacht basin. Ski Beach is on the east side and is the favorite spot in the bay for waterskiing. **Fiesta Island** is situated on the southeast side of the park. It's ringed with soft sand swimming beaches and laced with jogging, cycling, and skating paths. A favorite spot for fishing from the quieter coves and for kite flying. On the south side of Fiesta Island sits **South Shores**, a large boat launching area.

Over on the **East Shore**, you'll find landscaped picnic areas, a physical fitness course, playgrounds, a sandy beach for swimming, and the park information center. **De Anza Cove**, at the extreme northeast corner of the park, has a sandy beach for swimming plus a large private campground. **Crown Point Shores** provides a sandy beach, picnic area, nature study area, physical fitness course, and a waterski landing.

Sail Bay and **Riviera Shores** make up the northwest portion of Mission Bay and back up against the apartments and condominiums of Pacific Beach. Sail Bay's beaches aren't the best in the park and are usually submerged during high tides. Riviera Shores has a better beach with waterski areas.

Santa Clara and **El Carmel Points** jut out into the westernmost side of Mission Bay. They are perfect for water sports: swimming, snorkeling, surfing, waterskiing, windsurfing, and boating. Santa Clara Point is of interest to the visitor with its recreation center, tennis courts, and softball field. A sandy beach fronts San Juan Cove between the two points.

Just about every facility imaginable can be found somewhere in the park. There are also catamaran and windsurfer rentals, playgrounds and parks, frisbee and golf, and restaurants and groceries. ~ Located along Mission Boulevard between West Mission Bay Drive and East Mission Bay Drive; 619-221-8900, fax 619-581-9984.

▲ The finest and largest of San Diego's commercial camp-grounds is **Campland On The Bay** (2211 Pacific Beach Drive; 800-422-9386; www.campland.com), featuring 600 hookup sites for RVs, vans, tents, and boats; $49 to $175 per night.

MISSION BEACH PARK 🚲 ⛵ 🏊 The wide, sandy beach at the southern end is a favorite haunt of high schoolers and college students. The hot spot is at the foot of Capistrano Court. A paved boardwalk runs along the beach and is busy with bicy-clists, joggers, and roller skaters. Farther north, up around the old Belmont Park roller coaster, the beach grows narrower and the surf rougher. The crowd tends to get that way, too, with heavy-metal teens, sailors, and bikers hanging out along the sea wall, ogling and sometimes harassing the bikini set. This is the closest San Diego comes to Los Angeles' colorful but funky Ven-ice Beach. Facilities include restrooms, lifeguards, and a board-walk lined with restaurants and beach rentals. Surfing is popu-lar along the jetty. ~ Located along Mission Boulevard north of West Mission Bay Drive.

Point Loma Area

The Point Loma peninsula forms a high promon-tory that shelters San Diego Bay from the Pacific. It also provided Juan Rodríguez Cabrillo an excellent place from which to contemplate his 16th-century discovery of California. For those of us today interested in contemplating life—or just zoning out on a view—Point Loma peninsula presents the perfect opportunity.

SIGHTS

Heading south from Mission Beach, the first thing you'll encoun-ter on your way to Cabrillo National Monument is **Ocean Beach**, whose reputation as a haven for hippie hold-outs is not entirely undeserved. One of San Diego County's most dramatic coastlines then unfolds as you follow Sunset Cliffs Boulevard south.

After making a left on Hill Street, take a right on Catalina Boulevard. You'll enter the monument through the U.S. Navy's Fort Rosecrans, home to a variety of sophisticated military fa-cilities and the haunting **Fort Rosecrans National Cemetery**. Here, thousands of trim, white markers march down a grassy hillside in mute testimony to San Diego's fallen troops and deep military roots.

Naturally, **Cabrillo National Monument** features a statue of the navigator facing his landing site at Ballast Point. The sculpture itself, a gift from Cabrillo's native Portugal, isn't very impressive but the view is outstanding. With the bay and city spread below, you can often see all the way from Mexico to the La Jolla mesa. The visitors center includes a small museum. The nearby **Old Point Loma Lighthouse** guided shipping from 1855 to 1891. Admission. ~ 1800 Cabrillo Memorial Drive, Point Loma; 619-557-5450, fax 619-226-6311; www.nps.gov/cabr.

On the ocean side of the peninsula is **Whale Watch Lookout Point**, where, during winter months, you can observe the southward migration of California gray whales. Close by is a superb network of tidepools.

LODGING

Ensconced in a red, two-story former church building, the **Hostelling International—San Diego Point Loma** is filled up with 53 economy-minded guests almost every night during the summer. Comfortable bunk beds are grouped in 16 rooms housing from two to eight persons in youth-hostel fashion. Family rooms and private rooms are also available, and there is a common kitchen and dining area. The courtyard has Ping-Pong and other recreational activities. ~ 3790 Udall Street, Point Loma; 619-223-4778, fax 619-223-1883; www.sandiegohostels.org, e-mail point loma@sandiegohostels.org. BUDGET.

A rare beachfront find in residential Point Loma is the **Inn at Sunset Cliffs**. This trim, white, two-story, 24-room apartment hotel sits right on the seaside cliffs. Rooms are neat and clean but very basic. You can practice your swing on a miniature putting green, or lounge by the pool. There are also bachelor and studio apartments (with kitchenettes). ~ 1370 Sunset Cliffs Boulevard, Point Loma; 619-222-7901, 866-786-2543, fax 619-222-4201; www.innatsunsetcliffs.com, e-mail info@innatsunsetcliffs.com. DELUXE TO ULTRA-DELUXE.

Manmade Shelter and Harbor Islands jut out into San Diego Bay, providing space for several large resorts. For a relaxing, offbeat alternative to these mammoth hotels try **Humphrey's Half Moon Inn**. Surrounded by subtropical plants, this nautical 182-room complex overlooks the yacht harbor and gives the feeling of staying on an island. The rooms are tastefully decorated with a Polynesian theme. There is a pool, spa, putting green, a concert venue, and restaurant. ~ 2303 Shelter Island Drive, Point Loma; 619-224-3411, 800-542-7400, fax 619-224-3478; www.half mooninn.com, e-mail res@halfmooninn.com. ULTRA-DELUXE.

DINING

A marine view and whirling ceiling fans at **Humphrey's by the Bay** suggest Casablanca. California coastal cuisine is the fare, which means lots of fresh seafood. Breakfast, lunch, and dinner

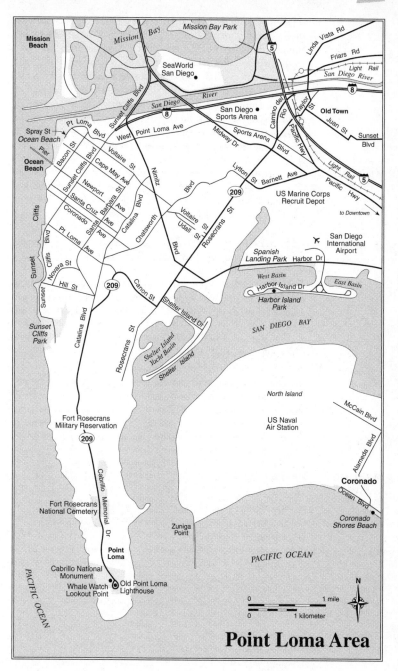

Point Loma Area

are served. ~ Adjacent to the Half Moon Inn, 2241 Shelter Island Drive, Point Loma; 619-224-3577, fax 619-224-9438; www. humphreysbythebay.com. DELUXE TO ULTRA-DELUXE.

The air at **South Beach Bar & Grille** is decidedly salty, with fishing trophies, a long wooden bar overlooking the pier, and a fun-loving sun-bronzed crowd. It's the perfect environment in which to enjoy grilled fish tacos (mahi, shark, wahoo), steamed clams and mussels, and other mouth-watering choices—washed down with a selection from the 24 beers on tap. ~ 5059 Newport Avenue, Ocean Beach; 619-226-4577. BUDGET.

SHOPPING **Newport Avenue** in Ocean Beach is the area's best bet for shopping. The blocks closest to the beach are lined with stores exuding a bohemian air: eclectic clothing and jewelry, black-light posters, smoking paraphernalia. Farther down is arguably San Diego County's largest antique district.

In addition, the 4900 block of Newport Avenue hosts a **farmer's market** every Wednesday afternoon.

NIGHTLIFE Alternative rock and pop bands, mainly local, perform Wednesday through Saturday to a young crowd at **Dream Street**. Cover. ~ 2228 Bacon Street, Ocean Beach; 619-222-8131; www.dream streetlive.com.

A mellower mood can be had nightly at nearby **Winston's**, where live blues, rock, and reggae are the preferred sounds. Cover. ~ 1921 Bacon Street, Ocean Beach; 619-222-6822.

Even musicians head outdoors during San Diego summers. **Humphrey's by the Bay** hosts the city's most ambitious series of jazz, comedy, funk, and mellow rock shows, which include an impressive lineup of name artists in a beautiful oceanview concert venue. ~ 2241 Shelter Island Drive, Point Loma; 619-224-3577; www.humphreysconcerts.com.

BEACHES & PARKS **OCEAN BEACH** 🏊 ⚓ 🚻 🐾 Where you toss down your towel at "OB" will probably depend as much on your age as your interests. Surfers, sailors, and what's left of the hippie crowd hang out around the pier; farther north, where the surf is milder and the beach wider, families and retired folks can be found sun-

---

HAM IT UP

Aside from being a popular restaurant and lounge, **Tom Ham's Lighthouse** is a real lighthouse and the official Coast Guard–sanctioned beacon of Harbor Island. ~ 2150 Harbor Island Drive; 619-291-9110; www.tomhamslighthouse.com.

bathing and strolling. At the far north end is San Diego's first and only dog beach, complete with a doggie drinking fountain. There are picnic areas, restrooms, and restaurants. Fishing is good from the surf or the fishing pier. Swimming and surfing is very popular here. ~ Take Ocean Beach Freeway (Route 8) west until it ends; turn left onto Sunset Cliffs Boulevard, then right on Voltaire Street; 619-235-1100.

SUNSET CLIFFS PARK The jagged cliffs and sandstone bluffs along Point Loma peninsula give this park a spectacular setting. High-cresting waves make it popular with expert surfers, who favor the rocky beach at the foot of Ladera Avenue. Tidepools evidence the rich marine life that attracts many divers. Winding staircases (at Bermuda and Santa Cruz avenues) and steep trails lead down to some nice pocket beaches. ~ Located off of Sunset Cliffs Boulevard south of Ocean Beach; 619-235-1100.

SHELTER ISLAND Like Harbor Island, its neighbor to the northeast, Shelter Island functions primarily as a boating center, but there's a beach facing the bay for swimming, fishing, and picnicking. A landscaped walkway runs the length of the island. There are picnic areas, a children's playground, restrooms, a fishing pier, and restaurants. ~ Located on Shelter Island Drive near Rosecrans Street; 619-235-1100.

HARBOR ISLAND There are no sandy beaches on this manmade island, but there is a walkway bordered by lawn and benches along its entire length. You'll get fabulous views of the city. Facilities here include restrooms and restaurants. ~ Located south of San Diego International Airport on Harbor Island Drive; 619-686-6200, fax 619-686-6400.

SPANISH LANDING PARK This is a slender sandy beach with walkways, a grassy picnic area, and a children's playground. Situated close to San Diego International Airport, the park overlooks Harbor Island Marina and offers lovely views of the bay and city. Restrooms are available. ~ Located just west of the airport on North Harbor Drive; 619-686-6200, fax 619-686-6400.

Old Town Area

Back in 1769, Spanish explorer Gaspar de Portolá selected a hilltop site overlooking the bay for a mission that would begin the European settlement of California. A town soon spread out at the foot of the hill, complete with plaza, church, school, and the tile-roofed adobe casas of California's first families. Through the years, Spanish, Mexican, and American settlements thrived until an 1872 fire destroyed much of the town, prompting developers to relocate the commercial district nearer the bay.

SIGHTS   Some of the buildings and relics of the early era survived and have been brought back to life at **Old Town San Diego State Historic Park**. Lined with adobe restorations and brightened with colorful shops, the six blocks of Old Town provide a lively and interesting opportunity for visitors to stroll, shop, and sightsee. ~ Park headquarters, 4002 Wallace Street; 619-220-5422, fax 619-220-7389.

The state historic park sponsors a free walking tour at 11 a.m. and 2 p.m. daily, or you can easily do it on your own by picking up a copy of the *Old San Diego Gazette*. The paper, which comes out once a month and includes a map of the area, is free at local stores. You can also hop aboard the **Old Town Trolley** for a delightful two-hour narrated tour of Old Town and a variety of other highlights in San Diego and Coronado. It makes ten stops, and you're allowed to get on and off all day long. Fee. ~ 4010 Twiggs Street; 619-298-8687, 800-868-7482, fax 619-298-3404; www.historictours.com.

As it has for over a century, everything focuses on **Old Town Plaza**. Before 1872 this was the social and recreational center of the town: political meetings, barbecues, dances, shootouts, and bullfights all happened here. ~ San Diego Avenue and Mason Street.

Casa de Estudillo is the finest of the original adobe buildings. It was a mansion in its time, built in 1827 for the commander of the Mexican Presidio. ~ Located at the Mason Street corner of the plaza.

Seeley Stables is a replica of the barns and stables of Albert Seeley, who operated the stage line. Nowadays it houses a collection of horse-drawn vehicles and Western memorabilia, and has a video presentation. ~ At Mason and Calhoun streets.

The **San Diego Union** building was Old Town's first frame building and the place where the *San Diego Union* was first printed in 1868. It has been restored as a 19th-century printing office. ~ Located at San Diego Avenue.

Shoppers seem to gravitate in large numbers toward the north side of the plaza to browse the unusual shops comprising **Bazaar del Mundo**. Built in circular fashion around a tropical courtyard, this complex also houses several restaurants.

About one and a half blocks east of Old Town lies **Heritage Park**, an area dedicated to the preservation of the city's Victorian past. Seven historic 1880s-era houses and an old Jewish temple have been moved to the hillside site and beautifully restored. ~ Juan and Harney streets.

The original mission and Spanish Presidio once stood high on a hill behind Old Town. This site of California's birthplace now houses the **Junipero Serra Museum**, a handsome Spanish Colonial structure containing an excellent collection of American Indian and Spanish artifacts from the state's pioneer days and relics from the Royal Presidio dig sites. Admission. ~ Presidio Drive; 619-297-3258, fax 619-297-3281; www.sandiegohistory.org, e-mail web.1@sandiegohistory.org.

Within five years after Father Serra dedicated the first of California's 21 missions, the site had become much too small for the growing numbers it served. So **Mission San Diego de Alcala** was moved from Presidio Hill six miles east into Mission Valley. Surrounded now by shopping centers and suburban homes, the "Mother of Missions" retains its simple but striking white adobe facade topped by a graceful *campanario*. There's a library (open 10 a.m. to 12 p.m., Tuesday and Thursday) containing mission records in Junípero Serra's handwriting and a lovely courtyard with gnarled pepper trees. Admission. ~ 10818 San Diego Mission Road; 619-281-8449; www.missionsandiego.com, e-mail info@missionsandiego.com.

LODGING

A good bet in the lower price categories is the appropriately named **Old Town Inn**. Strolling distance from Old Town, and across from the Old Town Trolley and Transit Center (the transportation hub), this spiffy little 74-room family-owned motel has economy units and handicapped-accessible deluxe rooms, some of which have partial kitchens. A guest laundry is available, as is a heated outdoor pool, and a complimentary deluxe breakfast buffet every morning. ~ 4444 Pacific Highway; 619-260-8024, 800-643-3025, fax 619-296-0524; www.oldtown-inn.com. MODERATE TO DELUXE.

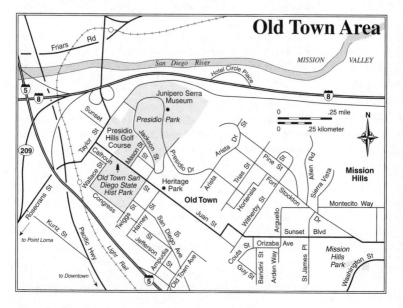

For the romantic, **Heritage Park Inn**, a storybook 1889 Queen Anne mansion with a striking turret, is an enchanting bed and breakfast. Set on a grassy hillside, it provides a tranquil escape. Choose from 12 distinctive chambers (all with private baths), each furnished with museum-quality antiques. Most feature ornate brass or four-poster canopy beds and old-fashioned quilts; three have jacuzzi tubs. ~ 2470 Heritage Park Row; 619-299-6832, 800-995-2470, fax 619-299-9465; www.heritage parkinn.com, e-mail innkeeper@heritageparkinn.com. DELUXE TO ULTRA-DELUXE.

For a choice of motels with a variety of prices, try looking for accommodations along **Hotel Circle**, on the north side of Presidio Park. The road loops under a portion of Route 8. Most properties around the circle are large chain hotels designed for vacation travelers, with resort facilities including large pools, tennis courts, and spas or fitness centers; many share the use of the 27-hole Riverwalk Golf Club. Rates are generally lower than at downtown hotels.

Among them is the 417-room **Crowne Plaza Hotel**, whose tall palm trees, courtyard, and tiki-style bar aim for a Polynesian ambience. ~ 2270 Hotel Circle North; 619-297-1101, 800-972-2802, fax 619-297-6049; www.cp-sandiego.com, e-mail sales@cp-sandiego.com. ULTRA-DELUXE.

The **Handlery Hotel Resort** is a lowrise 217-room complex adjacent to the golf course, with an outdoor pool, jacuzzi, and poolside gym. ~ 950 Hotel Circle North; 619-298-0511, 800-676-6567, fax 619-298-9793; www.handlery.com, e-mail sales @handlery.com. MODERATE.

The **Town and Country Hotel** is geared toward travelers who mix business with pleasure, featuring its own convention center as well as four swimming pools and an adjacent shopping mall. ~ 500 Hotel Circle North; 619-291-7131, 800-772-8527, fax 619-291-3584; www.towncountry.com, e-mail res@towncountry.com. ULTRA-DELUXE.

Hawthorn Suites San Diego has 50 one-bedroom and two-bedroom, two-bath suites ideal for traveling families, as well as an outdoor barbecue area. ~ 1335 Hotel Circle South; 619-299-3501, 888-591-1199, fax 619-294-7882; www.hawthornsuites sandiego.com. ULTRA-DELUXE.

The 280 rooms at **Days Inn–Hotel Circle,** which holds the distinction of being the largest Days Inn in California, feature video games for kids, as well as ironing boards and irons; some rooms have kitchenettes. ~ 543 Hotel Circle South; 619-297-8800, 800-227-4743, fax 619-298-6029; www.daysinnhc.com. DELUXE.

DINING

Old Town charmer **Berta's** specializes in Latin American cuisine. *Vatapa* (coconut sauce over mahimahi, scallops, and shrimp) and *cansado* (a plate of pinto beans, rice, salsa, plantain, and green salad) are wonderfully prepared. Closed Monday. ~ 3928 Twigg Street; phone/fax 619-295-2343. MODERATE.

Fresh, innovative seafood is the calling card at **Café Pacifica**, where a billion points of light sparkle from the wood-beamed ceiling and candles create a warm, intimate setting. California cuisine meets Pacific Rim panache, with preparations such as ginger-stuffed seared halibut and swordfish with soy-peanut glaze. Seating is also available at the bar and, in warm weather, the patio with removable roof. No lunch Sunday through Tuesday. ~ 2414 San Diego Avenue; 619-291-6666, fax 619-291-0122; www.cafepacifica.com, e-mail info@cafepacifica.com. MODERATE TO ULTRA-DELUXE.

Less than a mile from Old Town lies a pair of excellent ethnic take-out shops that few visitors ever find. **El Indio** opened in 1940 as a family-operated *tortillería*, then added an informal restaurant serving quesadillas, enchiladas, tostadas, burritos, tacos, and taquitos. Quality homemade Mexican food at Taco Bell prices; you can sit indoors, out on the patio, or order to go. Open for breakfast, lunch, and dinner. ~ 3695 India Street; 619-299-0333; www.el-indio.com. BUDGET.

Another one-of-a-kind fast-food operation with an equally fervent following, **Saffron Chicken** turns out zesty Thai-grilled chicken on a special rotisserie. The aroma is positively exquisite and so is the chicken served with jasmine rice, Cambodian salad, and the five tangy sauces. Eat on an adjacent patio or take a picnic to the beach. ~ 3731-B India Street; 619-574-0177. BUDGET TO MODERATE. Next door is **Saffron Noodles**, owned by the same restaurateurs. ~ 3737 India Street; 619-574-7737. BUDGET TO MODERATE.

Historic Old Town is blessed with several exciting bazaars and shopping squares. By far the grandest is the **Bazaar del Mundo**, Old Town's version of the famous marketplaces of Spain and Mexico. Adobe casitas house a variety of international shops. Here, **Design Center, Inc.** (619-296-3161) offers up a huge se-

SHOPPING

CROSS-CULTURAL CUISINE

"Nuevo Latino" is the theme at the spacious and contemporary **Zócalo Grill**, where the menu merges food cultures from Central and South America, Mexico, and the Caribbean: spicy Sonoran shrimp scampi, honey-beer-braised carnitas, grilled swordfish with pineapple-serrano salsa, honey-chipotle-glazed salmon, and pork chop with chile negro sauce. On Sunday, only brunch is served. ~ 2444 San Diego Avenue; 619-298-9840; www.zocalogrill.com. MODERATE TO DELUXE.

lection of furniture, home decor and gifts from the American Southwest and Mexico, and **Ariana** (619-296-4989) features clothing and wearable art. ~ 4133 Taylor at Juan streets; www.bazaardelmundo.com.

From Friday through Sunday, **Kobey's Swap Meet** converts the parking lot of the San Diego Sports Arena into a giant flea market where over 1000 sellers hawk new and used wares. Admission. ~ Sports Arena Boulevard; 619-226-0650.

Unlike other antique stores in the area, **Circa a.d.** offers anything but American antiques. It proudly displays a vast assortment of Asian, European, and African art, jewelry, textiles, and pottery, specializing in goods from around the Pacific Rim. It even carries bonsai trees. ~ 5355 Grant Street; 619-293-3328; www. circaad.com, e-mail info@circaad.com.

NIGHTLIFE   The prevailing culture in Old Town is Mexican, as in mariachis and margaritas. The **Old Town Mexican Café**, a festive, friendly establishment, has a patio bar. ~ 2489 San Diego Avenue; 619-297-4330; www.oldtownmexcafe.com.

O'Hungry's, a nearby restaurant, features an acoustic guitarist on Friday and Saturday nights. ~ 2547 San Diego Avenue; 619-298-0133.

For country-and-western dancing, try **In Cahoots**, which has free dance lessons Tuesday through Saturday. Closed Monday. Cover Wednesday through Saturday. ~ 5373 Mission Center Road; 619-291-1183, fax 619-291-1723; www.incahoots.com.

▼▼▼▼▼▼▼▼▼▼▼▼▼▼

Hillcrest & San Diego Gay Scene

Ironically, it's thanks to the strong presence of the U.S. Navy that San Diego has such a significant gay scene. After World War II, thousands of newly discharged men and women who had discovered their sexual identities during their military service opted to remain in places like San Diego and San Francisco instead of returning home. The long-time military presence contributed to the fairly conservative personality of San Diego's gay community, but a more liberalizing effect began to take place in the 1960s with the arrival of the University of California in La Jolla. Today, San Diego's gay and lesbian community is more out than it's ever been, and the center of attention is the section of town just to the northwest of Balboa Park called Hillcrest.

The '50s architecture and neon give the area a retro feel (a neon sign, which works intermittently, hangs across University Avenue at 5th Avenue and signals entrance into Hillcrest). Bookstores, trendy boutiques, innovative restaurants, and coffeeshops line University Avenue, 5th Avenue, and Robinson Street—all within easy walking distance of one another.

Since many of its guests hail from outside the U.S., the **Hillcrest Inn Hotel** considers itself an international hotel. Right in the hub of Hillcrest activity, the 45 modestly furnished rooms, outfitted with microwaves and refrigerators, provide guests with a comfortable stay. Fatigued wayfarers will appreciate the sun patio and spa after long days of sightseeing. ~ 3754 5th Avenue; 619-293-7078, 800-258-2280, fax 619-293-3861; www.hillcrestinn. net, e-mail info@hillcrestinn.net. MODERATE.

Just across from Balboa Park, in a converted 1926 apartment building, is the **Park Manor Suites**, long popular with gay visitors. The city has designated the Italian Renaissance–style structure a historical landmark. The spacious rooms and Old World touches, such as antique furnishings, set a gracious if somewhat time-worn tone. Several rooms have grand views of the park and skyline. ~ 525 Spruce Street; 619-291-0999, 800-874-2649, fax 619-291-8844; www.park manorsuites.com, e-mail info@parkmanorsuites. com. MODERATE TO ULTRA-DELUXE.

Built in 1915 for the Panama–California Exposition, the **Balboa Park Inn** is a popular caravansary with gays and straights alike. Its 26 rooms are decorated in different themes; you can choose to luxuriate in *Gone With the Wind*'s "Tara Suite," get sentimental in 1930s Paris, or go wild in Greystoke. Some suites boast jacuzzi tubs, kitchens, and faux fireplaces, and *everyone* can request a continental breakfast served in bed. A courtyard and sun terrace round out the facilities of this winsome getaway. Reservations recommended. ~ 3402 Park Boulevard; 619-298-0823, 800-938-8181, fax 619-294-8070; www.balboaparkinn.com, e-mail info@balboaparkinn.com. DELUXE.

> Like Balboa Park nearby, the four-building Balboa Park Inn was built in 1915 for the Panama–California Exposition.

There's a steady crowd day and night at **Urban Mo's**, the favored hamburger joint in the Hillcrest. Draped with flags and streamers that change seasonally and featuring two full bars and a dancefloor, you can be assured of something interesting to watch while you wait for your food. Besides hamburgers, you'll find steak, vegetarian plates, and salads, which can be eaten outdoors on the patio. If you dare, try the Kick-Ass Margarita and take a line dance lesson. Sunday brunch. ~ 308 University Avenue; 619-491-0400, fax 619-491-0160; www.urbanmos.com. BUDGET.

Bread lovers will think they have landed in paradise when they enter **Bread & Cie**. The aroma of fig, jalapeño, cheese, and rosemary breads lingers in this amazing bakery, which also serves sandwiches, pastries, and cappuccinos. Be prepared to wait at lunchtime. ~ 350 University Avenue; 619-683-9322, fax 619-683-9299. BUDGET.

◀ *HIDDEN*

Attracting attention has never been a problem for the **Corvette Diner**. Although it's usually crammed full of families and high school kids, the decor is not to be missed. Cool 1950s music, a soda fountain (complete with resident jerks), rock-and-roll memorabilia, dancing waitresses, and a classy Corvette have proven a magnetic formula for this Hillcrest haven. The place is jammed for lunch and dinner. Simple "blue-plate" diner fare includes meatloaf, chicken-fried steak, and hefty burgers named for 1950s notables like Dion, Eddie, and Kookie. ~ 3946 5th Avenue; 619-542-1476; www.cohnrestaurants.com. MODERATE.

Around the corner and up the block is another diner complete with black-and-white tile, neon, shiny chrome and naugahyde booths. **City Delicatessen & Bakery**, however, whips up Jewish deli treats such as matzo ball soup, lox and bagels, and beef brisket. You'll also find burgers, steaks, salads, and sandwiches; breakfast is served all day. A popular late-night spot. ~ 535 University Avenue; 619-295-2747, fax 619-295-2129. BUDGET TO MODERATE.

Located in the heart of Hillcrest, **California Cuisine** offers sumptuous dishes for your discriminating palate. Beef tenderloin and New Zealand lamb loin are among the many items on their ever-changing menu, as are pasta, salads, and vegetarian fare. You also get a taste of promising local artists whose original work adorns the walls. Dinner only. ~ 1027 University Avenue; 619-543-0790, fax 619-543-0106; www.californiacuisine.cc, e-mail info@californiacuisine.cc. DELUXE TO ULTRA-DELUXE.

Be transported to France without the airfare at **La Vache**, a neighborhood bistro that serves up French delicacies in a romantic setting. Velvet window coverings, mirrored walls and wooden wine racks surround diners who savor such creative dishes as salmon with crayfish sauce and a salad of walnuts, pears, olives, Roquefort, parmesan and goat cheese. A three-course prix-fixe dinner—offered Tuesday and limited hours the rest of the week—is a bargain. ~ 420 Robinson Avenue; 619-295-0214, fax 619-295-1833; www.lavacheandco.com, e-mail lavache@sbcglobal.net. MODERATE TO DELUXE.

AUTHOR FAVORITE

Searching high and low for that Betty Page calendar? How about some sweater-girl paper dolls? **Babette Schwartz**, the local drag queen, has a store that carries an array of novelty items and retro toys, including Wonder Woman lunchboxes and Barbie dolls. ~ 421 University Avenue; 619-220-7048; www.babette.com.

Obelisk carries gay, lesbian, and bisexual reading material, as **SHOPPING** well as gift items to tickle your fancy—jewelry, shirts, and cards —to name a few. ~ 1029 University Avenue; 619-297-4171.

Appeasing vinyl junkies and casual listeners alike, **Off the Record** is jam-packed with new, used, and out-of-print CDs, LPs, and singles (both vinyl and plastic). You'll also find T-shirts, books, magazines, and other music-related paraphernalia. ~ 2912 University Avenue; 619-298-4755.

The **Brass Rail**, which opened in 1958, is one of San Diego's old- **NIGHTLIFE** est gay bars. The bartenders' famed congeniality keeps the primarily male clientele coming back year after year for more— more drinks and more dancing (which is in full swing every weekend). Saturday is Latino night. Cover on weekends. ~ 3796 5th Avenue; 619-298-2233.

A few doors down from the Brass Rail and next to the Hillcrest Inn Hotel is **David's Coffee House**. Designed to look like a living room with a couch and antique furniture, this popular coffeehouse is a home away from home for travelers and locals alike; pets are also welcome. Aside from knocking back espresso and admiring the passing scenery, you can engage your neighbor with a board game or surf the web. David's Coffee House donates a portion of its proceeds to local AIDS organizations. ~ 3766 5th Avenue; 619-296-4173.

Also in this same stretch of 5th Avenue, **The Loft** is a gay bar offering jukebox music and pool playing. ~ 3610 5th Avenue; 619-296-6407.

The short trek to University Avenue brings you to Urban Mo's restaurant, home of **Kickers**. This C&W bar keeps gay, lesbian, and straight folks kickin' with free line dancing and two-step lessons Thursday through Saturday. Disco Wednesday features a drag show. ~ 308 University Avenue; 619-491-0400; www.urbanmos.com.

The real action on University Avenue is over at the Rainbow Block. First there's **Flicks**, a video bar that flashes visual stimuli on its six big screens while playing dance and progressive music. ~ 1017 University Avenue; 619-297-2056; www.sdflicks.com.

At the far end of the block, **Rich's** heats up with high-energy dancing until 2 a.m. The deejay-mixed music sets the beat: groove, techno, house, and tribal rhythms. Music isn't the only stimulation; your eyes will be dazzled by the specially created visual effects. Each night has a different theme. Wednesday has a hot boy contest (no cover) and Thursday is ladies' night; the dancefloor will be packed all week-end long. Cover. ~ 1051 University Avenue; 619-295-2195; www.richssandiego.com.

Other gay bars around town include **Bourbon Street**, a French Quarter–style bar that features an outdoor patio and nightly entertainment. Live music Thursday through Sunday. ~ 4612 Park Boulevard; 619-291-4043; www.bourbonstreetsd.com. The action at the **Chee Chee Club**, a local cruise bar and the oldest gay establishment in San Diego, revolves around shooting pool and playing pinball. Occasional performers present shows for the mostly male crowd. ~ 929 Broadway; 619-234-4404.

▼ ▼ ▼ ▼ ▼ ▼ ▼ ▼ ▼ ▼ ▼ ▼
Balboa Park and the San Diego Zoo

It's unclear as to whether it was intelligent foresight or unbridled optimism that prompted the establishment of Balboa Park. Certain that a fine neighborhood would flourish around it, city fathers in 1868 set aside 1400 acres of rattlesnake-infested hillside above "New Town" as a public park. The park's eventual development, and most of its lovely Spanish Baroque buildings, came as the result of two world's fairs: The Panama–California Exposition of 1915–16 and the California–Pacific International Exposition of 1935–36.

Today Balboa Park ranks among the largest and finest of America's city parks. Wide avenues and walkways curve through luxurious subtropical foliage leading to nine major museums, three art galleries, four theaters, picnic groves, the world's largest zoo, a golf course, and countless other recreation facilities. Its verdant grounds teem with cyclists, joggers, skaters, picnickers, weekend artists, and museum mavens.

SIGHTS

The main entrance is from 6th Avenue onto Laurel Street, which becomes El Prado as you cross Cabrillo Bridge. Begin your visit at the **Balboa Park Visitors Center**, located on the northeast corner of Plaza de Panama. They provide plenty of free pamphlets and maps on the park. ~ House of Hospitality, 1549 El Prado; 619-239-0512; www.balboapark.org.

From here you can stroll about, taking in Balboa Park's main attractions. To the right, as you head east on the pedestrian-only section of El Prado, is the **Casa de Balboa**. This building houses several worthwhile museums, including the **San Diego Model Railroad Museum** 619-696-0199, fax 619-696-0239; www.sdmrm.org, e-mail info@sdmrm.org), which features the largest permanent model railroad layouts in North America. Children under 15 enter free. Closed Monday. Here, too, is the **San Diego Historical Society's** extensive collection of documents and photographs spanning the urban history of San Diego. The **Museum of Photographic Arts** (619-238-7559, fax 619-238-8777; www.mopa.org, e-mail info@mopa.org) has exhibits of internationally known photographers. Admission except on the second Tuesday of the month.

Continuing east to the fountain, you'll see the **Reuben H. Fleet Science Center** on your right. Among the park's finest attractions, it features one of the largest planetariums and San Diego's only IMAX dome theater. The galleries offer various hands-on exhibits and displays dealing with science, technology, and natural phenomena. Admission. ~ 619-238-1233, fax 619-685-5771; www.rhfleet.org.

Balboa Park's museums charge an admission fee but every Tuesday select museums can be visited free.

Across the courtyard is the **San Diego Natural History Museum** with displays devoted mostly to the natural heritage of Southern and Baja California, including a hands-on display of San Diego archaeology. Traveling exhibitions and giant-screen films cover more global topics. Admission. ~ 619-232-3821, fax 619-232-0248; www.sdnhm.org, e-mail admissions@sdnhm.org

Going back along El Prado, take a moment to admire your reflection in the Lily Pond. With the old, latticed **Botanical Building** in the background, the scene is a favorite among photographers. The fern collection inside is equally striking.

Next is the **Timken Museum of Art**, considered to have one of the West Coast's finest collections of European and Early American paintings. The displays include works by Rembrandt and Copley, as well as an amazing collection of Russian icons. Closed Monday and the month of September. ~ 619-239-5548, fax 619-531-9640; www.timkenmuseum.org, e-mail info@timkenmuseum.org.

Right next door on the plaza is the **San Diego Museum of Art**, with an entrance facade patterned after the University of Salamanca in Spain. The museum treasures include a permanent collection of Italian Renaissance, Dutch, and Spanish Baroque paintings and sculpture, a display of Asian art, a gallery of impressionist paintings, contemporary art, and an American collection, as well as touring exhibitions. Closed Monday. Admission. ~ 619-232-7931, fax 619-232-9367; www.sdmart.org, e-mail information@sdmart.org.

Across El Prado from the Museum of Art is the **Mingei International Museum**. The Mingei (which means "art of the people" and is pronounced *min-gay*), has a superb collection of world folk art, craft, and design from countries around the world. Closed Monday. Admission. ~ 1439 El Prado; 619-239-0003, fax 619-239-0605; www.mingei.org, e-mail mingei@mingei.org.

◄ HIDDEN

The grandest of all Balboa Park structures, built as the centerpiece for the 1915 Panama–California Exposition, is the 200-foot Spanish Renaissance **California Tower**. The **San Diego Museum of Man**, at the base of the tower, is a must for anthropology buffs and those interested in Egyptian mummies and American Indian cultures. Admission. ~ 619-239-2001, fax 619-239-2749; www.museumofman.org.

Another museum not to be missed is the **San Diego Air & Space Museum**, several blocks south of the plaza. It contains over 65 aircrafts including a replica of Charles Lindbergh's famous *Spirit of St. Louis*, the original of which was built in San Diego. Admission. ~ 619-234-8291; www.aero spacemuseum.org.

On display at the San Diego Air & Space Museum is *Black Bird*, the world's fastest plane.

En route you'll pass the **Spreckels Organ Pavilion.** Those 4416 pipes make it the world's largest outdoor instrument of its kind.

Sports fans will want to take in the **Hall of Champions Sports Museum** in the historic Federal Building. It houses the Breitbard Hall of Fame and exhibits that feature world-class San Diego athletes from more than 40 sports. The museum also has an interactive media center. Admission. ~ 2131 Pan-American Plaza; 619-234-2544, fax 619-234-4543; www.sdhoc.com.

You'll want to attend a play at the **Old Globe** to absorb the full greatness of this Tony Award–winning stage, but for starters you can stroll around the 581-seat theater, famed for its Shakespearean presentations. Located in a grove on the north side of California Tower, the **Old Globe** is part of the trio of theaters that includes the **Cassius Carter Centre Stage** and the outdoor **Lowell Davies Festival Theatre.** Admission. ~ 619-234-5623; www.oldglobe.org, e-mail tickets@theoldglobe.org.

SAN DIEGO ZOO   North of the Balboa Park museum and theater complex is San Diego Zoo, which needs no introduction. It quite simply is the world's top-rated zoo. The numbers alone are mind-boggling: 4000 animals, representing 800 species, spread out over 100 acres. Most of these wild animals live in surroundings as natural as man can make them. Rather than cages there are glass enclosures where orangutans roam free on grassy islands and multihued birds fly through tropical rainforests. All around is a manmade jungle forest overgrown with countless species of rare and exotic plants.

Of particular merit is "Polar Bear Plunge." Here you can watch the polar bears as they gracefully swim underwater in their deep saltwater bay. At "Ituri Forest," Funani and Koboko delight all with their infamous underwater hippo ballet. The zoo's state-of-the-art primate exhibit, the "Gorilla Tropics," is a two-and-a-half-acre African rainforest that is home to eight lowland gorillas and hundreds of jungle birds. Within this area is "Pygmy Chimps at Bonobo Road," home to frolicsome troupes of pygmy chimps and Angolan colobus monkeys. One of the first pandas to be born and survive in captivity can be seen at the "Panda Research Station."

At the **Children's Zoo,** where there are just as many adults as kids, you can watch a large variety of bugs crawling around, and there's a petting zoo. Don't miss the pygmy marmosets. They are the world's smallest monkeys, weighing in at only four ounces when full grown. Admission. ~ Located off Park Boulevard; 619-234-3153, fax 619-231-0249; www.sandiegozoo.org.

My vote for the prettiest and most hospitable of San Diego's bed and breakfasts goes to the **Keating House Bed and Breakfast**. This historically designated 1888 Victorian home in a sunny hillside residential neighborhood between Balboa Park and downtown offers nine comfy-cozy rooms—six in the main house and three in the cottage out back. With its gabled roof, hexagonal window turret, and conical peak, this beautifully restored Queen Anne is every bit as nice inside. A garden completes the homey scene. ~ 2331 2nd Avenue; 619-239-8585, 800-995-8644, fax 619-239-5774; www.keatinghouse.com, e-mail inn@keatinghouse.com. MODERATE TO DELUXE.

LODGING

Another attractive bed and breakfast in the Balboa Park area is **Carole's B&B Inn**, built in 1904 and situated on a quiet residential street. The main house has four antique-furnished guest rooms (some with shared bath), while an annex across the street contains two garden studio apartments with private baths and kitchenettes, a one-bedroom cottage, and a two-bedroom apartment. In addition to a sitting room with player piano and a conference room, the inn has a swimming pool. ~ 3227 Grim Avenue; 619-280-5258, 800-975-5521; www.carolesbnb.com. DELUXE.

The best value for your dollar among reasonably priced hotels in the area is the 67-room **Comfort Inn**. They feature wood furniture, designer color schemes, and high-grade carpeting. The inn has a pool-sized jacuzzi and serves a continental breakfast. Conveniently located near Balboa Park just a few blocks from the civic center. ~ 719 Ash Street; 619-232-2525, 800-404-6835, fax 619-687-3024; www.comfortinnsandiego.com. MODERATE TO DELUXE.

Dmitri's Guesthouse offers five rooms (two with shared bath) close to Horton Plaza. Each suite comes with a ceiling fan and a refrigerator (one includes a full kitchen). Feel free to shed your clothing on the sundeck and immerse yourself in the hot tub or swimming pool. Situated in a century-old house, Dmitri's serves a continental breakfast poolside every morning. Reservations recommended. ~ 931 21st Street; 619-238-5547; e-mail dmitris@netzero.com. MODERATE TO DELUXE.

Located in Balboa Park's House of Hospitality is the **Prado Restaurant**, surrounded by lovely Spanish terraces and burbling fountains. Pasta, seafood, poultry, and meat dishes here blend Latin and Italian flavors. For lunch, you may find fancy panini sandwiches, pasta, and fish tacos, while dinner choices might include wild-mushroom risotto, orechette pasta with gorgonzola cream sauce, and osso buco with sweet potato mash. The dessert

DINING

menu is equally mouth-watering. Patio seating and a pitcher of sangria is a must during the warm months. No dinner on Monday. ~ 1549 El Prado; 619-557-9441, fax 619-557-9170; www.pradobalboa.com. MODERATE TO ULTRA-DELUXE.

When you're visiting the San Diego Zoo, consider **Albert's Restaurant**. Named for the gorilla who once occupied the area, this sit-down eatery offers a variety of salads, sandwiches, fresh pastas, and fish and meat entrées. No dinner except in summer (late June through Labor Day). ~ 2920 Zoo Drive, San Diego Zoo; 619-685-3200, fax 619-685-3204; www.sandiegozoo.org. MODERATE TO DELUXE.

HIDDEN ► Located north of the park in, well, North Park, **Hawthorn's Restaurant** presents an array of tasty dishes, specializing in fresh seafood ranging from calamari to Alaskan halibut. Usually available is filet mignon with green peppercorn and cabernet sauce. Dinner only. Sunday brunch. Closed Monday. ~ 2895 University Avenue; 619-544-0940, fax 619-544-0941. MODERATE TO DELUXE.

SHOPPING A haven for art lovers is **Spanish Village Art Center**. Over 35 studios are staffed by artists displaying their work and giving daily demonstrations. For sale are original paintings, sculpture, handblown glass and fine jewelry. ~ 1770 Village Place, near the San Diego Zoo entrance; 619-233-9050, fax 619-239-9226; www.spanishvillageart.com.

NIGHTLIFE The **Old Globe Theatre** presents classic and contemporary plays, including Shakespeare with innovative twists, in three Balboa Park theaters. ~ Balboa Park; 619-234-5623; www.theoldglobe.org.

Bertrand at Mr. A's is the critics' choice for "best drinking with a view." The atmosphere at this elegant restaurant is one of monied luxury, and gentlemen are expected (but not required) to wear jackets. ~ 2550 5th Avenue, 12th floor; 619-239-1377; www.bertrandatmras.com.

Also on the western edge of the park but on a quiet block, you'll likely find a line out the door at **Extraordinary Desserts**. The reason? An agonizing array of decadent, French-style creations that will sate any sweet tooth. Tables, both indoor and patio, are often in short supply so don't be shy about nabbing the first one you see. ~ 2929 5th Avenue; 619-294-7032.

Downtown San Diego

At one time downtown San Diego was a collection of porn shops, tattoo parlors, and strip-tease bars. Billions of dollars invested in a stunning array of new buildings and in the restoration of many old ones have changed all that. Within the compact city center there's Horton Plaza, an exciting example of avant-garde urban architecture, and the adjacent Gaslamp Quarter, which reveals how San Diego looked at the peak of its Victorian-era boom in the 1880s.

Horton Plaza is totally unlike any other shopping center or urban redevelopment project. It has transcended its genre in whimsical, rambling paths, bridges, towers, piazzas, sculptures, fountains, and live greenery. Fourteen different styles, ranging from Renaissance to postmodern, are employed in its design. Mimes, minstrels, and fortune tellers meander about the six-block complex performing for patrons. The success of this structure sparked downtown's renewal by revamping local businesses and attracting more tourists.

SIGHTS

Horton Plaza was inspired by European shopping streets and districts such as the Plaka of Athens, the Ramblas of Barcelona, and Portobello Road in London. ~ The Plaza is bounded by Broadway and G Street and 1st and 4th avenues.

The **Gaslamp Quarter** is one of America's largest national historic districts, covering a 16-block strip along 4th, 5th, and 6th avenues from Broadway to the waterfront. Architecturally, the Quarter reveals some of the finest Victorian-style commercial buildings constructed in San Diego during the 50 years between the Civil War and World War I. This area, along 5th Avenue, became San Diego's first main street. The city's core began on the bay where Alonzo Horton first built a wharf in 1869.

> The redlight district was called the Stingaree, after the dangerous sting rays in San Diego Bay—in either place, you were bound to get badly stung.

It was this same area that later fell into disrepute as the heart of the business district moved north beyond Broadway. By the 1890s, prostitution and gambling were rampant. Offices above street level were converted into bordellos and opium dens. The area south of Market Street became known as the "Stingaree," an unflattering reference coined by the many who were stung by card sharks, con men, and of course, con ladies.

Rescued by the city and a dedicated group of preservationists, the area not only survived but played a major role in the massive redevelopment of downtown San Diego. The city added wide brick sidewalks, period street lamps, trees, and benches. In all, more than 100 grand old Victorian buildings were restored to their original splendor. See "Walking Tour" in this chapter for more details.

Make a point to visit the **Villa Montezuma–Jesse Shepard House**, situated a few blocks east of the Gaslamp Quarter. This ornate, Queen Anne–style Victorian mansion, magnificently restored, was constructed by a wealthy group of San Diegans in 1887 as a gift to a visiting musician. Culture-hungry civic leaders actually "imported" world-famous troubadour Jesse Shepard to live in the opulent dwelling as something of a court musician to the city's upper crust. Shepard stayed only two years but decorated his villa to the hilt with dozens of stained-glass windows and elaborate hand-carved wood trim and decorations. Currently closed for restoration; call ahead for information. Admission. ~ 1925 K Street; 619-239-2211, fax 619-232-6297; www.sandiego history.org, e-mail admissions@sandiegohistory.org.

Providing contrast to all this preserved history is the **Museum of Contemporary Art San Diego**'s downtown space, adjacent to the American Plaza Trolley Transfer Station. Two floors and four galleries showcase an internationally renowned collection and temporary exhibits featuring cutting-edge contemporary art. Educational tours and a well-stocked bookstore complement the exhibits. Closed Wednesday. ~ 1001 Kettner Boulevard; 619-234-1001, fax 619-232-4875; www.mcasd.org.

LODGING   Treat yourself to a nice dinner with the money you save staying at **Hostelling International—San Diego Downtown**, centrally located in the Gaslamp Quarter. Featuring a blue-and-yellow trompe l'oeil mural on the outside, this Mediterranean-style hostelry has 25 sex-segregated dorm facilities and 17 private rooms, as well as a fully equipped kitchen and common area. Unlike other hostels, there is no curfew. Reservations recommended. ~ 521 Market Street, 619-525-1531, 888-464-4872, fax 619-338-0129; www.sandiegohostels.org, e-mail downtown@sandiego hostels.org. BUDGET.

Located in the heart of the Gaslamp Quarter, the **Bristol Hotel** is an elegant boutique hotel that leaves a lasting impression. Ultra-modern in decor, its clean, minimalist lines are boldly accented with vivid splashes of color. The 102 rooms offer one king-sized or two double beds, and art lovers will revel in the hotel's art collection, which includes works by Peter Max, Andy Warhol, Roy Lichtenstein, and other Pop art greats. ~ 1055 1st Avenue; 619-232-6141, 800-662-4477, fax 619-232-0118; www.thebristolsandiego.com. DELUXE TO ULTRA-DELUXE.

No downtown hotel has a more colorful past than the **Horton Grand Hotel**. This 132-room Victorian gem is actually two old hotels that were disassembled piece by piece and resurrected a few blocks away. The two were lavishly reconstructed and linked by an atrium-lobby and courtyard. The 1880s theme is faithfully executed in the hotel's antique-furnished rooms, each of which has a fireplace. Such amenities as a concierge and afternoon tea (served Saturday) combine with friendly service and perfect location to make it one of the city's best hotel values. ~ 311 Island Avenue; 619-544-1886, 800-542-1886, fax 619-544-0085; www.hortongrand.com, e-mail info@hortongrand.com. com. DELUXE TO ULTRA-DELUXE.

Built in 1910 in honor of the 18th president by his son Ulysses S. Grant, Jr., the **U.S. Grant Hotel** reigned as downtown San Diego's premier hotel for decades. The U.S. Grant is a showcase boasting 317 rooms, a restaurant, and a lounge. It is quite possibly the most elegant and certainly the most beautifully restored historic building in the city. There's a marble-floored lobby with cathedral-height ceilings and enormous crystal chandeliers. Rooms are richly furnished with mahogany poster beds, Queen Anne–style armoires, and wing-back chairs. ~ 326 Broadway; 619-232-3121, 800-996-3426, fax 619-232-3626; www. usgrant.net. ULTRA-DELUXE.

Housed in a historic 1913 building now listed on the National Register of Historic Places, **Gaslamp Plaza Suites** evokes another era of coffered ceilings, etched-glass windows, and intricate carpentry. The rooms are smallish, as one would expect, but they have been recently remodeled and include pillow-top mattresses, wi-fi, microwaves, and mini-fridges. ~ 520 E Street; 619-232-9500, fax 619-238-9945; www.gaslampplaza.com. MODERATE TO DELUXE.

A recommended midtown hotel is the **Best Western Bayside Inn**. Small enough (122 rooms) to offer some degree of personalized service, this modern highrise promises nearly all the niceties you would pay extra for at more prestigious downtown hotels,

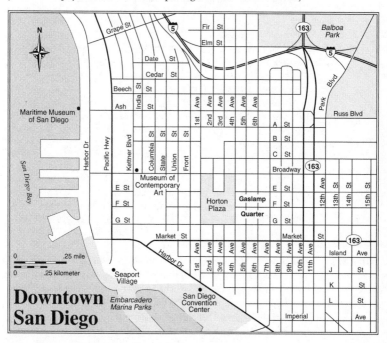

WALKING TOUR
The Gaslamp Quarter

History buffs and lovers of antique buildings should don their walking shoes for a tour of the Gaslamp Quarter, accompanied by a map available at the William Heath Davis House Museum. The 16-block district contains over 90 historic buildings, most of which now house galleries, shops, restaurants, and upscale hotels. Here are a few of the highlights.

WILLIAM HEATH DAVIS HOUSE   Start your tour at the William Heath Davis House, the oldest surviving wooden structure in the downtown area, this 1850 "saltbox" prefabricated family home was framed on the East Coast and shipped around Cape Horn to San Diego. It is now filled with museum exhibits recounting the house's history. Call for museum hours. Admission. ~ 410 Island Avenue; 619-233-4692, fax 619-233-4148; www.gaslampquarter.org, e-mail tracey@gaslampquarter.org.

ROYAL PIE BAKERY   Just down the street from the William Heath Davis House is what was once the Royal Pie Bakery. Almost unbelievably, a bakery was on this site from 1871 until 1996. Around the turn of the 20th century, the bakery found itself in the middle of a red-light district, but it didn't stop turning out cakes and pies even though a notorious bordello operated on the second floor. It's now a restaurant. ~ 554 4th Street.

FIFTH AVENUE   Go back down Island Avenue to 5th Avenue and turn left. Not only was this block part of the Stingaree, but it was the heart of San Diego's Chinatown. The **Nanking Café** (now Royal Thai) was the only restaurant on the street when it was built in 1912; today there are 95 restaurants in the district. ~ 467 5th Avenue. The nearby **Timken Building**, notable for its fancy arched brick facade, was erected in 1894. ~ 5th Avenue and Market Street. Across the street is the **Backesto**

including a harbor view. Furnishings and amenities are virtually on a par with those found in the typical Hilton or Sheraton. There is a pool and spa, plus a restaurant and cocktail lounge. ~ 555 West Ash Street; 619-233-7500, 800-341-1818, fax 619-239-8060; www.baysideinn.com, e-mail info@baysideinn.com. MODERATE.

DINING   Visitors to Horton Plaza are bombarded with dining opportunities. But for those who can resist the temptation to chow down on pizza, french fries, and enchiladas at nearby fast-food shops, there is a special culinary reward. On the plaza's top level sits **Panda Inn**. Here the plush, contemporary design alludes only subtly to Asia with a scattering of classic artwork. But the menu

Building, a beautifully restored late-19th-century structure. The tall, Romanesque Revival **Keating Building** was one of the most prestigious office buildings in San Diego during the 1890s, complete with such modern conveniences as steam heat and a wire-cage elevator. ~ 5th Avenue and F Street. Next door is the **Ingersoll Tutton Building**. When this 90-foot-long structure was built in 1894 for $20,000 it was the most expensive building on the block! ~ 832 5th Avenue.

COMMERCE ROW   Most of the block on the other side of 5th Avenue, from F up to E streets, represents the most architecturally significant row in the Gaslamp Quarter. From south to north, there's the **Marston Building** on the corner of F Street. Built in 1881, it was downtown San Diego's leading department store. Next is the 1887 **Hubbell Building**, originally a dry goods establishment. The **Nesmith-Greeley Building** next door is another example of the then-fashionable Romanesque Revival style with its ornamental brick coursing. Featuring twin towers and intricate Baroque Revival architecture, the 1888 **Louis Bank of Commerce** is probably the most beautiful building in the quarter. It originally housed a ground-floor oyster bar that was a favorite haunt of Wyatt Earp. The famous Western lawman-turned-real-estate speculator resided in San Diego from 1886 to 1893 and operated three Gaslamp Quarter drinking establishments. Be sure to go to the fourth floor to see the beautiful skylight.

CHINESE BENEVOLENT SOCIETY   As you return south through the Gaslamp District, take a short detour west (right) along G Street, then south (left) on 3rd Avenue, to see the Chinese Benevolent Society, established in 1920, when police had shut down the bordellos and the Gaslamp District had become completely Chinese. Today, Chinese holidays are still celebrated in the street in front of the Benevolent Society. ~ 428 3rd Avenue. Continue south to Island Avenue and turn east (left) to return to your starting point.

is all-Chinese. Three dishes stand out: Mongolian beef, wok-seared scallops, and chicken with garlic sauce. Lunch and dinner menus together present more than 100 dishes. Dine on the glassed-in veranda for a great view of the harbor. Closed Sunday. ~ 506 Horton Plaza; 619-233-7800, fax 619-233-5632; www. pandainn.com. BUDGET TO DELUXE.

There are no shortages of restaurants in the Gaslamp either, with the majority offering sidewalk tables from which to watch the passing parade of horse-drawn carriages, bike taxis and pedestrians.

Fans of the late Jim Croce ("Bad, Bad Leroy Brown," "Time in a Bottle") will surely enjoy a visit to **Croce's Restaurant and**

Bar. Located in the heart of the Gaslamp Quarter and managed enthusiastically by Jim's widow, Ingrid Croce, the restaurant features an eclectic mix of dishes served in a friendly setting. Daily dinner specials vary and are best described as contemporary American ranging from salads to pasta, beef, chicken, and fresh fish dishes. No breakfast or lunch on weekdays. ~ 802 5th Avenue; 619-233-4355, fax 619-232-9836; www.croces.com, e-mail info@croces.com. ULTRA-DELUXE.

Just down the block, **Dakota Grill & Spirits** occupies two floors of San Diego's first skyscraper (1913). Black-clad, bolo-tied waitstaff bustle around with woodstone-fired pizza, hearty rotisserie meats, and grilled seafood whipped up by cooks in the open kitchen. Among the offerings: grilled pork prime rib with apricot mustard glaze, rotisserie chicken with honey-mustard sauce, and artichoke–pine nut linguini. There's piano music Thursday through Saturday. ~ 901 5th Avenue; 619-234-5554, fax 619-234-5321; www.cohnrestaurants.com. DELUXE TO ULTRA-DELUXE.

History, atmosphere, and great cooking combine to make dining at **Ida Bailey's Restaurant** a memorable experience. Located in the Horton Grand Hotel, Ida's was once a brothel, operated back in the 1890s by a madam of the same name. Things are tamer now, but the rich Victorian furnishings serve as a reminder of San Diego's opulent past. Breakfast and tea are served. ~ 311 Island Avenue; 619-544-1886, fax 619-239-3823; www.horton grand.com, e-mail info@hortongrand.com. MODERATE TO DELUXE.

Nearby, a suit of armor marks the entrance to **Sevilla**. Inside, clouds float across the ceiling, red-tiled roofs and striped awnings extend from walls with shuttered windows, and gaslamps dot the dining room, evoking the festive atmosphere of a Spanish plaza. Diners combine plates of *tapas* (*bocadillos*, marinated lamb, *empañadas*) over glasses of sangria, or indulge in full-sized traditional meals such as *zarzuela* (a savory seafood stew) and paella. Save room for the equally marvelous desserts. Dinner only. ~ 555 4th Avenue; 619-233-5979; www.cafesevilla.com. DELUXE.

SHOPPING   The **Westfield Shoppingtown Horton Plaza** is anchored by three department stores and a flood of specialty and one-of-a-kind shops complete the picture. Along the tiled boulevard are shops and vendors peddling their wares. ~ Between Broadway and G Street, 1st and 4th avenues; 619-239-8180; www.westfield.com.

On the third level, the **San Diego City Store** (619-238-2489) sells retired street signs, keychains and the like. There are men's apparel shops, shoe stores, jewelry shops, and women's haute couture boutiques, dozens of stores in all.

The **Gaslamp Quarter**, along 5th Avenue, is a charming 16-square-block assemblage of shops, galleries, and sidewalk cafés in the downtown center. Faithfully replicated in the quarter are Victorian-era street lamps, red-brick sidewalks, and window displays thematic of turn-of-the-20th-century San Diego.

Intriguing Gaslamp Quarter shops include **Le Travel Store**, which sells innovative and hard-to-find travel gear, packs and luggage, guidebooks, maps, and travel accessories—there's even a travel agency inside the store. ~ 745 4th Avenue; 619-544-0005; www.letravelstore.com. **Palace Loan & Jewelry** offers top-of-the-line pre-owned merchandise at bargain prices in a building that once housed a saloon and gambling parlor owned by Wyatt Earp. Closed Sunday. ~ 951 4th Avenue; 619-234-3175.

You can watch Cuban exiles roll *panatelas, toropedos, presidentes,* and *robustos* from Cuban-seed tobacco grown in other parts of the Caribbean at the **Cuban Cigar Factory**. ~ 551 5th Avenue; 619-238-2496; www.cubancigarfactory.com.

Chocolaholics won't want to miss **Chi Chocolat** in Little Italy. ◀ *HIDDEN* Whether you're popping creamy bonbons or sipping a chocolate-sweetened espresso drink, a trip to this upscale chocolatier is a thrill for your sweet tooth. Closed Monday. ~ 2021 India Street; 619-501-9215, fax 619-501-9216; www.chichocolat.com.

The sun is certainly the main attraction in San Diego, but the city **NIGHTLIFE** also features a rich and varied nightlife, offering the night owl everything from traditional folk music to high-energy discos. There are piano bars, singles bars, and a growing number of jazz clubs.

Call the **San Diego Performing Arts League** for its monthly arts calendar and information about inexpensive events. ~ 619-238-0700; www.sandiegoperforms.com. KIFM Radio (98.1 FM) hosts **Jazz Hotline**, a 24-hour information line that provides the latest in jazz happenings. ~ 619-543-1401.

> Lawman Wyatt Earp once ran three gambling halls in the Gaslamp Quarter.

If you're a culture vulture with a limited pocketbook, try **Arts Tix**, a 24-hour recording listing half-priced theater, music, and dance tickets. ~ 619-497-5000.

THE BEST BARS **4th & B** features national musical acts and well-known comedians. ~ 345 B Street; 619-231-4343; www.4thandb.com

It's a non-stop party at the **Bitter End**, a three-level bar and nightclub that has something to offer everyone. Top-40 music complete with videos is blasted on the first level, high-energy dance music can be found on the second, and a more mellow crowd kicks back to jazz on the top level. Cover. ~ 770 5th Avenue; 619-338-9300; www.thebitterend.com.

Fans of the immortal Jim Croce will love **Croce's Jazz Bar** (619-233-4355), built as a memorial to the late singer-songwriter by his wife, Ingrid. Family mementos line the walls in tribute to a talented recording artist. Live entertainment nightly. Just next door, **Croce's Top Hat Bar** (619-233-6945) is a snazzy New Orleans–style club featuring live R&B. Closed Sunday through Thursday. Cover. ~ 802–820 5th Avenue; www.croces.com.

Karl Strauss Restaurant and Brewery Downtown may well have the best beer in town—San Diego's original microbrew. ~ 1157 Columbia Street; 619-234-2739; www.karlstraus.com.

Plaza Bar, at the distinctive Westgate Hotel, is a graceful period French lounge where prominent locals and visitors enjoy classy piano entertainment nightly. ~ 1055 2nd Avenue; 619-238-1818, www.westgatehotel.com.

For cocktails and some dazzling views of the city, head up to **Altitude Skybar & Garden Lounge**, 22 stories atop the Marriott Gaslamp Quarter. ~ 660 K Street; 619-446-6024; www.altitudeskybar.info.

THEATER In addition to performances of the San Diego Opera, the **San Diego Civic Theatre** presents a variety of entertainment ranging from pop artists to plays to dance performances. ~ 1100 3rd Avenue; 619-570-1100; www.sdcivic.org, e-mail info@sandiegotheatres.org.

The **San Diego Repertory Theatre** performs dramas, comedies, and musicals. ~ At the Lyceum Horton Plaza; 619-544-1000; www.sandiegorep.com.

OPERA AND DANCE With performances at the San Diego Civic Theatre, the **San Diego Opera** presents such international stars as Patricia Racette, Ferruccio Furlanetto, and Anja Henteros. The season runs from January through May. ~ 1200 3rd Avenue; 619-533-7000, fax 619-231-6915; www.sdopera.com.

California Ballet Company and School presents a diverse repertoire of contemporary and traditional ballets at area theaters. ~ 4819 Ronson Court; 858-560-5676; www.californiaballet.org, e-mail info@californiaballet.org.

▼▼▼▼▼▼▼▼▼▼▼▼▼
San Diego Harbor

San Diego's beautiful harbor is a notable exception to the rule that big-city waterfronts lack appeal. Here, the city embraces its bay and presents its finest profile along the water.

SIGHTS The best way to see it all is on a harbor tour. A variety of vessels dock near Harbor Drive at the foot of Broadway. **San Diego Harbor Excursion** provides leisurely trips around the 22-square-mile harbor, which is colorfully backdropped by commercial and naval vessels as well as the dramatic cityscape. Ferry service to Coronado Island from downtown is also operated by Harbor Excursion. My favorite sunset harbor cruises are aboard the 150-foot yacht *Spirit of San Diego*. Admission. ~ 1050 North

Harbor Drive; 619-234-4111; 800-442-7847; www.sdhe.com, e-mail george@sdhe.com.

All along the cityside of the harbor from the Coast Guard Station opposite Lindbergh Field to Seaport Village is a lovely landscaped boardwalk called the **Embarcadero**. It offers parks where you can stroll and play, a floating maritime museum, and a thriving assortment of waterfront diversions.

The **Maritime Museum of San Diego** is composed of six vintage ships and a Soviet submarine; most familiar is the 1863 *Star of India*, the world's oldest iron-hulled merchant ship still afloat. Visitors go aboard for a hint of what life was like on the high seas more than a century ago. You can also visit the 1898 ferry *Berkeley*, which helped in the evacuation of San Francisco during the 1906 earthquake, and the 1904 steam yacht *Medea*. Admission. ~ 1492 North Harbor Drive; 619-234-9153, fax 619-234-8345; www.sdmaritime.com, e-mail info@sdmaritime.com.

Kid-friendly vendors at Seaport Village include a face painter, a balloon artist and a caricaturist.

Nautical buffs or anyone concerned about American naval power will be interested in the **U.S. Navy** presence in San Diego harbor. As headquarters of the Commander Naval Base, San Diego hosts one of the world's largest fleets of fighting ships—from aircraft carriers to nuclear submarines. Naval docks and yards are off-limits but you'll see the sprawling facilities and plenty of those distinctive gray-hulled ships during a harbor cruise. Naval vessels moored at the Broadway Pier hold open house on weekends.

The Marine Center presents colorful **military reviews** most Fridays. Marching ceremonies begin at exactly 10 a.m. at the Marine Corps Recruiting Depot (619-524-1772). ~ The center may be reached from downtown by going north on Pacific Highway to Barnett Avenue, then follow the signs.

The city's newest harbor attraction is the **San Diego Aircraft Carrier Museum**. USS *Midway*, the nation's longest serving aircraft carrier, with active service since the late 1950s, has been turned into a naval aviation museum. Visitors can check out the many exhibits, wander around the second hangar and flight decks, and experience an airplane's lift-off from the carrier in a flight simulator. ~ 1355 North Harbor Drive; 619-544-9600, fax 619-238-1200; www.midway.org.

Near the south end of the Embarcadero sits the popular shopping and entertainment complex known as **Seaport Village**. Designed to replicate an Early California seaport, it comprises 14 acres of bayfront parks and promenades, shops, restaurants, and galleries. You'll also find a carousel, free weekend concerts, and magicians and musicians entertaining the masses. ~ Kettner

Boulevard and West Harbor Drive; 619-235-4013, fax 619-696-0025; www.seaportvillage.com.

On the south side, overlooking the water, is the 45-foot-high **Mukilteo Lighthouse**, official symbol of the village, a recreation of a famous lighthouse located in Washington state. Nearby is the **Seaport Village Carousel**, a hand-carved, turn-of-the-20th-century model built by renowned carousel craftsman Charles Looff.

Nearby, the **San Diego Convention Center** looks like an erector set gone mad. An uncontained congeries of flying buttresses, giant tents, and curved glass, it is fashioned in the form of a ship, seemingly poised to set sail across San Diego Harbor. This architectural exclamation mark is certainly worth a drive-by or a quick tour. ~ 111 West Harbor Drive; 619-525-5000, fax 619-525-5005; www.sdccc.org.

DINING

For quality seafood by the harbor, try **Anthony's Fish Grotto**, whose menu includes fresh catch-of-the-day, seafood kabobs and lobster thermidor. ~ 1360 North Harbor Drive; 619-232-5103, fax 619-232-1877; www.gofishanthonys.com. BUDGET TO DELUXE.

A macho kind of establishment, famous for being used as a location in the movie *Top Gun*, **Kansas City Barbeque** is one of San Diego's most happening places. It is also *the* place in the city to eat barbecue, whether it's huge platters of chicken or ribs with all the sides or enormous barbecue beef sandwiches. ~ 610 West Market Street; 619-231-9680; www.kcbbq.net. BUDGET TO MODERATE.

SHOPPING

Seaport Village was designed to capture the look and feel of an early California waterfront setting. Its 57 shops dot a 14-acre village and include the usual mix of boutiques, galleries, clothing stores, and gift shops. ~ Kettner Boulevard and West Harbor Drive; 619-235-4013; www.seaportvillage.com.

NIGHTLIFE

There's a wonderful view of San Diego Bay from the Seaport Village restaurant **Edgewater Grill**, where a tropical setting creates a lovely relaxed atmosphere. ~ 861 West Harbor Drive; 619-232-7581; www.edgewatergrill.com.

BEACHES & PARKS

EMBARCADERO MARINA PARKS The center city's only real waterfront park is a breezy promenade situated on the bay and divided into two sections. The northern part has a nicely landscaped lawn and garden, picnic tables, and benches. The southern half features a fishing pier, basketball courts, and an athletic course. Restrooms are available. ~ Enter at the southern end at Harbor Drive and 8th Street; at the northern end, from Seaport Village shopping center; 619-686-6225, fax 619-686-6200; www.portofsandiego.org.

An isolated and exclusive community in San Diego Bay, Coronado is almost an island, connected to the mainland only by the graceful San Diego–Coronado Bay Bridge and by a long, narrow sandspit called the Silver Strand. Long a playground of the rich and famous, the city's hotels reflect this ritzy heritage.

Coronado

SIGHTS

Once known as the "Nickel Snatcher," the Coronado Ferry for years crossed the waters of San Diego Harbor between the Embarcadero and Coronado. All for five cents each way. That's history, of course, but the 1940-vintage, double-deck *Silvergate* still plies the waters. The **San Diego Bay Ferry** leaves from the Bay Café on North Harbor Drive at the foot of Broadway on the hour and docks 15 minutes later at the Ferry Landing Marketplace on the Coronado side. ~ San Diego Harbor Excursion; 619-234-4111, fax 619-522-6150; www.sdhe.com.

The town's main attraction is the **Hotel del Coronado**, a red-roofed, Victorian-style, wooden wonder, and National Historic Landmark. Explore the old palace and its manicured grounds, discovering the intricate corridors and cavernous public rooms. It was Elisha Babcock's dream, when he purchased 4100 acres of barren, wind-blown peninsula in 1888, to build a hotel that would be the "talk of the Western world." Realizing Babcock's dream from the beginning, it attracted presidents, dignitaries, and movie stars. You might even recognize it from the movie *Some Like It Hot.* ~ 1500 Orange Avenue; 619-435-6611, fax 619-522-8262; www.hotel del.com, e-mail delinquiries@hoteldel.com.

A farmer's market is held at Ferry Landing Marketplace on Tuesday afternoons.

Although shadowed by its noted neighbor, the **Glorietta Bay Inn** is a worthy landmark in its own right. It was built in 1908 as the private mansion of sugar scion John D. Spreckels. Tours are offered Tuesday, Thursday, and Saturday mornings. From here you can cruise the quiet neighborhood streets that radiate off Orange Avenue between the bay and the ocean, enjoying the town's handsome blend of cottages and historic homes. ~ 1630 Glorietta Boulevard; 619-435-3101, 800-283-9383, fax 619-435-6182; www.gloriettabayinn.com, e-mail info@gloriettabayinn.com.

LODGING

El Cordova Hotel is in the heart of Coronado. Originally built as a private mansion in 1902, El Cordova's moderate size (40 rooms) and lovely Spanish-hacienda architecture make it a relaxing getaway spot. A pool and patio restaurant are added niceties. ~ 1351 Orange Avenue; 619-435-4131, 800-229-2032, fax 619-435-0632; www.elcordovahotel.com. ULTRA-DELUXE.

Nothing can detract from the glamour of the **Hotel del Coronado**. With its turrets, cupolas, and gingerbread facade, it is one of the great hotels of California. The last in a proud line of extravagant seaside resorts, the Hotel del Coronado has long been the relaxing place of Hollywood stars and ten United States presidents. Remember, however, this celebrated Victorian landmark is a major tourist attraction, so in addition to guests, who usually fill its 679 rooms to capacity, a large number of visitors crowd the lobby, grounds, and shops every day. Be aware, too, that many rooms are in two structures adjacent to the original building and though more comfortable are not the real thing. "Hotel Del" has two pools, a long stretch of beach, nine eating areas, a fitness center, a spa, and a gallery of shops. Reservations recommended. ~ 1500 Orange Avenue; 619-522-8000, 800-435-6611, fax 619-522-8262; www.hoteldel.com, e-mail delinquiries@ hoteldel.com. ULTRA-DELUXE.

Across the street rises the **Glorietta Bay Inn**, the 1908 Edwardian mansion of sugar king John D. Spreckels which has been transformed into an elegant 100-room hotel. Rooms and suites in the mansion reflect the grandeur of Spreckels' time; more typical accommodations are available in the contemporary inn buildings that surround the mansion. Continental breakfast, ladies and gentlemen, is served on the mansion terrace. ~ 1630 Glorietta Boulevard; 619-435-3101, 800-283-9383, fax 619-435-6182; www.gloriettabayinn.com, e-mail info@gloriettabayinn.com. DELUXE TO ULTRA-DELUXE.

The **Coronado Victorian House** is quite possibly the only hotel anywhere to offer dance, exercise, and gourmet cooking classes with a night's stay. Located in an 1894 historic building near the beach and downtown Coronado, the decor of this seven-room bed and breakfast includes Persian rugs, stained-glass windows, and private baths with clawfoot tubs; rooms are named after artists and dancers. Those guests not interested in the extracurricular activities are invited to relax and enjoy such healthy and home-cooked specialties as baklava, stuffed grape leaves, and homemade yogurt. Two-night minimum. ~ 1000 8th Street; 619-435-2200, 888-229-2822, fax 619-435-4760; www.coronadovictorianhouse.com. ULTRA-DELUXE.

DINING

Visitors crossing over to Coronado invariably tour the famous Hotel del Coronado, and many are lured into the **Crown Room**. Its grand Victorian architecture and enormous domed ceiling (the chandeliers were designed by *Wizard of Oz* author L. Frank Baum) set a tone of elegance and style unmatched anywhere on the Pacific Coast. The place is so magnificent the food seems unimportant, but the Sunday brunch at the Crown Room will never disappoint. Sunday brunch only. Reservations recommended. ~ 1500 Orange Avenue; 619-435-6611, fax 619-522-8262; www.hoteldel.com. ULTRA-DELUXE.

Locals looking to avoid the crowds at "Hotel Del" usually head for **Chez Loma**. Set in a charming 1889 Victorian house, it serves a lovely Continental/French dinner—excellent *canard rôti* (traditional roast duck with cherry, green peppercorn, and burnt orange sauce). Dinner only. ~ 1132 Loma Avenue; 619-435-0661, fax 619-435-3770; www.chezloma.com, e-mail info@chezloma. com. DELUXE TO ULTRA-DELUXE.

Peohe's, located at the Ferry Landing Marketplace, is primarily praised for its panoramic views of San Diego Bay and for its tropical decor. The dinner menu is mostly fresh fish plus lobster, shrimp, and a daily featured "catch." There are also prime rib, chicken, and lamb. Sunday brunch is another option. ~ 1201 1st Street; 619-437-4474, fax 619-437-8471; www.peohes.com. DELUXE TO ULTRA-DELUXE.

SHOPPING

Coronado's fancy Orange Avenue in the village center harbors an assortment of unusual shops in the **El Cordova Hotel**. ~ 1351 Orange Avenue; 619-435-4131; www.elcordovahotel.com.

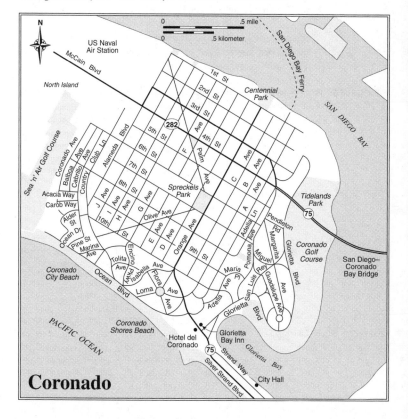

Coronado

The **Ferry Landing Marketplace** is a modern shopping area complete with boutiques, specialty shops, galleries, and eateries. ~ 1201 1st Street; 619-435-8895.

The **Hotel del Coronado** is a city within a city and home to many intriguing specialty shops, such as **The Spa Shop**, which has a selection of bath and body products, kitchenware, and gardening accessories. ~ 1500 Orange Avenue; 619-435-6611; www.delshop.com.

NIGHTLIFE   If you're out Coronado way, stop for a cocktail in the Hotel del Coronado's **Babcock & Story Bar**. Live entertainment Wednesday through Sunday night. ~ 1500 Orange Avenue; 619-435-6611; www.hoteldel.com.

Check out the boisterous Irish scene at **McP's**, a full swinging bar and grill with shamrock-plastered walls and a bartender with the gift of gab. McP's is a Navy SEAL hangout, so as one glib bartender noted, it's the most likely place in town to pet a seal. Entertainment includes live rock and jazz bands on a nightly basis. ~ 1107 Orange Avenue; 619-435-5280; www.mcpspub.com.

The historic Spreckels Building in Coronado is a vintage-1917 opera house that has been restored to a 347-seat venue called the **Lamb's Players Theatre**. ~ 1142 Orange Avenue; 619-437-0600; www.lambsplayers.org.

BEACHES & PARKS   **CORONADO SHORES BEACH** It's the widest beach in the county but hardly atmospheric, backed up as it is by a row of towering condominiums. Still, crowds flock to this roomy expanse of clean, soft sand where gentle waves make for good swimming and surfing. The younger crowd gathers at the north end, just south of the Hotel del Coronado. There are lifeguards. ~ Located off Ocean Boulevard.

CORONADO CITY BEACH That same wide sandy beach prevails to the north. Here the city has a large, grassy picnic area known as **Sunset Park** where frisbees and the aroma of fried chicken fill the air. Facilities include firepits, restrooms, and lifeguards. The beach offers good fishing and swimming. Surfing is restricted to the north end during the busy summer months; it's generally safe, but be wary of unpredictable breaks. ~ On Ocean Boulevard north of Avenue G.

South San Diego County

Linking downtown with the Mexican border city of Tijuana, 20 miles south, a string of seaside cities straddle Route 5. While thriving as manufacturing, commercial, and residential communities, Imperial Beach, Chula Vista, and National City are beginning to develop as tourist industries.

The **Chula Vista Nature Center** is located in the Sweetwater Na-   **SIGHTS**
tional Wildlife Refuge on San Diego Bay and, through interactive exhibits especially appealing to children, offers a close-up
look at the history and geology of Southern California wetlands.
There is a shark and ray tank, birds of prey exhibits, sea turtle
lagoon, and a composting garden. Closed Monday. Admission.
~ 1000 Gunpowder Point Drive, Chula Vista; 619-409-5900, fax
619-409-5910; www.chulavistanaturecenter.org, e-mail tina@
chulavistanaturecenter.org.

Visitors to Chula Vista also have an opportunity to glimpse
Olympic athletes in training at the **U.S. Olympic Training Center**. Self-guided tours are available daily, from 10 a.m. to 5 p.m.,
and guided tours at 1 p.m., Tuesday through Saturday. ~ 2800
Olympic Parkway, Chula Vista; 619-482-6148, fax 619-482-
6200; www.usolympicteam.com.

Along this southern coastline is the **Tijuana River National
Estuarine Research Reserve**, which comprises the county's largest
and most pristine estuarine sanctuary (Tijuana
Slough National Wildlife Refuge) and a two-mile   San Diego has been the
stretch of sandy beach (Border Field State Park).   backdrop for a number
For nature lovers, this haven of salt marsh and sand   of Hollywood films in-
dunes is a must-see diversion: more than 370 species   cluding, *Charlie's Angels:*
of birds are found there. The visitors center features   *Full Throttle*, *Bruce*
exhibits and a library (closed Monday and Tuesday).   *Almighty*, *Traffic*, and
Trails lead to the beach and wildlife refuge at this fasci-   *The Scorpion King*.
nating wetland (see the "Beaches & Parks" and
"Hiking" sections in this chapter for more information).
~ Visitors center: 301 Caspian Way, Imperial Beach; see "South
San Diego County Beaches & Parks" for directions to the state
park; 619-575-3613, fax 619-575-6913; www.tijuanaestu
ary.com, e-mail cphillip@parks.ca.gov.

Among all those identical motels grouped around the freeway   **LODGING**
exits in Chula Vista, **The Traveler Inn & Suites** is perhaps your
best bet. Conveniently located just a block from the highway, this
family-owned 85-unit motel is early Holiday Inn throughout, but
its rates hark back to 1960s. Not that you would really expect
them, but extras include two pools, a spa, laundry facilities, and
cable TV. Continental breakfast is served. ~ 235 Woodlawn Avenue, Chula Vista; 619-427-9170, 800-748-6998, fax 619-427-
5247. MODERATE.

The **Seacoast Inn of Imperial Beach** is the only hostelry located directly on the sands of Imperial Beach. Decked out with
a heated outdoor pool and hot tub, this 38-room complex looks
good inside and out. Beachside units are especially nice and have
full kitchens. It helps to make summer reservations well in ad-

vance. ~ 800 Seacoast Drive, Imperial Beach; 619-424-5183, 800-732-2627, fax 619-424-3090; www.theseacoastinn.com. DELUXE TO ULTRA-DELUXE.

DINING

There's no shortage of fast-food joints along Broadway. **Roberto's Taco Shop** has served up cheap and tasty Mexican fare since the early 1980s. Rolled tacos, burritos bursting with juicy shredded beef, savory chicken fajitas—it's hard to go wrong here. Open 24 hours. ~ 444 Broadway, Chula Vista; 619-425-0444. BUDGET.

La Bella Pizza Garden is like an annex to Chula Vista's town hall, and owner Kitty Raso is known as the "Mayor of Third Avenue." But the food will interest you far more than the latest political gossip. Besides pizza, there's great lasagna, rigatoni, and ravioli. La Bella features tender veal dishes, too, from a menu that amazingly rarely strays beyond budget prices. Best Italian food for the money in San Diego, and it's open from 7 a.m. to 1 a.m. or later every day. ~ 373 3rd Avenue, Chula Vista; 619-426-8820, fax 619-426-1302; www.labellapizza.com. BUDGET.

SHOPPING

The pastel-colored, open-air **Chula Vista Center** is anchored by Macy's, Mervyn's, and Sears, and comprises over 60 chain stores as well as unique boutiques. Kids love the carousel. ~ 555 Broadway, Chula Vista; 619-427-6700; www.chulavista.com.

For something more unique, you might peruse the eclectic offerings on 3rd Avenue between E and G streets. This historic strip harbors shops laden with antiques, religious curios and books, and kitschy knickknacks.

NIGHTLIFE

If you're looking for nighttime entertainment in these areas, you'll probably want to consider a trip downtown or to Tijuana (see the "South of the Border" feature in this chapter). Otherwise, be content with scattered restaurant bars and local pubs.

BEACHES & PARKS

SILVER STRAND STATE BEACH This one-mile strip of fluffy white sand fronts a narrow isthmus separating the Pacific Ocean and San Diego Bay. It was named for tiny silver sea shells found in abundance along the shore. The water here is shallow and fairly calm on the ocean side, making it a good swimming beach. Things are even calmer and the water much warmer on the bay shore. Silver Strand State Beach is also popular for shell hunting. Facilities include picnic areas, restrooms, lifeguards (summer only), showers, and food concessions (summer only). Parking fee, $8. ~ Located on Route 75 and Coronado Cays Boulevard between Imperial Beach and Coronado; 619-435-5184.

▲ There are 130 sites for self-contained RVs and trailers (no hookups); $25 to $30 per night.

Text continued on page 518.

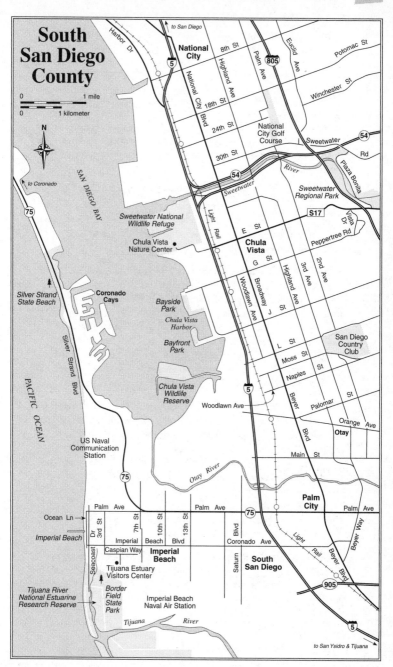

South San Diego County

0   1 mile

0   1 kilometer

N

to San Diego

Harbor Dr

National City

8th St

Highland Ave

National City Blvd

18th St

24th St

30th St

Palm Ave

Euclid Ave

Potomac St

Winchester St

National City Golf Course

Sweetwater

54

Rd

Plaza Bonita

River

Sweetwater

54

to Coronado

75

SAN DIEGO BAY

Light Rail

Sweetwater National Wildlife Refuge

Chula Vista Nature Center

Sweetwater Regional Park

S17

Vista Dr

E St

Peppertree Rd

Chula Vista

G St

3rd Ave

2nd Ave

Silver Strand State Beach

Coronado Cays

Bayside Park

Chula Vista Harbor

Bayfront Park

Woodlawn Ave

Broadway

Highland Ave

J St

L St

Moss St

Naples St

San Diego Country Club

PACIFIC OCEAN

Silver Strand Blvd

Chula Vista Wildlife Reserve

Woodlawn Ave

5

Beyer Blvd

Palomar St

Orange Ave

Otay

US Naval Communication Station

Main St

Otay River

Palm City

Palm Ave

75

Palm Ave

Palm Ave

Ocean Ln

3rd St

Dr

7th St

10th St

13th St

Palm Ave

Blvd

Coronado Ave

Light Rail

Beyer Way

Imperial Beach

Imperial Beach Blvd

Saturn

South San Diego

Caspian Way

Tijuana Estuary Visitors Center

Imperial Beach

Seacoast Dr

Tijuana River National Estuarine Research Reserve

Border Field State Park

Imperial Beach Naval Air Station

905

Tijuana River

5

to San Ysidro & Tijuana

South of the Border

Tijuana, a favorite day-trip destination for San Diego visitors, has been amazingly transformed in recent years from a bawdy border-town to a modern, bustling city of more than two million people. Gone, or very well hidden, are the borderline attractions that once lured sailors and marines. In their place is a colorful center of tourism suitable for the entire family.

A major revitalization effort brought highrise buildings, broad boule-vards, huge shopping centers, and classy shops and restaurants. But don't get the idea Tijuana has become completely Americanized. It still retains much of its traditional Mexican flavor and offers visitors an exciting outing and some surprising cultural experiences.

Perhaps the most impressive attraction, ideal for learning about Mexico, is the **Centro Cultural Tijuana**. Here the striking 85-foot-high Omni-max Space Theater is a silvery sphere held up by a stylized hand that symbolizes the earth housing a world of culture. Inside, the giant 180° screen shows various films pertaining to Mexico. The complex, designed by Pedro Ramírez Váquez, architect of Mexico City's famous Anthro-pological Museum, houses five exhibit halls, a restaurant, a bookstore, and a multilevel cultural and historical museum. Admission. ~ Paseo de los Héroes at Calle Mina; 52-66-46-87-96-00; www.cecut.gob.mx.

No doubt a major reason to visit "TJ" is to shop. The central shopping district is downtown, along Avenida Revolución, where arcades, stalls, and hawkers line the boulevard promoting the usual selection of tourist trinkets, piñatas, colorful flowers, serapes, pottery, and lace. There are numerous shops featuring quality merchandise such as leather goods, designer clothes, perfumes, artwork, and jewelry at incredible savings. A good one-stop shopping center for Mexican *artesanía* is the **Bazar de Mexico**. ~ Avenida Revolución at Calle 7; 52-664-638-4737. **Tolán** offers authentic Mexican folk art and fashions. ~ Avenida Revolución between Calles 7 and 8; 52-664-688-3637.

American currency is accepted everywhere but small bills are recom-mended since getting change can sometimes be a problem. U.S. residents receive a duty and federal tax exemption on the first $400 in personal goods purchased in Mexico. One liter of alcoholic beverage is allowed for those 21 years and older.

Spectator sports are a popular pastime for Tijuana visitors, including greyhound racing at **Caliente Race Track**. ~ Boulevard Agua Caliente at Avenida Salinas; 52-664-682-3110 in Tijuana, 619-231-1919 from San Diego; www.caliente.com.mx. Or catch a colorful bullfight at **Plaza Monumental**. ~ Located six miles west via Highway 1D; 52-664-680-1808. Call **Five Star Tours** for tickets and information. ~ Located in the Amtrak Santa Fe station, 1050 Kettner Boulevard, San Diego; 619-232-5040, 800-553-8687 from the U.S.; www.fivestartours.com.

Call the **Baja Visitors Information** for information about all events. You can also visit their office in Mission Valley and pick up helpful literature. Closed Sunday. ~ 6855 Friars Road #26, San Diego; 619-298-4105.

Tijuana has some exceptional restaurants. For some of the freshest, most unusual seafood dishes in the city, go to **Los Arcos**, a bright, family-style restaurant. ~ Boulevard Salinas 1000; 52-664-686-4757. MODERATE.

La Fonda de Roberto boasts a friendly, contemporary upstairs dining room that is best known for its specialty, *chiles en nogada*, poblano chiles stuffed with meat and fruit and smothered in walnut sauce topped with pomegranate and cilantro. Closed Monday. ~ Boulevard Cuauhtémoc 2800; 52-664-686-4687. DELUXE.

Should you decide to stay longer than a day, enjoy Tijuana's stylish hotel, **The Grand Hotel Tijuana**. This 422-room luxury complex boasts dramatic city views from its 28-story glass towers and offers three restaurants, two bars, a gallery of shops, tennis courts, swimming pool, and a health club. ~ Boulevard Agua Caliente No. 4500; 800-026-6007 in Tijuana, 866-472-6385 in San Diego; www.grandhoteltij.com.mx, e-mail reservaciones@grandhoteltij.com.mx. DELUXE TO ULTRA-DELUXE.

Just a little farther south of Tijuana along the coast, the small towns of Rosarito Beach and Ensenada provide a less commercial glimpse of Mexico. A modern highway makes the trip easy and comfortable.

If you venture down south, remember to bring your valid passport or identification for return to the U.S. and a copy of *Hidden Baja* (Ulysses Press). If you do not want to drive across the border, you can take a trolley to the border, walk on a pedestrian overpass across the International border, and then take a taxi into town for about $7 per person.

IMPERIAL BEACH ≈ 🏊 🚲 ➡ A wide, sandy beach, popular at the south end with surfers; boogie-boarders and swimmers ply the waters between the two jetties farther north, just past the renovated fishing pier. The crowd is mostly young with many military personnel. There are restrooms and lifeguards. There is also a deli nearby. Surfing is very popular on both sides of the pier and rock jetties. ~ Take Palm Avenue exit west off Route 5 all the way to the water; 619-686-6200, fax 619-686-6200.

Each July Imperial Beach hosts the annual U.S. Open Sandcastle Competition, attracting huge crowds.

BORDER FIELD STATE PARK 🚶 🚲 🐎 True to its name, this oceanfront park within the Tijuana River National Estuarine Research Reserve actually borders on Mexico. It features a two-mile-long stretch of sandy beach, backed by dunes and salt marshes studded with daisies and chaparral. Equestrian and hiking trails crisscross this unsullied wetlands area which adjoins a federal wildlife refuge at the mouth of the Tijuana River. Sounds idyllic except for the constant racket from Border Patrol helicopters and the ever-present threat of untreated sewage drifting north from Mexico. Picnic areas and restrooms are available, and a visitors center houses exhibits and a library. Fishing and swimming are not recommended because of pollution. Closed weekdays. ~ Take the Dairy Mart Road exit off Route 5 and go west. The name changes to Monument Road about a mile before reaching the park entrance. The visitors center is at 301 Caspian Way, Imperial Beach; 619-575-3613, fax 619-575-6913; www.tijuanaestuary.com.

Outdoor Adventures

SPORT-FISHING

The lure of sportfishing attracts thousands of enthusiasts to San Diego every year. Yellowtail, sea bass, bonito, and barracuda are the local favorites, with marlin and tuna the prime objectives for multiday charters. Most outfitters provide bait and rent tackle.

For deep-sea and local sportfishing, contact **Helgren's Sportfishing**; five-day excursions lead down into Mexico. ~ 315 Harbor Drive South, Oceanside; 760-722-2133; www.helgrensportfishing.com. **Seaforth Sportfishing** uses 36- to 85-foot boats for their runs. Longer trips in summer head out to Mexican waters for albacore. ~ 1717 Quivira Road, Mission Bay; 619-224-3383; www.seaforthlanding.com. **Islandia Sportfishing** offers trips for albacore, mackerel, and skipjack. ~ 1551 West Mission Bay Drive, Mission Bay; 619-222-1164; www.islandiasportfishing.com. **H & M Landing** arranges half-day jaunts to local kelp beds or up to 21-day expeditions past the tip of Baja for giant yellowfin tuna. ~ 2803 Emerson Street, Point Loma; 619-222-1144; www.hmlanding.com. Call **Fish 'N Cruise** for custom-designed charters. ~ 1551 Shelter Island Drive, San Diego; 619-224-2464; www.sandiegoyachts.com. **Point Loma Sportfishing** operates a fleet of ten boats. Their daytrip goes down to Mexico for tuna. ~ 1403 Scott Street, Point Loma; 619-223-1627; www.pointlomasportfish ing.com. Also in Point Loma is **Fisherman's Landing**, which takes groups of 6 to 35 on fishing excursions. The 23-day charter winds up in Cabo San Lucas. ~ 2838 Garrison Street, Point Loma; 619-222-0391; www.fishermanslanding.com.

Spearfishing is very popular off La Jolla beaches, especially south of La Jolla Cove. Contact **San Diego Divers Supply** for supplies, tours, and information. ~ 4004 Sports Arena Boulevard, San Diego; 619-224-3439; www.comedivewithus.com. Note: Spearfishing is not allowed in protected reserves from La Jolla Cove north.

WHALE WATCHING

The stately progress of our fellow mammalians in migration is a wonderful sight to behold. To get an even closer look at these mammoth cetaceans, book a charter with one of the many whale-watching companies; most outfitters guarantee marine sightings. The season generally runs from late December through late February (mid-January is the best time).

Helgren's Sportfishing sets sail from mid-December to mid-April—that's when you'll see California gray whales. ~ 315 Harbor Drive South, Oceanside; 760-722-2133; www.helgrensport fishing.com. **Islandia Sportfishing** serves the Mission Bay area, accommodating up to 150 guests. ~ 1551 West Mission Bay Drive, Mission Bay; 619-222-1164; www.islandiasportfishing.com. In Point Loma, **H & M Landing** takes you out on 65- to 85-foot boats in search of whales. ~ 2803 Emerson Street, Point Loma; 619-222-1144; www.hmlanding.com. **Point Loma Sportfishing** offers three-hour trips through local waters. ~ 1403 Scott Street, Point Loma; 619-223-1627; www.pointlomasportfishing.com. **San Diego Harbor Excursion** provides three-hour whale-watching tours during winter. ~ 1050 North Harbor Drive; 619-234-4111, 800-442-7847; www.sdhe.com.

DIVING

San Diego offers countless spots for diving. The rocky La Jolla coves boast the clearest water on the California coast. Bird Rock, La Jolla Underwater Park, and the underwater Scripps Canyon are ideal havens for divers. In Point Loma try the colorful tide-pools at Cabrillo Underwater Reserve; at "No Surf Beach" (located on Sunset Cliff Boulevard) pools and reefs are for experienced divers only.

For diving rentals, sales, instruction, and tips, contact **Under-water Schools of America**. ~ 225 Brooks Street, Oceanside; 760-722-7826; www.usascuba.com. **San Diego Shark Diving Ex-peditions** offers one-day trips off the coast of San Diego to dive within the safety of a shark cage and observe (or photograph) free-swimming white, tiger, and hammerhead sharks. For the less adventurous, there are two-tank trips to kelp beds or Wreck Alley and three-tank trips to the Coronado Islands. Reservations are a must. ~ 6747 Friar's Road, Suite 112, San Diego; 619-299-8560; www.sdsharkdiving.com. **Ocean Enterprises** teaches a variety of diving classes. They also rent and sell gear. ~ 7710 Balboa Avenue, San Diego; 858-565-6054; www.oceanenterprises.com. You can also arrange dives with **San Diego Divers Supply**. They provide instruction, sell gear, and do repairs. ~ 4004 Sports Arena Boulevard, San Diego, 619-224-3439. In Pacific Beach, the **Diving Locker** offers open-water certification. They also rent and sell gear. Closed Tuesday. ~ 1020 Grand Avenue, Pacific Beach; 858-272-1120; www.divinglocker.com.

A free whale-watching station at Cabrillo National Monument on Point Loma features a glassed-in observatory.

SURFING & WIND-SURFING

The surf's up in the San Diego area. Pacific, Mission, and Ocean beaches, Tourmaline Surfing Park, and Windansea, La Jolla Shores, Swami, and Moonlight beaches are well-known hangouts for surfers. Sailboarding is concentrated within Mission Bay. Oceanside is home to annual world-class boogie-board and surfing competitions.

For surfboard, bodyboard, wetsuit, and snorkel rentals and sales, try **Mitch's**. ~ 631 Pearl Street, La Jolla; 858-459-5933. **Surfride** rents and sells surfboards, boogieboards, bodyboards, fins, and wetsuits. ~ 1909 South Coast Highway, Oceanside; 760-433-4020; www.surfride.com. **Hansen Surfboards** rents recreational gear such as snorkel equipment, surfboards, and bodyboards, as well as wetsuits. ~ 1105 South Coast Highway, Encinitas; 760-753-6595; www.hansensurf.com. **C. P. Water Sports** has windsurfing rentals and lessons. ~ 1775 East Mission Bay Drive, Mission Bay; 619-275-8945. Surfboards, boogieboards, and sailboards are available at **Mission Bay Sportscenter**. They have wetsuits and surfing instruction as well. ~ 1010 Santa Clara Place, Mission Bay; 858-488-1004; www.missionbaysportcenter.com.

BOATING & SAILING

Fabulous weather allows plenty of opportunities to sail under the Coronado Bridge, skirt the gorgeous downtown skyline, and even get a taste of open ocean in this Southern California sailing mecca.

Several sailing companies operate out of Harbor Island West in San Diego, including **Harbor Sailboats**. They offer instruction as well as sailboat rentals. ~ 2040 Harbor Island Drive, Suite 104, San Diego; 619-291-9568; www.harborsailboats.com. For sailboat rentals and party yacht charters, try **San Diego Yacht Charters**. ~ 1880 Harbor Island Drive, San Diego; 619-291-7245; www.sdyc.com.

Motorboat, sailboat, and kayak rentals can be found at **Action Sport Rentals**. ~ 1775 East Mission Bay Drive, Mission Bay; 619-

275-8945. Powerboat, sailboat, catamaran, and kayak rentals are also available from **Mission Bay Sportscenter**. In addition, they can teach you how to sail and waterski. ~ 1010 Santa Clara Place, Mission Bay; 858-488-1004; www.missionbaysportscenter.com. **Seaforth Mission Bay Boat Rental** rents motorboats, sailboats, jet skis, paddleboats, canoes, and kayaks. Sailing lessons are available. ~ 1641 Quivira Road, Mission Bay; 619-223-1681; www.seaforthboatrental.com. The **Coronado Boat Rentals** has motorboats and sailboats. ~ 1715 Strand Way, Coronado; 619-437-1514.

Charter a yacht through **Hornblower Cruises & Events**. ~ 1066 North Harbor Drive, San Diego; 619-686-8700; www.hornblower.com.

HANG GLIDING

Torrey Pines Glider Port is an expert-rated hang-gliding and paragliding site, located atop a towering sandstone bluff overlooking Black's Beach. Lesson packages and half-hour tandem flights are available. If you're not yet an expert, there is a great vantage point to watch from. ~ 2800 Torrey Pines Scenic Drive, La Jolla; 858-452-9858; www.flytorrey.com, e-mail info@flytorrey.com.

GOLF

You don't have to look far for a green to practice your swing. Most courses in San Diego rent clubs and carts so you're in luck if you didn't plan ahead.

NORTH SAN DIEGO COUNTY The 18-hole **Emerald Isle Golf Course** is a public executive green. ~ 660 South El Camino Real, Oceanside; 760-721-4700; www.emeraldislegolf.net. Tee off at **Oceanside Golf Course**, a public, 18-hole course. At the 13th hole, take a minute to admire the view of rolling hills, and majestic mountains. ~ 825 Douglas Drive, Oceanside; 760-433-1360. You'll have to caddy your clubs by pull cart at the executive, public **Rancho Carlsbad Golf Course**, a par-56, 18-hole green. ~ 5200 El Camino Real, Carlsbad; 760-438-1772.

LA JOLLA Beautiful **Torrey Pines Golf Course** is famous for its two 18-hole, par-72 championship courses. ~ 11480 North Torrey Pines Road, La Jolla; 619-570-1234.

MISSION BAY PARK AREA **Mission Bay Golf Resort** is a public, 18-hole executive course. It's San Diego's only night-lighted course. ~ 2702 North Mission Bay Drive, Mission Bay; 858-581-7880.

BALBOA PARK A duffer's delight, the 18-hole **Balboa Park Municipal Golf Course** is a par-72 championship course. It also features a nine-hole executive course. ~ Golf Course Drive, Balboa Park; 619-570-1234.

CORONADO The **Coronado Municipal Golf Course**, an 18-hole green, runs along Glorietta Bay. ~ 2000 Visalia Row, Coronado; 619-435-3121.

TENNIS

SAN DIEGO   San Diego has many private and public hardtop courts. The **Barnes Tennis Center** has 25 outdoor courts, 19 of which are lighted. Fee. ~ 4490 West Point Loma Boulevard, San Diego; 619-221-9000; www.barnestenniscenter.com. You'll find two unlighted courts at the **Cabrillo Recreation Center**. ~ 3051 Canon Street, Point Loma; 619-531-1534. If you're in Ocean Beach, try the 12 courts at **Peninsula Tennis Club**, which are outdoor and lighted. Fee. ~ 2525 Bacon Street, Ocean Beach; 619-226-3407. Some of the nine outdoor courts at the **La Jolla Tennis Club** are lighted. Fee. ~ 7632 Draper Avenue, La Jolla; 858-454-4434.

CORONADO   The **Coronado Tennis Center** has eight outdoor courts, three of which are lighted. ~ 1501 Glorietta Boulevard; 619-435-1616.

BIKING

North County's **Old Route 101** provides almost 40 miles of scintillating cycling along the coast from Oceanside to La Jolla. Traffic is heavy but bikes are almost as numerous as autos along this stretch. Bike lanes are designated along most of the route.

Cycling has skyrocketed in popularity throughout San Diego County, especially in coastal areas. The **Mission Bay Bike Path** (18 miles) starts at the San Diego Convention Center, winds along the harbor, crosses Mission Bay, and heads up the coast to La Jolla. **Balboa Park** and **Mission Bay Park** both have excellent bike routes (see the "Balboa Park and the San Diego Zoo" and "Mission Bay Park Area" sections of this chapter). Check with Regional Transit about their special "biker" passes.

Bike Rentals   To rent a bicycle (mountain, road, or kid's) in downtown San Diego, contact **Pennyfarthings Bicycle Store**. ~ 630 C Street; 619-233-7696. **Holland's Bicycles** sells, rents, and repairs cruisers, mountain bikes, and tandems. Rentals come with helmets and locks. ~ 977 Orange Avenue at 10th Street, Coronado; 619-435-3153; www.hollandsbicycles.com.

HIKING

Most of the San Diego County coastline is developed for either residential or commercial purposes, limiting the hiking possibilities. There are some protected areas set aside to preserve remnants of the county's unique coastal chaparral communities and tidelands. These reserves offer short hiking trails. Inland San Diego County, particularly in the Palomar and Laguna mountains, also provides backpacking opportunities. A trail map packet is available from the San Diego County Department of Public Works. ~ 858-694-3215.

Serious hikers might consider taking on the San Diego section of the **California Coastal Trail**. It follows the shoreline from the Mexican border to San Onofre State Beach.

All distances listed for hiking trails are one way unless otherwise noted.

NORTH SAN DIEGO COUNTY Three Lagoons Trail (5 miles) originates on the beach in Leucadia and heads north along the sand past three saltwater lagoons, ending in Carlsbad. The best place to begin is at the beach parking lot at Grandview Street in Leucadia.

LA JOLLA Without a doubt, the 1750-acre **Torrey Pines State Park and Reserve** offers the county's best hiking. It was named for the world's rarest pine tree *(Pinus torreyana)* which the reserve was established to protect. An estimated 6000 of the gnarled and twisted trees cling to rugged cliffs and ravines, some growing as tall as 60 feet.

Several major trails offer hikers a variety of challenges and natural attractions. Most are easily walked loops through groves of pines, such as **Guy Fleming Trail** (.6-mile loop), which scans the coast at South and North overlooks, and **Parry Grove Trail** (.5-mile loop), which passes stands of manzanita, yucca, and other shrubs. There are more strenuous treks such as the **Razor Point Trail** (.6 mile), which follows the Canyon of the Swifts, then links up with the **Beach Trail** (.8 mile); and the south fork of **Broken Hill Trail** (1.3 miles), which zigzags to the coast past chamiso and scrub oak (the north fork is 1.2 miles).

Del Mar Beach Trail (3 miles) leads from the Del Mar Amtrak Station along the beach past flatrock tidepools and up to the bluffs of Torrey Pines State Reserve.

POINT LOMA AREA Cabrillo National Monument offers the moderate **Bayside Trail** (1 mile). It begins at the Old Point Loma Lighthouse, beautifully restored to its original 1855 condition, and meanders through the heart of a scenic coastal chaparral community. A wide variety of native plants including prickly pear cactus, yucca, buckwheat, and Indian paintbrush grow along the path. In addition to stunning views of San Diego, there are remnants of the coastal defense system built here during World Wars I and II. ~ 619-557-5450; www.nps.gov/cabr.

AUTHOR FAVORITE

The one-mile **La Jolla Coastal Walk**, a dirt path atop La Jolla Bluffs, affords some of the most spectacular views anywhere on the San Diego County coastline. It begins on Coast Boulevard just up the hill from La Jolla Cove and continues past a sea cave accessible from the trail.

SOUTH SAN DIEGO COUNTY   Four miles of hiking trails criss-cross the dunes and marshes of the largely undeveloped **Tijuana River National Estuarine Research Reserve**, which forms the coastal border between the United States and Mexico. Trails lead through dunes anchored by salt grass, pickleweed, and sand verbena. The marshy areas, especially those in the wildlife refuge around the Tijuana River estuary, provide feeding and nesting grounds for several hundred species of native and migratory birds, including hawks, pelicans, plovers, terns, and ducks.

Border Field to Tijuana River Trail (1.5 miles) is a level beach walk past sand dunes and the Tijuana River Estuary.

Transportation

Even though it is located in California's extreme southwest corner, San Diego is the hub of an elaborate highway network. The city is easily reached from north or south via **Route 5**; **Route 8** serves drivers from the east; and **Route 15** is the major inland freeway for travelers arriving from the mountain west. **Route 76** runs inland from Oceanside to the Palomar Mountains, then becomes **Route 79**, which leads to Julian. From Carlsbad, **Route 78** connects the coast with inland communities like Escondido.

CAR

AIR

San Diego International Airport (Lindbergh Field) lies just three miles northwest of downtown San Diego and is easily accessible from either Route 5 or Route 8. The airport is served by most major airlines, including Alaska Airlines, America West Airlines, American Airlines, Continental Airlines, Delta Air Lines, Frontier Airlines, JetBlue Airways, Northwest Airlines, Southwest Airlines, United Airlines, and US Airways.

Taxis, limousines, and buses provide service from the airport. **San Diego Transit System** bus #992 carries passengers to downtown. ~ 619-233-3004. Or try the **Southwest Shuttle**, which travels to major points in the city as well as to Orange County and Los Angeles. ~ 619-758-9808.

UP, UP AND AWAY

Hot-air ballooning is a romantic pursuit that has soared in popularity in the Del Mar area. A number of companies provide spectacular dawn and sunset flights, most concluding with a traditional champagne toast. Contact **A Skysurfer Balloon Company** for daily sunset flights over the coastal valley area. The hour-long affair includes on-board champagne and soft drinks, and concludes with a first-flight certificate. ~ 2658 Del Mar Heights Road, Del Mar; 858-481-6800, 800-660-6809; www.sandiego hotairballoons.com.

Greyhound Bus Lines (800-231-222; www.greyhound.com) ser- **BUS**
vices San Diego from around the country. The terminal is downtown at 120 West Broadway and 1st Avenue; 619-239-3266. Greyhound also carries passengers inland from San Diego to Escondido
at 700 West Valley Parkway, 760-745-6522; and El Cajon at 250
South Marshall Avenue, 619-444-2591. There's also an Oceanside
station at 205 South Tremont Street; 760-722-1587.

Chugging to a stop at historic Santa Fe Depot, located at 1050 **TRAIN**
Kettner Boulevard and Broadway downtown, is a nice and convenient way to arrive in San Diego. **Amtrak** offers several coast-
hugging roundtrips daily between Los Angeles and San Diego,
with stops at Oceanside and Solano Beach. ~ 800-872-7245;
www.amtrak.com.

Much like the rest of Southern California, San Diego is spread **CAR**
out over a wide area and is best seen by car. Car rental compa- **RENTALS**
nies abound. Most major rental agencies have franchises at the
airport. These include **Avis Rent A Car** (800-831-2847), **Dollar
Rent A Car** (800-800-4000), **Hertz Rent A Car** (800-654-3131),
and **National Car Rental** (800-227-7368).

For better rates (but less convenient service) try agencies lo-
cated near the airport that provide pick-up service: **Thrifty Car
Rental** (800-367-2277), **Rent A Wreck** (800-535-1391), and
Budget Car & Truck Rental (800-527-0700).

North County Transit District, or NCTD, covers the general area **PUBLIC**
from Camp Pendleton to Del Mar along the coast. NCTD oper- **TRANSIT**
ates numerous North County bus routes that service the communities of Oceanside, Carlsbad, Encinitas, Leucadia, Cardiff,
Solana Beach, Del Mar, and Rancho Santa Fe. ~ 760-967-2001.
800-266-6883 (San Diego County only); www.gonctd.com.

Several modern and efficient public transportation systems
operate throughout San Diego. Information and schedules are
available for all systems by calling **Metropolitan Transit System**.
~ 619-233-3004, 800-266-6883 (San Diego County only); www.
sdcommute.com.

The Metropolitan Transit bus system is the city's largest public transportation network, with lines linking all major points.
All Regional Transit stops are marked with a blue rectangle.

The city's newest and most venturesome mode of public transportation is the **San Diego Trolley**. The light rail system's line operates daily. Understandably, the line running between Mission
San Diego and the Mexican border is known as the "Tijuana
Trolley," or the Blue Line. It also serves Old Town and the south
bay cities of National City, Chula Vista, and Imperial Beach. The
Orange Line travels between Santee and downtown, including

Seaport Village and the Gaslamp Quarter. The Green Line travels from Old Town to Santee. ~ 619-233-3004.

National City Transit serves National City. ~ 619-233-3004. **Chula Vista Transit** serves Bonita and the city of Chula Vista. ~ 619-233-3004. **Violia Transportation** runs from downtown San Diego to National City and Chula Vista and on to the San Ysidro international Otay Mesa borders. In addition, Violia runs from Coronado along the Silver Strand to Imperial Beach. ~ 800-858-0291.

TAXIS

In North County (Del Mar to Carlsbad), call **Yellow Cab of North County** (760-722-4217).

San Diego is not a taxi town in the usual big-city sense, but there's a cab if you need it—just a telephone call away. Leading companies include **Silver Cab** (619-280-5555), **Yellow Cab** (619-234-6161), **Orange Cab** (619-291-3333), and **USA Cab** (619-231-1144).

WALKING TOURS

Several San Diego organizations and tour operators offer organized walks: **Gaslamp Quarter Historical Foundation** conducts two-hour, docent-led walking tours of the restored downtown historic district on Saturday at 11 a.m. Fee. ~ 410 Island Avenue; 619-233-4692; www.gaslampquarter.org.

Walking tours of **Old Town San Diego State Historic Park** are offered at 11 a.m. and 2 p.m. through park headquarters. ~ 4002 Wallace Street; 619-220-5422.

Join **Coronado Touring** for a leisurely one-and-a-half-hour guided stroll through quaint Coronado. Tours leave from the Glorietta Bay Inn (1630 Glorietta Boulevard) at 11 a.m. on Tuesday, Thursday, and Saturday. Fee. ~ 619-435-5993.

Index

Lodging Index

LODGING SERVICES

HOSTELS

Dining Index

HIDDEN GUIDES

Adventure travel or a relaxing vacation?—"Hidden" guidebooks are the only travel books in the business to provide detailed information on both. Aimed at environmentally aware travelers, our motto is "Where Vacations Meet Adventures." These books combine details on unique hotels, restaurants and sightseeing with information on camping, sports and hiking for the outdoor enthusiast.

THE NEW KEY GUIDES

Based on the concept of ecotourism, The New Key Guides are dedicated to the preservation of Central America's rare and endangered species, architecture and archaeology. Filled with helpful tips, they give travelers everything they need to know about these exotic destinations.

PARADISE FAMILY GUIDES

Ideal for families traveling with kids of any age—toddlers to teenagers—Paradise Family Guides offer a blend of travel information unlike any other guides to the Hawaiian islands. With vacation ideas and tropical adventures that are sure to satisfy both action-hungry youngsters and relaxation-seeking parents, these guides meet the specific needs of each and every family member.

Ulysses Press books are available at bookstores everywhere. If any of the following titles are unavailable at your local bookstore, ask the bookseller to order them.

You can also order books directly from Ulysses Press
P.O. Box 3440, Berkeley, CA 94703
800-377-2542 or 510-601-8301
fax: 510-601-8307
www.ulyssespress.com
e-mail: ulysses@ulyssespress.com

HIDDEN GUIDEBOOKS

____ Hidden Arizona, $16.95
____ Hidden Baja, $14.95
____ Hidden Belize, $15.95
____ Hidden Big Island of Hawaii, $13.95
____ Hidden Boston & Cape Cod, $14.95
____ Hidden British Columbia, $18.95
____ Hidden Cancún & the Yucatán, $16.95
____ Hidden Carolinas, $17.95
____ Hidden Coast of California, $18.95
____ Hidden Colorado, $15.95
____ Hidden Disneyland, $13.95
____ Hidden Florida, $19.95
____ Hidden Florida Keys & Everglades, $13.95
____ Hidden Georgia, $16.95
____ Hidden Hawaii, $19.95
____ Hidden Idaho, $14.95
____ Hidden Kauai, $13.95
____ Hidden Los Angeles, $14.95
____ Hidden Maine, $15.95
____ Hidden Maui, $14.95
____ Hidden Miami, $14.95

____ Hidden Montana, $15.95
____ Hidden New England, $19.95
____ Hidden New Mexico, $15.95
____ Hidden Oahu, $14.95
____ Hidden Oregon, $15.95
____ Hidden Pacific Northwest, $19.95
____ Hidden Philadelphia, $14.95
____ Hidden Puerto Vallarta, $14.95
____ Hidden Salt Lake City, $14.95
____ Hidden San Diego, $14.95
____ Hidden San Francisco & Northern California, $19.95
____ Hidden Seattle, $14.95
____ Hidden Southern California, $19.95
____ Hidden Southwest, $19.95
____ Hidden Tahiti, $18.95
____ Hidden Tennessee, $16.95
____ Hidden Utah, $16.95
____ Hidden Walt Disney World, $13.95
____ Hidden Washington, $15.95
____ Hidden Wine Country, $14.95
____ Hidden Wyoming, $15.95

PARADISE FAMILY GUIDES

____ Paradise Family Guides: Kaua'i, $17.95
____ Paradise Family Guides: Maui, $17.95
____ Paradise Family Guides: Big Island of Hawai'i, $17.95

Mark the book(s) you're ordering and enter the total cost here ☞ [   ]

California residents add 8.75% sales tax here ☞ [   ]

Shipping, check box for your preferred method and enter cost here ☞ [   ]

❑ BOOK RATE   **FREE! FREE! FREE!**

❑ PRIORITY MAIL/UPS GROUND   cost of postage

❑ UPS OVERNIGHT OR 2-DAY AIR   cost of postage

Billing, enter total amount due here and check method of payment ☞ [   ]

❑ CHECK   ❑ MONEY ORDER

❑ VISA/MASTERCARD _____EXP. DATE_____

NAME _____PHONE_____

ADDRESS _____

CITY_____ STATE _____ ZIP _____

MONEY-BACK GUARANTEE ON DIRECT ORDERS PLACED THROUGH ULYSSES PRESS.

ABOUT THE AUTHORS

RAY RIEGERT is the author of eight travel books, including *Hidden San Francisco & Northern California*. His most popular work, *Hidden Hawaii*, won the coveted Lowell Thomas Travel Journalism Award for Best Guidebook as well a similar award from the Hawaii Visitors Bureau. In addition to his role as publisher of Ulysses Press, he has written for the *Chicago Tribune*, *Saturday Evening Post*, *San Francisco Chronicle* and *Travel & Leisure*. A member of the Society of American Travel Writers, he lives in the San Francisco Bay area with his wife, co-publisher Leslie Henriques, and their son Keith and daughter Alice.

CAROLYN PATTEN, the update author for this edition, is the author of *The Insider's Guide to Palm Springs*. She has worked as a tourism public relations professional and freelance writer, specializing in the off-the-beaten path delights of California and Oregon. She lives in Portland, Oregon.